GREAT LIVES
FROM
HISTORY

GREAT LIVES FROM HISTORY

Ancient and
Medieval
Series

Volume 5
Soc-Z

Edited by
FRANK N. MAGILL

SALEM PRESS
Pasadena, California   Englewood Cliffs, New Jersey

Library of Congress Cataloging-in-Publication Data
Great lives from history. Ancient and medieval
series / edited by Frank N. Magill.
    p. cm.
Includes bibliographies and index.
Summary: A five-volume set of biographical
sketches, arranged alphabetically, of 459 individ-
uals whose contributions influenced world culture
and the social development of societies flourishing
in earlier centuries.
    Biography—To 500. 2. Biography—Middle
Ages, 500-1500. [1. Biography—To 500. 2. Biog-
raphy—Middle Ages, 500-1500. 3. World history.]
I. Magill, Frank Northen, 1907-   .
CT113.G74 1988   920'.009'01—dc19   88-18514
[B]
[920]
ISBN 0-89356-545-8 (set)
ISBN 0-89356-550-4 (volume 5)

LIST OF BIOGRAPHIES IN VOLUME FIVE

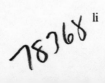

GREAT LIVES FROM HISTORY

LIST OF BIOGRAPHIES IN VOLUME FIVE

GREAT LIVES
FROM
HISTORY

SOCRATES

Born: c. 470 B.C.; Athens, Greece
Died: 399 B.C.; Athens, Greece
Area of Achievement: Philosophy
Contribution: Socrates combined his professional philosophical life with his private life in an exemplary fashion. He was a leader in the intellectual advancement that drew attention to human and social questions (in addition to physical questions) and bequeathed to posterity the Socratic method of learning by question and answer.

Early Life
The lives of many philosophers are quite undramatic: They write books, they do not lead eventful lives. Yet Socrates is a striking exception. First, he wrote no philosophy at all. He walked through the public places of Athens and engaged people of all types in philosophical discussions. In this way, he came to have many followers, especially among the young. Second, he acquired strong enemies, and eventually his enemies had him condemned to death.

Socrates—who was said to have had a broad, flat nose, bulging eyes, and a paunch—was a powerful and eccentric individual. His philosophy is intensely personal. More than any other philosopher, he successfully united his personal character with his professional career. For Socrates, there was ultimately no difference between his private life and his public career.

Socrates was the son of a stonemason (or sculptor) and a midwife. He does not appear to have spent much time in his father's line of work, although it was traditional for sons to do what their fathers did and Socrates was probably trained in stoneworking. He later claimed that he was following in his mother's footsteps, that he was an intellectual midwife. That is, he said, he assisted other people with the birth of the ideas they carried, while he himself had none. Clearly, he had ideas too; such a statement can be understood as an expression of typical Socratic irony.

Socrates was born, lived, and died in Athens. The only significant amount of time he spent outside the city was during his military service, when he earned a reputation for bravery, steadfastness in battle, and a general toughness of character. While on military campaigns in the northern parts of Greece, he reportedly went barefoot over ice and snow. In Athens, he became known for his unkempt appearance, his moral integrity, his probing questions, his self-control, his ability to outdrink anyone (while not himself becoming drunk), and his use of questions and dialogue in the pursuit of wisdom.

A friend of Socrates once asked the Delphic oracle—which was believed by the Greeks to speak with the divine authority of Apollo—whether anyone was wiser than Socrates. The answer was that no one was wiser. When Socrates heard this, he was confused. The oracle often spoke in riddles, and Socrates wondered what this saying could mean. He believed that he knew nothing and was not wise at all. He went to those who had a reputation for wisdom— to political leaders, authors, and skilled craftsmen—and questioned them. He found, to his surprise, that they really were not wise, although they thought that they were. He reasoned that since they were no wiser than he (as the oracle had said) but he knew nothing except that he was not wise, then they must know even less. Socrates' conclusion was that while others mistakenly believed that they were wise, his own wisdom consisted in knowing that he was not wise.

Life's Work

Socrates was a central figure in the revolution in fifth century Greek thought that turned attention away from the physical world (of stars and eclipses) and toward the human world (of the self, the community, the law). It has been said that Socrates brought philosophy down to earth.

Since Socrates wrote nothing himself, the evidence for his views must be somewhat indirect. Even if other sources are useful, scholars generally agree that the early, or Socratic, dialogues of Plato are the most important sources of information about Socrates' philosophy. Himself one of the foremost philosophers in the Western tradition, Plato was a personal student of Socrates. Moreover, although all the early dialogues were written after the death of Socrates, they were written while many of those who knew him were still alive, and Plato presumably would not paint a false picture of Socrates before the eyes of those who knew him.

The inquiries of Socrates, as represented dramatically in the dialogues of Plato, generally revolve around a particular concept, usually a moral concept. In the dialogue called the *Laches* (399-390 B.C.), for example, Socrates inquires into the definition of courage; in the *Euthyphro* (399-390 B.C.), he asks what piety is; and in the *Theaetetus* (388-366 B.C.), he examines the nature of knowledge. Often, the dialogues follow a pattern. At first, Socrates' partners in conversation are confident of their knowledge of the subject at hand. Socrates claims to seek enlightenment and asks them seemingly simple questions, such as "What is courage?" The speaker gives an example to which the concept applies, but Socrates replies that if the item given is only an example then the speaker should know the larger concept which it represents; he says that it is precisely this relationship between the example and the concept that should be explained. The speaker then considers one definition after another, but Socrates, by a skillful use of questioning, is able to show the speaker that the definitions are unsatisfactory. The speaker often complains that Socrates has robbed him of the confidence he once had. Yet Socrates, although he had been claiming that he only wanted to learn from the speaker, has all the while been orchestrating this very result by means of his questions. The speaker is led to see for himself that he really does not know what he thought he knew. The speaker, thus divested of false notions, is in a position to become a partner of Socrates in the quest for positive knowledge and wisdom. The ancient Greek term for this sort of question-and-answer testing of ideas is *elenchus*.

It is sometimes noted that in the dialogues Socrates refuses to suggest any positive ideas but only questions others and destroys their views (and sometimes their composure). Indeed, that is often the case. Yet there are some positive views that Socrates is willing to defend. For example, he defends the thesis that virtue is knowledge, and thus that all wrongdoing stems from ignorance, and he claims that it is far more important to care for one's soul than for one's body. These statements require some explanation, however, especially in their English and other non-Greek versions.

Socrates and other Greeks asked "What is virtue?" The Greek word that is generally translated as "virtue" is *aretē*. Another translation for this term is "excellence." (Virtue is a poor translation if it suggests ideas such as Christian charity, humility, and the like, since Socrates lived prior to Christianity and the Greeks themselves did not greatly admire charity and humility.) It was Socrates' belief, then, that human excellence consists in knowledge. If a person knew what was the best thing to do, for example, then the person would do it. Some critics have objected that this idea might be true for Socrates, who had great self-control, but that other, more ordinary people might see one course of action as superior to another and yet choose to do that which was not superior. The other side of the coin, according to Socrates, is that if a person has done something wrong, then it must be concluded that the person did not have the knowledge that what was being done was wrong. All wrongdoing, Socrates holds, is really the result of ignorance.

Socrates continually compares questions about man's nature, the purpose of life, and the nature of virtue (or excellence) to considerably more down-to-earth and sometimes humble questions. He discusses carpenters, shoemakers, horse trainers, and others. One could say that Socrates' discussions are dominated by a craft analogy. For example, the shoemaker's function is to make shoes, and he fulfills his function well when he makes good shoes. The shoemaker must know what he is doing; otherwise, he will probably produce poor shoes. Similarly, a person must know what his business in life is. "Know thyself," a Greek saying inscribed on the temple walls of Delphi, was a prominent theme of Socrates. He is also credited with saying that for a human being "the unexamined life is not worth living." A person will be an excellent human being only if that person subjects his life to examination and attains self-knowledge. Like excellence in shoemaking, excellence in human life is indeed an achievement, and it follows upon training from others and self-discipline from within.

Finally, Socrates believed that the disposition of the soul is more important than the body or any material thing. The word translated as "soul" here is the Greek *psychē*. Other translations might be "inner self" or "mind." It is the inner self that Socrates sees as inhabiting the body, just as a body can be thought of as inhabiting clothes. This *psychē*, or inner self—and not the appetites or passions or demands of the physical body—is what should give direction to one's life.

In 399, Socrates was tried in Athens on two charges: for not worshipping the Athenian gods (and introducing new divinities) and for corrupting the young. The first charge was unfair. It was a standard charge used to persecute threatening individuals, but Socrates had in fact been rather faithful in his observance of local religious customs. The only grain of truth in the charge was that he did claim to hear a voice within him—a daimon, or supernatural voice, that warned him not to do certain things. (The voice never encouraged particular actions, but sometimes stopped Socrates when he considered doing or saying something.) Yet Socrates and his fellow Greeks believed in many such divine signs and had little trouble accepting oracles and dreams as bearers of supernatural messages. The inner voice of Socrates did not replace the traditional gods; rather, it was supposed to be an additional source of divine messages.

The second charge was quite serious and, in some respects, plausible. As youths, Alcibiades, Critias, and Charmides had heard Socrates. As men, Alcibiades became a ruthless traitor and opportunist, and Critias and Charmides overthrew Athenian democracy (for a time) with a violent revolution, instituting a bloodthirsty regime. Moreover, Socrates himself had been a vocal critic of democracy.

It could be that this last charge was only a case of guilt by association. Socrates was not responsible for the fact that a few of his students proved troublesome. He certainly did not encourage violent revolution and bloodthirstiness; he stressed argument and discussion. In fact his criticism of Athenian democracy reflects this very point. He criticized the way Athenian democracy awarded some positions by lot (as potential jurors are selected even today) and some by vote. The random lottery method is unreasonable precisely because it is not responsive to argument. In general, Socrates believed that those who know, those who are wise, should rule. Why should a community leave important social and political decisions in the hands of voters—who may well be ignorant and are likely to be swayed by their own self-interest or by smooth-talking politicians—rather than in the hands of those who have wisdom and knowledge?

At his trial, Socrates was not contrite. He asserted that he would never stop asking his questions, the questions that some Athenians found so bothersome, and refused to accept the idea that he be banished to another place. He would stay in Athens and would remain who and what he was. The jury condemned him to death by drinking hemlock.

While Socrates was being held in prison, but before he was to drink the hemlock, he was visited by a friend who proposed to get him out of prison—bribing the guards if necessary—and to arrange for him to live at some distance beyond the reach of Athenian law. Socrates investigated this option with his usual methods and concluded that there were better arguments in favor of conforming to the legal judgment and drinking the hemlock—which, when the time came, he did.

Summary

To the philosophers who came after him, Socrates not only left the example of his life but also a new sort of inquiry (that is, social inquiry) and a new way of pursuing that inquiry, namely through the use of the Socratic method of question and answer.

Several schools of philosophers claiming to follow Socrates arose after his death. One of the best known, Cynicism, took up the view that virtue is an inner knowledge that has nothing to do with externals, such as material things or even other people. Diogenes, the most prominent Cynic, rejected conventional values and is said to have lived in a tub. He claimed that the life of the dog ("Cynic" comes from a Greek word that means "like a dog"), free and unfettered by human conventions, was a good model for the natural life. The Cynics invented the concept of the cosmopolitan (citizen of the cosmos or universe) when they claimed allegiance only to the universe at large and not to particular humanly instituted and local political units—such as Athens.

The Cyrenaics, also claiming to follow Socrates, held that inner, subjective experiences were far more important for life than the existence and nature of external objects. From this view, they derived the conclusion that the best life was one that was directed by subjective feelings of pleasure and pain. This school practiced a form of hedonism that was in many respects at odds with Cynicism. The Megarics, another minor Socratic school, practiced the art of refutation, which they modeled after Socrates' destructive criticism of the views of others. In this way, several schools of thought emerged, at variance with one another but all claiming to follow Socrates. One could say that each school followed some strands of thought in Socrates but that no school was able to capture him completely.

That is one reason that Socrates remains a giant in philosophy. It is possible to go back to the stories of his life and practice many times and each time discover some new aspect or line of thought. Moreover, the Socratic method of inquiry can be used by those less wise than the giant himself. Each new generation is enabled by this method to question received opinion, alleged wisdom, and even its own values.

Socrates said that he was a gadfly who stimulated his fellows to think more clearly. This applies both to his fellow citizens in Athens and to his fellow philosophers, or seekers after wisdom. With respect to his fellow citizens, it might be said that Socrates failed, since in the end they turned on him and had him condemned to death. With respect to philosophers who have come after Socrates, however, it could well be said that his mission has proved successful, for he has had a permanent effect on the direction of philosophy, an effect that can never be undone.

Bibliography

Guthrie, W. K. *Socrates*. Cambridge: Cambridge University Press, 1971. This work, which was originally published as part of volume 3 of Guthrie's *History of Greek Philosophy* (1969), is a thorough and scholarly treatment of Socrates' life, character, philosophy, and influence.

Kraut, Richard. *Socrates and the State*. Princeton, N.J.: Princeton University Press, 1984. Focuses on Socrates' rationale for not escaping from prison and from an unjust sentence. Kraut seeks to refute the contention that Socrates was a political authoritarian who believed that all laws must be obeyed without regard to consequences.

Plato. *The Last Days of Socrates*. Translated by Hugh Tredennick. Baltimore: Penguin Books, 1959. The translator provides an introduction and notes, but this work is mainly a rendering into English of four of Plato's Socratic dialogues, including Socrates' speech at his trial, his conversation in prison, and his last conversations and death.

Santas, Gerasimos X. *Socrates: Philosophy in Plato's Early Dialogues*. Boston: Routledge and Kegan Paul, 1979. A contribution to the Arguments of the Philosophers series, this volume emphasizes the logical reconstruction of the arguments of Socrates and sometimes uses formal logical symbolism. The book focuses on the Socratic method and Socrates' views on ethics.

Stone, I. F. *The Trial of Socrates*. Boston: Little, Brown and Co., 1988. Stone attempts to get behind the scenes at the trial of Socrates. He aims to show that political motivations, largely stemming from Socrates' negative attitude toward democracy and his friendships with those who supported a contrary regime, were powerfully at work in the trial, even though they were not openly acknowledged.

Vlastos, Gregory, ed. *The Philosophy of Socrates: A Collection of Critical Essays*. Notre Dame, Ind.: University of Notre Dame Press, 1980. A wide-ranging collection of articles by scholars in Socrates' philosophy. Consideration is given to the problem of the reliability of the various ancient sources for Socrates' views, the thesis that virtue is knowledge, and problems associated with the Socratic denial that one can do wrong willingly and knowingly.

Zeller, Eduard. *Socrates and the Socratic Schools*. 3d ed. New York: Russell and Russell, 1962. A reissue of a translation of the work on Socrates by Zeller, a renowned nineteenth century German scholar of Greek philosophy. A thorough investigation of the background of Socrates' life, his character, his methods of inquiry, his philosophical positions, and his influence on various ancient groups that claimed to be following in his footsteps.

Stephen Satris

SOLOMON

Born: c. 991 B.C.; Jerusalem, Israel
Died: 930 B.C.; Jerusalem, Israel
Areas of Achievement: Government and religion
Contribution: Through the application of his famous wisdom and the construction of the Temple, Solomon not only made a major contribution to the Judeo-Christian tradition but also forged the twelve tribes of Israel into a true nation, giving them an identity that would survive succeeding dispersions and persecutions.

Early Life
Solomon was the second child born to King David and Bathsheba and the fifth of David's sons. Although the sources are silent about Solomon's childhood, it is known that the prophet Nathan, who had enormous court influence, was his tutor. Accordingly, Solomon would have received a very thorough grounding in Jewish civil and religious teachings. His position at the court was enhanced by his mother, a remarkably intelligent figure with great influence over the king.

Although David had promised the throne to Solomon, David's eldest surviving son, Adonijah, harbored the ambition to be king, an ambition that to him seemed perfectly justifiable. His older brothers, Amnon, Absalom, and Chileab, had died, so should not the throne naturally devolve to the next oldest son? In order for him to secure the throne for himself, Adonijah needed allies. Through intrigue, he gained the support of his other brothers and of Joab, the commander of the army, and Abiathar, the high priest in Jerusalem. These were powerful people, but Solomon had an even more potent group backing his claim. These included Zadok, the high priest at Gilbeah, Benaiah, commander of David's mercenaries (David's "Mighty Men," who had fought with him since the king's early days and had never lost a campaign), Nathan, and Bathsheba.

To have any hope of success, Adonijah, then, had to act boldly before Solomon was consecrated king. As David lay on his sickbed, Adonijah, with an escort of fifty men and his supporters, had himself anointed king in the royal gardens at Enrogel. Nathan quickly learned of this and, alarmed, informed Bathsheba. It was vital that David reaffirm his oath concerning Solomon and have him anointed king immediately, or Solomon and his supporters would be killed. Confronted by Nathan and Bathsheba with Adonijah's acts, David ordered Benaiah and the royal troops to escort Solomon on the king's donkey and to have him anointed king by Zadok. When Adonijah and his followers realized that this had occurred, their coup attempt collapsed. His guests scattered, and Adonijah fled to the sanctuary altar and would not leave until Solomon promised not to harm him.

Solomon was now king. Shortly before David died, he advised Solomon on how to deal with his enemies, counseling him to stay true to the Lord's commandments. It was useful advice, for Adonijah quickly tried another tactic. Through Bathsheba, he asked Solomon's permission to marry Abishag, who was a member of David's harem. If this marriage were permitted, it would establish Adonijah's rightful claim to the throne. Solomon reacted swiftly. Adonijah was immediately executed, as was Joab. Abiathar was removed from his priestly office and exiled to Anathoth, fulfilling the prophecy regarding Eli's descendants (1 Sam. 2:27-37). Three years later, Shimei, an opponent whom Solomon had confined to Jerusalem, violated the terms of his punishment and was executed.

Life's Work

With his throne now secure, Solomon could concentrate on consolidating his kingdom, in order to secure the empire that his father had created. To achieve this end, Solomon initiated a sophisticated program based on three policies: There would be no further territorial conquests for the Israelite Empire, he would take advantage of the economic opportunities presented by Israel's strategic location, and he would build the Temple in Jerusalem to provide a unifying political and spiritual focal point for his people.

Although there were no significant foreign threats during his reign, Solomon realized that to attain his goals he needed to secure his borders through a combination of peaceful dealings with his neighbors and a modernized army at home. Accordingly, he launched a bold foreign policy initiative: an alliance with Egypt. After some difficult negotiations, the alliance was confirmed by Solomon's marriage to Pharaoh Siamon's daughter—a clear indication of the importance Egypt gave to the alliance, for Egyptian princesses were rarely given in marriage to foreign potentates. Solomon received the fortified city of Gezer as a dowry after the pharaoh had taken and plundered it. The land route for the transport of goods from Phoenicia to Egypt thus secured was mutually beneficial for Egypt and Israel. The main advantage with which this alliance provided Solomon, however, was that it gave him access to Egypt's building expertise and military technology: chariots, horses, and technical advisers to train the Israelites in their proper use.

Solomon could now proceed to modernize his army. This involved creating a large chariot force of fourteen hundred chariots and twelve thousand horsemen and constructing forts with stables at strategic points around the kingdom. For example, excavations at the thirteen-acre site at Megiddo, which controlled the vital highway running through the Plain of Esdraelon between Egypt and Syria, show that this fortress could house 450 horses and 150 chariots. Similar fortresses were apparently built at Beth-horon, Baalath, Hamath-zobah, and Tadmor.

Solomon also cemented relations with Hiram of Tyre. Tyre was a vital maritime city with colonies in Cyprus, Sicily, Sardinia, and southern Spain. Hemmed in by the Lebanon Mountains, Tyre had to depend on commerce for survival. Solomon needed cedar lumber as well as skilled artisans and architects from Tyre for his building projects; in return, Hiram received food and protection for his city.

Solomon's political program required not only safe borders backed by a military force capable of protecting important trade routes but also a firm revenue base. To meet this need, Solomon divided the nation into twelve districts. The official in charge of each district had to provide the supplies for the central government for one month of the year. The rest of the time, he collected and stored the necessary provisions. The required items for a single day's supply for the king and his court are enumerated in 1 Kings 4:22-23; though the list appears excessive, it is similar to the daily victual lists for other kingdoms in Mesopotamia.

Central to Solomon's overall policy was his building program. He built not only forts and cities but also ports, mines, highways, and shipyards. Solomon is most famous, however, for two major projects completed by the middle of his reign: the construction of the royal palace and of the Temple. These two undertakings played a major role in his plan of consolidation. The palace, which in addition to the king's personal residence included the complex of buildings housing the various governmental offices, took thirteen years to complete. Cedar, gold, ivory, and silver were liberally used; the resulting grandeur would have been a source of national pride. The building that was the cornerstone of Solomon's political program, however, was the Temple.

The erection of the Temple was the most important event in the Israelites' religious history since they had left the Sinai; accordingly, Solomon must have overseen every detail of construction. With a work force of 150,000 men, the project took seven years. The Bible gives a very detailed description of the finished Temple. Though it was once thought that it was a unique structure in the ancient world, recent archaeological finds have revealed that the Temple was quite similar to other temples in Mesopotamia.

It is difficult to overstate the deep significance of the Temple for Israel. Moses had prophesied that a kingdom would be created; with the construction of the Temple, divine confirmation of the Davidic throne was established. Thus, Solomon, by the act of building the Temple, firmly cemented his mandate to rule. Further, by placing the ark in the Temple, he focused the religious fervor of his people on the Temple, making Jerusalem their holy city and their national center. Solomon also was able to control the Temple and therefore gained a reputation for piety.

While the Bible says much about the Temple, it gives little space to discussion of the commercial ventures of Solomon. These played a significant part, however, in financing his other programs, and archaeological evidence indicates that they were extensive. Solomon was the middleman in the region's lucrative horse and chariot market. His involvement in and control of the major caravan routes passing through the Negev have been well documented. Excavations at Ezion-geber have shown that Solomon was also very involved in shipping and shipbuilding. His ships carried copper and iron ore (and their related products) dug from his mines throughout the Wadi al-'Araba (biblical Arabah) as far as Yemen and Ethiopia, returning with gold, silver, ivory, and monkeys.

His shrewd commercial activities made Solomon incredibly wealthy. Anxious to meet this legendary and successful king, other rulers came to Jerusalem bearing gifts and riches to establish relations with Solomon. The Queen of Sheba may have come to learn his wisdom, but she also wanted to create trade relations with Israel.

Solomon's power and grandeur were believed to have arisen from his exceptional wisdom. The Bible states that immediately after Solomon assumed the throne, the Lord, appearing to him in a dream, granted his request for wisdom and added that he would also receive riches, honor, and long life, as long as he obeyed the Lord's commandments. Eventually, Solomon became world renowned for his sagacity. His decision regarding the two women fighting over the custody of one living child is an example of his judicial wisdom. Because Solomon's reign was a time of peace, literature and scholarship flourished; much of Israel's history, up to that point preserved orally, was set down in writing during this period. Solomon himself is credited with the authorship of the Song of Songs, the Book of Proverbs, and Ecclesiastes. While there is some question regarding Solomon's authorship of the Song of Songs, there is little doubt that he did write most of Proverbs, and the weight of evidence leans toward him as the author of Ecclesiastes. These works of genius, stamped with the character of Solomon, reveal a deep spiritual insight and have formed a vital part of the Judeo-Christian tradition.

Summary

The final years of Solomon's reign present an interesting historical problem. Chapter 11 of 1 Kings makes it clear that Solomon, King of Israel, recipient of godly wisdom, vast wealth, and international recognition, ended his reign amid predictions of failure. Indeed, immediately after his death, the kingdom was split into the kingdoms of Israel and Judah. Some of the causes that have been advanced to explain the stresses that finally fractured Solomon's empire include the increasing bureaucratization of government, the excessive taxes needed to support Solomon's programs, the use of Israelites for forced labor, the unequal distribution of wealth, and the Israelites' inability to identify fully with their king's vision of a united Israelite state. According to the biblical interpretation, however, these problems were only symptoms of the disease. The root cause was Solomon's religious apostasy.

Early in his reign Solomon had followed the Lord's commandments, but eventually he fell into disobedience in two important areas. First, he violated the command not to take foreign wives (Deut. 17:17). At the height of his power he reputedly had seven hundred wives and three hundred concubines. The wives were usually taken for diplomatic or political reasons, but concubines were given as sexual gifts that Solomon could have refused but did not. These wives and concubines were his downfall, for in his efforts to please them, Solomon fell into idolatry.

Solomon not only tolerated idolatry but indeed officially recognized it. He gave official sanction for the worship of the fertility goddess Ashtoreth (Astarte) and constructed altars near Jerusalem for the worship of Moloch and Chemosh. During his reign, a valley just outside Jerusalem became known as the site of child sacrifices to Moloch; its name, Gê Hinnom, in later years was rendered Gehenna, which became a synonym for the word "hell."

Such religious apostasy, then, clearly moved Solomon away from the sound principles of rule that had governed the first half of his reign and induced him to adopt methods that in the eyes of his people undermined the legitimacy of his vision of a permanent, unified state. As a result, Solomon suffered rebellion at home by Jeroboam, son of Nebat, and the loss of various parts of his realm, and the welfare and prosperity of the kingdom would be endangered.

Despite his failings, however, Solomon was a great king. Without his efforts, one of the great achievements of history would have been impossible: that despite unprecedented persecutions, invasions, and sufferings, the Jews would retain their distinct national identity. Furthermore, Solomon's contributions to the Old Testament have proved to be a valuable legacy to countless generations and must be counted as one of the pillars of Western civilization.

Bibliography

Barker, Kenneth, ed. *The New International Version Study Bible*. Grand Rapids, Mich.: Zondervan Bible Publishers, 1985. In this edition, each book is preceded by a detailed introduction, and there are verse-by-verse explanations on each page. There are also indexes, essays, notes, time lines, colored maps, and charts. For an excellent archaeological supplement, see the *Thompson Chain-Reference Bible*, also published by Zondervan.

Beers, V. Gilbert. *The Book of Life*. Vol. 12, *The Nation Divides*. Grand Rapids, Mich.: Zondervan Bible Publishers, 1980. Beers combines the accounts of 1 Kings and 2 Chronicles to provide a cogent picture of Solomon and his times. Excellent photographs, illustrations, and text bring the period and people alive for the reader. A superior introduction to the topic.

Maly, Eugene H. *The World of David and Solomon*. Englewood Cliffs, N.J.:

Prentice-Hall, 1966. Consistently cited by later works, this book makes excellent use of twentieth century archaeological findings and interpretations. It is designed to be read by people not well acquainted with the Bible; the author's style is scholarly yet accessible. The chapter on Solomon provides valuable insights into his political program and commercial activities. Brief bibliography at the conclusion of each chapter; contains an index.

Schultz, Samuel J. *The Old Testament Speaks: Old Testament History and Literature*. 2d ed. New York: Harper and Row, Publishers, 1970. This is an outstanding book in which to begin one's research on Solomon. The author fully comprehends the deep significance of the spiritual aspect of Solomon and his reign. Makes use of other scholarly works and archaeological revelations to fill in the biblical gaps. His discussion of Solomon's decline is highly perceptive. Short bibliography at the conclusion of each chapter; indexed.

Thieberger, Frederick. *King Solomon*. Oxford: East and West Library, 1947. One of the few books in English that focus exclusively on Solomon. The author did not have the benefit of later archaeological discoveries, but he does depend greatly on the extensive textual research into the Old Testament that was done in Germany in the late nineteenth and the first third of the twentieth centuries. For that alone the book is worthwhile. It is well written, with excellent detail and interesting interpretations. Extensive notes and index.

Ronald F. Smith

SOLON

Born: c. 630 B.C.; probably Athens, Greece
Died: c. 560 B.C.; probably Athens, Greece
Areas of Achievement: Government, law, and literature
Contribution: Through his law code, Solon averted a civil war at Athens and established the political and social foundations for the development of classical Athenian democracy.

Early Life

The ancient sources include many details about Solon's life before 594 B.C., but most of these are probably romantic inventions about what the life of a great man ought to have been like. The fragments of Solon's own poems tell little about his early life. Plutarch, in his biography of Solon (c. A.D. 105-115), writes that Solon's mother was the cousin of the mother of Peisistratus, the tyrant of Athens who ruled between 561 and 527 B.C. This is one of many probably spurious attempts to link Solon's and Peisistratus' families. There is a stronger argument that Solon's father was Execestides, a member of one of Athens' noblest families. Execestides could trace his ancestry back to Codrus, a semilegendary king of Athens, and even to Poseidon, a wholly legendary god. Plutarch maintains that Execestides exhausted his wealth through lavish gift giving and that Solon traveled widely as a trader to recoup his fortunes, even though there were many Athenians who would have repaid his father's gifts. Another possibility mentioned by Plutarch is that Solon traveled solely to visit foreign lands.

Solon won a reputation as a poet, and several of his works are quoted at length by Plutarch and in the *Athenaiōn politeia* (c. 335-323 B.C.; *The Athenian Constitution*), attributed to Aristotle. Many early Greek statesmen were poets; poetry had an important role in politics, and Plutarch writes that Solon used his verse to catapult himself into political prominence, probably around 610. Plutarch further relates that Solon used a ruse to be put in charge of a war against Megara to win back the island of Salamis. The Athenians were so humiliated by their defeat some years before that they passed a law forbidding anyone even to mention their claim to Salamis. Solon circumvented this restriction by feigning insanity and then publicly reciting poems urging revenge. The Athenians were inspired by this act and soon won the island back. Like many other incidents in Solon's early life, however, this story may be attributing to Solon events which really happened later in the sixth century.

According to a second story, around 600 Solon had the Alcmaeonid family put on trial for the massacre of the followers of Cylon, who staged an unsuccessful coup in Athens in the 630's. The murders had ritually polluted Athens, and Solon supposedly brought in the semilegendary seer Epimenides of Crete to help purify the state. Yet it is quite likely that this event was made up to provide a Solonian precedent for the expulsion of the Alcmaeonids during political strife around 500. A third account links Solon to the possibly fictitious First Sacred War in the 590's, fought for control of the oracle at Delphi.

Life's Work

Whatever the truth of these stories about political crises, one thing is certain: Around 600, Athens was torn by social unrest. In the words of Aristotle:

> For a long time there was strife between the rich and the poor. For the state was oligarchic in all ways, and the poor, along with their wives and children, were enslaved to the rich. And they were called "clients" and "sixth-parters," for it was at this rate that they worked the fields of the rich. All the land belonged to a few people; and if the poor did not render these dues, they and their children could be sold overseas. And before Solon, all loans were made on the security of the person; but he became the first champion of the people.

Fearing civil war, the Athenian nobles elected Solon chief magistrate (archon) in 594, to draw up new laws to avert the crisis.

Other than Solon's own poems, which are often obscure, the earliest source for his laws is Herodotus' *Historiai Herodotou* (c. 425 B.C.; *The History*), which simply mentions that "at the request of his countrymen he had made a code of laws for Athens." Yet Solon's laws were publicly displayed on wooden boards, and it is believed that these boards survived for later writers such as Aristotle to consult. The laws fall into three main groups: economic reforms, political reforms, and other laws.

In an economic reform known as the "shaking off of burdens" (*seisachtheia*), Solon cancelled all debts and forbade enslavement for debt. He said he would try to bring back to Athens all those who had been sold as slaves overseas. He also addressed land tenure, removing from the soil certain markers called *horoi*, which probably stood on mortgaged fields. The meaning of the *horoi* is unclear, but by this act Solon claimed "I have made free the dark earth, which was enslaved." These reforms led to the disappearance of the serflike statuses of "clients" and "sixth-parters." Solon is also credited with a reform of weights, measures, and coinage, but that is probably a later fabrication (coinage only appeared at Athens circa 550 B.C.).

Solon also instituted political reforms. He divided the adult male population into four groups, based on the annual agricultural production of their land. The top class, the "five hundred bushel men" (*pentakosiomedimnoi*) monopolized the highest political offices. The next class was called the *hippeis* or "knights," who could produce three hundred to five hundred bushels, and the third class was the *zeugitai* ("infantrymen," or perhaps "yoke-men"), who could produce two hundred to three hundred bushels. These two groups could hold lesser political offices. Below them were the *thetes* (usually translated as "laborers," although most of these men probably owned some land), who could vote in the assembly and sit in the law courts but not hold office.

It is difficult to uncover the details of other political reforms because of later fabrications. In 403, the Athenians were forced by the Spartans to abandon their democracy and to return to an undefined "ancestral constitution." In the years that followed, various Athenians tried to project their own political programs back onto past statesmen, claiming that their own ideology was taken from the ancestral constitution. Solon was commonly said to have founded the democracy. According to Aristotle, Solon established the Council of Four Hundred to prepare measures to be voted on by the assembly of all citizens and set up the law courts as the central democratic organ. These institutions are uncannily like those of the fourth century B.C. and were possibly falsely attributed to Solon by propagandists at that time.

Solon is said to have legislated on all aspects of life, from mourning at funerals to the placing of trees near field boundaries and the digging of wells. While some of the laws attributed to him can be proved to have originated centuries later, the scope of his code reflects the general tendency of early Greek lawgivers to assume responsibility for every dimension of life.

According to his own notes, Solon had enough support to set himself up as a tyrant over Athens, but because of his moderation, he chose not to do so. This moderation made his position difficult after 594: The poor demanded a complete redistribution of land, which he resisted, while the rich believed that he had already relinquished too much power. It is said that he left Athens for ten years of travel, making the Athenians agree not to tamper with his laws while he was away. Similar stories are attributed to other early Greek lawgivers, however, and this story may be no more than a literary flourish.

Summary

Solon's moderation probably saved Athens from a self-destructive civil war. The greatness of his achievement was recognized in his status as one of the so-called Seven Sages of early Greece. He did not resolve all Athens' social, economic, and political troubles (unrest continued during the sixth century), but he did lay the foundations on which Athenian greatness was built. By freeing the poor from their serflike status and from the threat of bondage resulting from debt, he provided the basis of a relatively unified citizen body. His time also marked the beginning of one of the great paradoxes of Athenian society: the interdependence of democracy and slavery. Legally unable to reduce fellow Athenians to bondsmen after 594, wealthy men were forced to look elsewhere for labor to work their fields, workshops, and mines and began to import increasing numbers of non-Greeks, mainly from the Black Sea area, as chattel slaves. By the fifth century B.C., as much as one quarter of the resident population of Athens may have been slaves completely lacking civil rights.

Solon is one of the most important figures in Greek history, but also one of the most obscure, hidden beneath layers of later fabrications. Almost no detail in his biography is beyond question, but his overall contribution—averting civil war and setting Athens on the path to democratic rule—was a decisive one.

Bibliography

Andrewes, Anthony. "The Growth of the Athenian State." In *The Cambridge Ancient History*. Vol. 3, part 3, *The Prehistory of the Balkans, and the Middle East and the Aegean World, Tenth to Eighth Centuries B.C.* 2d ed. Cambridge: Cambridge University Press, 1982. A concise and balanced assessment of the literary sources for the political and social development of the Athenian state, from the earliest times to the reforms of Solon. *The Cambridge Ancient History* is the standard reference work for Greek history.

Aristotle. *Aristotle: "The Athenian Constitution."* Translated by P. J. Rhodes. Harmondsworth, England: Penguin Books, 1984. Fine translation, with excellent introduction and notes, of one of the main sources for Solon's reforms. Rhodes is the leading authority on this text, and his rendering is readable and reliable. This work was one of a collection of 158 constitutions of ancient states written by Aristotle and his students.

Edmonds, John Maywell. *Greek Elegy and Iambus.* Vol. 1. Cambridge, Mass.: Harvard University Press, 1931, reprint 1968. Parallel edition of the original Greek texts with a fairly literal translation of all the surviving fragments of several early Greek poets' works, including Solon. A few new fragments have been found and new readings made, but this volume remains the most convenient collection.

Finley, Moses I. *The Ancestral Constitution.* Cambridge: Cambridge University Press, 1971. Finley's sparkling inaugural lecture at Cambridge, reprinted in his work *The Use and Abuse of History* (1975), looks at the reinterpretation and invention of Solonian laws in Athens around 400 B.C. and compares this practice to similar distortions of past politics in seventeenth century England and early twentieth century United States.

_____. *Ancient Slavery and Modern Ideology.* London: Chatto and Windus, 1980. Reprint. Harmondsworth, England: Pelican Books, 1983. Brilliant discussion of modern attitudes toward ancient slavery and the logic of slave economies, including an analysis of the relationships between Solon's reforms and the rise of both slavery and the ideology of citizen equality in ancient Athens. Finley goes on to compare Solon's laws to similar developments in fifth century B.C. Rome.

Forrest, William George Grieve. *The Emergence of Greek Democracy: 800-400 B.C.* London: Weidenfeld and Nicolson, 1966. Classic, beautifully written, and well-illustrated overview of the rise of democratic institutions in Athens, setting the Solonian agrarian crisis in the context of similar problems in a number of other states in seventh century Greece.

Gallant, T. W. "Agricultural Systems, Land Tenure, and the Reforms of Solon." *Annual of the British School of Archaeology at Athens* 77 (1982): 111-124. A sophisticated discussion of the archaeological data relating to Solon's economic reforms, drawing on comparative anthropological evidence from modern societies facing similar problems of agrarian debt. With an extensive bibliography.

Hignett, Carl A. *A History of the Athenian Constitution.* New York: Oxford University Press, 1952. A very detailed study of constitutional developments. Hignett works within the very critical tradition of nineteenth century German scholarship and offers penetrating discussions of the sources. He is best known for his attempt to date Solon's reforms to the 570's.

Murray, Oswyn. *Early Greece.* Berkeley: University of California Press, 1981. General and highly readable account of Greek history from 800 to 480 B.C., combining the literary and archaeological evidence with judicious use of comparative material. Highly recommended as an introductory text.

Plutarch. *Plutarch: "The Rise and Fall of Athens."* Translated by Ian Scott-Kilvert. Harmondsworth, England: Penguin Books, 1960. Translations of nine of Plutarch's lives, including that of Solon, along with a brief introduction. Solon was of interest to Plutarch mainly as a moral example. His writing includes many clearly fictional elements but has remained popular through the ages for its lively style and content.

Woodhouse, W. J. *Solon the Liberator.* Oxford: Oxford University Press, 1938. Reprint. New York: Octagon Books, 1965. Rather dated, but still one of the best critical analyses of the ancient literary evidence for Solon's economic reforms. Particularly strong on the range of meanings of some of the obscure words (for example, *misthosis*, *hektemoros*, and *horos*) in Solon's poems and Aristotle's account of the unrest in seventh century Athens.

Ian Morris

SOPHOCLES

Born: c. 496 B.C.; Colonus, near Athens, Greece
Died: 406 B.C.; Athens, Greece
Area of Achievement: Literature
Contribution: One of the most important ancient Greek tragedians, Sophocles was an innovative and skilled master of character development and dramatic irony.

Early Life

Sophocles' life is known from a variety of ancient sources but especially from an Alexandrian biography included in the manuscript tradition of his plays. The playwright was born about 496 B.C. in Colonus, a suburb of Athens, which Sophocles commemorated in his last play, *Oidipous epi Kolōnōi* (401 B.C.; *Oedipus at Colonus*). His father, Sophilus, was a wealthy industrialist who owned many slaves and operated a prosperous weapons factory. The young Sophocles was given a good education. He won several prizes in school for music and wrestling, and his music teacher, Lamprus, was famous for a sobriety and restraint in composition which would later be noted in the style of his student.

The childhood of Sophocles parallels his city's long conflict with Persia, which began shortly after his birth with Darius' invasion, continued with Darius' defeat at the Battle of Marathon in 490, and climaxed in 480 with Xerxes' capture of Athens and defeat in the sea battle of Salamis. Sophocles was probably too young to have seen action at Salamis, but his family status—as well as his own personal talent and beauty—may account for his selection as a chorus leader in the public celebration which followed Athens' unexpected defeat of the Persian fleet.

Record of Sophocles' dramatic career begins in 468, when he entered an annual competition at Athens with a group of plays. It is not known if the young Sophocles was competing for the first time in this year, but his victory over the established playwright Aeschylus at this festival must have raised a sensation among the Athenians, especially if, as is recorded, the officiating public servant requested Cimon and nine other generals to replace the judges usually chosen by lot. Sophocles did not compete in the following year, but a papyrus fragment discovered in the twentieth century suggests that in 463 Sophocles was defeated by Aeschylus, who produced his Danaid trilogy.

Sophocles performed in many of his earlier plays, none of which survives. His appearance as the ball-playing heroine in one play and his lyre playing in another are recorded in his ancient biography. Later in his career, Sophocles abandoned such performances, perhaps because his voice was weakening or because the roles of actor and playwright became increasingly specialized in the second half of the fifth century.

Life's Work

The second half of Sophocles' life was dedicated to public service, both in the theater and in government. In general, the several civic offices held by the mature Sophocles are better documented than are the dates of Sophocles' extant tragedies. The most difficult extant plays to put in a chronology are probably *Aias* (*Ajax*), datable on stylistic grounds to about 448 to 445, and *Trachinai* (*The Women of Trachis*), usually placed somewhere between 435 and 429.

In 443 or 442, Sophocles served as a *Hellenotamias*, one of the financial officials in the Delian League of the Athenian empire. This appointment may have been the result of the great wealth of Sophocles' family. It may also be attributable to the well-known patriotism of Sophocles, who did not follow the example of many contemporary artists, including Aeschylus and Euripides, in leaving Athens for the court of a foreign patron.

In 441 or 440, Sophocles was elected to serve as general along with the great Athenian leader Pericles during the rebellion of Athens' ally Samos. Since the ancient *hypothesis*, or introduction, to *Antigonē* (441; *Antigone*) says that his election was encouraged by the success of this play, Sophocles' military service is often considered to have been more honorary than practical, but it is almost certain that the playwright traveled with the fleet on the campaign.

In 438, Sophocles was back in Athens, where he defeated Euripides' entry, including *Alkēstis* (438; *Alcestis*), with an unrecorded group of plays. Sometime in this decade Sophocles may also have produced a group of plays, now lost, although it is doubtful that these plays were connected thematically in the same way that the plays of Aeschylus' *Oresteia* (458 B.C.) were linked. When Euripides' *Mēdeia* (431; *Medea*) was defeated in a competition of 431 by Euphorion, the son of Aeschylus, Sophocles received second place with unknown plays.

Shortly after the beginning of Athens' long conflict with Sparta known as the Peloponnesian War and following the Athenian plague recorded in the histories of Thucydides, Sophocles produced his most famous play, *Oidipous Tyrannos* (*Oedipus Tyrannus*), probably in 429, and was voted second place to Philocles, the nephew of Aeschylus. In the following year Sophocles made no production, and around 427 he was probably elected general again, this time with Nicias.

A combination of patriotism and piety may have again motivated Sophocles in 420 to help introduce to Athens the worship of Asclepius, the deified physician and son of Apollo. Sophocles is also known to have composed for Asclepius a paean, or hymn of praise, which survives in fragments. The playwright was also a priest of Halon, a hero connected ritually with Asclepius, and was honored after his death with Halon's epithet, *dexion*, or "receiver."

Based on comparison with Euripides' *Ēlektra* (413; *Electra*), Sophocles' extant play of the same name is variously dated by scholars between 420 and 410, except for 415, when Sophocles made no entry in the dramatic competitions. In the same decade, the octogenarian Sophocles was once again called to public office. In 413 he was one of the ten *probouloi* elected to deal with the crisis caused by the disastrous defeat of the Athenian fleet in Sicily.

In the last years of his life, Sophocles continued to produce plays. The extant *Philoktētēs* (*Philoctetes*) is known to have won first prize in 409. Three years later, Sophocles apparently again entered the competition, where he displayed a chorus in mourning for the dead Euripides. Sophocles himself died within a few months. He was certainly dead by early 405, when Aristophanes produced *Batrachoi* (*The Frogs*), in which Sophocles' death is mentioned.

The ancient biographers were not content to accept Sophocles' advanced age as sufficient cause of death—but recorded several more colorful versions, including choking on a grape, overexertion while reciting *Antigone*, and overexcitement after a dramatic victory. At the time of the dramatist's death, Spartan garrisons were in control of the road to Decelea, where the family burial plot was located, and the family had to seek special permission from the Spartan general Lysander to complete the funeral.

Like many of his contemporaries, Sophocles appears to have had two families. He had one son, Iophon, by a lawful wife, Nicostrata, and another son, Ariston, by a Sicyonian *hetaira*, or mistress, named Theoris. Iophon followed his father into the theater, where he even competed with Sophocles at least once. In *The Frogs*, Aristophanes suggests that Iophon was often helped in his career by his more famous father, but that may be an example of comic exaggeration. Of Ariston, all that is known is that he produced a son named Sophocles, who was favored by his grandfather; Ariston produced his grandfather's last play, *Oedipus at Colonus*, in 401 and won first prize.

Iophon brought a suit of senility against his elderly father, perhaps because of the attentions shown to a cherished, but illegitimate, grandson. At the trial, Sophocles is said to have told the jury, "If I am Sophocles, I am not insane; if I am insane, I am not Sophocles" and to have proven his sanity to the jury by reciting lines from his current work, perhaps *Oedipus at Colonus*.

In his long life Sophocles was associated with many of the great men of fifth century Athens. His political sentiments are difficult to verify because of strong links with both the pro-Spartan and aristocratic Cimon, who may have assured Sophocles his first dramatic victory in 468, and with the democratic champion Pericles, with whom Sophocles served as general in the early 440's. Other members of Sophocles' circle of friends included Polygnotus, an outstanding painter who produced a famous portrait of the dramatist holding a lyre; Archelaus of Miletus, the philosopher and teacher of Socrates; the dramatist Ion of Chios, whose home Sophocles is said to have visited during the Samian Revolt; and the historian Herodotus of Halicarnassus. With some of these men, Sophocles may have formed the *thiasos*, or religious guild in honor of the Muses, which is mentioned in his ancient biography.

Summary

To the ancients, Sophocles' career as civil servant, as priest of Asclepius, and, especially, as dramatist at the festival in honor of the god Dionysus, proved he was a man of great patriotism and piety, although some modern scholars have tried to find a different, more questioning Sophocles in the extant plays. Certainly this man called by his ancient biographer *phil-athenaiotatos*, or "a very great lover of Athens," exhibited throughout his life a high level of personal involvement in his beloved city.

During his career, Sophocles is known to have written more than 120 plays, always produced in groups of three tragedies plus one satyr play. Sophocles, therefore, competed dramatically at least thirty times, perhaps every other year during the course of his career. If his ancient biography is correct that he won first prize twenty times, second prize many times, and third prize never, then Sophocles may have won first prize in two-thirds of the competitions he entered—a great testimony to his contemporary popularity.

There is some evidence that Sophocles was interested in literary theory. Besides his book, now known as "On the Chorus," which does not survive, Sophocles' analysis of his own dramatic style is recorded in Plutarch. Here, Sophocles suggests that there were three stages in his work. The first was influenced by "the majesty and pomp of Aeschylus." The second displayed an originality in the creation of painful effects. In the third he had characters speak in languages appropriate to their personalities. Since the date of this statement is unknown and since so few of Sophocles' plays survive, it is not possible to follow these stages in Sophocles' seven extant plays.

Traditionally, in addition to abandoning the practice of a playwright acting in his own plays, Sophocles may have introduced several important innovations to the theater. He is said to have increased the size of the tragic chorus from twelve to fifteen members and to have added a third actor, scenery, and other dramatic paraphernalia. Sophocles received particularly high commendation in Aristotle's *De poetica* (c. 334-323 b.c.; *Poetics*), in which *Oedipus Tyrannus* was praised for displaying the Aristotelian ideal of tragic plot and character. In the modern world Sophocles has become known for his masterful and dramatic development of character and irony.

Bibliography

Bates, William Nickerson. *Sophocles: Poet and Dramatist*. Philadelphia: University of Pennsylvania Press, 1940. A good biographical sketch. With several plates and figures depicting scenes from Sophocles' plays.

Bowra, C. M. "Sophocles on His Own Development." *American Journal of Philology* 61 (1940): 385-401. The playwright's comments about changes in his dramatic style are discussed in this article.

Helmbold, W. C. "The Mad Sophocles." *Classical Journal* 45 (April, 1950): 342. This short article argues that the trial of Sophocles for senility originated as the joke of a comic poet and has no basis in fact.

Lefkowitz, Mary. *The Lives of the Greek Poets*. Baltimore: Johns Hopkins University Press, 1981. A translation and discussion of the Alexandrian biography of Sophocles are included in this book, which also includes a bibliography.

Lenz, F. W. "The Athenian Strategoi of the Years 441/40 and 433/32." *Transactions of the American Philological Association* 72 (1941): 226-232. While the discussion does not specifically focus on Sophocles, this article considers the evidence for the list of Athenian generals in the year 441-440, when Sophocles served with Pericles.

Lesky, Albin. *Greek Tragedy*. New York: Barnes and Noble Books, 1965. A scholarly introduction to Aeschylus' dramaturgy, with a brief summary of his life. A bibliography is included.

_____. *A History of Greek Literature*. New York: Thomas Y. Crowell, 1966. Sophocles' place in the literature of ancient Greece can be traced in this standard history, which includes biographical evidence and a bibliography.

Scodel, Ruth. *Sophocles*. Boston: Twayne Publishers, 1984. A good introduction written for the general reader, this book includes a chronological chart and a select annotated bibliography.

Webster, T. B. L. *An Introduction to Sophocles*. Oxford: Clarendon Press, 1936. An excellent and carefully documented life of Sophocles can be found in the first chapter of this standard study.

Thomas J. Sienkewicz

SOSIGENES

Born: c. 90 B.C.; place unknown
Died: First century B.C.; place unknown
Areas of Achievement: Astronomy and mathematics
Contribution: Sosigenes advised Julius Caesar on the development of the Julian calendar, which, with only slight modification, is still in use today.

Early Life

Virtually nothing is known about the life of Sosigenes, an Alexandrian astronomer and mathematician who flourished in the first century B.C. Even the place of his birth is disputed. Some sources maintain that he was born in the Roman-controlled Egyptian city of Alexandria; others say that he came to Alexandria from Greece. Regardless of how he got to Egypt, Sosigenes must have found it an exciting, if turbulent, place.

Since the ancient days of the pharaohs, Egypt had been besieged by foreign powers. Its people had been conquered by the Assyrians, then the Persians, and finally, in the fourth century B.C., by Alexander the Great, for whom the city of Alexandria is named. In the years just before Sosigenes' life, the Ptolemies, who ruled following the collapse of Alexander's realm, had made Alexandria into a world center for commerce and cultural development. Trading vessels arrived from lands as diverse as Britain and China. Science and art flourished. The city had several parks, a university, and a library with 750,000 volumes. It became a mecca for philosophers and scientists, producing such great scholars as Hipparchus, Ptolemy, Euclid, and Hero. It is no wonder, then, that Sosigenes ended up in Alexandria.

Interest in Alexandria was not limited, however, to intellectuals. Foreign leaders continued to see Egypt as a prize. During the century before the birth of Sosigenes, the ruler of Macedon, Philip V, conspired with the king of Syria to conquer and divide Egypt. This move attracted the attention of the great and expanding Roman Empire. Though the Romans were currently embroiled in the Second Punic War with Carthage, they managed to send an army east to punish the two rulers. After both countries had been conquered, the Romans set up a protectorate in Egypt. Thus, the Alexandria of Sosigenes' time was under profound Roman influence. The Romans did not, however, interfere with the growth and development of the city, which now held more than half a million inhabitants—more than Rome itself.

After ending a bloody civil war in 48 B.C., Julius Caesar rested a year in Egypt before returning to Rome to become dictator. Perhaps it was during this visit that he became acquainted with Sosigenes, who by that time had come to be considered an authority on astronomy. One of Caesar's goals, as ruler of the Roman Empire, was to make radical reforms to the calendar in use at that time. The Roman republican calendar was so out of synchronization with the natural year that the vernal equinox, the springtime event when the sun's path crosses the celestial equator, had occurred months later, in early summer. Caesar called on Sosigenes to advise him on this matter and to develop a new calendar to replace the problem-ridden one of old.

Life's Work

The earliest calendars were lunar in that they followed the phases of the moon. Each month was designed to chart a complete cycle of lunar phases, from new moon to full moon and then on to the next new moon. Lunar calendars were easy to use, especially since they were tied to readily observable astronomical events. Their main problem was that they were independent of important phenomena on Earth. Most notably, they did not follow the seasons. The progression of seasons follows the solar year, the time it takes Earth to complete a revolution around the sun, roughly 365 days. The phases of the moon, however, follow the synodic period (the time between successive new moons) of about thirty days. A lunar year might consist of twelve such cycles (twelve months), or 360 days. The five-day discrepancy meant that seasonal events (monsoons, river flooding, snowfall, and the like) would drift five days forward each lunar year. Thus, by the time a calendar had been in use for two decades, the cold-weather days of winter would occur three months later, in the "spring" months.

Agricultural concerns dictated a need for a calendar that would closely follow the seasons. Farmers would then know when to plant and when to harvest. Such seasonal, or solar, calendars would be based on the observed motion of the sun through the constellations of the sky (ancient astronomers did not realize that this drifting of the sun through the constellations was actually caused by the revolution of Earth). The difficulty with solar calendars was that they did not follow the phases of the moon—which were important for setting the dates of religious feasts and events.

It seemed impossible to reconcile these two demands. Egypt, at the time of Sosigenes, had no fewer than three calendars in use. The oldest calendar was actually a very good one, by modern standards. It was a lunar calendar but was corrected each year by the rising of the star Sirius (the day on which a given star rises at the moment the sun sets is a seasonal year constant). Thus, this calendar—lunar, but regulated by the solar year—accurately predicted seasonal events such as the flooding of the Nile, an important consideration for farmers. Governmental and administrative personnel, however, wanted something more: a calendar which would not vary from year to year, so that they could set predictable dates for treaties and business contracts. Therefore, a true seasonal calendar was developed. It consisted of twelve months, each of which contained exactly thirty numbered days. Since this worked out to 360 days, the Egyptians then intercalated five extra days at the end of each year. At first, this calendar worked as well as the lunar calendar.

As the decades passed, however, the seasonal calendar grew out of synchronization with the seasons. Farmers went back to the Sirius-regulated lunar calendar. Astronomers tried to determine the reasons for the failure of the seasonal calendar. They developed a new lunar calendar. This one, instead of being corrected by Sirius, was tied to the civil year (the seasonal calendar). This helped the religious leaders set their events but was of no use to the farmers, who continued to use the old calendar.

Sosigenes realized that the reason for the problems that developed in the civil calendar was that the solar year did not consist of exactly 365 days. His calculations revealed that the year actually consisted of 365.25 days, so that any calendar based on a 365-day year would lose a whole day every four years. He decided that the way to solve the problem would be to intercalate an extra day every fourth year. Though the Egyptian government did not listen to his proposals, his work attracted the attention of Julius Caesar, who sought his advice on amending the Roman calendar.

This task proved quite a challenge, for the calendar of the Roman Republic was in a shambles. It consisted of twelve months, each having either twenty-nine or thirty-one days except for February, which had twenty-eight. The year ended up having 355 days, far too few to be in step with the seasons. A Roman administrative office known as the Pontifices was assigned to intercalate whole months when necessary to reconcile the calendar with the seasons. Sosigenes must have seen this solution as a rather messy one—and it was not made any better by the actual practice of the Pontifices. It seems that these officials chose to add extra months not as needed by the solar year but instead to increase the time in office of their favorite politicians. As a result, when Sosigenes took the job, the Roman calendar was several months off the solar year.

Sosigenes' task was twofold. First, he had to correct the current year, 46 B.C., so that it would align itself with the seasons. Second, he was to develop a new calendar which would keep synchronization with the solar year. A fixed system of intercalation would also be helpful, to prevent the Pontifices from changing the calendar according to their whims. Sosigenes accomplished the first task by intercalating a full ninety days into the year 46, making that year have 445 days. Then he designed a new calendar, which was to start on the first of January in 45 B.C. For this calendar, which came to be called the Julian calendar after Caesar himself, Sosigenes used his knowledge of the problems with the Egyptian calendars. He made each standard year consist of 365 days, with each of the twelve Roman months having either thirty or thirty-one days, except for February, which he left at twenty-eight days. In order to keep the calendar in precise synchronization with the solar year, he required that every fourth year an extra day should be intercalated in February.

This calendar, with its extremely simple and fixed method for intercalation, should have finally ended all the confusion and discrepancies caused by the old calendar and the meddling Pontifices. Sosigenes and Caesar seemed to have considered everything in their new calendar. They even prescribed that the intercalary day, the *punctum temporis*, should be inserted between the twenty-third and the twenty-fourth of February (Roman custom for adding days in the past) and that persons born on the intercalary day would, for legal purposes, be considered to have been born on the twenty-fourth.

Unfortunately, both men completely overestimated the capabilities of an ignorant bureaucracy. The Pontifices managed to misinterpret the command to add the extra day every fourth year. They counted the year in which they added the day as the first year of the cycle and thus managed to insert the extra day every three years. Julius Caesar was assassinated in 44 B.C., and Sosigenes had no authority over the Pontifices. It was not until 8 B.C. that Augustus remedied the problem and enforced the correct observance of the Julian calendar. It is probable, however, that Sosigenes did not live to see this accomplished.

Summary

The Julian calendar that Sosigenes developed has survived to the present time. The names of a few months have been changed, and the extra day is now inserted at the end of February rather than after the twenty-third. Still, the basic structure of the calendar has changed little through the centuries. In fact, the only significant difference between the modern calendar and the Julian one has to do with how often the extra day is intercalated. For the most part, the four-year rule is still followed; the years of 366 days are referred to as leap years. After several centuries of using the Julian calendar, however, it was noticed that the seasonal events were again out of synchronization with the dates. This problem was traced to Sosigenes' figure of 365.25 for the length of the year. Advances in astronomy were able to determine the number more precisely, finding it to be 365.24219 days. Sosigenes was only off by eleven minutes per year, but over the centuries this error propagated into several days. It was finally corrected in 1582 by Pope Gregory XIII, who omitted ten days from the calendar that year to bring the dates back into alignment with the vernal equinox. Then he instituted the policy of making centurial years (1600, 1700, 1800, and so on) common years instead of leap years, unless they were evenly divisible by four hundred. Thus, 1900 was not a leap year, but 2000 is.

Besides his achievement with the Julian calendar, little is known of Sosigenes. The few bits of available information are intriguing. It is known that he wrote three treatises on astronomy. One of them, on "revolving spheres," was likely a primary source for Pliny the Elder's chapters on the sky in the second book of his massive *Historia naturalis* (A.D. 77; *Natural History*). Unfortunately, none of Sosigenes' texts is extant. All that has survived is a few isolated fragments. One of these fragments indicates that Sosigenes believed that the planet Mercury revolved about the sun—a truly remarkable insight. Hipparchus, the great Alexandrian astronomer who lived before Sosigenes, maintained that all celestial objects revolve about Earth, and Ptolemy, the great Alexandrian astronomer who lived after Sosigenes, developed a model of the solar system based on Hipparchus' data and ideas. Sosigenes' view was ignored. It would be some fourteen centuries before anyone would advance such a notion again.

Bibliography

Michels, Agnes Kirsopp. *The Calendar of the Roman Republic*. Princeton, N.J.: Princeton University Press, 1967. The best work available on the pre-Julian calendar. It includes a discussion of the peculiarities of the Roman enumeration of dates, which continued into the Julian calendar of Sosigenes.

Mommsen, Theodor. *The History of Rome*. Translated by William P. Dickson. 4 vols. New York: Charles Scribner's Sons, 1887. This work gives the political background for the calendar reform of Julius Caesar and Sosigenes.

Packer, George. *Our Calendar*. Williamsport, Pa.: Fred R. Miller Blank Book Co., 1892. This work describes the Julian calendar and Pope Gregory's reform. Though out of date, the book is useful for anyone who seeks a mathematical examination of the calendar.

Philip, Alexander. *The Calendar: Its History, Structure, and Improvement*. Cambridge: Cambridge University Press, 1921. The best overarching discussion of Sosigenes' work with the Julian calendar. It explains, in accessible terms, both the astronomical and the anthropological concerns that influenced the development of the modern calendar.

Pliny the Elder. *Natural History*. Translated by John Bostock. London: Henry G. Bohn, 1855. Has extensive annotations; one of the most useful translations of Pliny's great work. In the second book, Pliny writes of Sosigenes' work on the planet Mercury. He discusses the calendar reform in his eighteenth book.

Greg Tomko-Pavia

SSU-MA CH'IEN

Born: c. 145 B.C.; Lung-men, Han-ch'eng hsien, China
Died: c. 86 B.C.; China
Area of Achievement: Historiography
Contribution: As principal author of the *Shih chi*, a monumental historical
work of 130 chapters which covers the history of the Chinese people from
earliest times to the late first century B.C., Ch'ien is the chief source of
nearly all subsequent historical knowledge of the dynasties of ancient
China. For helping to fill this gap in scholarship, Ch'ien ranks with Thucydides and Herodotus as an important ancient historian.

Early Life

Ssu-ma Ch'ien was born about 145 B.C. in the county of Han-ch'eng hsien
in what is modern Shensi Province, China. Nearly all information concerning
his life comes from his lifework, the *Shih chi* (c. 90 B.C.), which has been partially translated in a number of editions but remains best known by its original title. As was customary, Ch'ien traced his genealogy to legendary figures
of high station and high repute. In the mid-ninth century B.C., however, the
family suffered a loss of position and became known by the name Ssu-ma.
Ssu-ma T'an, his father, had been appointed the Grand Historian of the Emperor Wu's court early in his reign in 141 B.C. Prior to Ch'ien's birth, his father had commenced collecting materials and writing a major historical
work, his motive being to ensure his immortality. Thus, on his deathbed,
T'an charged his son with completion of the history.

Little is known of Ch'ien's specific training for this task. While Ch'ien was
a child and before, his father was made court astrologer and historian; his
family apparently earned a living farming and keeping livestock in the hills
south of the Hwang River. Ch'ien's early education purportedly consisted of
village schooling, which was continued after his father had been appointed to
serve in the court around 140 B.C. By his tenth year, Ch'ien reportedly was
reading old texts, although what texts they were is unclear.

Between his young boyhood and his twentieth year, Ch'ien traveled extensively. He reported going south to the Yangtze and the Huai rivers. He
climbed Hui-chi, where the mythical Emperor Yü, a great cultural hero who
had saved man and Earth from flooding, supposedly had died, and searched
for a fabled cave atop the mountain. He saw the famed Nine Peaks, where
the legendary Emperor Shun, whose reign had brought mankind un-
matchable happiness, was interred, and then sailed down the Yuan and
Hsiang rivers. Farther north, he crossed the Wen and the Ssu rivers. He traveled onward to study in Lu, Confucius' home state, and in Ch'i, the home
state of Mencius, making obvious his interest in Confucianism. He also
participated in an archery contest at a famed mountain near Confucius'

home—an appropriate anecdote, since the role of ancient historians had been collecting arrows representing the emperor's best shots—and he encountered local toughs in Hsueh and P'eng-ch'eng. After passing through Liang and Ch'u, he returned home to Lung-men probably around 122 B.C.

There, his father's influence, careful training, and good grades brought him into government service as a Lang-chung, one of the emperor's traveling court attendants. In this capacity, he wrote of having participated in imperial expeditions—one important one, for example, that was launched in 111 B.C. to southwest China, where he became acquainted with several of the tribes of that region—as well as many other journeys, which made him one of the most widely traveled men of his era and immensely enriched his capacities as a historian.

The event critical to his career occurred in 110 B.C., as Wu prepared for the sacred Feng Sacrifice, symbolic of the divine election of the Han Dynasty. Having already reported to the authorities in Ch'ang-an, the capital, on his recent mission, Ch'ien traveled eastward to join the emperor at Lo-yang. On his way, he saw his father, who apparently had become too feeble to participate in the sacrifice. Dying, his father asked Ch'ien, for the sake of the family's glory, to succeed him as Grand Historian, thereby ensuring continuation of his historical research and writing. Ch'ien did have a family, although nothing is known of his wife and only brief mention is made of a daughter.

Life's Work

What had begun as the private initiative of Ssu-ma T'an, the court astrologer-historian whose official duties lay in divination, became in the hands of his son and successor one of the acknowledged masterworks of historical writing. Creation of most of the *Shih chi* absorbed Ch'ien for twenty years, almost until his death. In carrying out the spirit of his father's injunction, however, he produced a history that was not only monumental but also unique in the implementation of its creative perceptions. Previous "histories" had consisted essentially of genealogical records, bland chronicles of a single regime, mere cautionary tales, essays propagandizing current political morality, or, as his father had expected, work dedicated to individual or institutional glorification.

Contrary to these precedents, Ch'ien sought to depict, as far as his sources allowed, the entire past of the Chinese people—basically a universal history, but one which fortunately illuminated the presence of many non-Chinese of whom no written record would otherwise have existed. His purpose was to record what had happened—the good, the bad, and the indifferent—with judicious objectivity. While the assumption of objectivity was not novel in Ch'ien's day (objectivity had been the goal of previous chroniclers, T'an included), the degree of objectivity with which Ch'ien wrote, together with the chronological span and geopolitical range of his study, was unparalleled.

The *Shih chi* is organized into five extensive sections. The "Basic Annals" are composed of a dozen chapters relating the histories of early dynastic families—back to the mythic Yellow Emperor—and, in the instance of the Han, the lives of individual emperors. Ten "Chronological Tables," graphing and dating important events of the past, follow. Subjects such as astronomy, rites, pitch pipes, music, the calendar, religion, and political economy subsequently are discussed in eight "Treatises." In turn, there follow thirty chapters on "Hereditary Houses," which cover political and diplomatic events before the Ch'in Dynasty. The next seventy chapters relate the "Accounts," or biographies, of famous men—including invaluable information on kings, ministers, sages, rebels, Confucian scholars—as well as reports on foreign governments and "barbarian" peoples with whom the Chinese had contact. Internally, the organization of sections and chapters is chronological, although some mixing of events and biographies leads to repetition of the narrative and a dispersal of information. Such confusions notwithstanding, the singularity of the organization is undoubtedly a result of Ch'ien's research, imagination, and sheer capacity for work.

Because of losses sustained in uprisings, wars, or the Hans' wanton destruction of documents relating to their predecessors, the Ch'in, sources for early dynasties were scarce and Ch'ien's narrative was parsed out by legends. Indeed, these sections belie the fact that Ch'ien disliked superstitions. In possession of more abundant and substantiable sources in dealing with events and personalities of the Ch'in and the Han dynasties, including those of his own lifetime, he wrote fairly accurate, three-dimensional portrayals.

Yet, while evoking plausible historical personages, he rarely obtruded his own personality directly, although almost the entire work (some sections may be later emendations) bears his imprimatur. Similarly, as was the case with most Chinese historians, he avoided forthright insertion of his own opinions. He was also inclined to present the most favorable aspects of his subjects first while introducing harsher facts later in the text.

For dramatic effect, like the historians of ancient Greece and Rome, Ch'ien also composed speeches for his principal characters, though not, as was the case in the West, so that they could be declaimed publicly. He wrote of the past as a sequence of dramas; hence, the narrative portions of the *Shih chi* are actually speeches by the principal figures instead of the author's descriptions of the action. In fact, very little pure description exists in the text. The Chinese preferred the directness of speech, as readers of Thucydides, Herodotus, or Cornelius Tacitus did. The terseness of the classical Chinese language, however, lends a fluidity to the *Shih chi* that is not present in analogous Western writings.

Scholars have sought to discover the personality and beliefs of Ch'ien beneath his literary devices. Although Ch'ien may have been objective in many respects, his purpose was often didactic. Concentration on heroes, important figures, and grand events insofar as his sources allowed, was designed subtly to convey moral judgments. He doubtless believed that goodness triumphs over evil. In this respect, he was at one with Confucius, whom he admired and whose *Ch'un ch'iu* (c. 480 B.C.; *Spring and Autumn Annals*) he partly imitated. He was also Confucius' first full-length biographer in the *Shih chi's* section on the "Hereditary House of Confucius." It seems unlikely, however, that Ch'ien extended his admiration for Confucius to all Confucianists or to Taoists.

Whether Ch'ien as a historian believed in an evolutionary process, in the inevitability of decline, in cycles, or in continuous flux, is uncertain. His selection of emperors, sages, ministers, bandits, rebels, and even nonentities (as well as his structuring of events) is too complex to suggest a firm conclusion. If, as he explained, his motive in writing was to glorify Wu, then the universal history that he produced was unnecessary. This obeisance to his emperor aside, it appears that he intended to create a new form of history.

Ch'ien was engaged in his private historical enterprise while officially attending to observance of rites, the arrangement of the calendar, and other courtly duties. He suffered as a result of a dispute with Wu over the actions of Ch'ien's friend, a general named Li Ling. Li Ling had fought brilliantly on the western frontier but, failing to receive the support essential to saving his army, went over to the enemy. For his efforts to explain Li Ling's behavior, Ch'ien was castrated in 99 B.C. and imprisoned. Contemplating suicide, he consoled himself with the past: Confucius had written a great work while in distress, Ch'u Yuan had composed a great poem while in exile, Tso-ch'iu Ming wrote while blind, and Sun Tzu produced his classic on the art of war after amputation of his feet. Persevering in order to continue his history, Ch'ien was restored to favor and completed his great work around 90 B.C. Still a minor and largely unrecognized court official, he died shortly afterward, probably in 86 B.C., presumably near the Han capital. The *Shih chi* remained unknown until the Marquess of P'ing-t'ung, Yang Yun (mid-first century B.C.), Ch'ien's grandson, succeeded in having it widely circulated.

Summary

Ssu-ma Ch'ien's *Shih chi* provides the principal written source of knowledge about ancient Chinese history and culture: its major and minor figures from many walks of life, its major events. As such, it continues to be an invaluable resource for understanding and interpreting a substantial portion of China's past. While it embodies many dramatic elements and important writings already familiar to his predecessors, it remains unique for its scope, substantive richness, and literary distinction. It must also be regarded as a fresh form of historical writing. Unlike previous historians, who had been content with the production of dynastic or personal eulogies and cautionary or moralizing tales in which a recounting of the past was merely a convenient vehicle for their views, Ch'ien sought to offer an objective perspective on the whole experience of the Chinese people. Scholarly difficulties in ascertaining precisely what his final estimates of many personalities and events were and in determining what his philosophy of history might have been tend to reaffirm his objectivity. This objective cast to the *Shih chi* has lent it a timeless quality, despite Ch'ien's obvious inventions and despite later and inferior emendations. In subsequent generations, the *Shih chi* continued to be admired for its organization, execution, and objectives.

Bibliography

Gardner, Charles S. *Chinese Traditional Historiography.* Cambridge, Mass.: Harvard University Press, 1938. A brief but brilliantly suggestive synthesis of the general ideas that shaped Ch'ien's intellectual environment. Intended for the fledgling sinologist but easily read, since complex technical questions are kept to the notes. Includes footnotes and a good, useful index.

Loewe, Michael. *The Cambridge History of China.* Vol. 1, *The Ch'in and Han Empires, 221 B.C.-A.D. 220.* Edited by Denis Twitchett and John K. Fairbank. New York: Cambridge University Press, 1986. An outstanding collection of scholarly syntheses that offer all the necessary background for understanding Ch'ien's work. Chapter 2, "The Former Han Dynasty," is a good place to begin; Loewe's introduction, which deals with sources for Han study, is a fine complement to that chapter. With footnotes throughout. Includes a superb forty-page bibliography, a sixty-page, double-columned glossary-index, and essential maps.

Ssu-ma Ch'ien. *Records of the Grand Historian of China.* Translated by Burton Watson. 2 vols. New York: Columbia University Press, 1961-1968. The most extensive translation of Ch'ien's work in English, but it is a select translation, so portions regarded as less rewarding by the translator do not appear. Includes few but useful maps, scattered footnotes, and an excellent master index in volume 2.

Watson, Burton. *Ssu-ma Ch'ien: Grand Historian of China.* New York: Columbia University Press, 1958. The only full-length, English-language biography of Ch'ien. The author does a fine job of placing the subject in the context of his times and of examining the beginnings of Chinese historiography, the structure of his work, and the subject's thought. Includes two informative appendices, more than forty pages of detailed, instructive notes, and a brief bibliography and glossary. Unless supplemented by other works, differences between the author's interpretations and those of other scholars may be missed.

Wilhelm, Hellmut. "The Scholar's Frustrations: Notes on Type of 'Fu.'" In *Chinese Thought and Institutions.* Chicago: University of Chicago Press, 1957. A brief but provocative essay on problems of political criticism confronting Ch'ien's contemporaries and the deployment of sophisticated literary devices to overcome them. Since most Chinese scholars were dependents of rulers, their survival depended on skill in indirect commentary. Aids an understanding of the style of the *Records*. With detailed notes at the end of the volume and an extensive general index.

Clifton K. Yearley
Kerrie L. MacPherson

SSU-MA KUANG

Born: 1019; Hsia, Hunan, China
Died: 1086; Pien Lian, Hunan, China
Areas of Achievement: Literature, historiography, and government
Contribution: Ssu-ma Kuang was a scholar, statesman, and poet who compiled the *Tzu-chih t'ung-chien*, one of the outstanding works in Chinese historiography. He was also a significant political figure in the Northern Sung Dynasty.

Early Life

Ssu-ma Kuang is one of the prominent individuals in early Chinese history. Born in Hunan Province in 1019, he was intensively educated in the Confucian classics and influenced by the historical writings of Kao Chün and the commentaries of the *Tso-chuan* (Tso tradition). Early in his life, he developed a passion for historical studies which motivated him to read widely. He completed his education in 1038, passed the civil service examinations, and moved rapidly into public office.

From 1038 to 1060, Ssu-ma Kuang established a distinguished and productive record in a variety of high positions. An excellent writer and speaker, he built a reputation as a fiscal conservative, opposing high taxes and extravagance in public office. He was firmly committed to the Confucian emphasis on the correct understanding of the past as a guide to proper life and preparation for service to the state, and, as a consequence, he served to promote the growth of schools and academies in Sung China. Ssu-ma Kuang is frequently represented as a hero in Chinese children's books. This reputation stems from his having saved a young friend from drowning by breaking the water tank into which the child had fallen.

Life's Work

It is as one of China's greatest historians that Ssu-ma Kuang is most remembered. In 1064, he presented to Emperor Yang-tsung a chronological table of Chinese history from its origins to the beginnings of the Sung Dynasty. His purpose was to organize the scattered records and existing information into a convenient and manageable form. Two years later, he presented the emperor with a chronicle of the history of the Warring States (403-221 B.C.), which he titled the *T'ung-chih* (comprehensive record). The emperor was so impressed with this work that he gave Ssu-ma Kuang a mandate to compile the records of all the emperors, rulers, and ministers prior to the Sung Dynasty. Two distinguished scholars were appointed to assist in the work.

In 1067 Ssu-ma Kuang was directed to read his work in the emperor's presence. The emperor titled it *Tzu-chih t'ung-chien* (1084; comprehensive mirror for aid in government) and wrote a preface that would later be included with the completed work.

At approximately the time Ssu-ma Kuang began his historical project, the celebrated reformer Wang An-shih rose to power as literary councillor, vice grand councillor, and in 1070, grand councillor. The two acquaintances were philosophically opposed to each other and had vigorously debated their differences on national policies. When Wang An-shih's reform program received imperial support from 1070 to 1085, Ssu-ma Kuang emerged as the leader of the opposition to Wang's sweeping reforms. His vigorous opposition forced Ssu-ma out of government during this period. He retired to Loyang with a comfortable sinecure and dedicated himself to his historical endeavor.

Between 1070 and 1084, Ssu-ma Kuang directed the collection and writing of his great history. He began with a chronological outline of the 1,362 years of Chinese history preceding the Sung Dynasty. Next, he had all available sources, family records, biographies, anecdotes, document collections, inscriptions, dynastic histories, and literary works reviewed and cited in the outline in the appropriate places. From this outline he created what he called the "long draft." If the cited accounts all agreed, the draft was so written; if there were varying interpretations, the most logical explanation was used with the conflicting accounts noted and an explanation offered as to the inclusion or exclusion of the account.

Ssu-ma Kuang then began the process of summarizing and reducing the text to the most essential details. He reduced the long draft (originally several hundred manuscript rolls) to 294 rolls. As each phase of the project was finished it was presented to the emperor. In 1084 the final work, along with a thirty-roll outline and a thirty-roll examination of the differences between the sources, was completed. This work was the first of its kind in the discipline of historiography and one of the most significant efforts in world history.

The inherent disadvantages of the chronicle nature of the project were overcome, in large measure, by subsequent works. In the twelfth century, a scholar, Yüan Shu, rewrote the history by tracing 239 topics from beginning to end, creating the first topical history in the Chinese experience. Also in the twelfth century the philosopher Chu Hsi completed a digest of the *Tzu-chih t'ung-chien*, selecting the most significant historical events included and developing them in narrative fashion so as to convey the moral lessons of history from the Confucian perspective. According to many historians, it is unfortunate that it was Chu Hsi's version of the history that became the most widely used in China, resulting in a moralism that stifled intellectual life for some time.

Ssu-ma Kuang's work brought a new emphasis to Chinese dynastic history, fitting it into the cyclical idea of history that had emerged with Ssu-ma

Ch'ien in the Han Dynasty. Ssu-ma Kuang interpreted the rise and fall of dynasties as a part of an established rhythm but was of the opinion that wise leaders could learn from past cycles and make moral choices that would extend the life of the dynasty.

This perspective led Ssu-ma Kuang to assume the leadership of the conservative opposition to Grand Councillor Wang An-shih and his reform program. The fierce power struggle between these two brilliant scholars developed into one of the most famous political conflicts in Chinese history.

The reign of Emperor Shen-tsung (1068-1085) coincided with Wang An-shih's reform program and Ssu-ma Kuang's writing of the *Tzu-chih t'ung-chien*. It had been the emperor's support for Wang that had driven Ssu-ma Kuang to his scholarly efforts. In the third month of 1085, however, the emperor died and was succeeded by his ten-year-old son, Che-tsung. The young emperor's grandmother, Hsuan Jen, was appointed to act as his regent. Opposed to many of Wang's reforms and impressed with the *Tzu-chih t'ung-chien*, she immediately called Ssu-ma Kuang to the capital. In the fourth month of 1085, the famous historian made a triumphant return to power. He was determined to eliminate all Wang's programs, which were, in his view, the result of wrong ideas. Within a year, Ssu-ma Kuang had rescinded every one of Wang's reform measures. Boards and agencies were abolished, supporters of Wang were transferred out of the capital, and laws were canceled. Nearly every trace of Wang's reforms was removed. Wang An-shih was a southerner and a reformist; Ssu-ma Kuang was a northerner and a conservative: The struggle was both philosophical and political.

Wang An-shih lived until 1086, long enough to see his reform program destroyed. Five months later, Ssu-ma Kuang, having achieved his desire to rescind Wang's program, died in Pien Lian. From every account, his funeral was a national event. The emperor and empress dowager attended, all routine business in the capital city was suspended for the day, and memorial services were conducted in all parts of the country.

Although the two factional leaders were gone, the struggle continued long after their deaths. With every subsequent change of leadership, the battle lines were redrawn. Liberal forces would restore Wang An-shih's reforms while conservatives would call up the image and history of Ssu-ma Kuang and rescind them again. For years the two men and their supporters were alternately defamed and restored. Perhaps this inability to maintain a steady course may have significantly weakened the Sung Dynasty and contributed to its decline.

Summary

Ssu-ma Kuang was one of the outstanding historians of China. He is important because of the critical intelligence used in the examination and evaluation of sources, the understanding and development he contributed to the historical process, the great skill he demonstrated in narration, the preservation and organization of early Chinese records that he accomplished, and the enormous scope of *Tzu-chih t'ung-chien*, which many consider the finest single historical work in Chinese history. Ssu-ma Kuang sought to develop history as a means of understanding the present. He is deserving of a prominent place in the history of China and in the writing of history in general.

Bibliography

de Bary, William Theodore, Wing-tsit Chan, and Burton Watson, comps. *Sources of Chinese Tradition*. New York: Columbia University Press, 1960. Contains several passages from the writings of Ssu-ma Kuang with editorial analysis of not only his work but also the work of other historians and political leaders of the Sung Dynasty.

Liu, James T. C. *Reform in Sung China: Wang An-shih (1021-1086) and His New Policies*. Cambridge, Mass.: Harvard University Press, 1959. A careful analysis of the reform program of Wang An-shih with reference to the philosophical differences between Wang and his antagonist Ssu-ma Kuang.

Pulleyblank, E. G. "Chinese Historical Criticism: Liu Chih-chi and Ssu-ma Kuang." In *Historians of China and Japan*, edited by W. G. Beasley and E. G. Pulleyblank. New York: Oxford University Press, 1961. An important work that offers exceptional insight into Ssu-ma Kuang's personal life, political struggles, and, most significant, his writing of the *Tzu-chih t'ung-chien*.

_____ . "The Historiographical Tradition." In *The Legacy of China*, edited by Raymond Dawson. New York: Oxford University Press, 1964. A concise article that brilliantly places Ssu-ma Kuang in historical perspective. Urges Western historians to direct attention to the importance of Chinese historiography and to the work of Ssu-ma Kuang.

Sariti, Anthony W. "Monarchy, Bureaucracy, and Absolutism in the Political Thought of Ssu-ma Kuang." *Journal of Asian Studies* 32 (November, 1972): 53-76. A highly focused article that addresses the political philosophy of Ssu-ma Kuang. Explains Ssu-ma Kuang's opposition to the reforms of Wang An-shih as a philosophical issue rather than as a simple power struggle.

Williamson, H. R. *Wang An Shih: A Chinese Statesman and Educationalist of the Sung Dynasty*. 2 vols. London: Arthur Probsthain, 1935-1937. A detailed biography of Wang An-shih. Places great emphasis upon Ssu-ma Kuang. Williamson effectively develops the power struggle between the two and includes quotations from their correspondence and debate. Provides important insight into the political dimension of Ssu-ma Kuang.

Frank Nickell

STEFAN DUŠAN

Born: 1308; central Serbia
Died: December 20, 1355; near Prizren, Serbia
Area of Achievement: Government
Contribution: The greatest ruler of medieval Serbia, Stefan Dušan extended his kingdom's borders at the expense of the Byzantine Empire. He successfully defended Serbia against its enemies, promulgated an important law code, and was crowned Czar of the Serbs and the Greeks in 1346.

Early Life

Stefan Dušan (also known later as Stefan Uroš IV Dušan) was the son of Stefan Uroš III Dečanski and his first wife, Theodora. He was born during the reign of his grandfather, the Serbian king Stefan Uroš II Milutin (reigned 1282-1321), who was successfully waging war with the Byzantine Empire and expanding Serbian rule in the Balkans. Dušan's father was the governor of the maritime provinces of Serbia on the Adriatic coast, but he rebelled against Milutin and tried to seize royal power. The revolt was unsuccessful and Dečanski was captured and subsequently blinded by Milutin to make him unfit for succession. Around 1314, Dečanski was sent into exile to Constantinople with his wife and young son. For nearly seven years, Dušan lived in the imperial capital, where he received an excellent education and came to understand and appreciate Byzantine government and traditions. These were to be important influences upon his later policy.

About 1320, Dušan's father and grandfather were reconciled, and the family returned to Serbia. The following year, Milutin died, and Dečanski made a successful bid for the throne. He claimed that his blindness had been miraculously cured (other sources suggest that he had always been able to see a little but had hidden that fact), and the Serbian nobility accepted him from among three claimants as their new king. At an assembly in January, 1322, Dečanski was crowned by Serbian archbishop Nikodim, and Dušan was proclaimed coregent or junior king (in Serbian, *mladi kralj*). The exact significance of this title is difficult to determine, but it may have been partly based on reservations that the nobility expressed about Dušan's father. From the beginning of Dečanski's reign, Dušan played an important role in the kingdom. He was appointed to govern the crucial region of Zeta, in modern Montenegro, and he participated actively in several important military campaigns. The most crucial of these was against the Bulgarians and resulted in a great Serbian victory at Velbužd (Kjustendil) on July 28, 1330. This battle established Serbian control over Macedonia and became the foundation upon which Dušan's later Balkan hegemony was based.

In the aftermath of the Battle of Velbužd, the Serbian nobility revolted against Dečanski. They resented his cautious and pacific policy, especially toward Byzantium. There may also have been conflict between Dušan and his father, either from natural rivalry or because the nobility influenced Dušan. The son marched against the king and captured him on August 21, 1331. Early in September, Dušan was crowned king. His father was subsequently murdered and eventually canonized by the Orthodox Church. Before Dušan could embark upon the great work that justified posterity in calling him Serbia's greatest medieval ruler, he had to suppress a revolt in Zeta, probably based on provincial bitterness felt by the local nobility, who did not achieve the degree of influence over the new king that they had expected. By the end of 1332, Dušan's position was secure.

Life's Work

The major focus of Dušan's foreign policy was the Byzantine Empire. Before he could begin the process of further territorial expansion to the south into the Greek lands of Byzantium, however, he had first to consolidate relations with Bulgaria and his other neighbors. During the spring of 1332, Dušan signed a peace treaty with the new Bulgarian ruler, Czar John Alexander. Throughout his reign, Dušan was able to count upon good relations with Bulgaria and to rely upon there being no Byzantine-Bulgarian alliance directed against Serbia. To the north, Dušan adopted a two-part policy toward Charles Robert of Anjou, King of Hungary, and toward his son and successor, Louis the Great. On the one hand, Dušan's stance was militarily defensive, and he prevented Hungary from pursuing its territorial interests south of the line of the Sava and Danube rivers. On the other hand, he was diplomatically aggressive, forcing the Angevin rulers of Hungary to protect their other European interests rather than focusing upon Serbia. Dušan was also careful not to antagonize Bosnia to the northwest and the powerful maritime city of Dubrovnik on the Adriatic Sea. Though Serbia had territorial interests and claims in this region, especially the district of Hum, which it had lost during the reign of Dečanski, Dušan chose not to pursue these. He correctly judged that the support of the nobility for any ventures in this area was lacking. In 1333, he reached a settlement with Dubrovnik, which brought substantial revenues to the Serbian royal treasury. In the following year, he concluded an agreement with Bosnia. To the east, the north, and the northwest, therefore, Dušan was assured of peace and had a free hand to pursue his southern policy.

In the spring of 1334, the Serbian king launched an attack into the Byzantine territory of Macedonia. Dušan's efforts achieved early successes, in part through the help of the Byzantine general Syrgiannes, who was the governor of the region and who had earlier revolted against Emperor Andronicus III Palaeologus. The Serbian army captured several important fortified cities, but the campaign ended when Syrgiannes was killed and the Byzantines mounted a counteroffensive. In a peace treaty signed on August 26, 1334, a compromise was reached. The Serbs withdrew, but the Byzantines confirmed many of their conquests. The border established between the two states at this time was nearly identical to the modern border between Yugoslavia and Greece.

The next phase of Dušan's southward expansion came following the death of Andronicus III in 1341. Quarrels over the succession in Byzantium brought the empire near to civil war. One of the leading parties was John VI Cantacuzenus, who had been Andronicus III's leading general and close adviser but whose own ambitions had been shunted aside in 1341. He led his army to Serbia to seek Dušan's support in ousting his opponents in Constantinople.

An agreement was forged between the two in July, 1342, in which the Serbs expected to be rewarded with imperial territory. Dušan invaded southern Macedonia and also captured large portions of Albania. After early cooperation which benefited both sides, the alliance between Dušan and Cantacuzenus dissolved over conflicting interests. The Serb advance in the Balkans continued, however, and by the end of 1345, Dušan controlled all Macedonia, except Thessaloniki, east to the straits of Chrysopolis. In the following three years, Dušan added to his empire, conquering Epirus and the region of Thessaly from Byzantium. These conquests extended his control south to the Gulf of Corinth.

Even before these successes, Dušan had changed his title. After 1343, he called himself King of Serbia, of Albania, of the Coast (that is, the Dalmatian coast), and of the Greeks. Late in 1345, he began to style himself czar, the Slavonic equivalent of emperor. To reflect this enhanced status, he arranged for the Archbishop of Serbia to be raised to the rank of Patriarch, and then, in April, 1346, Dušan was himself crowned Czar of the Serbs and the Greeks. In his next years, the czar turned his attention primarily to consolidating and administering his royal lands and his multiethnic empire.

To regularize practice, he introduced a system of titles and ranks which he modeled upon the Byzantine structure of government. He also reorganized the imperial chancery, again using the Byzantine model. His greatest achievement, however, was the law code that was prepared at his direction during the late 1340's. It was promulgated by a council in Dušan's capital of Skoplje in 1349. It consisted of 201 articles which specialized in public and criminal matters. It did not deal with issues of civil legislation, which were addressed in other ways. In general, the code reflected Dušan's great reliance upon his nobility as a base of political support for the monarchy, for it significantly enhanced their authority over lands and villages given them as fiefs. Byzantine elements may be found in the code, especially in matters relating to the church, but it was primarily based on previous Serbian practice and codes. The code was modified slightly in 1353 or 1354.

In his last years, Dušan's relations with the imperial court in Constantinople worsened. Emperor John V Palaeologus and his coruler, Cantecuzenus (Dušan's former ally), sought to recover parts of Macedonia. By allying themselves with Turkish auxiliaries, the Byzantine rulers defeated Dušan in 1352. In retaliation, the Serbian czar planned an invasion of Byzantium; he was most likely preparing for an expedition which would reach Constantinople itself when he unexpectedly died in December, 1355. As his successor he left his son Stefan Uroš V, who was, however, unable to maintain Dušan's accomplishments.

Summary

One measure of the magnitude of Stefan Dušan's territorial expansion is the fact that he doubled Serbia's size and conquered the parts of Macedonia and the south which his predecessors had either not been able to annex or had not even attempted to acquire. During his reign, he was able to transform his position from that of a semipuppet placed upon the throne by a rebellious nobility into that of a strong and effective ruler whom later centuries remembered as "Dušan the Mighty." His military and territorial successes were, however, not his only claim to be regarded as the greatest of medieval Serbia's rulers. His legislative skill, his administrative reforms, and his law code also contribute to this reputation.

Another measure of Dušan's greatness is found in the fact that his attention was by no means limited narrowly to Serbian affairs. He developed cordial ties with Popes Clement VI and Innocent VI in Avignon with two policies in mind. First, he was sympathetic to the possibility of church reunion between Latin West and Orthodox East, especially since the Patriarch of Constantinople had anathematized Dušan and the Serbian church after 1346. Second, he needed support from the west against the Ottoman Turks. They had significantly expanded their empire in Anatolia (modern Turkey) during the early part of the fourteenth century and in 1354 had established themselves in Europe by conquering Gallipoli. Dušan recognized them as a danger not only to Serbia but indeed to all Christians, whether Catholic or Orthodox. He hoped to be named to head a great crusade against the Turks. That he thought he might be able to use such a campaign also to conquer Constantinople and establish his rule there is clear from some of his preliminary negotiations with the Venetians.

All of these ambitions came to naught. Within twenty years of Dušan's death, Serbia had been reduced to a territorial extent smaller than when he had ascended the throne. In the Battle of Kosovo on June 15, 1389, Serbia was decisively defeated by the Ottomans, who were thereby firmly established in the Balkans. Nevertheless, Dušan may fairly be credited with having fundamentally established the predominance of the Serbian state in the region. This accomplishment was, in subsequent generations, to be an important and enduring fact of Balkan history.

Bibliography

Dinić, M. "The Balkans, 1018-1449." In *The Cambridge Medieval History*, edited by Joan M. Hussey, vol. 4. Cambridge: Cambridge University Press, 1966. Based solidly in nineteenth and twentieth century Balkan scholarship, this reliable study treats Stefan Dušan's reign in the context of both Balkan history and Byzantine relations with the region. The treatment of Dušan's law code is very superficial, but political and diplomatic details are reliable. The analysis of the fate of Dušan's empire is particularly good.

Dušan, Stefan. "The Code of Stephan Dušan." Translated by Malcolm Burr. *Slavonic and East European Review* 28 (1949-1950): 198-217, 516-539. A full translation of the text of the czar's law code, originally issued in 1349. The English rendering is fluid and readable, and there are helpful annotations with regard to technical terms and obscure references. There is, unfortunately, no additional commentary which places the code in the context of Stefan Dušan's reign. Especially lacking is any analysis of the relationship of this translated text to previous Serbian legal collections and to Byzantine elements included in the code.

Fine, John V. A. *The Late Medieval Balkans: A Critical Survey from the Late Twelfth Century to the Ottoman Conquest*. Ann Arbor: University of Michigan Press, 1987. An authoritative study on all aspects of Balkan history in the era covered in its subtitle. Two long chapters are devoted to the period of Stefan Dušan's life and rule. They are particularly good with regard to social conditions in Serbia and to Serbia's relations with its other Balkan neighbors. This work contains one of the very few presentations of Serbian-Albanian relations.

Soulis, George Christos. *The Serbs and Byzantium During the Reign of Tsar Stephen Dušan (1331-1355) and His Successors*. Washington, D.C.: Dumbarton Oaks Library and Collections, 1984. The most thorough study in English of Stefan Dušan's career. The focus is upon Serbian-Byzantine relations, but this is treated broadly enough to include detailed analyses of other aspects of the czar's foreign policy. One chapter is devoted to Dušan's internal policy in his conquered Byzantine lands, and there is a full discussion of the law code of the czar. It is based upon a comprehensive knowledge of the primary sources. The text is largely unchanged from the 1958 doctoral dissertation the author presented at Harvard University, though the notes have been somewhat updated by editors who prepared this manuscript for publication after the author's death in 1966.

_____. "Tsar Stephen Dušan and Mount Athos." *Harvard Slavic Studies* 2 (1954): 125-139. A specialized study which focuses upon the monastic communities of the arm of the Chalcidian peninsula which is dominated by the holy mount, Mount Athos. The communities there were of great antiquity, even in Dušan's time, and represented many of the major Christian traditions. Dušan sought the support of the monastic groups on Mount Athos for the creation of a Serbian patriarch and his own eventual coronation as czar. He was, in addition, a patron of considerable importance for several of the monasteries. An important work for understanding Dušan's ecclesiastical policy.

Paul W. Knoll

SAINT STEPHEN

Born: c. A.D. 5; Samaria
Died: c. A.D. 36; Jerusalem
Area of Achievement: Religion
Contribution: By means of his innovative theology, his personal courage, and his martyrdom, Stephen helped to universalize the early Christian Church by encouraging its expansion beyond the doctrinal confines of Judaism and the political confines of Jerusalem.

Early Life

All that is known of Saint Stephen's life and thought is derived from chapters 6 and 7 of Saint Luke's Acts of the Apostles. The former chapter tells of Stephen's rise to prominence in the early Christian Church, his election to the protodiaconate (the earliest board of deacons), his theological disputations with the Jews, and his arrest on trumped-up charges of heresy. The latter chapter relates his impassioned and provocative defense before the Sanhedrin, a group of Jewish leaders who became so enraged at his ideas that they stopped his defense short and dragged him away for execution. His death at their hands made Stephen the first in a long line of Christian martyrs.

From his Greek name and the ecclesiastical task to which he was elected, on the one hand, and from his idiosyncratic theological beliefs, on the other, scholars believe that Stephen was both a Hellenist and a Samaritan prior to his conversion to Christianity. A Hellenist was not only a Greek-speaking Jew but also one who was influenced by Greek (Hellenic) culture and open to Greek ideas. That is, Hellenists had a broader outlook and a more liberal education than did those Jews whose persuasion and practice were more separatistic. That Stephen was a Hellenist is deduced from the fact that his parents gave him a Greek name (Stephanos—the other deacons also had Greek names) and that the segment of Christian people he was elected to serve were Hellenists themselves. The Samaritans, those who came from Samaria (in central Palestine, between Judea and Galilee), were known for their unorthodox religious beliefs: Though they were Jews, they deplored the temple worship conducted at Jerusalem. They opted instead for worshipping at Mount Gerizim in Samaria. Besides an intense messianism, they also had their own version of the five books of Moses, a version known as the Samaritan Pentateuch, which, though it is largely the same as the standard Pentateuch, differs in a few significant ways. Stephen's recorded defense not only contains a Samaritan-like attack on the Temple and a presentation of Jesus as Messiah, it contains allusions to numbers and events found only in the Samaritan Pentateuch. This remarkable fact underscores not only his Samaritanism but also the historical reliability of Saint Luke's account, which in all other places employs a different version of the Old Testament Scriptures. Thus, Stephen appears to have been a Hellenist and a Samaritan.

Because no record of Stephen's conversion to Christianity has been preserved, scholars are unable to date it precisely or to identify its causes. A late and unreliable ecclesiastical tradition, however, numbers Stephen among the seventy evangelists sent out by Jesus.

Life's Work

According to the second chapter of Acts, the early Church experienced periods of remarkable growth. On the day of Pentecost alone, for example, approximately three thousand people were converted to the faith. As time passed, the Church's numbers continued to swell. While desirable, this growth brought with it some knotty organizational problems, among them the problem of how the small band of twelve apostles could oversee the distribution of the Church's extensive program of charitable outreach while still devoting sufficient time and energy to teaching and preaching the Christian message, a task they considered their supreme assignment.

Especially needy among the early converts were the Hellenistic widows. Financially, they were in a precarious position. With no husbands as breadwinners, and faced with a language barrier that seems to have prevented them from making their needs known to the Church, they faced severe difficulties. In an effort, therefore, to free the apostles for teaching and preaching, and in order to relieve the Hellenistic widows' distress, the Church appointed "seven men of honest report, full of the Holy Spirit and wisdom," among whom Stephen, as the subsequent biblical narrative shows, was most prominent.

From Luke's account, it is clear that Stephen did not restrict himself to the duties attached to the care of the poor. Stephen was an impressive theological debater, one who carried his Christian message into the Hellenistic synagogues in and around Jerusalem, one whom his opponents found difficult to gainsay.

Added to his Hellenism and his Samaritanism, his Christianity aroused the ire of the established Jewish leaders. His theological adversaries, bested in argument and distressed at what they deemed his unconscionable heresies, resorted to arousing opposition to him by distorting his teachings. They raised charges against him which they not only exaggerated but also corroborated with what Luke calls "false witnesses." By prearrangement, these false witnesses testified before the Sanhedrin to Stephen's "heresies." He was accused (like Jesus before him) of advocating the destruction of the Temple and of the overthrow of the Jewish law. The former idea they extrapolated from his Samaritanism and the latter from his Christianity. That is, like the Samaritans, he opposed worship in the Jerusalem Temple, and like Saint Paul after him (who now, as Saul, was in charge of the proceedings against

Stephen), he was opposed to trying to achieve salvation through observance of the Jewish ceremonial laws.

Stephen's defense before the Sanhedrin was not so much a defense of himself as a defense of the early Christian message and a counterattack against his accusers and judges. He spoke against the Temple and the system of sacrifices followed there by maintaining that, because God was not confined to buildings made by human hands, the true worship of God was not a temple-based function. Furthermore, by condemning Jesus to death, Stephen asserted, the Jews of his day had merely acted in accord with the spiritual failures of their ancestors, who had also resisted the revelation of God. In his view, the will of God had been made known by means of the prophets, and the prophets had been killed by their own people. The fate of the Messiah whose coming the prophets had predicted was no different: He too suffered at the hands of His own people. Thus, Stephen's defense chastised the Jews for what he believed to be their spiritual intransigence and wickedness. They did not grow closer to God or obey Him, even though they had the spiritual light to do so.

Quite predictably, such a speech served only to enrage his judges. In the midst of the ensuing turmoil, the council bypassed the normal procedures for passing a sentence. As they began to converge on him, Stephen offended his opponents even more by declaring that he saw, at that very moment, the heavens opened up and Christ, as if to welcome Stephen or to assist him, standing at the right of His Father. To Stephen's accusers, this was rank blasphemy. He was dragged unceremoniously out of the chambers to a place now known as Stephen's Gate, where he was stoned to death. Remarkably, in the midst of this torture, he knelt to pray aloud for his executioners. This startling sight, many believe, was the catalyst behind the conversion of Saul, soon to be the Apostle Paul, perhaps the greatest theologian and missionary of the apostolic era. As Saint Augustine later wrote, "If Stephen had not prayed, the Church would not have had Paul."

As is the case with many other notable ancient Christians, pious but unhistorical legends grew up around Saint Stephen's memory. The apocryphal apocalypse known as "The Revelation of St. Stephen" is unquestionably false and bears no genuine connection to the first Christian martyr, either by its content or by its authorship. This book purports to be a narrative of Saint Stephen's reappearance after his death; it was popular among Manichaean heretics and survives only in garbled segments. The discovery of Stephen's alleged relics occurred early in the fifth century.

Summary

Saint Stephen's not inconsiderable influence can be summarized under four important headings. First, he was the Paul before Paul. His personal conviction and courage in the face of death and his unique combination of

Samaritanism and Hellenism in a dynamic system of Christian belief undoubtedly influenced the zealous Pharisee Saul of Tarsus in his pilgrimage toward a new identity as Saint Paul the Apostle. Second, Stephen's death was the immediate impetus behind the Church's leaving its nest in Jerusalem and spreading itself and its message, as Luke writes, from Jerusalem, to Judaea, to Samaria, and to "the uttermost parts of the earth." Third, Stephen's defense was the basis of an effective strategy of theological defense, one that seems to have been employed in various segments of the early Church. Fourth, Saint Stephen has served as a stimulus to piety. Christians in all ages have been strengthened by his courage and spirituality. The Roman Catholic church celebrates the feast of Saint Stephen on December 26.

Bibliography

Barnard, L. W. *Studies in the Apostolic Fathers and Their Background*. New York: Schocken Books, 1966. Chapter 6, "St. Stephen and Early Alexandrian Christianity," is a technical examination of Stephen's theology and his influence upon one segment of the early Church. Barnard argues that *Barnaba epistolē* (*The Epistle of Barnabas*, 1719) contains significant strands of Stephenic theology, especially with regard to the Temple, the Torah, and Christ. The extensive bibliography is of use primarily for biblical and theological specialists.

Bruce, F. F. *Peter, Stephen, James, and John: Studies in Non-Pauline Christianity*. Grand Rapids, Mich.: Wm. B. Eerdmans Publishing Co., 1980. Chapter 2, "Stephen and the Other Hellenists," is a well-balanced and well-documented account of the theology of Saint Stephen, especially as it is seen in the context of Jewish Hellenism. Apart from the biblical account itself, this chapter is perhaps the best and most easily accessible introduction to the man, his life, his beliefs, and his theological tradition.

Kilgallen, John. *The Stephen Speech: A Literary and Redactional Study of Acts 7, 2-53*. Rome: Biblical Institute Press, 1976. Easily the most extensive treatment of Stephen's defense before the Sanhedrin, this book is both thorough and demanding. Though specialists will benefit from its detailed analysis (and will be able to detect its weaknesses), the beginning student will quickly be overwhelmed. The bibliography is quite inclusive, but unannotated.

Munck, Johannes. *The Acts of the Apostles*. Garden City, N.Y.: Doubleday and Co., 1967. Appendix 5, "Stephen's Samaritan Background," notes thirteen reasons why scholars identify him as a Samaritan. It also explains how the presence of these Samaritanisms in the Stephen account underscores Luke's historical reliability and clarifies Luke's use of sources.

Schmithals, Walter. *Paul and James*. Translated by Dorothea M. Barton. Naperville, Ill.: Alec R. Allenson, 1965. Chapter 1, "Stephen," is an idiosyncratic examination, from a theologically radical point of view, of the beliefs and practices of the Jewish Hellenists. Schmithals' bibliographical citations are quite numerous and quite technical, and almost all reflect a theologically liberal stance.

Simon, Marcel. *St. Stephen and the Hellenists in the Primitive Church.* London: Longmans, Green and Co., 1958. Unlike Munck's book (cited above), this text emphasizes the Greek aspects of Stephen's background. Though carefully argued, Simon's conclusions are speculative and therefore open to criticism. While the documentation is extensive, no separate bibliography is given. Like most works dealing with Stephen, this book is written for specialists.

Michael E. Bauman

STEPHEN I

Born: 975; Esztergom, Hungary
Died: August 15, 1038; Royal Alba, Hungary
Areas of Achievement: Religion and government
Contribution: Stephen I zealously spread the Christian faith to his largely pagan people, taking a great interest in the welfare of the poorest of his subjects and establishing numerous churches and monasteries both at home and abroad to place Christianity at the center of Hungarian life.

Early Life

Stephen was born with the name of Vajk at Esztergom, Hungary, in 975 to Geza, the fourth duke of the Hungarians, and Sarloth. Stephen was baptized by the renowned missionary to the Hungarians, Saint Adalbert, Bishop of Prague, the man responsible for converting his father to Christianity. Adalbert educated young Stephen in the mysteries of the Christian faith, a religion with few Hungarian adherents. Stephen was also strengthened in the faith by his tutor, Count Theodatus of Italy, whose piety mirrored that of Adalbert. Together these men impressed upon Stephen that by taking Christianity as its guide, a pagan and therefore ungodly nation could be transformed into a nation dedicated to peace and inner harmony.

Both Adalbert and Theodatus believed that Stephen had the potential to lead his country by applying Christian principles, and great time and effort were therefore given to his education. When Geza died in 997, Stephen became duke and assumed leadership of the state and its army. An able military leader who deplored bloodshed and prayed that his soldiers would not harm the enemy, Stephen made peace with neighboring states. By establishing a peaceful relationship with others, Stephen was able to make missionary work, which he had seen Adalbert doing in Hungary, his chief preoccupation. He gathered a band of itinerant ministers of the gospel to preach to anyone who would listen to their message. In their company, Stephen traveled extensively throughout his dukedom, proclaiming God's liberation of mankind through Jesus' death on the Cross at Jerusalem. Such proclamations, Stephen hoped, would convert the pagans to Christianity and free them from their bondage to superstition and fear.

Stephen's efforts in converting the masses to Christianity were so successful that a number of pagan chieftains were angry with him and discussed making war on Stephen's entourage. The most important of these chieftains, Count Zegzard, took action and attacked Stephen's forces at the town of Vesprin. Stephen's army, though badly outnumbered by Zegzard's forces, was able to rout and kill many pagan troops. Zegzard was captured and executed, thus ending the most serious threat to Stephen's attempt to impose his religion upon unbelievers. In celebration of this impressive victory, Stephen founded a monastery, which became widely known throughout Christendom as Martinsberg, in honor of Saint Martin. Subsequently, Stephen invited many holy men from surrounding countries not only to visit but also to live permanently at Martinsberg and help him establish the Christian religion as the nation's singular faith.

Life's Work

As a result of his victory against Zegzard, Stephen was crowned King of Hungary. Moreover, the title he bore was not merely "king" but "Apostolic Majesty." To his subjects he became known as Stephen, the Apostle of Hungary. He was crowned on August 15, 1000, by Pope Sylvester II. The pope admired Stephen's dedication to the Vatican and included him among the preferred monarchs, upon whom many favors were bestowed. At the time of his coronation, Stephen dedicated his kingdom to Mary, the Blessed Virgin, the patroness of Hungary, and made veneration of her a centerpiece of the Catholic faith in that country.

As king, Stephen took his high office seriously and worked from the outset of his reign to change Hungary into a humane, Christian kingdom where the dignity of the individual was of central importance. He created a new constitution, which survived into the twentieth century, that advocated and promoted Christian standards of conduct and provided for punishment of those who violated the strictures. At Royal Alba, Stephen built a great church that was to serve as the burial place of all Hungarian kings and a center of national religious life. He built another imposing monastery, named for Saint Peter and Saint Paul, in the city of Buda, and created the Church of Saint Stephen in Rome near the inn which he constructed for Hungarian pilgrims. Under his guidance, many smaller churches and monasteries were established throughout Hungary.

In a politically important move, Stephen married Gisela, sister of the German king and emperor-to-be, Henry II, known as Saint Henry. Henry was an administrative genius who divided his German territory into counties to be administered by people he appointed. By so doing, he made certain that the provinces were ruled by the monarchy rather than the often-rapacious local gentry. Applying these ideas and others given to him by Henry II, Stephen did much to bring order to his kingdom, which added to his popularity. In near-total control of the kingdom, Stephen was not only able to make illegal pagan religious observances and practices but was also empowered to put an end to the lawlessness that had been the hallmark of pre-Christian Hungary. Murder, robbery, assault, and other crimes were punished severely, but impiety and acts against the newly established church received ferocious punishment.

On a few occasions, Stephen had to resort to the threat of warfare in order to safeguard his kingdom from incursions by neighboring states. One marauder who brought his army into Hungary was Stephen's cousin, the Prince of Transylvania, who, after being defeated in battle, divested of his lands, and taken prisoner, was released unharmed on the condition that he allow Christianity to be preached in his domain. Stephen's kingdom was also confronted by Bulgarian forces, who mysteriously retreated without fighting, which Stephen attributed to his prayers to God for protection against bloodshed. In general, however, Stephen ruled over a tranquil kingdom that was unblemished by large-scale war or threats of war. His constitution, which guaranteed the rights of citizens, proved to be a sound basis for a society, for Hungary flourished under its protection. Stephen was well loved by his people, who regarded him as an ideal monarch.

The latter part of Stephen's reign, however, was marred by personal tragedy. All of his children died of various conditions, including his much-relied-upon eldest son, Emeric, who had greatly assisted Stephen in governing the kingdom. After the death of Henry, Stephen again had to contend with the possibility of war, this time the invasion of Hungary by the Germans under Henry's successor, Conrad II. Stephen was said to have again prayed to God that there would be no conflict, and, as in the past, the invader did an about-face and retreated to its territory. No blood had been spilled. This seeming miracle added to Stephen's reputation as a saintly king who had a close relationship with God.

At the end of his life, Stephen was the object of a murder plot created by knights who wanted to usurp his power. The plot was not carried out because the man who was to strike the killing blow against Stephen fell to his knees and begged the king's forgiveness. He was forgiven, but his fellow conspirators were executed. Stephen, reminded by this murder attempt that his life was coming to a close, commended his kingdom to the care of the Virgin Mary and was then given the last rites of the Catholic church. He died on August 15, 1038, having reigned over Hungary for a remarkable forty-one years. His remains were enshrined by request of Saint Ladislaus within the latter's own chapel at Buda. Stephen was later canonized by Pope Benedict IX.

Summary

Stephen I was a ruler who did much for his country during his long and relatively peaceful period of rule. One of his most illustrious achievements from a historical perspective was that he created the nation of Hungary from an assortment of miniature states. Without Stephen's unifying genius and the guidance from Henry II, Hungary may have remained a divided nation or fallen under the sway of more powerful neighboring states. As an administrator, Stephen devised a fair, comprehensive, and consistent constitution which endured for many centuries. As an apostle, he succeeded in spreading Christianity throughout his kingdom. Not only did Stephen preach Christian ideals, but he also put them in practice in his daily life, even to the extent of washing the feet of the poor people whom he invited to his palace. His unusual degree of sympathy for the poor helped make him a widely popular and beloved king.

Stephen is perhaps most important as a source of national pride for Hungarians during the past ten centuries, for he was one of the most humane, resourceful, and brave monarchs of his time. His humility, love of peace, hatred of impiety, and compassion for the least fortunate members of society make him one of history's most admirable figures.

Bibliography

The Book of Saints. Compiled by the Benedictine Monks of St. Augustine's Abbey, Ramsgate. New York: Macmillan, 1947. An informative assessment of the major accomplishments of Stephen I that places him within the context of the Europe of his time.

Englebert, Omer. *The Lives of the Saints*. Translated by Christopher and Anne Freemantle. New York: David McKay Co., 1951. A good summary of what Stephen I did to extend the power of the Catholic church in Europe, especially Eastern Europe, where the Church needed to assert its authority.

Hoyt, Robert S. *Europe in the Middle Ages*. 2d ed. New York: Harcourt Brace and World, 1966. Hoyt discusses Stephen's successes as short-lived, destroyed by the inept kings who followed him.

Poulet, Dom Charles. *A History of the Catholic Church*. Edited by Sidney A. Raemers. St. Louis: B. Herder Book Co., 1940. A solid discussion of the struggle of Stephen I against the pagans and his victory over them.

Thurston, Herbert, and Donald Attwater. *Butler's Lives of the Saints, Complete Edition*. Vol. 3. New York: P. J. Kenedy and Sons, 1956. Extensive discussion of how Stephen I made Hungary a thoroughly Christian country before he died, with special emphasis on his saintly character and application of the Christian virtues to his dealings with the poor and disenfranchised.

John D. Raymer

FLAVIUS STILICHO

Born: c. 360; Eastern Roman Empire, perhaps near Constantinople
Died: August 22, 408; Ravenna, Italy
Area of Achievement: Warfare
Contribution: For a period of some fifteen years, Stilicho acted as the generalissimo of the Western Roman Empire (and as much of the Eastern as he was allowed), repeatedly staving off barbarian assaults on Rome and on Constantinople.

Early Life

Flavius Stilicho's father was a Vandal cavalry officer, his mother a Roman. The Vandals at that time did not have the reputation for ferocity and destruction which they were later to acquire. Nevertheless, it was never forgotten that Stilicho was a "half-barbarian." He was never fully trusted by all of his Greek or Roman civilian masters and colleagues. He began his career as a protector, a member of the personal bodyguard of Theodosius the Great (c. 347-395). Following the normal course of events, he was presumably made a tribune, attached to the imperial general staff, and sent on a diplomatic mission to Persia in 383 or 384.

Shortly after this, an unexpected event took place which catapulted Stilicho firmly into prominence: He married Serena, niece and adopted daughter of Theodosius. It has been suggested that this was a love match instigated by Serena, and though historians have been reluctant to accept this sentimental theory, no more plausible one exists. Stilicho was at that time quite undistinguished, had no important relatives, and was not a likely candidate for a diplomatic marriage. The poet Claudian (c. 370-c. 404), who is admittedly totally biased in favor of Stilicho, nevertheless wrote that his hero surpassed the demigods of antiquity in strength and size; wherever he walked, the crowds moved out of his way. This must have some basis in fact and could explain how the young officer attracted the attention of the emperor's niece.

Naturally, after the marriage promotion was rapid. Stilicho was made "count of the stable," then chief of the imperial guard. He seems to have held independent command in a campaign in Thrace in 392, and from 393 onward he was called *magister utriusque militiae*, meaning "master of both arms," that is, of the infantry and the cavalry. While still firmly under the wing of Theodosius, he had become the approximate equivalent of field marshal, a position from which many earlier and later generals aimed at seizing imperial power. (Stilicho never tried that.) In 394, he marched with Theodosius from the eastern half of the Empire toward Italy, to put down the revolt and usurpation of the general Arbogast and his puppet emperor Eugenius, installed in 388. In early September, 394, the armies of the Eastern and Western Empires clashed at the Battle of the Frigidus River, and after initial failure the easterners won a decisive victory. Both enemy leaders were killed. Theodosius marched toward Rome but died soon after, on January 17, 395. He left Stilicho in charge of both the Eastern army and the pardoned survivors of the Western army. Remote from the control of Constantinople and related by marriage to the imperial house, Stilicho was in a position of unusual power.

Life's Work

One certainty about Stilicho's life is that he did not use his power to the full. He never made himself emperor, though no one was in any position to stop him. For the rest of his life he claimed that Theodosius had appointed him guardian of both his sons, Arcadius (c. 377-408), the Eastern Emperor, and Flavius Honorius (384-423), declared Emperor of the West by his father in 393. It seems that no one else was present at Theodosius' deathbed, so naturally people have been skeptical about Stilicho's mandate. The fact remains that Stilicho always obeyed imperial orders, even foolish ones, and made no move against his former master's children (although Honorius, at least, was widely disliked).

Stilicho was left, however, with at least two problems. One was the division now accepted between the two halves of the Empire. This was dangerous and unproductive, as neither side was willing to help the other very much, and there was always danger of civil war—for example, over the border province of Illyricum, the modern Balkans. Yet neither half of the Empire could afford civil war, for both were hard-pressed by constant waves of barbarian invasion. In the immediate background of all events of Stilicho's life was the disaster of Adrianople, August 9, 378, when the Goths, driven on by fear of the Huns and fury at imperial treachery, had totally destroyed the main imperial army and killed Emperor Valens (c. 328-378). The barbarians then knew that the Romans were not invincible.

Stilicho had a difficult hand to play. In 395, he led his joint army out of Italy toward Constantinople, again threatened by the Goths under Alaric (c. 370-410). No decisive battle was fought, but the Goths withdrew, and Stilicho—with apparently characteristic selflessness—released the Eastern army from his control, returning it to Arcadius. The year following, he led an expedition into the West, along the Rhine River, possibly as a demonstration of force and to "show the flag." In 397, Alaric once again moved into Greece, and Stilicho launched an amphibious expedition against him. Alaric was beaten, but in some unexplained way—there were accusations of treachery—he managed to make an orderly withdrawal. Stilicho then returned to Italy, only to find that North Africa had broken its allegiance to Rome and cut off the corn supply on which Rome depended—and had done so under the pretense of authorization from the Eastern Emperor, whom Stilicho had just rescued. Stilicho dispatched a naval force against North Africa which rapidly brought the province back under control.

In late 401, Alaric invaded Italy; it was the start of a series of barbarian invasions which led to the sack of Rome itself in 410. Alaric and Stilicho fought a bloody battle at Pollenza in 402 which both sides claimed as a victory; Alaric withdrew, however, and was decisively beaten at Verona in the summer of the same year. Once again Alaric escaped; Claudian ascribes this to the poor discipline of Stilicho's auxiliaries. In early 406, a later invasion under one Radagaisus, with a mixed force of less well-disciplined barbarians, was defeated outside Florence, with very few Roman casualties (Claudian claims that there were none at all).

Matters soon worsened: The Rhine froze, Gaul was invaded by hordes of German barbarians (Vandals, Burgundians, Swabians, and Alans), the army of Britain elected the usurper Constantine as emperor and launched a cross-Channel invasion, Alaric reinvaded, and, in 408, Arcadius died, leaving the Eastern Empire insecure and leaderless. Stilicho could hardly have known which way to turn. What he did, in fact, was to leave Gaul to itself; he persuaded the bitterly resentful Roman senate to buy off Alaric with four thousand pounds of gold and dispatch him against Constantine. Stilicho then prepared to leave for Constantinople to take charge of Arcadius' seven-year-old heir, Theodosius II (401-450). Yet these measures were too pragmatic for the Roman people to accept. Thus Stilicho was accused of treachery. Honorius launched a massacre of his supporters: His Hunnish bodyguard was murdered, and Stilicho himself was arrested at Ravenna. It is clear that even then Stilicho could have fought and probably cracked Honorius' stronghold on power. Instead, he obeyed orders and surrendered to execution.

Summary

Flavius Stilicho has long proved a puzzle to historians. It is very tempting to see him as the noble upholder of an impractical and decadent imperial ruling class which rewarded his support and obedience only by murder. There is a kind of justice, in this view, in the sack of Rome by Alaric's Goths two years later. The Roman senate and emperor did not realize how much they had relied on Stilicho until they had killed him. In favor of this view is the unswerving loyalty which Stilicho himself displayed, almost to the point of quixotism.

Yet there are odd features in Stilicho's career. He hardly ever won a major battle, except against the unimportant Radagaisus. Alaric always seemed to slip away from him. Did Stilicho in fact retain a kind of alliance with the Gothic king, who had been his ally at the Frigidus River in 394? Or should Stilicho be seen as essentially a warlord, whose trade was war and whose capital was soldiers? Could it be that Stilicho would not risk casualties and did not particularly want a major victory which would only bring peace? It has also been noted that rivals of Stilicho—such as the commander of the North

African expedition in 408 or Arcadius' main adviser in 395—were inclined to meet with strange accidents or be openly murdered. Stilicho was also very quick to marry his daughters to Honorius and seems to have planned to marry his son into the imperial family also. As a "half-barbarian," he could not be emperor, but his design may have been to have a grandson as ruler over a reunited empire. In this way, he was quite capable of ruthlessness.

The questions are insoluble, but one final point may be made. Stilicho may not have had as much choice as modern historians tend to suppose. Accusations of "letting people off" and military ineptitude rest on the assumption that Roman armies were competent and reliable. After Adrianople, this may not have been the case. Stilicho had continuous trouble in recruiting good Roman troops, and the barbarians he used instead were often badly disciplined and unreliable. He was fencing with a brittle weapon and may in fact have done as well as anyone could expect. Possibly his underlying weakness was something as elementary as a desperate shortage of real Roman drill sergeants.

Bibliography

Bury, John B. *A History of the Later Roman Empire*. London: Macmillan, 1889. Rev. ed. *A History of the Later Roman Empire from the Death of Theodosius I to the Death of Justinian (A.D. 395 to A.D. 565)*. London: Macmillan, 1923. This volume may be considered the nineteenth century alternative to Gibbon, cited below. It is strong on dates and events and determinedly personal in interpretation. Lacks the twentieth century awareness of social forces demonstrated, for example, by Jones, below.

Cameron, Alan D. E. *Claudian: Poetry and Propaganda at the Court of Honorius*. Oxford: Clarendon Press, 1970. This work attempts to distinguish truth from flattery in the work of Stilicho's greatest propagandist. Perhaps by inevitable reaction from its subject, this book takes a severely negative view of Stilicho.

Claudian. *Claudian*. Translated by Maurice Platnauer. New York: G. P. Putnam's Sons, 1922. This edition and translation, in the familiar Loeb Classical Library series, makes it possible for students to see both what data can be extracted from Claudian's poems on Stilicho and how carefully data are at times concealed. The information Claudian does not mean to give is more revealing than his surface intention.

Gibbon, Edward. *The Decline and Fall of the Roman Empire*. 6 vols. New York: E. P. Dutton, 1922-1926. This set of volumes in the Everyman series is only one of innumerable reprints of Gibbon's classic work, first published from 1776 to 1788. In spite of their age, chapters 29 and 30 are well worth reading, for their style and recondite learning. Gibbon succeeded at an early stage in catching the ambiguous quality of Stilicho's achievement.

Isbell, Harold, trans. *The Last Poets of Imperial Rome*. Harmondsworth,

England: Penguin Books, 1971. Among other poems, this volume offers Claudian's *Raptus Proserpiae* (c. A.D. 397) and the *Epithalamium* (A.D. 398) for the marriage of Honorius and Stilicho's daughter Maria. The former poem is valuable as a reminder that there was still an important pagan faction among the Roman aristocracy.

Jones, A. H. M. *The Later Roman Empire 284-602: A Social, Economic, and Administrative Survey*. 3 vols. Oxford: Basil Blackwell, 1964. These volumes provide essential data for considering the complicated social, administrative, and military structures within which Stilicho functioned. This work does not make for easy reading, and careful use of the index and table of contents is advised.

O'Flynn, John M. *Generalissimos of the Western Roman Empire*. Edmonton: University of Alberta Press, 1983. The three chapters of this work devoted to Stilicho give an able summary of what is known and attempt to answer some of the riddles of his career in terms of the power structures of the time. There is some interest in the comparison with Stilicho's successors, who appear to have shed some of his inhibitions and solved some of his problems.

Randers-Pehrson, Justine D. *Barbarians and Romans*. Norman: University of Oklahoma Press, 1983. This work is organized geographically, but the chapters on Milan, Rome, and Ravenna all have relevance to Stilicho's career. Includes good illustrations: for example, a photograph of the monument celebrating the victory at Pollenza, with Stilicho's name carefully removed.

T. A. Shippey

STRABO

Born: 64 or 63 B.C.; Amasia, Pontus, Asia Minor
Died: After A.D. 23; probably Amasia or Rome
Areas of Achievement: Geography and history
Contribution: Building on the work of his predecessors, Strabo wrote a description of the known inhabited world, valuable for its philosophy of geography, its historical digressions, and the current scientific notions it contains. Although not always accurate in details, the seventeen books of the *Geography* stand out for their diverse subjects, encyclopedic scope, and contemporary view of the ancient world at the dawn of the Christian era.

Early Life

Strabo was born at Amasia in Pontus, about ninety kilometers inland from the southeastern shore of the Black Sea. Formerly a royal capital of Pontus, Amasia was located in a deep valley on the Iris River. It was a well-fortified place, with striking mountains towering above the town. Located there were the tombs of the kings of Pontus. Amasia controlled the river valleys and villages about itself, which doubtless contributed to its wealth. It is inferred that Strabo belonged to a rich family that could afford to give their son a good education. Although his lineage was a mixture of Asiatic and Greek, Strabo's training and language were purely Greek.

The area had been conquered by the Romans immediately before Strabo's birth. In the generation before, Mithradates the Great of Pontus had extended the kingdom's borders through Asia Minor, the islands of the Aegean Sea, and the southern and eastern shores of the Black Sea. He fought the Romans Lucius Cornelius Sulla, Lucius Licinius Murena, and Lucullus before succumbing to Pompey the Great. A most formidable foe of Rome, he died about the time Strabo was born.

Strabo thus grew up appreciating both the power of Rome and the legacy of Pontus. His mother's ancestors had been on close terms with the royal house, and one of them, the general Dorylaus Tacticus, had been a friend of King Mithradates V Euergetes. Mithradates the Great patronized Strabo's great-grandfather Lagetas and granduncle Moaphernes, appointing the latter to a governorship. The king also made Dorylaus' nephew the priest of Ma at Comana, a position that gave him power second only to Mithradates himself.

Strabo's education in grammar and rhetoric at Nysa (in southern Asia Minor) included lessons from Aristodemus, who was also the tutor of Pompey's sons. When he was nineteen or twenty years old, he went to Rome and was instructed by Tyrannio, a tutor of Cicero's sons and an expert on geography. It is likely that Strabo got his passion for the subject from this master. Also in Rome, Strabo learned from Xenarchus, who, like Tyrannio, was an Aristotelian. Nevertheless, references throughout the *Geōgraphica* (c. 7 B.C.; *Geography*, 1917-1933) indicate that Strabo himself became a follower of the Stoics, perhaps under the influence of Augustus' teacher and friend Athenodorus. In addition to his early educational trips, Strabo made other visits to Rome, most likely in 35 and 29 B.C.

As a youth, Strabo read widely and became especially enamored of Homer, as shown by his later passionate defense of the epics' historical and geographical accuracy. He also read Herodotus' *Historiai* (c. 425 B.C.; *The History*), which he did not value, and the work of Polybius, which he considered useful and accurate. He became familiar with the historical, scientific, and geographical works of Posidonius, Eratosthenes of Cyrene, Hipparchus, Artemidorus, and Ephorus. In addition, Strabo read the works of the historians of Alexander the Great, especially concerning Alexander's eastern travels.

By adulthood, Strabo had visited a good portion of Asia Minor and made several trips to Rome. He had met influential Romans and Greeks and had been introduced to the best in literature and history—all of which were to influence his later writings.

Life's Work

Probably between 25 and 19 B.C., Strabo resided in Alexandria, Egypt. At the beginning of his sojourn there, he accompanied his friend Aelius Gallus, the Roman prefect of Egypt, on a trip up the Nile River, reaching the border of Ethiopia. His time in Egypt gave him opportunity to observe the country—and perhaps to use the library at Alexandria. Afterward, he returned to Rome for an undetermined amount of time.

Strabo's travels continued through his life and reached as far west as Etruria and as far east as the border of Armenia, south to the northern edge of Ethiopia, and north to the Black Sea. Around 26, Strabo wrote a historical work, now known as *Historical Memoirs*, none of which has survived, although Plutarch and Flavius Josephus refer to it. It comprised forty-three books, covering the period from the destruction of Corinth and Carthage in 146 B.C. to (perhaps) the Battle of Actium in 31 B.C., thus forming a continuation of Polybius' history.

Strabo's magnum opus was the *Geography*, a work in seventeen books describing the inhabited world of the three continents Europe, Asia, and Africa. Its scope included mathematical, physical, political, and historical aspects of geography. His was a general treatise on the subject: the first ancient attempt to synthesize all known geographical knowledge.

The first two books of the *Geography* deal with the history of the discipline, including attacks on the ideas of Eratosthenes and others, whom Strabo considered to have made mistakes in their published works on geography.

He discourses at length on Homer, naming him the first geographer. (Strabo was often at pains to "prove Homer right" and saw the ship catalog in the second book of the *Iliad*, transcribed c. 800 B.C., as preserving historical locales and the voyages of Odysseus and Jason's quest for the Golden Fleece as actual events.) Strabo also suggests that since the inhabited world which he knows only makes up one-third of the temperate zone, it is likely that other continents exist.

Apparently not relying on Roman writers, Strabo addresses Spain in book 3, drawing mainly on Greek sources in his description of the natural resources and physical traits of the country. This book also makes mention of the mythical island home of Geryon and the Tin Islands, which Strabo does not recognize as connected with Britain in any way.

Relying heavily on the *Commentaries* (written 52-45 B.C.) of Julius Caesar, Strabo wrote the fourth book about Britain, France, and the Alps. Although he used Caesar's description of the Gaulish tribes, for some reason Strabo ignored his descriptions of the dimensions of Britain, thereby making the island much broader and shorter than it actually is. Strabo believed that Ireland lay to the north of Britain. His description of the Alps is somewhat accurate, including discussions of trade, alpine passes, and avalanches.

Since maps of Italy and the surrounding islands were common in his day, Strabo probably had one before him while writing about this area in his fifth and sixth books. In addition, Strabo was personally familiar with Italy and aware of several Greek and Roman writers on the subject. Impressive in this section is his description of Mount Vesuvius, which he describes as having every appearance of a volcano, although it had not erupted in living memory. His words were oddly appropriate, for Vesuvius erupted in A.D. 79. Strabo never visited Sicily, so his description is not as accurate as that of Italy proper, but his descriptions of the volcanic activity of Mount Etna and the Aeolian Islands are well done.

Northern Europe forms the bulk of the seventh book, and the lack of information handicapping Strabo is very evident in this section. It is strange that Strabo ignores things which the Romans knew about these regions: the amber trade and the testimony of Herodotus about the region. When he describes the area north of the Black Sea, however, his accuracy increases, probably because of Mithradates' recent conquests in the area.

The next three books deal with Greece and its islands and is surprisingly lacking in geographical information; Strabo probably assumed that his readers were familiar with the area, and Strabo knew little of it at first hand. In addition, his preoccupation with identifying sites mentioned in the Homeric catalog of ships skewed Strabo's account here. Finally, Greece's diminished status in the period left little outstanding to describe. Many cities lay in ruin, while others were reduced to the status of sleepy villages in Strabo's lifetime. His interest in volcanoes does not flag in this section, which describes the volcanic activity of mountains at Thera and near Methone.

Books 11 through 16 deal with Asia. Strabo's accounts of Asia Minor—especially the northern sections—are rather accurate, for he had seen much of it, his home being in Pontus. The section includes a discussion of the site of Homeric Troy. Strabo believed that the Caspian Sea connected to the northern ocean, and even describes what a sailor would see as he sailed southward into this arm of the surrounding sea. Strabo admits that he knows nothing about the extreme north of Asia, and, although he knows the name of silk producers, he does not mention the silk trade at all, although it had already become quite important. He provides an interesting account of India, derived from the lost works of those who accompanied Alexander the Great to that land. Strabo concentrates on the customs of the inhabitants there—at the expense of the actual geography of the territory. Africa, the subject of the seventeenth book, is well described along the Nile because of Strabo's personal acquaintance with the territory. He describes the antiquities of the land and gives an account of the Ethiopians. The rest of Africa is not as well delineated; in fact, Strabo reduced its size by more than two-thirds, having no idea how far to the south it actually extended. In fact, Strabo seems to have ignored or not to have known of the works of his younger contemporary Juba II, King of Mauretania, who had written extensively on North African geography and history.

Strabo died some time after completing the *Geography*, possibly in his homeland. His acquaintance with eminent Romans of his time and the admiration for the Roman Empire which he consistently shows in his writing could not ensure instant success at Rome for his work, which came to be appreciated only by later generations.

Summary

Strabo said that his work would be useful to administrators and generals, calling geography a practical and philosophical science. He thus avoids tedious listings of the insignificant in favor of major points relating to places under discussion. His work is encyclopedic and comprehensive—a storehouse of information about his world.

The date and place of composition are uncertain. The latest date in it is A.D. 23, but few believe that he began his work in his eighties. It has been argued that he composed it while in his fifties, around 7 B.C., and later revised, for it lacks references to events between 3 B.C. and A.D. 19. Rome seems a likely place for its publication, but some have argued that Strabo returned to Amasia to write it, because Pliny the Elder and Ptolemy ignored the work. Had it been published in Rome, one would expect that it would have gained some attention. In fact, however, there are only a few minor references to the *Geography* before Stephanus of Byzantium made frequent use of it at the end of the fifth century A.D. Other possibilities for Strabo's residence at the end of his life include the eastern Mediterranean region or Naples.

Although Strabo boasts of his wide travels, he evidently did not make detailed studies of all the places he visited. He probably saw Cyrene in Libya only as he sailed by and likely did not even visit Athens. In Italy, he kept to the main roads leading to and from Rome.

Strabo assumed a spherical Earth at the center of the universe. An island surrounded by ocean, it was admissible of being divided into five zones, uninhabitable at the extreme north because of the cold and at the extreme south because of the heat. Aside from assuming a geocentric universe, Strabo made a number of mistakes, mainly resulting from the lack of accurate observations and reliable sources of information. Where data were available, they were often misleading. As a result, he distorted the shape of the whole of the Mediterranean and Europe. Other mistakes include the assumption that the northern coast of Africa was practically a straight line, and that a line from the Pillars of Hercules to the Strait of Messina was equidistant from Europe and Africa. Also in error are his statements that the Pyrenees form a line from north to south, that Cape St. Vincent is the most westerly point of Europe, and that eastern Crete does not extend much to the east of Sunium Promontorium (when in fact four-fifths of the entire island lie east of it). Describing Palestine, he asserted that the Jordan River flowed into the Mediterranean, being navigable for ships sailing east from the sea.

In spite of its inaccuracies, Strabo's *Geography* is the most important geographical treatise from the ancient world. Its great value lies not only in his own observations—which, when firsthand, are accurate and lucid—but also in the preservation of so many previous authors whose work it summarizes, especially Eratosthenes and Posidonius.

Bibliography

Bunbury, E. H. *A History of Ancient Geography Among the Greeks and Romans from the Earliest Ages Till the Fall of the Roman Empire.* New York: Dover Publications, 1959. Originally published in 1879, this work is the standard handbook on the subject of ancient geography. Putting Strabo in historical perspective, it has four long sections on the *Geography*, with detailed discussions of each book, commenting on Strabo's sources, errors, and value. With maps, notes, and an index.

Dilke, O. A. W. *Greek and Roman Maps.* Ithaca, N.Y.: Cornell University Press, 1985. Evidence for cartography in the ancient world, from the work in Mesopotamia to the Renaissance. Chapters on ancient Greece and geographical writers, the latter containing a section on Strabo: his cartographic terms, construction of a globe, contribution to mapmaking, use of myth, and lack of scientific accuracy. Contains numerous maps, charts, photographs, notes, appendices, a bibliography, and an index.

Keane, John. *The Evolution of Geography: A Sketch of the Rise and Prog-*
ress of Geographical Knowledge from the Earliest Times to the First Cir-
cumnavigation of the Globe. London: Edward Stanford, 1899. The chapter
on ancient geography covers material from the Bible to Ptolemy. Substantial discussion of Strabo and his contribution, including his sources, life,
travels, and observations. With maps and an index.

Kish, George. *A Source Book in Geography.* Cambridge, Mass.: Harvard
University Press, 1978. Selections from Strabo and other ancient geogra-
phers, putting the *Geography* in context. Casts light on the geographical
theory. Includes selections from Plato, Aristotle, Greek travelers'
reports, Greek heliocentric theory, and selections from Strabo on geography in general, the inhabited world, changes in the earth, volcanoes, Asian
lands.

Magie, David. *Roman Rule in Asia Minor to the End of the Third Century*
After Christ. 2 vols. Princeton, N.J.: Princeton University Press, 1950.
Exhaustive historical discussion of Strabo's homeland. Essential for under-
standing the geographer's background. A chapter on "The Rise of the
Power of Pontus," chapters on Mithradates, Pompey, and the years of
Strabo's youth. Told from the Roman perspective, it is dependent on
Strabo's *Geography* as the copious notes show.

Richards, G. C. "Strabo: The Anatolian Who Failed of Roman Recognition." *Greece and Rome* 10 (1940): 79-90. Brief introductory piece about
the major events of Strabo's life, including short discussions of the controversies involved. Covers his visits to Rome, dates of his works, location
of his retirement, and his Roman connections. Also discusses the importance of his Stoicism and his use of sources, both scientific and poetic
(Homer).

Strabo. *The "Geography" of Strabo with an English Translation.* Translated
by Horace Leonard Jones. 8 vols. London: Heinemann, 1917-1933. Contains the complete Greek text and English translation, with notes and bibliography. Includes diagrams illustrating complex mathematical discussions, maps, and index. Useful introduction discusses Strabo's life and
works. Identifies the sources of Strabo's many quotations, contains useful
cross-references, and points out textual variations.

Thompson, J. Oliver. *History of Ancient Geography.* New York: Biblo and
Tannen, 1965. Originally published in 1948 as an update to Bunbury, this
work is arranged chronologically, with an emphasis on theory and regions
rather than individual authors. Numerous useful maps and pertinent chapters on geography in the Roman Republic, theory in the same period, and
the great days of the Roman Empire. With a brief section on Strabo. Contains an index and addenda.

Tozer, H. F. *Selections from Strabo.* Oxford: Clarendon Press, 1893. Of great value for its fifty-page introduction on Strabo's life and works, including estimates of his style, interests, audience, defects, methods, sources, text, and date. Excellent introductions to and commentary on the most important sections of the *Geography*. With notes, maps, and an index.

Daniel B. Levine

SU TUNG-P'O
Su Shih

Born: December 19, 1036; Mei-shan, Szechwan, China
Died: July 28, 1101; Ch'ang-chou, China
Areas of Achievement: Government, literature, and art
Contribution: One of China's most famous poets and scholars, Su Tung-p'o
was also an important government official during the Sung Dynasty (960-
1279). He figured prominently in the political controversies surrounding
the attempted imposition of state capitalist programs.

Early Life

Su Shih (he took Su Tung-p'o as his pen name) was the eldest son of an
upper-class, landowning family living in the western Yangtze Province of
Szechwan during China's Sung Dynasty. His clan was one of the most distinguished literary families in the history of China. He, his father, Su Hsün, and
his younger brother, Su Tse-yu, all were famous scholars and government
officials. In the eleventh century, Szechwan Province produced a high percentage of scholar-officials, noted for their cosmopolitan prose and poetry. Su Tung-p'o grew up in a cultured, sophisticated home which prepared
its sons to take the imperial civil service examinations. Success in these exams would guarantee for the family official positions and access to wealth and
power.

Su Tung-p'o and his brother Su Tse-yu were both brilliant students. Lifelong friends, their careers in scholarship and government were inextricably
linked. Their personalities were different but complementary: Su Tse-yu was
serious, stable, and cautious whereas Su Tung-p'o was impetuous, volatile,
and excitable. They stayed in continuous contact with each other, even when
their official duties separated them by hundreds of miles, communicating in
poetry at least monthly throughout their lives.

In 1056 the brothers went to K'ai-feng in northern China to take the imperial exams. This city was the metropolis of China, cloaked in imperial
grandeur. The wealth, talent, and beauty of the nation centered on the court.
The brothers were not dazzled by the city's splendor, however, and passed
the exams with high honors. Su Tung-p'o's main examination essay, which
developed the principle of simplicity and leniency in the administration of a
country, caught the attention of the imperial examiner and the emperor himself. On April 14, 1057, at the age of twenty, Su Tung-p'o was officially designated a *chin-shih* (the highest ranking academic honor), second in a class of
388 successful candidates. He thus achieved instant fame and recognition as
one of the leading scholars of China. Normally he would have entered immediately into government service, but his mother died during the examinations
and he had to go into a compulsory period of twenty-seven months of mourn-

ing. He already was known as a literary genius, however, and he emerged from the mourning ready to assume his public life.

Life's Work

Su Tung-p'o's life was notable for three reasons. First, he was a brilliant, if somewhat impetuous, scholar-bureaucrat who figured prominently in the political disputes of the early Sung Dynasty. Because he took controversial stances on important issues, he frequently found himself in serious conflict with his bureaucratic superiors and opponents. Second, he was one of China's most gifted poets and literary figures. His contemporaries compared him to China's greatest men of letters, and succeeding generations have continued to honor his genius. He was equally versatile in prose and poetry, writing in a beautiful classical style. He experimented with a common form of poetry, the *tz'u*, which had been previously confined to love songs composed in cabarets, and turned it into a vehicle for discourse on Buddhist and Taoist philosophy. Third, he developed a theory of calligraphy and painting resembling modern impressionism. The purpose of painting, according to Su Tung-p'o, was to paint the inner spirit rather than the form of an object. The painting should reflect not only the spirit of the object but also the artist's inner essence.

In the early phase of his career, from 1062 to 1079, he achieved fame as both a government bureaucrat and a poet. After a brief posting as a minor provincial official, he returned to the capital (K'ai-feng) in 1064. Thereafter, he and his brother were swept into the center of a political storm surrounding the efforts of the statesman Wang An-shih (1021-1086) to reform Chinese government and society.

To most of its inhabitants, the Sung Dynasty seemed peaceful, prosperous, and humane. China had agricultural wealth, busy commercial cities, and great public works such as canals, walls, and roads. Beneath the surface, however, lay chronic national difficulties. Barbarian tribes in the north and west constantly threatened invasion, forcing the Sung to maintain large armies, which overtaxed the imperial treasury. Despite the country's apparent productivity, the government rarely had sufficient revenues to meet its obligations. It was clear to many officials, if not the majority, that fundamental reform was necessary to save the dynasty. Yet the questions of the shape the reforms should take and who should lead them caused acrimonious bureaucratic conflicts.

Between 1069 and 1077, Wang An-shih served as the chief imperial adviser and initiated institutional reforms designed to change fundamental fiscal, economic, and bureaucratic practices. First, he instituted state capitalist schemes to increase government revenues. One such program, for example, provided government loans to farmers at an actual interest rate of 30 percent. Second, he levied numerous new taxes. Finally, he established methods of registration to regiment and control the people. The *pao-chia* system, for example, organized the people into groups of ten and sixty, from which able-bodied men were called up for military training and duty. While these reforms seemed capable of resolving some of the government's fiscal woes, the methods by which they were implemented alarmed Su Tung-p'o and his colleagues.

In essence, Su Tung-p'o contended that Wang's methods were too authoritarian and resulted in exploitation of commoners by arbitrary central officials. Su Tung-p'o risked his career by writing a nine-thousand-word letter to the emperor in June, 1071, criticizing Wang's reforms, which had been authorized by the emperor. He was particularly concerned about the farm-loan program. Participation in this was supposedly voluntary, but in order to please Wang, provincial and local bureaucrats frequently forced peasants to take out loans even if they did not need them. When Wang's critics noted this fact, he had them demoted or removed from office. Su Tung-p'o's memorial argued that, contrary to what the emperor had been told, public opinion was solidly against Wang. He reminded the emperor that his power derived from the people and that he ignored their will at his peril. Unfettered dissent, he claimed, was vital to the health of the government. The emperor did not take his advice, however, and demoted Su Tung-p'o from the capital to the Hangchow area, where he served as governor of three cities between 1071 and 1080. Eventually, in 1076, Wang was forced out of office, but the doctrinal disputes fired by his reform continued to plague Su Tung-p'o and China for the remainder of the Sung era.

The years Su Tung-p'o spent in the Hangchow area saw his greatest activity as a poet. His distaste for the internecine political squabbles in the capital drove him to seek solace in his poetry, in which he explored the beauties of nature and the highest reaches of the human spirit. By this time, Su Tung-p'o had assumed his mature temperament and appearance. From his portraits, he had a muscular build, stood five feet, eight inches in height, and had a dominating face with prominent cheekbones and an imposing forehead. He wore a long, tapering mandarin beard and regarded the world through wide-set, brilliant eyes. His chief personality fault was his propensity to speak his mind too freely among people who had no loyalty to him.

He loved the Hangchow area and wrote such beautiful poetry about it that he has been regarded ever since as the city's poet laureate. It was there, between 1071 and 1074, that he mastered and transformed the *tz'u* form of poetry. This poetic form had originated in houses of entertainment (disguised brothels) where female entertainers sang songs arranged in such a way that each succeeding line contained a definite number of syllables. In time, the *tz'u* became an honorable form of literary expression. Su Tung-p'o took the lead in transforming the *tz'u* from love poetry to a vehicle fit to express the highest sentiments of the human spirit. He freed the *tz'u* from its sentimentality and infused it with power and grace.

Yet the poet's life was not untouched by strife in these years, for political disputes about Wang An-shih's reforms continued to rage and Su Tung-p'o could not ignore them. He wrote numerous poems of protest satirizing the government officials. He did not overtly criticize the Sung leadership or advocate rebellion, but his subtle satire thoroughly annoyed his enemies. In all, his poetry, whether *tz'u* or protest, crackles with life and depth. Eventually, in 1079, he was impeached for his veiled attack on officialdom, and he was exiled in 1080 to a small, poor town near Hankow on the Yangtze. By then, however, he had proved his administrative skills, saving the city of Süchou from a disastrous flood in 1077 by building huge dikes, and ruling equitably over a series of districts. His literary reputation and his commitment to virtue were also well established.

The next period of his life, from 1080 to 1093, continued this pattern of official success followed by degradation and demotion. During his periods of demotion and exile, he studied Buddhist and Taoist philosophy, which profoundly shaped his writing and thinking. He was one of the first Confucian scholars to incorporate these ideas into the official philosophy and he played a leading role in creating Neo-Confucian philosophy, which dominated Chinese life into the twentieth century.

Between 1084 and 1093, Su Tung-p'o's party was in power at the capital, and he rose to the post of secretary to the emperor. Nevertheless, he managed eventually to lose his job, since his propensity to attack corruption even within his own party gained for him many enemies.

He remained close to the seat of power, however, until a new emperor ascended the throne in the autumn of 1093 and Su Tung-p'o's enemies regained power. Thereupon he was again dismissed from office and was eventually exiled to the far southern island of Hainan, from which he returned only in time to die in July of 1101. This last phase of his career, from 1094 to 1101, was the saddest time of his life.

Summary

The Sung Dynasty was noted for its versatile intellectuals, and Su Tung-p'o stands out as one of the most prominent. His position in history is secured by his poems and prose and by his courageous stand for his political and ethical principles. Although he was a respected patriot and hero, his life provides a study of national degeneration through factional strife. His party's clash with Wang An-shih set in motion the forces that undermined the dynasty, as ineffective, corrupt administrators controlled the dynasty and sapped its vitality.

He is best remembered, however, as a poet, writer, and artist. He incorporated Buddhist philosophy into Confucianism and was the central figure in the formulation of the theory of "literati painting" as a coherent body of doctrine. His fundamental contention was that a painting should be a revelation of the nature of the artist who painted it, and of his mood and feelings at the moment of creation. Under the influence of Buddhism, Su Tung-p'o delved into problems of the mind and the universe. He believed that nature was spiritually alive and that an artist should catch that inner spirit in painting. The essence of things had to be seized by the eye and the imagination. To paint a fish, for example, the artist must imagine swimming with it in the water and share its reactions to current and storm. Only then could he paint the salmon leaping the rapids. Su Tung-p'o's theories informed the Chinese approach to painting thereafter.

Su Tung-p'o ranks as one of China's greatest poets, painters, and prose writers. He also was an able administrator, containing floods, building causeways, and struggling against bureaucratic corruption. He was one of China's greatest men of letters as well as a great man of action.

Bibliography
Bush, Susan. *The Chinese Literati on Painting: Su Shih (1037-1101) to Tung Ch'i-ch'ang (1555-1636)*. Cambridge, Mass.: Harvard University Press, 1971. This monograph describes Su Tung-p'o's incorporation of Buddhist metaphysics into his theory and practice of painting and calligraphy. While the focus is on painting, it provides an important investigation of Su Tung-p'o's intellectual and artistic achievements.
Chaffee, John W. *The Thorny Gates of Learning in Sung China*. New York: Cambridge University Press, 1985. Su Tung-p'o, like his scholar-bureaucrat friends and enemies, entered China's governmental elite through the examination system. This book provides a social history of the examinations and details Su Tung-p'o's experience with them, as both a student and a chief examiner.
Li, Dun J. *The Ageless Chinese: A History*. New York: Charles Scribner's Sons, 1978. A general survey of Chinese history, this well-written book provides a sensitive account of the history of the Sung Dynasty. Li details the cultural movements of the era, discusses the emergence of Neo-Confucianism and *tz'u* poetry, and places Su Tung-p'o in larger historical context.
Lin Yutang. *The Gay Genius: The Life and Times of Su Tungpo*. New York: John Day Co., 1947. This book remains the best biography of Su Tung-p'o in English. It is clearly written and is based on original Chinese sources. Lin feels a strong attraction for Su Tung-p'o but presents a balanced account of his life and ideas. An indispensable source.
Meskill, John, ed. *Wang An-shih: Practical Reformer?* Boston: D. C. Heath and Co., 1963. This book presents the clash of historical opinion regarding Wang An-shih's personality and reforms. It excerpts Wang's ideas in his own words, the judgments of his Sung critics and supporters, and modern

reappraisals. There is no more convenient book for placing the Wang An-shih/Su Tung-p'o controversy in perspective.

Wright, Arthur F., ed. *The Confucian Persuasion*. Stanford, Calif.: Stanford University Press, 1960. This is a book of essays on various aspects of Confucian thought and practice. It includes an article on Confucian elements in the Chinese theory of painting, which places Su Tung-p'o in perspective. James F. Cahill argues in his essay that Su Tung-p'o was the central figure in formulating the theory of literati painting.

_____. *Studies in Chinese Thought*. Chicago: University of Chicago Press, 1953. A series of essays on various aspects of Chinese thought, this volume contains a valuable article by W. T. deBary on Neo-Confucianism. In it, deBary labels Su Tung-p'o "the outstanding literary figure of his time" and fixes his place in the history of Neo-Confucianism.

Loren W. Crabtree

SUGER

Born: 1081; Saint-Denis, near Paris
Died: January 13, 1151; Saint-Denis
Areas of Achievement: Government and architecture
Contribution: A lover of peace, order, and political harmony, Suger defined and popularized the centralizing and peacekeeping mission of the Capetian monarchy, increasing its prestige and assisting its rise to dominance in medieval France. As abbot of Saint-Denis he rebuilt the abbey church according to principles which make him the founder of the Gothic style.

Early Life

Suger was born of villein parentage in or near Saint-Denis, just outside the city of Paris. He entered the monastery as a student in 1091; one of his fellow pupils, who became his lifelong friend and patron, was Louis Capet, afterward King Louis VI (Louis the Fat). Suger was an outstanding student, practical and efficient as well as intelligent. He described himself as "small and frail," but he was also energetic and untiring. He was amiable and discreet, with a talent for peacemaking; he was also an enthusiastic defender of the privileges and prestige of his own monastery. In 1106, he was made secretary to abbot Adam.

Saint-Denis was a royal monastery, and many of the kings of France were buried there. It possessed relics of the Passion of Christ and of Saint Dionysius, the apostle of France, but much of its prestige came from the belief, historically untrue, that this Saint Dionysius was identical with Dionysius the Areopagite, the disciple of Saint Paul mentioned in Acts 17:34 (a further misunderstanding, which was to have important consequences, was the belief that Dionysius was the author of a mystical treatise, now known to be an anonymous composition of the fifth century and referred to as Pseudo-Dionysius, proclaiming the manifestation of God to human beings in the form of light). The king and his entourage often lodged at the monastery, allowing the abbot and his staff proximity to the center of royal politics.

In 1109, the monastery obtained from the king the right to hold the famous Lendit fair, to which merchants came from great distances; during the event, the monastery displayed its relics to crowds of pilgrims, and the fair became an important religious as well as commercial occasion.

In 1107, Suger was made provost of one of the monastery's dependent houses in Normandy; there he saw at first hand both Norman experiments in church architecture and the efficient organization of the duchy under Duke Henry Beauclerc (who was also King of England), the most effective feudal overlord of the time. In 1118, he was sent by King Louis on the first of a series of missions to the papal court. The Investiture Controversy between the Papacy and Emperor Henry V had turned into open warfare, and the

King of France was a strong supporter of the Papacy. Suger was in Rome in 1122 when this conflict was at last resolved by the agreement known as the Concordat of Worms; it was there that he received the news that the monks of Saint-Denis had elected him abbot upon the death of Adam. He did not return to France at once but spent several months visiting pilgrimage churches in Italy. Pope Calixtus II summoned him to the papal court again in order to make him a cardinal but died before Suger reached Rome. His future was to lie with the royal rather than the papal court.

Life's Work

The first great crisis of his career came in 1124, when the emperor, seeking vengeance for the French king's support of the Papacy, invaded France. Louis convened an assembly of clerics and lay magnates at Saint-Denis and there, in an elaborate ceremony organized by Suger, took from the altar the banner of Saint Dionysius and formally declared himself a vassal of the saint. He then appealed to the assembled dignitaries to join him in defense of the Church and the realm. This appeal succeeded even among barons who were the king's rivals, and the appearance of Louis and his vassals in arms persuaded the emperor, who had anticipated no such united opposition, to depart without giving battle.

In gratitude for the saint's support during the invasion of 1124, the king gave the monastery entire control of the Lendit fair. Suger hoped to make Saint-Denis a major pilgrimage center during the season of the fair; in this he was successful, and the church rapidly became overburdened by the crowds of pilgrims coming to see the relics. He devised an ambitious program of rebuilding, using the profits from the fair; he also reorganized the estates of the abbey to make them more profitable, replacing customary fixed rents by a percentage of the annual yield and encouraging more intensive agriculture.

Suger's intention to rebuild the church took shape soon after 1124, but actual work did not begin until 1137. Two factors, in addition to his close attendance upon the king, seem to have been responsible for the delay. One was a reaffirmation of his own sense of religious mission. Suger had long been an admirer of Saint Bernard of Clairvaux and had come under increasing pressure from Bernard to reform Saint-Denis on Cistercian principles. The monastery's wealth and the crowds of courtiers and pilgrims had eroded much of its discipline and made the traditional monastic life almost impossible. There is a famous letter of Bernard's in which he sneers at an unnamed abbot whom he had seen riding in state with sixty horsemen attending him; this is usually taken as a denunciation of Suger, intended to shame him into reform, but it may well have been aimed instead at his predecessor Adam, whose sense of religious vocation seems to have been less intense than Suger's. In 1127, Suger undertook the reform of the monastery, reaffirming the Benedictine rule but stopping short of imposing the full rigors of Cistercian discipline. This task occupied much of his time for the next several years.

In 1137, Louis VI died and was succeeded by his son Louis VII, a young man of hotter temperament, who wanted independence from his father's policies and advisers. Suger lost his influence at court until harsh experience proved that he was indispensable. In the meantime he began the building campaign that was to revolutionize medieval architecture.

After centuries of decay, destruction, and restoration, disappointingly little of Suger's building remains today; what does remain, however, as interpreted from his own writings, allows one to understand the magnitude of his achievement. The western front of Saint-Denis, the first part of the work to be undertaken, is still Norman in appearance; there is an unprecedented rose window, however, flooding the interior with light, and the architectural elements are arranged to emphasize the central doorway, identified by an inscription as the gate of Heaven. The church, built according to rule in harmonious proportion, is a model of the Kingdom of Heaven. Church architecture was said to have an anagogical purpose, guiding the beholder by visible signs to the perception of divine reality. This purpose becomes more explicit in the choir at the east end of the church, a theological treatise in architecture putting into practice the mystical vision of Pseudo-Dionysius. The cross-ribbed vault and pointed arch, both of which had been known to the Normans but not combined by them, are employed together for the first time to allow a maximum of height with a minimum of masonry, dissolving the walls and filling the space with stained glass; the interior columns radiate from a central point to avoid obstructing the light entering through the windows.

The divine light, according to Pseudo-Dionysius, does not appear directly to human beings; rather, it shines "through a veil" of created objects. Suger therefore made his windows translucent, not transparent. Some are plain gray (grisaille); others are brightly colored "sermons in glass" illustrating biblical passages important to Dionysian theology.

Suger then decided to rebuild the nave in the same style as the choir, but the pace of construction slowed in 1147 when Louis VII decided to take part in the Second Crusade. Suger attempted to dissuade him, arguing that his absence would be used by the barons as an opportunity for violence and plunder. He could not, however, change the king's mind. Instead, Louis appointed him regent, and Suger was effectively ruler of France for two years during the king's absence. He governed firmly, suppressing a baronial revolt aimed at deposing the absent king. When Louis returned in 1149, his crusade a humiliating failure, he gave Suger the title "father of his country" in recognition of his services. Though approaching seventy, Suger determined to renew the crusade himself, financing it out of the revenues of Saint-Denis, but he died before he could embark for the East.

Summary

Suger wrote four books, which are the principal sources for the knowledge of his career and policies. His biographies of Louis VI and Louis VII (the latter unfinished) are masterpieces of medieval biography, but there is no complete English translation of either. Two others, *De rebus in administratione sua gestis* (the accomplishments of his administration) and *De liber alter de consecratione ecclesiae Sancti Dionysii* (*Abbot Suger on the Abbey Church of St. Denis and Its Art Treasures*, 1946), are accounts of his career as abbot and of the rebuilding of the church. While he shows considerable modesty in writing about himself, one would occasionally like to see him through someone else's eyes. There is no doubt, however, that he is one of the founding fathers of the medieval French monarchy. The kings might on their own have pursued some of the policies which he advocated; there is no evidence, however, that they had considered them, perceived them clearly, or would have followed them systematically. Suger encouraged the kings to take seriously the promise of their coronation oath to protect the poor and the helpless and to do justice; he urged them to invited the barons themselves to seek justice at the king's court in return for accepting the obligations of vassalage. He saw in the ties of lord and vassal an orderly framework within which disputes could be resolved by conciliation rather than violence: An ordered hierarchical society was the earthly image of the Kingdom of Heaven.

The impact of his other great achievement, the architecture of Saint-Denis, was even more widely felt than his political artistry. The Gothic style spread rapidly from Saint-Denis to Paris, inspiring the larger-scale use and refinement of its techniques in the great cathedral of Notre-Dame and then around the Île-de-France (at Chartres, for example) and elsewhere, sometimes as the official style of the French monarchy, sometimes as an advance messenger glorifying French culture by its own intrinsic merits. Suger was buried in Saint-Denis, but his tomb was desecrated during the French Revolution. In one sense, however, every Gothic cathedral is his monument, and his work makes him the medieval figure whose influence is most widely felt and most highly visible today.

Bibliography

Crosby, S. M. *The Abbey of Saint-Denis*. New Haven, Conn.: Yale University Press, 1942. Discusses the construction history of Saint-Denis, including Suger's building campaigns, as revealed by archaeological investigation; good on details but somewhat outdated in its interpretation of their relationships. Indispensable for tracing the fate of Suger's work through centuries of neglect, vandalism, and overenthusiastic restoration.

Fawtier, Robert. *The Capetian Kings of France*. New York: St. Martin's Press, 1960. A translation of a French work originally published in 1941. Discusses the French monarchy as an institution, with chapters focusing on topics rather than developing a narrative history. References to Suger are scattered throughout, and his overall contribution is difficult to assemble. Nevertheless, this is the best work of its kind.

Kelly, Amy. *Eleanor of Aquitaine and the Four Kings*. Cambridge, Mass.: Harvard University Press, 1950. A detailed, thoroughly researched, well-written popular history, frequently reissued in paperback. Contains an extensive discussion of Suger's attempts to exert a positive influence on Louis VII at the time of his marriage to Eleanor, his unfortunate crusade, and the breakup of his marriage. The focus of the book is on personalities rather than institutions or ideas.

Male, Émile. *Religious Art in France of the Thirteenth Century*. London: E. P. Dutton, 1913. Still one of the great classics of art history, this volume initiated the modern study of Gothic art as theologically programmed visual sermons. It contains no systematic discussion of Saint-Denis but analyzes the themes of its sculpture and stained glass in relation to those of other Gothic churches.

Panofsky, Erwin. *Abbot Suger on the Abbey Church of Saint-Denis and Its Art Treasures*. Princeton, N.J.: Princeton University Press, 1946. A translation of Suger's account of his building campaigns, with a long introduction which is now the starting point for the study of Gothic architecture as an expression of religious symbolism. There is not much attention to the revolutionary engineering techniques of Gothic building, because Suger himself makes little mention of them.

_____. *Gothic Architecture and Scholasticism*. New York: Latrobe Books, 1951. An elaboration and expansion of the ideas contained in Panofsky's earlier work, relating Suger's intellectual and religious objective at Saint-Denis to the planning and execution of other Gothic buildings; Panofsky makes clear for the first time the systematic and deliberate connection between Scholastic philosophy and Gothic architecture as logical, ordered intellectual systems.

Petit-Dutaillis, Charles. *The Feudal Monarchy in France and England from the Tenth to the Thirteenth Century*. London: Routledge and Kegan Paul, 1936. A translation of an important French work, this volume is older than Fawtier's translation, but more readable and narrative in its approach. A comparative study of the two major feudal monarchies and the influence of Norman feudalism upon both. There is considerable attention to the lessons Suger drew from his Norman experience, which he urged the King of France to apply within his own territories.

Rockwell, Anne. *Glass, Stones, and Crown: The Abbé Suger and the Building of Saint-Denis*. New York: Atheneum Publishers, 1968. The only book in English which claims to be specifically a biography of Suger, but it is apparently aimed at a juvenile audience. A brief popularizing account, readable but superficial, containing no original research or analysis.

Von Simson, Otto. *The Gothic Cathedral: Origins of Gothic Architecture and the Medieval Concept of Order.* 2d ed. Princeton, N.J.: Princeton University Press, 1962. A very thorough treatment, taking into account all previous scholarship, much of it in other languages. There are two long chapters on Suger, one on his career, one on the rebuilding of Saint-Denis. Von Simson emphasizes the intellectual consistency between Suger the statesman and Suger the builder. This volume is the definitive work on Suger's church as an embodiment of the ideas of Pseudo-Dionysius, and on the influence of Saint-Denis on other major French Gothic buildings.

Robert I. Willman

LUCIUS CORNELIUS SULLA

Born: 138 B.C.; Rome
Died: 78 B.C.; Puteoli
Areas of Achievement: Government and warfare
Contribution: Sulla played an extremely important historical role in the transformation of the Roman Republic into the Roman Empire. While attempting to prevent others from using force to influence Roman politics, Sulla became the first Roman to use the military to gain a political end.

Early Life

Lucius Cornelius Sulla was born into an old Roman patrician family in 138 B.C. Although not much is known of his youth, Sulla did receive an excellent education in the Greek and Roman classics. He grew to be a handsome man with golden red hair and sharp piercing blue eyes. Sulla had a very pale complexion, and a severe skin condition badly scarred his face. Because his family had little wealth and his father left him nothing when he died, Sulla had to live on the income from a relatively small investment. As a consequence of his modest means, Sulla lived in a small apartment in one of the less desirable neighborhoods of Rome, a circumstance he found demeaning. To an ambitious patrician, wealth was a necessary prerequisite to participation in politics.

Sulla's life changed, however, when he inherited the estates of both his stepmother and his mistress, allowing him to pursue his dream of public service. Although Rome had been at war with Jugurtha in North Africa since 111, the Roman army had not made much progress toward victory. In 108, Gaius Marius was elected consul for the following year, and the people voted to transfer the command of the war from Quintus Caecilius Metellus to Marius. In the same election, they elected Sulla quaestor and chose him to serve under Marius.

During his years of military service in Africa, Sulla proved himself an able and courageous soldier, popular with common soldiers as well as officers. Although Marius was more successful against Jugurtha than Metellus had been, he was unable to capture the elusive enemy leader. Sulla was entrusted with the task of convincing Bocchus (King of Mauretania and father-in-law of Jugurtha) to betray Jugurtha to the Romans. Through skillful diplomacy, Sulla was able to win the friendship of Bocchus, capture Jugurtha, and end the war.

After the war, Marius returned to Rome in triumph on January 1, 104. Although Sulla captured Jugurtha, Marius claimed the triumph as his. Sulla, as a military subordinate, was in no position to dispute Marius' claim. Immediately after their victory in Africa, the Romans faced a new war against two German tribes, the Cimbri and the Teutons. Because of his recent triumph, the Romans now elected Marius consul to defend Italy. Sulla served as a legate of Marius and once again used his diplomatic skills to detach the Marsi from the German alliance.

After his latest tour of duty, Sulla returned to Rome in 99 to stand for the praetorship. Despite his military successes, Sulla failed to win office. Yet the next year, the people elected Sulla urban praetor. The senate assigned Sulla to Cilicia for his propraetorial governorship. On reaching his province, Sulla received a senatorial order to restore Ariobarzanes to the throne of Cappadocia. After his success in Cappadocia, Sulla had the opportunity to negotiate Rome's first diplomatic relations with the Parthians.

Life's Work

Sulla now returned to Rome to seek the consulship. When his political enemies prosecuted him in an unsuccessful campaign to discredit him, Sulla had to postpone his canvassing for office. With the failed campaign for the consulship came public notice of Sulla's feud with Marius. Many of the Roman aristocracy viewed Marius as an upstart (*novus homo*) who did not know his proper place. Sulla's capture of Jugurtha, his military successes, and his patrician background made Sulla the perfect man to challenge Marius. When Sulla received sufficient backing, he gained the consulship for 88.

Because of the territorial expansion of Mithradates the Great, King of Pontus, the senate decided to give Sulla the command of the war against Mithradates. The tribune Publius Sulpicius Rufus, however, introduced a bill in the Tribal Assembly to transfer the command to Marius. Since no public business could be conducted during a public holiday, Sulla and a consular colleague declared a public holiday to prevent the vote from taking place. Sulpicius claimed that this was illegal and incited the people to riot. To save himself from the mob, Sulla rescinded the holiday decree and pretended to accept the transfer of his command. Sulla then went to address his troops gathered in Campania for the war against Mithradates. After he explained the political developments in Rome, the troops urged Sulla to lead them to Rome to reclaim his rightful command. With the backing of his soldiers, Sulla marched on Rome and took the city by force.

Although these events marked the first time in history a Roman army had violated the *pomerium* (the sacred boundary of Rome), Sulla believed that he was defending legally constituted authority and that he was saving Rome from tyrannical demagogues. Once in control of Rome, Sulla had the senate declare Marius and Sulpicius public enemies, subject to immediate execution. Although Marius managed to escape from Rome, Sulpicius was captured and killed. After having the senate annul the laws of Sulpicius, Sulla sent his army away and allowed the election of the consuls for the next year. Gnaeus Octavius (a supporter of Sulla) and Lucius Cornelius Cinna (an enemy of Sulla) were elected consuls for the year 87. Sulla, anxious to fight the war with Mithradates, left for Greece.

With Sulla out of Italy, Cinna declared Sulla a public enemy but did nothing to hinder him in the East. After pushing the forces of Mithradates out of Greece and defeating them in Asia Minor, Sulla made peace with Mithradates. On hearing that Cinna had been murdered by his own troops, Sulla invaded Italy in the spring of 83. Within a year, Sulla defeated all the forces ranged against him. He massacred the Italians who sided with Cinna and who were still in rebellion and confiscated some of their lands.

Having Rome firmly in his control, Sulla ordered the execution of all magistrates and high military officers who had served Cinna's government. To limit the executions to those guilty, Sulla published proscription lists of those subject to the death penalty. Sulla confiscated the properties of those proscribed and auctioned them to his supporters. Motivated by greed, some Sullan supporters arranged for the proscription of certain wealthy individuals in order to acquire their money and lands. The death toll among the upper classes included seventy senators and sixteen hundred equestrians. The sons and grandsons of those proscribed were barred from holding public office in the future.

From Sulla's point of view, he meted out various punishments under his authority as proconsul. The drawback to being a proconsul, however, was that Sulla could not enter Rome. When the death of Gnaeus Papirius Carbo, Cinna's former consular colleague, became known, Sulla suggested that the dictatorship be revived after a lapse of 120 years. Although the usual term of office for a dictator in Rome was six months or less, Sulla wanted no time limit placed upon him. Accordingly, the people elected Sulla dictator and granted him complete immunity. Sulla's having the title of "Dictator for the making of laws and the settling of the Constitution" allowed his every decree to become law immediately.

As dictator in 81 Sulla instituted a constitutional reform which placed the senate in total control of the state. Sulla increased senate membership from the traditional number of three hundred to six hundred by including pro-Sullan equestrians and by automatically making all former quaestors members of the senate. The number of praetors was increased to eight and the number of quaestors to twenty. To create an orderly career ladder, Sulla established a strict *cursus honorum* in which politicians had to hold the quaestorship and praetorship before holding the consulship (the minimum age for holding this office was to be forty-two). Because tribunes had caused so much political turmoil in the past, men holding the tribuneship were now limited in the use of the veto and were barred from holding any higher office. In addition, prior senatorial approval was required before bills from a tribune could be introduced into an assembly.

At the height of his power, Sulla stepped down from the dictatorship and restored constitutional government. Sulla was elected consul for 80, after which he retired to one of his villas in Puteoli (in Campania) to write and to relax by hunting and fishing. In his extensive memoirs, Sulla minimized the humble circumstances of his early years and emphasized his career from the time of the war with Jugurtha. Sulla wanted to create the image of having possessed *felicitas* (good luck) from childhood. After a lifetime spent in active service to Rome, Sulla died of liver failure in 78. His body was taken to the Forum in Rome, where it lay in state. After thousands of Sullan veterans and ordinary people passed the funeral bier to pay their respects, the body was cremated. So great was Sulla's following that the matrons of Rome mourned Sulla for a full year, just as they would have done for their own fathers.

Summary

Although Lucius Cornelius Sulla was not a talented orator, he had the ability to establish an immediate personal rapport with people. Whether commanding troops, leading the state, or managing delicate diplomatic negotiations, Sulla was always able to earn the respect of the people with whom he dealt. Sulla's contemporaries of all classes were most impressed by his personal charm and by his highly developed sense of humor. In addition, Sulla believed that he possessed a special divine gift, *felicitas*. With his natural abilities and his good luck backing him, Sulla was always confident.

Unknowingly, Sulla played an important historical role in Rome's transition from a republic to an empire. Despite his passionate belief in Rome's republican form of government, Sulla felt compelled to defend the state by being the first to use military force against it. As Roman politics became more polarized, adversaries used violence as the means to a political end. Although angered at the prospect of losing his command against Mithradates, Sulla looked upon Marius, Cinna, Carbo, and Sulpicius as men intent on violating the Roman constitution. Sulla, therefore, saw his actions in a broader context than a mere factional dispute. As a patriotic Roman, Sulla could not stand by and watch the subversion of the Republic.

When Marius allowed the Roman legions to recruit from among the urban proletariat, he made possible the rise of a man such as Sulla. Generals now recruited armies whose only loyalties were to their commanders. When Sulla's men believed their general to have been wronged, they rose to his defense, not to that of the state. Although Sulla exercised absolute power over Rome, he did not use his power to establish a Hellenistic-style monarchy. Sulla viewed the senate as representing traditional republican government: He attempted to restore it to its former central role. In short, Sulla tried to repair the Roman constitution after self-serving politicians had damaged it.

Using as many historical precedents as possible, Sulla tried to resolve Rome's problems in a constitutional manner. In reviving the dictatorship with no time limit, Sulla was harking back to 387 B.C., when Marcus Furius

Camillus required more than six months to save Rome from the Gauls. Just as the Romans thought Camillus the savior of Rome, Sulla hoped for the same recognition. When the Romans needed a thorough revision of their laws in 451, they turned to the *decemviri* for leadership. In Sulla's view, the Romans needed a new constitutional reform.

Despite his great talents and his extreme patriotism, Sulla ultimately failed to accomplish what he had set out to do. The Sullan reforms were not permanent, and they did not stop the Roman constitution from changing. By 70, Sulla's own supporters, Marcus Licinius Crassus and Pompey the Great, annulled or changed much of Sulla's work. Although his efforts to preserve the Republic were well-meaning, they demonstrated that Sulla did not understand Rome's deep-seated problems. The very situation he sought to prevent, the use of force in politics, became the established norm as a result of Sulla's own march on Rome and his use of proscription lists. Rome did not achieve political stability until Augustus established the Empire in 27 B.C.

Bibliography
Appianos. *Appian's "Roman History."* Translated by Horace White. 4 vols. New York: Macmillan, 1912-1913. Appian's "The Civil Wars," "The Mithridatic Wars," and "Numidian Affairs" cover the time periods for Sulla's participation in these events. Although Appian lived during the late first and early second centuries A.D., he preserved some very valuable information from an unknown early imperial annalist. This work is part of the Loeb Classical Library series.
Badian, E. "Waiting for Sulla." *Journal of Roman Studies* 52 (1962): 47-61. The author attempts to bring modern critical historiographical analysis to the study of the period of Sulla. Through a reexamination of the sources, Badian maintains that Sulla's ambition drove him into rebellion against lawful authority. Sulla's contemporaries did not, according to Badian, believe that Sulla was a champion of the Roman nobility.
Keaveney, Arthur. *Sulla: The Last Republican.* London: Croom Helm, 1982. The first full-scale biography of Sulla to appear in English. The author gathered and analyzed all the available evidence on the life of Sulla and presents it in a most convincing manner. A very favorable interpretation of Sulla.
Plutarch. *Fall of the Roman Republic, Six Lives: Marius, Sulla, Crassus, Pompey, Caesar, Ciero.* Translated by Rex Warner. Harmondsworth, England: Penguin Books, 1958, rev. ed. 1972. This volume contains a chapter on Sulla together with other chapters on some of his political rivals. Because Plutarch used many sources unavailable today, he preserved much anecdotal material which may be contemporaneous with Sulla. Although Plutarch's work lacks historical perspective and is very moralistic, it portrays Sulla vividly.

Sallust. *"The Jugurthine War" and "The Conspiracy of Catiline."* Translated by S. A. Handford. Baltimore: Penguin Books, 1963. A useful and interesting but brief account of Marius and Sulla in the war against Jugurtha. Despite his prejudice against the Roman nobility and his inaccuracies in chronology and geography, Sallust is an important source of information. It is highly probable that Sallust used Sulla's memoirs as one of his sources.

Scullard, H. H. *From the Gracchi to Nero: A History of Rome from 133 B.C. to A.D. 68.* London: Methuen and Co., 1959, 2d ed. 1963. This book contains two chapters, "The Rise and Fall of Marius" and "The Rise and Fall of Sulla," which give an exceptionally clear account of this most crucial period in Roman history. Points of interpretative discussion with secondary source citations are included in the notes at the back of the book.

Peter L. Viscusi

SUNDJATA

Born: c. 1215; near the confluence of the Niger and Sankarani rivers in Guinea, West Africa
Died: c. 1255; near Niani, Guinea, West Africa
Area of Achievement: Government
Contribution: Founder of the thirteenth century empire of Mali in the western Sudan, Sundjata has become the unifying cultural figure for the Mandingo peoples of West Africa.

Early Life

Sundjata is mentioned in written sources by medieval Arabs, but his life is best known from the oral epic poetry of his descendants, the Mandingo peoples of West Africa. That poetry, sung by hereditary performers commonly known as griots, or as *(d)jeli* in Mandingo, is filled with contradictory and mythical accounts of Sundjata's life and deeds. While many details of this tradition must be dismissed as exaggerated, a biographical sketch of the historical Sundjata emerges from the griot's song.

Great attention is given to names and their meanings in Mandingo epic, where names may vary in form from region to region and version to version. Sundjata's name, for example, is alternately spelled "Soundiata," "Sundiata," "Son-Jara," and "Sun-Jata." According to various interpretations, "Sundjata" means Lion Prince or Lion Thief. In the Arabic sources, he is known as Mari Jata, or Lion Lord. Association with the lion gives Sundjata the power and authority of this beast, which is considered both physically and spiritually powerful in Mandingo culture. Other names in the tradition illustrate a similar variation and significance.

Genealogies are also important for the Mandingo. The oral tradition of Sundjata associates his lineage with Islam and with certain families, such as the Konnatés, Keitas, and Kondés, who are still prominent in the modern Mandingo world. Thus, Sundjata's father, whose name is usually given as some variation on Maghan Kon Fatta, or Magan the Handsome, can trace his ancestry back to the African Bilali, Companion of the Prophet Muhammad and one of the first converts to Islam. The immediate predecessor of Sundjata's father is sometimes said to have been the first Muslim ruler of the area and a maker of a hajj, or pilgrimage to Mecca. Through his mother, Sugulun, Sundjata is related to the Kondés and associated with traditional African religious beliefs, such as fetishism and animism.

Sundjata's father was a local ruler in the Mandingo heartland on the border between the modern nations of Guinea and Mali. He took Sugulun as one of his several wives. She is described in the tradition as a deformed or ugly woman from the region of Du (Do) near the modern city of Ségou, Mali. Sundjata, born about 1215, is usually said to have been a younger son of his father but his mother's firstborn.

In his infancy and childhood, Sundjata was a weak and crippled youth who did not walk until an advanced age and showed little promise. The death of his father during this period left the lame Sundjata and his foreign mother vulnerable to the scorn and mistreatment of his older half brothers. At the same time, his whole family suffered from the cruel oppression of Sumanguru Kanté, king of the Susu, near modern Bamako, at whose hands all Sundjata's elder brothers are said to have been killed or defeated in battle. As a teenager, Sundjata left his home to escape either the dangers of family rivalry or, perhaps, Sumanguru. After a period of wandering, he was a guest of Tunkara, who was the king of Mema, a Soninke state located on the border of modern Mauritania and Mali.

Life's Work

In the late twelfth and early thirteenth centuries, West Africa experienced a severe population upheaval and political fragmentation caused by the waning of the power of Wagadu. Located on the borders of the Sahara Desert, Wagadu is often identified with the great empire of ancient Ghana. This major movement of peoples, often called the Soninke dispersion, included the migration of the Susu from Ghana—where the ancestors of their ruler, Sumanguru, were said to have been members of the slave class. As the strongest king in the region, Sumanguru took advantage of the power vacuum, according to Arabic sources, by attacking Ghana and reducing it to slavery around 1203. He then moved to subdue the region to the south, including Sundjata's homeland. In this conflict, Sumanguru defeated Sundjata's older half brother Dankaran, who then sought refuge in the region of Kissidougou in Guinea, where many inhabitants still claim descent from him.

Sumanguru's ruthlessness and cruelty is illustrated in the tradition by two crimes, the theft of Sundjata's griot and the abduction of the wife of his own nephew, Fa Koli. Both these actions galvanized opposition to Sumanguru, encouraged Fa Koli to break with his uncle, and sent some Mandingo to seek the help of the exiled Sundjata.

From exile, Sundjata organized an army against Sumanguru. His allies included Fa Koli and Fran Kamara from the mountainous Fouta Djallon region of modern Guinea. Sundjata's sister, Sukulung Kulukang, is also thought to have played an important role in her brother's war by marrying Sumanguru and robbing state secrets from her husband. Around 1235, Sundjata's army defeated the forces of Sumanguru, and Sumanguru himself is said to have disappeared mysteriously in the hills near Koulikoro. After this victory, many Susu refugees fled to the region of modern Sierra Leone, where their descendants still live.

Following the defeat of Sumanguru, Sundjata oversaw a great gathering of the clans at Ka-ba, the traditional center of the Mandingo world. There, each chief swore allegiance to Sundjata as *mansa*, or king, and was granted authority over his own province. For the first time, the various Mandingo peoples were organized under one head; this assembly is thus considered to mark the beginning of the ancient empire of Mali. About this time, Sundjata also established a new capital for his empire, probably near modern Niani, Guinea. This city was well-known to medieval Arab travelers and was inhabited for several hundred years. Its exact location, however, remains the subject of scholarly debate.

Sundjata's position in West Africa's great religious conflict between Islam and animism is uncertain. The Arabic sources consistently refer to Sundjata as a Muslim, but in the oral tradition he exhibits both Islamic and animistic features. As a result, some twentieth century scholars have referred to Sundjata as an animist, while others consider him a champion of Islam against fetishism.

Circa 1240 Sundjata led a successful military expedition against the weakened power of Ghana and incorporated this kingdom into his growing empire. During his reign, Sundjata may also have begun a policy of commercial and political expansion along the Gambia River. After the defeat of Sumanguru, Tira Makhang, Sundjata's greatest general, is said to have gone as far west as The Gambia and to have founded several towns in that area.

In later life, Sundjata apparently led no military campaigns but pursued the life of a farmer, a noble occupation which has remained for centuries the mark of a free Mandingo warrior. There are several versions of his death circa 1255, many mythical in nature. The most common tale is that he was accidentally killed by an arrow at a festival held in his capital city. In Mandingo oral tradition, the deaths of great men are usually shrouded in mystery, but cult shrines in Sundjata's memory have long existed along the Sankarani River near Niani.

Sundjata founded not only an empire but also a dynasty. According to Arab sources, Sundjata was succeeded by his son Mansa Uli, who is said to have made a hajj circa 1260-1277. Since succession from brother to brother rather than from father to son is not unusual in Mandingo culture, Uli was followed in succession by each of his two brothers. Sundjata's greatest descendant was Mansa Mūsā, who reigned from 1312 to 1337 and whose pilgrimage to Mecca was so spectacular that word of it reached even contemporary Europeans. Members of the Keita family, as descendants of Sundjata, continued to rule in this region for centuries after his death. The first president of modern Mali, Modibo Keita, was also a member of this important family.

Summary

Sundjata was a great military leader and conqueror. His victories over Sumanguru and Ghana mark the beginning of the Malian Empire, which, at its height in the fourteenth century, stretched from Senegal and The Gambia on the Atlantic Ocean to Gao and Es-Souk on the Sahara Desert and controlled the gold and salt trade across the desert. The empire of Mali lasted until the fifteenth century, when its authority was replaced by the Songhai of Gao, under the leadership of Sonno Ali. The Mandingo heartland and Sundjata's capital of Mali remained independent until a Bambara prince seized the region circa 1670.

As founder of the empire of Mali, Sundjata is known as the father of the Mandingo world. His military conquests and policy of political expansion began the great geographic growth of the Mandingo, who form a major cultural and linguistic group in modern West Africa. As the victor over the ruthless Sumanguru, Sundjata is considered by the Mandingo to have been their first great liberator and champion of the oppressed.

Sundjata has continued to serve as a major unifying element in Mandingo culture. His genealogy has established a system of kinship and interfamily obligations upon which Mandingo society has operated for centuries. For example, the ancient conflict between Sundjata and Sumanguru still affects relationships between their descendants, the Keitas and the Kantés. The religious ambiguity of Sundjata, who can be seen as both animist and Muslim in the oral tradition, reflects West Africa's tendency toward religious assimilation. Through the oral poetry linked with Sundjata's name, the Mandingo, who live in wide areas of modern Mali, Senegal, The Gambia, and Guinea, have managed to preserve an intense sense of cultural cohesion over great spatial and temporal distances.

Bibliography

Fage, J. D. *A History of West Africa: An Introductory Survey*. 4th ed. New York: Cambridge University Press, 1969. A standard history of the region with specific discussion of the rise of the empire of Mali and the life of Sundjata. Several excellent maps are included as well as a useful annotated bibliography arranged according to period.

Innes, Gordon. *Sunjata: Three Mandika Versions*. London: University of London, 1974. This publication contains three versions of the story of Sundjata from The Gambia in the original Mandingo with parallel English translation, introduction, and explanatory notes.

Johnson, John William. *The Epic of Son-Jara: A West African Tradition*. Bloomington: Indiana University Press, 1986. An English translation of an oral performance of the epic transcribed under careful ethnographic conditions. Includes an excellent introduction to Mandingo culture and epic poetry, explanatory notes, genealogical charts, illustrations, and an extensive annotated bibliography.

_____. *The Epic of Sun-Jata According to Magan Sisòkò*. Bloomington, Ind.: Bloomington Folklore Publications Group, 1979. An oral performance of *Sunjata* is here translated and annotated. The singer of this version is the son of the performer of Johnson's 1986 variant. Many notes found in this version are repeated word for word in the 1986 text.

Laye, Camara. *The Guardian of the Word*. New York: Vintage Books, 1984. This literary reworking of the epic by an important Guinean author was first published in French in 1978. One map is included.

Levtzion, Nehemia. *Ancient Ghana and Mali*. New York: Methuen and Co., 1973. This detailed history of the area pays particular attention to the rise of the empire of Mali and its founder and includes a good summary of the oral tradition of Sundjata's life along with a comprehensive bibliography.

Niane, Djebril T. "Mali and the Second Mandingo Expansion." In *UNESCO General History of Africa*. Vol. 4, *Africa from the Twelfth to the Sixteenth Centuries*. Paris: UNESCO, 1984. Part of an excellent universal history of Africa, this article analyzes the history of the empire of Mali, the life of Sundjata, and the archaeological evidence for his capital at Niani with maps and photographs of sites and archaeological finds.

_____. *Sundiata: An Epic of Old Mali*. Translated by G. D. Pickett. London: Longmans, Green and Co., 1965. An eminent scholar of early Mali, publishing this literary version of the epic at the time of the African independence movement, introduced the epic into the mainstream of Western literature. A map and some explanatory notes are included in this English translation of Niane's French adaptation of the oral epic.

Pageard, Robert. "Soundiata Keita and the Oral Tradition." *Présence africaine* 8 (1961): 53-72. An essay review of Niane's book in the English edition of this periodical with a highly politicized but thorough analysis of the oral tradition of Sundjata.

Thomas J. Sienkewicz

SYLVESTER II
Gerbert of Aurillac

Born: c. 945; Aurillac, Aquitaine
Died: May 12, 1003; Rome
Areas of Achievement: Education and politics
Contribution: Gerbert was the most outstanding teacher of the tenth century; his brilliant pedagogy contrasted sharply with the cultural darkness of his age. After he became pope under the name Sylvester II, he furthered papal-imperial cooperation during his short pontificate.

Early Life
Gerbert was born to poor parents in Aurillac, in Aquitaine, which was then part of the late Carolingian West Frankish kingdom. He was educated in grammar at the Benedictine monastery near his birthplace by the monk Raymond, under whose teaching he developed a thorough knowledge and appreciation of Latin literature. Gerbert may himself have taken monastic vows, and he certainly would have spent his life in obscurity if he had not come to the attention of Count Borrell of Barcelona, the Carolingian ruler of the Spanish march, who visited Gerbert's monastery in 967. Raymond, by then abbot, asked Borrell to take Gerbert with him to Spain to continue his education, for schools there were regarded as superior to those in Aquitaine. During the next three years, Gerbert studied in Christian Spain with Bishop Hatto of Vich and may have come in contact with Arabic learning. He became particularly expert in mathematics.

About 971, Borrell took Hatto to Rome in an effort to have Vich raised to the level of an archbishopric. Gerbert accompanied them, and he was introduced to Pope John XIII, who was impressed with his mathematical skills. The pope, who was closely allied with the Holy Roman Empire, brought Gerbert to the attention of Emperor Otto I, called "the Great." This marked an important moment in Gerbert's career; henceforth he was to have very close association with the imperial family, which came from Saxony. Otto I appointed Gerbert to teach students at the imperial court, including his son and successor, the eventual Otto II.

Gerbert was not satisfied, however, for—as he told the emperor—he would rather learn what he did not know (that is, philosophy) than teach what he did. In 972 Gerbert met Archdeacon Gerann of Reims, a well-known philosopher, at the imperial court. With the emperor's permission, Gerbert returned to France with Gerann to study logic (dialectic), while also teaching the archdeacon mathematics. Gerbert quickly surpassed his teacher in philosophy. His accomplishments attracted the attention of Archbishop Adalbero of Reims, who in 973 appointed him to direct the cathedral school. This appointment initiated the most fruitful period of Gerbert's life.

Life's Work

For a decade, Gerbert taught brilliantly at Reims. His reputation extended throughout Europe, and his successful efforts to gather together a first-rate library at the school ensured that in subsequent generations Reims would continue to be an important cultural center. From the numerous letters Gerbert left, one can follow the process by which he obtained copies of the best books available on each subject he taught. His knowledge and appreciation of the work of classical authors, especially Cicero, was extensive.

One of the most important aspects of Gerbert's educational accomplishment was that he taught all seven of the courses in the trivium and the quadrivium, the two groups of three and four subjects which together constituted the seven liberal arts of medieval education. None in his own day and few in subsequent generations could match this pedagogical omnicompetence. Gerbert began with grammar, which he defined as "the art of explaining the poets and historians and speaking and writing correctly." Next came the teaching of dialectic, beginning with introductory works and commentaries by Porphyry and Boethius, then using more advanced works by Aristotle, Cicero, and Boethius. These constituted all the treatises on logic available in Gerbert's day and represented a standard of accomplishment not to be matched for a century and more. In the teaching of rhetoric, Gerbert made sure that his students understood both the wisdom and the style of the ancient and Christian authors whose works were studied, so that they would be prepared for an active life.

The four subjects of the quadrivium were taught with both textbooks and visual aids. In arithmetic, Gerbert himself wrote two works (completing a third after he became pope) and made use of the abacus for computational purposes. He was probably the first in Western Europe to make use of an early form of Arabic numerals (really Hindu-Gobar numerals) from one to nine, without the use of the zero. It is possible that Gerbert had picked up an imperfect knowledge of these numerals while studying in Spain—not from direct contact with the Arabs, but from secondary contacts with merchants and the like.

Gerbert's teaching of music was done in such a way as to emphasize the practical and mathematical aspects of the subject. He utilized a monochord with a sliding bridge, which could be positioned so as to create all the overtones from the root note, thus showing the mathematical qualities and relationships of sounds. One of his students implies in his description of Gerbert's teaching that a symbol was placed over each note on manuscript music corresponding to the position of that note on the monochord; thus, each pupil could pick out melodies without Gerbert's help. In order to present geometry, Gerbert also wrote a textbook of his own. It emphasized classical elements from Euclid's work as filtered through Boethius, but it drew in addition upon the surveying methods of the Romans. Little is known about the details of Gerbert's actual teaching of this subject.

It was in the teaching of astronomy that Gerbert was at his best and was most creative. He was familiar with a variety of astronomical hypotheses, but he opted for the geostatic theories of the Roman authority Pliny, probably on the pragmatic grounds of simplicity. To teach the principles of astronomy, Gerbert constructed a celestial globe, made of polished wood covered with horsehide, on which were marked the poles, the celestial circles, and the constellations of the Northern and Southern hemispheres. He also constructed an intricate planetarium, in which the planets were mechanically moved, and at least two complex viewing instruments which allow modern viewers to conclude that his astronomy not only was theoretical but was based on observation as well.

The range of Gerbert's interests extended beyond the curriculum of the arts. He had a solid acquaintance with medical literature, was familiar with scientific and astrological literature in the Islamic world, and wrote a philosophical treatise which dealt with issues beyond those treated in the study of dialectic. In his learning and his teaching, he had no equal in his time.

It was perhaps this reputation which aroused the jealousy of another well-known teacher, Otric of Magdeburg. After sending one of his own students to spy on Gerbert's teaching, Otric accused him of a pedagogical error relating to the relationship between the disciplines, which was of considerable importance in the constructing of an educational curriculum. The dispute was important enough and the personalities sufficiently well-known that the matter was eventually referred to the imperial court of Otto II. After an extended debate, recorded in the careful notes taken by Gerbert's pupil Richer, the emperor decided the issue in favor of his former teacher, Gerbert, who returned to Reims with many imperial gifts. In 983 the emperor further rewarded Gerbert by appointing him abbot of the famous monastery at Bobbio. Even though he continued to teach there, he was unhappy, for local disputes and controversies distracted him. Bobbio was a monastery where corruption had been particularly extensive, and Gerbert's efforts at reform met aggressive resistance. After the death of Otto II on December 7, 983, Gerbert returned to his school in Reims. There, however, he was unable to resume his teaching career, instead becoming involved in political disputes between the French and imperial parties. He was elected Archbishop of Reims in 991, but the circumstances were irregular and he was opposed by the new Capetian dynasty in France. Gerbert returned to Italy, where he was dependent upon the favor of Emperor Otto III, to whom he was close. Otto named Gerbert Archbishop of Ravenna in 998. A year later, when the incumbent pope suddenly died, Gerbert was elected his successor, taking the pontifical name Sylvester II.

This choice was significant, for it consciously looked back to the pontificate of the first Sylvester, pope at the time of the first Christian emperor,

Constantine. Between this fourth century pair there was supposed to have been close cooperation; Gerbert and his youthful patron Otto (born 980) intended their era to be one of papal-imperial partnership. Despite this ideal and despite some concrete steps to bring about a period of perfect peace, the reality proved to be different. Otto died prematurely in January, 1002, and Sylvester followed him less than a year and a half later.

Summary

Even if Sylvester and Otto had lived longer, it is doubtful that their goal could have been accomplished. Despite the appearance of equal partnership, the Papacy was in reality a subordinate element. Sylvester and his predecessors had, for the most part, been puppets to an imperial policy which was predicated upon theocratic assumptions. Sylvester had a sharply circumscribed sphere of independent action. Even in the city of Rome itself, he was closely controlled by the emperor, who modeled himself upon the Byzantine tradition of the superiority of the state over the church (caesaropapism).

Practically the only act Sylvester undertook during his pontificate which was even slightly at variance to imperial policy was in his relations with Poland and Hungary. Otto III was a close friend of Duke Bolesław of Poland (nicknamed "Chrobry"—the brave) and had gone to Gniezno in 1000 to worship with the Polish duke at the shrine of the martyred Bohemian missionary Adalbert of Prague and to establish an archiepiscopal see for Poland at Gniezno. There had also been some talk at that time of a royal crown for Bolesław. The emperor clearly conceived that his goal of a sanctified Christian commonwealth was predicated upon Germany, the Papacy, and the Western Slavs, especially the Poles. (Indeed, there is a contemporary manuscript illustration which shows Otto being waited upon by three figures labeled *Germania*, *Romania*, and *Sclavinia*.) Sylvester, however, was more inclined to reward the Hungarians for their recent conversion to Christianity. The crown that had been intended for Poland was instead given by him in 1000 to Stephen of Hungary. While Otto could not object, for the Hungarians were fully deserving, Sylvester's initiative was not precisely what he intended.

For the most part, however, Sylvester was a pliant pontiff who did not challenge imperial authority. It was to be another three-quarters of a century before the Papacy would emerge as an independent force. In other respects, Sylvester's pontificate was characterized by a high moral tone, which was reflected in his efforts to eliminate simony (the buying and selling of church offices), and by an administrative efficiency which set a standard for decades to come. His numerous extant letters clearly reflect these concerns. Yet despite these accomplishments, Sylvester's importance does not lie in the history of his pontificate. It rests instead on his pre-papal career as Gerbert.

As the leading scholar and educator of his time, Gerbert shone with a brilliance all the more bright because of the way he contrasted with the darkness of his age. In the larger picture of medieval and European civilization and culture, he does not seem to merit the reputation for learning he possessed in his own day. One should not forget, however, that he established a tradition which continued. His pupil Richer was in turn the teacher of figures whose importance and influence extended into the generation that brought about the cultural revival known as the "medieval Renaissance" or the "Renaissance of the twelfth century."

In his own time, Gerbert's accomplishments were so astonishing to his contemporaries they could explain him only by resorting to legends. Some medieval chroniclers, for example, told stories about Gerbert having stolen a book of magic while in Spain, having conjured up the Devil, having sold his soul to gain knowledge and power, and—at his death—telling his servant to cast his body into the street to let the Devil "have the service of my limbs . . . for my mind never consented to that oath." All of this reflects the awe in which Gerbert, the peasant boy who became pope, was held.

Bibliography
Allen, Roland. "Gerbert, Pope Sylvester II." *The English Historical Review* 7 (1892): 625-668. A detailed treatment of the biography of Gerbert Sylvester II, tracing his career as student, teacher, and ecclesiastical leader. The emphasis is upon his political problems at Reims and Bobbio and upon his program as pope. Relatively little attention is paid to the academic content of his teaching, although there is a good description of his astronomical instruments.
Dales, Richard C. *The Intellectual Life of Western Europe in the Middle Ages*. Washington, D.C.: University Press of America, 1980. In many ways the best intellectual history of the Middle Ages in English. The chapter which treats tenth century developments is especially well done, and the author's analysis of Gerbert's teaching and his philosophical thought is clear and thorough. The notes and bibliographical suggestions are very helpful. There is little on the details of politics and ecclesiastical developments.
Duckett, Eleanor Shipley. *Death and Life in the Tenth Century*. Ann Arbor: University of Michigan Press, 1967. An excellent study of the politics, culture, and religious life of the period. The major figures, including Sylvester II, are treated against the background of their times. The description of Sylvester's relations with the three Ottos is particularly effective, and the analysis of his teaching and cultural influence is very good.
Lattin, Harriet. *The Peasant Boy Who Became Pope: Story of Gerbert*. New York: Henry Schuman, 1951. This is the only full-length biography of Gerbert in English. It is based on the primary sources and makes good use of the scholarly literature in other languages. While the tone of the book is

somewhat romanticized, the author is a serious scholar whose narrative is generally reliable, especially in matters of detail and in tracing the political issues in which Sylvester was involved.

Poole, Austin Lane. "Germany: Henry I and Otto the Great" and "Germany: Otto II and Otto III." In *The Cambridge Medieval History*, edited by J. B. Bury, vol. 3. Cambridge: Cambridge University Press, 1922, reprint 1957. A detailed treatment of the political history of the Empire during the lifetime of Sylvester. These two chapters of a multivolume, collaborative work are especially good at showing the policies and ambitions of the Saxon emperors. The relations between the Ottos and Gerbert/Sylvester II are traced carefully. This standard work is useful for presenting the larger picture of European and imperial politics in which Sylvester was involved.

Sylvester II, Pope. *The Letters of Gerbert, with His Papal Privileges as Sylvester II*. Translated by Harriet Lattin. New York: Columbia University Press, 1961. A fluid translation of 264 extant letters which fully reflect the intellectual, educational, political, and religious interests and activities of Gerbert/Sylvester II. The introduction by the translator is a briefer version of her earlier biography, but it also adds interesting new details. The appendices in this volume are important to the scholar, but add little to the details of Gerbert's life or Sylvester's pontificate.

Taylor, Henry Osborn. *The Mediaeval Mind: A History of the Development of Thought and Emotion in the Middle Ages*. 4th ed. 2 vols. Cambridge, Mass.: Harvard University Press, 1966. A rather old-fashioned intellectual history of the Middle Ages, originally published in 1911, which contains much that has been outdated by subsequent scholarship. The author's chapter on Gerbert, however, is still useful, particularly since it contains the best treatment in English of the dispute with Otric and a fine analysis of Gerbert's philosophical works.

White, Lynn T., Jr., ed. "Symposium on the Tenth Century." *Medievalia et Humanistica* 9 (1955): 3-29. A series of short articles by several authors focusing upon the vitality and dynamism of the tenth century. Various aspects of the period are treated, but Gerbert receives especial attention within the context of learning. His contributions in astronomy are well treated and placed within the European astronomical tradition. Little attention is paid to political matters.

Paul W. Knoll

AL-TABARI

Born: c. 839; Amol, Tabaristan (modern Iran)
Died: 923; Baghdad, Iraq
Areas of Achievement: Historiography and religion
Contribution: The premier historian on the first century of the Islamic empire and a renowned commentator on Koranic tradition, al-Tabari established a model of universal history and a corpus of religious tradition crucial to the development of later Islamic theology and scholarship.

Early Life

Abu Ja'far Muhammad ibn Jarir al-Tabari was born to a moderately wealthy family. He demonstrated all the traits of a child prodigy and began formal study at an extremely early age. Legend has it that he memorized the entire Koran by the time he was seven. Al-Tabari's father, realizing the extent of his son's talents and the limitations of his hometown, provided financial support for the travel so crucial to a broad education in those days.

After visiting centers of learning in northern Iran, al-Tabari, while still a teenager, set out for Baghdad in hopes of studying under the great Muslim jurist Ahmad ibn Hanbal, who, unfortunately, died just before al-Tabari's arrival in the city. Nevertheless, the youth remained briefly in Baghdad and also visited the important traditional Iraqi Muslim centers of Basra and Kufa. There followed a trip to Syria to study *hadith*, the traditions attributed to Muhammad. Al-Tabari also spent some time in Egypt before returning to Baghdad around 872, where he would pass the remaining half century of his long life as an increasingly renowned scholar, teacher, and writer.

Al-Tabari's Baghdad career was one of modest means and stupendous productivity. Despite his family's largesse in providing travel money in his early life, al-Tabari endured what some have described as a life of extreme poverty in Baghdad. There is a story that he was once reduced to selling the sleeves of his shirt in order to buy bread. To some extent, al-Tabari placed himself in these dire straits by rejecting several lucrative offers of government posts and commissions. His independence may have helped free him from official drudgery, making possible his voluminous literary output. Some early writers claim that al-Tabari customarily wrote or copied forty manuscript pages each day.

There was, however, one brush with politics and notoriety. After breaking with the uncompromising literalism of Hanbali religious law, al-Tabari attempted to form his own school of Muslim jurisprudence. This enterprise brought a pro-Hanbali mob to his door and required police intervention to ensure his safety. Little of the nature of al-Tabari's legal essays is known, since these works are among a considerable number of his writings which have been lost. (Some scholars have concluded that his proclivity for iconoclastic thinking and the catholic nature of his works—a quality that probably made them less attractive to specialists—may have been responsible for the disappearance of so much of his output.)

Life's Work

Al-Tabari's career spanned many fields of study, including history and Koranic commentary, poetry, lexicography, grammar, ethics, mathematics, and medicine. He was an unparalleled collector of *hadith*, devoting most of his early years to gathering and copying material wherever he went. His commentary on the Koran was the first to bring together sufficient material from different regions of Islam to make it a standard work, upon which later generations of commentators could draw. Even for modern scholars, al-Tabari is an important source of information on Koranic tradition. Although he was concerned with the structure and syntax of oral traditions, al-Tabari seldom introduced his own conclusions or opinions on religious or historical questions.

The most important surviving work of al-Tabari is his world history, *Ta'rikh al-rusul w'al-muluk* (annals of the apostles and the kings; partial translation as *Selections from the Annals of Tabari*, 1902). It is an enormous work; a late nineteenth century edition fills thirteen volumes, and numerous authorities assert that in its final form *Ta'rikh al-rusul w'al-muluk* was ten times that long. (Some scholars, however, doubt this claim, noting that the language of the work does not lead one to suspect large amounts of missing material or any sort of abridgment, and that, in any case, a work of such dimensions would have been beyond the capacity of a single man in the ninth century.)

Ta'rikh al-rusul w'al-muluk is more than simply a history of Islam. By al-Tabari's time, Islam was a vast aggregation of civilizations and cultures, and the work considers the pre-Islamic history of many of them. It begins with a history of the patriarchs, prophets, and rulers from early Semitic cultures, followed by a history of Persia and Iraq during the Sassanid period (226-637). Then comes the era of Muhammad and the first four caliphs (570-661), the Umayyad Dynasty in Damascus (661-750), and, finally, the 'Abbasid period in Baghdad. The coverage stops in 915.

The style of the annals changes from a somewhat disconnected narrative for pre-Islamic times to a yearly chronology of events for the Muslim era. The source material came from both oral traditions and written accounts. Throughout *Ta'rikh al-rusul w'al-muluk*, a connected narrative is sacrificed in the interest of compiling accounts of the same events from a variety of sources. Not surprisingly, the work is full of contradictions. In declining to make judgments between variant accounts, al-Tabari may perhaps be subject to criticism from modern historians. On the other hand, *Ta'rikh al-rusul w'al-muluk* provides an unsurpassed record of primary sources on given events, to be winnowed by later scholars.

In a supplement, al-Tabari provides biographical information on most of his informants, evidently to aid the reader in discerning the true versions of events. This method is closely related to the early Muslim technique of testing the veracity of *hadith* by examining the character and known biographies of individuals who transmit them. Early Muslim legists used this system to determine authentic *hadith* and to arrive at a codified Muslim system of law. Al-Tabari does the same, or rather invites the reader to exercise such discretion, by providing the necessary data.

The structure of al-Tabari's historical work, confusing though it may be to a general reader, is especially helpful for scholars, since there is relatively little trustworthy material on the first century of Muslim history, one in which Islam grew from a local system in western Arabia into a monumental imperial organization. Most other Arabic sources on this period, in fact, were produced much later, after religious and political divisions had led to civil war and competitive dynasties in Islam. Many Islamicists regard these later histories, which are far more interpretive and judgmental than al-Tabari's annals, as untrustworthy because their information often was selected for political or sectarian ends. It is unfortunate that *Ta'rikh al-rusul w'al-muluk* deals mainly with Iraq and Iran and has only scant material on Syria, center of the area ruled by the Umayyad Dynasty, or other parts of the Muslim West.

Many later Muslim historians emulated al-Tabari's method of presentation. They not only depended heavily upon his work for the early period but also often extended the annalistic coverage into their own eras. As a result, numerous "Tabariesque" works which recount Islamic history, and often events in other civilizations, were produced into the early thirteenth century. Some of these historians attempted to reconcile variant accounts in al-Tabari's annals, and they occasionally supply additional information of which al-Tabari himself apparently was not aware.

The value of *Ta'rikh al-rusul w'al-muluk* as a universal history, not a record of Islamic developments only, is evident in the fact that it was translated into Persian in 963.

Summary

Al-Tabari's voluminous collections of *hadith* and Koranic commentary are crucial to modern understanding of the evolution of Muslim thought in its formative period. He epitomizes the early Muslim practice of seeking exemplary truth and Koranic exegesis through a careful examination of genealogical and historical components. Though a traditionalist in this sense, al-Tabari also represents a break in the Islamic tradition of regarding history as a simple dichotomy between the pre-Islamic "Days of Ignorance" and the era of Muhammad and his community, or between Muslims and non-Muslims. He took a major step toward the development of world history by transcending these early limitations in the Muslim worldview. Al-Tabari also appreciated the importance of source preservation and criticism. His career was that of a pioneer on the road that would lead to modern historical scholarship. No other early Muslim historian would be so widely imitated by students and successors.

Bibliography
Butler, Alfred Joshua. *The Treaty of Misr in Tabari: An Essay in Historical Criticism*. Oxford: Clarendon Press, 1913. Reprinted as an addendum to the author's *The Arab Conquest of Egypt and the Last Thirty Years of the Roman Dominion* (Oxford: Clarendon Press, 1978). A brief essay concerning the sources used by al-Tabari in forming his account of the Arab conquest of Egypt. Focuses on the textual problems presented by such early materials.
Dahmus, Joseph. *Seven Medieval Historians*. Chicago: Nelson-Hall Publishers, 1982. Contains an excellent synopsis of the career and intellectual antecendents of al-Tabari. The discussion incorporates some lengthy translated passages of his work as illustrative material.
Dodge, Bayard, ed. and trans. *The Fihrist of al-Nadim: A Tenth-Century Survey of Muslim Culture*. 2 vols. New York: Columbia University Press, 1970. Contains a brief biography of al-Tabari in traditional Muslim form, also listing some of the scholars associated with him, by a tenth century chronicler. A good example of biographical treatment at the time, it provides a sense of the intellectual environment in which al-Tabari lived and worked.
Hodgson, Marshall G. S. *The Venture of Islam: Conscience and History in a World Civilization*. Vol. 1. Chicago: University of Chicago Press, 1974. This volume includes one of the best descriptions in English of al-Tabari's methods and technique, exemplified by his account of the murder of the caliph Uthman in 656. Shows how the study of history and that of Koran and *hadith* intermingle in al-Tabari's thought.
Marin, Elma. *The Reign of al-Mu'tasim*. New Haven, Conn.: American Oriental Society, 1951. This book, volume 35 in the American Oriental Series, includes a rare translation into English of a small portion of al-Tabari's annals.

Ronald W. Davis

CORNELIUS TACITUS

Born: c. A.D. 56; place unknown
Died: c. A.D. 120; probably Rome
Areas of Achievement: Government and historiography
Contribution: Combining a successful career in the Roman civil service with
a lifelong interest in his nation's past, Tacitus devoted his mature years to
exploring the many facets of history. His portraits of the famous and the
infamous, especially during the early years of the Roman Empire, are
among the most vivid and influential descriptions in all Roman literature.

Early Life

Cornelius Tacitus, considered by many scholars to be Rome's greatest historian, is an enigma. Neither the exact date of his birth nor that of his death is known. His *praenomen*, that name which distinguished each Roman from his relatives, is a mystery, as is his birthplace. Tacitus never mentioned his parents or any siblings in any of his writings. He imparts to his readers much information about his contemporaries and a number of historical personages, but he never reveals a single solid fact about himself.

Almost everything that is known about Tacitus has been gleaned from the writings of his close friend Pliny the Younger, an author in his own right and the nephew of the great scientist and historian, Pliny the Elder. The friendship seems to have been of long duration, a fact which has led authorities to speculate that Tacitus was actually the son of one Cornelius Tacitus, who served as a financial agent of the government in Gallia Belgica and was a friend of Pliny the Elder. The public career of Tacitus is a matter of record, and by carefully noting the dates of his terms of office in each position it is possible to place his birth early in the reign of Nero, probably the year 56.

Clearly, Tacitus received an excellent education with special emphasis on rhetoric, because he was recognized in later life as a fine public speaker and an outstanding lawyer. He may have studied with the great Quintilian, who taught Pliny the Younger, but Tacitus never mentions his teachers or his fellow students. The elegance of his prose and his reputation denote one of good birth who received all the advantages belonging to his class, but the actual details must remain speculation. From natural modesty, Tacitus may have thought it unnecessary to repeat facts well-known to his readers or he may have done so out of caution. Most of his youth was spent during troubled times when the slightest notoriety might mean death.

In his late teens Tacitus probably had the opportunity to hold his first public offices. Usually, young men at this age were assigned minor posts in one of the four minor magistracies. During these brief terms of service it was possible to judge their preparation as well as their potential for success in government service. Having tested his mettle as a civilian, a young man then entered the military for a brief time to experience the rigor and discipline of the Roman army. This tour of duty was usually performed under a relative or close friend of the family. If a career in the military were not his choice, a young Roman of good birth reentered civilian life by selecting a wife and offering himself for a place in the civil service. Since a candidate with a wife was given priority, marriage at an early age was not unusual. In 77, Cornelius Tacitus, his military service completed, was betrothed to the daughter of the noted general Agricola.

Life's Work

Tacitus took the first step in the *cursus honorem*, or the Roman civil service, in 82, when he was chosen a quaestor. He was one of twenty young men who for a year had the opportunity to prove their potential for a political career by fulfilling the duties of the lowest regular position in the civil service. If the quaestor's command of the law earned for him the commendation of the consul under whom he served, he might be offered another year under a proconsul in one of the imperial provinces.

For Tacitus, the next rung in the ladder of preferment was probably the position of aedile. These magistrates might perform any number of duties in Rome. Some of them saw to the care of the city and supervised the repair of public buildings. Others were responsible for regulating traffic within the capital. The organization of public games or the supervision of the morals of the populace might prove more difficult than the checking of weights and measures, but all these duties could fall to an aedile during his term of office, and each was a test of his ability. Tacitus obviously succeeded, because he was elected a praetor in 88.

Originally a military title, the office of praetor was by the time of the empire essentially a legal position. The experience gleaned during his term as an aedile would prepare the praetor for dealing with offenses from oppression and forgery to murder and treason. During his term as praetor, Tacitus was elected to the priesthood of one of the sacerdotal colleges, quite an honor for one so young. This election may have indicated not only his aristocratic birth but also the possession of the patronage of the influential and the powerful, including the emperor. The following year, Tacitus left for a tour of duty somewhere in the provinces.

He probably spent the next three years serving in the army, and he may have commanded a legion. During his last year abroad, Tacitus may have served as a proconsul in one of the lesser provinces of the empire. In 93, the year that he returned to Rome, his father-in-law, Agricola, died. Requesting permission to write a biography of Agricola, Tacitus was rebuffed by Domitian, who had already begun the judicial murder of anyone who he believed threatened his position or his life. While many of his friends and colleagues were slaughtered, Tacitus buried himself in his research and the subsequent writing of the forbidden biography, which he finished in 96, the year in which Domitian was assassinated.

De vita Julii Agricolae (c. 98; *Agricola*, 1793) was more than a simple biography. While recounting the various stages in the career of Agricola and imparting to the reader varied details about the Britons, their history, and their country, Tacitus began to examine a theme on which he would comment for the next twenty years: the conflict between liberty and the power of the state. He also had the opportunity to serve the state in the aftermath of the reign of terror of Domitian; in 97, he was elected consul during the first year of the reign of Nerva, a distinguished and respected senator.

In 99, Tacitus' public career reached its zenith when he and Pliny the Younger successfully prosecuted the case of Marius Priscus, who had used his government position to abuse the provincials of Africa. Both men received a special vote of thanks from the senate for their preparation of the case for the state. Tacitus also received much attention for his second book, *De origine et situ Germanorum* (98; *Germania*, 1793). Based on his observation and research while serving with the army, it was an immediate success. While Tacitus saw the Germans as a potential threat to the security of the empire, he was impressed with their love of freedom and the simplicity of their lives when contrasted to the servility and decadence of his fellow Romans. With few flaws, *Germania* is an impressive and persuasive work of scholarship.

Having embarked on the study of the past, Tacitus devoted his next work, *Dialogus de oratoribus* (c. 98-102; *Dialogue on Orators*, 1793), to the apparent decay of the art of oratory. Quintilian had addressed the problem a generation earlier, and while he may have had a strong influence on Tacitus' thoughts on the subject, it was to Cicero that Tacitus turned for stylistic inspiration. The culprit appeared to be the decline of education, but as Tacitus developed his theme using the time-honored device of the dialogue, it became apparent that the age of the Antonines was not suited to great oratory because it lacked the tension and turmoil that inspires great public speakers. The consolation for the decline of this discipline was the universal peace that had replaced the chaos of the reign of Domitian.

In 115, after serving as proconsul of the province of Asia, Tacitus finished his narration of the events between 69, when Servius Sulpicius Galba assumed the *imperium*, and the death of Domitian in 96. *Historiarum libri qui supersunt* (c. 109; *Histories*, 1793) was followed the next year by *Ab excessu divi Augusti* (c. 116, *Annals*, 1793), which concentrated on the period from the beginning of the reign of Tiberius in 14 through the death of Nero in 68. As examples of historical scholarship, these works are flawed, punctuated with misinformation which might have been easily corrected had Tacitus troubled to do so. Tacitus was a student of human nature, not of politics, a moralist who sometimes reshaped history to suit his narrative. Having chosen the most turbulent period in Rome's history for his subject, Tacitus filled both works with his own prejudices, but his delineation of his characters is at times brilliant and redeems the *Histories* and the *Annals* from being mere gossip. Unfortunately, neither work exists intact. Tacitus died several years after completing the *Annals*, around 120, probably in Rome.

Summary

Reared in the tradition of sacrifice and service to Rome that had characterized the republic, Cornelius Tacitus dedicated himself to the best interests of the state, and he distinguished himself as a man of great promise from the beginning. At the age of forty, he witnessed the beginning of a three-year-long nightmare in which many of his friends and colleagues were murdered on the orders of Domitian because they espoused and publicly proclaimed many of those same principles that Tacitus held dear. For the rest of his life, Tacitus was haunted by the events of those years, and their memory runs like a dark thread through everything he wrote.

Either consciously or unconsciously, Tacitus sought to ease his fears, his guilt, and his confusion through the study and writing of history. The past held the key to Rome's gradual decay as well as the source of her possible salvation, and to reveal both was a duty Tacitus could not avoid. In his first book, *Agricola*, Tacitus not only celebrated the deeds of his father-in-law but also explored for the first time the conflict between liberty and the power of the state. The theme of freedom is also a strong element in his second book, *Germania*. Much of what is known about the early Britons and Germans is found in these two works, and while there may be some doubt about the accuracy of some facts, it would be hard to question the admiration of Tacitus for those who prized liberty above life.

His third work, *Dialogue on Orators*, seems a pleasant interlude between his earlier works and his histories of contemporary Rome, the *Histories* and the *Annals*. Tacitus was able to unleash a flood of criticism of the imperial system and question the character of a number of his fellow countrymen, because the Antonine emperors under whom he served, Nerva, Trajan, and Hadrian, were willing to tolerate free inquiry. Thus, his vivid portraits have colored the opinions of countless generations of writers and historians. They are boldly drawn to serve not only as records of past deeds but also as warnings to the future leaders of the Roman state. Tacitus accepted the imperial system as inevitable, but he believed that it could be revitalized by a return to the noble virtues that had made the republic unique. It is as a moralist more than as a historian that Tacitus has had his most positive and enduring effect.

In the years following his death, the scholars and writers who succeeded Tacitus as the guardians of the traditions of the Roman state created a vogue for everything pre-imperial, and the republic, despite its violent history, was idealized as a golden age. The emperor Marcus Claudius Tacitus, who reigned briefly at the end of the third century, sought to claim descent from the great historian. As an act of filial piety, he ordered statues of his supposed ancestor to be erected in every public library and ten copies of his works to be produced every year. The latter edict certainly was a fitting memorial to perhaps Rome's greatest historian.

Bibliography
Chilver, G. E. F. *A Historical Commentary on Tacitus' Histories I and II.* Oxford: Clarendon Press, 1979. Containing a wealth of information, this work will prove very helpful to students of the period, because the author takes great care to trace each source and reference used by Tacitus.
Löfstedt, Einar. "Tacitus as an Historian" and "The Style of Tacitus." In *Roman Literary Portraits*, translated by P. M. Fraser. Oxford: Clarendon Press, 1958. This posthumously published collection of essays by a noted Swedish classical scholar contains two chapters which are extremely useful in understanding the personality as well as the work of Tacitus.
McDonald, A. H. "The Roman Historians." In *Fifty Years and Twelve of Classical Scholarship*, edited by Maurice Platnauer. New York: Barnes and Noble Books, 1968. This excellent essay compares and contrasts Tacitus with the other Roman historians and places him in the context of his time. It also contains an excellent bibliography.
Syme, Ronald. *Tacitus.* 2 vols. Oxford: Clarendon Press, 1958. This superb biography is a remarkable work of scholarship which examines the life and work of Tacitus against the background of Rome in the first century. Its bibliography is an excellent resource for the student.
Tacitus, Cornelius. *Agricola.* Translated by M. Hutton and revised by R. M. Ogilvie. Cambridge, Mass.: Harvard University Press, 1970. Part of the Loeb Classical Library, this volume also contains the *Germania*, translated by M. Hutton, and the *Dialogue on Orators*, translated by Sir W. Peterson. With the original Latin as well as line-by-line English translations. Enriched with excellent notes and scholarly essays.
——————. *Annals.* Translated by John Jackson. 2 vols. Cambridge, Mass.: Harvard University Press, 1937. Contained in these volumes are books 4 through 6 and books 11 through 14 of the *Annals*. Also included is an index to the other volumes in the Loeb Classical Library containing parts of the *Histories* and the *Annals*. With excellent maps.
——————. *Histories.* Translated by Clifford H. Moore. Cambridge, Mass.: Harvard University Press, 1925. Another volume in the Loeb series, this bilingual text contains an excellent introductory essay to the life and works of Tacitus, as well as the first three books of the *Histories*.
——————. *Histories.* Translated by Clifford H. Moore. Cambridge, Mass.: Harvard University Press, 1931. Contains fragments of the *His-*

tories, books 4 and 5, as well as books 1 through 3 of the *Annals*, translated by John Jackson.

Clifton W. Potter, Jr.

T'AI TSUNG
Li Shih-min

Born: January 23, 599; Wo-hung County, Shensi Province, China
Died: May, 649; Ch'ang-an, Shensi Province, China
Area of Achievement: Government
Contribution: The second ruler of the T'ang Dynasty, T'ai Tsung brilliantly
consolidated his regime through administrative reorganization and centralization, codification of laws, extension of hegemony over domestic enemies and menacing foreign powers, stabilization of commerce, and cultivation of the arts. Throughout East Asia, his regime continues to be
regarded as the exemplar of civic order and military might.

Early Life

Li Shih-min (T'ang T'ai Tsung was his imperial name) was born on January 23, 599, in Wo-hung County, Shensi Province, China, the second son of
the first T'ang emperor, Kao Tsu. A member of the influential Tou clan, his
mother was equally aristocratic, having been reared in the Northern court of
an imperial uncle.

Since his father's reign did not begin until Li Shih-min was seventeen, he
was reared without special preparations. He received an upper-class Confucian education, exposing him to historical and classical learning. Buddhist
beliefs, important to his family, were also passed on to him, and he persisted
in observance of Buddhist rituals. His northern frontier upbringing centered
upon development of the martial arts—pertinent training in view of the
political rivalries, rebellions, and warfare that marked Chinese history after
the imperial unity of the Han and the Ch'in dynasties shattered.

Traditional accounts of Li Shih-min stress his youthful military prowess.
While an adolescent, he accompanied his father and brothers on campaigns
against the Turks. Apparently, he was a superb presence: forceful, histrionic,
imperious in bearing, and awesome in his rages: qualities requisite for survival in a northern frontier family of landholding, fighting aristocrats.

Ruthless cunning characterized his responses to the conniving of his eldest
brother, Li Chien-ch'eng, the heir apparent to the T'ang throne, and his
younger brother, Li Yüan-chi, who supported the crown prince. Reacting decisively to these fraternal plots, to which his father, in some measure, ac-
quiesced, he ambushed and killed his brothers at the gate of the capital city,
Ch'ang-an. Li Shih-min then humiliated his father, the emperor, constraining
him to abdicate after designating him as heir to the T'ang throne in January,
627. T'ai Tsung would reign for twenty-three years, a period which, at the
outset, he named *Chen-kua*, the reign of "True Vision."

Life's Work

T'ai Tsung endeavored to mark his rule with an indelible personal style.

Unlike most educated Chinese, he was preeminently a rationalist. The shaping of human destiny, in his view, was the consequence of human actions and not the uncertain result of magical rituals, superstitions, or intractable mandates of Heaven. Unlike his predecessors, he developed his own role as a leader whose initiatives or failures would be evaluated by history rather than by spirits or gods. To this end, the advice he sought, his consultations with officials, and the manner in which he arrived at decisions were open and carefully recorded. Anxious to place his imprimatur upon his times, he was capable of sublimating his convictions the better to ensure the approbation of those around him and to avoid the risk of historical rebuke or misjudgment. For much of his reign, he acted out a drama of which he perceived himself to be the principal author. If T'ai Tsung's style deemphasized the accomplishments of previous reigns, while exaggerating claims for his own, his problems nevertheless were immense and his assaults upon them were impressive, often unprecedented.

Once renowned for his military prowess, after assuming power he affected the role of the humble scholar, anxious to remedy his lack of administrative skills. By virtue of his high intelligence and inexhaustible energies, however, he swiftly reordered imperial administration and soon evidenced increasing confidence in his mastery of administrative affairs. Officials, like himself, were expected to be continuously accessible. He valued their frank criticisms and strove to convince them that they had a share in policymaking, thus in improving the lot of the people—those to whom he and his officials were ultimately responsible.

Confucian frugality marked the early years of his reign. Public works were curtailed or abandoned in order to lessen the burdens of corvée labor and of taxation. Though he had been an ardent hunter, he forbade great formal hunts, principally because, like military maneuvers, they were expensive and destructive of property. Similarly, he at first restrained the elaborate construction of palaces. Such measures brought him wide popularity.

Selection of his chief ministers brought him great respect. He valued ability and dedication over personal compatibility. Wei Cheng and Wang Kuei, two of T'ai Tsung's principal ministers, for example, had served against him with the slain crown prince. Generally, he sought to minimize nepotism and, despite exceptions, preferred his own appointments to the continuation of inherited ministers. A notable deviation from this preference was the installation of his brother-in-law, Chang-sun Wu-chi, as vice-president for the department of state affairs, a figure who remained his confidante throughout his reign, despite allegations of excessive influence over the emperor. It was Chang-sun Wu-chi who was entrusted with a codification of T'ang laws and with settlement of the future question of succession to the throne.

The appointment of Fang Hsuan-ling, who for thirteen years helped direct the department of state affairs, was another splendid ministerial choice. A practical man of affairs, though intellectually precocious, Fang, an easterner from Shantung, brought many of the emperor's former enemies from the east into high office. In company with Tu Ju-hui, scion of a famed northwestern clan of officials, Fang developed a brilliantly balanced executive administration respected for its efficiency and fairness. Similarly, the humorless Confucian moralist Wei Cheng, a southerner and former enemy of the emperor, was chosen for his diplomatic skills and served superbly in negotiations with external opponents of the regime.

Appointments of this caliber not only brought singular talents into T'ai Tsung's service but also lent geographical breadth and social cohesion to the government. Fearless critics were made integral parts of policymaking and administration. Aided by such experts, T'ai Tsung reordered and consolidated administrative changes begun by his father. Where Kao Tsu, however, had greatly increased the number of government positions to increase his patronage support, T'ai Tsung reduced them. China was divided into ten *tao*, or circuits, which were overseen by imperial commissioners. In tightening and centralizing authority, T'ai Tsung, through his ministerial galaxy, also attempted an upgrading of provincial bureaucracies by special education in law, calligraphy, and civil administration—establishing the School of the Sons of State, the School of Calligraphy, and the Superior School—and by means of rigorous examinations. Endemic under his father's regime, bribery and corruption were substantially diminished or made disreputable.

Isolated on the northcentral Chinese frontier, T'ai Tsung, like his father, was ringed by real and potential enemies with their own bases of political and social power. Therefore he gave priority to centralization of authority, through combinations of diplomatic and military action. The broad geographical representation of his officials, their obvious contributions to T'ang policy, plus their cultivation by the emperor, drew many of his enemies' followers under his rubric. Establishment of more than six hundred provincial militias led by loyal aristocrats or solid citizens contributed to this process of ensuring the ascendancy of Ch'ang-an over neighboring regions, without necessity of quartering alien troops and without the imposition of financial burdens on local populations.

The reunification of China was T'ai Tsung's most formidable objective. Not since the Han Dynasty had China been united, although the Sui and Ch'in rulers, and T'ai Tsung's own father, had taken steps in that direction. While T'ai Tsung consolidated his own authority, he initially sought détentes with menacing neighbors, but direct military actions were unavoidable. In 630, when the collapse of the khanate of the Eastern Turks eliminated his most dangerous foreign rivals and opened a political vacuum along the northern frontier, he seized the chance for expansion. Whereas his father had been obliged to declare himself a vassal of the Eastern Turks, T'ai Tsung so effectively defeated them that the new khan acknowledged his vassalage to the

T'ang, dramatically altering the Asian power equilibrium for half a century.

The Western Turks, however, had grown stronger with the collapse of the Eastern Turks, dominating a vast stretch from the Great Wall to the western borders of Sassanid Persia and from Kashmir in the south to the Altai Mountains in the north. Using "barbarians" to control "barbarians" and exploiting their internal dissensions, T'ai Tsung defeated them in the 640's, liberating the Silk Route from China to the Western world and extending his hegemony over most of central Asia. Subsequently, he added the oasis states and eventually nearly all states in the Tarim basin, either through military occupation or by accepting their tribute.

Bitter opposition by his chief ministers worried about military expenditures, as well as the employment of Chinese troops among foreigners, did not alter T'ai Tsung's imperial ambitions. The powerful and expansive Tibetan state, which eventually, he defeated in battle, he allied to the T'ang by marriage. By 646, he had also crushed and received the submission of the chief Turkish tribes in northern Sinkiang. Anxious to redeem his father's failures, he found pretexts for the reconquest of Koguryo (Korea) in 644, although in this venture he succeeded no better than his predecessors.

Such attempts at grandeur curtailed prosperity at home. Commerce was made safe and, not least for maintaining an open Silk Route, flourished. While great agricultural problems remained unresolved, he sought to prevent the growth of large estates, partly to maintain revenues and partly to increase peasant proprietorships. Although an effervescence of fine arts and letters awaited T'ai Tsung's successors, historical scholarship, long neglected, prospered under his aegis. Directed by Wei Cheng and Fang Hsuan-ling, histories of the Liang, Ch'en, Ch'i, Chou, and Sui dynasties were begun in the 630's. Work on the Northern Wei recommenced after 636 and a fresh history of the Ch'in was completed by 646. While they promoted T'ai Tsung's historical prejudices about his own regime, these works nevertheless proved invaluable to subsequent generations. In spite of neo-Confucian pressures upon him to extirpate Buddhism, T'ai Tsung reformed aspects of the religion's relationships to the state and, though publicly observing its rituals, tried to meliorate criticisms by bringing it under official control.

Undeniably the quality of T'ai Tsung's regime degenerated in the latter years of his reign. He became arrogant, self-satisfied, and spendthrift. He relapsed into extravagant palace-building, indulged in memorializing his horses and dogs, rediscovered the delights of expensive and destructive hunts, and shaped major policies contrary to ministerial advice. In addition, efforts to extend his fiscal system throughout his realms were aborted; despite numerous battles and lengthy sieges, Korea escaped incorporation; and his own succession was mismanaged. Debilitated by a disease incurred during his Korean campaigns and thereafter dependent on the heir apparent, T'ai Tsung died in May, 649, in his capital, Ch'ang-an.

Summary

The weaknesses of T'ai Tsung's rule are easily listed because they were few and natural. Expansions of his fiscal system failed, and a larger proportion of the population than ever before eluded taxation; the growth of landed estates slowed but did not cease; codifications and revisions of the law remained incomplete; state-sponsored historical scholarship tended to exaggerate the emperor's attainments; Confucians who wanted Buddhism eradicated saw it merely controlled; the emperor's foreign policy burdened the nation's manpower and resources and the Korean adventure failed; and finally, his personal virtues degenerated.

His weaknesses or failures, however, were but the obverse of T'ai Tsung's great achievements in the face of immense difficulties. He consolidated a precarious T'ang rule, carrying to fruition initiatives of his father. He brilliantly rationalized China's administrative system both formally and stylistically. Ministerial selections based on talents and character brought the highest capacities to bear in governance, discouraging sycophancy and venality. Emphasis on the emperor as the people's servant set a high tone for the times and for future generations. His ideal of service was enhanced by legal codifications, as was his restoration of China's historical record. Subordination of Buddhist influences to those of the state, while keeping an open arena for other religions, was important for China's spiritual and intellectual needs. Combinations of astute diplomacy and decisive military action against opponents brought the Chinese domestic tranquillity and prosperity. Finally, his virtual reunification of China restored an important part of China's heritage.

T'ai Tsung's regime represents an unprecedented high point in Chinese history. It approximated the Confucian ideal of *wu* and *we*: a harmonious combination of civil order and military strength. It was a regime centered on securing the people's welfare. For later generations, the *Chen-kuan cheng-yao* (705) embodied the wisdom accumulated by T'ai Tsung and his ministers, while the *Li Wei-kung wen-tui*, also compiled after his death, summarized the military strategies of the emperor and his principal general, Li Ching. Both works have continued to be reminders throughout Asia of the principles of wise and effective government.

Bibliography

Bingham, Woodbridge. *The Founding of the T'ang Dynasty: The Fall of Sui and Rise of T'ang, a Preliminary Survey*. New York: Octagon Books, 1970. Concentration is on the fall of the Sui Dynasty; of T'ang rulers, only Kao Tsu is examined. The study lacks critical balance but identifies the period's important problems. Useful appendices.

Fitzgerald, Charles P. *Son of Heaven: A Biography of Li Shih-min, Founder of the T'ang Dynasty*. Cambridge: Cambridge University Press, 1933. The first work in English on the T'ang. Uncritical, inferior to foreign studies, and superseded by recent, broader scholarship.

Latourette, Kenneth S. *The Chinese: Their History and Culture.* 4th ed. New York: Macmillan, 1966. Standard and generally authoritative. Excellent for broad contextual understanding. Chapter 5 deals with the T'ang. Fine end-of-chapter bibliographies, summary, glossary, and index.

Wechsler, Howard J. "The Founding of the T'ang Dynasty: Kao-tsu" and "T'ai-Tsung (626-649), the Consolidator." In *The Cambridge History of China: Part 1*, edited by Denis Twitchett. Cambridge: Cambridge University Press, 1979. Authoritative scholarship by a leading Sinologist. Useful footnotes. Excellent glossary and index, but no bibliography.

Wright, Arthur F. "T'ai-Tsung: The Man and the Persona." In *Essays on T'ang Society*, edited by John C. Perry and Bardwell L. Smith. Leiden, Netherlands: E. J. Brill, 1976. Critical and authoritative interpretations. Superb annotated bibliography. Includes an index.

Clifton K. Yearley
Kerrie L. MacPherson

TAIRA KIYOMORI

Born: 1118; Japan
Died: March 21, 1181; Heian-kyo, Japan
Area of Achievement: Government
Contribution: A warrior who rose to power in the last years of aristocratic
government in Japan, Kiyomori used political connections and the mar-
riages of his daughters to control the imperial court. Shortly after his
death, his family was destroyed, marking the most dramatic rise and fall in
Japanese history.

Early Life

Taira Kiyomori was the son of the great warrior Taira Tadamori, whose
military family had formed an alliance with retired emperors at the Japanese
court. Both sides prospered from this alliance as the aristocratic Fujiwara
family, which had dominated imperial government for generations, declined
in power.

Actually, there is some doubt about Kiyomori's parentage on both sides. It
may well be that he was the son of the emperor Shirakawa II, who asked that
Tadamori rear him as a warrior. His mother was said to be Lady Gion, a favorite mistress of Shirakawa. She was apparently very pious, for she commissioned costly Buddhist services, but little is known about her influence or
the early training of the young Kiyomori. Imperial patronage helped gain for
him important appointments and governorships in southwest Japan and the
Inland Sea. These areas were important sources of revenue, because trade
with Sung China flowed through their harbors, many of which Kiyomori
developed.

In twelfth century Japan, the aristocratic court in the imperial capital of
Kyoto retained its prestige, but real power had fallen into the hands of warrior clans in the provinces. Some of these warriors realized that their ignorance of classical learning and lack of refined taste made them inferiors in
the eyes of the nobility. The Ise branch of the Taira (the characters can also
be pronounced "Heike" or "Heishi") was particularly aware of this problem,
as it was based near the capital. Kiyomori's reputed father, Tadamori, took
an interest in cultivating the arts and gained the favor of the court, including
influential women. His rise in rank and privilege was a result of his provincial
power base and successful currying of favors at the court. When Tadamori
died in 1153, Kiyomori was ready to take his place.

Life's Work

Kiyomori led his family to its peak of power in the 1170's, but his stubborn
temperament also created many enemies who would crush the Taira family in

1185. He played a central but unsuccessful role in the transition from aristocratic to warrior rule in medieval Japan.

When Kiyomori took over the leadership of his powerful family in 1153, a complicated power structure existed in Japan. Retired emperors appointed a share of the country's provincial governorships in return for protection of their private estates, and Taira estate managers profited from this imperial patronage system. Kiyomori was able to strengthen his influence at the court during two brief but important factional struggles.

The first was the Hōgen War of 1156. Kiyomori and Minamoto Yoshitomo defended Shirakawa against a coup attempt. Yoshitomo was less generously rewarded than Kiyomori, so he attempted to rectify this slight in another coup attempt in 1160 directed against Shirakawa, who was then a retired emperor, and Kiyomori. Unfortunately for the Minamoto warrior clan, Kiyomori was able to crush their uprising and make himself dominant as the most powerful military family at the court.

Because he now had military control of the capital and court, Kiyomori was able to place Taira family members and supporters in many important posts for the next twenty years. Until he finally crushed all opposition to his position in 1179, however, there was an uneasy sharing of power with Shirakawa, his former sponsor. In fact, Japanese scholar Ishimoda Sho has argued that in sharing authority, Shirakawa had the upper hand until 1179 and that Kiyomori, far from being in control of Japan, had yet to emerge as the clear ruler even of Kyoto.

It is clear that Kiyomori continued to receive official appointments from the retired emperor, continuing the patron-client relationship. For his part, Shirakawa was able to build up a huge landed base to support the imperial family. Facing no real military threat from the defeated Minamoto or other warrior clans, Kiyomori could have seized complete power, but he preferred to work within the old system of court alliances, marrying his daughters into the aristocracy and leaving the influential Fujiwara family their hereditary posts.

In 1160, Kiyomori received the rank of imperial adviser, and he was appointed to the Grand Council of State. He also was given the office of chief police commissioner in the capital. None of these positions had ever been held by a warrior from the provinces, and the nobility resented his rise to prominence. As Kiyomori placed his sons and followers in more and more official posts, nearly all political factions turned against him in the 1170's. Plots were frequent, as hostility toward the perceived arrogance of the Taira clan grew. Kiyomori had suffered an illness in 1168, and that, or a lack of discretion, led him to abandon the delicate compromise at the court.

In 1177, discontent surfaced in a plot by several of Shirakawa's followers. The incident was precipitated by the assignment of a military title coveted by one of Shirakawa's advisers to Kiyomori's heir, Shigemori. This Shishigatani affair, named after the valley where the conspiracy was hatched, was revealed by one of Kiyomori's spies. Kiyomori rebuked his former patron, Shirakawa, replaced high officials with Taira clansmen, seized Fujiwara land, and executed many of his enemies.

Despite the ruthlessness of his suppression of the Shishigatani plot, opposition to Kiyomori's control continued to grow. In 1179, his enemies and Shirakawa sought to take advantage of two misfortunes that befell the Taira house. Kiyomori's daughter, who had married into the Fujiwara family to gain control of their land, died. The land was seized by the retired emperor. Only two months later, Kiyomori's heir, Shigemori, also died, and Echizen Province was confiscated.

It appeared that the court was getting out of control, so once again Kiyomori ordered his troops into the capital in December, 1179. He placed Shirakawa under house arrest, dismissed all officials opposed to his rule, and appointed his kinsmen in their place. Although Kiyomori's personal power was greatly enlarged by the takeover of the capital, it destroyed the fragile balance of court power and threatened the economic and political interests of major Kyoto institutions, including the powerful monasteries.

In 1180, discontent surfaced yet again when Prince Mochihito, a son of Shirakawa who had been passed over for succession, joined with Minamoto Yorimasa and several temples to overthrow the Taira. They were soon pursued by Taira troops to the banks of the Uji River where Yorimasa, an ally of Kiyomori in the 1150's, committed hara-kiri within the grounds of a peaceful temple. Mochihito was also killed, but his call to arms against the Taira had reached the eastern provinces of Japan, where Minamoto Yoritomo, a son of Yoshitomo who was spared by Kiyomori in 1160, gathered around him a powerful military alliance that would destroy the Taira in 1185.

Kiyomori's last years were therefore ones of danger and growing animosity to his rule. He had to rely on an army of informers and spies and was surrounded by troops at all times. To help forestall further plots, Kiyomori moved the court to his base at Fukuhara (modern Kōbe) in late 1180, but he was forced to return the court to Kyoto after six months. Not long after the return to Kyoto, Kiyomori took to his deathbed, dying of a fever on March 21, 1181. His last request was not for a Buddhist service but that Yoritomo be killed and his head be placed on his tomb. Kiyomori's own death was not mourned by the court, and the official histories do not treat him sympathetically.

His son Munemori, a man of limited abilities, was left in charge, but the days of Taira power were already numbered. Early in 1180, Kiyomori's grandson had become the Emperor Antoku. Kiyomori was fond of the infant and hoped that he would perpetuate the Taira line, but he was destined to die a tragic death, one which is deeply ingrained in the Japanese mind through the classic war epic that depicts the military defeat of the Taira by the revived Minamoto clan, the *Heike monogatari* (c. 1240; *The Tale of the Heike*, 1918-1921).

This work is Japan's greatest medieval war chronicle, and it tells of the Minamoto victories which drove the Taira from the capital in 1183 and forced them away from their base of power in the Inland Sea in 1184. The clan was destroyed in 1185 with the drowning of Kiyomori's grandson Antoku in the last stand of the Taira in the famous sea battle of Dannoura.

Then and now *The Tale of the Heike* is a reminder of the pride that comes before a fall, reflecting Buddhist fatality and the sense of destiny. In the opening paragraph of the epic, Kiyomori's fate is predicted: "The brave and violent man—he too must die away in the end, like a whirl of dust in the wind."

Summary

Although he is not treated with sympathy in *The Tale of the Heike*, Taira Kiyomori played an important role in the transition from aristocratic court government in Japan to the warrior rule of the Kamakura (1185-1334) and later periods. Kiyomori at first ruled in cooperation with retired Shirakawa, but his nepotism and provincial origins were resented and finally resisted by a court full of pride but with little real power beyond tradition.

It was the continuing prestige of that tradition that attracted Kiyomori to the court and created a military coalition centered in Kyoto. His very success in gaining control over official positions and adopting the values of the court may have separated him from his warrior followers in the provinces. In any case, it was the resurrected Minamoto clan, led by Minamoto Yoritomo, that represented the new power of the provincial warrior class that would rise and destroy Kyoto-centered political authority in Japan.

Much has been written by court officials about the errors of Kiyomori and his character defects, yet the message that comes down through the ages is a tragic tale of the impermanence of glory. It was not only the Taira clan that perished in 1185 but also the last vestiges of the Heian court-dominated society and most of the refined aristocratic values that the aristocratic age embodied. Perhaps the greatest tragedy of Kiyomori and his clan was that they were crushed in the transition from one great period of Japanese history to the next.

Bibliography

Arnesen, Peter Judd. *The Medieval Japanese Daimyo.* New Haven, Conn.: Yale University Press, 1979. A study of the Ouchi, a local warrior family in Sue and Nagato. Chapter 1 provides a good overview of the decline of nobility and the rise of the warrior class.

_____. "The Struggle for Lordship in Late Heian Japan: The Case of Aki." *The Journal of Japanese Studies* 10 (Winter, 1984): 101-141. A local case study of a warrior family during the period of Kiyomori's ascendency.

Hall, John W., and Jeffrey P. Mass, eds. *Medieval Japan: Essays in Institutional History*. New Haven, Conn: Yale University Press, 1974. Eleven essays and an epilogue by scholars of medieval Japan. The chapters on *insei* government by G. Cameron Hurst and on the emergence of the Kamakura government by Mass have insights on Kiyomori.

Hurst, G. Cameron. *Insei: Abdicated Sovereigns in the Politics of Late Heian Japan, 1086-1185*. New York: Columbia University Press, 1976. An important study of the institution of *insei*, or retired emperors, who made the important decisions of state. Retired emperors such as Shirakawa could ignore the sitting emperor (often an infant) and established channels of imperial government. Chapter 7 analyses the complicated relationship between Kiyomori and Shirakawa.

Kitagawa, Hiroshi, and Bruce T. Tsuchida, trans. *The Tale of the Heike*. 2 vols. Tokyo: Tokyo University Press, 1975-1977. A careful translation of the *Heike monogatari*, Japan's greatest war chronicle. This thirteenth century epic is composed of stories spread by minstrels. It culminates in the three battles that destroyed the Taira. It is the most important source for Nō drama, and its tales are found in Kabuki and puppet theater, as well as modern film and television.

McCullough, Helen Craig, trans. *Yoshitsune: A Fifteenth-Century Japanese Chronicle*. Stanford, Calif.: Stanford University Press, 1966. A translation and introduction to a medieval war tale that depicts the life of the most famous figure of his time, Minamoto Yoshitsune, who defeated the Taira and was in turn killed by his brother Yoritomo.

Mass, Jeffrey P. "Patterns of Provincial Inheritance in Late Heian Japan." *Journal of Japanese Studies* 9 (Winter, 1983): 67-95. A technical but important study of the complicated evolution of landholding rights in medieval Japan.

_____. *Warrior Government in Early Medieval Japan: A Study of the Kamakura Bakufu, Shugo, and Jito*. New Haven, Conn.: Yale University Press, 1974. Analysis of how power shifted from the court to local power bases of warrior clans. Mass argues that until 1179 Kiyomori shared power and benefits with his patron, the retired emperor Shirakawa.

_____, ed. *Court and Bakufu in Japan: Essays in Kamakura History*. New Haven, Conn.: Yale University Press, 1982. Nine articles consider the development of feudal institutions in Japan following the demise of the Taira.

Morris, Ivan. *The Nobility of Failure*. New York: New American Library, 1975. A highly readable survey of failed heroes in Japanese history. Chapter 5 deals with Minamoto Yoshitsune.

Sansom, George. *A History of Japan to 1334*. Stanford, Calif.: Stanford University Press, 1958. A classic study of early Japanese history that is still valuable for its lucid style, although many of the details and interpretations have been revised by later studies. Contains a chapter on Kiyomori that discusses his character, the Shishigatani affair, the dangers of monastic armies, and Kiyomori's enemies.

Richard Rice

TAMERLANE

Born: 1336; Kesh (modern Shahr-i Sabz), Transoxiana, Central Asia
Died: 1405; Otrar, Turkistan, Central Asia
Areas of Achievement: Government and patronage of the arts
Contribution: Tamerlane combined extraordinary military talent with strong
   administrative leadership to create the first large independent Central
   Asian state to throw off the domination of the Mongols. In the process, he
   altered the regional balance of power and revived Central Asia's main
   cities as international trading and cultural centers.

Early Life

Ahmed ibn Arabshah, captured by Tamerlane at Damascus in 1401, later
composed a generally critical history about him, entitled *Kitab aja'ib al-
maqdur fi akhbari timur* (1410; *Tamerlane: Or, Timur the Great Amir*, 1936).
Writing soon after the death of Tamerlane, the historian described him as a
brave, big-hearted youth friendly with the sons of the viziers, main advisers
to the ruler at court. Contemporaries and later Central Asians called the formidable ruler "Timur" or "Timur Lang" (Timur the Lame), from which Europeans derived the form Tamerlane. His skeleton, found buried at Samarkand below a royal mausoleum, the Gur-e Amir, showed his damaged right
leg attached to a tall, sturdy frame.

Tamerlane's Barlas tribal origin sharply defined his outlook and behavior.
Like the other nomadic tribesmen of the region, he virtually lived and usually
fought on horseback. Habits of nomadic life kept the youth from any inclination toward ease and settled existence. Emulating the former Mongol masters of the area, Tamerlane displayed a distaste for urban residence. Mi-
gratory life also probably accounted for the almost ceaseless campaigning he
undertook, starting from young adulthood. In his early years, aggressive opposition repeatedly drove Tamerlane into retreat with only a handful of
followers.

Life's Work

By the time Tamerlane reached the age of twenty-four, however, he had
begun to acquire a reputation as an effective chieftain. He became prince of
the Barlas clan in 1360 and continued to expand his influence during the next
decade. Within Central Asia, he repeatedly had to fight the deadly rivals who
held Khwarizm, just south of the Aral Sea, and the nomadic Moghuls (then
called Jata or Jattah) of the plains and mountain passes east of Transoxiana.
In his drive to ascendancy, he sanctioned the killing of his superior, the Emir
Husayn of Transoxiana, and then married the emir's widow. This royal link
improved Tamerlane's political position and added the honorific *gurakan*
(son-in-law of the ruler's family) to the new leader's title. At Balkh in 1370,

he took the throne of Central Asia.

Tamerlane's idea of his natural domain apparently encompassed the sub-regions of Transoxiana, Khorasan, Afghanistan, Turkistan, Iran, and the Transcaucasus, in whose Karabakh region he preferred to pass the winter. These areas served the Chaghatay and other tribal warriors as summer and winter pasturage. Within that periphery, his settled subjects found irrigable lands for farming and safe routes for travel.

Perhaps the most salient feature of Tamerlane's leadership was his ability to employ the mobile military might of the Turkic Chaghatay tribes to build a state. With this tribal support, Tamerlane checked internal opposition. From Samarkand, his splendid capital, the Central Asians thrust into Kashgar (several times from the 1370's to the 1390's), southern Russia (1395), Delhi (1398), Baghdad and Damascus (1401), and the environs of Ankara (1402). After widespread destruction, enslaving, and plundering, however, they remained in none of these places. Unlike earlier conquerors of the same region, such as Alexander the Great and Genghis Khan (whose relative Tamerlane proudly but on tenuous grounds claimed to be), Tamerlane chose not to colonize or govern these distant lands.

In campaigns north of the Caspian and Aral seas, Tamerlane's forces routed the vast armies of the Golden Horde, commanded by Toktamish Khan. Two great battles in 1391 and 1395, along with numerous lesser skirmishes, broke the hold of the Golden Horde. For some one hundred years, these offensive victories gave Central Asia a defense against the incursions of nomads north of Transoxiana. Equally significant, Tamerlane's success released the Russians from the tight grip imposed by the Mongols' Tatar successors, who had been centered at Sarai, near the great bend in the Volga River.

The emir spoke both the Turkic and Persian languages of Central Asia, but he never learned to read or write. To overcome this handicap and to satisfy his keen interest in history, he established the post of official Reader of Manuscripts (*qissakhan*). Despite his illiteracy, the conqueror learned the Koran and Islamic teachings so well from his spiritual counselors that he could discuss controversial points of dogma with them. Later historians, including Ibn Arabshah, accused him of ruthlessly using religion for political purposes. In Syria, opponents regarded Tamerlane and his Central Asian forces as zealous Shi'is, whereas in parts of Iran, Shi'i defenders knew him to be a devout Sunni. He demonstrated his merciless commitment to Islamic doctrine when he drove into India. There, his troops slaughtered Hindus by the thousands as a pious act in response to the commandment to convert or kill infidels. Had his planned invasion of the Far East run its course, non-Muslims there might have suffered a similar fate.

In 1405, Tamerlane initiated a campaign directed toward China. Pushing eastward from his capital, he had scarcely reached Turkistan (regarded then as stretching beyond the Syr Darya River) when he died, not in combat but from illness. His successors fell to struggling for power in clashes that soon diminished Timurid authority and territory.

Summary

Tamerlane's principal achievement fulfilled what he considered to be the normal responsibilities of a sovereign: to establish and maintain a large, secure, prosperous state and to embellish it with artistic and cultural institutions of the highest quality. At the heart of his empire, Samarkand, Bukhara, Herat, and smaller cities were graced with large numbers of talented intellectuals, artisans and artists, theologians and teachers, many of them foreigners, for whom Tamerlane served as a demanding patron. The civilization under the Timurid Dynasty that Tamerlane founded set the highest standards in western Asia in literary composition, miniature painting, and historiography.

Great architectural monuments of the fourteenth and early fifteenth centuries still demonstrate his accomplishment in such fields. The most magnificent of the structures designed and built by Tamerlane's order served religious purposes. A grand mosque rose in his birthplace, Kesh, and another, dedicated to a favorite wife, Bibi Khanum, in Samarkand. Tamerlane's architects constructed a huge mausoleum in Yasi, Turkistan, to honor the sainted Ahmed Yesevi (died 1166).

Politically, the durability of the state of Tamerlane and his successors was determined by certain factors characteristic of medieval Central Asia. Political power at that time was founded primarily on the military might of the nomadic tribesmen; at the same time, these tribes posed the greatest threat to a ruler. Tamerlane was able to bring the tribes under his control by replacing the potentially dangerous tribal chieftains with individuals personally loyal to him. As long as this practice was maintained, the stability of the state was assured. No one of his successors, however, could completely command the loyalty of these factions, and the unity of the realm gradually broke up during the century following Tamerlane's death. Despite this factionalism, Samarkand continued to flourish as a great cultural center under the Timurid Dynasty until it was overrun by the Shaybanid Uzbeks at the beginning of the sixteenth century. Tamerlane's longest-lasting legacy was the Turkic literary language called Chaghatay, which emerged during his rule and supplanted Persian. It survived as the primary language of the literary arts in Central Asia down to the twentieth century.

Bibliography

Barthold, Vasilii V. *Four Studies on the History of Central Asia*. Translated by V. Minorsky, and T. Minorsky. 2 vols. Leiden, Netherlands: E. J. Brill, 1956. Volume 1 consists of a history of Turkistan and Semirechie. It places

Tamerlane in the historical context, based on Barthold's authoritative interpretation. Notes, index, and chronological table. Volume 2 treats the origins of the Timurid state, the lives of Tamerlane and his successors, emphasizing his grandson Ulugh Beg. Notes, index, chronological table, and a few illustrations.

Gonzalez de Clavijo, Ruy. *Embassy to Tamerlane, 1403-1404*. Translated by Guy Le Strange. London: G. Routledge and Sons, 1928. Gives a firsthand account of the author's voyage in an embassy from Castile to the court of Tamerlane. It offers abundant description of the region, anecdotes from the court of the emir, and observations of life in Samarkand. Indexed, with notes.

Grousset, Rene. *The Empire of the Steppes*. Translated by Naomi Walford. New Brunswick, N.J.: Rutgers University Press, 1970. A general chronological history of the Eurasian Plains empires through the eighteenth century. Chapter 11 surveys the history of Tamerlane's conquests and the fate of his successors. Based on fifteenth and sixteenth century histories, with little analysis provided. Index, notes, and maps.

Howorth, Henry H. *History of the Mongols, from the Ninth to the Nineteenth Century*. 4 vols. London: Longmans, Green and Co., 1876-1927. Volume 2 contains Howorth's discussion of Toktamish, Khan of the Golden Horde, perhaps Tamerlane's most formidable adversary. Genealogical tables and extensive index.

Ibn Arabshah, Ahmed. *Tamerlane: Or, Timur, the Great Amir*. Translated by J. H. Sanders. London: Luzac, 1936. Reprint. Lahore, Pakistan: Progressive Books, 1976. A translation of the medieval historian's account of Tamerlane's life. Written after the emir's death, it is based on the works of earlier historians and on Ibn Arabshah's own experience. The author took a very negative view of Tamerlane's actions. Appendices give a conversion table for the Islamic calender and a list of tribal names. There is also a chronological table of the main events in Tamerlane's career.

Ibn Khaldun, Abd al-Rahman ibn Muhammad. *Ibn Khaldun and Tamerlane: Their Historic Meeting in Damascus, 1401 A.D. (Kitāb al-'Ibar al-Ta'rif)*. Translated by Walter J. Feischel. Berkeley: University of California Press, 1952. A short work supplemented with many explanatory remarks and notes. It gives Ibn Khaldun's account of his meeting with Tamerlane during a siege at Damascus, and of his later service with the emir.

Jackson, Peter, and Laurence Lockhart, eds. *The Cambridge History of Iran*. Vol. 6, *The Timurid and Safavid Periods*. Cambridge: Cambridge University Press, 1986. Contains chapters devoted to the history of Tamerlane and his successors. Analyses also of science, religion, architecture, other arts, and literature in the period, primarily in Iran. Many explanatory notes, a long bibliography, and thorough index.

Lamb, Harold. *Tamerlane: The Earth Shaker*. New York: Robert M. Mc-

Bride and Co., 1928. A readable history tracing Tamerlane's life from his rise to power until his death. Written in the style of a historical novel, based upon nineteenth century interpretations of primary and secondary sources. There is some discussion of Tamerlane's world, but Lamb slips into an uncritical use of primary documents. Illustrations, brief bibliography, and index.

Timur, the Great. *The Mulfuzat Timury*. Translated by Major Charles Stewart. London: J. Murray, 1830. This work purports be Tamerlane's autobiography. Some historians have doubted its authenticity; scholars, especially in Central Asia, however, continue to refer to it as a source for the study of Tamerlane's life.

Edward Allworth
William McCabe

T'AO CH'IEN

Born: A.D. 365; Hsin-yang, China
Died: A.D. 427; Hsin-yang, China
Area of Achievement: Literature
Contribution: T'ao Ch'ien's insistence upon directness and simplicity in both form and content, although largely unappreciated during his lifetime, was in subsequent generations recognized as a major contribution to the development of Chinese poetry.

Early Life

T'ao Ch'ien was born on his parents' farm near the city of Hsin-yang in what is now the province of Kiangsi. His family had once been prominent among the local gentry, but by T'ao Ch'ien's time their property had shrunk to a few acres. In an autobiographical sketch written for his sons, he described himself as a bookish youth, fond of quiet and never happier than when observing the changing of the seasons. He received a conventional education in the Confucian Classics and upon completing his studies was awarded a minor position in the civil service.

It did not take him long, however, to become bored with this post, and he resigned to return to the life of a small farmer. He married and soon found himself with several young children to support; the unremitting toil of farming soon took its toll on his health. In 395, when he was thirty, his first wife died, and for a short time he was employed as a general's secretary. Once again, he found that he could not abide the life of an official, and he was soon back tilling his meager farm.

After remarrying and having more children, thus putting additional pressure on his already straitened circumstances, T'ao Ch'ien made one final attempt at occupying the sort of position for which his education had prepared him. In 405, an uncle with influence at court arranged for him to be appointed magistrate at P'eng-tse, not far from his home. Before long, however, he had to resign, because "my instinct is all for freedom and will not brook discipline or restraint." For the remainder of his life, he would eke out a subsistence living on his farm and refuse all further offers of government employment, while exercising the poetic gifts that would not be widely acknowledged until well after his death.

Life's Work

China was racked by dynastic warfare during much of T'ao Ch'ien's life, and some commentators have suggested that his reluctance to assume official positions was caused by an awareness of the punishments which awaited those who supported the losing side. It is far more probable, however, that it was his profound dislike of being at a superior's beck and call that made it impossible for him to take on the kinds of responsibilities society expected of him. His independent attitude was incomprehensible to most of his peers, and as a result it was commonly assumed that T'ao Ch'ien must be some sort of hermit or recluse.

This he was not, although it is true that he studiously avoided anything which carried with it formal duties or organizational affiliations. He was at one point on the verge of accepting an invitation to join the Lotus Society, an exclusive group of Buddhist intellectuals and literary men, but at the last moment he declined when he realized that no matter how convivial its members might be, it was still an organization with rules and regulations. T'ao Ch'ien was not antisocial—he was reputed to have been well liked by his neighbors, and he knew quite a few of his fellow poets—but he definitely was an advocate of the simple life, which for him meant staying close to home and nature and ignoring almost everything else.

It is this fundamental love of simplicity that distinguishes T'ao Ch'ien's verses from the works of court poets of his time, who utilized obscure allusions and complicated technical devices to fashion verses that appealed only to the highly educated. T'ao Ch'ien, by way of contrast, seldom made any literary allusions whatsoever, and he wrote for the widest possible audience. As a consequence, he was slighted by his era's critics and only fully appreciated by later generations of readers. It was more than a century after his death before a complete edition of his works appeared. The first writers to champion seriously his reputation were the T'ang Dynasty poets Meng Hao-jan (689-740) and Wang Wei (701-761), who ensured that his name would not be forgotten by honoring him as a spiritual predecessor of what would become one of the most brilliant periods in Chinese literary history.

The charms of T'ao Ch'ien's poetry are subtle. The fifth poem in his series of poems on drinking wine is perhaps as good an example as any of how simple words and thoughts can yield complex emotions:

> I built my cottage among the habitations of men,
> And yet there is no clamor of carriages and horses.
> You ask: "Sir, how can this be done?"
> "A heart that is distant creates its own solitude."
> I pluck chrysanthemums under the eastern hedge,
> Then gaze afar towards the southern hills.
> The mountain air is fresh at the dusk of day;
> The flying birds in flocks return.
> In these things there lies a deep meaning;
> I want to tell it, but have forgotten the words.

The irony resides in the concluding line's apparent confession of failure, which is superficially true—the poem's meaning has not been formally defined in words—but in a more profound sense false, since meaning has been suggestively expressed in the cumulative interaction of these direct and vivid images. Such images might strike self-consciously sophisticated readers, which was how many of the court officials of T'ao Ch'ien's time viewed themselves, as nothing more than bucolic snapshots. For those who approach them without patronizing preconceptions, however, their evident simplicity is resonant with intimations of elemental natural forces.

In order to appreciate the full impact of T'ao Ch'ien's decision to concentrate on realistic description of his humble surroundings, the reader needs to compare his approach with that of the dominant aristocratic and scholarly poets of the period. Their ideal was the mannered evocation of court life in lyrics that were rigidly controlled by parallel structures and recurring tonal patterns. A literal translation of one of Shen Yo's poems reads:

> slackening reins, dismounts carved carriage,
> changing clothes, attends jade bed.
>
> slanting hairpin, reflects autumn waters,
> opening mirror, compares spring dresses.

Each line contains two—and no more or fewer than two—parallel images, the Chinese ideograms follow a set sequence of tones, and the content is characteristically taken from upper-class life.

Compare the above to the third section of T'ao Ch'ien's "Returning to the Farm to Dwell":

> I planted beans below the southern hill
> The grasses flourished, but bean sprouts were few.
> I got up at dawn to clear away the weeds
> And come back now with the moon, hoe on shoulder.
> Tall bushes crowd the narrow path
> And evening dew soaks my clothes.
> Wet clothes are no cause for complaint
> If things will only go as hoped.

Here the conversational tone of the narrative, the way that content is restricted to the mundanities of farm life, and the *in medias res* beginning all work together to convey an impression of natural reality that is the polar opposite of Shen Yo's sort of poetry.

T'ao Ch'ien was not, however, averse to enlivening his rural existence with an overindulgence in the pleasures of wine. He was renowned for his drinking, which in the social context of his period was an acceptable way of temporarily escaping worldly preoccupations rather than a sign of moral weakness. T'ao Ch'ien's name is thus often linked with those of two other poets who were also serious imbibers: Ch'u Yuan (c. 343 B.C.-c. 289 B.C.) and Li Po

(701-762). Some of his best poems were written while enjoying this favorite pastime.

T'ao Ch'ien's life ended in the same pastoral setting in which it had begun, with no dramatic anecdote to set the day of his death apart from the days that had preceded and would follow it. During his final twenty-two years, he had become both a material and a spiritual part of his natural environment. In a prose sketch written just before he died, T'ao Ch'ien described how, as was the custom, his old friends gave him a farewell banquet in honor of what he had meant to their lives. With typical unhurried deliberation, he enumerated the foods and wines that were served as he prepared "to depart from this lodging house to return for all time to his own home," where he would become one of the immortal figures of Chinese literature.

Summary

It is the high value T'ao Ch'ien set upon immediacy and immanence that has led many literary historians to see his work as pivotal in the development of Chinese poetry. Although there were advocates of simplicity who came before him and apostles of aestheticism still to come after him, it was his lyrics, more than any others, that served as a continuous source of inspiration for succeeding ages and would be rediscovered whenever poetry seemed in danger of becoming too mannered and removed from common experience.

In addition to his importance as a literary model, T'ao Ch'ien is admired for his decision to remain true to himself rather than subordinate his feelings to the demands of conventional life-styles. The writers and intellectuals of his day were, broadly speaking, split into the opposing camps of conformist Confucians and antiauthoritarian Taoists, and when T'ao Ch'ien rejected the former it would have been normal for him to have gravitated to the vagabond life of the latter. He chose, however, to pilot his own idiosyncratic course between these polar opposites, and he suffered much personal hardship in so doing.

Even more important than his position in literary history or his personal qualities, however, is the candid beauty of his poetry. The freshness of his images, his homespun but Heaven-aspiring morality, and his steadfast love of rural life shine through the deceptively humble words in which they are expressed, and as a consequence he has long been regarded one of China's most accomplished and accessible poets.

Bibliography

Cotterell, Yong Yap, and Arthur Cotterell. *The Early Civilization of China.* London: Weidenfeld and Nicolson, 1975. Chapter 6, "The Age of Disunity: The So-Called 'Six Dynasties,'" gives a good general account of historical developments during T'ao Ch'ien's time. This chapter also includes useful sections on the religion and art of the period.

Hightower, James Robert. "Allusion in the Poetry of T'ao Ch'ien." *Harvard Journal of Asiatic Studies* 31 (1971): 5-27. The received view of T'ao Ch'ien is that he only rarely made use of allusion as a literary technique, an interpretation which Hightower here argues is only partially accurate. This brief discussion is much more fully elaborated in the notes to Hightower's translation of T'ao Ch'ien's poetry.

————————. "T'ao Ch'ien's 'Drinking Wine' Poems," In *Wen-lin: Studies in the Chinese Humanities*, edited by Chow Tse-tung. Madison: University of Wisconsin Press, 1968. A fuller treatment of a subject also addressed in *The Poetry of T'ao Ch'ien*. This article is more extensively documented and offers a fuller discussion of the poems' important theme of the conflict between public service and private retirement.

T'ao Ch'ien. *The Poems of T'ao Ch'ien*. Translated by Lily Pao-hu Chang and Marjorie Sinclair. Honolulu: University of Hawaii Press, 1953. This beautifully produced volume includes original brush drawings reminiscent of a deluxe Chinese-language edition. Chang and Sinclair opt for inclusiveness in translating all the poems attributed to T'ao Ch'ien, several of which are the objects of scholarly debate. The translations themselves are reliable if not always idiomatic. A brief biography of the poet is included in an appendix.

————————. *The Poetry of T'ao Ch'ien*. Translated and edited by James Robert Hightower. Oxford: Clarendon Press, 1970. The standard edition in English. The translations themselves are not noticeably superior to those of his predecessors, but Hightower's notes make the book an essential reference for anyone doing serious work on T'ao Ch'ien. It is by far the best guide to its subject's use of traditional elements of the Chinese literary tradition.

————————. *T'ao the Hermit: Sixty Poems by T'ao Ch'ien (365-427)*. Translated by William Acker. London: Thames and Hudson, 1952. None of the three readily available English translations of T'ao Ch'ien's poetry seems to have influenced the others. Acker's have an unassuming dignity that is quite in keeping with what is known of T'ao Ch'ien, although they can sometimes seem stiff and unidiomatic as well. The well-annotated selection he offers includes about 40 percent of T'ao Ch'ien's poetry.

Paul Stuewe

TERENCE
Publius Terentius Afer

Born: c. 190 B.C.; Carthage
Died: 159 B.C.; en route to Greece
Area of Achievement: Literature
Contribution: As a Roman comic playwright whose innovative adaptations of Greek dramas depicted in graceful Latin the social realities operating in his ancient world, Terence strongly influenced the development of sophisticated theater in the West. His psychologically accurate portraits brought integrity to his craft.

Early Life
Ancient materials reporting Terence's life frequently present contradictory information; certain facts, however, fall into the realm of probability: Publius Terentius Afer (Terence) was born at Carthage and came to Rome as the slave of Terentius Lucanus, a senator who educated him and set him free. Since Terence's life fell between the Second and Third Punic Wars, he could not have been a slave captured in combat; thus, he may have been owned and sold by a Carthaginian trader.

Of average height, medium build, and with a dark complexion, Terence was a shade of brown which could range in hue from olive to Moorish, his cognomen "Afer" further indicating his African birth. Yet one cannot be completely certain that Terence was actually ever a slave, for Roman biographers, who often wove a web of fiction around their subjects, commonly recorded playwrights as having sprung from slavery, and "Afer" need not positively establish African birth. Nevertheless, many commentators have marveled at the significant achievement of the onetime slave who learned Latin as a second language and who came to use it with such outstanding artistry and precision.

In Rome, the young man's intelligence and talent soon gained for him entry into the Scipionic circle of study, a group of patrician literati behind a philhellenic movement. So close was the involvement of Terence and particular associates in this group—including Scipio Africanus and Gaius Laelius—that rumors circulated suggesting that Terence was simply a front for these august patrons of the arts who had really authored the plays. Terence, in fact, inadvertently helped the malicious gossip along by never definitively attempting to refute the charges. Indeed, in the prologues to his plays he concentrated on stating his theories of dramatic art, trying to deflect the scurrilous accusations. Yet, unfortunately, Terence's short life came to be plagued by constant innuendo.

When Terence offered his first drama to the aediles, the officials at the public games where the performances were held, he was ordered to show his work to Caecilius Statius, a revered comic playwright of an earlier era whose successes had been, in part, a result of the abilities of noted actor Lucius Ambivius Turpio. Legend describes the youthful Terence, poorly dressed, arriving at the dramatist's home during the dinner hour, sitting himself on a bench near the old man's couch, and beginning to read from his first effort. It took only a few minutes for Caecilius to recognize the genius of his young visitor, and Terence was invited to take a seat at the table. Not only did his career as dramatist begin at that moment but also the actor Turpio, now in old age, performed in Terence's plays, giving them the same public notice and authoritative support he had given to Caecilius. Thus promoted, Terence appeared an assured success from the beginning.

Life's Work

Terence looked to the New Comedy of Greece for his major literary resource and composed, therefore, in the tradition of *palliatae*, plays derived from Greek models, and acted in Greek dress, or *pallium*. Of the twenty-six complete plays surviving from the second century B.C. Roman stage, six are the work of Terence, whose chief model was Menander, an artist with a reputation in the ancient world superseded only by Homer and Vergil. While the Old Comedy had dealt with affairs of state, the New Comedy exemplified by Menander focused on domestic issues, particularly on wealthy youths and the tangled dilemmas of their often-complicated love lives. Filial duty, which on occasion ran counter to the young man's casual self-indulgence, and the devious machinations of crafty slaves helped generate comic situations at times to farcical extremes.

Terence found his métier in these intricate plots and, by artfully adapting the Greek models, brought with his distinctive translations a conscious artistry to the Roman stage. He developed prologues which articulated literary principles and which did not simply explain the action to follow. He developed a "doubling technique" to balance Menander's character creations. Alongside these innovations, Terence sensitively rendered the impact of behavioral fashion on the ethical values of his time. While Terence realized that in his models the characters were standard, the action was predictable, and the themes were formulaic; under his original touch the plays not only embody a vivid realism but also detail a sociological compendium of the age.

The complete works of Terence, produced over a six-year period, include the following extant plays: *Andria* (166 B.C.; *Andria*), *Hecyra* (165 B.C.; *The Mother-in-Law*), *Heautontimorumenos* (163 B.C.; *The Self-Tormentor*), *Eunuchus* (161 B.C.; *The Eunuch*), *Phormio* (161 B.C.; *Phormio*), and *Adelphoe* (160 B.C.; *The Brothers*). While the dramas themselves—all of them based on the work of either Menander or Apollodorus of Carystus—reveal the extent of Terence's achievement during his short, productive life, of greater significance to his biography are the *didascaliae* (production notes attached to the dramas) and the prologues, for these writings candidly reveal information which chronicles the way Terence's creative life was progressing. These statements sometimes indicate his strategy for dealing with the hurtful charges of plagiarism and the jealous accusations of *contaminatio*, that is, adulterating his literary sources.

Even before the presentation of his first play, Terence was forced to defend his unorthodox, innovative literary practices. Luscius Lanuvinus, a jealous competitor who had either seen *Andria* in rehearsal or read it in manuscript, began a vendetta of slander by accusing Terence of contaminating the plays he had used in his adaptation. During the next few years, these accusations were repeated and, apparently, escalated into charges of plagiarism. Terence went about defending the legitimacy of his literary methods as well as the originality of his artistry, going so far as to point out the Roman historical precedent for adapting work from the Greek stage. On one occasion, Terence flatly charged that his accuser was simply trying to force him into early retirement, to drive a young competitor from the theater by wounding him with invective. Insisting that he would prefer to exchange compliment for compliment rather than engage in verbal skirmishes, Terence urged his audiences to enjoy his plays, to be fair in their assessments, and to disregard the gossip of an evil-tempered old man, especially one whose talent was weak.

Another difficulty in his career Terence accepted with benign amusement: the problem with presenting *The Mother-in-Law*, a drama which suffered two failures before its eventual success. The first time Terence offered the play (165 B.C.), his audience rushed out of the performance to view a prizefight and a tightrope walker. Trying again five years later, Terence watched as the audience hurriedly left to watch some gladiators. A few months later, the play was successfully performed, with Terence in his prologue requesting courteous support for his efforts and urging his audience to abstain from irreverent behavior that might expose him to more unfair criticism by his enemies.

In his plays, Terence used the stock themes—boastful soldiers, crafty slaves, kindly prostitutes, professional parasites, confused sons, all involved in innocent mistakes and switched identities—and held the mirror up for the examination of moral and ethical principles, touching such concerns as the limits of filial duty, the question of a slave's loyalty, the role of women in Roman society, and the proprieties of legal deportment. While comedy did not readily lend itself to didacticism, Terence's plays, nevertheless, were epitomes of both entertainment and instruction, especially in portraying the emotional and psychological complexities involved in all human relationships.

Summary

As Terence's brief life was filled with controversy and speculation, so were the events surrounding his death. The playwright left Rome for Greece and never returned. He had undertaken the journey possibly to study at first hand the culture from which his plays were derived or to scrutinize the work of Menander—maybe even to discover other works modeled after Menander's or to escape for a time the Roman atmosphere of jealousy and acrimony which had spawned the petulant attacks of his rivals as they jockeyed for favor among patrons of the arts and theater audiences. Terence died in 159 B.C., either of an illness in Greece or in a shipwreck which also may have destroyed more than one hundred adaptations from Menander that he was bringing home.

Terence's reputation as a master dramatist has clearly withstood the passage of centuries; his accomplishments in the development and advancement of world theater are clear. His painstaking artistry in portraying psychological motivation and social reality set benchmarks for dramatists to follow in establishing the seriousness of comedy. In eliminating the prologue as simply a means to explain plot, Terence ensured that the drama had to depend upon characterization and dialogue. When sophisticated theatrical tastes came to govern the stage, Terence became a major literary source. During the Restoration in England, when the comedy of manners reigned supreme, Terence's work influenced such masters as William Congreve and Thomas Otway. In France, Molière looked to Terence for inspiration. In addition, the expository prologue as a means for critical expression and advancement of dramatic theory came to be a mark of identity for George Bernard Shaw.

The facts of Terence's life will be forever clouded by rumor and hearsay, for speculation and gossip were often freely intermingled with fact among ancient biographers. On Terence's death, records Suetonius, he left a twenty-acre estate on the Appian Way; Licinus Porcius, however, asserts that at the end of his life Terence possessed not even a rented house where his slave might announce his master's death.

Bibliography

Beare, W. *The Roman Stage: A Short History of Latin Drama in the Time of the Republic.* London: Methuen and Co., 1950. An authoritative study of the Roman stage particularly useful for revealing the stage practices, customs, and techniques of the time. Includes a detailed examination of the charge of contamination leveled against Terence. With extensive notes, bibliography, and appendices.

Copley, Frank O. *The Comedies of Terence.* Indianapolis: Bobbs-Merrill Co., 1967. Translations of each play with a useful, informative introductory note on each drama. A fourteen-page essay surveys the problems encountered in attempting to reconstruct Terence's life and in trying to analyze his art.

Duckworth, George E. *The Nature of Roman Comedy: A Study in Popular*

Entertainment. Princeton, N.J.: Princeton University Press, 1952. A vital source for learning about the ancient stage and its conventions as well as for the contribution of Terence to the "Golden Age of Drama at Rome." This work is a detailed study of themes, treatments, methods, and influences of Terence, including the critical problems in studying his texts and the biographical problems in studying his life. With an extensive index and bibliography.

——————, ed. *The Complete Roman Drama*. 2 vols. New York: Random House, 1942. This work includes Terence's production notes, which date the performances, describe some of the staging techniques, identify some of the actors, and generally help both in setting the Terentian ambience and establishing the plays' chronologies. A general introduction provides a sound overview of the entire era and gives important information on ancient stage discipline.

Forehand, Walter E. *Terence*. Boston: Twayne Publishers, 1985. A sound, basic work which outlines the major controversies surrounding Terence's life and productions. Contains a full account of Terence's literary career, surveying the plays and illuminating the theater background of the times. An excellent introduction to Terence and his stage. Includes a selected bibliography.

Goldberg, Sander M. *The Making of Menander's Comedy*. Berkeley: University of California Press, 1980. A study of Menander's art important for the light it sheds upon Terence, whose adaptations came mainly from this Greek model. Terence's work in relation to Menander is discussed in detailed, analytical fashion throughout.

——————. *Understanding Terence*. Princeton, N.J.: Princeton University Press, 1986. A perceptive, analytical study focusing on Terence and the Latin tradition of New Comedy rather than on Terence as an adapter of Menander; this work analyzes the prologues and the plays for their language and themes. The critical problems in dealing with Terence are studied. Contains a bibliography for the individual plays as well as for further study of ancient Greece.

Harsh, Philip Whaley. *A Handbook of Classical Drama*. Stanford, Calif.: Stanford University Press, 1944. Contains an informative survey of Terence's life and work set within the context of the total range of classical drama. Extensive notes as well as full bibliographies for Terence and his peers are included.

Konstan, David. *Roman Comedy*. Ithaca, N.Y.: Cornell University Press, 1983. An examination of the New Comedy genre within contexts of the ideology and the institutions of the Roman state. With a reading of Roman plays—including Terence's—from the social and philosophical perspective to determine how the plays defined and revealed the ethical standards and moral imperatives of the age. Includes an extensive bibliography.

Norwood, Gilbert. *Plautus and Terence*. New York: Cooper Square Publishers, 1963. Five of the nine chapters address Terence's life and work, emphasizing his style, characterizations, plot structure, and basic thought. Contains an appendix outlining specific influences of particular Terence plays on English drama. Examined also are the disputes over Terence's methods of adaptation. Includes a selective bibliography.

Abe C. Ravitz

TERTULLIAN

Born: c. A.D. 155-160; at or near Carthage, North Africa
Died: After A.D. 217; probably near Carthage, North Africa
Areas of Achievement: Religion and literature
Contribution: Eloquent and aggressive, Tertullian was the most outstanding spokesman for Christianity in the Latin West before Saint Augustine; his polemical treatises set the direction for much of Western theology.

Early Life
Quintus Septimius Florens Tertullianus, though he left a strong mark on the history of Latin literature and exercised more influence than anyone but Augustine on the development of theology in the Western church, left but few scraps of biographical information. A short paragraph in Saint Jerome's *De viris illustribus* (392-393; on famous men) yields a few assertions, and several deductions can be made from Tertullian's writings, which are remarkable for their lack of self-revelation. Each item has been closely examined by scholars, and while virtually nothing can be said with certainty about the man, the following picture emerges from a cautious balancing of ancient tradition and modern skepticism.

Tertullian was certainly born and reared in Roman North Africa, in or near the proconsular capital of Carthage, to a prosperous pagan family. His father was probably a career military officer attached to the staff of the proconsul, and several relatives were active in the literary life of the city. Any birth date assigned to Tertullian (usually A.D. 155-160) is reached by subtracting from A.D. 197, the secure date of one of his earliest works, the *Apologeticus (Apology)*, enough years—roughly forty—to account for its character as a mature masterpiece of style, argumentation, and Christian apologetics.

Tertullian received the standard education of a well-to-do Roman, culminating in extensive rhetorical training, in which he must have excelled, judging from his subsequent literary career. It is difficult to avoid identifying Tertullian of Carthage with Tertullian the jurist, whose writings are quoted in later Roman law codes. The men were contemporaries; the jurist wrote on questions of military law, and the Carthaginian had a penchant for legalistic language and argument and was declared by Eusebius of Caesarea to have been eminent at the Roman bar. If they were indeed the same person, Tertullian of Carthage traveled to Rome, became a pupil of the great jurist Pomponius, and established among legal scholars of the Empire a reputation that was later vindicated by his apologetic works.

It was probably in early middle age, not long before 197, that Tertullian converted to Christianity. He never discusses his conversion, though he expresses repeatedly an admiration for the constancy of Christian martyrs, their steadfastness in persecution, and their stubborn defiance of Roman authority in the face of death. It was he who coined the saying "The blood of Christians is seed." He may have been ordained a priest, as Jerome claims, for some of Tertullian's works are clearly sermons. While Tertullian uses two or three turns of phrase which place him among the laity, these may be rhetorical poses—devices which he uses more frequently than any other Latin writer. He was certainly married, but though he addressed several treatises to his wife, they reveal nothing of her personality or of their relationship. This opacity is characteristic of Tertullian's writings: He turned consistently outward toward problems and enemies but seldom inward to reflect on himself or friends.

Life's Work

In the first three or four years of his career as a Christian, Tertullian devoted his rhetorical talents to apologetics—for example, in *Ad nationes* (A.D. 197; *To the Nations*) and the *Apology*—defending Christianity against pagan hostility with the aim of ending official persecution. These writings provide an invaluable window on primitive Christian belief and practice, but they are so self-righteous and vehement that they must have increased the pagans' animosity rather than diminishing it. Tertullian's strategy is often to argue that pagan Romans do not live up to their own beliefs, values, laws, and civic traditions as well as Christians do. This pose claims for the writer a privileged ability to interpret the texts and traditions of others. He denies repeatedly the right of Roman magistrates to judge Christians, on the ground that God's law is higher than man's, and he makes the claim, remarkable for a lawyer, that no law has binding force unless it is accepted by the individual's conscience. Such claims to unfettered autonomy of belief and action recur throughout Tertullian's works.

Tertullian's theological vision centered initially on the Church, seeing it as the community mediating between God and humans and thus the authoritative interpreter of Scripture and channel of God's grace. He argued against certain rigorists that postbaptismal sins could be forgiven by the Church, but his lawyer's training led him to think of sin chiefly in terms of Roman law, the categories of which he introduced into Christian theological vocabulary. He uses the term *delictum* (crime) much more often than *peccatum* (sin) and demands confession before a judge, and the imposition of a penalty, to complete the process of expiating wrongdoing. Correspondingly, penances or good deeds "hold God a debtor" and oblige Him to grant the doer forgiveness, favor, and eventually salvation.

Tertullian's logical prowess and penchant for fine distinctions served him well in dogmatic theology. He was the first to use the term "trinity" to describe the relation of Father, Son, and Spirit, and he pioneered the description of Jesus as one person with a divine and a human nature. These positions antedate the Nicene Creed by more than a century and have become standard in all the main branches of Christianity.

Not long after the year 200, Tertullian's energies turned to polemical treatises against Gnostics and other heretics, especially the ascetic Marcionites. In these contentious and angry pieces he seems to take on many of the characteristics of his opponents, sinking deep into moral rigorism and antisocial attitudes. He was forced consequently to make ever more contorted and idiosyncratic interpretations of Scripture to score points against them. By around 210, he had drifted away from the mainstream of orthodox Christianity into Montanism, a sect which claimed that its private revelations superseded those of the New Testament and which opposed a pure, invisible, "spiritual" Church to the corrupt, visible church of the bishops and clergy. Thereafter, Tertullian increasingly stressed the role of private illuminations from the Spirit and the ability of each Christian to interpret Scripture for himself, outside, or even against, the tradition of the Church.

Though he is famous for comparing classical philosophy unfavorably with Christian theology—"What . . . has Athens to do with Jerusalem?"—he does not reject the formulations and arguments of philosophy, but only their claim to compel assent—so strong was his determination to be utterly unfettered in his choice of belief. In fact, he formulates his own positions much more often in philosophical than in biblical terms, quoting Scriptures more for slogans and proof texts than to develop any genuine biblical theology. His major treatise *De anima* (*On the Soul*), for example, is based on Stoic theory, affirming that the substance of the cosmos is all one, with no distinction of matter and spirit. Tertullian drew the explicit conclusion that soul-substance, as well as body-substance, is passed on from parents to children and laid thereby the foundation for the doctrine of Original Sin, unknown previously.

Having always tended toward absolutism, Tertullian became more extreme and rigorist in his Montanist phase. He reversed his earlier position that sins could be forgiven, claimed that anything which is not explicitly commanded by Scripture is forbidden, and became so confident of his own interpretations as to revoke divine commands from the Old Testament and apostolic counsels in the New. In his last writings his tone is bitterly antisocial and misanthropic; here he pictures himself as living in a world bound for damnation and gloats over the impending deaths of his enemies. Apparently he broke with Montanism in his last years to found his own sect, the Tertullianists, which survived some two centuries until the time of Augustine. His last datable writing was done in 217; according to Jerome, however, he lived to an advanced age.

Summary

Tertullian's Latin prose style is the most vehement, tortuous, and pyrotechnic ever produced, the ultimate flower of the genre of controversy, lush with innovative vocabulary and quotable phrasing. This power, however, was in the hands of a tortured spirit, a man who was hostile, suspicious, and self-righteous, alienated from the world, from others, and, ultimately, from himself. His writings exhibit many of the traits associated with the authoritarian personality. Rejecting first pagan religion, then the Roman Empire, then orthodox Christianity, and finally the Montanist heresy, he ended his days in an idiosyncratic splinter group defined solely by himself.

Though Tertullian's writings were condemned by the Church in the sixth century, his genius blazed theological paths which are followed to this day: the doctrine of Original Sin, the Trinity of Persons in God, and the dual natures of Jesus. His legalism and penchant for *quid pro quo* justice set the tone for Western Christianity's outlook on sin, forgiveness, grace, and salvation for fourteen centuries, until Martin Luther supplied a corrective. His insistence on the validity of philosophical concepts led to the Roman Catholic tradition of reasoning from natural law, as his rejection of the binding force of philosophical conclusions on his absolute God led to the primacy of scriptural authority in Protestantism. His early argument that Scripture belongs to the Church and can only be interpreted rightly by the Church in accord with its traditions is still a mainstay of Catholic and Eastern Orthodox thinking. His later emphasis on private interpretation of scriptural texts provided a strong impetus to the Protestant Reformation; combined with his moral rigorism and rejection of a visible Church in favor of a "spiritual" or personally defined one, it has exerted continuing influence on Fundamentalism.

Bibliography

Barnes, T. D. *Tertullian: A Historical and Literary Study*. Oxford: Clarendon Press, 1971. This specialized work presents all the evidence ever likely to be available concerning Tertullian's life and the dates of his writings, but Barnes subjects the material to an extremely narrow and skeptical criticism, ignoring or dismissing ancient testimony. His largely negative conclusions must be taken into account, but their radical denials should be balanced by the recognition that ancient authorities had available to them more and better sources than do modern scholars.

Bray, Gerald L. *Holiness and the Will of God: Perspectives on the Theology of Tertullian*. Atlanta: John Knox Press, 1979. This is probably the best overview of Tertullian's thought. It is particularly helpful in synthesizing his positions, which often appear fragmentarily in scattered works and which changed drastically during his writing career.

Morgan, James. *The Important of Tertullian in the Development of Christian Dogma*. London: K. Paul, Trench, Trubnar, 1928. Classic work surveying Tertullian's contributions in various areas, and thus somewhat superficial in each. Bray's work (see above) supplies more up-to-date interpretations.

Roberts, A., and J. Donaldson, eds. *The Ante-Nicene Fathers*. Vols. 3 and 4. Reprint. Grand Rapids, Mich.: Wm. B. Eerdmans, 1956. This is a reprint of the 1925 American edition of the nineteenth century British *Ante-Nicene Christian Library*. The translation is somewhat archaic, and it is sparsely annotated, but these volumes offer the only English versions of many of Tertullian's works, including *Ad Scapulam*.

Tertullian. *Treatises on Penance*. Translated by W. P. LeSaint. New York: Newman Press, 1959. A modern translation of two representative works, with extensive introduction and meticulous annotation, theological, philosophical, philological, and literary. This annotation draws out well the depth and fertility of Tertullian's genius and situates him in the intellectual climate of his time.

Tertullian and Minucius Felix. *Apology, De spectaculis, Octavius*. Translated by T. R. Glover and G. H. Rendall. Cambridge, Mass.: Harvard University Press, 1931. A serviceable and widely available translation of Tertullian's best-known work, with Latin text. The text of Minucius Felix is interesting since he is the only known Christian Latin writer before Tertullian and the only author from whom Tertullian borrows extensively. "Minucius" may in fact be a pseudonym used by Tertullian for his first Christian work.

Warfield, B. B. *Studies in Tertullian and Augustine*. Reprint. Westport, Conn.: Greenwood Press, 1970. This monograph-length essay on Tertullian gives the best treatment of his power and originality as a theologian, using his Trinitarian doctrine as focus for the study.

John D. Madden

THALES OF MILETUS

Born: c. 624 B.C.; Miletus, Ionia, Asia Minor
Died: c. 548 B.C.; Miletus, Ionia, Asia Minor
Areas of Achievement: Philosophy and science
Contribution: Through his various theories, Thales countered supernatural and mythical explanations of nature, attempting to replace them with empirically derived answers. He became a transitional figure between the worlds of philosophy and science.

Early Life
Few details are known about the life of the man many call "the father of philosophy." Ancient tradition often fixed a person's birth date by a major event. According to Apollodorus, an Athenian historian of the second century B.C., the major event in Thales' life was the solar eclipse of 585-584 B.C., when he was forty years old. If this is correct, then Thales was born circa 624. He was a member of a distinguished family from the port city of Miletus, Ionia, on the west coast of Asia Minor. Thales' upper-class background meant that he had the luxury of spending his life engaged in intellectual pursuits.

Although probably from Phoenicia originally, Thales' family most likely lived in Miletus for several generations. Besides his social standing, his place of birth is also significant. Miletus was the major trading center of the Aegean Sea in the sixth century B.C. The coastal city entertained merchants from Egypt, Greece, and the Persian Empire. It possessed both a frontier spirit and a cosmopolitan, intellectual environment. A thriving economic center with a rich mixture of Near Eastern and Greek cultures, Miletus had no traditional, government-imposed beliefs that it sanctioned; life in Miletus was unconventional.

The body of knowledge familiar to the young Thales came principally from two sources: the earliest Greek writers and the scholars of Egypt and Babylon. These ideas played a significant role in the philosophy of Thales, not because of their influence on him but rather because of his departure from them. Among the first ideas Thales encountered were those from the writings of Homer and Hesiod. Both these important Greeks speculated on the origins of the world and certain natural phenomena. Their answers, however, were always found within the realm of the Olympian gods. Homer and Hesiod did gather some factual data which they incorporated into their writings, but scientific advancement was impossible as long as nature was interpreted as the supernatural caprices of the gods. Greek thinkers before Thales had some knowledge of natural occurrences but never moved toward a more rational analysis. Theirs was an anthropomorphic world. Mythology served both as science and history prior to the revolution in thought which occurred in Miletus during the mid-sixth century.

The other information common to men such as Thales came from the Near East. The ancients of Egypt and Babylon had long experimented with their own forms of science and mathematics. The wonders of the Egyptian pyramids and other structures interested the Ionians, and the Babylonians claimed the attention of scholars for their study of the stars. While the achievements of these Near Eastern civilizations were remarkable, they were also limited in their scope. The Egyptians never converted their practical knowledge of mathematics and engineering into theories and principles. The Babylonians compiled volumes of notes on the heavens and developed astrology, a discipline hardly resembling astronomy. This was the intellectual climate, complete with preconceptions and misconceptions about natural "science," into which Thales was born.

Life's Work

The philosophy Thales espoused must be gleaned from the excerpts and comments of other authors. Herodotus, Aristotle, and Diogenes are the most notable ancient writers who included Thales in their works, and Thales' contributions are represented consistently in all three accounts. Thales bridged the gap between superstition and reason. Aristotle credited Thales with being the first recorded Milesian in a line of pre-Socratic philosophers who attempted to define nature in terms of nature itself. The questions Thales asked and the assumptions he proposed changed philosophy and science and laid a rational foundation upon which others could build.

Thales searched for the "stuff," as the ancients referred to it, which composed all existing matter. He assumed that among the infinite variety of things on Earth there must be one underlying source of their existence. Though the stuff might change its form, it essentially retained its properties. Through observation, Thales concluded that the first principle of the world must be water. It was the prime substance of all things, and Earth floated on a cushion of it.

The matter of Thales' theory also possessed the quality of fluidity. It was to some degree alive and caused the change perceived in the visible world. Thales compared the inner power of water to a magnet that moves a piece of iron. This animism was typical of sixth century philosophy. It compelled Thales to conclude that all things are "full of gods." Although he used religious language, Thales did not adhere to a prevalent religious system—nor did he attempt to deify water in the traditional sense of ancient custom. To Thales, that which gave continual life must, in the vernacular of the time, be to some extent divine. Water was that life-giving substance which in one form or another composed everything and thus merited the term "god," not an anthropomorphic Olympian god but a new secular and rational god of Thales' making.

There is no extant record of the reason Thales chose water as the stuff of the world. Certainly the importance of water was not lost on ancient man. Water was central in the mythology of Greece, Egypt, and Babylon, as well as in the Hebrew creation account. Some historians suggest that these myths exerted the greatest influence on Thales. In the epics of the Near East, Earth rises out of primeval water. The principal focus of these myths, however, was the origin of the world, not a common substance underlying all things in the world; thus, Thales probably did not draw from them. Further, none of the ancient commentators on Thales mentions any influence of Near Eastern thought on Ionian philosophy developing in the sixth century B.C.

Many modern scholars have asserted that there is a rational explanation for Thales' choice of water. Since Thales' theory was founded on observation only, not experimentation, the three phases of water would have been readily apparent to him. Water, appearing in such numerous forms, fits the description of the stuff which changes but is fundamentally constant. From the sources on Thales, however, it is never established that he even understood the three states of water.

Aristotle postulated another reason which led Thales to his conclusion. It is a variation of the rational explanation fashioned by modern scholars. Given the proximity of Aristotle to Thales, this may be the closest to the latter's own thinking. As Aristotle suggested, there existed a close link in the ancient mind between water and life. There were the rivers and seas without which man could not nourish himself. Trees contained sap, and plants had liquid within their stems. Growth, and therefore change, was inextricably tied to water—and nowhere was this clearer than in the ancient world. Even the human body testified to the importance of moisture. From conception to death, water was an integral part of human existence. As Aristotle observed, when the body died two things occurred: It became cold, and it dried up. Even that which was hot and dry required water. A popular fifth century B.C. idea held that the sun drew water to itself for nourishment and then rained it back to Earth to complete the cycle. Whether myth or logic influenced Thales, his attempt to look outside the divine process for answers to the puzzles of nature was monumental. By so doing, he attributed an orderliness to the cosmos which had heretofore been regarded as the disorderly and mystical playground of the gods.

Contemporaries hailed Thales as a politician, diplomat, civil engineer, mathematician, and astronomer, but his achievements in those roles are uncertain. Among the more important feats attributed to Thales was his prediction of a solar eclipse in 585-584 B.C. During a significant battle between the Medes and Lydians, Thales is said to have forecast a solar eclipse which, when it occurred, caused such trepidation among the combatants that they ceased fighting and called a truce. The ancients certainly believed the tale, but modern scholars doubt that Thales could predict an eclipse (such a prediction requires sophisticated astronomical calculations). A more likely astronomical achievement attributed to Thales is his idea of steering ships by the constellation Ursa Minor.

Tradition also credited Thales with introducing Egyptian principles of geometry to Greece. In Egypt, Thales is said to have taken the practical knowledge of Egyptian scholars and devised a method for accurately measuring the pyramids by their shadows. Altogether, five theorems are attributed to Thales. It is impossible to know the exact contribution of Thales to mathematics; it is likely, however, that he made some fundamental discoveries that enabled later mathematicians to build a framework for a variety of theorems.

In the minds of his contemporaries, Thales was not only a philosopher but also a sage. The Greeks named him one of the Seven Wise Men, because he urged the Ionian states to unite lest they fall easy prey to the Persian Empire. Thales was so respected by his countrymen that it is difficult to determine to what extent the legends which surround him are apocryphal. In antiquity, attributing great discoveries or achievements to men with reputations for wisdom was a common practice. The ancient authors themselves often recorded conflicting accounts of the accomplishments of Thales. It seems that they chose whatever Thalesian story would substantiate the more general point they were trying to make. Whatever the veracity of the stories enveloping Thales, it seems logical that his reputation for rational thinking would spread from his cosmological interests to such fields as mathematics, astronomy, and politics.

Summary

Were all the legends surrounding Thales false, his speculations on the principal substance of the world would be enough to accord him special recognition. It is not the theory itself that is so significant but the revolution in thinking that it produced. Thales placed the study of nature on a new plane: He lifted it from the realm of the mythical to the level of empirical study. Scholars began to evaluate and analyze theories on the basis of the factual data available. Thales was the first of what has been called the Milesian group of the Ionian school of philosophy. Anaximander and Anaximenes, who followed him, produced more sophisticated philosophical systems, but they regarded Thales as the master.

To the modern scholar, the limitations of Thales' thinking are apparent. There remained elements of anthropomorphism and mythology in the work of Thales and the other pre-Socratic philosophers. While Thales rejected a universe controlled by the gods with his assertion "all things are water," he did not anticipate an atomic theory, as Democritus did. Thales attributed to nature an animism which prevented him from seeing it as a neutral agent in the world. In this sense, his ideas are less abstract than the ideas of those who came after him. Thales does not properly belong to the world of modern science, and yet he is equally misplaced when his ideas are classified with the cosmologies of Homer and Hesiod. Thales transcended, through rational analysis, the established supernatural explanations of nature, laying the foundation for major advances in philosophy and science in the following centuries.

Bibliography

Brumbaugh, Robert S. *The Philosophers of Greece*. New York: Thomas Y. Crowell, 1964. Evaluation of Greek philosophy from Thales to Aristotle. Brumbaugh draws his information mainly from ancient authors themselves. Takes a "romantic" approach to the subject which depicts Thales as a Renaissance man. Includes an extensive bibliography.

Burnet, John. *Early Greek Philosophy*. London: Adam and Charles Black, 1892, 4th ed. 1930. An older work and somewhat out-of-date, but still considered one of the first major pieces on the subject. Emphasizes the Greeks as the earliest scientists and philosophers. The extensive use of Greek in the footnotes and to a lesser degree in the text limits the book's usefulness for less advanced scholars. Includes elaborate notes on source material.

Guthrie, William Keith Chambers. *A History of Greek Philosophy*. Vol. 1, *The Earlier Presocratics and Pythagoreans*. Cambridge: Cambridge University Press, 1962. A standard, sound, general account of the subject, beginning with Thales and continuing through to the works of Heraclitus. Concentrates on how early Greek writers of myths and theogonies influenced the early ideas of the pre-Socratic philosophers and adheres to the traditional claim of Thales as the first European philosopher. Contains a large bibliography.

Hussey, Edward. *The Pre-Socratics*. New York: Charles Scribner's Sons, 1972. An introduction to early Greek thought designed for the reader with no background in Greek. This volume provides a general account with less detail about historiographical controversies. Deals with philosophy and science within the political and cultural setting of the ancient world and stresses the importance of political development on the emergence of the ideas of Thales. Includes a few helpful maps and an extensive annotated bibliography.

Jones, W. T. *The History of Western Philosophy*. Vol. 1, *The Classical Mind*. 2d ed. New York: Harcourt Brace Jovanovich, 1970. First volume of a four-volume work. Deals with Thales and the pre-Socratics through the late classical period of Roman philosophy. A limited coverage of Thales that places more emphasis on the philosophical and scientific foundation he laid for those who followed him than on his actual theories. Includes a small bibliography and a helpful glossary of philosophical terms.

Nahm, Milton C., ed. *Selections from Early Greek Philosophy*. New York:

F. S. Crofts and Co., 1934. Short translated excerpts from the works of ancient authors on various personas in early Greek philosophy. Book spans the period from the Milesians through the atomists. Includes the commentaries on Thales by Diogenes, Aristotle, and Plutarch.

Wightman, William P. D. *The Growth of Scientific Ideas*. New Haven, Conn.: Yale University Press, 1951. Critically explores the advance of science from the Ionians through Charles Darwin. Less concerned with the philosophical aspects of the Milesian thinkers than with their contributions to science. Somewhat critical of Thales' theories, even within the context of the ancient world. Contains a limited annotated bibliography of general works, but a more specific list of sources concludes each chapter. Includes several illustrations and a helpful chronology of scientific discoveries and innovations.

Linda Perry Abrams

THEMISTOCLES

Born: c. 524 B.C.; Athens, Greece
Died: c. 460 B.C.; Magnesia, Asia Minor
Areas of Achievement: Government and military
Contribution: Themistocles engineered the naval defeat of the Persians at
Salamis and thus made possible the subsequent Age of Pericles in ancient
Athens.

Early Life

Themistocles was born about 524 B.C. to an Athenian father, Neocles, and
a non-Athenian mother. His father's family, the Lycomidai, was respected,
but his father achieved no great prominence. No details of his early life antedate Plutarch, who six centuries later related a number of anecdotes showing
him to be clever, resourceful, and interested in politics from the start. In one
of these stories, Themistocles was coming home from school when he saw
coming toward him the tyrant Peisistratus. When the boy's tutor cautioned
him to step aside, Themistocles answered, "Isn't the road wide enough for
him?"

The political and military events of the final decades of the sixth century B.C. shaped the course of Themistocles' life. Even before he was born,
the rapidly expanding Persian Empire had entrenched itself in Lydia, directly east from Athens across the Aegean Sea, with its countless islands
available as stepping stones to the Greek mainland. In his teenage years, Themistocles would have heard older Athenians discussing the ominous Persian
advance across the Bosporus into Thrace and Macedonia to the north as well
as into the easternmost Greek islands.

He was growing up in an increasingly commercial culture fostered by
Peisistratus and maintained by his successors until Sparta, the strongest
Greek state, expelled Hippias in 510 and enrolled Athens in its Peloponnesian League. Athens found herself the focus of a struggle between the mili-
tant Spartans and the advancing Persians. It might have occurred to Themistocles early in his manhood that a strong naval force might become the key to
Athenian defense.

The career of Hippias must have seemed particularly instructive. Having
fled to Persia after his deposition, Hippias was first offered reinstatement as
the price Athens must pay for Persian neutrality. Sparta later brought
Hippias back and offered to restore him in Athens to block any increase in
Persian influence. Given these political realities, freedom was precarious,
and Themistocles certainly would have learned how participation in such
maneuvers could impair the credibility of a leader. Despite achievements
much more brilliant than those of Hippias, he would eventually face both exile and suspicion himself.

Life's Work

By 493, Themistocles had attained sufficient stature to be chosen an archon in Athens, then a post of considerable authority. Nothing is known of his role in the famous Battle of Marathon in 490, which resulted in victory for the Athenian general Miltiades the Younger, and because the whereabouts of Themistocles are unknown until 483, some historians doubt the earlier archonship. In the latter year, however, he manifested his leadership by persuading the Athenians to use the proceeds of a newly discovered silver mine to modernize the navy and expand its fighting strength to two hundred vessels. Accepted as the unquestioned leader of Athens, Themistocles directed the campaign against the great Persian commander Xerxes I. Ordering a series of strategic retreats as the Persians, fresh from their victory at Thermopylae, swept down on Athens from the north, Themistocles at length committed the newly enlarged fleet to battle at Salamis, off the Attic coast, in 480. He used deception—at which he excelled—to lull the Persian fleet into overconfidence, and he used eloquence to bolster Athenian morale. Along with its Greek allies, the Athenian navy maneuvered the larger Persian fleet into a narrow strait and decisively defeated the invaders, who fled back across the Aegean.

Themistocles being a man who needed recognition, he resented the Athenian failure to honor him sufficiently and went to Sparta, where he was given an olive crown and a chariot described by the historian Herodotus as the most beautiful in Sparta. After a shower of praise, Themistocles enjoyed an escort of three hundred Spartan soldiers who accompanied him to the border. Back in Athens, which had borne the brunt of the Persian offensive, only remnants of the city wall stood, and a massive rebuilding project loomed. A Spartan delegation tried to persuade the Athenian leaders not to reconstruct the wall, ostensibly so that no foreign invader could capture the city and hold it as the Persians had before Salamis. In reality, as Themistocles saw it, Sparta and its other allies to the south feared that with its new naval eminence, a fortified Athens itself represented too strong a potential foe. Regarding the rebuilding as essential, Themistocles persuaded his fellow Athenians to send him back to Sparta to negotiate the matter and meanwhile to put all men, women, and children to work at the reconstruction. In Sparta, Themistocles used all of his wiles to postpone the talks. He explained that he could not proceed without his colleagues, who had been unaccountably delayed. When reports came back that the wall was already rising, he labored to convince the Spartans of their falsity. Eventually he suggested that a trustworthy inspection team be sent, while at the same time he secretly sent instructions to delay the visitors in every possible way.

With the hastily constructed wall in place, Themistocles admitted the deception but defended it stoutly. The Athenians, he pointed out, had abandoned their city in the first place on their own; furthermore, they had devised the strategy that had lured the invaders to their defeat. Whenever they had consulted with their allies, the Athenians had displayed good judgment. Now it was the Athenian judgment that without walls Athens could not contribute equally with other walled cities of the alliance. Sparta had no doubt expected such arguments from Themistocles, though not after the fact; nevertheless, he extricated himself from Sparta without drawing any overt hostility. Through his deception, he had obtained improvements which he never could have negotiated, for the workers had substantially increased both the thickness of the walls and the area they enclosed. Following Themistocles' advice, they had also fortified the "lower city," Piraeus, in accordance with his theory that as long as Athens maintained naval superiority, safety lay. in the lower city, with its natural harbors on both sides of the peninsula that it straddled.

Within five years of the victory at Salamis, a reaction set in against Themistocles. He probably contributed to this reaction through boasting and heavy-handed attempts to exact payments toward the cost of his military campaign from Athenian allies. He appears to have had little to do with the ascendancy of Athens in the Delian League, formed in 477 to combat future Persian aggression. It is difficult to determine whether Themistocles' absence from leadership in this important defensive alliance springs from distrust on the part of his colleagues or his own perception that Sparta, not Persia, represented the most likely future enemy. While the new leaders, Cimon and Aristides, supported Sparta and the alliance, Themistocles opposed any extension of Spartan influence. In this respect, he showed more foresight than the men who had replaced him in power.

Themistocles had obvious faults. Herodotus depicts him as constantly seeking personal gain; even if his assiduous fund-raising went largely for the common good, suspicions to the contrary were bound to arise. He appears to have been vain and egotistical. Even his wiliness, so valuable against enemies, posed a threat. Like Homer's Odysseus, Themistocles had built his reputation not so much on valor as on duplicity. In the Athens of the 470's, it would not have been difficult to see this devious man with his unpopular anti-Spartan bias as dangerous to Athenian security.

For whatever reason, around the year 472, he was ostracized. Many prominent citizens were exiled without specific accusations or formal trials in that era, and ostracism was only temporary, but Themistocles never returned to Attic soil. He first chose anti-Spartan Argos as his refuge, but in his absence he was condemned as a traitor. He found it necessary to flee to the island of Corcyra in the Ionian Sea, but he found no welcome there and continued to Epirus in northwestern Greece. His odyssey continued in the land of the Molossians to the east and then to Pydna on the Aegean coast. Thucydides reports him to have sailed on a merchant ship to Ionia, but a storm carried the ship to Naxos, an island then under Athenian siege. Bribing the captain,

Themistocles persuaded him to sail to the coast of Asia Minor, and there he applied to his old enemies the Persians for refuge. He was granted not only refuge but also honors, in fact the governorship of Magnesia, in what is now west-central Turkey, probably after the death of his old adversary Xerxes in 465. Magnesian coins bearing his imprint have survived.

One story of Themistocles' death has him committing suicide by drinking bull's blood to avoid the necessity of leading a military expedition against the Greeks, but it is much more likely that he died a natural death around 460.

Summary

An Odyssean leader, Themistocles excelled at outwitting his military and political opponents. He demonstrated the true leader's capacity to resist the popular mood and to redirect popular energy toward prudent ends. His decision to devote windfall profits from silver mines, which others wanted to divide up among the populace, to naval defense, saved Athens from almostsure defeat at the hands of the Persians and preserved Athenian autonomy in the face of Spartan ambition. Although Themistocles did nothing personally to promote Athenian democracy, its later flowering surely depended on his actions in defense of a strong and independent city-state.

Not always a good man, Themistocles was an indisputably great leader. Despite the fact that at various times he opposed all of them, the three major states of his region—Athens, Sparta, and Persia—all heaped honors on him. Thucydides reports that the Magnesians, whom he led in his last years, erected a monument to him in the marketplace. They saw him not as a former enemy but as a man whose talent for governance, frustrated in his own land, needed scope and opportunity. His brilliance and energy in public projects outweighed the devious means by which he achieved them and his penchant for boasting of them afterward. Thucydides regarded him as an intuitive genius who could operate successfully in matters for which neither his training nor his experience had prepared him. Adversity brought out the best in him and inspired him to bring out the best in the troops and citizens whom he led.

Bibliography

Forrest, W. G. "Themistokles and Argos." *The Classical Quarterly* 10 (1960): 221-241. From admittedly scanty evidence, Forrest attempts to reconstruct the period of Themistocles' exile. He summarizes succinctly the most likely causes of his ostracism and argues for a longer period in Argos than most historians have been willing to concede.

Frost, Frank J. "Themistocles' Place in Athenian Politics." *California Studies in Classical Antiquity* 1 (1968): 105-124. Frost questions the labels often applied to Themistocles of "new man," "democrat," and "radical" and suggests that they involve a misapplication of Aristotelian political theory to a period of Greek politics too little known to permit their application. He finds Themistocles working within an aristocratic culture by skillful manipulation of the powerful families that controlled Athens in the early fifth century B.C.

Gomme, A. W. *A Historical Commentary on Thucydides*. Vol. 3. Oxford: Clarendon Press, 1945. One section of Gomme's learned commentary on the work of the most respected ancient Greek historian deals with Themistocles. Gomme is particularly interested in the gap between his archonship and shipbuilding activity a decade later. Skeptical of the theories advanced to explain the gap in Themistocles' career, Gomme is inclined to doubt the archonship and places his rise to power in the 480's rather than the 490's.

Herodotus. *The Persian Wars*. Translated by George Rawlinson. New York: Random House, 1942. Of the two great ancient Greek historians who write of Themistocles, Herodotus is more likely than Thucydides to accept fanciful sources of information and shows less understanding of military affairs, but his subject encompasses the years of Themistocles' most notable exploits. Furthermore, Herodotus lived and wrote at a time when many witnesses of the Persian Wars were still living.

Lenardon, Robert J. *The Saga of Themistocles*. London: Thames and Hudson, 1978. This is the only true biography in book-length form for English-speaking readers. Lenardon's method is to place before the reader the full variety of evidence, with many substantial quotations from ancient sources, and encourage readers to draw their own conclusions in cases of dubious or conflicting evidence. His cautious approach can be maddening to anyone looking for an authoritative assessment of his subject, but his presentation of the facts could not be more scrupulous.

McGregor, Malcolm F. "The Pro-Persian Party at Athens from 510 to 480 B.C." In *Harvard Studies in Classical Philology*, Supp. 1. Cambridge, Mass.: Harvard University Press, 1940. McGregor emphasizes Themistocles' political cunning in his accession to power. He sees Themistocles as a "new man" who cultivated Miltiades the Younger, the hero of Marathon and an Athenian aristocrat, as a fellow hater of Persia and thus created an anti-Persian momentum in Athens.

Plutarch. *Themistocles and Aristides*. Translated by Bernadotte Perrin. New York: Charles Scribner's Sons, 1901. Plutarch is the ancient biographer most skillful at conveying a sense of his subjects' personalities. There can be little doubt that many of his anecdotes are inventions, but others may have a basis in fact. His semi-fictionalized life of the Athenian leader makes absorbing reading.

Thucydides. *History of the Peloponnesian War*. Translated by Richard Crawley. New York: E. P. Dutton, 1910. Only the first of Thucydides' eight books, giving the historical background for his subject, deals with Themistocles, but this early historian's general reliability and his relative closeness to Themistocles in time (his birth came close to Themistocles' death) make his account preferable wherever, as often happens, early authorities disagree.

Robert P. Ellis

THEODORE OF MOPSUESTIA

Born: c. A.D. 350; Antioch (modern Turkey)
Died: 428; Mopsuestia, Cilicia
Area of Achievement: Religion
Contribution: The most important representative of the Antiochene school of biblical exegesis and theology, Theodore served as Bishop of Mopsuestia from 392 until his death in 428. Primarily because of alleged similarities with Pelagianism and Nestorianism, Theodore's theological views were condemned by the Emperor Justinian and by the Fifth Council of Constantinople in 553.

Early Life

Theodore, generally known by the name of his bishopric as "of Mopsuestia," was born at Antioch about 350. Little is known about his parents or family, except that his father held an official position at Antioch and the family was reportedly wealthy. Theodore's brother, Polychronius, eventually became Bishop of Apamea on the Orontes; a cousin, Paeanius, held an important civil post at Constantinople.

Since Theodore belonged to the nobility in Antioch, his early education was under the most renowned professor of rhetoric of his day, the Sophist Libanius. Theodore was an early companion, fellow student, and friend of John Chrysostom, also born in Antioch, a few years before Theodore. John, usually known simply as Chrysostom, became famous for his eloquent preaching and eventually became Patriarch of Constantinople.

Theodore and Chrysostom enjoyed an excellent philosophical education along with another friend and fellow student, Maximus, who later became Bishop of Isaurian Seleucia. It seems, however, that the three friends came to enjoy the luxurious life of polite Antioch as well. Chrysostom was the first to turn back from the pleasures of that world, and he then succeeded in winning back his fellow students, Theodore and Maximus. The three friends shortly thereafter sought a retreat in the Asketerion, a famous monastic school of Diodore (later Bishop of Tarsus) and Carterius, near Antioch.

According to Chrysostom, Theodore's conversion was sincere and fervent, and he threw himself into the monastic discipline with characteristic zeal. He may have been baptized at this time as well. His days were spent in study, his nights in prayer. He practiced almost every conceivable form of ascetic self-discipline, including lengthy fasts and sleeping on the bare ground. He is reported to have found inexpressible joy in the service of Christ as a Christian celibate until "the world" beckoned to him again.

Theodore had become fascinated by the charms of a beautiful young girl named Hermione, and he was seriously contemplating marriage and a return to the secular life. This proposal became a matter of great concern to his fellow ascetics in the monastery, with many prayers offered and various efforts made for his "recovery" from his "fall." Such efforts included the earliest known literary compositions of Chrysostom—two letters appealing to Theodore to abandon his infatuation and remain true to his monastic vows. Theodore was not yet twenty years of age, but the appeal of his friends prevailed, and he remained true to his vow of celibacy throughout his life.

From 369 to 378, Theodore remained under the spiritual leadership of Diodore, who was at that time elevated to the See of Tarsus. Theodore probably became closely acquainted with both Scripture and church doctrine during these years. He may also have developed his principles of interpretation of the Bible and his views of the person of Christ, which eventually led him into theological controversy. He subsequently came under the influence of Flavian, Bishop of Antioch, who ordained him as a priest in 383, three years before his friend Chrysostom was ordained. Chrysostom almost immediately rose to the full height of his oratorical powers in the pulpit of Antioch. Theodore may have felt himself eclipsed by his friend's greater power as a preacher, or a visit from his old master Diodore to Antioch may have caused him to move to Tarsus, where he stayed until 392, at which time he was elevated to the See of Mopsuestia, in Cilicia, where he remained for the final thirty-six years of his life.

Life's Work

Nothing is known about the physical appearance or general health of Theodore. He died in 428, at the age of seventy-eight, reportedly exhausted from more than fifty years of literary and pastoral work. Most of his later years were marked by theological controversy, but he died peacefully with a great reputation from his many books and other writings. His long episcopate was marked by no outstanding incidents, and his many friends and disciples left few personal recollections. He impressed the Emperor Theodosius I, however, who heard him preach once, and Theodosius is said to have declared that he had "never met with such a teacher." (Theodosius had also heard Saint Ambrose and Saint Gregory of Nazianzus.) A letter from Chrysostom when he was an exile also reveals that the two friends always retained a high regard for each other. Chrysostom declared that he could "never forget the love of Theodore, so genuine and warm, so sincere and guileless, a love maintained from early years, and manifested but now." He assured Theodore that, "exile as he is, he reaps no ordinary consolation from having such a treasure, such a mine of wealth within his heart as the love of so vigilant and noble a soul."

Theodore wrote widely on a great variety of topics. Active in the theological controversies of his time, he is said to have written at least fifteen books on the Incarnation of Christ before he began his serious exegetical work in 402. Unfortunately, many of Theodore's writings have not survived, and those that have do not give a true indication of the scope of his work. He began with a commentary on the Psalms and eventually wrote commentaries on practically every book of the Bible. In addition, he wrote at least thirty-seven other works on a variety of theological, ecclesiastical, and practical problems: the Incarnation, the sacraments, the Holy Spirit, exegetical method, monasticism, and other topics.

Theodore is doubtless best known today as a theologian, and in particular for his views on Christology and anthropology. Although his theological ideas were condemned by the Fifth Council of Constantinople more than a century after his death, during his lifetime he enjoyed the reputation of an orthodox teacher. It is ironic that this untiring foe of theological heresies was later condemned as a heretic himself. In his opposition to heresy, Theodore's attention was particularly directed toward the Christological views of Apollinaris of Laodicea. His fifteen-volume *On the Incarnation* was primarily directed against Apollinaris, and Theodore's (admittedly) extreme views on the "two natures" of Christ were largely by way of response to Apollinaris' teachings concerning the subordination of the human nature of Christ.

Theodore insisted on the complete manhood of Christ and roundly condemned the theory of Apollinaris that the divine Logos had taken the place of Christ's rational soul. Theodore reasoned that if the Godhead had replaced human reason, Jesus would not have experienced fear or any other human emotion. He would not have wrestled in prayer or needed the Holy Spirit's assistance; the story of the temptations of Christ, for example, would have been meaningless. Christ would have had nothing in common with humanity, which would render the Incarnation itself devoid of meaning.

Theodore also insisted that the two natures of Christ, human and divine, were perfect and always remained two. He refused to contemplate the spiritual and material as confused in any manner. His emphasis on this theological point may have been derived from a careful analysis of human personality. Since only elements of the same substance can become unified, Theodore could not conceive of any sort of union between the two natures of Christ. This view, later held in somewhat modified form by Nestorius, was condemned by the Third Ecumenical Council at Ephesus in 431.

Summary

By his insistence on maintaining the human nature of Christ along with the divine, Theodore of Mopsuestia held his own against the ontological speculations of the Alexandrian school, which were, in fact, derived primarily from philosophical abstractions. In principle, his position was vindicated by the great Council of Chalcedon in 451, which recognized in Christ two natures "without confusion, change, division, or separation in one person and subsistence." Through his emphasis on the human nature of Christ and his keen awareness of the biblical evidence, Theodore may have saved Christendom from falling into endless theological speculation.

As the greatest exegete and spiritual leader of the Antiochene school, Theodore became the acknowledged leader of numerous ecclesiastical figures of the fourth and fifth centuries. In his theological writings he also stressed the importance of free will and the human contribution to salvation. Human achievements were ascribed to free will; thus, Theodore opposed the doctrines of predestination and original sin. Because of such views Theodore was regarded by some as a forerunner to Pelagius, whose views were also condemned by the council at Ephesus in 431.

Theodore's theological views, considered orthodox during his lifetime, became controversial after his death, particularly when Nestorians and Pelagians appealed to his writings. In the end the Alexandrian school succeeded in bringing Theodore and his writings under ecclesiastical anathema. Indeed, the primary reason so few of his writings survive today is that many of them were intentionally destroyed by church authorities. Rabboula, Orthodox Syriac Bishop of Edessa from 411 to 436, vehemently attacked Theodore and his teachings and ordered all existing copies of his works confiscated and burned. It may have been Monophysite reaction to the Council of Chalcedon that first brought Theodore's theological views into question. He was condemned as a heretic by the Emperor Justinian in 544. Under imperial pressure Pope Vergilius condemned sixty propositions from Theodore's writings as heretical, and the Fifth Council of Constantinople in 553 placed his writings under anathema.

As an interpreter of Scripture, Theodore stood out among the scholars of his day. His scholarship is said to have astounded his contemporaries. In thoroughness, accuracy, and consistency of thought he had no peer, not even Chrysostom. His followers called him simply "the interpreter." He became the most remarkable and original representative of the Antiochene school of exegesis, noted for its insistence on the plain, literal meaning of Scripture and its opposition to the fanciful, allegorical interpretations so typical of Origen and the Alexandrian school.

Theodore was also a pioneer in the use of critical methods of Bible study unheard of in his day. He made careful use of scientific, critical, philological, and historical methods, thereby anticipating by more than a millennium the rise of modern historical-critical methods of Bible study. He consistently tried to take into account the historical circumstances under which biblical books were written; subsequently, he rejected several books as uncanonical, including Job, Chronicles, the Song of Songs, Ezra, Revelation, and the Catholic Epistles (except 1 Peter and 1 John). The few of his writings that survive demonstrate something of the power and authority of his work. The only commentary that survives in the original Greek is *On the Twelve Prophets*, but many of his writings were translated into Syriac very early and have been preserved, at least in part, primarily by Nestorians. His commentary on John has long been known, but recent discoveries include commentaries on the Lord's Prayer, the Nicene Creed, and the sacraments. His massive work on the Incarnation was discovered early in the twentieth century in a codex in Seert, Turkey, but unfortunately seems to have been destroyed during World War I.

Bibliography

Dewart, Joanne McWilliam. *The Theology of Grace of Theodore of Mopsuestia*. Washington, D.C.: Catholic University of America Press, 1971. An important study of Theodore's teachings about the grace of God. Emphasizes Theodore's scriptural understanding of grace as divine benevolence, best understood against the background of the Pelagian controversy. Demonstrates Theodore's insistence on the cooperation of divine grace and the human will.

Greer, Rowan A. *Theodore of Mopsuestia: Exegete and Theologian*. London: Faith Press, 1961. A sympathetic assessment of the theology of Theodore from the point of view of biblical criticism. Greer uses Theodore's *Commentary of St. John* as representative of his critical and exegetical work and as a vantage point from which to illustrate the basic differences between the Antiochene and Alexandrian schools. He concludes that Theodore was a biblical critic first of all; his theology sprang from his study of the Bible.

Norris, Richard A. *Manhood and Christ: A Study in the Christology of Theodore of Mopsuestia*. Oxford: Clarendon Press, 1963. A thorough survey of Theodore's anthropological presuppositions and their impact on his Christological thought. This highly recommended theological analysis contains valuable appendices on fifth and sixth century discussion of Theodore as well as more recent treatment of his thought.

Patterson, Leonard. *Theodore of Mopsuestia and Modern Thought*. London: Society for Promoting Christian Knowledge, 1926. Although dated, this is an important study of Theodore's life and thought. Particularly interesting is Patterson's discussion of Theodore's relation to modern thought (for example, evolutionary theory and the mind-body relationship).

Sullivan, Francis., S. J. *The Christology of Theodore of Mopsuestia*. Rome: Apud Aedes Universitatis Gregorianae, 1956. A careful study of Theodore's thought concerning the unity of Christ. Sullivan treats some of the problems involved in making use of existing fragments of Theodore's works, mostly in Syriac translation. He concludes that Theodore was indeed, despite his orthodox intentions, the "father of Nestorianism."

Swete, Henry B. "Theodore of Mopsuestia." In *A Dictionary of Christian Biography, Literature, Sects and Doctrines During the First Eight Centuries*, edited by William Smith and Henry Wace, vol. 4. London: John

Murray, 1887. Dated but extremely valuable and sympathetic study of Theodore's life and work. Excellent use made of primary sources, despite the fact that many of Theodore's writings had not yet been discovered when Swete prepared this article.

C. Fitzhugh Spragins

THEODORET OF CYRRHUS

Born: c. A.D. 393; Antioch, Roman Syria
Died: c. A.D. 458; Cyrrhus, Roman Syria
Area of Achievement: Religion
Contribution: Theodoret served as the Bishop of Cyrrhus for forty-one years. Aside from carrying out an effective and sensitive bishopric, he authored works on practically every aspect of Christian thought and practice. He is perhaps best remembered for his contribution to the Christological debates that led to the Council of Chalcedon.

Early Life

Theodoret was born in Antioch in the Roman province of northern Syria circa A.D. 393 to moderately wealthy Christian parents. He spent the first twenty-three years of his life in the city of Antioch, leaving in 416/417 for the monastery at Nicerte. While Theodoret wrote sparingly of these formative years in Antioch, his remarks as well as what can be deduced from his later writings reveal that he drew deeply from both the rich Greco-Roman culture of the city and the monks who lived on the fringes of Antioch. His writings reflect the education typical of the privileged population of large Greco-Roman cities in late antiquity. Such an education would have entailed training in Greek grammar, speech, and the classics of Greek literature and philosophy from Homer to Demosthenes.

From his parents, Theodoret inherited a fondness for the monks who lived in the caves and wilderness surrounding Antioch. Theodoret's mother had sought out these monks to cure an eye ailment, and his father had sought help when after thirteen years of marriage no child had been conceived. In both cases, the monks were given credit for solving the problem; from childhood, Theodoret was taken on weekly visits to them. Theodoret fondly recalled his visits to the monks Peter of Galatia and Macedonius and noted that Peter had given him a piece of linen girdle which was treasured by the family when it proved a remedy for a variety of physical afflictions.

Upon the death of his parents, Theodoret left Antioch to become a monk himself. He joined the monastic community at Nicerte near Apamea and there enjoyed some seven years of quiet seclusion. It was during his tenure at Nicerte that Theodoret composed his celebrated apology for the Christian religion, *Therapeutica* (c. 424; *A Treatise of Laws*, 1776). This apology displays the breadth of his knowledge of Greek philosophy and religion as he juxtaposes the claims of Christianity to those associated with a host of Greek philosophical schools and religious cults.

Life's Work

After seven years in the monastery at Nicerte, Theodoret was called to assume the duties of bishop of the diocese of Cyrrhus. Theodoret says he "unwillingly assumed" the office, as it meant leaving behind the beloved tranquillity of the monastery and taking on the demands of an exceptionally large and unruly diocese on the eastern edges of the Roman Empire. Theodoret's reluctance did not prevent him from fulfilling his appointed task: He served as bishop there from the year 424 until his death in 458.

The boundaries of the diocese were the same as those of Cyrrhestica, a territory of the province of Euphatensis in eastern Syria. The diocese was subject to the Metropolitan at Hierapolis and covered sixteen hundred square miles. Theodoret described the diocese as mountainous and bare. This bleak landscape had not, however, discouraged the establishment and spread of Christianity; Theodoret also refers to the existence of eight hundred parishes, each with its own church. The area also contained a significant population of monks, with whom Theodoret maintained a cordial relationship.

The town of Cyrrhus, where Theodoret was to reside, was located approximately sixty-five kilometers northeast of Antioch at the confluence of the Aphreen and Saboun Souyou rivers. Cyrrhus had been an important Roman military outpost, but, like many other Roman frontier towns, it was in a state of decline by the fifth century. Theodoret called it "a solitary and ugly village." Over the course of his residence, he spent much time and energy in rebuilding and improving Cyrrhus. Using funds collected from the diocese, he constructed two bridges and public galleries, rebuilt a major aqueduct, and improved the public baths. The bishop also paid to have skilled physicians move to the town and secured the service of educators and engineers.

Theodoret's responsibilities were numerous. He describes such tasks as visiting and encouraging the monks living in the diocese, driving out heretics, playing ecclesiastical politics, and writing a number of tracts on practically every aspect of Christian life and thought. Aside from the apology mentioned earlier and the treatises on Christology to be discussed below, the extant works from Theodoret's vast corpus include historical studies, biblical commentaries, a series of sermons on Providence, and a collection of letters.

While Theodoret's interests and contributions were wide-ranging, his place in the history of Christianity has consistently been recorded in terms of his role in the Christological controversies that began with the Council of Ephesus in 431 and culminated with the Council of Chalcedon in 451. In 431, Theodoret was called upon to represent the Antiochene interpretation of Christ (the two-nature Christology) against the Alexandrian interpretation as it was put forth by Cyril of Alexandria. Theodoret's response took the form of a tract entitled *Reprehensio duodecim capitum seu anathema anathematismorum Cyrilli* (431), in which he stressed the biblical foundation for the fullness of the two natures of Christ and argued that Cyril's formula implicated the divine Christ in the passion and suffering of the Crucifixion. The Council of Ephesus was called to resolve the differences between Cyril and

Theodoret; it decided in favor of Cyril.

In the years between the First Council of Ephesus and the Council of Chalcedon, Theodoret continued to be involved in the debates over the proper interpretation of the nature of Christ. In 447, he composed a work entitled *Eranistes seu Polymorphus* (*Dialogues*, 1892) as an attack on the position held by the monk Eutyches, who had succeeded Cyril as the leader of the Alexandrian one-nature school of interpretation. This work and the ensuing debate led to the Second Council of Ephesus in 449; Theodoret again lost and was deposed from his bishopric in Cyrrhus. He was apparently restored soon thereafter and the Council of Chalcedon in 451 closed the chapter on Theodoret's involvement in the Christological debates. In fact, from the end of the Council of Chalcedon till his death in 458, Theodoret must have lived a comparatively quiet and uninvolved life as bishop, as there is no record of any further writing or involvement in ecclesiastical politics.

Summary

Theodoret of Cyrrhus was one of the most prolific writers and influential voices for Christianity in the East during late antiquity. He wrote against a rich and complex background which was at once deeply indebted to the language, ideas, and ideals of the long-established, Greco-Roman culture and which at the same time increasingly felt the influence of Christianity and its otherworldly monks and theological squabbles. Theodoret labored as a bishop in the eastern provinces of the later Roman Empire to improve the life and resources for his congregation, to establish the proper interpretation of the Bible, to chronicle the history of the Church and its monks, and to clarify what the Church taught about the person and work of Christ. While in the end, Theodoret found himself on the losing side of the Christological debates, his contributions to those debates have been judged the clearest and most profound statements on the two-nature view of the person of Christ.

Bibliography

Ashby, Godfrey William Ernest Candler. *Theodoret of Cyrrhus as Exegete of the Old Testament*. Grahamstown, South Africa: Rhodes University Press, 1972. One of the few English-language studies of Theodoret, this book provides, in largely summary fashion, a guide to Theodoret's exegesis of the Old Testament. While the author provides few critical insights, the work nevertheless proves valuable as it offers an entry into an enormous collection of biblical commentary, most of which is available only in Greek or Latin.

Chesnut, Glenn F. *The First Christian Histories*. Paris: Éditions Beauchesne, 1977. A well-researched work which compares the ecclesiastical histories of Eusebius, Socrates, Sozomen, and Theodoret. The author demonstrates how each brought to his historical studies a distinct theological and philosophical bias and shows the extent to which these early Christian historians were dependent on classical Greco-Roman models of history writing.

Grillmeier, Alois. *Christ in Christian Tradition.* Vol. 1, *From the Apostolic Age to Chalcedon.* Translated by John Bowden. Rev. ed. Atlanta: John Knox Press, 1975. This book provides a thorough treatment of the development of Christology in the early Church and includes a long and helpful discussion of Theodoret's contribution. The book has an extensive bibliography of works in English and European languages.

Jones, A. H. M. *The Later Roman Empire.* 2 vols. Norman: University of Oklahoma Press, 1964, reprint 1975. The standard work on this period, it provides not only an account of the major events and persons but also useful insights into the contemporary social world.

Theodoret of Cyrrhus. *"The Ecclesiastical History," "Dialogues," and "Letters" of Theodoret.* Translated by B. Jackson. Grand Rapids, Mich.: Wm. B. Eerdmans Publishing Co., 1975. This English translation of the letters and two of Theodoret's works was originally published in 1892. In the case of *Ekklēsiastikē historia* (c. 449; *The Ecclesiastical History*, 1612) and *Dialogues*, new editions of the Greek text have recently been published. The translations are competent and since they are the only modern English translations of these works of Theodoret, they are invaluable for those wishing to read his words who are limited to reading publications in English. A brief historical and theological introduction has been appended to the collection.

_____. *A History of the Monks of Syria.* Translated by R. M. Price. Kalamazoo, Mich.: Cistercian Publications, 1985. One of the rare English translations of a work by Theodoret, the text and translation are based on the French edition of Pierre Canivet. The history itself offers a rare glimpse into the provocative world of Syrian monasticism. The translation is clear and the introduction and notes do a splendid job of situating the work historically and literally.

Young, Frances M. *From Nicaea to Chalcedon: A Guide to the Literature and Its Background.* Philadelphia: Fortress Press, 1983. This is a clearly written handbook intended as an introduction to the major figures and writings of Christianity from the period between the Council of Nicaea and the Council of Chalcedon. Many of Theodoret's works are discussed, with special attention paid to *The Ecclestiastical History* and his Christological treatises. There is a substantial bibliography.

C. Thomas McCullough

THEODORIC THE GREAT

Born: c. 454; probably Hungary
Died: August 30, 526; Ravenna, Italy
Area of Achievement: Government
Contribution: For a third of a century, Theodoric gave Italy strong, stable governance and its longest period of peace and prosperity in more than a century. His promotion of Roman ideals of justice and civic virtue led to the preservation of Roman law, administration, learning, and urban life. These formed the groundwork for the structure of medieval Italian society.

Early Life

Theodoric the Great was the eldest son of Theodemir, a warrior king of the Ostrogoths. The family traced its ancestry back to a legendary Ostrogothic king, Amal, who lived around A.D. 200. In the late fifth century, the Amal kingship was shared by three brothers—Valamir, Vidimir, and Theodemir—but the Ostrogoths lived under the domination of the Hunnish king Attila. After Attila died, the Amal kings revolted, defeating the Huns in 454. News of the victory supposedly reached Theodemir's home on the day of Theodoric's birth, considered an auspicious sign for the new prince. The Ostrogoths then moved westward into the Roman province of Pannonia (now western Hungary, eastern Austria, and Slovenia). They entered into a treaty with the Eastern Roman emperor Leo I, pledging to defend the Roman frontiers in return for financial subsidies.

When Theodoric was about seven years old, the subsidies failed to arrive. After the Ostrogoths raided a nearby Roman province, the alliance was renewed, the subsidies paid, and peace restored. Yet young Theodoric was taken to Constantinople as a hostage to assure the future good behavior of the Ostrogoths. For ten years, he lived in the imperial palace under the protection of Emperor Leo I. Not much is known of Theodoric's life or education during this decade. He almost certainly learned to speak Latin, still the official language of the government, and possibly some Greek. He must have observed the dynamics of imperial court politics and the character of late Roman society.

In 471, Leo sent the young prince home to his royal father with rich presents. Theodoric immediately won fame by leading a war party to seize the city of Singidunum (modern Belgrade) from the Sarmatians, who had recently taken it from the Romans. The victorious general was hailed as a true Amal king, and the conquered city was kept under Ostrogothic control.

In 473, famine forced the Ostrogoths to abandon Pannonia. Theodemir and his son marched south from Singidunum, eventually laying siege to Thessalonica, one of the most important cities in the Greek world. The Roman government was forced to renew the peace with the Goths and to agree to their resettlement in Roman territory. In return, the Goths undertook the defense of the lower Danube frontier as federates of the Roman Empire. Shortly after, Theodemir died, and Theodoric assumed sole rule at about age twenty.

During the next fourteen years, Theodoric was a key player in the game of Roman Balkan politics. Residing in the fortress city of Novae on the lower Danube, he supervised defense of the nearby Roman frontier. When Emperor Zeno was temporarily overthrown by a rival, Theodoric intervened to restore him to power. Later, Theodoric had to contend with treachery from Zeno, as well as opposition from a rival Ostrogothic army not related to his own royal tribesmen. After much fighting, diplomacy, and shifting of loyalties, Theodoric triumphed, and peace with the emperor was restored. He again resumed military defense of the Roman frontier.

In 483, Theodoric was named Master of Soldiers, and in 484 he was appointed consul, the most prestigious office in the empire. Yet the peace was frequently broken, as the Ostrogoths continued plundering the provinces whenever supplies were short. While Theodoric continued to live at Novae, his warriors sought adventure and loot where they could. In these circumstances, it is likely that Theodoric developed his plan to invade Italy to assure his people a permanent home.

Life's Work

The main achievement of Theodoric was to create a Romano-Gothic regime that brought more than thirty years of peace, prosperity, cultural revival, and some justice to the peoples of Italy.

In 488, Theodoric was elevated to the rank of patrician and commanded by Emperor Zeno to march into Italy and overthrow Odovacar, the German general who had overthrown the last Western Roman emperor in 476 and ruled Italy ever since. Theodoric, with his tribal army, was to rule in Italy until Zeno's arrival. The emperor may have thought that the Goths were less dangerous to him in Italy than in the Eastern Empire. Both Theodoric and Zeno recognized Italy to be a Roman province—and Theodoric to be a military subordinate of the Roman emperor. Yet the Gothic general was essentially the hereditary king of a warrior nation. He is sometimes called "king" in Byzantine sources, but that seems to have been a courtesy title for any Germanic war leader who signed a formal contract with the Romans to provide military services for pay.

Invading Italy in 489, Theodoric won a series of hard-fought battles against Odovacar's armies. A central factor in the 476 coup had been the demand of Odovacar's soldiers that they be given landed estates in Italy as recompense for their defense of the country. When the demand was refused by the Roman government, Odovacar had seized power and distributed "thirds" of large Roman estates among his followers.

Following Odovacar's surrender in 493, Theodoric murdered him at a banquet in his palace in the old imperial capital at Ravenna. Theodoric then distributed the *tertia* (thirds) of the estates previously held by Odovacar's soldiers to his own faithful troops. Those whose lands were not seized paid a special tax to the Gothic treasury. While the military affairs of the new regime were the exclusive province of the Ostrogoths, the civil affairs of Italy continued to be directed by Roman administrators. The senate continued to govern in Rome, and local Roman councils governed in the cities. Roman law prevailed in all cases where both litigants were Romans; a Gothic court heard cases if one litigant was non-Roman. Among themselves, the Goths maintained their own national legal customs.

Theodoric maintained the capital in Ravenna, although he also kept royal palaces in Pavia and Verona, areas where many Goths had settled, whence they could be mobilized quickly to defend the frontiers of Italy. Other groups were settled thinly throughout the Italian peninsula, where they provided local garrisons for police and defense purposes. The number of Goths under Theodoric's command in 490 has been variously estimated at forty thousand to one hundred thousand, of whom one quarter were full-time soldiers. Since Italy had a population of several million, the Goths did not constitute an overwhelming addition to its total population and yet were enough to give it adequate order and defense.

One problem for Theodoric was that he and the Goths were considered heretics by orthodox Christians. As Arians, they denied the orthodox Christian doctrine of the Trinity. Theodoric's solution was to practice religious toleration. He was particularly insistent on protecting Jews from religiously inspired violence. When a schism arose as a result of a disputed papal election, he refused at first to decide the case, ultimately granting legal recognition to the candidate elected first and with the most votes. At a later time, he refused to sit in judgment on a pope accused by his enemies of adultery. He insisted that the matter be decided by a council of bishops. Yet he was frequently persuaded to change his policies through the influence of saintly bishops acting as defenders of the weak or persecuted.

Under the Ostrogothic regime, new buildings were constructed and older monuments and public works restored. The king and the bishops took the lead in this work and were helped to some extent by senatorial aristocrats. In 500, Theodoric celebrated the tenth year of his rule in the city of Rome with traditional games, ceremonies, and distribution of gifts. The walls of the imperial city were repaired, as was the principal road leading south, the Appian Way. The old imperial palace on the Palatine Hill was renovated. At his capital in Ravenna, he restored the broken aqueduct and repaired the imperial palace. He also built a new church, now called St. Appollinare Nuovo, richly decorated with brilliant mosaics on its walls and inlaid gold plates on its roof. Other palaces and baths were built in Pavia and Verona.

Public offices were still the goal of ambitious Romans seeking power and social prestige. The Gothic king occasionally reached out beyond the local Roman aristocracy to Romans from the Eastern Empire or even to fellow Goths for appointees to high civil offices, but mostly he relied on the local elites. The king also intervened in the traditional imperial task of organizing relief during local famines and promoted reclamation work in the Pontine Marshes south of Rome and in the plain north of Spoleto.

Theodoric's foreign policy was successful in defending Italy from invasions and in expanding Ostrogothic control over the strategic approaches to Italy from beyond the mountains to the north, west, and east. Through prudent diplomacy, limited military interventions, and Amal dynastic marriages with the ruling Visigothic, Frankish, Burgundian, Vandal, and Thuringian royal families, Theodoric sought peace and unity among the Germanic peoples ruling the former Western Roman Empire. He expanded the areas of his direct rule from Italy eastward to the Danube River and westward to the lower Rhone River. Theodoric's de facto rulership in Italy was recognized by successive Eastern Roman emperors: Zeno, Anastasius I, and Justin I. Theodoric, in turn, recognized the right of Roman imperial sovereignty over Italy by nominating consuls each year and notifying the Eastern emperor for his approval.

Only in the last three years of his life were Theodoric's political relations with Emperor Justin and the neighboring Germanic kings suddenly shaken by events beyond his control. In 522, his son-in-law and heir Eutharic died, leaving an infant son as heir to Theodoric's realm. An older grandson, Sigeric, heir as well to the Burgundian kingship, was murdered the same year. Theodoric's alliances with both Vandals and Thuringians also broke down because of dynastic changes. When the Roman emperor Justin began a systematic persecution of Arians within his realm, it seemed a calculated challenge to Theodoric, who responded with threats against the Catholics of Italy. In the midst of this crisis, Theodoric was persuaded that two of the highest Roman officials in his regime, Symmachus and Boethius, were plotting against him with the Eastern Roman emperor. In 525, both were executed, probably without a fair trial. Theodoric, aged and seeing his life's work unraveling around him, died the following year.

He designated his ten-year-old grandson, Athalaric, as his heir, under the regency of the boy's mother, Amalasuntha. Within a decade, Athalaric was dead and his mother forced to open negotiations with Justin, bringing about the Gothic-Byzantine war which ravaged Italy in the mid-sixth century and ultimately led to the destruction of the Ostrogothic nations.

Summary

The principal policies Theodoric the Great used in governing Italy were already in place during the rule of his predecessor Odovacar: religious toleration, cooperation with the local Roman aristocracy, Germanic control of all military power, respect for the existing Roman law and political institutions, and efforts to seek legitimacy from the Eastern Roman emperor.

Like most Goths, Theodoric was an Arian Christian, a heretic in the eyes of his Catholic Roman subjects. Following a policy of religious toleration and avoiding interference in the religious quarrels which beset the orthodox Christian church in his time, Theodoric managed to defuse the religious disputes in Italy. He won the cooperation of the Roman aristocracy by allowing it to govern the city of Rome and hold the higher civil offices. He also sustained the customary operations of Roman law. Theodoric believed that the best way to govern the two peoples under his control was by respecting their cultural distinctiveness and leaving to each as wide an area of autonomy as seemed compatible with Gothic military supremacy. Theodoric's sense of justice was famous in a society in which litigation was frequently used as a weapon of oppression by the powerful. The king used Gothic special agents called *saiones* to investigate injustices, supervise special projects, and exercise the royal will against recalcitrant bureaucrats. Taxes were collected with efficiency and greater fairness than before. Commerce, manufacturing, and reconstruction were encouraged, and famine relief was effectively organized.

Theodoric also demonstrated the greatest respect for Roman culture and encouraged the efforts of such Roman intellectuals as Boethius, Symmachus, and Cassiodorus to preserve and promote the Greek scientific and philosophical learning among the Latin-speaking population of Italy. Cassiodorus wrote a history of the Goths, now lost, which served as the principal source of a later history of the Goths by Jordanes. Boethius' textbooks on Greek arithmetic, geometry, music, and Aristotelian logic became the basis for the curriculum of the medieval Latin schools. Boethius' father-in-law, Symmachus, supported a revival of Neoplatonic philosophy, and Boethius' last work, *De consolatione philosophiae* (*The Consolation of Philosophy*), is considered the finest expression of Greek humanistic philosophy of late classical civilization and was very influential in the early medieval schools. Symmachus also patronized many poets, rhetoricians, and the Latin grammarian Priscian, whose works were authoritative for medieval Latin scholars. This intellectual revival, so important for the future direction of European culture, would have been impossible without the personal patronage and atmosphere of peace and stability provided by the great Ostrogothic ruler.

Although Theodoric's heretical Arian religious views and his brutal execution of both Symmachus and Boethius have tempered the enthusiasm of some historians for his judgment and moral excellence, even the hostile Byzantine historian Procopius treated the king with respect.

When the armies of Justin invaded Italy after Theodoric's death, the Goths put up stiff resistance and received considerable support from their Roman subjects. The Gothic-Byzantine wars devastated Italy and ended what most Italians later looked back upon as the last good times their country would see for the next two centuries. Nevertheless, the reign of Theodoric allowed the structure of Roman society to survive the fall of the empire and become the foundation for the new, vibrant, and creative Italy of the Middle Ages.

Bibliography
Bark, William. "The Legend of Boethius' Martyrdom." *Speculum* 21 (1946): 312-317. The author argues that Boethius and Symmachus should not be viewed as Catholics martyred for their faith, victims of Theodoric's alleged sudden outburst of religious prejudice. He believes it much more plausible that both were guilty of treasonable acts designed to undermine the Ostrogothic regime.

Burns, Thomas S. *A History of the Ostrogoths*. Bloomington: Indiana University Press, 1984. An American scholar's extensive synthesis of the history and culture of the Ostrogoths, using original documentary and archaeological and modern monographic sources. The focus is the Ostrogoths' culture and achievements—from their first mention in Roman records of the third century to their extinction as a nation in the sixth century. The author uses a mixed chronological and topical approach. References to Theodoric the Great are scattered throughout the text. Illustrated. With index, bibliography, maps, and dynastic tables.

Chadwick, Henry. *Boethius: The Consolations of Music, Logic, Theology, and Philosophy*. Oxford: Clarendon Press, 1981. A masterful study of the career and literary works of the greatest intellectual of the court of Theodoric the Great. The first chapter describes the revival of Greek classical learning in the West stimulated by the Roman statesman Symmachus, his son-in-law Boethius, and others under the patronage of Theodoric. Later chapters deal with Boethius' literary and philosophical works. Examining the causes which led to Theodoric's brutal execution of both men, the author finds religious as well as political reasons for the sudden reversal of favor. Includes bibliography and index.

Duckett, Eleanor S. *The Gateway to the Middle Ages: Italy*. Ann Arbor: University of Michigan Press, 1961. A rich portrait of the cultural life of the leading intellectuals of Theodoric's Gothic-Roman Italy. After an introduction to broader historical events, the author offers two chapters on the leading Roman intellectuals Boethius and Cassiodorus and another chapter on two historians, Ennodius and Jordanes. The interaction of each with Theodoric is emphasized throughout the text. With bibliography and index.

Jones, A. H. M. "The Constitutional Position of Odovacar and Theodoric." *Journal of Roman Studies* 52 (1962): 126-130. Lack of clear evidence has made the exact constitutional relationship between Theodoric and the

Eastern Roman emperors a matter of controversy among historians. Jones argues that both Odovacar and Theodoric were no more than typical Germanic kings without formal status under Roman law. They were accepted as de facto leaders until circumstances permitted otherwise. Jones's views have been challenged.

O'Donnell, James J. *Cassiodorus*. Berkeley: University of California Press, 1979. A top official in the government of Theodoric, Cassiodorus collected a book of official letters, *Variae*, which are a principal source for the history of the Ostrogothic ruler. His history of the Goths, now lost, was the basic source used by the later historian of the Goths, Jordanes. The author has made a detailed study of Cassiodorus' life and works; chapters 2 and 3 focus on Cassiodorus' role as a courtier of Theodoric the Great.

Thompson, E. A. *Romans and Barbarians: The Decline of the Western Empire*. Madison: University of Wisconsin Press, 1982. In chapter 4, the author discusses the Ostrogothic conquest of Italy and its consequences, the popularity of the government of Theodoric, and the constitutional character of the regime with respect to the Roman imperial government in Constantinople. He also compares the Ostrogothic regime with its predecessor, headed by the Germanic general Odovacar.

Joseph R. Peden

THEODOSIUS THE GREAT

Born: January 11, A.D. 346 or 347; Cauca, Gallaecia
Died: January 17, A.D. 395; Milan
Area of Achievement: Government
Contribution: Theodosius restored peace to the Eastern Roman Empire after the Roman defeat at Adrianople and established a dynasty that held the throne for more than seventy years. His settlement of Visigoths as *federati* inside the Empire may have contributed to the fall of the western part of the Empire, and his religious policies were a major step in the development of a theocratic state in the East.

Early Life

Flavius Theodosius, known as Theodosius the Great, was the son of Count Flavius Theodosius, a Hispano-Roman nobleman whose family estates were located at Cauca in northwestern Spain. Theodosius' father distinguished himself in commands in Britain and North Africa. The younger Theodosius probably served under his father in Britain. He became military commander on the Danube River, in what is now Yugoslavia, and made a name for himself by winning victories over the Sarmatians, non-Germanic peoples who had been filtering into the Danube area from southern Russia since the first century A.D.

Theodosius' career ended suddenly in 376, when his father, who had just suppressed a revolt in North Africa, was accused on some charge and executed at Carthage. The whole incident seems to have occurred just after the death of the emperor Valentinian I, and it is assumed that Valentinian's young son Gratian, the new emperor, was persuaded to authorize the execution by a newly powerful faction at court which included enemies of Count Theodosius. The younger Theodosius may have been in danger himself; at any rate, he retired to the family estates in Spain, his official career apparently over. He married Aelia Flavia Flacilla and had a son, Arcadius, during the two years spent in Spain.

A crisis in the Eastern Empire brought Theodosius from retirement to the highest responsibility. The Germanic Visigoths had been defeated by the Huns as the latter advanced westward. The Visigoths asked for and received from the Romans permission to cross the Danube River and find refuge inside the Empire. When Roman officials sent to supervise their reception abused the Goths, they revolted and in August, 378, defeated and killed the emperor Valens in a great battle at Adrianople in Thrace. The Goths were then free to pillage the Balkans and Thrace.

Gratian, who had broken off wars with Germanic tribes in eastern Gaul to assist Valens, only to find that Valens had gone into battle without waiting for his aid, now had to find someone to restore Roman control in Thrace.

The men who had accused Theodosius' father were now out of favor; a new faction made up of friends and connections of the Theodosian family had the emperor's ear. They suggested the younger Theodosius as a good candidate for emperor of the East. Gratian summoned Theodosius from Spain and apparently first gave him a military command, in which he again won victories against the Sarmatians, and then named him emperor. Theodosius officially took power on January 19, 379.

Life's Work

Theodosius' next few years were spent in campaigns against the Goths, first from headquarters at Thessalonica in northeastern Greece and then, after November, 380, from Constantinople. Very little is known about these wars, but Theodosius was unable to destroy the Goths or even to drive them out of the Empire, in part, perhaps, because of a manpower shortage caused by the losses at Adrianople. As part of an attempt to conciliate at least some of the Goths and perhaps disunite them, the emperor welcomed the Gothic chieftain Athanaric to Constantinople on January 11, 381, and, when the Gothic leader died two weeks later, gave him an elaborate state funeral. Such treatment impressed the Goths and may have disposed them to negotiate.

In October, 382, Theodosius, apparently having concluded that victory was not attainable, ordered one of his generals to make a treaty with the Goths. By its terms, they were allowed to settle in Thrace as *federati*. They owed military service to the Empire, but unlike earlier settlements of barbarians inside the Empire, the Goths were allowed to retain their arms as well as their own rulers and laws. In effect, they were a separate nation inside the imperial borders. Many contemporaries criticized this arrangement; some modern scholars have even suggested that it was a factor in the fall of the Western Empire.

On the other hand, Theodosius reorganized the eastern armies in a way that greatly contributed to the internal security of the Eastern Empire. He set up five separate armies, each with its own commander who reported directly to the emperor. No single commander could concentrate power in his own hands as was still possible in the West.

In the same years in which he was engaged in campaigns against the Goths, Theodosius involved himself in religious affairs. He was baptized in the autumn of 380, when he was believed to be near death from illness. Many people in this period preferred to delay baptism, since it absolved sins committed before the sacrament. There is no way of knowing whether baptism on threat of death caused Theodosius to have some sort of conversion experience or whether it only intensified an already strong adherence to the Church. Certainly he took vigorous steps shortly after his recovery to demonstrate his support of the Nicene Creed (which maintained that Father and Son were of the same substance). The Arians, who were especially powerful in the Eastern Empire, believed that the Son was not divine, but only a creature, and thus subordinate to the Father.

Within two days after entering Constantinople on November 24, 380, Theodosius expelled the Arian bishop Demophilus and established his own candidate, the orthodox Catholic Gregory Nazianzus, as bishop. On February 28, 380, he had issued an edict requiring everyone to accept the Trinity. Yet the new decree was enforced mainly against bishops and priests, who lost their churches if they refused to accept it. It did not, apparently, represent an attempt to force all laymen to adhere to the Nicene Creed.

Toward paganism, Theodosius adopted a more conciliatory approach, at least in the early years of his reign, even reopening a pagan temple on the Euphrates River in 382 as long as no sacrifices took place there. In January, 381, he issued another edict ordering that all churches be turned over to the Nicene Catholics, and in May through July he held the Council of Constantinople, at which about 150 eastern bishops reaffirmed the divinity of Son and Holy Spirit.

Soon Theodosius was faced with a situation in which his loyalty to the Church conflicted with the duty he owed to the man who had made him emperor. In 383, Magnus Clemens Maximus in Britain proclaimed himself emperor of the West and invaded Gaul, where Gratian's army went over to the usurper and Gratian himself was killed, perhaps by his own men. Magnus Maximus controlled Britain, Spain, Gaul, and North Africa. In Italy and the middle Danube provinces Valentinian II, Gratian's younger brother, ruled under the tutelage of his mother, Justina, an Arian. Theodosius was placed in something of a dilemma. Loyalty to Gratian would have demanded that he avenge his patron's death and restore all the western provinces to Valentinian. Religion complicated the picture, however, since Magnus Maximus was presenting himself as a champion of orthodox Catholicism. How could the defender of orthodoxy in the East put down a Catholic ruler in the West in order to put an Arian in his place?

There may also have been personal ties between Theodosius and Magnus Maximus; Maximus came from Spain, was apparently some sort of dependent of the Theodosian family, and may have served in Britain alongside Theodosius under Count Theodosius. His concern for his eastern frontier could have increased the emperor's reluctance to divert his armies to a campaign in the West. When the envoys of Magnus Maximus arrived in Constantinople to ask for official recognition, the King of Persia, Ardashir II, had just died, and it was not known whether his successor planned to attack the Romans. A revolt of tribes on the Arabian frontier, in modern Jordan, complicated the situation. Religion, personal ties, and military concerns apparently decided the issue. Theodosius not only made no attempt to get rid of Magnus Maximus but also gave him official recognition as ruler of Britain, Spain, and Gaul.

Many of the difficulties which had held Theodosius back in 383 were resolved in the next few years. In 384, the new ruler of Persia sent envoys to Constantinople with lavish gifts for the emperor, presumably to signal friendly intentions. The tribes in revolt on the eastern frontier had submitted in 385, and in 387 a treaty was signed with Persia. In an agreement similar to those made by Rome and Parthia in earlier centuries, Theodosius allowed the Persians to name a ruler for most of Armenia, a mountainous area in eastern Asia Minor which controlled the roads between Roman Asia Minor and Persia. This Persian treaty and the earlier one with the Goths gave the Eastern Empire a long period of peace in which to rebuild its forces.

Although repeated incursions by bands of Huns and other tribes kept the frontier forces on the alert, the only major wars Theodosius fought in the remainder of his reign were against usurpers in the West, the first not until about ten years after Adrianople. In those ten years, he had succeeded in rebuilding his armies to a point where they could win victories over other Roman armies. Whether Theodosius' decision to make peace with foreign enemies but to fight internal rivals was best for the whole Empire in the long run is a question fundamental to any assessment of his accomplishments as ruler.

In the same year in which the Persian treaty was signed, Maximus invaded Italy, causing Valentinian II, his mother, and his sister Galla to flee to Theodosius for help. Theodosius was now militarily in a much better position to confront Maximus, and by marrying Galla he could claim that family loyalties outweighed the claims of religion. In June, 388, he led an army from the East, defeated Maximus twice in Pannonia, at Siscia and Poetovio, and forced him to retreat to Aquileia, at the head of the Adriatic Sea. There, Maximus surrendered and was killed by Theodosius' soldiers, who feared that the emperor might pardon him. Indeed, Theodosius punished very few of Maximus' supporters and issued a general pardon for the rest. He installed Valentinian as emperor in the West under the supervision of Arbogast, an army commander of mixed Germanic and Roman parentage. Valentinian converted from Arianism to Catholicism at Theodosius' urging and established his court at Vienne in southern Gaul.

Theodosius spent considerable time in Italy between 388 and 391. On June 13, 389, he made a formal entry into Rome with his younger son Honorius. By generous gifts, reforms in the laws, and deference to powerful individuals, he cultivated the support of the senate. While in Italy, Theodosius himself came under the influence of Bishop Ambrose of Milan, one of the Fathers of the Church. If Theodosius had given orders to church officials in the East, he now found himself submitting to the demands of a western bishop. In 390, after the people of Thessalonica murdered one of the emperor's German officers, soldiers were allowed to massacre thousands of spectators in the city's stadium. Ambrose demanded that Theodosius do penance for the massacre, and after long negotiations the emperor conceded. Stripping himself of the diadem and purple cloak which symbolized his power, he knelt before the bishop in the cathedral in Milan to ask for a pardon. It was a vivid demonstration of the western Church's power in relation to the government.

Having returned to Constantinople in 391, Theodosius found himself facing another western usurper in the following year. As Valentinian II grew into his late teens, the young man realized that Arbogast meant to keep real power in his own hands. In frustration, he apparently committed suicide, although many at the time and later accused Arbogast of murdering the young emperor. Arbogast named a teacher of rhetoric, Eugenius, as the emperor of the West.

Arbogast, a pagan himself, seems to have hoped for the support of the surviving pagan aristocracy, and a number of distinguished pagan nobles did rally to Eugenius' cause. Pagan support for Eugenius allowed Theodosius to present himself as the defender of Christianity. In 394, Theodosius again led his armies westward; on September 6, 394, at the Battle of the Frigidus, a river in Yugoslavia, he defeated Arbogast and Eugenius. On the first day of the battle, ten thousand Visigoths in Theodosius' army died in a frontal assault, and the emperor's officers advised retreat. Theodosius refused to give up and on the next day won a decisive victory with the aid of a sudden windstorm. Eugenius was captured and executed; Arbogast escaped but killed himself two days later. Many consider this final defeat of the forces of paganism in the Roman Empire to have been Theodosius' greatest achievement.

The emperor, however, had only a few months to enjoy the victory; he died in Milan in January, 395. He left the Empire to his sons Arcadius and Honorius—Arcadius to rule in the East and Honorius in the West. It has been argued that this division led to the fall of the Western Empire because the wealthier East not only did not send aid when barbarians attacked the West but also diverted invaders westward to save itself, in some cases.

Summary

Theodosius the Great brought peace to the eastern empire through diplomacy, rebuilt the eastern armies, and used them to win victories against western Roman armies. He ruled the East for fifteen years in which no one successfully disputed his authority and founded a dynasty which held power in the East until 450 and in the West until 455. In his zeal for Catholic orthodoxy, he issued orders to people and bishops on matters of doctrine, conciliated the senate with high offices, and won the people's favor. He made sure that Constantinople had a secure supply of grain, extended the walls, and embellished the city with a forum and a column depicting his victories. He even managed to lower taxes.

By most of the standards applied to earlier emperors, Theodosius was successful; the Church thought he deserved the title "Great." One could argue that the Eastern Empire benefited substantially from his rule, in both the short and the long terms. Whether his settlement of the Goths and his division of the Empire between his sons did not in the long run prove disastrous to the West is a question still disputed.

Bibliography

Baynes, Norman H. "The Dynasty of Valentinian and Theodosius the Great." In *The Cambridge Medieval History*. Vol. 1, *The Christian Roman Empire and the Foundation of the Teutonic Kingdoms*, edited by H. M. Gwatkin and J. P. Whitney. 2d ed. Cambridge: Cambridge University Press, 1957. This detailed account of the military and political aspects of Theodosius' reign includes an attempt to reconstruct the Gothic wars which occurred from 379 to 382.

Dudden, F. Homes. *The Life and Times of St. Ambrose*. 2 vols. Oxford: Clarendon Press, 1935. Scholarly but very readable account includes extensive material on Theodosius, emphasizing his relations with Ambrose but dealing with many other aspects of the reign as well. Contains frontispiece portrait of Ambrose, table of dates, bibliography, indexes.

Ferrill, Arthur. *The Fall of the Roman Empire: The Military Explanation*. London: Thames and Hudson, 1986. Chapter 4 on Theodosius is a careful evaluation of his military accomplishments, with a description of the Roman armies in 395. With table of emperors, bibliography, and illustrations, including a sculptural portrait of Theodosius and a map of the Battle of the Frigidus.

Gibbon, Edward. *The History of the Decline and Fall of the Roman Empire*. Edited by J. B. Bury. 7 vols. London: Methuen and Co., 1909-1929. This historical and literary classic includes two chapters on Theodosius. Gibbon's prejudice against religion colors his estimate of Theodosius' relations with the Church. Includes illustrations, maps, editor's appendices, bibliography of Gibbon's works and replies to it, indexes to text and appendices.

Hodgkin, Thomas. *Italy and Her Invaders*. Vol. 1, *The Visigothic Invasion*, 1880. Oxford: Clarendon Press, 1880-1899. A well-written chapter on Theodosius includes an introductory discussion of the primary sources, a chronological table of Theodosius' life, and a detailed account and evaluation of his Gothic policy, civil wars, internal administration, and religious policy. Old but still useful. With illustrations, maps, genealogical table of the Theodosian family.

Holum, Kenneth G. *Theodosian Empresses: Women and Imperial Dominion in Late Antiquity*. Berkeley: University of California Press, 1982. Part of chapter 2, "Theodosius the Great and His Women," provides a useful summary of some of the main issues of Theodosius' reign as well as a description of Theodosian Constantinople, a discussion of the position of the emperor's first wife, and an account of the implications of his second marriage for the war against Maximus. With detailed footnotes, a plan of Constantinople under Theodosius, a genealogical table of the Theodosian family, illustrations with an emphasis on coins, extensive bibliography, and an index.

Jones, A. H. M. *The Later Roman Empire, 284-602: A Social, Economic, and Administrative Survey.* 4 vols. Oxford: Basil Blackwell, 1964. Reprint. 2 vols. Norman: University of Oklahoma Press, 1975. Detailed authoritative treatment of the period includes material on Theodosius' reign, his religious policy, and his laws. Third volume contains notes, three appendices, lists of collections and periodicals cited and an exhaustive list of sources with abbreviations. With seven maps in a folder.

King, N. Q. *The Emperor Theodosius and the Establishment of Christianity.* London: SCM Press, 1961. Scholarly treatment of the relation of church and state under Theodosius viewed in the light of modern problems in this area. King argues that Theodosius, instead of imposing his own views on the Church, never acted in church matters without the support of an important group of bishops.

Matthews, John. *Western Aristocracies and Imperial Court: A.D. 364-425.* Oxford: Clarendon Press, 1975. Chapters 4 through 9 deal with Theodosius' reign in considerable detail, intermingled with extensive and occasionally digressive treatment of the social and cultural background of the aristocracies under his rule.

Carolyn Nelson

THEOLEPTUS OF PHILADELPHIA

Born: c. 1250; Nicaea (modern İznik, Turkey)
Died: c. 1326; Philadelphia (modern Alasehir, Turkey)
Area of Achievement: Religion
Contribution: As a spiritual writer, dynamic speaker, and respected teacher among medieval Greeks, Theoleptus played a major role in preventing the reunion of the Roman Catholic and Greek Orthodox churches. He also was influential in promoting Hesychasm, a mystical form of prayer and meditation.

Early Life

Theoleptus was born into a Christendom that was divided, long before the sixteenth century Reformation. Differences between the Latin Christianity of the West and the Greek Christianity of the East were long-standing. In the sixth century, the *Filioque* controversy had begun. The Western church, believing that the Christian Church could grow and unfold in time, and trusting in reason and the intellect, added this word to the Nicene Creed of the second century: "Credo ... in Spiritum Sanctum ... qui ex Patre Filioque procedit" (I believe ... in the Holy Spirit ... who proceeds from the Father and the Son). The Eastern church, believing the Christian Church to be fixed and immutable, and relying on tradition and mysticism, insisted that the Holy Spirit proceeded only from the Father and that this doctrine had been upheld by the early church fathers. Theologians of the West desired a more precise definition of the Godhead, while those of the East saw such a quest as producing legalistic interference. The *Filioque* doctrine had become entrenched in the West by the eighth century, but the Eastern church continued to oppose it and to claim true orthodoxy for its interpretation.

In addition to the *Filioque* issue, there were other doctrinal and liturgical differences. The Western church eventually came to forbid marriage of the clergy, while the East continued to allow it. The West forbade divorce; the Eastern church, never having completely cut its ties to the state, viewed marriage as a civil contract and tolerated divorce under certain conditions. The West had teachings on Purgatory, while in the East such things were thought to be unknowable. The Western church used cold water and unleavened bread in the celebration of the Eucharist, while the Eastern church used warm water and leavened bread.

All these matters reflected the deepest division, which centered on the question of authority: Would Rome or Constantinople lead Christianity? In 1054, a Western cardinal laid upon the altar of Hagia Sophia in Constantinople a decree excommunicating the Patriarch of Constantinople. The next day, the patriarch expelled the papal legate, and a schism between the two churches resulted. While Latin churches and monasteries in the East continued to maintain contact with local Orthodox bishops, the Western church increasingly came to view Constantinople as rigid and decadent, and the Eastern church came to see Rome as careless and arrogant.

The Crusades, which began in 1095 and which brought a massive Western presence into the Byzantine world, steadily reinforced these differences. During the Fourth Crusade (1202-1204), the Greeks, hating their emperor, Alexius III, for taking orders from Western Crusaders and the pope, resisted the emperor. Crusaders then overthrew Alexius; sacked, pillaged, and raped in Constantinople; made Baldwin, Count of Flanders, the Eastern Roman emperor; and divided Asia Minor among ten rulers and four national groups. This situation did not last; still, the Crusades, and particularly the events of 1204, served to solidify the differences between the Roman West and the Greek East.

During the latter half of the thirteenth century, when Theoleptus was a young man, the Eastern emperor, Michael VIII Palaeologus (reigned 1259-1282), sought reconciliation with the Western powers, for he feared the power of the encroaching Turks. He was joined by Patriarch John XI Becchus and certain other powerful Orthodox clergymen. The majority of the Orthodox clergy and people, however, remembering centuries of differences and the abuses of the Crusades, opposed such a reunion. Theoleptus would join the latter.

Life's Work

Reconciliation between the Roman and Byzantine churches was accomplished at the Council of Lyons in 1274. Opening on May 2, it was presided over by Pope Gregory X and attended by more than five hundred prominent Western clergymen, making it the largest ecclesiastical gathering since the Second Lateran Council of 1139. The Greek delegation, which did not arrive until June 24, consisted of Germanus, a representative of the Patriarch of Constantinople; Theophanus, Archbishop of Nicaea; the chancellor; and two high officials of the Eastern Empire. The Greek delegation also brought a letter of support signed by five hundred Greek clergymen. Nevertheless, most prominent Orthodox clergymen boycotted the council.

The council agreed on July 26, at its fourth session, to a plan of reconciliation. The council agreed to the *Filioque* doctrine—a determination that had been made even before the Greek delegation arrived on June 24. The reunion plan also upheld Western teachings on marriage of the clergy, Purgatory, and the celebration of the Eucharist. Finally, the plan called for the supremacy of the Roman pope in all disputes. Virtually every area of dispute was decided in favor of the Western teaching, and the Greek delegation accepted these decisions.

Shortly after the council's pronouncements had been promulgated, Theoleptus, an Orthodox church deacon, openly repudiated the council's stance. With the support of the majority of Orthodox clergy, he began to organize opposition to the decrees, principally in Bithynia, in northwestern Asia Minor near Constantinople. His polemics resulted in his excommunication by the Patriarch of Constantinople, and Emperor Michael VIII Palaeologus imprisoned and mistreated him. After his release in 1275, Theoleptus left the wife whom he had only recently married, abandoned the diaconate, and retired as a monk to Mount Athos in northeastern Greece, near the city of Thessalonica.

Mount Athos was a center of monasticism. Here Theoleptus practiced a form of prayer and spirituality known as Hesychasm, from the Greek word *hēsychia* (quiet). An early form of Hesychasm had been practiced by certain Greeks who had called for a solitary life and withdrawal from the world. At Mount Athos, Theoleptus was a student of Nicephorus the Athonite, who taught a variation on Hesychasm that did not require withdrawing into the wilderness. Under Nicephorus, Theoleptus learned a profound silence and spiritual vigilance brought about by fixing the eyes on the middle of the body, controlled breathing, and concentrating on a litany known as the "Jesus prayer." These disciplines elevated the mind from the world and human passions and were believed to result in an intuition of God in the form of light. Theoleptus' writings on Hesychasm exerted a profound influence on the fourteenth century Hesychast and contemplative Saint Gregory Palamas. Theoleptus remained at Mount Athos, first as a student and later as a spiritual teacher, for ten years, and his reputation grew throughout the Byzantine world.

With the 1282 accession of Andronicus II as Eastern Roman emperor and of Gregory II Cyprius in 1283 as Patriarch of Constantinople, the antiunionists among the Greeks once again gained ascendancy. To Theoleptus' satisfaction, the Council of Lyons' decrees and union with the West were repudiated. Because of his earlier opposition to reunion and his reputation as a spiritual leader at Mount Athos, Theoleptus was made Archbishop of Philadelphia in 1285. Philadelphia, in southeastern Asia Minor, eighty miles east of the port city of Smyrna (modern İzmir), had been Christian since apostolic times. It was the titular see of the province of Lydia, but during the fourteenth century its jurisdiction came to extend over other neighboring sees as well. Theoleptus would be the spiritual leader here for at least thirty-five years, until his death; he did, however, frequently depart to spend long periods in Constantinople.

As Archbishop of Philadelphia, Theoleptus was once again thrust into controversy. He wrote a blistering attack against the Orthodox clergy who had followed the unionist Patriarch John XI Becchus. He even turned on the new patriarch, Gregory II. Gregory actually had wanted unity, but without a complete surrender to Western doctrines. In opposition to the Western *Filioque* doctrine—that the Holy Spirit proceeds from the Father and the

Son—the Orthodox followed Photius' teaching regarding the "eternal progression" of the Holy Spirit from the Father alone and the "emission in time" by the Son.

Gregory, seeing a need for delineating a clearer, more permanent relationship between the Father and the Son, attempted a compromise. In a tome written in 1285, Gregory proposed the "eternal manifestation" of the Spirit by the Son. After the publication of this treatise, Theoleptus and many other Orthodox clergy refused to mention Gregory's name during the enactment of the liturgy; later, however, Theoleptus pronounced Gregory orthodox, after the latter disavowed certain passages in the 1285 tome. Nevertheless, Gregory ultimately pleased no one; he came to be denounced by unionists and antiunionists alike, including Theoleptus, whose renewed attack was instrumental in persuading the emperor and a church synod to remove Gregory from the office of patriarch in 1289.

In 1303, Theoleptus reportedly helped to rally the residents of Philadelphia against a Turkish siege of the city, at a time when many bishops were deserting their sees because of the Turkish threat. The city would change hands many times between the eleventh and fourteenth centuries, succumbing permanently to the Turks—under Bayezid I's leadership—in 1390; at that time, it was renamed Alasehir.

Upon the death in 1308 of John Palaeologus, son of Emperor Andronicus II, Theoleptus became spiritual adviser to his widow, the Empress Irene, daughter of Nicephorus Choumnus. Widowed at sixteen, after four years of marriage, she entered a convent in Constantinople under the name Eulogia. Theoleptus was the spiritual director of this convent and also of an adjacent monastery. In about 1320, Eulogia's parents requested of Theoleptus that they be allowed to be near their daughter. Nicephorus Choumnus was permitted to enter the monastery, and her mother joined Eulogia's convent. Not long afterward, Theoleptus died, and it was Nicephorus who presented the funeral oration, which has been preserved as a valuable summary of Theoleptus' life. A generation after Theoleptus' death, Eulogia would take part in theological controversies against Gregory Palamas.

In his final years, Theoleptus is supposed to have skillfully defended Hesychasm against the attacks of one its most virulent critics, Barlaam of Calabria, a pro-Western Italo-Greek monk, theologian, and bishop. Because Barlaam first appeared as a teacher at the Imperial University in Constantinople in 1326, many believe that Theoleptus lived until that year. According to Nicephorus Choumnas, however, Theoleptus died shortly after 1320. In any case, Barlaam ridiculed Hesychasm, calling its practitioners *omphalopsychoi* (men with their souls in their navels). The written and oral debates of Barlaam with the monks of Mount Athos after the death of Theoleptus (in the 1330's and 1340's) actually helped bring Hesychasm into prominence.

Summary

Centuries before the Reformation, the most serious division in the medieval Church was the one that separated the church of Rome from the church of Constantinople. Theoleptus of Philadelphia played a major role during the late thirteenth and early fourteenth centuries in opposing, reversing, and keeping reversed the reunion of the Roman Catholic and Greek Orthodox churches.

Despite the centuries of division, the Orthodox were much closer to Rome dogmatically than were the individualistic Protestant sects that arose later. Paradoxically, Theoleptus actually spent his life upholding sacramentalism and the ideal unity of the Christian Church. According to Theoleptus, Christ never intended anything less than one faith, one doctrine, and one Church, united under Him. Theoleptus conceived of the monastic Hesychast life as having a prophetic mission to benefit the whole world, not merely as a means of individual salvation.

Theoleptus was a dynamic religious writer and orator, a charismatic teacher and spiritual leader, and a composer of hymns. Almost all of his works remain unedited. Despite his importance, his name is rarely mentioned even in histories of the Eastern Empire (Byzantium) or of the Greek Orthodox church. Scholars in the English-speaking world would do well to give attention to this influential teacher.

Bibliography

Geanakoplos, Deno John. *Emperor Michael Palaeologus and the West, 1258-1282: A Study in Byzantine-Latin Relations.* Cambridge, Mass.: Harvard University Press, 1959. A helpful work on the character of the Eastern emperor who sought reunion with the West. Chapter 2, "The Ecclesiastical Union of Lyons," contains an excellent summary of East-West differences, although it does not mention Theoleptus. The work is well annotated and indexed and contains a good bibliography.

Hughes, Philip. *The Church in Crisis: A History of the General Councils, 325-1870.* Garden City, N.Y.: Hanover House, 1961. While it does not contain information on Theoleptus, this work is a clear and concise description of the important Second General Council of Lyons in 1274, which reunited the Latin West and Orthodox East after more than two centuries of division. It was his repudiation of this council that gave Theoleptus historical importance. The work is indexed and has a fair bibliography.

Le Guillou, M. J. *The Spirit of Eastern Orthodoxy.* Translated by Donald Attwater. New York: Hawthorne Books, 1962. This monograph introduces the reader to the "church outside the Church," that is, the Byzantine (Orthodox) heritage in Christendom. Chapters 7 and 8 focus on the estrangement between Rome and the Orthodox churches of the East, concentrating on the two largest churches, the Greek and Russian Orthodox.

There is no index and only a select bibliography. The work is concise (150 pages) and readable.

Meyendorff, John. *A Study of Gregory Palamas*. Translated by George Laurence. London: Faith Press, 1964. This work, translated from the French, centers on the renowned contemplative Gregory Palamas, who was influenced by Theoleptus in the practice of Hesychasm and who was a spokesman for conservative Orthodoxy. There are numerous references to Theoleptus but only about four or five total pages of information on the man, which appear mostly in chapter 1. The bibliography is brief, but further sources are cited in the footnotes.

Runciman, Steven. *The Great Church in Captivity: A Study of the Patriarchate of Constantinople from the Eve of the Turkish Conquest to the Greek War of Independence*. Cambridge: Cambridge University Press, 1964. Chapter 4, "The Church and the Churches," is an excellent description of the differences between Latin West and Greek East just before and during the time of Theoleptus, although Theoleptus himself is only briefly mentioned. Thorough index and seven pages of bibliography.

John J. Hunt

THEOPHANES THE CONFESSOR

Born: c. 752; Constantinople
Died: c. 818; Samothrace
Area of Achievement: Historiography
Contribution: Theophanes the Confessor was a monk and author whose chronicle, *Chronographia*, is for modern scholars the main source for the history of the Eastern Roman (or Byzantine) Empire from about 600 to 813.

Early Life

Theophanes was born to a wealthy family sometime around 752. At this time, the Byzantine Empire was mired in the Iconoclastic Controversy. The iconoclasts were Christians who believed that all religious art was idolatry and should be destroyed. (The characteristic religious art form of East Christian churches is the icon, hence the name iconoclasts, or "icon breakers.") Those who defended the use of religious art were called iconodoules (icon servers) or iconophiles (icon lovers). At the time of Theophanes' birth, the imperial government was sympathetic to the iconoclasts, and iconophiles were being persecuted. Theophanes' parents were secret iconophiles. As he grew up, Theophanes followed their lead in concealing his iconophile sympathies; as a result, he held a number of government posts under Emperor Constantine V, who reigned from 741 to 775. After Constantine's death, government policy changed; iconoclasm ceased to enjoy official support. Theophanes could now openly reveal his iconophilism. He became a monk and founded a monastery near Constantinople, the capital of the Eastern Roman Empire.

Life's Work

Theophanes' importance lies principally in his authorship of *Chronographia* (c. 810-815), a chronicle covering the history of the Eastern Roman Empire to August, 813. Theophanes undertook this project at the suggestion of a friend, George Syncellus. George had written a chronicle that began with the creation of the world and continued through the beginning of the reign of the Roman emperor Diocletian (late 284). When he learned that he was dying, George requested that his friend Theophanes complete the chronicle down to their own day, and Theophanes agreed.

The *Chronographia* is marred by Theophanes' extremely negative depiction of people with views other than his own. He disliked Muslims and hated iconoclasts. His attitude toward the iconoclasts is understandable, for he and his family had suffered under their rule. Still, two of the most important iconoclastic emperors, Leo III (717-741) and Constantine V, had been mighty generals who won great victories over the Arabs, Bulgars, and Slavs.

The empire owed its survival to them.

Theophanes also made some errors in the chronology of his *Chronographia*. Today, virtually the entire world uses the Christian or common era system of dating, which dates everything before or after the approximate year Jesus Christ was born. In Theophanes' time, the B.C.-A.D. system was just coming into use, and he used it only occasionally and incorrectly, since he was not completely familiar with it. Eastern Christians and Jews most often used the *annus mundi* system (dating things from the year of the Creation), a system Jews still employ for religious purposes. In addition to the *annus mundi*, Theophanes dated events by the indiction, a fifteen-year cycle originally used by the imperial government for reassessment of property for tax purposes. From September, 610 (the Byzantine year began on September 1), through August, 773, except for the years between 715 and 725, Theophanes' *annus mundi* and the indiction were one year out of synchronization.

Yet another major problem with the *Chronographia* lies in its format. A chronicle is not a true history, but rather a year-by-year record of events. Because of its structure, a chronicle cannot give a proper account of events such as long wars that stretch over more than one year. A great Roman historian, Cornelius Tacitus, deliberately used a modified chronicle format for one of his books, *Ab excessu divi Augusti* (c. A.D. 116; *Annals*, 1793). In general, however, sophisticated historians avoid writing chronicles.

Theophanes, however, was neither sophisticated nor well educated. He lived in a time when the Byzantine Empire was fighting for its very life on three fronts. In the East, it was engaged in a great struggle with Muslim Arabs, who had already wrested Syria, Palestine, and North Africa (including Egypt) from the empire. In 717, the Arabs had besieged Constantinople with a huge army and fleet. This attack endangered the existence not only of the Eastern Roman Empire but indeed of Western civilization itself, for if the capital had fallen, the Arabs would have swept on into Europe. Emperor Leo III, however, managed to turn back the Arab armies and fleets. In the last year of his reign, he inflicted a second humiliating defeat upon the Arabs at Acroïnum, deep in Asia Minor (now eastern Turkey). The second threat to the Byzantines came from the Balkan peninsula. There, a people known as the Bulgars (ancestors of the modern Bulgarians) had seized much territory and were making their way toward Constantinople. Leo's son, Constantine V, fought several wars with the Bulgars and eventually brought them to a standstill. Other barbarian tribes, mostly Slavs, were also roaming about the Balkans, causing considerable damage. Finally, there was occasional warfare in Italy, the original homeland of the Romans, where the empire still had a few outposts, mostly in the south.

These terrible wars caused many changes in the Byzantine Empire. For example, in the year 600, the empire had been dominated by large estates called *latifundia*. Worked by slaves or tenant farmers, each estate grew one or two crops which were then sold on the open market for cash. By 800, however, the *latifundia* seem to have largely disappeared; by then, the agricultural scene was characterized by small family farms. Moreover, many cities disappeared, and the populations of those that survived declined. Finally, because the constant wars were a severe drain on the empire's resources, most schools closed and intellectual activity came to an almost complete halt. Thus, although Theophanes' parents could afford the best possible education for their son, he was not well trained by the standards of two centuries before or a century after his own day, when the empire was stronger and there were more schools.

Theophanes' work was used by all later Byzantine historians. Years after Theophanes died, his work was continued by a group of writers who are collectively known as Theophanes Continuatus (the Continuator of Theophanes); these writers were better historians than Theophanes himself. By the end of the ninth century, the empire had grown much stronger; schools reopened, and learning once again began to flourish. About fifty years after Theophanes died, the *Chronographia* was translated into Latin by Anastasius, a librarian who was one of the few Western scholars at the time to know Greek. As a result, Theophanes' work influenced not only the historians of the later Byzantine or Eastern Roman Empire but those of medieval Western Europe as well, for Latin was the language of all educated Western Europeans in the Middle Ages.

Theophanes' later life was not happy. After 800, iconoclasm revived briefly. Emperor Leo V (813-820), one of the last of the iconoclastic rulers, exiled Theophanes because of his position regarding icons. Already in poor health, Theophanes died in exile on the Aegean island of Samothrace around the year 818, probably of some kind of kidney disease. Theophanes is revered as a saint by both the Roman Catholic and the Greek Orthodox churches.

Summary

Today, many historians call the period from about 600 to 800 the Dark Age of the Eastern Roman Empire. Few Greek sources survive from this period. Therefore, scholars must frequently use the writings of Arab historians to piece together the story of what was happening in the Eastern Roman Empire at this time. Theophanes' *Chronographia* is thus a precious document, despite its many flaws. Without it, even less would be known about the Byzantine Empire during two centuries when it was undergoing profound political, social, economic, and cultural changes as a result of the wars it fought. Even the Latin translation of the *Chronographia* by Anastasius is useful. Anastasius used manuscripts which are now lost; consequently, his translation of Theophanes' work contains a few scraps of information which are not included in extant Greek manuscripts of the work.

Bibliography

Mango, Cyril. "Who Wrote the Chronicle of Theophanes?" *Zbornik radova vizantološkog instituta* 18 (1978): 9-17. Mango believes that George Syncellus, despite his poor health, did complete his work and that all Theophanes did was to polish the final draft. Therefore the *Chronographia* should be attributed to George, not Theophanes. While Mango's theory has been rejected by most other scholars, the article is interesting to read because it shows the methods by which specialists attempt to determine the authenticity of works such as the *Chronographia*.

Ostrogorsky, George. *History of the Byzantine State*. Translated by Joan Hussey. New Brunswick, N.J.: Rutgers University Press, 1957, 2d ed. 1969. Chapters 2 and 3 are most important for those interested in Theophanes and his time. Each chapter of Ostrogorsky's book starts with a section on the sources for the period covered by that chapter. Especially interesting are Ostrogorsky's comments on the chronological errors found in the *Chronographia*.

Theophanes. *The Chronicle of Theophanes*. Translated by Harry Turtledove. Philadelphia: University of Pennsylvania Press, 1982. This translation includes all entries in the *Chronographia* from September, 602, to the final one for September, 812, through August, 813. This is the most important section of the chronicle, since the period before 602 is known from other, better sources. Dr. Turtledove provides a useful, nontechnical introduction and helpful footnotes. One disadvantage of this translation is that it lacks maps.

—————————. *Chronographia: A Chronicle of Eighth Century Byzantium*. Translated by Anthony R. Santoro, with a preface by Martin Arbagi. Gorham, Maine: Heathersfield Press, 1982. This translation includes only the entries from September, 717, to August, 803. The introduction is much shorter and less informative than that of Turtledove, and there are no footnotes. This book does have an excellent set of full-color maps.

Vasiliev, A. A. Chapters 4 and 5 in *History of the Byzantine Empire*. 2 vols. 2d ed. Madison: University of Wisconsin Press, 1952. This book is more complete than that of Ostrogorsky, but it is older and not as well organized. Vasiliev's comments on Theophanes are not as informative as Ostrogorsky's.

Martin Arbagi

THEOPHRASTUS
Tyrtamus

Born: c. 372 B.C.; Eresus, Lesbos, Greece
Died: c. 287 B.C.; Athens?, Greece
Areas of Achievement: Science, philosophy, and literature
Contribution: Successor of Aristotle as head of his school, the Lyceum, Theophrastus became father of the sciences of botany, ecology, and mineralogy. He also wrote *Characters*, literary sketches of human psychological types.

Early Life

Theophrastus (originally named Tyrtamus) was born in Eresus, a small city-state on the Greek island of Lesbos, near the coast of Asia Minor. His father was Melantas, a cloth-fuller. He studied under the philosopher Alcippus in Eresus, later traveling to Athens to broaden his intellectual horizons. It is not known when he became Aristotle's student. It was Aristotle who called him Theophrastus, "he of godlike speech," a compliment to his polished Greek style. According to tradition, both men studied under Plato, but in Theophrastus' case this study must have been brief.

Theophrastus was in his mid-twenties when Plato died. Since Plato had not made Aristotle head of his school, the Academy, Aristotle moved to Assos at the invitation of its ruler, Hermias, and stayed three years. Theophrastus followed him there. When the Persians threatened Hermias, Theophrastus took Aristotle to the relative safety of his native island, Lesbos. The men were only twelve years apart in age, and the relationship between them was as much that of friends and colleagues as that of master and disciple. Soon Philip II, King of Macedonia, invited Aristotle to come there as tutor of his son, the future Alexander the Great. He accepted, and Theophrastus went with him, remaining until after Philip's death seven years later.

Life's Work

In 335, Aristotle returned to Athens and founded a school at the Lyceum, a cult center with a colonnade and park, where the Peripatetic philosophy flourished under his leadership for thirteen years. Theophrastus lived there, discussing, lecturing, and writing. It was a creative period. Alexander was conquering the East as far as India, and philosophers who went with him, at first including Aristotle's nephew, Callisthenes, sent back scientific specimens never seen before in Greece. Not least among these were seeds and living plants that were tended in the garden of the Lyceum and studied by Theophrastus. His books on botany thus contain descriptions of the plants of India. He traveled through Greece collecting plants and making observations of natural phenomena.

Around the time of Alexander's death in 323, Aristotle retired to Chalcis, and a few months later he also died. His choice of Theophrastus as his successor at the Lyceum proved to be a wise one. At this time Theophrastus was about fifty years old, and statues give some idea of his appearance. He was a vigorous, healthy man, but lines around his eyes and the hollows of his cheeks suggest the heavy responsibilities of leadership and the hard work of empirical research. He remained at the Lyceum as *scholarch* (senior professor) until his death in about 287. His will provided for the maintenance of the Lyceum garden, where he asked to have his body buried. He designated Strato of Lampsachus, known as "the physicist," his heir as head of the school.

Theophrastus taught some two thousand students, among them Demetrius of Phalerum, who became ruler of Athens and presented Theophrastus with the land on which the Lyceum and its garden were located. Thus the school came to possess its own real estate, instead of leasing its grounds from the city. This step was important, because many Athenians regarded Aristotle and his followers as pro-Macedonian; Theophrastus had even been charged with sacrilege in 319. He had managed to stay in the city, and the reestablishment of Macedonian power in Athens two years later had made Demetrius governor. Demetrius was not popular, and when his rule ended in 307 a law was passed forbidding the operation of philosophical schools without special permission. Theophrastus then had to leave Athens, but the law was repealed within a year, and he was able to return.

Theophrastus produced his most important writings during his years at the Lyceum. He continued to revise them until the end of his life. The titles of 227 works by Theophrastus have been recorded, but only a small fraction have survived. They fall into three major categories: scientific, philosophical, and literary.

It is in science that Theophrastus made his most significant contributions. Here he continued the work of Aristotle, achieving important insights of his own. He pointedly repeated Aristotle's statement that "nature does nothing in vain" and added his own comment, "anything which is contrary to nature is dangerous." In describing natural objects, Theophrastus established sets of opposing characteristics, such as cold and hot, wet and dry, male and female, wild and domestic. This method is typical of the Peripatetic school and is derived from Aristotle. In some respects, however, such as his emphasis on the autonomous purposes of living things and his avoidance of the ideas of final causation and the prime mover, he rejected Aristotle's authority and marked out an independent line of investigation.

His longest extant writings are the nine books of *Peri phytikōn historiōn* (translated in *Enquiry into Plants and Minor Works on Odours and Weather Signs*, 1916; often designated by the Latin title, *De historia plantarum*) and the six books of *Peri phytikōn aitiōn* (partial translation in *De Causis*

Plantarum, 1976-   ). Aristotle had written on animals; Theophrastus' works are the first careful treatment of botanical subjects. *Enquiry into Plants* describes the parts of plants and the characteristics of more than five hundred species, arranged in four groups: trees, shrubs, sub-shrubs, and herbs. *Peri phytikōn aitiōn* discusses generation, propagation, cultivation, and diseases of plants, as well as their tastes and odors. Theophrastus originated many terms in the botanical vocabulary and distinguished some of the main divisions of the vegetable kingdom. These works are also notable for their ecological viewpoint. Theophrastus always discusses a plant in the context of its relationships to the environment: sunshine, soil, climate, water, cultivation, and other plants and animals. His conclusions are sometimes wrong—for example, he believed in spontaneous generation—but even in such cases he showed caution and skepticism.

The works of Theophrastus dealing with other sciences are extant only in fragmentary form. Only excerpts remain of his *Peri physikōn* (on physics) and *Peri pyros* (*De Igne: A Post-Aristotelian View of the Nature of Fire*, 1971). Geology is represented by *Peri lithōn* (translated in *Theophrastus's History of Stones*, 1746; also as *On Stones*), a long fragment that investigates the properties of metals, minerals, gems, and substances whose animal origin he recognized, such as pearls, coral, and ivory. Fossils are handled in *Peri ichthyōn en xera katastasei* (on fishes in dry condition). Then there are fragments on meteorology such as *Peri semeiōn hydatōn kai pneumatōn kai cheimonōn kai eudiōn* and *Peri anemōn* (translated together in *On Winds and On Weather Signs*, 1894); the treatise on winds accurately describes many of the Mediterranean winds and goes beyond Aristotle in affirming that winds are moving air. Human physiology is discussed by Theophrastus in other treatises on sense perception, odors, weariness, fainting, paralysis, and perspiration. One called *Peri hypnou kai enypniōn* (on sleep and dreams) has disappeared.

The surviving philosophical work of Theophrastus is an important section of the *Ton meta ta physika* (*Metaphysics*, 1929), which criticizes Aristotle's doctrine that all things have a final cause, or *telos*. Aristotle said that the final cause of all living things is the service of the higher rational nature, that is, of human beings. Rejecting his teacher's excessive teleology, Theophrastus remarked,

> We must try to find a certain limit . . . both to final causation and to the impulse to the better. For this is the beginning of the inquiry about the universe, that is, of the effort to determine the conditions on which real things depend and the relations in which they stand to one another.

So he maintained that, by nature, each living thing always aims at assimilating its intake to its own goal, and the goal of a plant is not to feed humans or to give them wood, but to produce fruit containing seed for the perpetuation of its species—in other words, to produce offspring similar to itself. Aristotle would not have denied species perpetuation as a goal, but would have made it a subsidiary cause in his hierarchical organization of nature. For Theophrastus, it is the whole point.

Other authors often quoted from his now-lost reference works, *Physikon doxai* (doctrines of natural philosophers), a history of philosophical opinions about major problems, and the *Nomoi* (laws), a compilation of the statutes and traditions of Greek cities. *Charactēres ethikōi* (c. 319; *The Moral Characters of Theophrastus*, 1702, best known as *Characters*) is Theophrastus' only surviving literary work and his most famous writing. In it he sketches thirty aberrant human personality types, giving as much care to their description as he did to plant species in his botanical works. These are not objective treatises, but satirical, dryly humorous jabs at disagreeable people such as the flatterer, the faultfinder, and the miser. This genre established by Theophrastus was much imitated, particularly in Great Britain and France in the seventeenth and eighteenth centuries.

Summary

Theophrastus was, as Diogenes Laërtius wrote, "a man of remarkable intelligence and industry." His fame has suffered because he has remained in the shadow of Aristotle. Where he differed from his teacher, it was for the most part because he was more scientific, more dependent upon observation, and less ready to make universal statements of principle which could not be supported by perceptible facts. Aristotle had moved away from Plato in that direction; Theophrastus went even further.

In doing so, Theophrastus anticipated some of the methods of modern science. More than Plato's or Aristotle's, his philosophical stance was congenial with scientific discovery, emphasizing as it did efficient causes, not final causes. He has been recognized as the founder of the science of botany, having made many observations about plant for the first time and having established the basic terminology in that field. In modern times, he is also recognized as the first ecologist, for he viewed species not as isolated phenomena but in interaction with their physical environment and other species. He was distinguished as a perceptive investigator of lithology and mineralogy. Many of his ideas have been corrected in the light of later work; many others have so far withstood the test of time. It is hard to criticize him too severely, since he was among the first to set out on the journey of scientific inquiry. All told, he is impressive for his rationality and good sense and for his wish to depend on observations and to criticize the reports that he received. His practical attitude may be discerned in his rejoinder to those who advised him to plant and fell trees by the moon and signs of the zodiac: "One should not in fact be governed by the celestial conditions and revolution rather than by the trees and slips and seeds."

Among those who followed him were the researchers of the Museum and Library of Alexandria in Egypt in the second and first centuries B.C. The Latin natural historian Pliny the Elder quoted him extensively, and his influence can be traced in other ancient writers on sciences such as botany and medical pharmacology. Arabic commentators studied, preserved, and translated his writings during the medieval period. When interest in the sciences was reawakened in early modern Europe, the botanical works of Theophrastus were revived and printed. A Latin translation appeared in 1483, and the Greek text was published in Venice between 1495 and 1498. An English translation of the *Peri phytikōn historiōn* was published in 1916, and of the first two books of the *Peri phytikōn aitiōn* in 1976.

Bibliography
Diogenes Laërtius. "Theophrastus." In *Lives of Eminent Philosophers*, edited by R. D. Hicks., vol. 1. Cambridge, Mass.: Harvard University Press, 1925. Since Diogenes wrote his set of biographies about five hundred years after the death of Theophrastus, his work is not entirely reliable, but it does preserve many ancient traditions about him.
Fortenbaugh, William W., Pamela M. Huby, and Anthony A. Long, eds. *Theophrastus of Eresus: On His Life and Work.* New Brunswick, N.J.: Transaction Books, 1985. Volume 2 in the Rutgers Studies in Classical Humanities series, this volume is the fruit of Project Theophrastus, an international undertaking to collect, edit, and translate the fragments of Theophrastus. It contains numerous scholarly essays on the major issues in literary, philosophical, scientific, and historical research on Theophrastus. Three of these deal with the Arabic tradition.
Fortenbaugh, William W., and Robert W. Sharples, eds. *Theophrastus as Natural Scientist and Other Papers.* New Brunswick, N.J.: Transaction Books, 1987. Volume 3 in the Rutgers Studies in Classical Humanities series and a companion to *Theophrastus of Eresus*, this is another collection of articles on Theophrastus' shorter scientific works, and others on botany and ecology, metaphysics, ethics, religion, and politics.
Theophrastus. *The Character Sketches.* Translated with an introduction and notes by Warren Anderson. Kent, Ohio: Kent State University Press, 1970. The best recent translation of the *Characters*, with useful explanatory notes and an introductory essay on the development of the "character" as a literary genre.
──────────. *De causis plantarum.* Translated with an introduction by Benedict Einarson and George K. K. Link. Cambridge, Mass.: Harvard University Press, 1976- . This translation of the *Peri phytikōn aitiōn* has the Greek and English texts on facing pages and includes a fine introduction on the author and the work, Theophrastus' predecessors, his calendar, and more.

—————————. *Enquiry into Plants and Minor Works on Odours and Weather Signs*. Translated with an introduction by Sir Arthur Hort. 2 vols. Cambridge, Mass.: Harvard University Press, 1916. This has the Greek text and English translation on facing pages; it includes a short but useful introduction. The difficult Greek of Theophrastus is rendered accurately, but in an eccentric English style.

J. Donald Hughes

SAINT THOMAS

Born: c. early first century A.D.; Galilee, Palestine
Died: Second half of the first century; possibly Mylapore, India
Area of Achievement: Religion
Contribution: As one of the handpicked followers of Jesus, Thomas played a
  role in the epoch-making spread of the Christian message in the first cen-
  tury. He continues to be venerated in Christendom, especially among
  Christians of India, who plausibly claim that Thomas first brought the
  word of Jesus Christ to their ancestors and others in the Orient.

Early Life

Little specific information is available, but the general conditions of
Thomas' early life are reasonably secure. The signs point to his birth around
or slightly after the traditional date of Jesus' nativity (c. 4 B.C.). Also like
Jesus, he hailed from the area of Galilee, a district some sixty miles north of
Jerusalem. His Jewish heritage furnished him with knowledge of the history
of his race, respect for the religious customs of his forefathers, and familiarity with the Hebrew scriptures, perhaps in Aramaic or even Greek form.

Yet a Galilean Jew such as Thomas (also called Didymus in the New Testament, a Greek word meaning "twin") likely differed somewhat from his
countrymen in Jerusalem to the south. There are several reasons for this.
First, Galilee had long been extensively affected by foreign cultural influences and had a large non-Jewish population. Foreign merchants and settlers
were encountered everywhere. Second, the Galileans' dialect was different
from that spoken by Jews in Jerusalem (Matt. 26:73). Third, Jews of Galilee
were regarded with some disdain by their southern neighbors for their less
strict observance of the oral religious tradition which formed the basis for
faith and practice among the Pharisees, the most respected and influential
Palestinian Jewish sect of the day. Finally, Galileans would most likely have
been bilingual, both Aramaic and Greek being widely used throughout the
district. A Jewish male would probably have had some command of Hebrew,
the language of most of the Old Testament, as well.

Thomas' early years, then, would have been marked not only by thorough
grounding in Judaism but also by considerable exposure to non-Jewish language and culture. The radical separation of Jew from Gentile practiced by
some in Jerusalem would have been most difficult in Galilee. This cultural
background helps account for, though it does not totally explain, his apparent willingness to become a disciple of Jesus of Nazareth (a village in south-
central Galilee), whose views evidently met such forceful opposition from
certain more strictly traditional Jewish authorities based in Jerusalem.

Thomas' early years would also have instilled in him, along with the vast
majority of all Jews of his locale and time, a profound distaste for the pres-

ence of Roman military and political power, for Galilee was part of the Roman Empire throughout the first century. This loathing, which eventually erupted in the First Jewish Revolt (A.D. 66-70), was coupled in many persons with a distinct religiopolitical expectation, even longing. That is, the Jews hoped that the promises of the Hebrew Scriptures (understood quite literally as God's very words to his chosen people) were soon to come true in a new and dramatic fashion. God would send his designated deliverer, the Messiah (in Greek, *Christos*), to liberate the land from foreign domination and mightily bless his ancient covenant people, the Jews. The kingdom of God would one day soon arrive in tangible form.

Thomas was most likely an heir of such a theological and political outlook. His life's work as a disciple of Jesus was a response to what he understood as God's fulfillment, as promised in the Scriptures, of his and his nation's heartfelt longing.

Life's Work

The scanty available evidence points to Thomas' achievement in two settings: Galilee and surrounding districts during and after the life of Jesus of Nazareth, and areas to the east of the Roman Empire in the second half of the first century.

In his native Galilee, Thomas came into contact with Jesus, whose influence in the mid- to late 20s was felt from Roman Syria southward through Galilee and on to Jerusalem. Galilean Jews would have been aware of John the Baptist's prophetic proclamation; Jesus rode on John's coattails into the public arena, attracting followers such as Thomas.

Thomas was, according to available evidence, one of only a dozen persons selected by Jesus from a much larger group of followers to receive special instruction and responsibilities (Matt. 10:3, Mark 3:18, Luke 6:15). For a period of some three years, Thomas observed and participated in a religious movement (not without political implications, however) led by Jesus and bent on intensifying, if not ushering in, the earthly reign of Israel's covenant God, Yahweh ("the kingdom of God"). Thomas was among the twelve sent out to call his countrymen to repentance (Mark 6:7-13), a recognition of personal and corporate need for moral reform in the light of impending divine judgment. In this way he and his colleagues saw their mission, like that of John the Baptist and Jesus himself, as preparation for a decisive act of God in the near future (Luke 19:11, Acts 1:6).

Thomas was as disillusioned as his comrades were when Jesus' activity culminated in his arrest and execution by local and imperial authorities in Jerusalem. Like the other disciples, he fled the scene (Matt. 26:56), presumably to avoid being incriminated himself because of association with an alleged criminal. Were this the last hint of Thomas' activity, his name would long ago have been forgotten. Ancient sources, however, afford three specific glimpses into his life and thought which have for centuries enshrined him in the memories of those whose own personal religious experience resonates with that of Thomas. These traditions, all in the Gospel of John, merit specific mention as a result of their continuing religious relevance as well as their probable historical significance.

At the crucial point in Jesus' life, when his sense of destiny beckoned him from Perea (where he was fairly safe from arrest) to Jerusalem (where he was not), it was Thomas who rallied his comrades with the declaration, "Let us go with him so that we may die with him." Scholars debate whether this evinces a fatalistic or a courageous spirit. In either case, Thomas helped to galvanize the other disciples into accompanying Jesus, against their own better judgment (Mark 10:32), to the eventual site of his death. He models a stoic, or perhaps selfless, response to perceived duty.

Some days later, according to John's gospel, Jesus sought to console his disciples on the eve of his imminent betrayal. Again Thomas focused the collective spirit of his fellows. This time, however, his words betrayed not courage but curiosity, if not incredulity. Jesus spoke enigmatically of departing in order to make ready a place for his followers; Thomas observed: "We do not know where you are going; how can we know how to get there?" Thomas demonstrates here a searching if not critical temperament which articulates the heartfelt inquisitiveness, or even frustration, of many religious persons in the first century, and others since that time.

Thomas is most remembered, however, for the independent yet ultimately pliant spirit he exhibited during the days when, according to sources preserved in the New Testament, Jesus appeared to his disciples alive following his death by crucifixion (John 20:24-31). Thomas refused to give credence to hearsay evidence, saying that unless and until he had personal, tangible proof that Jesus had indeed somehow risen from the dead—which, one surmises, Thomas doubted he would receive—he refused to set any store by his friends' astonishing claims.

One week later, Thomas' skepticism was forced to contend with the corporeal presence of the person whose existence he had so roundly questioned: Jesus. Thomas was invited to satisfy his doubt and then draw the appropriate conclusions. In John's account, Thomas becomes the first person to affirm, in the wake of Jesus' resurrection, unqualified recognition of Jesus as master and deity.

Apart from his activity in Galilee, Thomas is also connected in ancient sources with missionary activity east of the Roman Empire. Evaluation of these sources is still in its early stages, and both literary and archaeological evidence awaits further sifting. *The Acts of Thomas*, dating from about the third century, speaks of Thomas' presence in India. (The second century *Gospel of Thomas* gives little if any information on Thomas and was in any case not written by him.) Much of the material in this apocryphal book may be safely regarded as fiction. There seems, however, to be a historical core which supports the view, held by several communities of Indian Christians to this day, that the Gospel was first brought to their ancestors by Thomas in the first century. According to traditions preserved in these communities, Thomas was fatally stabbed on July 3, 72, for refusing to worship Kali, a Hindu goddess.

Other ancient sources speak somewhat vaguely of Thomas' labors in Parthia, an ancient nation southeast of the Caspian Sea. Today scholars theorize that these reports reflect not an actual visit by Thomas to Parthia but written communication between Thomas and Christians in the Parthian city of Edessa. In any case, the Parthian tradition corroborates the assertion that in the early years of Christianity's expansion Thomas was instrumental in bearing the Gospel message to lands far to the east of his native Galilee.

Summary

Saint Thomas was hardly a pivotal figure in the history of early Christianity. It cannot even be said that he occupies a prominent place in the Gospel records where he receives direct mention. During Jesus' life he was overshadowed by Peter, James, and John, while his activity in the first decades of early church expansion is now nearly hidden.

Yet there is good evidence that he played a more integral role in the spread of Christianity to India—where thousands have revered his memory for centuries—and perhaps even farther eastward than Western Christendom and historians generally acknowledge. Thomas in his milieu may perhaps be compared to someone such as Martin Bucer in the Reformation: Both men played significant roles, but in historical perspective both are eclipsed by more dominant personages and events in which they had only tangential involvement. Still, the careful student of ancient Christianity will be as loath to overlook Thomas' place as will the student of the Reformation to overlook Bucer.

Wherever the New Testament has been read through the centuries, which is virtually everywhere in the West, Thomas has served as an example, both good and bad, for Christian faith. Commentators such as John Calvin, stressing his incredulity, have criticized his obduracy and contributed to a view of him epitomized in the expression "doubting Thomas." Augustine sees in Jesus' words to Thomas ("Blessed are they who have not seen, and yet believe," John 20:28) a commendation of those who in coming centuries and God's predestinating plan place personal trust in God through Jesus. Origen refutes the claims of Augustine's adversary Aulus Cornelius Celsus by adducing Thomas' testimony as proof of the corporeality of Jesus' resurrected body.

In these and many other cases, Thomas takes his place as a continuing witness to both the objective reality and the subjective impact of the person of

Jesus in the experience of one who examines his claims. Thomas himself would perhaps affirm an assessment of his contribution to religion, and even history, which would stress not his own achievement but the merit of the one whose reality convinced his questioning mind and, as a result, his heart.

Bibliography

Barclay, William. *The Master's Men*. London: SCM Press, 1959. Popular level but learned discussion. A renowned New Testament scholar devotes a chapter to an insightful, if slightly overimaginative, character sketch which attempts to assess all significant historical references to Thomas. Also discusses Thomas traditions in works by ancient historians as well as in *The Acts of Thomas*.

Barker, Kenneth, ed. *The New International Study Bible*. Grand Rapids, Mich.: Zondervan Bible Publishers, 1985. Makes available, in modern English translation, all extant first century references to Thomas (indexed in a concordance). Includes explanatory comments on Thomas' remarks in the Gospel of John and other Gospel references to him. Maps aid in picturing the geographical dimensions of the world in which Thomas lived.

Brown, Raymond. *The Gospel According to John*. 2 vols. Garden City, N.Y.: Doubleday and Co., 1966-1970. The most significant primary source for information on Thomas is the New Testament, especially John's gospel. This critically acclaimed entry in the Anchor Bible series is among the most competent and thorough investigations of John, and therefore of the Thomas traditions as they occur in the New Testament.

Eusebius of Caesarea. *Ecclesiastical History*. 2 vols. Translated by K. Lake and J. E. L. Oulton. Cambridge, Mass.: Harvard University Press, 1926-1932, reprint 1980. The classic ancient account of the rise and development of the early Church. Contains at least six references to Thomas (see index in volume 2) and furnishes an overall context for traditional understanding of his significance and the circles in which he moved.

Farquhar, J. N. "The Apostle Thomas in North India." *Bulletin of the John Rylands Library* 10 (1926): 80-111. A dated but still-relevant examination of extra-New Testament references to Thomas. Offers a creative reconstruction, based on documentary evidence, of how Thomas traveled to India. Seeks to reconcile the conflicting testimony of *The Acts of Thomas*, on the one hand, with traditions which speak of Thomas' presence in Parthia, on the other. This article and another by Farquhar are reprinted in J. Vellian, ed., *The Apostle Thomas According to the "Acts of Thomas"*: Kottayam, India, 1971.

Finegan, J. *Hidden Records of the Life of Jesus*. Philadelphia: Pilgrim Press, 1969. Contains a valuable discussion of the Gospel of Thomas with extensive bibliography. Cites portions in the original languages, then gives translation and analysis. Concludes with the verdict that alleged sayings of

Jesus in the Gospel of Thomas generally have little chance of being authentic. Implies that Jesus' disciple Thomas is not the author.

Freyne, Seán. *Galilee from Alexander the Great to Hadrian, 323 B.C.E. to 135 C.E.* Wilmington, Del.: Michael Glazier, 1980. The standard history of Galilee in the days of Thomas. Useful for general background on living conditions and social environment. Discusses the languages spoken in Galilee, the religious views of Galileans, and the political currents of the time. Useful maps and full bibliography.

Hennecke, E. *New Testament Apocrypha*. Edited by W. Schneemelcher. Translated and edited by R. M. Wilson. 2 vols. Philadelphia: Westminster Press, 1963-1965. Volume 1 contains extensive discussion of scholarly views on the Gospel of Thomas. Volume 2 contains the standard English translation of *The Acts of Thomas*, along with full discussion of its linguistic and literary distinctives. The discussion unfortunately fails to take cognizance of work by nonbiblical scholars (see studies listed elsewhere in this bibliography) which argues in favor of the probable historical core of portions of the narrative.

Medlycott, A. E. *India and the Apostle Thomas: An Inquiry, with a Critical Analysis of the "Acta Thomae."* London: David Nutt, 1905. The seminal study in English of the ancient extra-New Testament Thomas traditions in the light of modern historical and archaeological findings. Medlycott is among the first to furnish, and at times deny, solid historical footing for certain ancient ecclesiastical traditions concerning Thomas. His observations and arguments are foundational to subsequent discussion.

Mundadan, A. M. *History of Christianity in India*. Vol. 1, *From the Beginning up to the Middle of the Sixteenth Century (up to 1542)*. Bangalore, India: Theological Publications in India, 1982. Chapter 1 of this exhaustive critical history focuses primarily on the traditions which link Thomas to India. Mundadan's evaluation of both primary and secondary evidence in some respects supersedes all previous discussion in its breadth and depth of treatment. He concludes that the Indian community's ancient traditions of Saint Thomas are rooted in the historical fact of Thomas' first-century labors there. Exhaustive bibliography.

Perumalil, A. C. *The Apostles in India: Fact or Fiction?* Patna, India: Catholic Book Crusade, 1952. Elaborates on ancient traditions concerning both Thomas and Bartholomew. Not always sufficiently analytical and critical in dealing with historical evidence, but this is more than compensated for by the complete listing of all references to India in both Greek and Latin sources from the second to the thirteenth century.

Placid, Fr. "The South Indian Apostolate of St. Thomas." *Orientalia christiana periodica* 18 (1952): 229-245. This careful and informed investigation examines the claims of modern Christians in Malabar, South India, that their ancestors were converted to Christianity through the labors of

Thomas in the first century. Placid argues that ancient traditions in Syrian and Arabic literature substantiate this claim, while no compelling evidence requires its denial.

Robert W. Yarbrough

THOMAS À KEMPIS
Thomas Hemerken

Born: 1379; Kempen
Died: July 26, 1471; monastery of St. Agnietenberg, near Zwolle
Area of Achievement: Religion
Contribution: Thomas is credited by most historians with writing *The Imitation of Christ*, the most important piece of devotional literature produced by the late medieval pietistic movement called the *devotio moderna* and one of the most influential religious works in history. Some scholars claim that this work has been more widely read than any Christian work other than the Bible.

Early Life

Thomas Hemerken of Kempen—better known as Thomas à Kempis—was born in 1379 to a blacksmith named John Hemerken and his wife, Gertrude, who ran a school for children and apparently began her son's education. In 1392, at the age of thirteen, Thomas left his family to attend the chapter school in Deventer. That town was home to a number of the Brethren of the Common Life, followers of an ascetic religious movement known as the *devotio moderna* (modern devotion), founded between 1374 and 1384 by Gerhard Groote (1340-1384) and most prominent in Holland, the Rhineland, and central Germany. Thomas did not come to Deventer because of the movement, however, and—contrary to a common misconception—he never became a member of the Brethren. Still, he accepted the ideals of the *devotio moderna*, was befriended by Groote's successor, Florentius Radewyns (c. 1350-1400), and lived in a hostel which the Brethren owned. When he left the school in Deventer in 1399, on the verge of adulthood, he was well versed in Latin and knew some philosophy, though little of theology.

Thomas was reared at the end of the catastrophic fourteenth century, which brought to Europe famine, the Black Death (bubonic plague), economic disruption and decline, the Hundred Years' War (1337-1453), conflicts between inept monarchs and greedy aristocrats, and popular uprisings, such as the French Jacquerie and the English Peasants' Revolt. There were also disturbing problems within a church increasingly politicized during the Middle Ages. Its image suffered greatly between 1305 and 1376, when the Papacy was transplanted from Rome to Avignon and lay mired in corruption, and even more so when there ensued in 1378 a papal schism, with two rival (French and Italian) popes and then, from 1409 to 1417, three. Meanwhile, the upper clergy's wealth aroused criticism, while the reforming orders of recent centuries—the Cistercian monastics and the Dominican and Franciscan friars—had lost much of their original vitality. Disillusioned with ecclesiastics and demoralized by disasters which some attributed to God's wrath toward the Church, many Europeans clamored for reform or sought spiritual consolation outside ordinary avenues. Yet conciliarist reformers failed to replace the pope with a council, and the challenge which John Wyclif and Jan Hus posed to the Church's worldliness and to fundamental doctrines about revelation, the sacraments, and papal authority, the Church branded as heresy.

The *devotio moderna* avoided that stigma, despite its resemblance to an earlier generation of ascetic—and often heretical—spiritualists, the Beghards and Beguines. Its founder, Groote, the well-educated son of a wealthy cloth merchant, was loyal and orthodox. Following a serious illness in 1372, he lived for a time in a monastery near Arnhem belonging to the austere eremitic order of Carthusians, whose asceticism he adopted (although he did not become a monk). In 1374 he donated a house he had inherited in Deventer to a group of religious women who became known as the Sisters of the Common Life, and over the next decade a similar group of Brethren emerged. Both groups devoted themselves to a common life of poverty, chastity, and obedience, although they took no formal vows and belonged to no established order. In 1387, however, some adherents of the *devotio moderna* known as the Windesheim congregation adopted and rigorously observed the rule of the Augustinian canons. Thomas' older brother, John, became prior of St. Agnietenberg, one of the order's houses near Zwolle. In 1399 Thomas visited him there and became a monk, though he was not invested until 1406. Ordained a priest in 1413 or 1414, Thomas served unsuccessfully as procurator and subprior before moving on—with better results—to a career as a copyist, preacher, and writer of hymns and treatises. Aside from being exiled with his fellow monks to Ludingakerk from 1429 to 1431 and a brief stint in Mariaborn, he remained at St. Agnietenberg for the rest of his life.

Life's Work

As is illustrated above, the particulars of Thomas' long life (he died at the age of ninety-two) are well-known, something which often cannot be said for much less obscure figures in medieval history. The only important exception is the mistaken notion that he was one of the Brethren, when in fact he was a monk for his entire adult life. Whereas a Brother or Sister of the Common Life might abandon with comparative ease the life of poverty, chastity, and obedience, Thomas' vows were formal and permanent, though in any case he showed little inclination to return to the world once he had left it. Contemporary observers reveal that the adult Thomas, described as of medium build and dark complexion, was quiet by nature and most fond of reading, study, and contemplation. Indeed, the great value of a life of prayerful, meditative, monastic devotion is a theme found throughout his work. Even the limited involvement of the Brothers and Sisters of the Common Life in the ordinary world—which must have seemed particularly wicked to a monk living at the end of the fourteenth century and the beginning of the fifteenth—was more than Thomas wanted.

Given that the basic facts about Thomas' life are clear, it is ironic that the most important part of his life's work—his authorship of *Imitatio Christi* (c. 1427; *The Imitation of Christ*, c. 1460-1530)—is the one most subject to doubt and controversy. Ever since the fifteenth century, there have been those who question whether Thomas is, in fact, the author of *The Imitation of Christ*. His authorship is accepted by the late R. R. Post in *The Modern Devotion: Confrontation with Reformation and Humanism* (1968), generally considered the definitive work on the *devotio moderna*. Post notes, however, that claims have been made on behalf of a number of writers, often along essentially nationalistic lines. For a long time many French scholars favored Jean de Gerson (also known as Jean Charlier), the reform-minded chancellor of the University of Paris at the beginning of the fourteenth century, although by the twentieth century such claims had diminished. A number of Italians have suggested Giovanni Gersen (whose name, Post observes, is suspiciously like Jean de Gerson's); it is impossible, however, to prove even the existence of this man, who was supposedly abbot of Santo Stefano, a Benedictine monastery in Vercelli in northern Italy. The Belgians, Dutch, and Germans have generally accepted that Thomas wrote *The Imitation of Christ*, but a vocal minority has given credit instead to the founder of the *devotio moderna*, Gerhard Groote. Since the 1920's the application of textual criticism has given renewed vigor to the debate, with various scholars supporting Groote, Giovanni Gersen, and Gerard Zerbolt (one of the Brethren associated with Radewyns in Deventer), although Thomas is still the most commonly accepted author.

Thomas was in any case quite a prolific writer, producing biographies of Groote, Radewyns, and other important figures in the *devotio moderna*, as well as a number of devotional works—although none of the others was of the quality of *The Imitation of Christ*. In fact, it is the obvious superiority of the latter which has led some to doubt that Thomas wrote it, while his extensive work as a copyist has been used to suggest that he merely transcribed someone else's book (even a manuscript dated to 1441, written in Thomas' own hand and containing *The Imitation of Christ* and nine other treatises, is unsigned). It is doubtful whether the question will ever be settled to everyone's satisfaction. Yet regardless of the controversy about the author's identity, it is the attribution of *The Imitation of Christ* to Thomas which has lifted him out of obscurity, and—more generally—it is that work which has made the *devotio moderna* as influential as it has been since the fourteenth century. Thus, if Thomas' authorship is accepted—as it is here—*The Imitation of Christ* must be treated as the centerpiece of his life's work. (Conversely, if his authorship should ever be decisively disproved, Thomas' other work will merit considerably less attention from historians.)

The Imitation of Christ is actually not one treatise, but four, the first of which appeared no later than 1424, while all were completed by 1427. Thomas evidently never intended that the four treatises be seen as a unit, and indeed, in the century after their appearance, they were not always found together or in the same order as in more recent editions. Yet despite some differences among the four—and especially between the first three and the fourth—the treatises have several elements in common. As Post notes, all were written for monastics who shared Thomas' contemplative life-style, a rather narrow group. Thus it was not the author's purpose to address the concerns of the general populace, of adherents of the *devotio moderna* as a whole, of the secular clergy, or even of all the regular clergy (monks and nuns). That is not to suggest, however, that Thomas dealt with matters unfamiliar to other monastics or followers of the *devotio moderna* or that what he had to say could not be appreciated outside his small intended audience. In fact, notwithstanding his exhortation to despise the things of the world, Thomas' urgings that men seek comfort, consolation, and security in the love of God, the friendship of Jesus, and a turning to the inner self, or spirit, struck a responsive chord among many of his contemporaries living in the world, as they have for subsequent generations.

A common "weakness" of the treatises is that the author gives them almost no theological foundation: These are not learned works. Yet this unscholarly quality, at the same time, is one of the strengths of *The Imitation of Christ*, for it is the simplicity of Thomas' explication of Christian virtues and practices that has attracted so many readers to his work. In the sometimes frightening conditions of the fifteenth century, Thomas' straightforward, inspirational prose met the needs of many individual believers much more immediately and directly than the complex arguments of theologians or even the Latin liturgy of the local parish church, which they might understand only partially. All the treatises, particularly the first three, encourage the *contemptus mundi* (contempt for the world) associated with traditional medieval monasticism, in which the regular clergy sought to escape the temptations and sinfulness of the world by living in isolation from it. Yet while the monastic life was not an option which most of Thomas' contemporaries considered, a significant number shared his disdain for the vanities of the world, while his emphasis on remaining pure in heart is one of the central ideals of Christianity, in or out of the monastery. Another pervasive characteristic of the treatises is Thomas' disregard for secular learning, which at times seems rather anti-intellectual (although he encourages respect for the "wise").

The first treatise admonishes its readers to lead a more spiritual life by reading the Bible, the church fathers, and other holy works, by praying and meditating, by being humble in the presence of greater wisdom and obedient to authority, and by contemplating the life and holy sacrifice of Christ, as well as the reader's own life, sinful nature, and impending judgment by God. In the second treatise Thomas concentrates on the inner life—self-examination and self-knowledge, being at peace with oneself and accepting life's adversity, seeking the friendship of Christ and the comfort of God, and willingly following the way of the Cross. The longer third treatise stresses disregard of worldly desires, temporal honor, and the opinions of men, while emphasizing the need to accept humbly God's will and Christ's example, trusting not one's own wisdom and virtue. Unlike the first three treatises, the fourth deals explicitly with sacramental life, focusing on the Eucharist, the sacrament most frequently received by all medieval Christians (some weekly or even daily) and by no means limited in importance to monastics alone.

Summary

The overall significance of the *devotio moderna* outside its own age has been much debated. Post contends that its impact upon Christian Humanism and the Reformation was at most very slight. Yet while Post's account of the *devotio moderna* is considered to be in most respects the ultimate authority, other historians have discerned a substantially greater degree of influence upon such figures of the Reformation era as the Christian Humanist Desiderius Erasmus and the first great Protestant reformer, Martin Luther. Nor does it seem mere coincidence that pietism, asceticism, and mysticism of the type espoused by Thomas à Kempis and the Brethren remained characteristic of religious movements in the Low Countries and Germany, the heartland of the *devotio moderna*, during the Reformation and even into the Enlightenment. (Thomas and other followers of the *devotio moderna*, however, did not aspire to the ecstatic union with God sought by some late medieval and early modern mystics.)

Much more apparent, however, and thus less controversial, is the continuing importance of *The Imitation of Christ* from the fifteenth century onward. It is still widely read by Catholics and Protestants alike and is one of the most important devotional works available to modern readers. The translation of the entire work into English took some time. The first English version, done by an anonymous translator in 1460, and the first English edition, produced in 1502 by William Atkinson of the University of Cambridge, included only the first three books. The fourth was finally rendered in English in 1503 by, interestingly enough, Margaret Beaufort, the mother of the English king Henry VII (who reigned from 1485 to 1509). Thereafter, there were numerous editions containing all four treatises, the most important being that compiled in 1530 by Richard Whitford of Queens' College, Cambridge. This edition enjoys much the same status with regard to others in English as the King James Version of the Bible does relative to later English translations of the Scriptures. Like the King James Bible, it is thought to have been so widely read as to have had a formative influence on the modern English language.

There have, however, been many other English versions of *The Imitation of Christ* in print in modern times, a testimony to the book's continuing significance.

The Imitation of Christ has been translated into many languages; in fact, the bulk of scholarship which it has generated is found in non-English works (notably French, German, and Italian). Regardless of what tongue is spoken by its readers, the continuing popularity of this work is remarkable. Although written by a comparatively obscure adherent of a religious movement smaller and less organized than many others in the late medieval and early modern period, and directed not to Christian society as a whole or even all monastics but limiting its intended audience to monks whose life-style was primarily contemplative, it remains relevant to generation after generation. The work of Thomas à Kempis thus surpasses in longevity not only that of Gerhard Groote and Florentius Radewyns but also that of more famous figures of medieval Christianity.

Bibliography

Hyma, Albert. *The Christian Renaissance: A History of the "Devotio Moderna."* Hamden, Conn.: Archon Books, 1965. Unique among English-language works in that it rejects Thomas as author of *The Imitation of Christ* in favor of Zerbolt. It asserts perhaps more strongly than any work in any language that the *devotio moderna* was the source of all religious reform in the sixteenth century, whether manifested in Christian Humanism, Protestantism, or the Catholic Reformation.

Montmorency, J. E. G. de. *Thomas à Kempis: His Age and Book.* New York: G. P. Putnam's Sons, 1906. Reprint. Port Washington, N.Y.: Kennikat Press, 1970. A still-useful English-language biography of Thomas. Places Thomas and the *devotio moderna* in a wider historical framework, taking into account the very uneasy time in which both emerged. Montmorency examines the debate about authorship up to the beginning of the twentieth century, although he prematurely declares it at an end—with Thomas the author. He also discusses in detail the structure of *The Imitation of Christ* and examines its content in the context of medieval Christianity as a whole.

Oakley, Francis. *The Western Church in the Later Middle Ages.* Ithaca, N.Y.: Cornell University Press, 1978. Contains a chapter on modes of piety, which gives considerable attention to the *devotio moderna* and Thomas. This book is useful in relating both to other aspects of late medieval religious history, including the problem of order, doctrine and theology, heresy, reform movements, and spirituality. Oakley for the most part follows Post in his interpretation of the *devotio moderna* and Thomas' career.

Oberman, Heiko A. *Masters of the Reformation: The Emergence of a New Intellectual Climate in Europe.* Translated by Dennis D. Martin. Cambridge: Cambridge University Press, 1981. Contains a chapter on the *devotio moderna*, although Oberman, unfortunately, has relatively little to say about Thomas and *The Imitation of Christ*. With regard to the impact of the movement and Thomas on the Reformation, Oberman accepts the position taken by Post that it was slight.

Ozment, Steven E., ed. *The Reformation in Medieval Perspective*. Chicago: Quadrangle Books, 1971. Although not concerned primarily with Thomas or the *devotio moderna* as a whole, this book nevertheless examines the connection between late medieval reform movements and the Reformation, giving some attention to the influence of Thomas on subsequent reformers. Some of the authors featured here—Gerhard Ritter, Bernd Moeller, and so on—see a greater influence than Post, who is also represented in this collection.

Post, R. R. *The Modern Devotion: Confrontation with Reformation and Humanism*. Leiden, Netherlands: E. J. Brill, 1968. The essential English-language work on the *devotio moderna* and Thomas, all the more important because it discusses in considerable detail the very extensive non-English scholarly literature on both subjects and thus deals comprehensively with the controversies about the movement's influence on the Reformation and the authorship of *The Imitation of Christ*. Although he regards Thomas as the most likely author, Post examines in depth the earlier attempts to give credit for the work to Jean de Gerson, Giovanni Gersen, and Groote, as well as more recent scholarship. Devotes only one chapter to Thomas, but makes reference to his work in discussing various aspects of the *devotio moderna* and offers very valuable commentary on *The Imitation of Christ*.

Thomas à Kempis. *The Imitation of Christ*. Edited by Harold C. Gardiner. Garden City, N.Y.: Doubleday and Co., 1955. While this edition has no claim to authority greater than many other English editions, it is a nicely rendered version, based on the classic translation by Richard Whitford and influenced by the scholarly edition made in 1939 by Edward J. Klein. Gardiner's edition modernizes Whitford's translation, replacing archaic words and phrases with ones more intelligible to modern readers.

William B. Robison

SAINT THOMAS AQUINAS

Born: 1224 or 1225; Roccasecca, north of Naples, Italy
Died: March 7, 1274; Fossanova, Italy
Areas of Achievement: Religion and philosophy
Contribution: By adapting pagan philosophy as a handmaiden to Christian doctrine, Thomas created both a magisterial systematization of medieval Catholic faith and a philosophical system with implications for ethics, law, psychology, semantics, and the nature of reason itself.

Early Life

Thomas Aquinas (Tommaso d'Aquino) was the youngest son of Count Landulf (Landolfo) of Aquino and his second wife, Donna Theodora of Naples, who was descended from Norman nobility. Landulf, along with his older sons, had been employed as a soldier by Emperor Frederick II to defend Sicily from the Papal States to the north. Thomas was born in the family castle near the old city of Aquino in 1224 or 1225 (the testimony from Thomas' first biographers is conflicting). When he was five, he was taken to the nearby Benedictine monastery of Monte Cassino; there he received his early religious instruction. Hostilities between Frederick II and the pope had calmed for the moment, and it is thought that Thomas' parents hoped that their son would one day become an abbot. The feudal system brought little prospect of family stability; perhaps Thomas' eventual clerical influence would provide for the future.

The emperor was excommunicated in 1239; in return, he threatened Monte Cassino; most of the monks there were sent into exile. That year, Thomas returned to his parents, who sent him to the *studium generale* (later to become the university) in Naples, a school which had been founded by the emperor in 1224 to compete with similar church institutions. Frederick welcomed the introduction of Islamic as well as Christian scholarship into his university. Thomas' studies included logic, grammar, natural philosophy, and metaphysics, and it was probably at Naples that he began his first serious study of Aristotle. Portions of Aristotle's works were being translated from the Greek, making their way into the Latin West often accompanied by interpretations of Arabic scholars, most notably the twelfth century Islamic philosopher Averroës.

It was an age of ferment: Intellectually, the new learning, especially Aristotle's teaching on the eternity of the world, threatened Christian doctrine. Politically and militarily, with the continued clash of secular and ecclesiastical powers, the old feudal order was coming to an end.

At Naples, Thomas was drawn to the Order of Friars Preachers, the Dominicans, founded in France in 1216 by Saint Dominic. The Dominicans taught obedience and poverty (and thus the begging of alms), as did the

Franciscan Order (founded by Saint Francis of Assisi less than a decade earlier), but the Dominicans also put special emphasis on the life of study, preaching, and teaching. The order penetrated many of the universities of Western Europe, opening study houses devoted to theology and philosophy. Though reared to appreciate the Benedictine cycle of prayer, worship, sleep, and manual labor, Thomas found the new order better suited to his temperament.

His decision to join the Dominicans in 1244 was not without controversy. His mother, now a widow, persuaded Thomas' older brothers to abduct and imprison him until he changed his mind. There is a story, perhaps based in fact, that when his brothers brought a prostitute into Thomas' cell to break his resolve, he picked up a burning stick from the fire and drove her from the room. Taken to Roccasecca, Thomas remained steadfast, and after about a year of detention he was permitted by his family to join his Dominican brothers at the University of Paris in 1245. His novitiate was under the tutelage of the German Dominican theologian Saint Albertus Magnus.

An early biographer notes that in 1248 Thomas joined Albert in Cologne and a new *studium generale* there, where Thomas was often referred to as the "dumb ox." This sobriquet did not pertain to his intelligence, but to his massive physique: Though Thomas was a bit taller than his peers, he was corpulent, slow of movement, quiet, and often withdrawn. Yet Albert saw deeper; his mentor remarked that the bellowing of this ox would be heard throughout the world.

Life's Work

Upon Albert's recommendation, Thomas returned to the University of Paris in 1252 to prepare for his degree in theology. Not yet thirty years of age, Thomas would have little more than two decades of life remaining. In that time, he was to produce an enduring systematization of the Catholic faith, numerous commentaries on the works of Aristotle, liturgical works, and polemical pieces.

Already he was discussing theological issues in public disputations and lecturing on the era's standard theological textbook, *Sententiarum libri IV* (1148-1151; books of sentences) of Peter Lombard. The "sentences," or opinions, were collected from church fathers and medieval theologians and arranged by doctrines. Book 1, for example, treated God; book 2, the Fall of Man. Theology students, "bachelors of the Sentences," tried to harmonize the varying viewpoints and elucidate the fine points; nuance was everything. Thomas' own *Scriptum super "Libros sententiarum"* (1252-1256; writings on the books of sentences) joined more than a thousand other commentaries. The structure of Thomas' book was derived from the oral tradition of the public disputation. The master would employ his students in framing theological arguments, both pro and con, with debate sometimes lasting six or eight hours. The master then met in private with his students, analyzing the arguments and formulating a written version of the dispute. Many of Thomas' theological works are based on the form of the disputation and thus were not intended for lay audiences. In the multiplicity of distinctions and definitions, Thomas' writings exemplified a Scholastic style popular during the Middle Ages but stigmatized in later eras as hollow and pedantic.

In 1256, Thomas obtained his license to teach theology at the university. For three years thereafter, he continued to lecture, primarily on the Gospel of Matthew, and to participate in public disputations. During this time, he began work on a theological guidebook for Dominican missionaries as they engaged in disputes with Muslims, Jews, and heretical Christians in North Africa and Spain. This treatise, the *Summa contra gentiles* (c. 1258-1264; English translation, 1923), was completed after he returned to Italy to lecture at the papal court in 1261. In 1265, he left Orvieto and Pope Urban IV for a two-year stay in Rome. It was while he was in Rome, teaching Dominican students, that Thomas began his masterwork, *Summa theologiae* (c. 1265-1273; *Summa Theologica*, 1911-1921). He finished the first part, on God's existence and attributes, during his stay at the papal court of Clement IV in Viterbo, Italy, from 1267 to 1268. Here Thomas was apparently associated with William of Moerbeke, a Flemish Dominican who was working on more accurate translations of Aristotle than those that had come to the West via the Arabic. In 1268 or 1269, Thomas was sent back to the University of Paris for his second tenure as a professor—and found himself in the midst of a seething controversy.

Masters and students at the university had become fascinated not only with the speculative works of Aristotle but also with those of his Arab interpreter Averroës. Though at least nominally a Muslim, Averroës taught, contrary to Islam and certainly to Christianity, that there was a fundamental duality between reason and faith. That is, philosophy might conclude that the world existed from eternity (as Aristotle did), while faith might speak of Creation. Both assertions, though contradictory, would be "true" in their own realm. Averroës also brought into question the nature of the soul and, using Aristotle's writings, concluded that it was doubtful that each individual had a separate, immortal soul, as the Church taught. In 1266, the Latin Averroist Siger of Brabant had begun to popularize Averroës' understanding of Aristotle and to attract disciples among the university's faculty. Thomas plunged into dispute with Siger, attempting to argue that Averroës had misinterpreted Aristotle on matters of the soul and that though the eternity of the world might be a reasonable conclusion of science, such a conclusion was not absolute. Faith supplemented or fulfilled reason (not contradicting it) by teaching the Creation.

Nevertheless, Thomas was caught in the middle. When radical Averroism was officially condemned in 1270, Thomas' own reliance upon Aristotle's reasoning was also brought into question. Thomas was criticized by the followers of Saint Augustine's more mystical Platonism, who claimed that human reason had been hopelessly compromised in the Fall. While Thomas condemned the doctrine of double truth (believing, apparently mistakenly, that Siger and others were teaching it), he did maintain that natural reason can discover certain fundamental theological truths by studying the effects of God's working in the universe—thus the celebrated five proofs for God's existence. Reason, however, can take man only so far. Grace completes nature by revealing what cannot be learned from reason—for example, that God is Triune. There are not two truths here: Since God is responsible for both reason and revelation, the two can never be contradictory. Thomas sought to separate Aristotle from his heterodox interpreters, but at the same time was forced to defend his own use of the philosopher.

In the first three years of his return to the University of Paris, Thomas finished both the first and second sections of part 2 of *Summa Theologica*, dealing with happiness, virtue, sin, law, and grace and, in the second section, with specific moral questions. It is said that Thomas sometimes employed four secretaries at a time to take his dictation and that he would often dictate in his sleep. One story has Thomas sitting next to King Louis IX at a banquet. Completely forgetting himself, Thomas lifted his head from a trance, banged his hand on the table, and called for his secretary to dictate some prize answer to Christian heretics.

In 1272, Thomas returned to Naples to set up a Dominican study house at the university there. His attention was also given to completing part 3 of the *Summa Theologica*, on the person and work of Christ. Yet on December 6, 1273, three months before his death, he put aside his writing, explaining that all he had written seemed as straw and that he could not continue. It is not known whether Thomas suffered a stroke or received a mystical vision or whether his faculties simply collapsed as a result of overwork. In 1274, he was summoned to attend a church council at Lyons. In poor health to begin with, he found himself unable to complete his journey after he struck his head on a tree or branch which had fallen in the road. He stopped at his niece's castle near Fossanova; a few weeks later, he was taken to the nearby Cistercian monastery, where he died on March 7, 1274.

Though Thomas never completed the *Summa Theologica*, a supplement drawn from his earlier work was added to round out the presentation. In its two million words, the *Summa Theologica* contains more than five hundred questions, twenty-six hundred articles, and ten thousand objections and replies. The prolific Thomas had produced more than one hundred other works as well.

Though in 1277 an official church body in Paris condemned some 219 theological propositions which included twelve held by Thomas, by 1319, inquiries had begun concerning Thomas' possible canonization. Thomas Aquinas was canonized a saint in 1323 (the Paris condemnation concerning his teachings was canceled in 1325), and in 1567, he was named Doctor of the Church, his works sanctioned as a repository of orthodoxy.

Summary

For the Roman Catholic church, the thirteenth century was a time of synthesis. The writings of Aristotle and other ancients posed a new challenge to the Christian tradition, as did the influx of teachings from the Muslim world. It was the abiding passion of Saint Thomas Aquinas' life to integrate faith and reason, exploring systematically the teachings of the Church by taking natural reason as far as it might go and supplementing it with the reasonableness of revelation. To him, the Christian faith was both reasonable and rationally defensible.

Aristotle supplied many of the categories by which the nature and content of theology might be profitably organized. The philosopher maintained that the world was purposive, and Thomas adopted this idea of a final cause. Thomas also used Aristotle's conception of matter and form, and act and potentiality, in formulating his *Summa Theologica*. Moreover, although Thomas disputed with the Augustinians, he also adapted Neoplatonism for his purposes, much as he did Aristotelianism. Creation was ordered in a kind of chain of being, with man occupying a unique place, sharing earthly existence with other creatures but also possessing the capacity of receiving the vision of God after death and thus complete happiness. Critics have called the *Summa Theologica* the capstone of passionless Scholasticism, the last gasp of medieval society in its effort to hold the world together by outmoded categories. Others have called Thomas an elitist who preferred order to freedom, citing his description of women as naturally inferior to men, his preference for monarchy, and his attitude toward Jews as examples of his outmoded beliefs. In response, twentieth century Thomists have attempted to demonstrate that certain historically conditioned positions should not invalidate Thomas' method or his insights and that Thomistic thought can be modified in favor of freedom, human rights, and democracy. Through Jacques Maritain in France and Mortimer Adler in the United States, generations of intellectuals have been introduced to the thought of Thomas Aquinas. Thomas' influence in theology has diminished since the Catholic church ceased to promulgate Thomism after the Second Vatican Council ended in 1965; yet his contribution to philosophy as an interpreter of Aristotle continues to be widely recognized.

Bibliography

Chesterton, G. K. *St. Thomas Aquinas*. New York: Sheed and Ward, 1933.
　　Praised by Thomistic scholar Étienne Gilson, Chesterton's is a superb lay introduction to the life and thought of Thomas, "the Angelic Doctor."

Novelist Chesterton, a convert to Catholicism, at times takes great delight in contrasting what he considers positive Thomism with negative Protestantism (especially that of Martin Luther and John Calvin). In the main, however, the wry Chesterton takes aim at the irrationalities of the world, from whatever quarter, and scores elegantly.

Copleston, F. C. *Aquinas*. Harmondsworth, England: Penguin Books, 1955. A scholarly yet accessible discussion of the philosophy of Thomas Aquinas. Spends little time in dealing with Thomas the man, but rather considers God and Creation, body and soul, and morality and society. The discussion of modern Thomism is dated. Copleston's analysis provides insight into Thomas' use of Aristotle (he notes that the ancients were concerned with *how* things came into being; Thomas was concerned with *why*). No footnotes. The author has also written a multivolume, authoritative history of philosophy.

Gilson, Étienne. *The Christian Philosophy of St. Thomas Aquinas*. Translated by L. K. Shook. New York: Random House, 1956. A classic and scholarly treatment of Thomas as philosopher and theologian. Chapters fall under the headings of God, Nature, and Morality. The book contains a comprehensive bibliography of Thomas' works with descriptive details.

Kenny, Anthony. *Aquinas*. New York: Hill and Wang, 1980. This volume in the Past Masters series offers a semipopular introduction to Thomas in fewer than one hundred pages. Three chapters explore Thomas' life, his conception of Being (which Kenny believes is hopelessly flawed), and his notion of the nature of Mind (which Kenny praises for the questions Thomas asks). The latter two chapters introduce the reader to medieval categories of thought, but Thomas Aquinas the Christian is almost submerged.

McInerny, Ralph. *St. Thomas Aquinas*. Boston: Twayne Publishers, 1977. An accessible study of Thomas' thought in chapters dealing with Aristotle, Boethius (c. 480-524, through whose writings Aristotelian concepts first reached the Middle Ages), and Platonism. In a chapter on the tasks of theology, the author explains Thomas' distinction between believing and knowing. The book is replete with examples, a useful chronology of Thomas' life, and a short annotated bibliography.

Sigmund, Paul E., ed. and trans. *St. Thomas Aquinas on Politics and Ethics*. New York: W. W. Norton and Co., 1987. A wise and varied introduction to Thomas, with eighty pages devoted to pertinent excerpts of Thomas' work, newly translated by the editor. Selections are generally quite short and range from Thomas' writings on government to selections from his treatise on God in the *Summa Theologica*. Excerpts from background sources are also presented, with the remainder of the volume devoted to interpretations of Thomas. A short bibliography points out inadequacies in present translations of Aquinas and lists useful secondary sources. Extensive notes

and prefatory remarks make this book an indispensable introduction.
Weisheipl, James A. *Friar Thomas D'Aquino: His Life, Thought, and Work.*
Garden City, N.Y.: Doubleday and Co., 1974. A standard modern biography arranged in chronological order. The text is burdened by a continual sorting out of evidence supplied by earlier biographers of Thomas, and many of the discussions seem merely academic. A useful chronology is included, as well as an updated listing of Thomas' works. An index and a list of primary and secondary sources are also included. Useful for basic information about Thomas.

Dan Barnett

THUCYDIDES

Born: c. 459 B.C.; probably Athens, Greece
Died: c. 402 B.C.; place unknown
Area of Achievement: Historiography
Contribution: For the methods he employed in his account of the Peloponnesian War, Thucydides is considered one of the founders of the discipline of history.

Early Life

Thucydides was born around 459 into a wealthy and conservative Athenian family. He grew up in Periclean Athens, an exciting place for a young, intelligent aristocrat. He followed the traditional course of education founded on the study of Homer, but leavened it with the rational skepticism of the Sophists. Thucydides could listen to the teachings of Protagoras, Socrates, Herodotus, and other major intellectual and creative figures who lived in or visited Athens.

Little is known about Thucydides' personal life. His family was politically active and opposed the democratic forces led by Pericles, but Thucydides evidently did not involve himself in political intrigues. It is known that he inherited gold mines in Thrace and had an estate there. He married a Thracian woman and had a daughter. He seems to have been a slightly detached but observant young man, studying the social and political turbulence around him. He did not break openly with his family, nor did he enter actively into Athenian politics. Though he criticized the people when they acted as a "mob," he did not approve of oligarchy. He respected the wisdom and moderation of Athenian leaders such as Nicias but was stirred by the boldness of Pericles, Themistocles, and Alcibiades.

When the Peloponnesian War began, Thucydides perhaps first intended to record for posterity the events and the deeds of men in a dramatic conflict. He soon saw that the war provided instruction in something basic about human nature and the fortunes of nations. In 431, he started collecting material for his *Historia tou Peloponnesiacou polemou* (431-404 B.C.; *History of the Peloponnesian War*, 1550), at the outbreak of the twenty-seven-year conflict.

Life's Work

The victory of the Greeks over the Persians at Plataea in 479 B.C. ushered in the golden age of Athenian history. The city's economy flourished, its government became more democratic than in the past, its art, literature, and freedom of expression attracted creative people from throughout the Greek world, and its navy established it as a power over the Aegean Islands and many coastal cities. Though Athens and Sparta had cooperated against the

soon went separate ways. The slow-moving, conservative
d Athens build an empire and, under Pericles' leadership,
)ower and wealth. "What made war inevitable," Thucydides
wrote, "was the growth of Athenian power and the fear which this caused in
Sparta."

War began in 431. It opened with ten years of fighting, followed by some
years of shaky truce, before fighting continued for another ten years. After
Sparta established its power on land, the Athenians retreated into the city,
which was joined by the Long Walls to the port of Peiraeus. The Athenians
supplied themselves by sea and harassed the Spartans and their allies. The
war was brutal. Besieged cities turned to cannibalism, and conquerors sometimes put defeated males to death and enslaved their women and children.

Despite Thucydides' renowned objectivity—he was acclaimed at one time
as "the father of scientific history"—later military historians have seldom
matched the emotional intensity and striking visual images conveyed by his
calm prose. He described trapped Plataeans counting bricks in the besieging
wall to determine how high to build scaling ladders. They began a desperate
dash for freedom through a dark, rainy night, each man wearing only one
shoe for better traction in the mud. He gave a masterful clinical description
of the plague that hit Athens and chronicled the degeneration of morale and
morals as disease swept the hot, overcrowded city. People gave themselves up
to lawlessness and dissipation: "No fear of god or law of man had a restraining influence. As for the gods, it seemed to be the same thing whether one
worshipped them or not, when one saw the good and the bad dying indiscriminately." With the gods silent in the face of human tragedy and no one
expecting to live long enough to be punished for violating society's laws,
people took what pleasure they could.

Revolution also spread through the city-states, with war between democratic and oligarchic forces. Brutality within cities equaled that between
them. Thucydides wrote that in times of peace and prosperity most people
acted decently: "But war is a stern teacher; in depriving them of the power of
easily satisfying their daily wants, it brings most people's minds down to the
level of their actual circumstances." People of the turbulent twentieth century
found many occasions to quote his words about fanaticism:

What used to be described as a thoughtless act of aggression was now regarded
as the courage one would expect to find in a party member; to think of the future and wait was merely another way of saying one was a coward; any idea of
moderation was just an attempt to disguise one's unmanly character; ability to
understand a question from all sides meant that one was totally unfitted for
action.

With both sides battered by war and revolution, leaders of Athens and
Sparta negotiated a shaky truce in 421, but resolved none of the larger issues.

The first war had revealed something basic about human affairs, Thucydides believed. The Athenians had told the Spartans before the war opened that always the weak had been subject to the strong. When the Spartans raised questions of right and wrong, the Athenians answered: "Considerations of this kind have never yet turned people aside from the opportunities of aggrandizement offered by superior strength."

War started again. The Athenians mounted a disastrous expedition to Sicily. Soon, Thucydides wrote, the Athenians, intending to enslave, were totally defeated and themselves enslaved. Athens was in turmoil, and oligarchic leaders overthrew its democracy. Vicious bloodletting occurred as the two sides fought for control. Disaster followed disaster, and the Athenians surrendered in 404. The Spartans forced them to renounce their empire, destroy their navy, and tear down the Long Walls.

Thucydides was himself caught up in the war. In 424, Athens elected him a general but then exiled him for twenty years when he failed to prevent the brilliant Spartan general Brasidas from taking the strategically important city of Amphipolis. Exile meant withdrawing a short distance from Amphipolis to his Thracian estate, where he had time to think, write, and talk to Brasidas and other opponents and to central figures in Athenian politics, such as Alcibiades.

Unlike his older contemporary, the great historian Herodotus, Thucydides did not leave much room for the divine in human affairs; he believed that human activities could be understood in human terms. Like Herodotus, Thucydides displayed breadth of sympathy for all sides in the conflict. He weighed his oral evidence carefully, seeking accuracy and precision. He stated his purpose eloquently:

> It will be enough for me . . . if these words of mine are judged useful by those who want to understand clearly the events which happened in the past and which (human nature being what it is) will, at some time or other and in much the same ways, be repeated in the future. My work is not a piece of writing designed to meet the taste of an immediate public, but was done to last forever.

Thucydides found meaning in history, evidence of a pattern or cycle. Unless human nature changed, states would continue to overreach themselves, create defensive resistance, and then decline and fall. Even the second part of the Peloponnesian War repeated the first, with new actors making much the same mistakes for the same reasons. People could, however, use their intelligence and reason. They might not escape the cycle, but some few could at least come to understand what was happening and perhaps moderate the cycle. Thucydides did not believe that cycles were endlessly repeating series of events that allowed historians to predict the future, but he thought that people could use history to interpret their times.

It is unclear when Thucydides wrote his history. Most scholars believe that changes in style and conflicting statements about events suggest that it was written in stages; Thucydides died before putting it in final form. He probably died around 402.

Summary

Thucydides and Herodotus, the first historians, retain their rank among the very greatest. Few historians who followed would equal Herodotus' breadth of sympathy for the diversity of human culture, and seldom would they match Thucydides' clarity and precision and his emotional and intellectual power.

Thucydides found a scholarly audience more easily than did Herodotus. Thucydides' objective tone, rational skepticism, and focus on the military and on politics fit the modern temper. His writing on war and revolution seemed directed at the twentieth century. His message seemed clear, especially after World War II, when in the Cold War atmosphere it was easy for Americans to identify themselves with the free Athenians, confronting dour, warlike Spartans in the form of the totalitarian Soviets. Thucydides, viewed by some scholars as the father of realpolitik, seemed to have a clear warning: Democracies must be strong and alert in a dangerous world.

When the Vietnam War changed historians' understanding of the Cold War, Thucydides did not drop from favor among scholars, but his message came to seem different. To some scholars, he seemed to be the first revisionist, revealing Athens for what it was: an arrogant and aggressive state aimed at dominating and exploiting the weak and inciting fear of the Spartans to help keep Athenian allies in line.

Changing times will bring still another Thucydides. Like every genius, he speaks to some members of each generation, who find in him insights into human affairs that clarify their understanding of their own time.

Bibliography

Adcock, Sir Frank Ezra. *Thucydides and His History*. Cambridge: Cambridge University Press, 1963. A short, clear study of Thucydides' mind and personality by an admiring British historian who regards Thucydides as one of the first great adventurers in thought.

Connor, W. Robert. *Thucydides*. Princeton, N.J.: Princeton University Press, 1984. A meditation on Thucydides and an analysis of the text, especially to determine the source of Thucydides' emotional impact on his readers.

Edmunds, Lowell. *Chance and Intelligence in Thucydides*. Cambridge, Mass.: Harvard University Press, 1974. A study of Thucydides' theory of reason and chance in human affairs and of the interplay of pessimism and optimism in his work.

Hornblower, Simon. *Thucydides.* Baltimore: Johns Hopkins University Press, 1987. Places Thucydides in the intellectual atmosphere of Periclean Athens and carefully distinguishes the various influences on his thought.

Pouncey, Peter. *The Necessities of War: A Study of Thucydides' Pessimism.* New York: Columbia University Press, 1980. A study of Thucydides' theory of human nature and its influence on history; Pouncey finds an "essential pessimism" that holds that human nature carries within it drives that destroy human achievements.

Proctor, Dennis. *The Experience of Thucydides.* Warminster, England: Aris and Phillips, 1980. A careful analysis of the text of Thucydides to try to determine the phases of its composition.

Rawlings, Hunter R., III. *The Structure of Thucydides' History.* Princeton, N.J.: Princeton University Press, 1981. Provides insights into Thucydides based on an analysis of the structure of his work.

Thucydides. *The Peloponnesian War.* New York: Penguin Books, 1954. This translation by Rex Warner, with an introduction by M. I. Finley, is highly regarded and easily accessible.

William E. Pemberton

THUTMOSE III

Born: Late sixteenth century B.C.; near Thebes, Egypt?

Died: 1450 B.C.; near Thebes, Egypt?

Area of Achievement: Government

Contribution: During a reign of nearly fifty-four years, Thutmose III consolidated Egypt's position as primary power in the ancient Near East and North Africa. He laid the groundwork for some two hundred years of relative peace and prosperity in the region.

Early Life

Thutmose III, son of Thutmose II and a minor wife named Isis, became the fourth king of Egypt's Eighteenth Dynasty while still a child. It is very likely that Thutmose III was not the obvious heir to Egypt's throne. According to an inscription at Karnak carved late in his reign, the young Thutmose spent his early life as an acolyte in the Temple of Amon. Thutmose III asserted that the god Amon personally chose him as successor to his father: During a ritual procession of Amon's statue through the temple, the god sought out Thutmose; an oracle revealed that he was the god's choice to be the next king. Thutmose thus became his father's legitimate heir.

The historical value of this account has been doubted. It was recorded late in Thutmose III's reign. Furthermore, it closely parallels an earlier text describing the accession of Thutmose I. Whatever the historical value of this account for determining the legitimacy of Thutmose III's claim to succeed his father, he did ascend to the Egyptian throne upon the death of Thutmose II. Contemporary inscriptions make clear, however, that during the first twenty-one years of the reign, real power was held by Hatshepsut, the chief queen or "Great King's Wife" of his father.

The relationship between Thutmose III and Hatshepsut in these early years has been the subject of scholarly controversy. By year two of Thutmose III's reign, Hatshepsut had assumed all the regalia of a reigning king. Yet it is not at all certain that she thrust Thutmose III into the background in order to usurp his royal prerogative, as early twentieth century commentators have claimed. Hatshepsut probably crowned herself coregent to obtain the au- thority to administrate the country while Thutmose III was still a minor. Hatshepsut's year dates are often recorded alongside dates of Thutmose III. There is also evidence that his approval was necessary for significant decisions such as installing a vizier, establishing offering endowments for gods, and authorizing expeditions to Sinai.

In any case, there is no question that Thutmose's early years were spent in preparation for his eventual assumption of sole authority. His education included study of hieroglyphic writing. Contemporaries comment on his ability to read and write like Seshat, the goddess of writing. His military training must also have occurred during this time.

When Hatshepsut died in the twenty-second year of Thutmose III's reign, he assumed sole control of the country. Whether it was at this point that an attempt was made by Thutmose III to obliterate the memory of Hatshepsut is open to doubt. It is clear that Thutmose III emphasized his descent from Thutmose II as part of the basis for his legitimate right to rule Egypt.

The mummy of Thutmose III reveals a man of medium build, almost five feet in height. (For his time, he was relatively tall.) He appears to have enjoyed good health throughout most of his life, avoiding the serious dental problems common to other Egyptian kings.

Life's Work

The ancient Egyptians expected their pharaoh's career to follow a preconceived pattern which was ordained by their gods. This pattern was always followed in the historical texts which the Egyptians wrote describing the accomplishments of their kings. There is good reason to believe that Thutmose III became the prototype for a successful king. His achievements were emulated by his successors throughout most of the New Kingdom (c. 1570-1070 B.C.). The pattern included conquests abroad, feats of athletic prowess, and building projects at home.

Between the twenty-third and thirty-ninth years of his reign, Thutmose III undertook fourteen military campaigns. These campaigns are documented in a long historical text carved on the walls at the Temple of Karnak, called the Annals. Various stelae (inscriptions on upright slabs of stone) found in other Egyptian temples also provide information on his career. The most significant campaigns occurred in year twenty-three and in year thirty-three of his reign.

The campaign of year twenty-three was fought against a confederation of Syro-Palestinian states led by Kadesh, a Syrian city-state on the Orontes River. The forces allied with Kadesh had gathered at a city called Megiddo on the Plain of Esdraelan in modern Israel. The Egyptian description of the battle that took place in Megiddo follows a pattern known from other inscriptions yet contains many details that attest its basic historical value.

Thutmose III set out for Syria-Palestine with a large army. Upon reaching the town of Yehem, near Megiddo, Thutmose III consulted with his general staff on tactics and strategy. The general staff urged caution on the king, suggesting that the main road to Megiddo was too narrow and dangerous for the Egyptian army to pass safely upon it. They argued for an alternative route to Megiddo that would be longer, yet safer. Thutmose III rejected his staff's advice, judging that the bolder course was more likely to succeed. The staff acceded to the king's superior wisdom; the Egyptian army proceeded along the narrow direct path, surprised the enemy, and encircled Megiddo. The enemy emerged from the city only to be routed through Thutmose's personal valor. As the enemy retreated, however, the Egyptian forces broke ranks and fell on the weapons which the enemy had abandoned. This unfortunate break in discipline allowed the leaders of the Kadesh confederation to escape back into the city of Megiddo. Thutmose was forced to besiege the city. The siege ended successfully for the Egyptians after seven months, when the defeated chieftains of the alliance approached Thutmose with gifts in token of their submission.

This total defeat of the enemy became synonymous in later times with utter disaster. The name of the Battle of Megiddo—*Har Megiddo* (Mount Megiddo) in Hebrew—entered English as Armageddon, a word that designates a final cataclysmic battle.

Thutmose was equally wise in his handling of the defeated chieftains as he had been in war. The chieftains were reinstalled on their thrones, now as allies of Egypt. Their eldest sons were taken back to Egypt as hostages to guarantee the chieftains' cooperation with Egyptian policy. As the various Syro-Palestinian rulers died, their sons would be sent home to rule as Egyptian vassals. These sons, by that time thoroughly trained in Egyptian customs and culture, proved to be generally friendly to Egypt.

Thutmose's ambitions for Egyptian imperialism extended beyond Syria-Palestine. In the thirty-third year of his reign, he campaigned against the Mitanni, who occupied northern Mesopotamia (modern Iraq), the land the Egyptians called Nahrain. This battle also demonstrated Thutmose's mastery of strategy. He realized that his major problem in attacking the Mitanni would be in crossing the Euphrates River. To that end, he built boats of cedar in Lebanon and transported them overland 250 miles on carts. Once again, the element of surprise worked in Thutmose's favor. He was easily able to cross the river, attack the enemy, and defeat them.

Thutmose demonstrated his athletic prowess on the return trip from Nahrain. He stopped in the land of Niy, in modern Syria, to hunt elephants as had his royal ancestors. His brave deeds included the single-handed slaughter of a herd of 120 elephants.

Thutmose was responsible for initiating a large number of building projects within Egypt and in its Nubian holdings. The chronology of these projects is not understood in detail, but it is clear that he either built or remodeled eight temples in Nubia and seven temples in Upper Egypt. In the Egyptian capital of Thebes, he built mortuary temples for his father and grandfather as well as for himself. He added important buildings to the complex of temples at Karnak. These projects included the site of the Annals and a temple decorated with relief sculptures showing the unusual plant life Thutmose had observed during his campaigns to Syria-Palestine and Mesopotamia. Though it is difficult to identify the plants that interested Thutmose and his artists, this unusual form of decoration for a temple illustrates the king's interest in scholarly pursuits.

Thutmose's foresight included planning for his own successor. In the fifty-second year of his reign, his son Amenhotep II was designated coregent. The custom of naming and training an heir to the throne while the father still lived had been known since at least the Middle Kingdom (c. 2040-1782 B.C.). Thutmose showed wisdom in choosing as his successor Amenhotep, a son who would largely follow his father's policies.

The last twelve years of Thutmose III's reign passed relatively peacefully. The Annals for this period record only the yearly delivery of goods for the king's and the god's use.

Little is known of Thutmose III's personal life. Scholars are in disagreement as to whether he ever married Neferure, the daughter of Hatshepsut. His earliest wife was probably Sit-iakh; she was the mother of Amenemhat, a son who probably died young. A second wife, Meryetre-Hatshepsut II, was the mother of Amenhotep II. Nothing is known of a third royal wife, Nebtu, aside from her name. Four other royal children are known.

During the fifty-fourth year of a reign largely dedicated to war, Thutmose III died peacefully. He was buried by his son Amenhotep II in the tomb which had been prepared in the Valley of the Kings.

Summary

Despite the clichés and preconceived patterns which characterize the sources available for reconstructing the life of Thutmose III, he emerges as a truly remarkable man. His conquests in Syria-Palestine and Mesopotamia laid the groundwork for at least two hundred years of peace and prosperity in the ancient Near East. Vast quantities of goods flowed into Egypt's coffers from colonial holdings during this time. The royal family, the noblemen, and the temples of the gods came to possess previously unimagined wealth. The threat of foreign domination which had haunted Thutmose's immediate ancestors was finally dissipated. Egypt looked confidently toward a future of virtually unquestioned dominance over its neighbors.

Thutmose III himself was long remembered by Egyptians as the founder of their country's prosperity and security. Succeeding kings of Dynasties Eighteen and Nineteen modeled their reigns on the historic memory of the founder of the Egyptian Empire.

Bibliography

Gardiner, Alan. *Egypt of the Pharaohs: An Introduction*. Oxford: Clarendon Press, 1961. Contains a chapter on the triumph of Egyptian foreign policy under Thutmose III, emphasizing and including translations of many of the sources for modern knowledge of the period.

Grayson, A. Kirk, and Donald B. Redford, eds. *Papyrus and Tablet*. Englewood Cliffs, N.J.: Prentice-Hall, 1973. Introductory material and modern translations of Egyptian historical texts, including contemporary accounts of the campaigns of year twenty-three and year thirty-three and the elephant hunt.

Nims, Charles F. "The Date of the Dishonoring of Hatshepsut." *Zeitschrift für ägyptische Sprache* 93 (1968): 97-100. A ground breaking examination of the relationship between Hatshepsut and Thutmose III during the early years of his reign.

Steindorff, George, and K. C. Seele. *When Egypt Ruled the East*. Chicago: University of Chicago Press, 1942. An analysis of the rise and fall of the Egyptian Empire, with a chapter on the career of Thutmose III.

Wilson, John A. *The Burden of Egypt: An Interpretation of Ancient Egyptian Culture*. Chicago: University of Chicago Press, 1951. An interpretive essay on the culture of ancient Egypt which includes a chapter on the early Eighteenth Dynasty.

Edward Bleiberg

TIBERIUS

Born: November 16, 42 B.C.; Rome, Italy
Died: March 16, A.D. 37; Misenum, Italy
Area of Achievement: Government
Contribution: As the second emperor of Rome, Tiberius solidified and firmly established the new system of power—but not without devastating impact on his personal life and the Roman upper classes.

Early Life
Tiberius Claudius Nero, the second emperor of Rome, came from a very ancient family of Sabine origin, the Claudians, who had moved to Rome shortly after the foundation of the city. Among the most patrician of Rome's residents, the Claudians expressed an aristocratic disdain for the other, less ancient, less noble inhabitants of Rome.

Tiberius' father, also named Tiberius Claudius Nero, was an associate of Julius Caesar and served as a quaestor (a sort of deputy) under him. The elder Tiberius fought with Caesar during the campaign in Egypt which ended the civil war between Caesar and Pompey the Great, but after the murder of Julius Caesar in 44 B.C. went over to the side of the republicans.

This decision made the Claudian family enemies of Octavian (later Augustus), Marc Antony, and Marcus Aemilius Lepidus, the three men who formed the so-called Second Triumvirate which succeeded Caesar in power. The triumvirs were anxious to wipe out any traces of republican sentiment, and Tiberius the elder, his wife Livia, and his young son were forced into flight, often coming close to capture and death.

When Tiberius was only four years old, even stranger events happened. Augustus imposed a divorce between Livia and her husband, and soon married Livia—although she was pregnant at the time. Despite the adverse early influences, Tiberius was reared to be a loyal and dutiful servant of Augustus, ready to serve him in civil, military, and personal capacities. For twenty-two years Tiberius was an associate of Augustus; Tiberius was to be emperor himself for an equal period of time.

He began his service early. In 26 B.C., while only a teenager, he was sent to Spain on military service. Two years later, he was made quaestor in charge of the grain supply in Rome. Later, he served primarily in military positions, commanding armies in the east and in Europe. During several hard-fought campaigns, Tiberius subdued Illyricum and Pannonia (modern Yugoslavia and Hungary) and helped secure the empire's northern border with the dangerous German tribes. For these efforts, he was awarded a triumph, the highest honor bestowed upon a victorious general.

His personal life was less triumphant. He was forced by Augustus to divorce his beloved wife, Agrippina, and marry Julia, the daughter of Augustus. The match was arranged to strengthen the chance of succession of a descendant of Augustus to power; it failed, for Tiberius and Julia were incompatible and soon lived apart. For this reason, because Augustus was advancing his grandsons, and perhaps because of simple fatigue with his exhausting duties, Tiberius retired to the island of Rhodes in 6 B.C. He remained there for eight years, until the premature deaths of Augustus' grandsons forced his return, and he was adopted by the emperor as his son and heir.

There followed more campaigns in the north, interspersed with time at Rome. During the latter years of Augustus' reign, Tiberius seems to have been virtual co-emperor, and in A.D. 14, when Augustus died, Tiberius assumed sole power of the whole Roman world.

Tiberius was a large, strong man, well above average height. He had a fair complexion, which was sometimes marred by outbreaks of skin disease. According to the ancient historian Suetonius, he wore his hair long in back, an old-fashioned style perhaps adopted in memory of his distinguished ancestry.

For most of his life, Tiberius enjoyed excellent health, although he was reported to have indulged in excessive drinking and an astounding number and variety of sexual pleasures. He was stiff and formal in manner and seemed ill at ease in the senate chambers. He was quite well educated in Latin and Greek literature and was devoted to astrology.

Life's Work

Tiberius came to the throne at the age of fifty-six. He had served Augustus all of his adult life, helping to establish the political system of the Roman Empire, also known as the principate (after one of Augustus' titles, *princeps*, or first citizen). The new system was a delicate and highly personal one, in which Augustus balanced traditional Roman republican forms with the new reality of one-man rule; the creation and maintenance of this balance required considerable skill and tact.

Because of his nature, Tiberius found it impossible to adopt his predecessor's role completely. Although he assumed actual power, he seemed to do so unwillingly and refused most of the titles which the senate offered him. Many, including the eminent Roman historian Cornelius Tacitus, have seen this as hypocrisy; others believe that Tiberius was genuinely reluctant to become an autocrat. During the early years of his rule, he made a great show of consulting the senate on all matters, great and small. After years of Augustus' rule, however, the old methods were simply inadequate to govern a worldwide empire, and increasingly Tiberius was forced to assume and exercise absolute powers.

At first, these powers were used for the common good. In matters of religion and morals, Tiberius took firm steps against foreign beliefs which he believed threatened traditional Roman virtues: He expelled adherents of the Egyptian and Jewish religions from Rome and banished astrologers on pain of death—although he firmly believed in the practice himself. Perhaps he was protecting himself against possible conspiracies inspired by favorable horoscopes; such things were taken very seriously in ancient Rome.

Tiberius was also firm in his suppression of riots and other civil disturbances, which often afflicted Rome and the other large cities of the empire. Many of these problems were caused by an excessively large unemployed population, which was fed by the public dole and amused by public games; with little to lose, this group was easily incited to violence. As one measure against this violence, Tiberius established a central camp for the Praetorian guard in Rome, so this elite military unit could be called out to quell civil violence. At the same time, this concentration of troops gave enormous potential power to its commander, and soon that man, Lucius Aelius Sejanus, made a bold play for power.

Sejanus came from the equestrian order, the group below the senate in social standing and generally ineligible to hold the higher offices of the state. From about A.D. 23, however, Sejanus worked on the psychological and political insecurities of Tiberius, increasing his own hold over the emperor. It seems possible that Sejanus may even have aimed at the imperial power for himself—or, at least, as regent over Tiberius' successor. Sejanus aspired to marry Livia Julia, Tiberius' daughter, and worked to increase the emperor's fear and distrust of other members of his family. At the instigation of Sejanus, many senators (and others) were accused and condemned on charges of treason.

During this time, Tiberius left Rome, never to return. He settled on the island of Capri, off the coast of Naples. It was a spot well chosen for a man grown increasingly paranoid: No boat could approach it without being seen, and there were only two landing places, both easy to defend. By A.D. 31, Sejanus was named to a shared consulship with Tiberius and was at the height of his powers.

That same year saw the abrupt fall of Sejanus. Tiberius had become convinced that the Praetorian commander was aiming to become ruler of the state, and in a carefully worded letter to the senate, read while the unsuspecting Sejanus sat in the chamber, Tiberius bitterly denounced him. Sejanus' former lieutenants and others privy to the plot quickly acted, and Sejanus and his family were brutally executed, and his aspirations ended.

After this incident, Tiberius continued to rule Rome and the empire from the isolation of Capri. Important appointments were left unmade or, if made, were not allowed to be filled: Provincial governors sometimes spent their entire terms in Rome, having been denied permission to leave for their posts. Governing by letters, Tiberius often confused and mystified the senate, which was often unable to decipher his enigmatic messages.

His fears were clear enough, however, and resulted in an endless series of treason trials. During the latter years, a virtual reign of terror descended on the Roman upper classes, as they were accused of the vague but heinous crime of *maiestas* (roughly, treason). Executions of prominent Romans became commonplace, and many of those accused by professional informers chose not to wait for the show of a trial, committing suicide instead.

Meanwhile in Capri, Tiberius is reported by Suetonius to have engaged in a series of gaudy vices and perversions. His character, weakened first by years of hard work and worry and then the intense pressures of solitary rule, gave way to tyranny, debauchery, and paranoid suspicion. Having outlived his own sons, he settled the succession on his nephew Gaius (later the emperor Caligula). Tiberius died on March 16, A.D. 37; there was widespread rejoicing, instead of mourning, in Rome, and it was not until April 3 that his body was cremated and his remains interred in the imperial city he had vacated for so many years.

Summary

When Augustus adopted Tiberius as his son and heir, he took a formal oath that he did so only for the good of the Roman state and people. Historians have puzzled over this statement ever since. Some have argued that Augustus meant it as a sincere compliment, underscoring Tiberius' high qualifications for rule and indicating Augustus' confidence in his abilities. Others, however, have perceived a darker meaning in the words: that the action was one Augustus would have preferred not to take but was forced to by the lack of other, more preferable candidates.

Assessments of Tiberius as emperor similarly take two differing views. There are those who believe that on the whole he was a fairly good emperor, maintaining peace at home and security along the borders. While there is little doubt that after the fall of Sejanus Tiberius turned increasingly suspicious and vengeful, these dark elements cloud only the latter part of his rule, and the so-called reign of terror affected only a handful of the empire's inhabitants. It was only the senatorial and equestrian orders in Rome itself which felt the weight of the treason trials, and their hostility to Tiberius and the imperial system was to a large extent responsible for these events.

On the other hand, there are those who believe that from the first Tiberius was a cruel and tyrannical ruler, one who delighted in the suffering of his victims and whose life was given over to vice and debauchery. Foremost of these critics is the celebrated Roman historian Tacitus, whose brilliant writings paint a vivid portrait of Tiberius as a completely evil despot, a ruler who used his unlimited powers to destroy his supposed enemies. So great is Tacitus' genius that his version of history and his view of Tiberius seem almost irrefutable. Yet it must be remembered that Tacitus was a firm believer in the virtues of the vanished republic and hated the empire which replaced it. In a sense, he used Tiberius as a symbol of an entire system which he believed to be evil and unjust.

Those with a more balanced view maintain that Tiberius was a man of considerable abilities, both military and political. While serving under Augustus, Tiberius used these abilities to the benefit of Rome and, following his own succession to power, continued for many years to provide effective, proper rule for the empire. A series of causes—plots against him, the hostility of the upper classes, mental and physical exhaustion caused by overwork—wrought profound and disastrous changes in his personality. In the end, the task of ruling the Roman Empire proved too great a burden for one man to bear alone.

Bibliography

Grant, Michael. *The Roman Emperors: A Biographical Guide to the Rulers of Imperial Rome*. New York: Charles Scribner's Sons, 1985. For a fast-paced yet comprehensive introduction to Tiberius and his reign, the relevant section in this volume is unsurpassed. Grant, an outstanding historian of Rome, combines information and explanation in a narrative that provides as much pleasure as knowledge.

————. *The Twelve Caesars*. New York: Charles Scribner's Sons, 1975. Working from the base of Suetonius' historical scholarship, Grant approaches Tiberius from a combination of psychology, power politics, and common sense. He asks intriguing questions about what it must have been like to be the sole ruler of the vast Roman Empire, and his answers are thought-provoking. An excellent place to start a study of this enigmatic emperor.

Marsh, Frank Burr. *The Reign of Tiberius*. New York: Oxford University Press, 1931. Still the definitive modern biography of Tiberius, this volume brings together an impressive amount of scholarship in a generally readable and often entertaining fashion. Especially good in its knowledge of the detail and connections of ancient Roman political life.

Seager, Robin. *Tiberius*. Berkeley: University of California Press, 1972. A balanced and scholarly (but not pedantic) biography which shows how, under the early Roman Empire, the personality of the ruler had a profound impact on the state. Seager is careful to place Tiberius within the context of his times and his position, both of which were unique and difficult.

Smith, Charles E. *Tiberius and the Roman Empire*. Baton Rouge: Louisiana State University Press, 1942. Reprint. Port Washington, N.Y.: Kennikat Press, 1972. A work more concerned with Tiberius the ruler than Tiberius the man or tyrant, this book is strong on events and happenings outside the arena of Rome itself and is thus useful to counteract the popular image of that time created by Tacitus, that of unrelieved terror.

Suetonius. *Lives of the Twelve Caesars*. New York: Modern Library, 1959.
This is one of the enduring classics of the ancient world, and it combines
shrewd personal insight, revealing anecdotes, and a contemporary point of
view. The section on Tiberius also has a long-famous description of his
alleged sexual escapades on the isle of Capri; readers unfamiliar with Latin
should be careful to choose an unexpurgated version, such as this one.

Tacitus, Cornelius. *The Complete Works*. Translated by Alfred Church and
William Brodribb. New York: Modern Library, 1942. The *Annals* of Tacitus covers the period of Tiberius' reign, and this work is perhaps the most
impressive production of classical history. Tacitus has fashioned a Tiberius
who is a monster of deceit, hypocrisy, tyranny, and cruelty. This view may
be distorted, but its impact has profoundly influenced history and historians ever since its conception.

Michael Witkoski

TIGRANES THE GREAT

Born: c. 140 B.C.; Armenia
Died: c. 55 B.C.; Armenia
Area of Achievement: Government
Contribution: As King of Armenia between 95 and 55 B.C., Tigranes the Great defied the growing power of Rome and carved out a vast but short-lived empire which stretched from upper Mesopotamia to the Mediterranean.

Early Life

The Armenia of Tigranes the Great consisted of the uplands that run from the Black Sea to the Caspian Sea and from the Caucasus Mountains south to the upper Tigris and Euphrates rivers. Armenia had long been politically and culturally related, on the one hand, to the great civilizations of Mesopotamia and the Iranian Plateau and, on the other, to those of Asia Minor and the eastern Mediterranean. Centered on the fertile plain of the Araxes River between the alkaline Lake Van and Lake Sevan, Armenia had maintained a large measure of autonomy despite its status as a satrapy of the Persian Empire and, following the Macedonian conquest of Persia, a nominal part of the Seleucid Empire. After the Roman victory over Antiochus the Great at Magnesia in 190 B.C., the Seleucid Empire was stripped of its possessions north of the Taurus Mountains. In the resulting political vacuum, independent kingdoms were established in Lesser Armenia (known in antiquity as Sophene) and in Greater Armenia by the former governors of these regions, Zariadris and Artaxias, the ancestor of Tigranes the Great.

Practically nothing is known about the early life of Tigranes. Although the second century Greek writer Appian stated that Tigranes' father was also named Tigranes, the majority of scholarly opinion holds that Tigranes was the son of Artavasdes. Tigranes' birth date of circa 140 B.C. is deduced from the tradition that he was eighty-five years old at the time of his death in 55 B.C. It is known that, at some point in his early years, Tigranes was taken hostage by Mithradates the Great of Parthia when that king besieged Armenia. In 95 B.C. Mithradates placed Tigranes on the Armenian throne, having made Tigranes cede to Parthia seventy fertile valleys of eastern Armenia.

Tigranes came to power at a time which was ripe for the expansion of the Armenian kingdom. The apparently inexorable growth of Roman power in the east had been severely hampered by Rome's internal social problems and by the transformation of the Black Sea kingdom of Pontus into a significant military threat under the leadership of Mithradates VI Eupator. The Seleucid Empire had continued to disintegrate and was on the verge of total collapse.

Life's Work

Upon his accession to the throne of Greater Armenia in 95 B.C., Tigranes began immediately to enlarge his dominion. His first act as king was to invade Sophene and depose its ruler, thus uniting all Armenia under his rule. That same year, Tigranes made an extremely important political alliance by marrying Cleopatra, a daughter of Mithradates VI Eupator. For the next thirty years, the political and military fortunes of Tigranes and Mithradates were to be closely linked in their joint struggle against Rome.

The first conflict between Rome and the alliance of Tigranes and Mithradates was precipitated by Mithradates' struggle with Nicomedes III of Bithynia for the control of Cappadocia. To forestall a Roman attempt to intervene and appoint a pro-Roman king over Cappadocia, Tigranes overran the country with his Armenian army and secured it for his father-in-law. In 92 B.C., the Roman senate dispatched an army under the command of Lucius Cornelius Sulla, who cleared Cappadocia and installed the Roman candidate, Ariobarzanes I, as king. As soon as Sulla withdrew from Asia, however, Mithradates deposed both Ariobarzanes and the new Bithynian king, Nicomedes IV, from their thrones. In 89 B.C., with the support of another Roman army, both kings were reinstated, and Nicomedes, urged on by the Roman legates, provoked a full-scale war by invading Mithradates' Pontic homeland.

In 88 B.C., Mithradates the Great died, and Tigranes used the opportunity to recover the Armenian territory he had ceded to the Parthians in 95 B.C. Tigranes followed this success by invading northern Parthia, taking the important regions of Gordyene and Adiabene and the city of Nisibis. Tigranes then turned his attention to the east and annexed a large tract of Media Atropatene into his growing Armenian empire. Tigranes now called himself by the archaic title of "King of Kings" and had vassal kings wait upon him in his court.

At the same time, Tigranes' ally Mithradates responded to the provocation of Nicomedes IV and, taking advantage of the disruption of the Roman Social War, launched a major attack on the Roman province of Asia. After more than eighty thousand Roman officials and citizens were massacred in the Greek cities of Asia Minor, Mithradates invaded the Aegean. In 87 B.C., Sulla once again responded to this threat and swept Mithradates out of Roman territory. As a result of political troubles back in Rome, Sulla was unable to capitalize on his victory, and in 86 B.C. a peace between Mithradates and Rome was arranged.

With Mithradates in temporary retirement from active campaigning and with Asia Minor temporarily quiet, Tigranes moved against the tottering Seleucid dynasty. In 83 B.C., the Armenian army defeated the last Seleucid king, Antiochus Eusebius, and the entire eastern Mediterranean coast from Cilicia to the borders of Egypt became a part of Tigranes' empire. Tigranes was now at the height of his power. He divided his empire into 120 satrapies, following the old Persian model, and set an Armenian feudal lord as governor over each. As the evidence of his silver coinage shows, Tigranes now added the traditional Seleucid title "Divine" to the eastern "King of Kings."

With his kingdom stretching from the Caspian to the Mediterranean, the old Armenian capital of Artaxas on the Araxes River was far removed from the center of Tigranes' empire. Thus, Tigranes set about building a new capital in the west, near the head of the Tigris River, and named it Tigranocerta, for himself. Tigranes populated his city by forcibly displacing Greeks and natives from Syria (and later from Cappadocia), in addition to encouraging Jewish and Arab merchants to settle there.

For the next decade, Tigranes apparently was able to govern his massive empire without major incident. When trouble arose, it was once again caused by Mithradates, who dragged Tigranes into his struggle against Rome. In 74 B.C., Nicomedes IV died and willed his Bithynian kingdom to Rome. Mithradates responded by invading Bithynia, and Tigranes again invaded Cappadocia. Rome then sent out Lucius Licinius Lucullus, who, in a series of engagements from 74 to 72 B.C., was able to drive Mithradates out of Pontus.

When Mithradates fled to the safety of Armenia, Lucullus sent his brother-in-law, Appius Claudius, to Tigranes to ask him to turn over Mithradates. Initially, Tigranes employed a delaying tactic by refusing to give an audience to either Appius Claudius or his father-in-law, who was kept under virtual house arrest in an Armenian castle. When the Roman envoy finally did speak to Tigranes, Appius' haughty and preemptory tone so infuriated the king that he refused the Roman request. In 69 B.C., Lucullus invaded Armenia, with a force that Tigranes is said to have described as "too large for an embassy, too small for an army." Nevertheless, Lucullus was able to besiege Tigranocerta and, after Tigranes had fled into the Armenian hills and joined forces with Mithradates, to inflict a serious defeat on the combined Armenian and Pontic armies. Lucullus' army was unwilling, however, to fight further, and when the Roman garrison that had been left in Pontus revolted, Lucullus was forced to retire. Both Tigranes and Mithradates were able to recover much of the territory that had been seized, though Tigranes had lost Syria forever.

The final blow to Tigranes' imperial rule was soon to follow. In 67 B.C. Pompey the Great cleared the Mediterranean of pirates by destroying their bases in Cilicia; in the following year, he was awarded the command against Mithradates VI. When Pompey quickly moved against Pontus, Mithradates once again tried to seek refuge in Armenia. In the meantime, however, Tigranes was facing a new enemy. His third son, also named Tigranes, had married into the family of Phraates III, King of Parthia, and, urged on by his father-in-law, raised a revolt against his father.

As Pompey marched into Armenia, the elder Tigranes banished Mithradates from his kingdom and made overtures of submission to the Roman general. Perceiving that a weakened Tigranes would serve Roman interests, Pompey switched his support from Phraates to Tigranes, though he did set Tigranes' son on the throne of Lesser Armenia. The younger Tigranes soon intrigued again against his father, and Pompey thereupon took him prisoner and brought him back to Rome, where he perished. The next two years witnessed intermittent hostilities between Tigranes and Phraates until Pompey finally negotiated a peace between Armenia and Parthia. Tigranes the Great continued to rule as King of Armenia, albeit a king completely subservient to Rome, until his death.

Summary

The ancient Armenians themselves left no historical records, and the earliest extant Armenian history, written sometime between the fifth and eighth centuries A.D. by Moses of Khorene, presents only a very unreliable legendary account of the reign of Tigranes. Except for a single reference to Tigranes in a Parthian document and the evidence of Tigranes' coinage, all that is known about this king is what is preserved in the writings of a handful of Greek and Latin authors, who wrote from a Roman perspective; the main sources for the life of Tigranes are Strabo, Plutarch, Dio Cassius, Appian of Alexandria, and Justin. It is hardly surprising, therefore, that the Tigranes portrayed by these authors is an arrogant tyrant who through his own stupidity and hubris was unable to maintain his empire. In large part, this negative picture of Tigranes simply reflects a general Greco-Roman hostility toward absolute monarchs. In spite of his sincere philhellenism, which was shared by most of the eastern aristocracy of the Hellenistic age, Tigranes was above all an Oriental ruler.

After the death of Tigranes the Great, his descendants continued to rule as client-kings of Rome until 1 B.C., when Augustus attempted to put his own grandson, Gaius, on the throne. When Gaius was killed during an Armenian uprising in A.D. 4, the kingship was reinstated, and the Armenian throne continued to be a matter of contention between Rome and Parthia for another century. Finally, by A.D. 114, the usefulness of Armenia as a buffer state had ended, and Trajan annexed it as a Roman province.

Bibliography

Foss, Clive. "The Coinage of Tigranes the Great: Problems, Suggestions, and a New Find." *Numismatic Chronicle* 146 (1986): 19-66. A major reclassification of the silver and bronze coinage of Tigranes based on metrology, iconography, and style. Identifies mints and reassigns one type to Tigranes the Younger.

Lang, David M. *Armenia: Cradle of Civilization*. London: George Allen and

Unwin, 1970, 2d ed. 1978. Presents a general overview of Armenia from the Neolithic to the present. In general, the chapters on early Armenia are marred by historical errors and a strong pro-Armenian bias.

McGing, B. C. "The Date of the Outbreak of the Third Mithridatic War." *Phoenix* 38 (1984): 12-18. Suggests that the beginning of the war should be downdated from 74 B.C. to 73 B.C.

Musti, D. "Syria and the East." In *The Hellenistic World*, vol. 7 in *The Cambridge Ancient History*, edited by F. W. Wallbank and A. E. Astin. 3d ed. Cambridge: Cambridge University Press, 1984. The best general account available on the relations between the Seleucids and the Eastern kingdoms.

Ormerod, H. A., and M. Cary. "Rome and the East." In *The Roman Republic, 133-44 B.C.*, vol. 9 in *The Cambridge Ancient History*, edited by S. A. Cook, F. E. Adcock, and M. P. Charlesworth. 2d ed. Cambridge: Cambridge University Press, 1932. Still the best narrative on the Third Mithradatic War and Tigranes' battles against Lucullus.

Peters, F. E. *The Harvest of Hellenism*. New York: Simon and Schuster, 1970. In this massive history of the Hellenistic East, chapter 8, "The Romans in the Near East," presents a solid general account of the conflicts between Rome and the Eastern kingdoms from Cynoscephalae to Carrhae.

Murray C. McClellan

TRAJAN

Born: c. A.D. 53; Italica, Baetica
Died: c. August 8, A.D. 117; Selinus, Cilicia
Areas of Achievement: Government and warfare
Contribution: The first of the adoptive emperors of Rome, Trajan became one of the most successful, in both war and politics. During his reign, the Roman Empire reached its maximum territorial extent.

Early Life

Marcus Ulpius Traianus (Trajan) was born in Baetica, in what is now southern Spain, an area of Roman conquests and Latin influences for more than a century. By the time of Trajan's birth, circa A.D. 53, much of the population spoke Latin rather than the native Iberian language. Trajan's father, also Marcus Ulpius Traianus, was a native of Baetica who came from an Italian family that had been long established in Spain. The senior Traianus had a significant military and political career; he served as governor of Baetica and commanded a legion in the war Vespasian conducted against the Jews, then became a consul and a member of the patrician class before acting as governor of Syria and, ultimately, as imperial proconsul in the East. His attainments showed that most positions in the imperial hierarchy during the first century A.D. were open to non-Italians. His son, Trajan, would become the first provincial to become emperor.

Little is known of Trajan's early life. He served as a military tribune and accompanied his father to Syria during the latter's term as governor. Typically for one of his class, he held various judicial and political positions, but his primary experience was military. He held command in Spain, then in Germany, becoming governor of Upper Germany. Physically imposing, tall, and serious in manner, he was popular and successful in the military and also among the senators in Rome.

In 97, probably as a result of political pressure, Marcus Cocceius Nerva, emperor since the murder of Domitian the previous year, adopted Trajan as his successor. Nerva was a politician, not a warrior, who hoped to end the autocratic abuses of Domitian's reign. He was ill and had no children of his own, and his adoption of Trajan satisfied both the military and civilian powers. Four months after Trajan's adoption Nerva died, in January, 98, and Trajan, despite his provincial birth, became Emperor of Rome.

Life's Work

At the time of Nerva's death, Trajan was at Cologne, in Lower Germany. Before returning to Rome, he fought a series of engagements against nearby foes, both to impress upon them the might of Roman power and to establish plans for subsequent military action. His belated arrival in Rome, in the summer of 99, suggests the unchallenged position he had already achieved.

Like his predecessors, Trajan continued to wear the mantle woven by Augustus more than a century earlier. In reality he was an autocrat, but in theory he was merely the first citizen, the princeps. His power was nearly absolute, yet, unlike many of Augustus' successors, Trajan masked his powers so as to reassure rather than intimidate the former ruling body, the senate, and the aristocratic patricians who had governed during the era of the Republic. Republican sentiment still ran high, in spite of the many changes since the Republic's end, as reflected in the historical works of two of Trajan's contemporaries, Cornelius Tacitus and Suetonius. Trajan reconciled the reality of order with the appearance of freedom in a way that satisfied most people; the equilibrium sought by Nerva but established by Trajan ushered in an era which the English historian Edward Gibbon described as one of the golden ages of human history.

Trajan stressed moderation and reinforced the values of an earlier Rome. His family's upright reputation, his public generosity and private frugality, his lack of interest in excessive ceremonies glorifying himself, and his accessibility all contributed to the general popularity of his rule. As an administrator, Trajan was conscientious and hardworking rather than radically innovative; he was willing merely to improve existing practices inherited from his predecessors. If the senate remained powerless collectively, Trajan made good use of the abilities of individual senators. He created new patricians and made greater use of the class known as the knights rather than the services of freedmen, who often had attained considerable responsibility during the first century of the Empire. His judicial decisions favored the rights of slave owners rather than those of the slaves, although there is considerable evidence that Trajan's own sympathies were generally humanitarian. In his actions and demeanor, he conveyed the ruling-class virtues of the Republic.

As the Empire reached its maximum extent and its most notable era, public works projects continued to be of great importance. Roads were built or improved, particularly in the eastern part of the Empire, and road milestones from Trajan's reign have been discovered far south in Egypt. Aqueducts constructed around Rome greatly increased water supply to the city's populace. Harbors were improved, including Ostia, the port for Rome. New public baths were developed, and temples, libraries, and business facilities enhanced the city. Plans for many of the projects existed before Trajan became emperor, but he fulfilled and often expanded them. The Empire continued to become more urbanized, particularly in the East, and local municipalities also experienced considerable construction.

Trajan oversaw the reorganization of the traditional importation of grain so important to the Romans and increased the number of people qualified to receive it free. Public shows and games, a major part of urban life during his reign, were especially notable after his military victories. Trajan's interests in the plight of the lower classes possibly reflected his humanitarian concerns, but those actions were also simply good politics. He was fortunate to be able to reduce taxes—partially because of administrative dedication, but also because of the economic benefits which resulted from his military victories. Personally popular with the legions, Trajan successfully controlled his armies. He created a new mounted bodyguard, primarily made up of non-Italians, thus moving toward parity between Italians and those from the provinces. Concern for his personal security, given the record of violent deaths suffered by several of his predecessors, led to the development of a new secret service.

Trajan's religious beliefs, orthodox for members of his class and time, reflected his traditional and patriotic nature rather than a deep theological concern. He built and restored temples throughout the Empire, and like Augustus, he accepted the fact of emperor worship in the eastern part of the Empire but resisted its development in the West. Nevertheless, new religions, such as Christianity, were spreading throughout the Empire, and, although only a small minority of the population were Christians, questions arose about the new movement.

Pliny the Younger, a Roman aristocrat appointed by Trajan as governor of the province of Bithynia-Pontus, wrote often to ask for solutions to problems he faced, including how Christians were to be treated. Trajan seriously considered all such difficulties; he did not allow his subordinates to decide the many matters of governance. Given the intimate tie between the Roman gods and the Roman state, Trajan's instructions to Pliny were moderate and sensible. Fearing subversive threats which might affect the tranquillity of the Empire, Trajan ordered that Christians who would not recant should be punished according to the requirements of the laws, but Christians should not be sought out for special persecution, and anonymous accusations by others against them should not be accepted. Trajan's response was typical of his nature; he was not a religious fanatic, but he understood the necessity to uphold the laws which had traditionally been accepted by the society and which had been responsible for Roman well-being.

Predictably, war and military conquest, the enterprises that had led to his adoption by Nerva, became an important theme of Trajan's reign. In eastern Europe, the great rivers of the Rhine and the Danube had long served as the natural boundaries of the Empire. Yet, because of a great inward curve of the Danube, a portion of southeastern Europe, known as Dacia, had remained a dangerous enclave which threatened the security of the Empire. The Dacians had adopted at least part of the Greco-Roman culture, including certain military techniques; although the Romans considered them barbarians, they were not primitives, and periodically they aggressively raided Roman territory across the Danube.

Trajan waged two wars against the Dacians and their formidable king,

Decebalus. The first war, lasting from 101 to 102, resulted in Trajan leading the legions to victory over the Dacians, but Decebalus refused to abide by the terms of peace, and a second Dacian war was fought in 105. Again, Trajan was victorious, and Decebalus committed suicide. Most of the population of Dacia was removed and the area was colonized by Roman soldiers and civilians. The province became an important part of the Empire, until it was abandoned in the late third century after the invasion of the Germanic Goths. Trajan's conquest was celebrated by coins and inscriptions throughout the Empire, but the most famous monument stood in Rome. A hundred-foot-high column was constructed which portrayed the course of the Dacian wars; running counterclockwise from bottom to top, twenty-five hundred carved figures decorated the column, which was crowned with a statue of Trajan. It was dedicated in 113 and remains one of the most impressive remains of the Roman Empire at the time of its greatest power.

After the victory against Decebalus, Trajan spent the next several years in Rome before responding to another threat to Rome's supremacy, this time in the East, from Parthia, whose ancient borders spread at times from the Euphrates River to India. Rome and Parthia had been adversaries as far back as the late Republic, when Pompey the Great had extended the boundaries of the Empire into the area south of the Black Sea. Trajan, in 113, decided to annex Armenia to Rome, claiming that the Parthians had upset the existing arrangements in that territory. Trajan's motives have been variously interpreted; he may have acted for economic reasons, to secure the overland trade routes from the Persian Gulf and beyond, or because of ambitions for personal fame (although even the wars against Dacia resulted more from Dacian incursions than Roman aggression). Trajan was sixty years old when the war against Parthia began, and in 114 his armies easily conquered Armenia, making it a Roman province, with client kingdoms extending even farther to the east.

The Roman advance continued south the following year into Mesopotamia. Behind the Roman lines, however, there was unrest; businessmen were upset by the uncertain changes brought by the new Roman regime, and many Jewish communities in the East again rose up against Roman authority. At the same time the Parthians, previously disunited, came together, forcing the Romans back. The military situation stabilized, but Trajan's health declined; there were matters at Rome that needed his presence, and he turned west toward home. Before reaching Rome, he died at Selinus in Cilicia, in southern Asia Minor, probably on August 8, 117. His ashes were deposited in a golden urn at the base of his famous column in Rome.

Summary

Before he died, Trajan apparently adopted as his successor Publius Aelius Hadrianus (Hadrian), a distant relative who had been reared in Trajan's household. Trajan had no children of his own, and his wife, Pompeia Plotina, favored Hadrian's accession. One of the first acts of the new emperor was to reach an agreement with Parthia to have Rome withdraw from the advanced positions attained by Trajan. Hadrian's decision was both strategic and political. It is possible that under Trajan the Empire was overextended, that it lacked the resources necessary to hold the new territories, and for his own success Hadrian desired peace rather than a resumption of his predecessor's forward policy. Under Hadrian, and under his successors, the Roman Empire would never again reach the limits achieved by Trajan.

The adjustment made between the ruler as princeps and the ruler as tyrant distinguished Trajan's reign. Power resided solely in the emperor's hands, but he used that power responsibly. The practice of adopting one's successor, first established by Nerva, continued until 180, and during that period the Empire was governed by men of ability and much vision. It was not, however, a golden age; even under Trajan, increased centralization took place, Italy began to fall relatively behind other parts of the Empire, and the borders were never totally secure. The traditional governing classes of Rome turned more toward the literary life than toward politics and public service, while the Empire depended in large part on the labor of slaves for its prosperity.

Nevertheless, Trajan was one of the greatest of the emperors, both because of his military and territorial conquests and because of the standards he set as governor and statesman. Early in his reign he was hailed as *Optimus*, the best. Along with Augustus, Trajan was the standard by which later Romans measured the leadership of the Empire; their expressed hope, rarely attained, was that later emperors would be *felicior Augusto, melior Traiano*, or more fortunate than Augustus and better than Trajan.

Bibliography

Garzetti, Albino. *From Tiberius to the Antonines: A History of the Roman Empire, A.D. 14-192*. Translated by J. F. Foster. London: Methuen and Co., 1974. Until a full biography in English of Trajan is written, Garzetti's volume partially fills the vacuum. Trajan is one of the major figures and is the subject of a long chapter in the work. The author argues that Trajan was one of the best of all the emperors of Rome and that he successfully remained primarily princeps rather than dictator.

Gibbon, Edward. *The Decline and Fall of the Roman Empire*. 2 vols. New York: Modern Library, 1932. For Gibbon, the second century of the common era was one of humanity's golden ages. Trajan was one of the best of the emperors, whose only personal weakness was his military ambitions. Gibbon's own biases, however, were in favor of the Republic, not the Empire, and he would probably have agreed with Lord Acton's later dictum regarding the corrupting influences of power.

Grant, Michael. *The Army of the Caesars*. New York: Charles Scribner's

Sons, 1974. The author, one of the most prolific historians of ancient Rome, has produced a well-written study of the armies of Rome from the late Republic through the fall of the Western Empire in 476. Grant discusses the military conquests of Trajan in Dacia and against Parthia and argues that the latter was ultimately beyond the resources of the Empire.

——————. *The Roman Emperors: A Biographical Guide to the Rulers of Imperial Rome, 31 B.C.-A.D. 476*. London: Weidenfeld and Nicolson, 1985. The sketch on Trajan is brief but comprehensive of the subject's accomplishments and characteristics.

Harris, B. F. *Bithynia Under Trajan*. Auckland, New Zealand: University of Auckland, 1964. This brief monograph discusses the different but complementary views of the position and powers of the Roman emperor at the time of Trajan as expressed by the Roman governor in Bithynia, Pliny the Younger, and the Greek Dio Chrysostom.

Lepper, F. A. *Trajan's Parthian War*. London: Oxford University Press, 1948. The author discusses the last, and most controversial, of Trajan's activities and suggests the hypothesis that illness during the emperor's last years at least partially explains his excessive imperial exploits.

Millar, Fergus. *The Emperor in the Roman World*. Ithaca, N.Y.: Cornell University Press, 1977. This study of the emperors of Rome from Augustus to Constantine is one of the major works on the powers and responsibilities of the many rulers of the Empire. Long and not easily digested, it is still worth the effort because of its comprehensiveness and its insights. Although there is no single chapter on Trajan, he is frequently mentioned.

Rossi, Lino. *Trajan's Column and the Dacian Wars*. Translated by J. M. C. Toynbee. Ithaca, N.Y.: Cornell University Press, 1971. The author's historical interest is in warfare, Roman and modern. In this study, in the absence of written records, he uses one of the most famous monuments of the Roman Empire in order to dissect the course of Trajan's victorious wars against the Dacians, which represented one of the most important accomplishments of his reign.

Wilken, Robert L. *The Christians as the Romans Saw Them*. New Haven, Conn.: Yale University Press, 1984. Because of the lack of contemporary biographical works about Trajan, Pliny the Younger's letters to the emperor have continued to be one of the major sources for the era. Among other topics, Pliny wrote to Trajan regarding Christians in Bithynia. The author places that correspondence in historical context from the Roman perspective.

Eugene S. Larson

TU FU

Born: 712; perhaps Tu-ling, Shensi, China
Died: 770; Hunan, China
Area of Achievement: Literature
Contribution: Tu Fu is considered the greatest of Chinese poets as well as one of the giant figures of world literature.

Early Life

Tu Fu descended from the nobility, and his family tradition was both scholarly and military. He was the thirteenth-generation descendant of Tu Yu, a marquess and an army general who was married to a princess of the imperial family. Tu Fu's great-grandfather was Tu I-i, a mid-level government official. His grandfather was Tu Shên-yen, a *chin-shih* (literally, "entered scholar") who served in minor official positions and was a respected poet. Tu Fu's father, Tu Hsien, served in minor government posts. His mother was of imperial blood. She apparently died during his birth.

Little is known about Tu Fu's childhood or teenage years and the education he received. He studied the Confucian Classics to prepare himself to take the examination for the *chin-shih* degree, the gateway to officialdom for most men. Evidence also suggests that he attended private schools. Apart from his acquaintance with the *Szŭ-shu wu-ching* (the four books and the five classics), he probably also studied Sun Wu's military classic, the *Sun-tzŭ ping fa* (*Sun Tzŭ on the Art of War*).

What is known about Tu Fu's early life comes largely from his poems, many of which are autobiographical. In a poem written in 762, known as "Brave Adventures," he refers to himself at the age of seven when he writes, "My thoughts already concerned heroic deeds;/ My first song was on the phoenix, the harbinger of a sagacious reign." In the same poem, he refers to himself at the age of nine, when he began to practice calligraphy by writing "big characters" (that is, foot-square characters), which accumulated until there "were enough to fill a bag." He also remarks that his nature was "spirited," that he was already "fond of wine," that he "hated evil" unremittingly, and that he abandoned children his own age to associate exclusively with adults. At age fourteen or fifteen Tu Fu had entered into literary competition, and the local literati declared him a prodigy. In another poem written about the same time (c. 760), entitled "A Hundred Anxieties," Tu Fu reveals that despite his seriousness about learning and writing at this age, he was still very much a boy: At fifteen, his "heart was still childish," he was as "strong as a brown calf," and in one day he "could climb the trees a thousand times."

At age nineteen, Tu Fu began to see the world. He set forth in a southwesterly direction toward the lands of "Wu and Yüeh" (modern Kiangsu and Chekiang). His journey was to last four years (731-735). He described his visit to Su-chou, a city noted for its scenic wonders and rich past. In viewing the city's ancient ruins, Tu Fu recalled certain historical personages and the events associated with them. His journey completed, he returned northward by boat, eventually reaching his home in Ching-chao.

In the following year (736), Tu Fu, now in the prime of life at age twenty-four, was invited by his prefecture to Ch'ang-an to sit for the examination for the *chin-shih* degree. Yet, for reasons unknown, he failed the examination.

Life's Work

Tu Fu's failure in the examination practically put an end to his chances to have an official career. Although embittered, he never actually gave up this ambition and continually sought an official appointment by other means. In the meantime, he paid his respects to the prefect of Ching-chao and then left for his parents' residence at Yen-chou, where he would have to face their disappointment.

Soon, however, Tu Fu set out on another journey. This time he went to Ch'i and Chao (modern Shantung and southern Hopeh). This trip would occupy him for another four years (736-740). His activities during these travels are also described in "Brave Adventures." He employed himself mainly by honing his skills in falconry, horsemanship, archery, and hunting. He recalled this period of his life in another poem, written in 766, entitled "Song of the White-Headed." In this poem, he regrets that his present age no longer permits him to perform the exciting and adventurous feats of his youth:

> Suddenly I think of youthful days,
> When frosty dew froze on the steps and door.
> On a Tatar horse I clasped an ornamented bow;
> My humming string was not loosed in vain.
> My long shaft sped after the cunning hare;
> Its swift feathers fitted to the bow's full moon.
> Mournful, the Song of the White-headed;
> Deserted now, the haunts of the gallants.

Tu Fu's second journey was brought to a close by the death of his father in 740. He had to make the funeral arrangements, tend to his father's affairs, and find a place for the family to live. Tu Fu chose Yen-shih, northeast of Lo-yang, the eastern capital. There he built a house, which the family occupied in 741.

Soon Tu Fu took up residence in Lo-yang. There he met the older poet Li Po, who had just been dismissed from the court in Ch'ang-an. With Li Po and another distinguished poet, Kao Shih, Tu Fu made excursions to various historic sites in Honan. Tu Fu and Li Po met again—for the last time—the following year (745). At this time Tu Fu wrote two poems concerning their friendship. (Later, about 758, not having heard from Li Po since their parting, Tu Fu wrote his two famous poems entitled "Dreaming of Li Po—Two Poems.") Sometime between 742 and 745 Tu Fu had married and fathered a child. In 746 he and his family moved to Ch'ang-an. There, he once again sought an official appointment.

The years from about 730 to 745 may be taken as the formative stage, or First Period, of Tu Fu's poetic development. Yet only four of his poems written during this period are extant. Tu Fu's violation of conventional literary techniques can be seen in one of these poems, "A Poetry Contest After Dinner at the Tso Villa." Here he departs from the traditional decorum of subgenres and their themes, since his poem is both about meeting and about departing. He draws an extensive contrast in comparing the "firmament" to a "thatched roof . . . studded with stars." He also tries to balance the demands of "the book and the sword" (*shu chien*) in the statement "We consult books; . . . We reëxamine the sword. . . . "

In addition, Tu Fu affirms that his victory in the poetry contest (described in the poem) was, in effect, a conquest of Wu. (He wrote that the poem was chanted in the Wu dialect.) It was an action equal to the political and military feats of the heroes of China's antiquity. Tu Fu refers to the small boat of Fan Li (fifth century B.C.), the minister of K'u Chien, King of Wu. It is said that Fan Li, having enabled his king to gain a military victory, declined a reward for his service and sailed away in a small boat. From this poem, therefore, it is clear—as in "Brave Adventures" and "Song of the White-Headed"—that in the T'ang Dynasty there was no separation between the scholar and the man of action. Tu Fu was a *shih* in the older sense of the Chinese "scholar-knight."

Tu Fu spent the years from 746 to 759 in or near Ch'ang-an. For ten years he indulged in a frustrating effort to get a government post. The reigning emperor, Hsüan Tsung, was old and neglectful of public affairs. He left his rule entirely in the hands of a despotic minister, Li Lin-fu, who had many enemies—especially the heir apparent and his entourage. When Tu Fu arrived in the capital, he obtained the patronage of the prince of Ju-yang. Although this connection was politically harmless, Tu Fu also had ties with the heir apparent. Li Lin-fu eventually dispelled members of the heir apparent's entourage. Tu Fu had family ties with the despotic minister that saved him from also being banished. Nevertheless, his connection with the heir apparent blocked Tu Fu's chances for government service for some time to come.

In 747 Hsüan Tsung held a special examination to discover new talent. Tu Fu was again hopeful. Yet, fearful of the success of the examinees, Li Lin-fu arranged that all be failed. During the next three years Tu Fu tried to appeal to the emperor directly. He presented him with works of the *fu* genre that were accompanied by pleas for favor. Finally, he got the emperor's attention with his three *fu* on major rites. In 753 a special examination was prepared for him, and this time he passed. During the next five years, a turbulent period when the heir apparent finally assumed power, Tu Fu was given various ceremonial posts. In 758, however, he was ousted when one of his friends fell into disfavor with the emperor.

The years from 746 to 759 constituted the maturing stage, or Second Period, of Tu Fu's work as a poet. Generally, in this period he developed a new kind of "realism." His earlier tendency to combine, reconcile, and balance opposing elements—seen earlier in his merging of poetic subgenres and themes and in his balancing of the demands of "the book and the sword"—was expanded and developed in other directions. He mixed prose (*fu*) and verse (*shih*), introduced new "unpoetic"' subjects in combination with old "poetic" ones, merged private circumstances and concerns with public and national ones that embraced political, military, and economic factors, and transposed general descriptive judgments into specific ethical judgments that placed blame directly on specific persons.

Among Tu Fu's most outstanding poems of this period are "The Ballad of the War Chariots," "Frontier Duties: Nine Poems," and "Five Hundred Words to Express My Feelings When I Went from the Capital to Feng-hsien." These first two poems were written toward the end of 750, and the third was written near the end of 755, before Tu Fu knew of the outbreak of the rebellion which resulted in the heir apparent's rise to power. When Tu Fu was banished from court in 758, he was sent to Hua-chou, sixty miles east of the capital, to become commissioner of education.

In the early part of 759 Tu Fu was sent on a mission to Lo-yang. On his way home, he wrote two notable poems on recruiting officers at Hsin-an and Shih-hao. Yet not long after his return to Hua-chou, he resigned his position, probably because at this time he believed that his official services were futile. Then he and his family set out on a long journey, with pauses of some duration at Ch'en-chou (modern T'ien-shui) and T'ung-ku (modern Ch'eng-hsien). His journey finally ended by wintertime in Ch'eng-tu, where the following year he was to occupy his famous "thatched hut." Tu Fu was forty-eight years old, and he was not in good health. (He had had lung trouble since 754.) Although by this time he had written many distinguished poems, some of Tu Fu's greatest poems were yet to come.

During the years from 759 to 770, the Third Period, Tu Fu produced an abundance of mature poetry. Although he never actually gave up his ambition to perform public service, it seemed that age and bad health made him more content to devote himself almost entirely to his writings. He was much taken by his thatched hut, located on the outskirts of Ch'eng-tu, which he regarded as an ideal hermitage. At least two poems were inspired by the hut's location and completion: "Choice of a Domicile" and "The Hut Completed." "My Thatched Roof Whirled Away by an Autumn Gale" is one of his greatest poems, combining dismay, love, pathos, and the tragedy of aging.

Tu Fu's old friend and patron Yen Wu soon was appointed military commissioner of Ch'eng-tu. He, in turn, appointed Tu Fu to his military staff. Tu Fu served Yen as military adviser from 764 to 765, resigning probably because of age and poor health. His ambivalent attitude toward his position can be detected in his poems "Overnight at the General Headquarters" and "Twenty Rhymes to Dispel Gloom: Presented to His Excellency Yen."

Yen Wu died suddenly in 765. It appears that Tu Fu had left Ch'eng-tu just prior to his friend's death and at the time was sailing with his family down the Min River on his way to Jung-chou (modern I-pin), in Szechwan. His health failing, Tu Fu continued to travel, eventually arriving in K'uei-chou (modern Feng-chieh), Szechwan, to which he refers in his poetry as "the White Emperor's city." He found a generous patron there and stayed for two years. During this time he wrote a number of distinguished poems: his *lü-shih* series "Generals: Five Poems," "Thoughts on Historical Sites: Five Poems," and the series generally regarded as the finest of his masterpieces, "Autumn Thoughts: Eight Poems." He also wrote eight "in memoriam" poems, including a beautiful tribute to his deceased friend Yen Wu.

Old and sick, Tu Fu died in Hunan, in the winter of 770. David Lattimore nicely sums up the chief characteristics of Tu Fu's Third Period, pointing out that "though ill and isolated from literary centers," he tenaciously "undertook works of ever greater technical difficulty and perfection." The playful representation of the early poems gave way to the rich symbolism of the later ones, syntax became "more tortuous and more ambiguous," and realism was transformed into surrealism. The great works of this period are characterized by classical precision in versification and idiosyncratic freedom of diction and syntax.

Summary

Tu Fu's preeminence as a poet is unquestionable. He not only is the most celebrated poet in Chinese literature but also bears comparison to the chief figures of the various national literatures of the West. His literary accomplishment is a major contribution in the formation of literary values generally. Although no coterie formed around him during his time and the impact of his genius was not felt for decades after his death, once his preeminence was apparent, no later Chinese poet could afford to ignore his work.

Tu Fu is perhaps the most learned poet of China and its most complicated stylist. His poetry is characterized by recondite allusions; a feeling for the historicity of language; rapid stylistic and thematic shifts; social, political, military, and economic analysis; ethics, cosmology, aesthetics; and a decided interest in historical context. Indeed, this last interest gave him the designation of the *shih-shih*, or the "poet historian." In his view of old age and of art as timeless and distinct from the changes of life, he resembles William Butler Yeats. In his appreciation of nature, rusticity, and the common man (who, to

Tu Fu, may be good or evil, as an aristocrat may also be), he resembles William Wordsworth. In his treatment of society and his mockery, bitterness, and humor, he resembles François Villon. In his interest in history, government, and economics, he resembles Ezra Pound.

Bibliography

Davis, A. R. *Tu Fu*. New York: Twayne Publishers, 1971. A fine, short study of Tu Fu's life and poetry, with excellent translations of poems, whole or in part. Should be read in conjunction with William Hung's review in the *Harvard Journal of Asiatic Studies*, cited below.

Hawkes, David. *A Little Primer of Tu Fu*. Oxford: Clarendon Press, 1967. Written for readers who know little Chinese. The volume contains the texts of thirty-five of Tu Fu's poems in Chinese characters and Pinyin Romanization, with descriptions in English of titles, subjects, and poetic forms followed by exegeses and translations. Can be employed as a very useful textbook.

Hung, William. Review of *Tu Fu*, by A. R. Davis. *Harvard Journal of Asiatic Studies* 32 (1972): 265-284. An informative corrective to Davis' book.

_____. *Tu Fu: China's Greatest Poet*. Cambridge: Harvard University Press, 1952. Good but somewhat prosy translations of 334 poems together with a running account of Tu Fu's life and career. One of the best English-language sources, this work is essential to an understanding of Tu Fu's life and work. With supplementary volume of notes.

Lattimore, David. "Tu Fu." In *The Indiana Companion to Traditional Chinese Literature*, edited by William H. Nienhauser, Jr. Bloomington: Indiana University Press, 1986. An excellent short essay on Tu Fu's career and his qualities as a poet.

Liu, James J. Y. *The Art of Chinese Poetry*. Chicago: University of Chicago Press, 1962. A good, basic introduction to the forms and tropes of Chinese poetry.

Mei, Tsu-lin, and Yu-kung Kao. "Tu Fu's 'Autumn Meditations': An Exercise in Linguistic Criticism." *Harvard Journal of Asiatic Studies* 28 (1968): 44-80. An enlightening treatment of this great series of eight poems.

Owen, Stephen. "Tu Fu." In *The Great Age of Chinese Poetry: The High T'ang*. New Haven, Conn.: Yale University Press, 1981. An excellent criticism of Tu Fu.

Tu Fu. *Tu Fu: Selected Poems*. Compiled by Fêng Chih and translated by Rewi Alley. Peking: Foreign Languages Press, 1962. A handy volume of good translations of more than one hundred representative poems. The introduction by Fêng Chih is Marxist-oriented.

Richard P. Benton

UNKEI

Born: c. 1150; probably Nara, Japan
Died: 1223; probably Nara, Japan
Area of Achievement: Art
Contribution: Unkei established a new style of Buddhist sculpture during the Kamakura period in Japan.

Early Life

Unkei is the best-known sculptor in Japanese history. He was active in the early Kamakura period and was the son of Kōkei, who himself was probably a fifth-generation descendant of Jōchō, another influential Japanese sculptor. The date of Unkei's birth is unknown; nevertheless, scholars have speculated that it was around 1150, based on the birth date of his eldest child, Tankei, in 1173. Although there is no literary record of his early life, it is likely that Unkei was an apprentice to his father, who was chief sculptor of the Kei school (also called the Nara school) during the last half of the twelfth century. The Kei school, which began in 1096 with Jōchō's grandson, Raijo, had developed in Nara, Japan's oldest permanent capital, centering on the Kōfuku-ji (Kōfuku temple).

During the late twelfth century, the In and En schools (also known as the Kyoto schools) were prosperous in Kyoto and enjoyed aristocratic patronage. These two schools dominated the sculptural arts, preserving the traditional Jōchō style as their noble patrons desired. Unfortunately, this tradition was becoming overly refined in detail, no longer fresh and vivid as it had been under Jōchō. It was degenerating into a formalistic imitation.

To counter this stagnation the Kei school attempted to create a new style, one based on the more realistic expression found in art during the Late Nara period (724-794). Being less involved in important art commissions than the Kyoto schools were and thus freed from the constraints of aristocratic taste, the Kei school was allowed to establish a distinctive manner. Kōkei promoted this movement and his son Unkei completed the innovation by creating the Kamakura style.

The Amida triad in the Chōgaku-ji (Chōgaku temple) in Nara, sculpted in 1151, was one of the early experimental works, possibly made by Raijo's son, Kōjo. A monumental effort, it attempted to defeat the mannerism of the traditional Jōchō style by returning to the classic, naturalistic style of the Late Nara-period sculpture and adding a new technique: the creation of crystal eyes called *gyokugan*, which gave statues an increased realism.

Unkei's Buddha Dainichi at the Enjō-ji (Enjō temple) in Nara is one of the sculptures that seem to follow the style seen in the Chōgaku-ji triad. The Dainichi was made in 1176 and is the earliest of Unkei's extant works. The inscription on the pedestal states that the image was made by "true apprentice of Kōkei, Unkei." This inscription is usually interpreted by scholars to mean that Unkei was the son and disciple of Kōkei. Unkei, probably in his mid-twenties, appears to have carved the Buddha under the guidance of his father. The image's rounded cheeks and chin, wide, high knees, and strong articulation of folds reflect a sense of youthfulness. A high topknot and crystal eyes clearly follow the Chōgaku-ji Amida. Overall, the Dainichi retains the grace of the traditional Jōchō style, but Unkei's youthful vigor, seen in this image, indicates his future brilliant career.

Life's Work

Unkei lived during a time of social and political revolution in which power shifted from the aristocracy to the warrior class. In 1192, Minamoto Yoritomo, the leader of the Minamoto clan, which replaced the Taira clan, established its military government (*bakufu*) in Kamakura in eastern Japan. Prior to this action, Nara's most disastrous event had occurred during the war between the two clans: the destruction of the Tōdai-ji and Kōfuku-ji, two important temples, in 1180. The Kei school sculptors contributed their full energy to the reconstruction of the two temples.

Unkei's association with the warrior class began during this period. The Kei school needed powerful support in the new era, since the Kyoto and Kei schools were in conflict over the right to reconstruct the Kōfuku-ji. According to the *Azuma Kagami*, a record compiled in the Kamakura period (1192-1333), the sixth-generation descendant of Jōchō went to eastern Japan and made the temple images for Minamoto Yoritomo in 1185. Scholars are still debating whether Unkei went to the eastern region. Nevertheless, having been invited by two important politicians of the Kamakura *bakufu*, he made the images for two eastern Japanese temples.

In 1186, Unkei carved the images of the Ganjōjuin temple in the prefecture of Shizuoka. Yoritomo's father-in-law, Hōjō Tokimasa, commissioned the project, praying for the success of his northeastern expedition. The images consisted of an Amida, a Fudō, and a Bishamonten; the flanking bodhisattvas of the Amida do not remain. Four inscribed wooden tablets from each figure of the Fudō and Bishamonten prove the images to be Unkei's works.

In 1189, following the Ganjōjuin images, Unkei worked for the Jōraku-ji (Jōraku temple) in the prefecture of Kanagawa. The statues to be made were an Amida, a Fudō, and a Bishamonten. The patron was Wada Yoshimori, another important figure of the Kamakura *bakufu*. Inscribed tablets were also found in each of these statues. They state that these icons were made by Unkei with the help of ten *shōbusshi* (minor sculptors).

Both sets of temple images share common features: iconography, inscribed wooden tablets, and style. This style, which is characterized by a rough, massive body and complicated drapery folds, is dissimilar to his most important works, such as the Enjō-ji Dainichi and Hokuendō Miroku. Thus, the statues were not identified as Unkei's work until all the inscribed tablets were found.

By his mid-thirties, Unkei still had not acquired any honorable titles and the roughness and wildness of the Jōraku-ji and Ganjōjuin images were probably the results of one of his experiments in negating the aristocratic sense of beauty. These *bakufu* commissions were perfect opportunities for him to express himself artistically without any restrictions. Such a trend is particularly noticeable in the Ganjōjuin figures.

In the Ganjōjuin Amida, the work's massiveness and the triangular shape of the drapery on the leg, which is also seen in the Chōgaku-ji Amida, seem to derive from early Heian sculpture. Deeply undulating folds and the preaching mudra (symbolic position of the hands) are often found in work of the Nara period. Unkei's image is an extension of the Chōgaku-ji Amida and shows his study of the classical sculpture. Moreover, the power of the later Amida exceeds that of the classical figures and its realism appeals strongly to the viewer. The realistic facial expressions and movements of the Fudō and Bishamonten also seem to reflect the warrior class's taste and Unkei's interpretation of the people in the eastern region. The wild impression was reduced and became more organized in the later Jōraku-ji images.

Unkei perhaps went back to the Kōfuku-ji and Tōdai-ji reconstruction project after his commissions at Jōraku-ji. He was awarded the Buddhist rank of hōgen (eyes of law) in 1195 for his work at Tōdai-ji. The Kei school, which was treated less favorably than the Kyoto schools in the Kōfuku-ji project, was given great opportunities to work on the Tōdai-ji by the monk Chōgen (one of the men in charge of the restoration) and Yoritomo. While working at Tōdai-ji, Unkei acquired the position of chief sculptor for the Tō-ji (Tō temple) in Kyoto.

The works for Tō-ji were arranged by Mongaku, a monk who was closely associated with Yoritomo. Unkei's relationship with the warrior class was further strengthened by his ties to Mongaku. Unkei also worked on the images for Mongaku's temple, Jingo-ji. Through these works, Unkei learned more about early Heian sculpture; this influence appears in his later images.

In 1202, Unkei made a small Fugen bodhisattva for the regent Konoe Motomichi. This commission indicates that Unkei was finally being favored by the courtiers of Kyoto. During this period, Unkei's studio was located in Kyoto, and he was commissioned by both warriors and aristocrats. His success led to the prosperity of the Kei school.

Two of Unkei's masterpieces, the giant devas at the Tōdai-ji South Gate, were made in 1203 with the help of Kaikei in approximately seventy days. The statues, nearly twenty-eight feet high, present the essence of Kamakura sculpture. The expressions of rage, stances of the bodies, and flowing movements of the costumes are vigorous and tense.

The deities also display perfect studio work. Unkei, Kaikei, and two other *daibusshi* (major sculptors) made the statues in collaboration with sixteen *shōbusshi* (minor sculptors). Because of the statues' similarities, it is almost impossible to distinguish any one sculptor's techniques. Although the *A-gyō* (statue with an open mouth) can be ascribed to Kaikei because of the inscribed names inside it, the two statues were conceived by one person, probably Unkei. Unkei's ability to lead and the organized studio system of the Kei school made this high degree of stylistic consistency possible. Also in 1203 Unkei was promoted to the highest rank, hōin (seal of law), and Kaikei was awarded the hokkyō (bridge of law) rank.

Several years later, with his sons and other Kei school sculptors, Unkei began to work on his last project for Kōfuku-ji. Of these images, the Buddha Miroku and the monks Muchaku and Seshin remain in the Hokuendō hall of the temple. The Miroku, which was finished around 1212, presents a more mature style than the earlier Ganjōjuin and Jōraku-ji figures; this maturity is particularly noticeable in the Buddha's gentle, stable form and slenderness. The massive portrait statues of Muchaku and Seshin demonstrate Unkei's dedication to a more realistic technique, as may be seen in the heavy robes with their roughly carved folds, the static postures, the three-dimensional forms, and the sensitive movement of the hands. Despite this realism, like all Buddhist icons, these statues capture a spiritual truth as well: They represent the eternal truth in the human figure and move the viewer's soul with their ponderous, serious forms.

In his later years, Unkei is known to have worked primarily for the Kamakura *bakufu*. Despite his activity, however, no works remain extant after the Kōfuku-ji Hokuendō images. He is believed to have died in 1223.

Summary

The period from the end of the Heian to early Kamakura was a time of disturbance. The decline of the aristocrats and the rise of the warrior class required a new type of art. Quickly responding to this need, Unkei and other Kei school artists created a new style whose strong, masculine, realistic features were suitable to the taste of the new powers in the land. This realism was also a comment on the sculptors of Nara who had merely tolerated their inferior position. Unkei not only achieved a powerfully innovative individual style but also raised the social status of the entire Kei school with his great insight and leadership.

Historically, Japanese sculpture has almost always made rapid progress under intense foreign influence, particularly from China. Contrary to this trend, starting with the conversion of Jōchō's pure Japanese style, Unkei brought Japanese sculpture to fruition by recapturing the sculptural qualities of classic Japanese works and adding to this legacy a new realism.

Bibliography

Kidder, J. Edward. *The Art of Japan*. New York: Park Lane, 1985. A basic art survey book with rich illustrations. It describes the social, historical, and religious background in relation to the art of Japan.

——————. *Masterpieces of Japanese Sculpture*. Rutland, Vt.: Charles E Tuttle Co., 1961. Covers the development of Japanese sculpture with selected plates and explanatory paragraphs. It includes some of Unkei's most representative works.

Kuno, Takeshi, ed. *A Guide to Japanese Sculpture*. Tokyo: Mayuyama and Co., 1963. Useful for a survey of the major trends in the history of Japanese sculpture. Contains a helpful glossary and charts.

Moran, Sherwood F. "The Statue of Muchaku Hokuendō-Kōfukuji: A Detailed Study." *Arts Asiatiques* 1, no. 1 (1958): 49-64. A technical study of the statue of Muchaku, focusing on the structure and related features. Contains helpful diagrams.

Mōri, Hisashi. *Japanese Portrait Sculpture*. Translated by W. Chie Ichibashi. Tokyo: Kodansha International, 1977. Discusses the history of portrait sculpture from the Nara to the Kamakura periods. Useful for its references to the statues of Muchaku and Seshin.

——————. *Sculpture of the Kamakura Period*. Translated by Katherine Eickmann. New York: John Weatherhill, 1974. A good source covering the full range of Kamakura sculpture; pays special attention to the social and historical background.

Watson, William. *Sculpture of Japan from the Fifth to the Fifteenth Century*. London: Studio, 1959. This work provides a brief description of the styles and historical and religious backgrounds of Japanese sculpture to about 1500.

Yoshiko Kainuma

URBAN II
Odo of Lagery

Born: c. 1042, Châtillon-sur-Marne, France
Died: July 29, 1099; Rome
Areas of Achievement: Government and religion
Contribution: Through the practice of a quiet, astute diplomacy, Urban II laid the foundation for papal supremacy within the medieval church and lifted the papacy to the leadership of Western Christendom during the High Middle Ages.

Early Life

Urban II was born Odo (historians have also found his name referred to as Otto, Otho, or Eudes) in Châtillon-sur-Marne, France. Most scholars place his birth in the year 1042, others as early as 1035. Odo came from a knightly family. His father was Eucher, the lord of Lagery.

From the beginning of his education, Odo was destined to play a role in the reform movement that swept through the Church during the eleventh and twelfth centuries. He began his education for the clergy in the cathedral school at Reims, in northeastern France. There, he studied under Saint Bruno, a canon of the cathedral and master of the school, who later founded the strict Carthusian Order of monks.

Odo's character and administrative talents were recognized early by his superiors at Reims. He rose rapidly through the ranks. He served as canon and around 1055 was appointed archdeacon of the cathedral church. Perhaps following the example of his former teacher, Saint Bruno, Odo sought the more disciplined atmosphere of the monastery. Sometime between 1067 and 1070, he entered the famous monastery of Cluny, just north of Lyons, in central France.

Cluny was the birthplace and incubator of the reform movement. From Saint Hugh, leader of the order during Odo's tenure at Cluny, he learned the art of diplomacy that was to serve him so well later as one of the three reform popes to come out of Cluny. Again, Odo's talents were recognized and appreciated. In 1076, he was appointed prior of the monastery. In 1078, Pope Gregory VII, himself a former monk from Cluny, asked Hugh, then the abbot of Cluny, to send some monks to work under him at Rome. Odo was one of those sent in 1079 or 1080.

Gregory VII appointed Odo Cardinal-Bishop of Ostia. From then until Gregory VII's death in 1085, Odo served as one of his closest advisers. Although he remained close to the Pope, Odo occasionally sent on important missions as papal legate (1082-1085) to France and Germany. During one mission to Germany, Odo was held prisoner (1083-1084) by Emperor Henry IV, the chief opponent of the reform movement in the Church. So closely were Odo and Gregory VII in agreement on the principles and goals of the reform program that, prior to his death, Gregory VII recommended Odo as his successor.

Life's Work

Upon the death of Gregory VII, the cardinals chose as his successor Victor III, also a monk from Cluny. Although Odo opposed Victor III's election, the new pontiff bore him no malice. Indeed, as Victor III lay dying, he chose Odo as his successor. Victor III's choice, and that of Gregory VII, was honored by the cardinals when they met on March 12, 1088, at Terracina, south of Rome. There Odo was unanimously elected pope and took the name Urban II.

The circumstances surrounding Urban II's election exemplified the issues and problems which preoccupied his reign. The cardinals had to meet outside Rome, in Terracina, because Rome was occupied by the antipope Clement III, who enjoyed the support of Henry IV. Indeed, Urban spent most of his reign outside Rome, establishing the legitimacy of his election, upholding the authority of the Pope within the reformed Church, and defending the independence of the Church against the claims of the imperial party.

From the beginning of his reign, Urban II affirmed and pursued the reform policies of Gregory VII. He held a council at Melfi in southern Italy in September, 1089. There, he renewed Gregory VII's decrees against simony, clerical marriage, and lay investiture. He also anathematized both Henry IV and Clement III, an act he repeated several times during his reign. If Urban II agreed in principle with Gregory VII, however, his pursuit of reform was very different.

Urban II was in many ways different from his illustrious predecessor. Contemporary sources describe him as a tall, handsome, bearded man whose speech was eloquent and learned. In his relationships with friend and foe alike, he was friendly, gentle, and always courteous. The fact that he chose to pursue his goals through persuasion rather than direct confrontation did not mean that he was weak. Always uncompromisingly committed to the principles of reform, he cautioned church authorities to exercise reason in their implementation.

As a skillful diplomat, Urban II had few equals. He saw clearly that to maintain the program of reform begun by Gregory VII, it was necessary to win the support of the secular princes. To do so, he chose not to press the exaggerated claims to political sovereignty made by Gregory VII and instead emphasized the spiritual leadership of the Papacy. To combat Henry IV in Germany, Urban II allied himself with Matilda, Countess of Tuscany. He arranged a marriage between the forty-three-year-old countess and the seventeen-year-old Welf V, Duke of Bavaria, whose father had been deposed by Henry IV. By astute diplomacy, in 1093, Urban II was able to attract

Henry IV's son, Conrad, to the alliance with Matilda and Welf V.

Urban II was rewarded for diplomatic maneuvers. In 1093, he was able to enter Rome, and on Easter, 1094, he sat on the papal throne for the first time. His entry into the Lateran Palace was achieved by "diplomacy." The governor of the Lateran Palace offered to surrender it in exchange for a bribe supplied by a wealthy abbot. The event signaled the defeat of Henry IV's ambitions in Italy and, with them, those of Clement III.

Throughout his struggle with Henry IV, Urban II never ceased in his efforts to reform church government. His efforts were directed at increased centralization. His goal was a papal monarchy modeled after that of the secular princes. The role of the College of Cardinals, founded in 1059, was transformed. The cardinals henceforth had authority to excommunicate secular and ecclesiastical lords and to decide disputed episcopal elections. As with the king's council in England and France, the College of Cardinals became the Pope's supreme advisory body, participating in the highest levels of church government.

As the cardinals became a more integral part of the administrative structure of church government, political duties distracted them from their traditional religious functions. These were increasingly assigned to chaplains. Thus, Urban II gave birth to the papal chapel, which, like the new role of the College of Cardinals, was modeled after the chapels at the courts of the secular kings.

Similarly, Urban II reorganized papal finances and the papal secretariat. He chose Cluny as the model for the former and appointed a monk from Cluny as the first treasurer, or *camerarius*. Many scholars believe that Urban II's creation of the papal treasury (*camera*) was one of his most important innovations in church government.

Nothing demonstrated Urban II's success in enhancing the position of the Papacy more than his initiation of the Crusades. His call, at the Council of Clermont in 1095, for a crusade to rescue the Holy Land from the clutches of the Seljuk Turks was one of the key events of the Middle Ages. It was in part a culmination of efforts by Urban II to restore the unity between the Western and Eastern churches fragmented since the schism of 1054.

Soon after his election as Pope, Urban II opened negotiations with the Eastern Christians. He met with ambassadors from the Byzantine court at the Council of Melfi in 1089. There, in their presence, he lifted the ban of excommunication against the Emperor Alexius I. Another embassy from Alexius visited Urban II in 1090. It may be assumed that at these and other possible meetings, Alexius' desire for Western military aid against the Turks and Urban II's desire for unity between the two churches were discussed.

By March, 1095, Urban II felt secure enough to call the first great council of his reign at Piacenza, north of Rome. Ambassadors from Constantinople were present and may have addressed the assembly. For the first time,

Urban II called upon the Christian knights of Western Europe to go to the aid of the Eastern Christians. It was at the Council of Clermont in Auvergne, France, in November, 1095, however, that the effectual call went out—and the call was heard.

Some thirteen archbishops, two hundred bishops, more than ninety abbots, and thousands of nobles and knights assembled before Urban II at Clermont. It was the moment of triumph not only for Urban II but also for the reformed Church. Standing before the crowd on a specially constructed platform in an open field, Urban II, with all of his eloquence, called on the knighthood of Western Christendom to embark on an armed pilgrimage to Jerusalem. When he finished speaking, the crowd spontaneously broke out with shouts of "God wills it."

Following Clermont, Urban II continued to preach the crusade at subsequent synods and councils, while consolidating his control of the Church. A group of Crusaders stopped off at Rome on their way to the Holy Land and drove the antipope, Clement III, from the city. Clement retired to his archbishopric of Ravenna. Jerusalem fell to the first wave of Crusaders on July 15, 1099. Urban II never heard of the victory. He died two weeks later, on July 29, in Rome.

Summary

The Council of Clermont was the crowning achievement of Urban II's reign. His speech before the assembled ecclesiastical and secular lords has been ranked with the great orations of history. At Clermont, the Pope supplanted the Holy Roman Emperor as the leader of Western Christendom. Historians often view the Crusades as Europe's first imperialistic venture and note that economic greed played a key motivational role. In the context of the High Middle Ages, however, the Crusades were, above all, a religiously motivated pilgrimage. Proclaiming the Crusades brought unity to Western Christendom and elevated the Pope to the moral leadership of Europe for the next two centuries.

It may be argued that the Crusades eventually undermined papal leadership in European affairs. Renewed contact between Western Europe and the Levant awakened forces that had been dormant in Europe since the fall of the Roman Empire in the fifth century. The Renaissance of the fourteenth and fifteenth centuries, the scientific revolution of the fifteenth and sixteenth centuries, and the rise of the secular nation-state were all stimulated by the Crusades. Each in its own way contributed to the eventual fragmentation of the Church in the West and the loss of papal leadership in Europe.

Urban II's greatest achievement lay in his creation of the Papal Curia. By giving the Church a monarchical form of government, complete with an administrative structure modeled after the courts of the kings of England and France, Urban II placed the Papacy on an equal footing with the secular monarchs. As with the courts of the kings, the papal court was henceforth both a central administration and a court of law. The power and influence of the Pope has waxed and waned since Urban II's reign, but the Curia he founded has only grown stronger.

Bibliography
Barraclough, Geoffrey. *The Medieval Papacy*. New York: Harcourt, Brace and World, 1968. Chapter 3, "The Age of Reform," discusses Urban II's role as a reform pope. It is particularly helpful for understanding his contributions to the construction of the papal monarchy. The emphasis is on Urban II's pontificate as a turning point in the history of the medieval church.

Krey, August C. *The First Crusade: The Accounts of Eye-Witnesses and Participants*. Gloucester, Mass.: Peter Smith, 1958. This source is of particular value not only for its factual content but also for its ability to communicate a sense of participation. Urban II's role in the summoning of the First Crusade is seen through the words of those who were present.

Mourret, Fernand. *A History of the Catholic Church*. Vol. 4, *Period of the Later Middle Ages*. St. Louis: B. Herder Book Co., 1947. Chapter 6, "From the Death of St. Gregory VII to the Death of Urban II (1085-99)," deals with Urban II's reign as Pope. The emphasis is on his struggle to reform the Church and defend its independence from imperial control.

Runciman, Steven. *A History of the Crusades*. Vol. 1, *The First Crusade and the Foundation of the Kingdom of Jerusalem*. London: Cambridge University Press, 1968. Perhaps one of the best histories of the Crusades. Volume 1 provides an in-depth understanding of the background and course of the First Crusade. In addition to Urban II's role in the First Crusade, Runciman provides some information about his early life and election to the papacy.

Tanner, J. R., C. W. Previté-Orton, and Z. N. Brooke, eds. *The Cambridge Medieval History*. Vol. 5, *Contest and Empire*, edited by J. B. Bury. London: Cambridge University Press, 1968. Chapter 2, "Gregory VII and the First Contest Between Empire and Papacy," discusses the reform movement within the Church and the accompanying clash with imperial interests. Urban's role in initiating the First Crusade is examined in chapter 7, "The First Crusade."

Paul R. Waibel

VALDEMAR II

Born: May 9, 1170; Denmark
Died: March 28, 1241; Vordingborg, Denmark
Areas of Achievement: Government and conquest
Contribution: Valdemar II was a warrior, lawgiver, builder, and Crusader. He extended Danish control over North Germany, Scandia, and Estonia, leaving to his successors the dream of an empire extending over the Baltic Sea.

Early Life

Valdemar I (1157-1182) had brought to an end the long struggles between the Church and Crown for dominance in the north. Working with Absalon, the Archbishop of Lund, he began a crusading program which secured internal peace through external expansion, occupying the military talents of potentially rebellious nobles in defeating Wendish pagans on the Mecklenburg coast and islands and seizing Scandia (the southern part of modern Sweden), while establishing royal authority inside the kingdom. His defeat of the Wendish pirates made possible the rapid expansion of agriculture, the foundation of towns, and the growth of international trade. He secured his mainland conquests by wedding his sons, Canute (Knut) and Valdemar, to daughters of the Welf prince, Henry the Lion, Duke of Saxony.

Canute VI (1182-1202) continued this program, with his brother Valdemar's help, by occupying Mecklenburg, Holstein, and the archbishopric of Hamburg-Bremen. Canute was not a modern nationalist. He paid little attention to the ethnic origin of his subjects, and since his Danish-speaking subjects were hardly numerous enough to settle on the underpopulated mainland coast, the principal beneficiaries of his policies were German fishermen, peasants, burghers, and petty nobles. With Canute's encouragement, they founded towns, exploited the herring grounds, and traded in Gotland, Livonia (modern Latvia), and Russia. Canute's Wendish vassals introduced Germans into their lands in such numbers as to change the ethnic composition of Mecklenburg. Canute relied greatly on his vigorous younger brother, Valdemar, because he himself was too weak to lead armies in the field. Consequently, when Canute died childless at a relatively young age, Valdemar came to the throne well prepared for his duties and confident of his ability to continue the dynasty's program.

Life's Work

The political situation in 1202 was extremely favorable for Valdemar. The Holy Roman Empire was in political turmoil: Pope Innocent III was playing the Welf and Hohenstaufen factions against each other, encouraging the weaker of the two parties to continue its efforts to secure the throne. Valdemar intervened in the North, replacing some local rulers and rewarding others, thus consolidating his empire in Germany while winning papal thanks for his contributions to the Church's cause. Afterward, neither the Welf emperor, Otto IV, nor the Hohenstaufen, Frederick II, dared attack him. Frederick even confirmed his rights to the lands north of the Elbe in a Golden Bull.

Valdemar's policies on the mainland were not uniformly successful. His decision to send his sister, Ingeborg, to marry Philip Augustus of France was an embarrassing debacle. His decision to release Valdemar of Schleswig from prison cost him years of conflict in Hamburg-Bremen. He seemed, however, to have the golden touch in the Baltic.

Valdemar envisioned extending his rule over all the still-pagan shores of the eastern sea—over Pomerania, Prussia, Kurland (Courland), Livonia, and Estonia. His first step came in 1202, in his approval of the crusading mission of Bishop Albert to Riga in Livonia in return for recognition of Valdemar's overlordship. In 1206, Valdemar himself led a force to Oesel, the largest of the Estonian islands, to intimidate the fierce pirates there. In 1210, he raided Samland in Prussia. Still, he had to secure peace in North Germany before he could take a major force to the east. Peace came in 1215, followed quickly by the news that Bishop Albert's Crusaders were making such rapid headway in Livonia that they would soon overstep the agreed northern boundary of their conquests; moreover, they were refusing to recognize Valdemar as overlord.

In 1219, Valdemar sailed with a great army to Estonia. The overawed tribesmen surrendered so quickly that Valdemar became careless about his personal safety. When attacking natives penetrated right into the royal tent, they killed Valdemar's newly appointed bishop of Estonia and missed the king only because his modest clothing gave little clue as to his status. Valdemar, fighting courageously at the head of his Danish, German, and Wendish vassals, crushed the uprising, built a castle at Reval (Tallinn) and went home determined to humble Bishop Albert's unruly Crusaders. He brought home the *Dannebrog*, the distinctive red banner with a white cross, which had fallen from Heaven to encourage his Crusaders at a critical moment and which became the Danish standard.

A similar lapse of attention in May of 1223 cost Valdemar greatly. He invited Count Henry (Heinrich) of Schwerin to accompany him hunting on the island of Lyø. A few years earlier, Henry's brother had given a daughter as wife to Valdemar's eldest son. Though the couple died soon after their wedding, Valdemar was claiming half of Schwerin as the dowry. Henry, desperate to avoid this debt, kidnapped Valdemar and his eldest son—who had been made joint king in 1218—and imprisoned them in Dannenberg.

Papal threats failed to move Count Henry, who understandably feared Valdemar's revenge. Henry organized a coalition of local nobles and prelates which defeated Valdemar's allies in 1225, then expelled the Danish appointees to office and divided the spoils. Meanwhile, the news of Valdemar's fall had precipitated a rebellion in Estonia which was crushed by Livonian Crusaders, who henceforth occupied that land. Henry was then in a position to ransom the king for a large sum and his promise to surrender all territorial claims in North Germany. Valdemar retained control of Rügen and Estonia.

Valdemar sought to recover his losses by force of arms but was defeated on July 22, 1227, at Bornhöved, after which he abandoned his hopes of a mainland empire. He retained Estonia by diplomacy, through the Treaty of Stenby, in 1238.

The king contented himself with domestic affairs, particularly law reform. His codification of Jutland law was completed only a few days before his death in 1241. His children by Richza of Saxony and Margarete of Bohemia died before him. His sons by Berengaria of Portugal each, in turn, became king; Eric from 1241 to 1250, Abel from 1250 to 1252, and Christopher from 1252 to 1259. Their mutual hatred disrupted the kingdom and brought an end to the hard-won unity and internal peace of the Valdemar era.

Summary

The age of the Valdemars, from 1157 to 1241, was the most glorious era of Danish medieval history. For a short period, brilliant churchmen and monarchs ended the endemic civil wars, expanded trade, created a great empire, built churches and cathedrals, and established the kingdom on a hereditary basis.

Denmark profited greatly from the long era of internal peace and stability. The population grew steadily and more land was brought under cultivation. This provided the taxes and tithes which built palaces, cathedrals, and churches.

The king abandoned the common levy for raising troops, relying instead on prominent warriors and rich farmers, who were freed from taxation in return for serving as royal officials and mounted troops. These knights soon became a new nobility. Though bound to the king by an oath, in time they tended to work more for their own interests than those of the monarchy.

Another enduring accomplishment of the period was securing the safety of international trade across the Baltic Sea. Merchants from the Holy Roman Empire sailed east under Danish protection. Although Lübeck owed its rise to prominence to Valdemar II's policy of supporting merchants against local nobles, the merchants naturally chafed against any tax or interference in their affairs. Consequently, Lübeck joined Count Henry's coalition and made a significant contribution at the Battle of Bornhöved. The citizens' subsequent alliances with other growing mercantile communities were forerunners of the Hanseatic League. Valdemar's successors were to wage long wars against Lübeck and the League in an effort to re-create his Baltic empire, but with equal lack of ultimate success.

Valdemar II was a great warrior and an effective administrator, especially when he had the services of gifted vassals and churchmen. His self-confidence led him to be somewhat careless about his personal safety and less than thoughtful about the long-term results of his policies. His failure to instill brotherly love among his sons serves well to illustrate his shortcomings as man and ruler. Similarly, he failed to make the nobles more concerned for their country than for themselves or to reconcile his mainland subjects to Danish rule. These shortcomings were not made good by successors who modeled themselves on him.

Bibliography

Birch, J. H. S. *Denmark in History*. Westport, Conn.: Greenwood Press, 1975. This standard survey summarizes adequately the insights of the many historians who publish in Danish and German.

Christiansen, Eric. *The Northern Crusades: The Baltic and the Catholic Frontier, 1100-1525*. Minneapolis: University of Minnesota Press, 1980. Good background to the Wendish and Estonian Crusades, the origins of the Hanseatic League, and the long contest for hegemony over the Baltic Sea.

King, Wilson. *Chronicles of Three Free Cities: Hamburg, Bremen, and Lübeck*. London: J. M. Dent and Sons, 1914. An old-fashioned romantic history, but timeless good reading.

Lauring, Palle. *Denmark, a History*. Copenhagen: Host and Son, 1986. This is the seventh edition of a highly respected general survey.

Urban, William. *The Baltic Crusade*. DeKalb: Northern Illinois University Press, 1975. This volume describes the situation in the Holy Roman Empire before and after 1200 which made Valdemar's empire possible. There are detailed descriptions of Valdemar's policies, his crusades to Estonia, and his kidnapping and fall.

William L. Urban

VALENTINUS

Born: Probably early second century; Lower Egypt
Died: c. 165; Cyprus or Rome
Areas of Achievement: Religion and philosophy
Contribution: A second century religious genius, Valentinus synthesized concepts drawn from such disparate sources as Christian theology, rabbinic mysticism, Neopythagoreanism, Neoplatonism, Hellenistic mystery religions, and theosophy into an elaborate system of Gnostic thought that attracted large numbers of converts in the patristic period. His influence was so great that the patristic heresiologists singled him out as one of the most formidable enemies of orthodox Christianity.

Early Life

Very little is known of Valentinus' early life, except that he probably was born in Lower Egypt and obtained a Greek education in Alexandria. During his stay in Alexandria, he became a Christian; according to Irenaeus and others, he was taught by Theodas, one of the Apostle Paul's students.

Some authors have suggested that Gnosticism influenced Valentinus even during these early days in Alexandria and that Theodas himself may have preached a Christian gnosis. The Gnostic stress on salvation through a secret gnosis, or transcendental knowledge, must have appealed to Valentinus, whose teachings, to the extent that they can be reconstructed from the scattered information found in writings of the church fathers who came to oppose him (and perhaps also from the Nag Hammadi papyruses), reflect an exceptionally creative mind with a strong aesthetic bent.

Life's Work

Valentinus apparently taught in Alexandria before going to Rome during the bishopric of Hyginus (c. 136-c. 140). Tertullian states that Valentinus himself became Bishop of Rome but withdrew in favor of a man who was later martyred (probably Pius I). In fact, Valentinus also withdrew from the Christian community, for he had become a Gnostic; soon, the Church branded him a heretic. Subsequently, Valentinus gained a considerable following—he probably established his own school—and he remained in Rome for another twenty years, after which he may have gone to Cyprus; it is possible that he stayed in Rome until his death after 160.

Valentinus' move into Gnosticism may have been the result of a desire to go beyond the exclusivist teachings of Christianity and to integrate Jesus Christ's teachings with contemporary Hellenistic philosophies. Valentinus' teaching was done in the form of sermons, hymns, and psalms, as well as more formally through writing and lecturing.

Valentinian Gnosticism evolved so rapidly that it is difficult to disentangle the original Valentinian teachings from those of his disciples. Still, the Nag Hammadi works, combined with the heresiologies of the patristic writers, make it possible to describe the outlines of the Valentinian system.

As its core, it had a mythical cosmogony, offered as an explanation of the human predicament. This cosmogony was structured around "aeons": Everything that exists is an emanation of a perfect, primordially existent aeon, which is the origin and source of being for all subsequent aeons. The term "aeon" in the Valentinian system suggests eternal existence (*aei on*, "always being"). This means that in terms of temporal sequence there is no difference between the One and its progeny. The difference between them is, instead, ontological: All subsequent aeons are less perfect outpourings of the One's substance. The One is also called Proarche (First Principle), Propator (Forefather), and Buthos (Primeval Depth). The One is beyond conceptualization and is the storehouse of all perfections. In Buthos there is no difference of gender; it contains all the qualities of masculinity and femininity without distinction.

According to its inscrutable purpose, Buthos brings into being a sequence of secondary aeons. Unlike Buthos, this chain of beings is differentiated into gender pairs, or syzygies, arranged according to ontological perfection (relative perfection of being). Of these fifteen pairs, which together constitute the Pleroma (Fullness or Completion), only the first four and the last have significance in the Valentinian exposition of the ontological corruption of the universe.

The first syzygy is somewhat problematic, since Buthos transcends the qualities of masculinity and femininity yet is paired with Sige (Silence). From this first syzygy emanate Nous (Understanding) and Aletheia (Truth). From their union are produced Logos (Word) and Zoe (Life), and from the union of Logos and Zoe are produced Anthropos (Man) and Ekklesia (Church). Together, these four pairs (or two tetrads) form the Ogdoad (the Eight), from which issue the remaining eleven syzygies and, indeed, all the rest of reality.

According to the Valentinians, disharmony was introduced into reality in the following way. Of all the aeons, it was Nous who was best proportioned to understand the One and who took the greatest pleasure in this contemplation. Nous, in the abundance of his generosity, wished to share his knowledge with the other aeons, and the aeons themselves demonstrated a willingness to seek out and become more directly acquainted with the primacy and fullness of the One. Yet Nous was restrained from prematurely sharing this knowledge, for it was the desire of Buthos to lead the aeons to this awareness gradually, through steady application which might prove their worthiness. Buthos also was aware that the aeons had different capacities and therefore would have to be brought to this knowledge at different rates. The knowledge of Buthos' purpose was passed down through the successive aeons, and all except the malcontent Sophia (Wisdom) acceded to his will.

Sophia's desire could not be satisfied by either her station or her mate, Theletos (Will). She craved knowledge beyond her capacity: She wanted to comprehend the perfect wisdom of the Forefather. In her desire to grasp supernatural perfection, Sophia abandoned her station and stretched herself heavenward, nearly losing her distinctive character by being reabsorbed into the plentitude of the One, against its will. Alarmed by the hubris of Sophia, Buthos, in conjunction with Nous, generated Horos, the principle of limitation, who is also called Savior, One-Who-Imposes-Limitation, One-Who-Brings-Back-After-Conflict, and Cross. Horos was generated by Buthos for the purpose of restraining Sophia and stripping her of her presumptuousness. This was accomplished when Horos separated her from her passion and *enthumesis* (esteem, glory) and rejoined the purged Sophia to Theletos, while casting her passion in the abyss outside the Pleroma.

After the rebelliousness of Sophia was cast out, Buthos and Nous gave rise to another syzygy designed to perfect and strengthen the Pleroma. This syzygy is that of Christ and the Holy Spirit. Christ was sent to the aeons as a teacher to instruct them in the purpose of Buthos, leading them to be satisfied with the knowledge they possess by convincing them that only Nous can comprehend the One in its perfection. The aeon Christ thus was sent as a mediator of consoling knowledge concerning their stations and purpose. The Holy Spirit's function was to lead the aeons to give thanks for the knowledge revealed by Christ. Through contrition and thankfulness they were all brought into harmony.

The work of Christ, however, was not yet complete. The *enthumesis* and passion of Sophia had been banished from the Pleroma to smolder, a chaotic, self-consuming power without form and without purpose. The aeon Christ, seeing her state, did not forsake her but instead took pity on her. He extended himself beyond the limit of the Pleroma and imposed a substantial form upon her, to give her a definite nature; he withdrew, however, before providing transcendental wisdom. The dim reflection of Sophia was thus given character and definition as Achamoth (Hebrew for "wisdom"). The form Christ provided resulted in a regretful awareness of Achamoth's severance from the Pleroma and made her aspire to immortality with her limited intelligence. From the confusion of passions that boiled in Achamoth, the matter of the world issued, and from the desire to return to unity with the One, all souls (including that of the Demiurge) sprang into being.

From her own psychic substance, Achamoth formed the Demiurge, but she concealed herself from him. The Demiurge, not recognizing another greater than himself, deluded himself into believing that he was the only creator god, and he immediately began to make corporeal substances and to populate the realm below Horos with all manner of things. It is he who is responsible for the creation of the seven heavens and everything in or under them. All the while he was creating, however, he was unaware that Achamoth was working through him and was adding spiritual substances to the psychic beings (animals) he created. Humans are therefore composites of matter, psyche, and spirit, although the Demiurge is ignorant of their spiritual dimension.

Achamoth, feeling pity and responsibility for the spiritual beings she had generated, decided to bring them to knowledge of the aeons. To give this knowledge to the Demiurge and his creation, she imitated the production of the Christ aeon and contributed a spiritual substance to a body prepared by the Demiurge in ignorance. The resulting composite being was Jesus the Savior. Jesus' mission thus was primarily a ministry of teaching; his mission was to teach the gnosis of the aeonic hierarchy. His mission will be accomplished when all worthy creations below the Pleroma are brought to perfection in knowledge. Then Achamoth and her perfected children will ascend to places above the Horos. The Demiurge will ascend to the eighth heaven along with those beings of a purely psychic nature, and the purely corporeal humans will be consumed in a final conflagration.

From complicated cosmological speculations such as these, the Valentinians wove a fabric of doctrines that resembled Christianity but that were, in every instance, of a much higher speculative order. Like the traditional Christians, the Valentinians had a distinctive Christology. Whereas the former emphasized the sacrificial death of Jesus as the means of remission of sins, the Valentinians thought that the spirit of Jesus ascended before he could suffer, a belief consistent with their understanding of his aeonic mission of teaching.

Anthropologically, traditional Christianity interpreted all humans as being equally capable of finding salvation in Jesus, since he had died for all. The Valentinians, however, worked out a doctrine of election that in some ways anticipated Calvinist teachings. They believed that the salvation of a given individual depended upon whether Achamoth had implanted a bit of spiritual substance, a seed of light, in that individual. Those who are spiritual have the potential (if not certainty) of achieving gnosis and thus being raptured and carried aloft to the Pleroma. The best that other humans may hope for is either a place in the eighth heaven or to be burned as garbage at the end of time.

Ecclesiologically, Valentinians construed the body of Gnostics on earth as a dim reflection of the aeon Ekklesia. Basing their speculation upon certain passages in Saint Paul and upon obscure rabbinic doctrines, they saw the syzygy of Anthropos and Ekklesia as the Platonic archetype of the relationship which eventually will exist between Achamoth and the pneumatics. In the final rapture, Achamoth will be conjoined to her seeds of light in the nuptial chamber of the Pleroma. At that point, symmetry will be restored to the chain of aeons and the universe will exist in harmony, with the lower syzygies mirroring their higher paradigms and beings of all levels finding perfect satisfaction.

On the basis of this rich and intricate mythology and its resultant theology, the Valentinians taught a form of Christian theosophy which gained large numbers of converts in the second and third centuries. Of all the forms of Gnosticism it attracted the most followers. How such a complicated and seemingly arbitrary religious cosmology could have inspired droves to seek this brand of salvation is puzzling, but there are a few features which likely made it attractive.

First, it offered a kind of salvation that placed a premium upon knowledge and de-emphasized the moral rigor that was typical of the Christianity of the period. This, no doubt, appealed to the classes that Gnosticism attracted: the plebeians and the intellectual elite, who had no strong political or religious alliances but rather identified with their plebeian followers.

Second, although the Valentinians shunned the sacramentalism of many of the other Christian sects, they apparently practiced rituals of purification and made use of hymns and prayers, all of which were designed to culminate in a powerful ecstatic experience in which the individual would achieve spiritual intercourse with Achamoth in her nuptial chamber. In this way, Valentinian Gnosticism offered an experience which at least rivaled the charismatic experiences of the more traditional Christian groups.

Finally, a large part of the appeal of Valentinian theosophy was that it was continuous with other religious phenomena of the time. In that turbulent period when religious curiosity ran rampant and when contact with magicians, astrologers, and itinerant preachers of wisdom was the norm, Valentinian theosophy offered a model of the universe which allowed for the retention of a magical worldview. Unlike traditional Christianity, which was extremely strict in its rejection of alien gods and magic, the Valentinian system was syncretistic. It allowed its adepts to move freely between its sphere of concepts and other systems of theosophy and magic.

Summary

Valentinus had a very large following and probably was the most influential of the Gnostics. There is no doubt that his teaching affected orthodox Christianity. Many Christian theologians were forced to sharpen their rhetorical and theological skills as they undertook to refute the Valentinians, and, as they engaged in this dialogue, they began to formulate explicit orthodox Christian doctrines and creeds. Valentinus, as a representative of Gnosticism, spurred Christians toward the establishment of a canon of inspired Scriptures so that they might be able to avoid syncretism and heresy.

Valentinus was very much a man of the second century in his tendency toward religious syncretism, evidenced by his application of Neoplatonic and Neopythagorean concepts to Christian theology. Thus, Valentinus' thought was a representative form of the prototheology which developed dialectically in the early Christian milieu.

Bibliography

Jonas, Hans. *The Gnostic Religion: The Message of the Alien God and the Beginnings of Christianity*. Boston: Beacon Press, 1963. A classic (although somewhat dated) and thorough introduction to the nature of Gnosticism. Useful because it describes the Gnostic categories and discusses various Gnostic systems. Shows how Gnosticism is both an interruption and a continuation of classic Greek thought. Chapter 5 constitutes a helpful treatment of Valentinus' system. Thorough, multilanguage bibliography.

Lacarrière, Jacques. *The Gnostics*. New York: E. P. Dutton, 1977. Phenomenological treatment of Gnosticism, but only partly successful since the author regards Gnostics as Promethean heroes rebelling against established religion, and his bias is evident throughout. Valuable as a lively interpretation of the Gnostic mind-set. Chapter 6 deals with Valentinus in some detail. Contains a somewhat quirky bibliography.

Pagels, Elaine. *The Gnostic Gospels*. New York: Random House, 1979. Popular treatment, readable and interesting, but unsystematic. The feminist views of the author are evident. Tends to discuss the individualism of Gnostics in a manner inappropriate to the period and to impose twentieth century values on the second century. Valentinus is treated throughout rather than in a separate chapter. No bibliography.

Perkins, Pheme. *The Gnostic Dialogue*. New York: Paulist Press, 1980. In part a response and corrective to some extremes in Pagels' work, this is a scholarly attempt to contextualize Gnosticism in setting of particular scriptural traditions, with research based on texts. Investigates Gnosticism in dialogue with Christianity and other religions. Valentinus is treated throughout. Good selected multilanguage bibliography; especially helpful are the references to the Nag Hammadi, the New Testament, and patristic sources.

Robinson, James M., ed. *The Nag Hammadi Library*. New York: Harper and Row, Publishers, 1977. The single most revealing collection of Gnostic scriptures available in English translation. Particularly useful because it contains fragments of second century treatises of probable or certain Gnostic origin such as the *Gospel of Truth*, the *Treatise on Resurrection*, the *Tripartite Tractate*, the *Apocalypse of Paul*, *A Valentinian Exposition*, *On the Anointing*, *On Baptism*, and *On the Eucharist*.

Rudolph, Kurt. *Gnosis: The Nature and History of Gnosticism*. San Francisco: Harper and Row, Publishers, 1983. A comprehensive treatment by a specialist in Mandaean religion. Valentinus is cited frequently throughout, and the treatment of the Valentinian system is extensive. Extremely sensitive to all sources in all their complexity, though some Marxist bias is evident. Illustrations, photographs, maps, chronological table, and a multi-language bibliography of original texts and secondary sources.

Thomas Ryba
Ruth van der Maas

VARDHAMĀNA

Born: c. 599 B.C.; Kundagrama, Bihar, India
Died: 527 B.C.; Papa, Bihar, India
Areas of Achievement: Religion and monasticism
Contribution: By the example of his ascetic life and his charismatic leadership, Vardhamāna revived and systematized the religious tradition of Jainism.

Early Life

While the two sects of the Jains (Digambara and Svetambara) have differing traditions regarding the life of Vardhamāna, they are in agreement on the most essential features. Vardhamāna was born to Siddhartha, chieftain of a warrior (*ksatriya*) clan, whose wife Trisala was the sister of the king of Vaisali. Vardhamāna's conception was foretold to his mother in a series of dreams which are often described in Jain literature and represented artistically. About his youth virtually nothing is recorded, but probably he was trained in archery, horsemanship, and writing, as were other princes of his era. The two Jain sects disagree regarding one point concerning his adult life, the Svetambaras saying that Vardhamāna married and fathered one daughter, while the Digambaras say that he neither married nor had offspring.

By the age of thirty, Vardhamāna's parents had died. With the consent of his elder brother, he decided to abandon his royal position and become a wandering ascetic. He distributed his possessions, plucked out his hair, and renounced the life of the householder to pursue enlightenment. The most significant disagreement between the two sects of Jainism is highlighted by this incident in Vardhamāna's life, known as the Great Renunciation. Digambara ("sky-clad") Jains depict Vardhamāna as renouncing clothing as well as other possessions, choosing to remain nude and requiring this practice of his followers when they renounced the world. Svetambara ("white-clad") Jains depict Vardhamāna as wearing a single white cloth for thirteen months after the Great Renunciation, at which time he adopted nudity but did not require it of his followers after their renunciation. This difference in monastic practice has kept the two sects separate since about 300 B.C.

Life's Work

In the era in which Vardhamāna lived, dissatisfaction was growing with the then dominant religious tradition of Brahmanism, which was based on performance of sacrificial rituals and recitation of the sacred words of the Vedas. Asceticism—including endurance of hunger, thirst, pain, exposure to the elements, and celibacy—was an alternative way of being religious, by means of which individuals sought to accumulate power. It was widely believed that the actions (Karma) of one's life would cause one to be reincarnated but that the power accumulated through asceticism could enable one to destroy one's Karma and escape the otherwise endless cycle of rebirth.

Like a number of his contemporaries (such as the Buddha and ascetics of the Brahmanic Upanishads), Vardhamāna left his family to live as a homeless wanderer in the hope of escaping rebirth. For twelve years, subjecting himself to great hardship, including extended fasts, and engaged in deep meditation on the nature of the self, Vardhamāna single-mindedly persevered. Finally, after a fast of two and a half days during which he meditated continuously, he attained enlightenment accompanied by omniscience and was freed from the bondage of his Karma. According to the scriptures, following his enlightenment Vardhamāna taught large assemblies of listeners and organized the community of monks, nuns, laymen, and laywomen. He was acclaimed as Mahāvīra (Great Hero), a title by which he is best known.

Vardhamāna Mahāvīra taught others the means of attaining what he had attained. The ultimate objective was and is escape from the cycle of rebirth, with its suffering a result of the inevitability of disease, old age, and death. The infinite bliss of the cessation of such suffering was not to be attained by following the path of enjoyment of pleasures but by forsaking the finite pleasures and performing rigorous austerities. Restraint of body, speech, and mind and the performance of ascetic practices will destroy the effects of one's Karma, thereby freeing one from rebirth.

In Vardhamāna's view, Karma is a material substance which becomes attached to one's soul as a result of actions performed; Jainism is unique in its assertion of the material nature of Karma. The souls of individuals who are subject to the passions (desire and hatred) will be further defiled by the adherence of Karmic material, while the souls of those few individuals who are free from the passions will not be affected at all; Karma will not adhere to such a soul.

Absolutely necessary to the successful escape from rebirth is the avoidance of causing injury to living beings, a practice known as *ahimsa*. As a consequence of this strongly held belief, Jains are strict vegetarians. For the same reason, they have traditionally avoided occupations involving injury to living beings, including farming, and have instead often engaged in commerce. Avoidance of injury to life in all of its forms is the first vow of the Jains, ascetics and lay followers alike.

The path of the devout layman or laywoman differs from that of the monk or nun only in the extent to which ascetic self-denial is practiced. For the lay follower, eleven stages of spiritual progress are prescribed by which one is purified and prepares oneself for the ascetic life of the monk or nun. By passing through all eleven stages, the lay follower demonstrates that he or she has overcome the passions and is ready to become a monk or nun. As a result of the severity of the rules of conduct for the Jain lay follower, relatively few individuals in reality are willing or able to adhere to this ideal.

Most lay followers support the monks and nuns through donations.

All Jains regard Vardhamāna Mahāvīra as the twenty-fourth and last Jina (Conqueror) or Tirthamkara (Crossing-Maker) to have lived and taught in this world. His immediate predecessor, Parsva, apparently lived in Benares, India, in the ninth century B.C.; Western scholars, however, regard the other twenty-two saintly teachers in the Jain tradition as figures of myth rather than history. The parents of Vardhamāna are described as followers of Parsva's doctrine, and there are clear references in Buddhist scriptures to the existence of an established order of Jain ascetics. This information suggests the existence of a Jain community composed of ascetics and lay followers, a community older than that of the Buddhists and predating Vardhamāna himself. Vardhamāna's teachings are presented as eternal truths and the same path as has been taught by all the Jinas. Thus, Vardhamāna's contribution was the reviving and reactualization of this ancient tradition. As one who has "crossed over" the ocean of suffering and reached the other side, Vardhamāna has demonstrated the efficacy of the spiritual discipline of the Jinas.

At the age of seventy-two, Vardhamāna died, passing into the eternal peace of Nirvana. Although the Jain scriptures repeatedly state that the Jina was a human being, lay followers often have regarded him as superhuman and endowed with marvelous attributes. The exemplary life of Vardhamāna Mahāvīra has greatly influenced the Jain community, which continues to revere his memory.

Summary

Vardhamāna Mahāvīra was both a very able organizer and a thinker of striking originality. The social organization of Jain monks and nuns may well have been the world's first monastic orders. Thanks to the support of some Indian rulers and sympathetic lay followers, the monastic orders have been able to follow the example of Vardhamāna Mahāvīra for twenty-five centuries. Vardhamāna was one of the first to oppose the Brahmanic orthodoxy, a tradition of sacrificial ritual which was dominated by priests and aristocrats. In its place he offered a systematic explanation of the laws of the universe and humanity's place within it. Vardhamāna's teachings presented to everyone the possibility of attaining the ultimate state, whether female or male, regardless of social class.

The Jain insistence on *ahimsa*, refraining from injuring living beings, has influenced the whole of India and even some who are unfamiliar with Jainism. Vegetarianism, uncommon in India during Vardhamāna's lifetime, is now a way of life for many Hindus, and Jainism's uncompromising position is in part responsible for this change. The leader of India's independence movement in the first half of the twentieth century, Mahatma Gandhi, was profoundly influenced by a Jain layman named Raychandbhai Mehta, with whom he corresponded. He helped Gandhi realize the power of nonviolence, and Gandhi began to use nonviolent civil disobedience as a political weapon, agitating for India's independence from the British Empire. A generation later, Martin Luther King, Jr., with Gandhi as his inspiration, led similar nonviolent protests for civil rights in the United States. Vardhamāna's teachings, whether regarded as the ancient doctrine of all the Jinas or as his own unique contribution, are the core of a still-vital religious tradition.

Bibliography
Bloomfield, Maurice. *The Life and Stories of the Jaina Savior Parsvanatha*. Baltimore: Johns Hopkins University Press, 1919. An excellent collection of mythic and historical data on the predecessor of Vardhamāna within the Jain tradition and its probable founder in the ninth century B.C.
Jacobi, Hermann, trans. *Sacred Books of the East*. Vols. 22 and 44, *Jaina Sutras*, parts 1 and 2. Oxford: Oxford University Press, 1884, 1895. Reprint. New York: Dover Publications, 1968. A fine translation of selected scriptures of the Jain religious tradition, with an introduction by the translator which includes a brief treatment of the life of Vardhamāna. Volume 22 in the series contains Jain scriptures on the life of Vardhamāna, and volume 44 contains his teachings.
Jaini, Padmanabh S. *The Jaina Path of Purification*. Berkeley: University of California Press, 1979. An excellent treatment of the Jain religious tradition, both ancient and modern, including the life of Vardhamāna. Includes an extensive bibliography, illustrations, and thirty-two photographs.
Law, Bimala C. *Mahāvīra: His Life and Teachings*. London: Luzac and Co., 1937. A brief work with a wealth of references to Jain scriptures and other Indian literature, documenting the exemplary life and influential ideas of Vardhamāna Mahāvīra.
Schubring, Walther. *The Doctrine of the Jainas, Described After the Old Sources*. Translated by Wolfgang Beurlen. Rev. ed. Delhi: Motilal Banarsidass, 1962. A clear and concise presentation of Vardhamāna's teachings and the subsequent Jain scholastic traditions on cosmology, ethics, rebirth, and related topics.
Williams, Robert H. B. *Jaina Yoga: A Survey of the Mediaeval Sravakacaras*. London: Oxford University Press, 1963. This work presents the teachings of Jainism for lay followers, as found in the numerous texts specifically written as guides for laymen. The strict code of conduct reveals that Jainism's ascetic orientation applies even to the lay follower.

Bruce M. Sullivan

MARCUS TERENTIUS VARRO

Born: 116 B.C.; Reate
Died: 27 B.C.; Rome
Area of Achievement: Scholarship
Contribution: Varro contributed to every field of abstract and practical knowledge extant in his day, established the worthiness of intellectual pursuits such as linguistic study and encyclopedism, and left a body of knowledge that, directly or indirectly, has informed and influenced writers and scholars ever since.

Early Life
Marcus Terentius Varro was sometimes called Marcus Terentius Varro Reatinus because he was born in Reate, in the Sabine region of modern Italy. His family, which owned vast estates there, was considered to be of equestrian, or knightly, rank, although certain ancestors had attained noble rank by holding office in the senate. Varro's parents had the means to obtain for him the best education available at the time. This included a long sojourn in the capital, where he studied under the Stoic Stilo Praeconinus (who taught Cicero ten years later), and afterward a period in Athens during which he studied philosophy with Antiochus of Ascalon, the Academic. Stilo Praeconinus, the first Roman grammarian and philologist, was also a learned historian of Roman antiquity, and under his tutelage Varro soon showed an extraordinary aptitude for these pursuits.

Life's Work
As a gifted scholar, Varro could have kept himself apart from public life had he so chosen. Until he was nearly seventy, however, he remained deeply involved in both politics and the military. To people of his own era, this was not contradictory, for few of Varro's contemporaries were inclined to draw a strict boundary between intellectual and public life. Julius Caesar, during his march through the Alps to Gaul, composed a treatise on Latin grammatical inflections which he dedicated to Cicero. Indeed, political leaders such as Cicero and Caesar spent many adult years studying philosophy and ancient history, trying to draw lessons that would help them govern justly and wisely.

Varro's political and military career was closely allied with that of Pompey the Great. In 76, he served under Pompey in a military campaign against the rebel Quintus Sertorius in Spain. Afterward, Varro entered public office, serving first as tribune (a magistrate of the people with veto power over senate actions), then as curule aedile (roughly, superintendent of public works), and finally as praetor, or judicial officer. In 67, he held a naval command under Pompey in the war against the Cilician pirates, who, for a time, had virtually controlled the Mediterranean. From 66 to 63, Varro served, again under Pompey, in the third war against Mithradates the Great, King of Pontus. From 52 to 48, during the civil war between Pompey and Caesar, Varro commanded two legions for Pompey in Spain. On August 2, 48, two other Pompeian commanders in Spain capitulated to Caesar, and Varro, probably under pressure from his soldiers, was forced to follow suit. Afterward, like Cicero and Cato the Younger, he went to Dyrrachium, a sort of neutral corner, to await the outcome of the Battle of Pharsalus, which decided the entire conflict in Caesar's favor.

Varro and Caesar had remained on friendly terms during even the bitterest conflict between Caesar and Pompey. In 48, Pompey was murdered by agents of the Egyptian king, and the following year the victorious Caesar pardoned Varro and restored to him lands that had been seized by Marc Antony. Caesar also appointed Varro head of the great public library that was then being planned. Thus began the period of the works and accomplishments for which Varro is best remembered and which earned for him the title (bestowed by Quintilian in the first century A.D.) of "the most learned of Romans."

A profile of Varro, bearded and wearing a woolen, Greek-style cap, appears on an ancient coin now housed in the Museo Nazionale Romano. Most Roman men did not grow beards, although Greek men did, and Varro may have worn one along with the cap as a sign of his intellectual vocation, which was commonly associated with Greece rather than with Rome. Alternatively, regardless of Varro's actual appearance, the designer of the coin may have simply portrayed him in this fashion for symbolic purposes.

Varro is remembered, among many other reasons, for compiling in Rome what was to be the first library for public use. He concentrated on three types of prose works: the writings of the antiquarians, treatises by grammarians and philologists (by this time Stilo Praeconinus' new disciplines had come into their own), and works on practical subjects such as husbandry and domestic economy. His collection served as a kind of stylistic barometer for the times: The Ciceronian style dominated the prose of theoretical works, especially in philosophy, rhetoric, and history, while the sparser, more direct expression of Cato the Censor set the standard for practical treatises. In addition to Latin works in these genres, Varro acquired for his collection many volumes in Greek.

Although he seems generally to have ignored poetry (which was then in temporary eclipse), he is credited with establishing the canon of dramatic verse certifiably written by Plautus—some twenty-one plays, constituting what is called the *Fabulae Varronianae*—and, according to Aulus Gellius, Varro also wrote literary and dramatic criticism of Plautus.

Varro's unprecedented collection of books for public use proved of enormous benefit to contemporary scholars. As Rome passed from a republican to an imperial form of government, interest in Roman antiquity grew rapidly, and there developed a new fraternity of researchers and historians who made whatever use they could of the early records and works by the pioneering annalists of Rome. Yet before the formation of Varro's public library—as in Great Britain and the United States at comparable periods of their development—a literary worker had to depend upon the generosity of private library owners for a look at such rare works and records.

Though he now was devoted to the pursuits of scholarship and librarianship that were his forte, Varro had one remaining practical challenge to face. In 47, nearly seventy years old, he had retired altogether from political life when he accepted Caesar's appointment as librarian. Nevertheless, after Caesar was assassinated in 44 and Octavian, Marc Antony, and Marcus Aemilius Lepidus formed the Second Triumvirate, Antony declared Varro an enemy of the state and had him proscribed, that is, banished from the vicinity of Rome. Varro's home near the capital was destroyed, as was his private library, containing not only thousands of works by other writers but also many of the hundreds of volumes he himself had written up to his seventy-third year, when he was banished. If not for the proscription, with its destructive aftermath—an all-too-common occurrence in that period of Roman history—more might be known about the exact contents of the famous public library, for which Varro probably had earmarked many volumes in his private collection. Undoubtedly, too, many more of Varro's own works would have survived down to the present day.

Indeed, Varro nearly lost his life during Antony's proscription—the same proscription that actually did lead to the death of Cicero in 43 B.C. Yet with the help of friends, led by Quintus Fufius Calenus, Varro received a pardon from Octavian and spent the rest of his days peacefully in Rome.

The vigorous, hardworking old man now turned most of his energies to his own writing. Varro claimed to have composed, over his entire career, seventy-four works comprising more than six hundred volumes. This assertion is supported by commentators such as Aulus Gellius, Macrobius, and Nonius Marcellus, who all lived and worked within a few centuries after Varro. His work spanned virtually all areas of learning and all genres of writing then known to Rome: poetry, philosophy, history, literary criticism, grammar, philology, science and mathematics, practical handbooks, and the like. Among his lost books are a work on geometry, one on mensuration, and a nine-volume encyclopedia that helped form the basis for what became the medieval program of education.

On the other hand, what Varro did for his contemporaries, in the way of preserving and concentrating sources for antiquarian research, many later scholars have done for certain of his works. For example, it is thanks in large part to quotations by Nonius Marcellus (fl. fourth century A.D.) that some six hundred lines and ninety titles of Varro's 150 books which form the *Saturae Menippiae* (c. 81-67 B.C.; *Menippean Satires*) are preserved for the twentieth century. (According to Cicero, Varro himself composed much verse, although Varro allowed little room for poetry in his library collection.)

Actually, the satires were an intermixture of prose and verse in the style of Menippus, a Greek Cynic of the third century B.C. The extant titles are greatly varied, some named after gods or persons, some quoting Latin or Greek proverbs—for example, *Nescis quid vesper serus vehat* (You know not what the evening may bring forth) and the famous Socratic dictum "Know thyself." The subject matter also varies: eating and drinking, literature, philosophy, politics, and the "good old days." The general themes are the absurdity of much Greek philosophy and the preoccupation among Romans of Varro's day with luxury and leisure. Varro expressed his disapproval for the First Triumvirate in a satire he called *Trikaranos* (the three-headed).

Modern opinion, based on the surviving fragments, varies as to the literary merit of the *Menippean Satires*. The ancients, however, quoted them so frequently as to make quite evident their popularity with Varro's contemporaries. In addition to his own poetic compositions, Varro wrote several treatises on literature and literary history, including *De poematis* (of poetry), *De compositione saturarum* (on the composition of satire), and *De poetis* (about poets).

He also made many lasting contributions to science and education, chief of which was to introduce the Greek concept of the encyclopedia, meaning "general education," into Roman thought. This he did by way of his now-lost *De forma philosophiae libri III* (on philosophical forms) and *Disciplinarum libri IX* (liberal arts). The latter set forth all the known liberal arts gathered from Greek sources. It was the Greeks who had originally divided the liberal arts into a trivium (grammar, logic, and rhetoric) and a quadrivium (geometry, arithmetic, astronomy, and music), and the *Disciplinarum libri IX* contained a chapter on each, as well as on architecture and medicine. Later scholars removed these last two from the scheme and made them professional studies, retaining the others as the basic program of education in the Middle Ages. Meanwhile, the encyclopedia, incorporating excerpts from and synopses of writings by earlier authors, became a respectable genre among the Romans, particularly in scientific circles. Other scientific contributions included two works on geography, *De ora maritima* (of the seashore) and *De aestuariis* (of estuaries), as well as numerous works on meteorology and almanacs for farmers and sailors.

Varro brought innovation in yet another area: His fifteen-volume *Imagines*, also known as *Hebdomades*, published about 39 B.C., introduced the illustrated biography to Romans. (Crateuas, the physician of Mithradates the Great, had earlier published an illustrated book on plants written in Greek.) Varro's *Imagines* contained brief life histories of seven hundred famous Greeks and Romans, accompanied by a likeness of each. Varro's choice of precisely seven hundred biographies is also interesting: He had a powerful attachment to the number seven, and Aulus Gellius quoted him as saying that the virtues of that number are many and various.

By ancient estimates, Varro's greatest work was one of which no trace now remains: the forty-one volume *Antiquitates rerum humanarum et divinarum libri XLI* (of matters human and divine). Its importance lay in the complete account it gave of Roman political and religious life from the earliest times. Because the book displayed immense knowledge of the Roman past, the church fathers used it as a source of information about official Roman religion. Although this work is lost, much information from it is preserved in Gellius, Servius, Macrobius, and Saint Augustine.

Of those works by Varro that are preserved in the original, one, *De lingua Latina* (*On the Latin Language*), has come down in mutilated form. Only five of its twenty-five volumes survive, and even these are incomplete. Varro composed the work between 47 and 45 and published it before the death of Cicero, to whom it is dedicated. It has value not only as an early study of linguistic origins and development but also as a source of quotations from early Roman poets. Although some of the etymologies are a bit fanciful, many more evince true wit and insight. Perhaps most important, this work is a pioneering systematic treatment—starting with word origins and the evolution of meanings, moving to a defense of etymology as a branch of learning, treating abstract concepts such as ideas of time and the rare and difficult words that poets often use, then introducing the debate over "anomaly" versus "analogy" (a controversy that survives to modern times). Varro's approach, the product of independent thought despite its heavy debt to his teacher Stilo Praeconinus, made the subject worthy of attention from other scholars.

His other surviving work, *De re rustica* (36 B.C.; *On Agriculture*), has come down to the twentieth century almost completely intact. *On Agriculture* is a practical handbook rather than a theoretical treatise; Varro based it on his actual experience of running his family's three Sabine farms, as well as on lore and science drawn from ancient sources.

On Agriculture is important for several reasons: as an instance of the dialogue form, as a revelation of Roman agricultural ideas, as a source for Vergil's *Georgics* (c. 37-29 B.C.), and as a harbinger of at least one discovery of modern science. In this work, Varro cautioned farmers to choose a healthy site for their farmhouse and to avoid building near swamps because, as he wrote, "certain minute animals, invisible to the eye, breed there and, borne by the air, reach inside the body by way of the mouth and nose and cause diseases that are difficult to get rid of." Cicero and his circle, though friendly to Varro, apparently considered this theory of his absurd. Varro was possibly the only Roman who approached the germ theory of disease, which Louis Pasteur would fully develop more than eighteen hundred years later.

Summary

Even the briefest survey of his work reveals how pervasive Marcus Terentius Varro's influence was—not only on his own age but also on posterity. Cicero praised Varro with the words, "When we were foreigners and wanderers—strangers, as it were, in our own land—your books led us home and made it possible for us at length to learn who we were as Romans and where we lived." Through the sheer range of his undertakings, he influenced later authors and scholars as diverse as Vergil, Petronius, Gellius, Augustine, and Boethius.

Despite the enormous scope of his abstract knowledge, Varro was primarily a shrewd, practical thinker, and, because the Roman mind looked for the practical significance of all things intellectual, he attempted to absorb and then pass on to his fellow citizens all that could be learned. So intent was he on transmitting what was knowable that he summarized some of his longer works so that less-educated Romans could comprehend them more easily. In this capacity, he became perhaps the world's first intellectual popularizer.

Bibliography
Duff, J. Wright. *A Literary History of Rome in the Silver Age from Tiberius to Hadrian.* New York: Charles Scribner's Sons, 1927. Reprint. Westport, Conn.: Greenwood Press, 1964. Contains a discussion of Varro's place in Roman literature.

—————. *Roman Satire: Its Outlook on Social Life.* Berkeley: University of California Press, 1936. Includes a discussion specifically focusing on Varro's *Menippean Satires*, of which only fragments remain but which is thought by some scholars to have great literary merit.

Skydsgaard, Jens Erik. *Varro the Scholar: Studies in the First Book of Varro's "De re rustica."* Hafniae, Denmark: Munksgaard, 1968. A lucid discussion of the first part of Varro's *On Agriculture.* Written by a respected scholar.

Stahl, William H. *Roman Science: Origins, Development, and Influence to the Later Middle Ages.* Madison: University of Wisconsin Press, 1962. Reprint. Westport, Conn.: Greenwood Press, 1978. Includes a discussion of Varro's contributions to agriculture, mathematics, linguistic studies, geography, and encyclopedism.

Varro, Marcus Terentius. *On Agriculture.* Translated by William Davis Hooper and Harrison Boyd Ash. Cambridge, Mass.: Harvard University Press, 1934. Varro's only complete surviving work. Written in dialogue form, with great descriptive and dramatic power. Cato's *De agri cultura* (c. 160 B.C.; *On Agriculture*, 1913) is printed in the same volume.

—————. *On the Latin Language.* Translated by Roland G. Kent. 2 vols. Cambridge, Mass.: Harvard University Press, 1938. Contains the surviving fragments of Varro's twenty-five-volume work on the derivation, grammar, and popular usage of the Latin language. With the Latin original opposite each page of translation.

Thomas Rankin

JEAN DE VENETTE

Born: 1307 or 1308; probably the village of Venette, near Compiègne
Died: 1368 or 1369; probably Paris
Areas of Achievement: Literature and religion
Contribution: A friar who wrote a chronicle recording the political and social events of northern France between 1340 and 1368, Jean captured the sense of urgency and distress of the times in which he lived, while criticizing those whom he thought to be partially responsible for the troubles.

Early Life

Very little is known of Jean de Venette's life, except that which can be gleaned from references in his chronicle and the records of the Paris convent where he lived much of his adult life. He wrote that he was seven or eight years old when the famine of 1315 struck Europe, indicating that he was born in 1307 or 1308, most likely in the provincial village of Venette, approximately one mile from the town of Compiègne, about fifty miles northeast of Paris, on the banks of the Oise River. Of peasant stock, Jean was reared in the rolling and fertile countryside of northern France. In the years following the famine of 1315, it is probable that Jean, having shown interest and promise, began his formal education, learning the basics of reading and writing Latin at a local monastery. In all likelihood he was the only individual from his village to acquire training beyond the memorization of prayers and psalms which the parish priest might have provided.

At some point, probably in his teens, Jean decided to devote his life to the Church and joined the order of Carmelite friars. The Carmelites, also known as the White Friars for their white cloaks, had originated in Palestine, where in the twelfth century groups of hermits lived on the slopes of Mount Carmel, having dedicated their lives to prayer. Members of the group soon migrated to Western Europe, and, in 1250, Pope Innocent IV formally recognized the order and approved their constitution. Each friar pledged to devote himself to prayer, preaching, and study and to live a humble beggar's life in the urban centers of Europe. Rejecting the accumulation of property, the convents of Carmelites shared their meager resources and preached to townspeople about charity, humility, and the simple life of Christ. Jean's early years as a Carmelite have escaped the records of history, but in the 1320's or 1330's he joined the Parisian convent of Carmelites on the Place Maubert and studied theology at the University of Paris. After studying theology for several years, he became a master of theology; by 1339, he had become the prior, or head, of the Paris Carmelite convent.

Life's Work

As prior of a Carmelite convent in the capital city of France, Jean likely had many official duties to fulfill, such as running his own convent and inspecting the smaller convents in towns near Paris. He held this post until 1342, when the Carmelites selected him as the head of the order of the province of France, a post which he apparently held until his death. Despite his official duties, which undoubtedly consumed much time, Jean developed an interest in past events and historical accounts. He stressed the importance of historical study to the younger friars and likely enlisted their aid in collecting evidence and stories about the history of the Carmelite Order. In 1360, Jean compiled this information in a brief history of the order from its legendary founding by Elijah until the mid-twelfth century, when two English barons brought to Europe some Carmelite hermits from Palestine.

Jean's historical avocation further appears in *Chronicon* (*The Chronicle of Jean de Venette*, 1953), a book better known than the history of the order. The chronicle, which describes events from 1340 to 1368, contains many eyewitness accounts and tidbits of news that Jean received in Paris or on his travels to other convents throughout northern France. The chronicle's narrative—like most medieval chronicles—consists of entries for each of the years recorded by the author. In these yearly summaries, Jean wrote of weather conditions; political events; military campaigns, victories, and defeats; the wartime condition of the cities, villages, and countryside of France; and the social conflicts present in the France of his day. While parts of the book appear to have been written on a day-to-day basis, most of the Latin manuscript was written after Jean had spent some time reflecting on the dramatic events of the mid-fourteenth century. Throughout the text of the chronicle, Jean's sensitivity and humaneness are apparent. Coming from peasant stock, he understood the hardships and sufferings of peasants during times of war, famine, and plague and was clearly proud of the endurance and fortitude of his social class. As one who dedicated himself to a life of humility, he was sharply critical of the fourteenth century French nobility, whom he perceived as lax, vain, and impotent. Jean particularly criticized the aristocracy for their inability to protect the French from the English during the repeated invasions of the Hundred Years' War. Unlike many medieval chronicles or historical accounts, Jean's history comes alive with feeling, giving his audience the sense that Jean was often in the middle of the events he describes or was at least deeply concerned about their outcome.

Jean's history has a stately unity in that it begins and ends in years when Jean reported that a comet was observed in the skies above France. Despite this astronomical coherence, the years between 1340 and 1368 were years of social and political turmoil in the kingdom. Beginning in 1340, when the English king, Edward III, crossed the English Channel and invaded France to claim the throne that had belonged to his grandfather, Jean described a world that was increasingly unstable. He noted in 1340, for example, that men were beginning to wear unbecoming clothes and garments that were so short as to be indecent. Noblemen, except those of royal blood, grew their beards long and seemed to lose their courage in battle. Far from being prudish, Jean was seeking from the very beginning of his chronicle to provide an explanation for France's having nearly succumbed to English conquest in the 1350's and 1360's. Throughout the 1340's, Jean described the English military successes and depicted the incredible hardship that confronted the common people of France. Not only was the war difficult to endure when grainfields were trampled or set afire, but the king also seemed unable to protect his subjects from the depredations of his officials, who continuously levied taxes and altered the currency so that coins did not retain their true value. While the commoners thought that they were contributing their hard-earned pennies to the French war effort, Jean cynically and angrily noted that nobles and knights used the funds for their own pleasures, such as gambling.

The bubonic plague struck the kingdom in 1348 and ushered in a new era, in which, according to Jean, children developed only twenty or twenty-two teeth, instead of the normal thirty-two. Jean thought that humans had become more covetous and brawling, suing one another at every turn. Despite the vast mortality of the plague, however, the war between England and France continued, adding to the fear and suffering of those devastating years. In 1354, a nighttime political assassination ushered in new calamities for the French: With the murder of a leading royal official by Charles of Navarre, the son-in-law of King John, civil war erupted in the kingdom. On the heels of this tragedy followed the English capture of King John himself on the battlefield at Poitiers in 1356. With the king a captive in England, the States General attempted to provide some order in the kingdom, but its efforts were in vain, as noblemen utterly refused to cooperate with the representatives of the towns. In the ensuing confusion, aristocrats sought to exploit their subjects and refused to defend France from further English attacks. It seemed to many that the noblemen, who were charged with the responsibility of protecting the realm from its enemies, had severely neglected their duty. Revenge came when the exploited peasants rose up and slaughtered hundreds of these dissolute aristocrats. Seeking justice, the peasants became overzealous in their vengeance; they were then overpowered by noblemen who brutally restored a semblance of order.

Throughout the account of the calamities that befell France in the 1350's, Jean displayed not only his human sensitivity but also a deep love for his homeland. In 1359, when he wrote about the destruction of the region surrounding Compiègne, Jean emotionally described how vines were left unpruned and rotting, how the fields were not plowed or sown, how no hens called to their chicks, and how robbers and thieves freely wandered from village to village carrying off whatever they could find. The reader senses Jean's love of France and his recognition that France had the potential to be a great and rich kingdom, if only the noblemen responsible for its defense and protection would fulfill their duties. This attitude, prevalent among towns-people and peasants through the later 1350's, not only captured the frustration created by years of military misfortune but also condemned the upper classes for their corrupt life-style, their self-centeredness, and their exploitive greed.

Jean's sentiments about his kingdom and society, however, were not limited to sorrow and condemnation. In his accounts of the mid-1360's, after the captive King John's death in London and the accession of Charles V, Jean recorded the gradual process of reestablishing order and peace in France. After some lengthy negotiations, truces were arranged between the royal adversaries, the civil war between Charles of Navarre and the king ended, and noblemen began once again to fulfill their social role as the kingdom's protectors. Throughout these final annual accounts, Jean reflected the tentative hopefulness of his times and glorified the recently established Valois dynasty, which had the opportunity to create a powerful and peaceful France.

Summary

Although Jean de Venette was clearly a dedicated friar and capable administrator within the Order of Carmelites, he is best known for his chronicle of the mid-fourteenth century. While the veracity of a chronicle cannot always be judged from the distance of several hundred years, it is clear that Jean's writing has great historical value. Arising from the peasantry, Jean was an individual who understood and appreciated the value of learning and writing in an age when illiteracy was predominant. Using his skills, he recorded the passage of time, the events, the pleasures, and the tragedies of his era. Unlike many dry, emotionless records of the Middle Ages, however, Jean's work comes alive, reflecting his personality, his ideas, his dreams for France, and his moral judgment of the French people.

This living work offers the historian a special opportunity to comprehend the mentality of the fourteenth century. Understanding the war-weariness of France and the frustration of the lower classes provides a perspective that corrects the overly romantic idealization of the Middle Ages as a time of knights in shining armor performing feats to please a lady. Instead, Jean reveals a population gravely concerned about the fate of the kingdom and hopeful for the return of peace and order. Within Jean's writing, the reader can glimpse patriotic stirrings that were to give France a powerful cohesiveness in later centuries.

Bibliography

Fowler, Kenneth. *The Age of Plantagenet and Valois: The Struggle for Supremacy, 1328-1498*. New York: G. P. Putnam's Sons, 1967. A beautifully illustrated book which covers the origins of the Hundred Years' War, its key battles, and the political and social changes which the French and English kingdoms experienced.

Froissart, Jean. *The Chronicle of England, France, Spain, Etc.* Edited by Ernest Rhys. London: J. M. Dent and Sons, 1927. Another chronicle of the fourteenth century and the Hundred Years' War, Froissart's work incorporates much English evidence and gives the reader a slightly different perspective on the international conflict.

Lawrence, C. H. *Medieval Monasticism: Forms of Religious Life in Western Europe in the Middle Ages.* London: Longman, 1984. This survey of monasticism provides basic information on the monastic movement throughout the Middle Ages, including a chapter on the friars and mendicants such as the Carmelites.

Perroy, Edouard. *The Hundred Years' War.* Translated by D. C. Douglas. New York: Capricorn Books, 1965. The best survey of the late medieval conflict between the kings of England and France. This book describes not only the military conflict between the kingdoms but also the social upheavals in France caused by Charles of Navarre's civil war and the bubonic plague of 1347-1348.

Seward, Desmond. *The Hundred Years' War: The English in France, 1337-1453.* New York: Atheneum Publishers, 1982. A recent addition to the collection of popular books on the fourteenth century, Seward's volume presents a less detailed explanation of the war, its battles, and the misfortunes of France during the first phases of the conflict.

Tuchman, Barbara W. *A Distant Mirror: The Calamitous Fourteenth Century.* New York: Alfred A. Knopf, 1978. A very readable book which not only uses Jean de Venette's chronicle as one of its sources but also carefully explains the political and social turmoil experienced by France during the 1340's and 1350's.

Venette, Jean de. *The Chronicle of Jean de Venette.* Edited by Richard A. Newhall. Translated by Jean Birdsall. New York: Columbia University Press, 1953. The best English-language edition of the chronicle, this volume contains a good introduction to the life and times of the author, a very readable translation, and copious explanatory notes which help the reader understand some of the complexities of the fourteenth century.

David M. Bessen

VERGIL

Born: October 15, 70 B.C.; Andes, Cisalpine Gaul
Died: September 21, 19 B.C.; Brundisium
Area of Achievement: Literature
Contribution: Author of an epic poem celebrating the beginnings of the Roman race (the *Aeneid*), pastoral poems (the *Eclogues*), and a poem about the farmer's life (the *Georgics*), Vergil is among the greatest poets of all time.

Early Life

Publius Vergilius Maro (Vergil) was born in Andes, a village near Mantua in Cisalpine Gaul, in 70 B.C., a generation before the death of the Roman Republic. His origins were humble; his father eked out a living by keeping bees on the family's small farm. Though no record of his father's name remains, it is known that his mother's name was Magia Polla. It also seems likely that Vergil received his early education at Cremona and Mediolanum (Milan) and that he received the *toga virilis* (the toga of manhood) in 55 B.C., on his fifteenth birthday. Wearing the *toga virilis* would signify full rights and privileges of citizenship.

Vergil is said to have learned Greek at Neapolis (Naples) from Parthenius, a Bithynian captive brought to Rome during the war with Mithradates the Great. Supposedly, Vergil based one of his own poems, the *Moretum*, on a Greek model by Parthenius. The young poet also received instruction in Epicurean philosophy from Siron and training in rhetoric from Epidius. Most scholars believe that Vergil studied with Epidius at the same time as Octavian, the future emperor Augustus who would later become Vergil's champion and patron. In short, Vergil received a first-rate education in literature, philosophy, and rhetoric, and critics have discerned his broad learning in his *Georgics* (c. 37-29 B.C.), which deals with all elements relating to the farmer's work during the year. There is no indication that Vergil served in the military or engaged in politics. He was probably excused from these duties because of his fragile health and general bookishness.

About the year 45, upon completing his education, Vergil returned to his family's property near Mantua, but in 42, after victory at Philippi, Octavian, in assigning grants of land to his veterans, allowed his aide, Octavius Musa, to determine boundaries of lands assigned in the Cremona district, and Vergil's paternal estate was deeded to a centurion named Arrius. Vergil's influential friends Asinius Pollio and Cornelius Gallus advised Vergil to appeal directly to Octavian; that he did, and the family farm was restored. Vergil would celebrate Octavian's understanding and kindness in this matter in eclogue 1 of the *Eclogues* (43-37 B.C.). Unfortunately, a second attempt to appropriate the family's estate, led by a certain Milienus Toro, was successful several years later. (Vergil was almost killed by a ruffian named Clodius in the violence which ensued.)

Paradoxically, some good came from this sordid affair. Vergil took temporary refuge in a farmhouse owned by a neighbor named Siro but immediately thereafter moved to Rome, where he wrote the two collections of verse which attracted the notice of his first sponsor, Gaius Maecenas. The incident is referred to in section 10 of *Catalepton*, an ancient collection of poetry.

Life's Work

After Vergil's pastorals, the *Eclogues* (sometimes called the *Bucolics* and probably written with the countryside near Tarentum in mind), appeared, Maecenas became interested in Vergil's work. Maecenas led a literary circle, was influential in matters of state, and had the ear of Octavian, soon to be known as Augustus. Although Vergil did not recover his family's farm, Augustus saw to it that he was compensated with another estate, probably the one located near Nola in Campania to which Aulus Gellius refers in *Noctes Atticae* (c. A.D. 143; *Attic Nights*). Vergil also knew the poet Horace well by this time and was instrumental in admitting him to Maecenas' circle and securing a patron for him. Horace mentions his acquaintance with Vergil in the *Satires* (35, 30 B.C.), a description of a journey from Rome to Brundisium.

The *Georgics*, completed when its author had been fully accepted as a member of Maecenas' circle, is clearly the poem of which Vergil was most proud. It appears that he undertook its composition at Maecenas' suggestion and completed it at Naples sometime after the Battle of Actium (31 B.C.). Justifiably, the *Georgics* was compared with the idylls of Theocritus (c. 308-260 B.C.) and the *Works and Days* (c. 700 B.C.) of Hesiod, was found worthy of their Greek predecessors, and catapulted Vergil to prominence.

It is likely that for some time Vergil had considered writing the *Aeneid* (c. 29-19 B.C.), the epic poem for which he is best known. As early as 27, while Augustus was on military campaign in Spain, he wrote to Vergil suggesting composition of an epic which would celebrate Aeneas' founding of a so-called New Troy in Italy and set forth the ancient origins of the Roman people. It is likely that Vergil began the *Aeneid* soon thereafter. Dating composition of specific sections is difficult, but Vergil mentions the death of Marcellus, son of Octavia (the sister of Julius Caesar), in the *Aeneid*. Since it is known that Marcellus died in 23, one can assume that Vergil had outlined the entire poem by this time, the reference appearing almost exactly at the epic's midpoint. Octavia, supposedly present at Vergil's reading of this passage, is said to have fainted upon hearing the poet's allusion to her son as a young man of promise who died too young.

It is known that Vergil met Augustus in Athens late in the year 20. Possibly Vergil had intended to continue his tour of Greece, but his health, never strong, was rapidly declining, so he accompanied Augustus first to Megara, a district between the Corinthian and Saronic gulfs, then to Brundisium, on the tip of the Italian peninsula; he died there, at the age of fifty. His body was brought first to Naples, his summer residence, and supposedly interred in a tomb on a road between Naples and Puteoli (Pozzuoli), where, indeed, a tomb still stands. An epitaph, supposedly dating from Vergil's burial, reads: "Mantua me genuit, Calabri rapuere, tenet nunc Parthenope. Cecini pascua, rura, duces," meaning "Mantua bore me, Calabria ravished me, now Parthenope (the ancient name of Naples after the Siren of that name) holds me. I have nourished flocks, fields, generals." There is no evidence that Vergil himself composed this epitaph or even that it was on his tomb at the time of his death; nevertheless, the inscription is very old and has always been attributed to the poet.

One of the most dramatic events ensuing upon Vergil's death concerns his will. He left half his property to his half brother Valerius Proculus and named Augustus, Maecenas, and his friends Lucius Varius and Plotius Tucca as other legatees. His final request, however, was that Varius and Tucca burn the *Aeneid*, which he did not consider in its finished state. Tradition has it that Augustus himself intervened to save the poem and that it was published with the revisions of Varius and Tucca.

Vergil died a wealthy man, thanks primarily to the generosity of Augustus and Maecenas. His residence on the Esquiline Hill included a garden located next to that of Maecenas. Generous grants from his patrons had enabled Vergil to find the security and leisure he needed for writing his verse and enjoying the friendship of amiable fellow artists, such as Horace. Vergil was also fortunate in finding acceptance for his works, which, even during his lifetime, became an essential part of the school curriculum.

One wonders what this most celebrated of Roman poets might have looked like. Though many ancient renderings of Vergil survive, none dates to his own time and all are idealized. Artists, focusing on the certain frailty of Vergil's health, inevitably portray him as a youthful, frail, and sensitive man with hair covering the ears, longer than the close-cropped imperial style. In Renaissance paintings, he wears fillets or the poet's laurel crown and is often shown declaiming a passage from his works to an appreciative Augustus or Maecenas.

Summary

During his lifetime and even more so after his death, the *Eclogues*, the *Georgics*, and the *Aeneid* became classics, known well by every patriotic Roman. They were memorized, recited, and used for rhetorical training. Soon after Vergil's death, the poet's works were credited with every variety of mystical allusion. The fourth eclogue, for example, was taken as prophecy of the birth of Jesus Christ, though the boy whose birth will signal a new golden age is more likely the emperor Augustus. Others regularly consulted the *Aeneid* and collected its "hidden meanings" as the so-called *Sortes Vergilianae* (Vergilian allotments). This practice began as early as the period immediately after Vergil's death, becoming an obsession in the Middle Ages. The unusual *praenomen* (first name) of Magia Polla, Vergil's mother, implied for many that the poet was a gifted sorcerer as well. The alternate spelling of Vergil's name (Virgil) itself probably derives from the magician's *virga* (wand). That so many were able to see so much beyond the literal in Vergil's poems is testimony to their enduring value as masterpieces.

There is much information on Vergil's life, although much of it is embroidered with legend. Aelius Donatus' fourth century biography, appended to his commentary on Vergil's poems, is the most important ancient source, although it was derived in part from the rather random remarks in the *De viris illustribus* (second century A.D.; on famous men) of Suetonius. Suetonius is said to have derived his information from now-lost accounts by Varius (one of Vergil's literary executors) and from Melissus, a freedman of Maecenas. Other ancient biographies, less reliable, were written by Valerius Probus (first century A.D.) and Saint Jerome (c. A.D. 331-420). An unattributed life of Vergil is also attached to the Vergil commentaries of Servius (late fourth century A.D.).

Bibliography

Broch, Hermann. *The Death of Virgil*. San Francisco: North Point Press, 1983. This exceptional novel captures the drama of Vergil's last hours and describes his frustration at being unable to complete his revision of the *Aeneid*. Read symbolically, this work is a record of all human strivings against the limitations imposed by physical circumstances. It was originally written in German during World War II by an author thwarted by his own surroundings and first published in English in 1945.

Commager, Steele, ed. *Virgil: A Collection of Critical Essays*. Englewood Cliffs, N.J.: Prentice-Hall, 1966. This book of essays by well-known critics discusses everything from the landscape which gave Vergil his inspiration to important imagery in Vergil's poems. It is part of the Twentieth Century Views series and includes contributions by Bruno Snell, Jacques Perret, Brooks Otis, Adam Parry, Bernard Knox, and Viktor Pöschl, as well as a chronology of Vergil's life and a short bibliography. All essays which had been written in French or German appear in English translation.

Comparetti, Domenico. *Virgil in the Middle Ages*. Translated by E. F. M. Benecke. New York: G. E. Stechert and Co., 1908. Reprint. London: Allen and Unwin, 1966. This book remains the classic treatment of Vergil's literary legacy showing how it influenced both education and literature for centuries. It is still the best discussion of Vergilian bibliography available. A respected scholarly source.

Conway, Robert Seymour. _Harvard Lectures on the Vergilian Age_. Cambridge, Mass.: Harvard University Press, 1928. This study relates references in Vergil's poetry to locations which influenced him. In essence, it is an orthographic biography, accompanied by photographs. Fascinating and reliable despite its age.

Frank, Tenney. _Vergil: A Biography_. New York: Henry Holt, 1922. Reprint. New York: Russell and Russell, 1965. This standard biography discusses the poet's life through references to his works. Particularly interesting is Frank's use of the pseudo-Vergilian poems _Culex_ and _Cirus_, the influence of Epicureanism, and his discussion of the circle of Maecenas.

Knight, W. F. Jackson. _Roman Vergil_. Harmondsworth, England: Penguin Books, 1944. Reprint. New York: Barnes and Noble Books, 1968. How Vergil changed the literary world and how Augustus changed the political world are two important concerns in this biographical and literary study. There is also good discussion of Vergilian style, meter, and language, as well as appendices on how Vergil's poetry advanced Latin as a literary language and on the allegorical and symbolic applications of Vergil's poems.

Tilley, Bertha. _Vergil's Latium_. Oxford: Basil Blackwell, 1947. This small volume, with accompanying photographs, examines the landscape of Vergil's Italy and notes its influences on Vergil's poetry. A generalist reader or a traveler to Italy will find it worthwhile.

Robert J. Forman

MARCUS VERRIUS FLACCUS

Born: c. 60 B.C.; place unknown
Died: c. A.D. 22; place unknown
Area of Achievement: Education
Contribution: Emerging from a slave background, Verrius established at Rome an innovative method for the teaching of Latin language and literature and, through his studies of Roman antiquities, contributed to modern understanding of Latin literature and Roman history.

Early Life
The biographer Suetonius supplies the basic biographical information about Marcus Verrius Flaccus in his essay *De grammaticis et rhetoribus* (c. A.D. 120; *Lives of the Grammarians*). This work by Suetonius, a discussion of teachers active in Rome during the last half of the first century B.C., includes the statement "Marcus Verrius Flaccus the freedman was especially renowned for his method of teaching." Nothing of Verrius' background is known except for his freedman's status and the probable name of his former master, Marcus Verrius. (Manumitted Roman slaves normally took the first and family names of their former owner.)

The name Verrius points to the region about Naples, where others with precisely the same nomenclature and many of the same family name are known. Scholarly work which Verrius did late in his life for the Roman town of Praeneste (modern Palestrina), however, has suggested to some that Verrius may have had an early connection with this town twenty-three miles east and south of Rome.

Life's Work
During Verrius' time, several men of letters with similar backgrounds established private schools in Rome for the instruction of Latin language and literature. These schools normally took children at the age of eleven for several years of training in the reading, recitation, and writing of Latin, while other schoolmasters might also have trained the same students in Greek language and literature. Verrius' school was notable because he forced his students to compete in writing and recitation, with prizes of rare literary editions for the victors. Verrius thus attracted the attention of the emperor Augustus, who invited Verrius to move his school to the imperial palace and tutor—at a salary equal to that of a senior administrator—the emperor's young grandsons, Gaius and Lucius. The appointment of Verrius as imperial tutor must have occurred between 8 and 11 B.C. and is no doubt the reason for Saint Jerome's assertion that Verrius "flourished" in 8 B.C.

Verrius wrote on a variety of subjects. *Rerum memoria dignarum* (things worth remembering), to judge from references to this work by Pliny the

Elder and other ancient scholars, ranged from elephants to Roman religious lore and rituals. Other writings touched on the Etruscans and on Roman traditions. Several important works treated the Latin language: *De ortho-graphia* (on correct spelling) apparently urged a return to old-fashioned ways of spelling (and pronouncing) Latin words; *De obscuris Catonis* (difficult works in Cato) explained unusual words in the orations and writings of Cato the Censor (who died in 149 B.C.). Verrius' most influential work was his dictionary, *De verborum significatu* (on the meaning of words). This work, the first Latin lexicon, was an alphabetical list of Latin words with definitions, etymologies, and frequent quotations of examples of usage drawn from archaic Latin texts (c. 250-100 B.C.) otherwise unknown. For example, the dictionary's entry under *quartarios* reads:

> Romans used to call muleskinners hired on contract "fourth-parters" [*quartarios*] because the muleskinners customarily charged for their services a fourth part of the profit. Thus Lucilius [a Roman satirist who wrote at the end of the second century B.C.]: "And then the unspeakable men, like a bad fourth-parter, crashed against all of the tombstones."

None of Verrius' works has survived intact.

Suetonius also reports that the town of Praeneste dedicated a statue of Verrius to honor his work on a great calendar inscribed on marble and set up prominently in a public area of the town. Enough fragments of this calendar have been discovered at Praeneste to indicate its size (six feet high and more than sixteen feet wide) and the scope of Verrius' work. The calendar listed the days of each month, with remarks on the religious and legal nature of each day and with notes on the pertinent religious festivals and historical and legendary events associated with each day. For example, he included this information for January 30:

> A day on which legal business may be transacted, a day for religious rites. Festival decreed by the senate, because on this date the Altar of the Augustan Peace was dedicated in Mars' Field [at Rome], when Drusus and Crispinus were consuls [9 B.C.].

The calendar has been dated to between A.D. 6 and 9 and therefore would have been the fruit of Verrius' later years.

Verrius died sometime during the reign of the emperor Tiberius (A.D. 14-37). His rise from slave to acclaimed teacher and scholar illustrates well the social mobility possible for talented freedmen in ancient Rome.

Summary

Of Marcus Verrius Flaccus' teaching methods nothing more is known, although his practice of forcing his students to compete for literary prizes has clearly had a long (if unacknowledged) history.

Suetonius observed that Verrius' work on spelling was criticized by a fellow freedman and contemporary rival in teaching, one Scribonius Aphrodisius, who attacked Verrius' morals as well as his scholarship. Yet Verrius' writings, especially his dictionary and his treatise on Cato's vocabulary, were widely consulted and discussed in the second century A.D., when Roman literary scholars took a particular interest in Cato and other early writers of Latin. About the year A.D. 200, an otherwise unknown Latin scholar, Sextus Pompeius Festus, made an abridged edition of Verrius' dictionary. The first half of Festus' edition is lost, but a further abridgment of all Festus' work was made by Paul the Deacon, a historian and teacher of Latin at the court of Charlemagne (c. A.D. 800). Modern scholars, by studying what has survived of Festus' edition and Paul's condensed version of Festus, are thus able to judge the quality and content of Verrius' dictionary.

As Verrius' annotations to the Praenestine calendar have proved to be of significant value for those who study Roman history, so also Verrius' dictionary, even in the abridged editions in which it has survived, is a major source for students of the Latin language and early Roman literature.

Bibliography

Baldwin, Barry. *Studies in Aulus Gellius*. Lawrence, Kans.: Coronado Press, 1975. Chapter 4 ("Scholarly Interests") offers a lively discussion of Roman and Greek scholarship of the second century A.D. and of how students of Latin literature exploited previous studies, including the works of Verrius. Includes adequate notes citing the ancient and modern sources.

Bonner, S. F. *Education in Ancient Rome*. Berkeley: University of California Press, 1977. The standard discussion of education in the ancient Roman world. Chapters 5 and 6 provide a general discussion of the schools of literature, language, and rhetoric in Rome. Includes sparse notes, but a good bibliography.

Marrou, H. I. *A History of Education in Antiquity*. New York: Mentor, 1964. A broader and more detailed study than Bonner's, this volume is arranged along chronological lines. In part 3, chapters 2 through 7 discuss the emergence and development of schools at Rome; chapter 5, in particular, covers what is known of schools of the type that Verrius established. Includes complete bibliographic notes.

Michels, A. K. *The Calendar of the Roman Republic*. Princeton, N.J.: Princeton University Press, 1967. A technical discussion of calendars in ancient Rome, with particular attention to inscribed wall calendars such as that created by Verrius at Praeneste. Includes notes and fine schematic drawings of ancient wall calendars.

Rawson, E. *Intellectual Life in Ancient Rome*. Baltimore: Johns Hopkins University Press, 1985. Offers a concise discussion of the personalities

2236

associated with literary and language studies in ancient Italy in the time of Verrius and earlier generations. Contains detailed notes and a complete bibliography.

Scullard, H. H. *Festivals and Ceremonies of the Roman Republic*. London: Thames and Hudson, 1981. A good general introduction to the official religious holidays of ancient Rome. Scullard includes a brief discussion of Roman calendars and surveys the various types of calendars used in ancient Rome. A more general work than that by Michels, whose study should be consulted for specific details. Contains complete notes.

Suetonius Tranquillus, G. *Suetonius*. Translated by John Carew Rolfe. 2 vols. New York: Macmillan, 1914. These two volumes (often reprinted) contain a Latin text and the standard English translation of Suetonius' works. Volume 2 contains the text and translation of Suetonius' essay *De grammaticis et rhetoribus*. The bibliography and notes are now outdated.

Treggiari, S. *Roman Freedmen During the Late Republic*. New York: Oxford University Press, 1969. The standard discussion in English of the social and legal circumstances of manumitted slaves in Roman history before circa 30 B.C. Discusses the prominence in Roman life of freedmen in education and other learned professions. Includes notes and a bibliography.

Wallace-Hadrill, J. M. *Suetonius*. London: Duckworth, 1983. The best study in English of the ancient biographer. Treats Suetonius' essay on ancient teachers of literature and rhetoric. The author discusses fully the history of the profession of teachers and literary men such as Verrius and Suetonius himself in Rome. Includes generous notes and a bibliography.

Paul B. Harvey, Jr.

VESPASIAN

Born: A.D. 9; Reate (modern Rieti, Italy)
Died: June 23, A.D. 79; Aquae Cutilae (modern Bagni di Paterno, Italy)
Area of Achievement: Government
Contribution: After the chaos and civil war which followed the downfall of Nero, Vespasian restored peace and order to the Roman Empire and secured its survival as an enduring political and cultural institution.

Early Life
Titus Flavius Vespasianus, better known as Vespasian, came from a family whose origins were probably humble and certainly obscure. The Flavians were of Sabine stock, and Vespasian's grandfather and father were both tax collectors and moneylenders. His father never advanced above the equestrian order (the rank below the senate) but was an associate of several influential members of the court of the emperor Claudius; through them, he obtained a military commission for his son.

Vespasian was appointed a tribune of soldiers in Thrace and demonstrated his considerable abilities within a short period of time. He advanced fairly rapidly for a man of his position and won the office of quaestor, which meant that provinces could be assigned to him; he was given Crete and Cyrene.

He married Flavia Domitilla, and they had three children. The two sons, Titus and Domitian, would succeed their father as emperors; the daughter died at a young age. After the death of his wife, Vespasian resumed a relationship with a woman named Caenis, a former slave who had been secretary to the mother of the emperor Claudius. Vespasian lived with Caenis as his wife in all but official ceremony until her death.

During 43 and 44, Vespasian was in command of Roman troops in Germany, and then in Britain, where he distinguished himself through vigorous military actions, including the defeat of several powerful tribes and the conquest of the Isle of Wight. For these accomplishments he was awarded a consulship. He next served as governor of the Roman province of Africa (modern Tunisia) but was so honest that he left office without amassing the usual wealth. His career under Claudius' successor, Nero, took a disastrous turn in 66 when Vespasian fell asleep at one of the emperor's singing performances. For this heinous offense Vespasian narrowly escaped death and was instead banished from the court. Not until the outbreak of a serious revolt in Judaea, when an experienced general was required, was Vespasian rescued from oblivion.

Vespasian was strongly built, with a broad, sturdy frame. Throughout his life he enjoyed excellent health, partly because of his temperate habits and partly because of his active and energetic life. The coins and portrait busts of the period show a face that is humorous yet shrewd, with an expression that caused the ancient biographer Suetonius to compare it to a man straining to complete a bowel movement. Vespasian had a rough, often coarse humor, which was often directed at himself—in particular, at his well-known reputation for stinginess. His outstanding characteristics were hard work, administrative genius, and a profound fund of common sense.

Life's Work

In 67, Vespasian was recalled from exile to lead Roman forces against the Jewish revolt, which was a serious threat to Rome's eastern borders and a danger to the vital grain supply from Egypt. By the summer of 68, Vespasian had regained most of Judaea, and the remnants of the rebel forces were detained in Jerusalem, which he put under siege. It was at this point that Vespasian learned of the uprising in Rome and the death of Nero.

"The year of the four emperors" followed, as Servius Sulpicius Galba, Marcus Salvius Otho, and Aulus Vitellius successively aspired to and gained the throne. While seeming to accept each in turn as the legitimate ruler, Vespasian was secretly establishing contacts and making plans with other influential governors and generals in the east; most notable were those of the two key provinces of Syria and Egypt. In 68, the troops of Vespasian's army declared him emperor; troops throughout the region quickly followed, and soon the forces pledged to him were advancing upon Rome.

Vespasian himself reached Rome sometime in the fall of 70; his son, Titus, remained in Judaea to complete the reconquest of that territory. Later, the two would celebrate a splendid double triumph, which indicated that Titus was not only Vespasian's heir but also an important part of the government.

The disastrous end of Nero's reign and the fierce civil war and struggle over the imperial power had left their harmful mark on Roman life and society, and it was Vespasian's first and most constant task to repair this damage. He reintroduced strict discipline and order into the military, hoping to remove the threat of another emperor being created far from Rome by a discontented army. He began an extensive series of construction and renovation projects throughout the empire, especially in Rome, restoring years of neglect and destruction. At the rebuilding of the Forum in Rome, Vespasian himself carried away the first load of rubble.

A parallel effort was effected in the government and administration, as Vespasian assumed the title of censor and thoroughly revised the rolls of the senate and the equestrian orders. It was in his naming of new senators that Vespasian made one of his most innovative and lasting contributions to the Empire, for he included not only many Italians from outside Rome but also men from the provinces. Through this strategy Vespasian enlarged not only the senate but also the entire concept of the Empire itself, making it less a collection of territories conquered by Rome and more a unified, organic whole. It is impossible to determine if Vespasian was working from a coherent, deliberate plan or merely responding to the situation in a sensible, practical fashion; either interpretation is possible. The result, however, was to create a broader and more lasting base for Roman power.

This reconstruction of Roman life demanded much effort from Vespasian, and he proved to be an outstandingly diligent administrator. The work also required vast amounts of money, and it was in search of these funds that Vespasian acquired the reputation for greed. He was quite open and shameless in obtaining funds, buying and selling on the commodity market and placing a tax on the public restrooms. When his son Titus found this last measure distasteful and protested to his father, Vespasian held up a coin and asked if the smell was offensive. When Titus said that it was not, Vespasian answered, "And yet it comes from urine." Even today, public rest rooms in Italy are called *vespasianos*.

Although Vespasian was quick and crafty in gathering money, he was willing to spend it freely for worthwhile purposes. In addition to his extensive building projects, he was the first emperor to give grants and stipends to those who contributed to the liberal and practical arts: Teachers of rhetoric, poets, artists, and engineers received funds during his reign.

The years of Vespasian were marked by no major conquests or expansions of the Empire's boundaries. Even if he had aspired to such glories, the situation made the option highly dubious. Internally there was simply too much restoration to be done, as Rome was depleted from the recent succession of rival emperors and from the revolt in Judaea. Peace at home, rather than glory abroad, was the theme of Vespasian's reign.

This peace and the restoration it made possible were accomplished largely through Vespasian's abilities and innate common sense. Unlike the rulers who preceded him, he had little fear of conspiracies or plots, launched no treason trials, and encouraged no informers. Historians have generally accorded him a high place, naming him one of Rome's best emperors.

From the time of Julius Caesar it had become a tradition that rulers of the Empire were deified upon their deaths. When Vespasian was in his final hours, he took note of this practice and with rough good humor made his last remark: "Dear me, I seem to be turning into a god."

Summary

Vespasian's great achievements were the restoration of peace and political sanity to the Roman Empire and the enlargement of its imperial rather than strictly Roman foundations. After the disaster of Nero's final years and the almost fatal chaos of the struggle for power which followed, Vespasian was able to provide for domestic tranquillity, reassert military discipline, and establish a political framework which prevented, at least for a time, renewed outbreaks of self-destructive civil war.

At first glance, Vespasian might have seemed unlikely to be capable of such tremendous tasks: His origins were humble, his manner was common, even coarse, and his abilities, although genuine, seemed limited. Yet it is evident that these apparent defects, when allied with a solid basis of traditional Roman common sense and a broad view of the Empire, were in fact the very qualities needed to undo years of social uncertainty and internecine violence.

As an administrator Vespasian was diligent; his major concern was to ensure the proper functioning of those operations necessary to any state: tax collections, public works, defense, and commerce. Having achieved the imperial position, he was more concerned to execute it conscientiously for the state than to defend it obsessively for himself. Ancient historians are unanimous in their view that he displayed none of the crippling suspicions and paranoid actions of earlier rulers. Cornelius Tacitus, that bleak and perceptive observer of imperial Rome, gave Vespasian the rarest of praise when he wrote that he was the only ruler who became better, rather than worse, as time went on.

Vespasian's common origins were perhaps one reason that he could form a larger view of the Empire, including more of its population as citizens and senators. He was not trapped by the old views of patrician families seeking to retain their privileged status and their time-honored, yet ineffectual, control of the state. His wide-ranging experiences, from Britain to Judaea, also helped give him this expanded perspective; there was not much doubt that this new direction enabled later emperors to maintain one of the world's most lasting political systems.

In this view, Vespasian certainly ranks as one of the best of the Roman emperors. This judgment is based upon many factors, but focuses on Vespasian's renewal and expansion of the Empire, an expansion less in geographical territory than in political unity.

Bibliography
Grant, Michael. *The Roman Emperors*. New York: Charles Scribner's Sons, 1985. Vespasian's rule is best judged not alone but as counterpoint to the disorder which preceded it. The brief selections in this volume provide an overview of the decline of the Empire during the last years of Nero and the near-fatal chaos that followed. Vespasian's accomplishments are viewed as the more outstanding in the comparison.
_____. *The Twelve Caesars*. New York: Charles Scribner's Sons, 1975. Grant continues where Suetonius' *Lives of the Twelve Caesars* (see below) leaves off in using anecdotes of character and personality to establish underlying psychological and political motives. By placing Vespasian within the tenor of his times, Grant not only makes the emperor more human but also shows the impressive nature of his achievements.
Greenhalgh, P. A. L. *The Year of the Four Emperors*. London: Weidenfeld and Nicolson, 1975. A large part of Vespasian's reputation is linked to the

restoration of order to the Roman world after an intense period of chaos. This study concentrates on the events which brought him to power and reveals the extensive task of reconstruction he had to undertake.

Marsh, Henry. *The Caesars: The Roman Empire and Its Rulers*. New York: St. Martin's Press, 1971. A brisk narrative in this popular collection of biographical portraits shows Vespasian in his roles as soldier, administrator, emperor, and rough-edged individual. The nonscholarly style is admirably suited to the character of Vespasian, with his practical common sense and coarse humor.

Suetonius. *Lives of the Twelve Caesars*. New York: Modern Library, 1959. True to the standards of ancient biography, Suetonius shows the caesars less as actors on the grand political stage than as particular individuals with quirks and characteristics. This presentation, while missing much of importance, is still excellent for revealing the unmistakable individuality of a man such as Vespasian.

Michael Witkoski

GIOVANNI VILLANI

Born: c. 1275; Florence, Italy
Died: 1348; Florence, Italy
Area of Achievement: Historiography
Contribution: In his *Chronicle*, Villani conveys an empirical account of the Italian communes and lays the foundation for a historiography based on human will and action.

Early Life

Giovanni Villani was born into a wealthy merchant family in Florence, Italy. It may be assumed that Villani, like most sons of merchants, went to a grammar school to learn Latin and then to another school to learn computation on the abacus. Thereafter, he likely apprenticed with a merchant firm, perhaps the Peruzzi company, with which his name was first associated. He served as an agent and partner in this great merchant banking house in Flanders off and on from 1300 to 1307. From his intimate knowledge of the affairs of Philip IV, it has been conjectured that he had contact with the French royal court. In Florence, international trade and banking were integrally linked, and at some point Villani entered the guild of bankers. He witnessed and contributed to Florence's golden age of commerce when the city served as Europe's banker and one of its chief centers of trade. After 1308, Villani continued to act as a representative of the Peruzzi, but he was no longer a formal partner. In 1322, Villani became a member of the rival merchant company of the Buonaccorsi. His participation in the Buonaccorsi firm reflects his independence, for he appears to have been one of the principal partners, which would have required a sizable investment.

Life's Work

In a manner similar to that of other Florentine merchants, Villani served abroad in his early adulthood and accumulated knowledge and wealth. He thus possessed the leisure and experience to participate in the Florentine Republic from 1316 to 1341. In addition to numerous minor offices, including responsibility for coining money and for the city walls, Villani held the position of prior, the most prestigious and powerful in the Florentine government, in 1316, 1321-1322, and 1328. Though he apparently never fathered children, he married twice, his second wife being from the wealthy family of the Pazzi. This marriage into the highest echelon of Florentine society and his political offices best indicate Villani's social prominence in the city of Florence.

In 1338, Villani's economic and social fortunes suffered a disastrous blow—one that affected the entire Florentine merchant community. In that year, the Buonaccorsi suffered bankruptcy, as did the Bardi and Peruzzi companies. Villani was sent to the infamous Florentine prison, the Stinche, for his debts, and he never recovered his wealth or prestige. From 1342 to 1343, the Florentines experimented with rule by a dictator, which led to a more popular government composed of new citizens, many of them from the Florentine countryside. Villani held no offices after 1341 and felt alienated from the rule of the new governors. In his history of Florence, he frequently criticized these newcomers for their presumption and political ineptitude. Villani died in 1348 from the plague while describing in his history the devastating power of that terrible disease.

The fame of Villani derives from his *Croniche fiorentine* (*Chronicle*, 1896). The Italian edition was completed by F. G. Dragomanni in four volumes dated 1844 to 1845, though it has never been fully translated into English. Villani informs the reader that he was stimulated to write his history of Florence while on a pilgrimage in Rome for the Great Jubilee of 1300. Excited by the ancient monuments and the great deeds of Roman heroes and stirred by the belief that Florence was the daughter of Rome, Villani determined to memorialize the numerous accomplishments of his native city. On the basis of internal evidence, critics have judged that he began to write in the 1320's or even as late as the 1330's. He probably did conceive of writing the history in 1300, beginning to accumulate materials then or soon thereafter. He also may have sketched the chief events of the period of Florentine political conflict from 1301 to 1304, which he knew at first hand. It was only in 1322, however, that he began to treat Florentine history fully. From that year until his death, Villani appears to have written contemporaneously with the events and to have recorded all the important occurrences that came into his purview. In the 1330's or early 1340's, he decided upon the overall form of the work, to which he added chronicles of the final years.

The *Chronicle* is composed of twelve books, with the first six dealing primarily with events prior to Villani's lifetime. In the broadest analysis, Villani's *Chronicle* remains in the tradition of medieval histories because it places the events of fourteenth century Florence within a universal history that begins with the Tower of Babel as a dispersal of Adam's descendants. In the first book, Villani narrates the history of Rome intertwined with the mythical origins of Florence and its rival to the north, the small hilltop town of Fiesole. This Etruscan town was to serve Villani as the source of enmity and social conflict within Florence, a conflict which could be overcome only through the triumph of Roman virtues implanted within the Florentines by Julius Caesar's founding. Books 2 through 6 center on Florence's dealings with the two great medieval superpowers, the Roman Empire and the Papacy. Villani claimed that Charlemagne had refounded the city after the Gothic king Totila had destroyed it; Villani believed that Florence was to play an important role within the divine order by participating with the Papacy in the Guelph alliance.

Villani drew heavily from Roman and Christian legends as well as from a number of thirteenth and early fourteenth century Florentine chronicles. From the latter he took a knowledge of specific events and the ideology of Florence's preeminent place in Christendom and Christian history. Utilizing these earlier chronicles and his personal observations, Villani in books 7 through 12 recounted the history of Florence through 1348. Here he demonstrated an empirical knowledge of both the daily political and social life of his town and the larger political questions that troubled all of Europe.

Villani structured his narration of events upon the belief that history has several meanings. His history frequently illustrates the working out of divine judgment as sinful figures eventually come to earthly punishments after a season of success. Thus, God's will finds expression in historical time, often through the use of one historical personage to punish another. God's justice, however, triumphs in the world only to be tested again through another people's or individual's vices. Villani sought a confirmation of religious and moral beliefs in the events of history: In his chronicle, history is a stage for the conflict of moral forces and, insofar as historical individuals represent states and institutions, political forces.

Villani also recounted fully the round of natural events, particularly unusual storms, eclipses, and portents. The Florentine chronicler often explained the behavior of individuals and natural phenomena by the movement of comets, stars, and planets. Moreover, the Devil and Providence play important roles in the *Chronicle* by influencing both human decisions and the natural world. Next to these irrational explanations of behavior, however, are rational analyses of human will, thought, and act. At times these analyses are integrated with an intimate knowledge of the natural environment to yield a convincing explanation of human character and events. Villani is best and justly known for his empirical description of the world of the Florentine merchant of the fourteenth century. Historians have thoroughly explored his chronicle for information on Florentine life in the fourteenth century, in part because he describes it in intimate detail. His chapter on Florence in 1336-1338 demonstrates a statistical frame of mind. As one of the first demographers, he judged the size of the city's population; the number of adult males, foreigners, nobles, and knights; the number of males and females born each year; and the number of students in grammar schools, schools of computation with the abacus, and schools of Latin and logic. He noted the number of churches, abbeys, and parishes along with the names of their priests and friars. He celebrated the guilds, especially those of merchants and bankers, noted the number of members and shops, and estimated their output. He focused particularly on the achievements of the Florentine cloth industry. Though scholars have suggested that he exaggerated the number of shops and the amount of cloth they produced, Villani's account enables the reader to gain a sense of the complexity of cloth manufacturing and sale in a premodern city. He describes in considerable detail the amount of food brought into the city in 1280 and notes the quantities of wine, grain, cows, sheep, goats, pigs, and melons.

Villani initiated a family practice of writing chronicles. Soon after his death in 1348, Villani's brother, Matteo, took up the craft of writing history. Matteo continued many of Giovanni's practices, including an emphasis on morality (perhaps heightened in the new history because of the depression resulting from the Black Death), a chronological ordering of events, and a penchant for detailed description. Matteo's history of Florence also was ended by the plague when in 1363 he succumbed to the disease. Matteo's son Filippo continued the family tradition of writing history; he wrote one book that narrated the events of 1364.

Summary

The *Chronicle* of Giovanni Villani should be judged as the best expression of the writing of Italian history in the Middle Ages, combining two qualities of medieval historiography. In common with the chronicles of monasteries and towns it recounts in vivid detail the events that the chronicler believed deserved attention, from natural events to human accomplishments and viciousness. His chronicle also places these events within a divine ordering of nature and history. Villani could have borrowed this providential view of history from a variety of sources, but he ultimately draws it from the church fathers, particularly Saint Augustine.

Within these traditional qualities, Villani began several novel practices that came to fruition in Italian Renaissance history writing. Particularly significant was his close analysis of political motivation, a focus that came to be one of the hallmarks of Renaissance historiography. His explanations of human character and values often are complete and convincing, undermining his supernatural and magical explanations and rendering them superfluous. It is important to note, however, that his history does not demonstrate the influence of classical rhetoric, which added structure and a more complex awareness of audience to the histories of the Italian Renaissance Humanists.

Bibliography

Aquilecchia, G. "Dante and the Florentine Chroniclers." *Bulletin of the John Rylands Library* 48 (1965-1966): 40-51. This article argues that Villani stated that he was inspired to write his chronicle in 1300 in order to associate it with *The Divine Comedy*.

Becker, Marvin B. *Florence in Transition.* 2 vols. Baltimore: Johns Hopkins University Press, 1967-1968. The best account of the period of Villani's life, this work argues that Villani represents a corporate world in which the merchants and nobles attempted to rule through persuasion and with a minimum of law and punishment, though Villani emphasized both the vio-

lence of the nobles and the political immaturity of new citizens.
Green, Louis. *Chronicle into History: An Essay on the Interpretation of History in Florentine Fourteenth-Century Chronicles*. Cambridge: Cambridge University Press, 1972. In the chapter on Villani, Green contends that the *Chronicle* represents the fulfillment of the medieval chronicle tradition and fuses rational explanations of history with supernatural and magical elements. Subsequent Renaissance writers emphasized one or the other.
Schevill, Ferdinand. *Medieval and Renaissance Florence*. Vol. 1, *Medieval Florence*. Rev. ed. New York: Frederick Ungar Publishing Co., 1961. Discussion of medieval Florence that relies substantially on Villani's *Chronicle* and emphasizes Villani's empirical observation and rational analysis.
Wicksteed, Philip H., ed. *Selections from the First Nine Books of the "Croniche Fiorentine" of Giovanni Villani*. Translated by Rose E. Selfe. Westminster, England: Archibald Constable and Co., 1896. A translation of selected chapters of the *Chronicle* through 1321. Though the selections were intended to aid in understanding Dante's *The Divine Comedy*, they convey a good sense of the general ordering of the history and of the history of Florence in the medieval period and in the age of the great poet.

James R. Banker

GEOFFROI DE VILLEHARDOUIN

Born: c. 1150; near Bar-sur-Aube, France
Died: c. 1213; possibly Greece
Areas of Achievement: Warfare and literature
Contribution: After playing a significant role in the organization and conduct of the Fourth Crusade, Villehardouin wrote an original and valuable history of it.

Early Life

Geoffroi de Villehardouin, who was in all likelihood the son of Villain I de Villehardouin, was born circa 1150 to a family whose earlier history is virtually unknown. While little information exists about Villehardouin's youth, it seems that by 1172, the year that his name was entered on a list of the vassals of the Count of Champagne, he was already married and had children. The surviving records suggest that Villehardouin married twice and that he had, in all, five children.

In 1185, Villehardouin became Marshal of Champagne, which means that he assumed specific domestic and military responsibilities at a high level. In addition to overseeing the care of all the horses of his suzerain, Count Henry II of Champagne, Villehardouin's charge included the supervision of the military service and remuneration of the count's vassals. In time of war, Villehardouin's duty as marshal was to follow his overlord into battle, in the forefront of the army. Villehardouin may have done just that in 1190, when Henry left for the Holy Land to join in the Third Crusade, but there is no historical evidence establishing this as fact. While versed in Latin, theology, and music, Henry had little interest in works of literature written in the vernacular. It is quite possible, therefore, that Villehardouin's lack of enthusiasm for the courtly ideal, as later reflected in the generally sober style of his historical writing, was conditioned by the count's literary tastes.

Life's Work

Villehardouin achieved distinction both as a leader and as a historian of the Fourth Crusade. Unhappily, this dual distinction was to a certain degree tarnished by the abortive outcome of the Crusade itself, which, setting out to liberate the Holy Land from the Muslims, was diverted to the assaulting, capturing, and looting of Christian cities, such as Zara on the Dalmatian coast and Constantinople, the capital of the Byzantine Empire. Furthermore, Villehardouin's largely positive account of the expedition fueled the suspicion that he was primarily concerned with justifying his decisions and those of his fellow commanders rather than exposing the errors and the dubious motivations. In the final analysis, however, Villehardouin's achievement both as a participant in and as a chronicler of the Fourth Crusade proved to be outstanding.

Along with his new suzerain, Count Thibaut III of Champagne, Ville-hardouin became a Crusader in November, 1199, responding to the appeal launched the previous year by Pope Innocent III. From the outset, Ville-hardouin's role in the Fourth Crusade was prominent. He and Conon de Béthune, the celebrated poet, were among six envoys who went to Venice in February, 1201, in order to negotiate for the transportation of the Crusaders to the Holy Land. Subsequently, upon the death on May 24, 1201, of Thibaut, it was again Villehardouin who assumed an active role in the search for Thibaut's replacement. Indeed, at the Council of Soissons in June, 1201, Villehardouin argued in favor of Boniface of Montferrat as the new com-mander in chief of the Crusaders and saw his personal choice ratified.

After the Crusaders had captured Constantinople on July 17, 1203, and restored Emperor Isaac II Angelus, who had been deposed by his brother, Alexius III Angelus, Villehardouin was designated the spokesman among the four representatives sent to meet with the emperor. Villehardouin was charged with reminding the latter of the political and financial obligations that the emperor's son, young Alexius, had assumed when he had asked for the Crusaders' help for his father. Villehardouin's mission proved successful, and on August 1, 1203, the young Alexius was crowned coemperor, becom-ing Alexius IV. Later, however, because their fraternization with a Latin army of Crusaders had angered their Greek constituents, Isaac II Angelus and Alexius IV no longer seemed disposed to respect the agreement to pro-vide monetary assistance to the Crusaders. In November, 1203, Villehar-douin was again among envoys dispatched to the coemperors to convince them to honor their commitments.

Following the second conquest of Constantinople on April 13, 1204—in the course of which the Crusaders put to flight the usurper Alexius Ducas Murtzuphlus, who had strangled Alexius IV and seized power as Alexius V (Isaac II Angelus having died shortly before his son, apparently from a stroke)—an opportunity was afforded Villehardouin to display his skills as a conciliator. A dispute having arisen between the new emperor of Constan-tinople, Count Baldwin of Flanders, and Boniface of Montferrat over the kingdom of Thessalonica, Villehardouin brought about a face-saving truce by blaming the dispute on the bungling of the disputants' advisers. Emperor Baldwin then agreed to give Thessalonica to Boniface.

In 1205, with the Greeks in open revolt and the Bulgars and Vlachs invad-ing the Crusaders' strongholds, circumstances developed which permitted Villehardouin to display his military prowess. After Baldwin had laid siege to Adrianople and had in turn been attacked by King Ioannitsa of the Vlacho-Bulgarian state, Count Louis of Blois was killed, on April 14, 1205, when he unwisely left the main detachment of the Crusaders to pursue the enemy's Cuman archers. Baldwin himself was captured in this engagement, having followed Louis. Villehardouin halted the disorderly retreat of the Crusaders, reassembled them into a fighting unit—despite the constant harassment of the Bulgars—and effected an orderly withdrawal. Yet Villehardouin could not single-handedly stem the tide of military reverses. On September 4, 1207, Boniface was killed in an ambush by the Bulgars, thus dramatically marking, at least as far as Villehardouin was concerned, the official and tragic conclusion of the ill-fated Fourth Crusade.

Beyond being a trusted ambassador, an adroit conciliator, and an effective, courageous military commander, Villehardouin was also a chronicler of the momentous events of the Crusade. The portrait of Villehardouin the historian, however, is far more complex than that of Villehardouin the Crusader.

Villehardouin's work, written after 1207, was entitled *L'Histoire de Geoffroy de Villehardouin, mareschal de Champagne et de Roménie, de la conqueste de Constantinople par les barons français associez aux Vénitiens, l'an 1204* (1584; *The Chronicle of Geoffry de Villehardouin, Marshall of Champagne and Romania, Concerning the Conquest of Constantinople by the French and Venetians, Anno MCCIV*, 1829). More commonly known by the modernized French title *La Conquête de Constantinople*, Villehardouin's account seems at first glance designed not only to chronicle the deflection of the Fourth Crusade from its intended objective but also to justify that deflection. Thus the historian notes that the decision on the part of the Crusaders to help the Venetians invest Zara—which was taken on November 24, 1202—in return for the transportation of the crusading army to the Holy Land was inevitable: The defection of so many Crusaders had made it impossible to pay the Venetians as originally agreed, and the Zara diversion was a way of removing the debt. Villehardouin does not reveal, however, that he and other leaders of the Crusade had erred in their estimate of the number of Crusaders needing transportation and had thus contracted for an excessive quantity of ships. Since, of the estimated 33,500 men, only one-third actually appeared in Venice, even without the defections the error of calculation would still have loomed large.

At the same time, Villehardouin appears overly bent on justifying his choice of Boniface of Montferrat as leader of the Crusade on the basis of the latter's possession of the chivalric qualities of nobility, piety, generosity, loyalty, and courage. Villehardouin does not indicate that Boniface had a definite familial and political stake in the Crusade. His brother Conrad had kept Saladin out of Tyre in 1187, married Isabel, heiress to the kingdom of Jerusalem, and thought of himself as king until his assassination in 1192. Another brother, Renier, had married Maria, the daughter of Emperor Manuel I Comnenus of Constantinople, in 1180, and had been given Thessalonica. When, after the second conquest of Constantinople, Boniface demanded the kingdom of Thessalonica, it was therefore much more than a sudden whim. Indeed, another medieval French historian of the Fourth Crusade took stern and critical note of Boniface's private motives: In 1216, Robert de Clari accused the commander in chief of opportunism and hypocrisy in *Li Estoire de chiaus qui conquisent Coustantinoble de Robert de Clari, en Aminois, chevalier* (1868; *The Conquest of Constantinople*, 1936).

As for the initial conquest of Constantinople, Villehardouin again seems to have wanted to put the best possible construction on this additional attack on a Christian city. He maintains that the capture of Constantinople not only brought to an end the cruel reign of Alexius III Angelus and allowed the restoration to power of the dispossessed Isaac II Angelus and the future Alexius IV but also guaranteed that the new imperial authority would pledge fidelity to Rome and also support the Crusade. Villehardouin does not report that, beyond Boniface's personal stake in the matter as noted above, there was the special interest of the Venetians themselves. Having pressed for the move against Zara because it had been a Venetian vassal state until lured away by King Béla III of Hungary in 1186, Venice encouraged the assault on Constantinople because that city had long persecuted Venetian residents. Moreover, Constantinople had favored the Genoese and the Pisans, commercial competitors of the Venetians, in part by levying huge taxes on the latter. Finally, if the Doge of Venice, Enrico Dandolo, was half blind, it may have been because of the barbarity of his Greek "hosts."

Nevertheless, one must recognize that Villehardouin's failure to discuss the whole range of motives behind the diversion of the Fourth Crusade was neither demonstrably intentional nor substantially distortive. He appears genuinely to have believed that the leaders of the Crusade had no choice but to divert it from its original destination, given the circumstances. Villehardouin might be faulted for having overestimated the number of ships needed to transport the Crusaders. On the other hand, the majority of his actions seem to have been based on much more than narrowly partisan considerations. For example, the choice of Boniface as commander in chief, whatever his vested interest, was sound: He was widely recognized as one of the most accomplished men of his time, being a proven warrior who had fought against Saladin and a patron of the arts who encouraged troubadours at his court. Moreover, before deciding upon him, Villehardouin and others had approached two other candidates, the Duke of Burgundy and the Count of Bar-le-Duc.

As for the involvement of the Venetians, it had become common practice to seek maritime transportation to the Holy Land, in the light of the extended and complicated overland route. Although the Venetians were not exactly enamored of Byzantium, there is no evidence that, beyond seeking a fair financial return for their services, they actually conspired to steer the Crusaders away from the announced objective. Villehardouin's obvious respect for their organizational acumen, nautical skill, and courage did not appear suspect at a time when Venice was at the height of its prestige as a great maritime and commercial power. Even the portrait of the doge, admittedly epic, was not incompatible with the fame and glory of the aged but admired Dandolo.

If a more balanced view of the political and military realities of Villehardouin's time shows his history to be a worthy achievement in substantive terms, so a fair analysis of the work's place in the formal evolution of French historiography shows it to be a worthy achievement in stylistic terms. It is clear that Villehardouin's work owes much to the epic tradition of narration, as evidenced not only by the use of conventional techniques of anticipation, recapitulation, and transition, but also, and more fundamentally, by the attribution of legendary traits to the heroes of his narrative. In a manner reminiscent of the portrait of Charlemagne in the famous twelfth century medieval epic *La Chanson de Roland* (*The Song of Roland*), the Doge of Venice is characterized as *preuz* (valiant), *sages* (wise), and *vigueros* (vigorous) despite his years; his feats in the first Battle of Constantinople are attended by miraculous occurrences, as when the defenders of the city fled before this fearless brandisher of the standard of Saint Mark. Similarly, by its heroic loneliness, the death of Boniface—with which, significantly, Villehardouin chose to end his work—recalled that of Roland in *The Song of Roland*, without the subsequent redress of the situation featured in the medieval epic.

Yet in spite of being clearly indebted to the epic style, *La Conquête de Constantinople* broke new historical ground. Though primarily interested in the grand lines of strategy and combat, the historian, in dealing with specific events, often strove for the factual accuracy characteristic of the best Latin historical tradition, availing himself of eyewitness accounts when his own perspective—generally that of a direct participant—was inadequate. More significant still, Villehardouin chose to write his history in French prose, not in poetry. His work would be, in fact, the first known prose history in French. The nature of Villehardouin's prose, moreover, is itself remarkable for its straightforwardness, sobriety, and simplicity—qualities highlighted by a third-person narrative judiciously combined with moments of direct speech and marked by a more systematic use of the past tense than was typical of the epic style. In short, however great the temptation to be thoroughly partisan, Villehardouin appears, more often than not, to have made a real effort to move from fact to fact without rhetorical digressions—much in the manner of the modern historian.

If it is known that Villehardouin wrote *La Conquête de Constantinople* after 1207, that is practically all that is known about his last years. He is thought to have died between 1212 and 1218, at a site unknown.

Summary

Geoffroi de Villehardouin's skill in negotiating with the Venetians, his success in getting his personal choice approved as commander in chief of the Fourth Crusade, and his actions to avert total disaster after the failure of the siege of Adrianople testify amply both to the importance of his role in the organization of the Crusade and to the extent of his influence in determining its orientation and outcome. As a historian, however, Villehardouin's impact was perhaps even more impressive. With no known model to guide him, he composed a history in French prose which represented such a high standard of achievement that it would be matched only on rare occasions before the seventeenth century.

Bibliography
Beer, Jeanette M. A. *Villehardouin: Epic Historian.* Geneva, Switzerland: Librairie Droz, 1968. An insightful study of Villehardouin's stylistic technique, with particular attention given to his antecedents, the role in his work of biblical references, the influence upon him of the Latin historical tradition, and his employment of devices drawn from the medieval French epic. There are valuable vocabulary appendices and a useful selected bibliography of primary and secondary sources.
Godfrey, John. *1204: The Unholy Crusade.* New York: Oxford University Press, 1980. Motivated by a desire to approach the supposedly "criminal" Fourth Crusade from the more enlightened vantage of a deepened understanding of the medieval mind, the author of this work, without neglecting Villehardouin, seeks to place the Crusade within the broader framework of relations existing at the time between Constantinople and Western Europe, on the one hand, and Constantinople and Islam, on the other. Intended primarily for the general reader, this book nevertheless contains very interesting information of a specific nature, which is to be found in its chronological appendices relative to the imperial dynasties and in its notes.
Morris, Colin. "Geoffroy de Villehardouin and the Conquest of Constantinople." *History* 53 (1968): 24-34. Against the backdrop of data drawn from reliable sources, and with reference to critics both sympathetic and unsympathetic to Villehardouin's version, the author systematically and informatively compares what is known about the Fourth Crusade with Villehardouin's account of it in order to determine the extent to which the latter was writing a propaganda piece and the extent to which he took himself seriously as a historian.
Queller, Donald E. *The Fourth Crusade: The Conquest of Constantinople, 1201-1204.* Philadelphia: University of Pennsylvania Press, 1977. Written originally to fill the gap created by the absence of any modern scholarly work in English specifically dealing with the Fourth Crusade, this book finds its justification also in the fact that its author, adopting a perspective which is Western European rather than Byzantine, presents a view not commonly encountered in studies relating to the general area of his subject. The work is also useful because of its extensive bibliography of primary and secondary sources.

Villehardouin, Geoffroi de, and Jean de Joinville. *Memoirs of the Crusades.* Translated by Sir Frank Marzials. Reprint. Westport, Conn.: Greenwood Press, 1983. This work contains English translations of the chronicles of Villehardouin and Jean, Sire de Joinville, preceded by an introduction which discusses the chronicles from the standpoint of their political and literary importance. In the section on Villehardouin, the translator also provides a helpful summary of the earlier Crusades and, for both chroniclers, equally helpful annotations regarding earlier translations and their relative merits.

Norman Araujo

FRANÇOIS VILLON

Born: 1431; Paris, France
Died: 1463?; place unknown
Area of Achievement: Literature
Contribution: In his intensely personal, forthright verse, sordidly realistic yet devout, Villon was the greatest poet of medieval France.

Early Life

Born in Paris in 1431, François Villon was originally named François de Montcorbier et des Loges. Apparently his father died when the child was quite young, for François was sent to live with Guillaume de Villon, a priest who was chaplain to the church of Saint-Benoît-le-Bientourné, near the University of Paris. His protector gave the boy a home and an education; the grateful François adopted his name, Villon, and several times wrote fondly of him in his verse, calling him "more than father... who has been to me more tender than a mother and raised me from swaddling-clothes." Nothing is known of his real father, not even his first name; Villon called himself "of poor and obscure extraction." His mother, for whom he wrote "Ballade to Our Lady," he describes at the time as a poor old woman who knew nothing of letters.

Nothing is known of Villon's boyhood. Joan of Arc was burned at the stake the year he was born, and for the first five years of his life, Paris was in the hands of the English conquerors, while the ineffectual Charles VII nominally ruled the unoccupied part of France. Most of the country had been ravaged by the Hundred Years' War, and bands of freebooters were plundering whatever of value remained in the countryside or the capital. In 1434, there was the coldest winter in memory, followed in 1436 by a famine, which was succeeded in 1438 by an epidemic of smallpox that claimed some fifty thousand victims. Starving wolves invaded Paris and preyed upon children and the weak. It was a grim, harsh era, and as a child, Villon must have seen violence and famine and been surrounded by death.

When he was about twelve, Villon was enrolled at the University of Paris, from which he was graduated in March, 1449, as a bachelor of arts. He was tonsured and received minor holy orders, affording him some protection from the police—which he needed, as he was involved in student escapades that were typical of the medieval conflict between town and gown, including stealing boundary stones and house signs that were then carried off to the student quarter, which in turn was raided by the police. Despite his peccadilloes, Villon received a master of arts degree in August of 1452.

Life's Work

Despite his education and the opportunities that it might have provided him, Villon fell in with a group of criminals known as "Coquillards" and began a life of crime. Among his cronies, who are featured in his poems, were Colin des Cayeulx, described by the authorities as a thief and picklock, and Regnier de Montigny, a thief, murderer, and church robber. Both of them were hanged, and Villon wrote their epitaphs. Villon also prowled around Paris with Guy Tabarie, Jehan the Wolf, and Casin Cholet, all of them thieves, and spent much time at brothels and taverns such as the Mule and the Pomme de Pin, whose proprietor, Robin Turgis, was often a target of Villon's humor.

According to a poem of the time entitled "Repues Franches," thought to be by Friar Baulde de la Mare, Villon and his rascally friends had a genius for conning free fish, meat, bread, and wine from gullible victims. Soon Villon's picaresque career became more sinister. In the evening of June 5, 1455, the Feast of Corpus Christi, Villon was seated under the clock of Saint-Benoît-le-Bientourné, in company with a priest and a woman named Ysabeau, when another priest, Philip Chermoye, who had apparently been harboring a grudge, started a quarrel with Villon, drew a dagger, and slashed his upper lip. Bleeding copiously, Villon drew his own dagger and stabbed Chermoye in the groin; when Chermoye still attempted to injure him, Villon threw a rock that struck him in the face. After having his wound dressed, Villon fled from the city. Chermoye was taken to the Hôtel-Dieu, where he died after a few days. According to one account, Chermoye on his deathbed confessed that he had started the fight and forgave Villon. Thus Villon's friends were able to get him a pardon in January of 1456, and he then returned to Paris. There, he fell in love with Katherine de Vausselles, who may have been a kinswoman of a colleague of Guillaume de Villon. At any rate, she teased and tormented Villon and eventually left him for Noël Joliz, who beat him in her presence. Heartsick and purse poor, Villon resolved to leave Paris at the end of 1456 and wrote for the occasion his first important work of poetry, *Le Lais* (1489; *The Legacy*, 1878, also known as *Le Petit Testament, The Little Testament*), in which he bids an ironic farewell to his friends and mockingly bequeaths them his worldly goods.

Before departing, he and four of his Coquillard cronies, probably on Christmas Eve, climbed over the wall into the College of Navarre, broke into the sacristy, and stole five hundred gold crowns from the faculty of theology. With his one-fifth share, Villon left the city, going first to Angers and thence wandering for the next four and a half years. In the meantime, Guy Tabarie boasted of the crime, was arrested and tortured, and confessed the details. A wanted man, Villon stayed on the run, going at one time to the court of Blois, where he associated with the courtly poet Charles d'Orléans, to whose daughter Marie he wrote a poetic epistle. Otherwise, except for a few clues that he drops in his verse, his activities are unknown until the summer of 1460, when he was in a dungeon at Orléans under sentence of death, from which he was pardoned during the passage through the city of the Princess

Marie. A year later, at Meung-sur-Loire, he was tried at the ecclesiastical court of Thibault d'Aussigny, Bishop of Orléans, who chained him in a dungeon under the moat and inflicted the water torture on him. Villon's health was broken, but he once more received a pardon when King Louis XI made a royal progress through the town and freed the prisoners.

Hiding near Paris, during the winter of 1461, Villon wrote his major work, aside from some of the ballades, *Le Grand Testament* (1489; *The Great Testament*, 1878), which follows the form of the earlier *The Legacy* but has far more depth and texture and which also incorporates a number of ballades, chansons, and rondeaux. Back in Paris itself, he was arrested in November, 1462, for petty theft; before he was released, the authorities made him sign a bond promising to repay the money that was stolen from the College of Navarre. Shortly thereafter, following an evening of revelry, one of Villon's companions got into a brawl with a papal scribe and wounded the man with a dagger thrust. Though Villon had left at the first sign of trouble, he was identified, arrested as an accomplice, and imprisoned in the Châtelet, where he was tortured and sentenced to the gallows. While awaiting execution, he wrote an ironic "Quatrain" and his great "L'Épitaphe Villon," otherwise known as "Ballade of the Hanged," in which he imagines himself and six others rotting on the gibbet and prays to God to absolve them all. Yet once more Villon cheated the gallows. He appealed to Parliament, and since he had not taken part in the fight and the victim had not died, his sentence was annulled and changed to ten years' exile from Paris. In response, Villon wrote his "Panegyric to the Court of Parliament" requesting three days to prepare for his departure and his sardonic "Question to the Clerk of the Prison Gate." In January, 1463, he left Paris and vanished from history and into legend. Though only thirty-two years old, he may have died from the lasting effects of imprisonment and torture. In *The Great Testament*, he speaks of having the worn-out body of an old man and of "spitting white"—a hint that he may have had a lung disease, perhaps tuberculosis. A century later, François Rabelais recounts Villon's having gone to England and received the protection of Edward V; Rabelais also tells of Villon's having retired in his old age to Poitou. Without any corroborating evidence, however, Rabelais' accounts are probably fiction. At any rate, no more of Villon's poetry is recorded after he left Paris.

The Legacy is made up of forty octaves or *huitains* of octosyllabic lines; *The Great Testament* has 175 such octaves, among which are interspersed sixteen ballades, a triple ballade, three rondels, and *Belle Leçon*; in addition, there is Villon's codicil, containing other ballades, the quatrain written after his being sentenced to death, and a number of poems in thieves' jargon. The standard ballade consists of three stanzas of eight octosyllabic lines each, followed by a four-line *envoi* generally beginning with the vocative "Prince!"—though Villon's may be addressed to Fortune, a mistress, a fellow poet, or

God. The rhyme scheme is invariably *ababbcbc* in the octave and *bcbc* in the *envoi*. A difficult verse form with only three rhymes, the ballade went out of favor after Villon's time and was not revived until nineteenth century imitations of Villon.

The Legacy is minor apprentice work, but after his career of crime, five years of vagabondage, and several ordeals under torture, Villon emerged as a great poet in *The Great Testament*. In it, he re-creates with vivid intensity the underworld of medieval Paris—the same setting as Victor Hugo's *Nôtre-Dame de Paris* (1831; *The Hunchback of Notre Dame*, 1833). Writing sometimes in thieves' jargon, Villon takes the reader through the taverns, brothels, thieves' dens, and prisons. His is a world of ribald bawdry, crime, revelry, profanity, prostitution, disease, and the dance of death, but it is redeemed by sardonic wit, by an intense relish for life, and despite Villon's sacrilege, by a devout reverence for medieval Christianity and an awareness of the vanity of his riotous life. Outstanding among his poems are his "Ballade of Fat Margot"; "Lament of the Belle Heaulmière" (the beautiful armoress), about an aging prostitute; the ballades to the ladies and lords of bygone times, the first with its haunting refrain, "But where are the snows of yesteryear?"; the "Ballade of the Hanged"; the "Ballade as a Prayer to Our Lady," which he put into the mouth of his aged mother; the "Ballade Against the Enemies of France"; and "The Dialogue Between the Heart and Body of Villon."

Summary

The first critical edition of François Villon's poems was made in 1533 by Clément Marot, himself a major poet of the Renaissance. Thereafter, Villon's life and works fell into obscurity for the next three centuries. Not until the 1830's did Villon resurface, when Théophile Gautier began to write about him as a precursor to the Romantics and bohemians and to praise Villon's defiance of bourgeois values. In England, Villon was quite unknown until the 1860's, but during the rest of the century he received a considerable amount of attention, his work appearing in numerous translations, most notably by Dante Gabriel Rossetti and Algernon Charles Swinburne, both of whom tried to make the French poet fit into their Pre-Raphaelite aesthetic and who portrayed him as a rebel against middle-class morality. Following them, a number of lesser poets—Andrew Lang, Edmund Gosse, Walter Besant—did routine translations of some of Villon's poems as well as imitations of him. In 1878, John Payne published the first complete translation of Villon's work, issued to subscribers called "The Villon Society" to circumvent Victorian censorship. An edition for the public three years later was bowdlerized and expurgated of Villon's frank realism.

In 1877, Auguste Longnon published the first biography of Villon, following which a number of articles appeared in British periodicals providing a condensed account of Villon's life and exploiting the sensationalism of Longnon's discoveries. Several used Villon as a cautionary example to condemn bohemianism and aestheticism. Despite his own genteel bohemianism, Robert Louis Stevenson, in an article in 1877, presented Villon as an example of dissipation and degradation, one lacking the dignity of a Victorian gentleman, and condemned his "way of looking upon the sordid and ugly aspects of life," which he found becoming prominent in the work of such nineteenth century French writers as Émile Zola. Stevenson believed that one should bear one's sufferings stoically and complained that "Villon, who had not the courage to be poor with honesty, now whiningly implores our sympathy, now shows his teeth upon the dungheap with an ugly snarl." In the same year, Stevenson published his first short story, "A Lodging for the Night," about Villon's supposedly whining, cowardly behavior after his friend de Montigny murdered a priest. All the nineteenth century writers who saw in Villon a reflection of certain features of their own time oversimplify the man and his works and ignore the complexity of the medieval Christian not only indulging in debauchery, theft, murder, and sacrilege but also repenting and expressing a profound faith.

Reversing the portrayal by Stevenson and other nineteenth century writers, twentieth century fiction transformed Villon into the dashing and noble hero of swashbuckling romance. In 1901, Justin Huntly McCarthy's novel and play *If I Were King* turn Villon into a king of vagabonds who then becomes grand constable of France for a week and saves Paris from the invading Burgundians. The narrative is melodramatic and posturing; the characters speak what W. S. Gilbert calls "platitudes in stained-glass attitudes." The title poem, the best-known "verses" of Villon, are not by Villon at all but by McCarthy. *If I Were King* was turned into the popular operetta *The Vagabond King* (1925), with music by Rudolf Friml, which has been filmed twice, and a variation on the novel has been filmed three times, with William Farnum, John Barrymore, and Ronald Colman, respectively, playing Villon. It sounds an essentially false note but has colored the popular impression of Villon.

In a more serious vein, Villon influenced Ezra Pound, who wrote an opera about him, *The Testament of François Villon* (1926), an appreciative essay, "Montcorbier, alias Villon," and several "Villonaud" poems. Pound and T. S. Eliot also borrow for their own work the opening line of *The Great Testament*. Among Villon's other modern admirers was William Carlos Williams, who praised Villon's "intensity of consciousness," his psychological forthrightness and artistic integrity, his wit and daring realism, the immediacy and modernism of his personal note, so that of all the poets of the Middle Ages, Villon speaks most forthrightly to modern readers.

Bibliography
Anacker, Robert H. *François Villon*. New York: Twayne Publishers, 1968. A

critical survey in the Twayne World Authors series, Anacker's work follows the standard format for that series, with a chronology, a brief account of Villon's world and of his life, chapters analyzing *The Legacy*, *The Great Testament*, and other works, and an annotated bibliography. Dismisses the simplistic view of Villon as a "carefree vagabond," a "tavern minstrel," a bohemian, a Romantic lover, a forerunner of beatniks and hippies; tries to see him in the context of his times.

Fein, David A. *A Reading of Villon's Testament*. Birmingham, Ala.: Summa Publications, 1984. Fein reads the poetry on three levels: surface value, "that which Villon appears to be saying"; travesty, when Villon praises or blesses his enemies; and symbolic meaning. Quotes extensively from Villon, using Galway Kinnel's translation of the Longnon-Foulet text.

Lewis, D. B. Wyndham. *François Villon: A Documented Survey*. New York: Coward-McCann, 1928. The best biographical and critical study in English, Lewis' volume reconstructs in vivid detail the life of fifteenth century Paris. The biographical section is sometimes conjectural, as the author, writing in the first person, imagines the character of some of Villon's associates and dramatizes some of his escapades. Lewis also provides commentary on the works, followed by a variety of translations and an extensive bibliography of French sources.

Morsberger, Robert E. "Villon and the Victorians." *Bulletin of the Rocky Mountain Modern Language Association* 23 (December, 1969); 189-196. A study of the rediscovery of Villon, his influence upon such nineteenth century writers as Dante Gabriel Rossetti, Charles Algernon Swinburne, Robert Louis Stevenson, the interpretations and misinterpretations of him by the Victorian decadents and aesthetes, and his transformation in twentieth century fiction and films into a noble hero of romance.

Stevenson, Robert Louis. "François Villon, Student, Poet, and Housebreaker." In *Familiar Studies of Men and Books*. New York: Charles Scribner's Sons, 1905. A sometimes biased study, Stevenson's article condemns Villon for not having the traits of a Victorian gentleman but is important for showing the reaction of a leading Victorian writer. The article led to and parallels Stevenson's first short story,"A Lodging for the Night."

_____. "A Lodging for the Night." In *The Complete Short Stories of Robert Louis Stevenson*. Edited by Charles Neider. San Francisco: Windsor Press, 1969. The first treatment of Villon in fiction, it presents Villon as a whining, cowardly equivocator. The biased portrait of Villon is distorted by Stevenson's advocacy of the strenuous and stoical life and of noblesse oblige, which he thought Villon failed to exemplify.

Villon, François. *The Complete Works of François Villon*. Translated by Anthony Bonner. New York: Bantam Books, 1960. This edition gives the works in their original French, with Bonner's unrhymed translation on the facing page. The introductory material includes an appreciative essay by William Carlos Williams and a brief biography. The thirty-seven pages of notes are extremely thorough, identifying all the poems' characters, allusions, and historical details. A brief bibliography refers the reader chiefly to sources in French.

_____. *Poems*. Translated by John Heron Lepper. New York: Horace Liveright, 1926. A complete translation, following Villon's rhyme scheme, with an introduction by Lepper. Includes as well the first complete and unabridged translation by John Payne (also in Villon's rhyme scheme), as well as Payne's introduction to his 1881 edition and translations by Swinburne, Rossetti, Arthur Symons, and Ezra Pound.

Vitz, Evelyn Birge. *The Crossroads of Intention: A Study of Symbolic Expression in the Poetry of François Villon*. The Hague: Mouton, 1974. Vitz studies the symbolic expression in Villon's poetry—the process by which places, people, and things become symbolic. Considers the sexual symbolism, the symbolism in writing a will, and the contrast between Villon's self and the symbolic persona he assumes. Analyzes the medieval concept of psychology and cosmography.

Robert E. Morsberger

VINCENT OF BEAUVAIS

Born: c. 1190; Beauvais, Oise, France
Died: 1264; Beauvais, Oise, France
Areas of Achievement: Literature and historiography
Contribution: Vincent compiled the most comprehensive encyclopedia of the
Middle Ages, encompassing natural science, history, theology, philosophy,
and the liberal and mechanical arts.

Early Life

Very little is known about Vincent of Beauvais, except for his association
with the court of the French king Louis IX and inferences that can be drawn
from his writings. He never refers to his birthplace, but he often shows a
familiarity with people and events in Beauvais. No record of his birth exists,
and the approximate dates commonly given for it (usually between 1190 and
1200) stem partly from the assumption that he must have been a fairly young
man when he became a member of the newly formed Order of Preachers,
the Dominicans, in about 1220.

According to some sources, Vincent was based at the Dominican House
on rue St. Jacques in Paris and studied at the University of Paris in the
1220's. It seems likely that he participated in the founding of the Dominican
House in Beauvais in 1228-1229, perhaps in keeping with the Dominican custom of sending members of the order back to their hometowns to establish
convents. It was during this period of his life in Beauvais that he came to the
attention of Louis IX because of his early work on the compendium of
knowledge which finally became the *Speculum majus* (1244, revised 1256-
1259).

Life's Work

Although Vincent did not receive an official appointment from Louis IX
until about 1246, when he was made lector of the royally founded Cistercian
abbey at Royaumont (not far from Beauvais), he was probably in correspondence with the king in the early 1240's concerning his compendium, and he
received royal encouragement and financial support for some of the copying
and research on that immense project. The first version of the *Speculum
majus* seems to have been finished and ready for the king by 1244. From the
time of his appointment at Royaumont, however, Vincent was intimately
involved with the royal family, which was often in residence there. He became a kind of educational director for the king's children (although he did
not tutor them himself), and in 1260 he wrote, at the commission of the
queen, a work on the education of princes, *De eruditione filiorum nobilium*
(on the instruction of nobly born children). When one of the royal children,
the Dauphin Louis, died in 1260, Vincent wrote a personal consolation

(*Epistola consolatoria super morte filii*, or "letter of consolation on the death of his son") to the king. In the preface to this letter, Vincent mentions that he has preached before the king, a comment that offers further evidence of the respect he was shown by the royal family.

Vincent of Beauvais is chiefly remembered, however, for his tremendous three-volume encyclopedia, the *Speculum majus*. This work was begun probably in the 1230's and went through several stages before the revised version (covering material up to 1250) was made available sometime between 1256 and 1259. The Dominican emphasis on intellectual endeavors no doubt nurtured Vincent's desire to provide an all-inclusive reference book for the learned, but he devised the specific rationale and organization for the work, even though he presented himself as no more than an extractor of the wisdom of others. He saw the work as an aid to memory amid the bewildering abundance of materials one would have to consult to answer questions of theology, natural science, or history. He was a selector and arranger of knowledge, not an original thinker.

Nevertheless, what he produced was a monumental and influential treatise in three parts: the *Naturale*, the *Historiale*, and the *Doctrinale* (dealing, respectively, with the elements of nature, the acts of men, and the arts and sciences). The common purpose of these three parts (later editions added a spurious fourth book, the *Morale*) was to enable the readers more easily to observe, admire, and imitate the best in human wisdom up to that time; in other words, Vincent wanted to provide materials not only for intellectual instruction but also for moral improvement. The *Naturale* uses the six days of creation in Genesis as the basis of its organization, dealing with all aspects of the relationships among God, man, and nature. This line of thought leads into the next book, the *Historiale*, which through the account of fallen man's experiences shows the need for redemption through Jesus Christ. This redemption can be applied to man, however, by the process of education, and thus the arts and sciences discussed in the *Doctrinale* (*doctrina* means "instruction") serve to pull man out of the error imposed by sin and into the natural, uncorrupted knowledge of God's world.

With this emphasis on the value of human wisdom, the *Speculum majus* is one of the marvels of thirteenth century Scholasticism, ranking in its own way with the clearly more profound work of Saint Thomas Aquinas in his *Summa theologiae* (c. 1265-1273; *Summa theologica*, 1911-1921). Although Vincent did not share Thomas' exalted view of Aristotle, he did, like Thomas, show the usefulness of non-Christian sources of knowledge and affirmed the power of intellect to participate in the process of salvation.

Vincent's comments in the prologue to the *Speculum majus* indicate that he was a humble, unpretentious man, not bred to expectations of greatness. He wanted only to present the best of what others had said in the most usable form. When he wrote his smaller books of instruction, they were all commissioned, not volunteered. His last known work was *De morali principis institutione* (1263; of the order of moral principles for rulers), which he was entreated to write by Louis IX. An active and honored old man, Vincent of Beauvais died the next year after completing this book, his work assured of distribution through the patronage of his king, whom he had served as instructor, preacher, and friend.

Summary

Vincent of Beauvais was the most comprehensive of the medieval encyclopedists, going beyond the efforts of such others as Saint Isidore of Seville (c. 560-636), Lambert of St. Omer (*Liber floridus*, c. 1120), and Bartholomeus Anglicus (*De proprietatibus rerum*, c. 1230-1240; English translation, c. 1495). Vincent's authority was recognized well into the Renaissance. His treatment of the legends of Alexander the Great was the most extensive in the Middle Ages, and his lives of the saints and his other moral stories were drawn on or recommended by such well-known writers as Guillaume de Lorris and Jean de Meung in their *Roman de la Rose* (thirteenth century; *Romance of the Rose*), Jacob of Voragine (*Golden Legend*, late thirteenth century), Geoffrey Chaucer ("The Monk's Tale," late fourteenth century), and Christine de Pisan (early fifteenth century); even Sir Walter Raleigh, in *The History of the World* (1614), mentions Vincent as a source. The *Speculum majus* fell into disrepute as an emerging scientific age began to require more critical methods for ascertaining and presenting what purported to be facts, but Vincent's work remains an astounding intellectual feat and a monumental record of what medieval Europeans of the mid-thirteenth century regarded as their basic body of knowledge.

Bibliography

Aerts, W. J., E. R. Smits, and J. B. Voorbij, eds. *Vincent of Beauvais and Alexander the Great: Studies on the "Speculum Maius" and Its Translations into Medieval Vernaculars.* Gröningen, Netherlands: Egbert Forsten, 1986. A collection of essays, mostly on translations of Vincent's version of the Alexander story. The first two essays (by Smits and Voorbij) offer views of the Cistercian roots of the form, purpose, and function of the *Speculum majus* and of the probable chronology of the development of its parts. Includes a very complete bibliography.

Gabriel, Astrik L. *The Educational Ideas of Vincent of Beauvais.* Notre Dame, Ind.: University of Notre Dame Press, 1956, 1962. An excellent survey of Vincent's work, with special emphasis on his ideas on education as expressed in various parts of all of his writings. Documentation in footnotes is very thorough. Contains outlines of major works and a generous number of translated quotations.

Taylor, Henry Osborn. *The Medieval Mind: A History of the Development of*

Thought and Emotion in the Middle Ages. 2 vols. Cambridge, Mass.: Harvard University Press, 1966. Volume 2 deals with the relationship between Vincent's *Historiale* and the statuary at Chartres Cathedral and outlines and comments on the whole *Speculum majus.*

Tobin, Rosemary B. "Vincent of Beauvais' Double Standard in the Education of Girls." *History of Education* 7 (1978): 1-5. An exposition of the distinction made in Vincent's *De eruditione filiorum nobilium* between programs of education for boys and those for girls. Shows that girls' education is primarily moral, with the emphasis on preservation of chastity, whereas boys' education stresses intellectual development.

_____. "Vincent of Beauvais on the Education of Women." *Journal of the History of Ideas* 35 (July, 1974): 485-489. Tobin disputes the claim that Vincent's comments on women's education are more liberal than others of his time, concluding that Vincent's ideas on the education of women are quite consonant with other opinions in the thirteenth century.

Ullman, Berthold Louis. "A Project for a New Edition of Vincent of Beauvais." *Speculum* 8 (July, 1933): 312-326. In the context of demonstrating the need for a new edition of the *Speculum majus,* Ullman surveys what is known about Vincent and his work. Enumerates major figures influenced by the encyclopedia. Supported by sufficient, but not extensive, documentation.

Elton D. Higgs

SAINT VINCENT OF LÉRINS

Born: Late fourth century; probably in or near Toul
Died: c. 450; Lérins, Marseilles, or Troyes
Area of Achievement: Religion
Contribution: In his own time, Vincent was one of the leaders in the Gallic opposition to the concept of Augustinian predestination. After his death, Vincent came to be known primarily for his formula for distinguishing orthodoxy from heresy.

Early Life

Vincent was probably a native of Toul in northern Gaul and belonged to a well-to-do family. He and his brother, Lupus, would have received a classical education. Vincent also was learned in ecclesiastical literature: In the 490's, Gennadius of Marseilles described him as "a man learned in the holy scriptures and sufficiently instructed in the knowledge of ecclesiastical dogma." Sometime during his youth, Vincent held an unspecified civil or military secular office. Around 425-426, however, he and his brother, like many other young aristocrats, adopted the monastic life, going to the island of Lérins, near Nice. The abbot there, Honoratus, was another northerner; he perhaps came from near Dijon. Another monk who entered the monastery at about this same time was Honoratus' younger relative Hilary, whose sister Pimeniola had married Lupus.

Unlike many of the monks, who remained laymen, Vincent was ordained a priest. He was active in the quasi-familial atmosphere of the monastery. Along with Honoratus, Hilary, and the priest Salvian, later of Marseilles, he assisted in the education of Salonius and Veranus, the young sons of the monk Eucherius. Many of these monks went on to become bishops in their own right, Honoratus and Hilary at Arles, Eucherius at Lyons, and Lupus at Troyes. Vincent, however, remained a monk and may have spent time also at Marseilles as well as with his brother in the north: "Avoiding the turmoil and crowds of cities, I inhabit a little dwelling on a remote farmstead and within it the retreat of a monastery."

Life's Work

Vincent is known primarily for his involvement in ecclesiastical debates, especially in the controversy in Gaul surrounding some of the teachings of Saint Augustine. Augustine was much respected in Gaul, and every fifth century Gallic theologian cited him, at least on occasion, as an authority. Vincent himself compiled some *excerpta* from Augustine on the Trinity and the Incarnation. Augustine's opposition to Pelagianism, which denied original sin and the need for grace, was consistent with the prevalent Gallic orthodoxy. For example, according to a Gallic chronicler writing in 452, in 400 "the insane Pelagius attempts to befoul the churches with his execrable teaching."

The sticking point, however, was Augustine's concept of predestination, and according to that same source in the entry for the year 418, "the heresy of the predestinarians, which is said to have received its impetus from Augustine, once arisen creeps along." Predestination, which taught that only certain individuals were "predestined" for salvation, was seen as denying free will and as related to fatalism, Priscillianism, or Manichaean dualism.

The Gallic ambivalence toward Augustine ended in the mid-420's with the publication of his *De correptione et gratia* (426; *On Admonition and Grace*, 1873). In 426, John Cassian published an attack upon both Pelagianism and unconditional predestination. At about that same time, two of Augustine's supporters, the laymen Prosper of Aquitane and Hilarius, wrote letters to him, still extant, decrying the situation in Gaul. According to Prosper,

> Many of the servants of Christ who live in Marseilles think that, in the writings which Your Sanctity composed against the Pelagian heretics, whatever you said in them about the choice of the elect according to the fixed purpose of God is contrary to the opinion of the fathers and to ecclesiastical feeling.

In order to strengthen his case against the Gallic antipredestinarians, Prosper went so far as to accuse them of being Pelagians, referring to their "spirit of Pelagianism" and describing some of their teachings as the "remnants of the Pelagian depravity." Prosper's accusation has gained sufficient credence that the antipredestinarian party in Gaul has been given the misleading designation "Semi-Pelagian," in spite of the fact that all known influential Gallic theologians, including the Semi-Pelagians, condemned Pelagianism as heartily as did Augustine himself.

A more accurate depiction of Gallic sentiments is given by Prosper in the same letter to Augustine, when he reported on the short-lived Bishop Helladius of Arles: "Your Beatitude should know that he is an admirer and follower of your teaching in all other things, and with regard to that which he calls into question [predestination], he already wished to convey his own thoughts to Your Sanctity through correspondence. . . ."

In 430, Augustine died. Shortly thereafter, Prosper, seeing himself as the defender of Augustine in the struggle against the Gallic antipredestinarians, returned to the attack in three tracts, including the *Pro Augustino responsiones ad capitula objectionum Vincentianarum* (c. 431-434; *The Defense of Saint Augustine*, 1963). As a result, the Gauls also entered the pamphlet war; one of their most important writers was Vincent of Lérins. Although none of these anti-Augustinian works survives, Prosper's responses to them give a good idea of Vincent's objections. Augustine was accused of fatalism, of denying that all share the chance for salvation, and even of asserting that predestination compelled some to sin. The Gauls denounced Augustine for teaching that those predestined to salvation had no need to lead a Christian life, to be baptized, or to have free will.

It soon appeared to Prosper, however, that he was unable to sway his Gallic opponents with his rhetoric. He and Hilarius then exercised the increasingly popular last resort of so many disgruntled Gallic ecclesiastics: They went to Rome and appealed to the pope. As a result, Pope Celestine I, probably in 431, addressed a letter to several Gallic bishops, rebuking them for allowing the teaching of improper beliefs. Celestine, however, had been led to believe that the Gauls were infected with Pelagianism and on this basis were questioning the Augustinian interpretation of free will. Scholars have searched Celestine's letter in vain for any reference to the real reason that the Gauls opposed Augustine.

The definitive Gallic response to Celestine and Prosper came in 434, when Vincent, under the pseudonym Peregrinus (the pilgrim), wrote *Commonitoria* (*The Commonitory of Vincent of Lérins*, 1554), also known as *Adversus haereticos*, a tract ostensibly issued as a general guide for discerning heresy from orthodoxy. Vincent, stating that "the fraudulence of new heretics demands great care and attention," issued what would become the standard definition of orthodoxy, the so-called Vincentian canon: Orthodox belief was "quod ubique, quod semper, quod ab omnibus creditum est" (that which has been believed everywhere, always, and by all). Vincent therefore espoused a triple test—ecumenicity, antiquity, and universal consent.

Although Vincent taught that the true basis for orthodox belief lay in the Scriptures, he also placed great emphasis upon church tradition, because the Scriptures were capable of many different interpretations. How was one to distinguish between legitimate doctrinal evolution, which came with greater maturity and understanding, and heretical innovation? In Vincent's view, the established Church and all the orthodox church fathers were collectively the holders of dogmatic truth and stood as the guarantors of the proper interpretation.

Vincent soon, however, narrowed his discussion down to a consideration of "novelty" and "recent heresies, when they first arise." Vincent's particular concerns were to respond to Celestine's letter and to defend the Gallic antipredestinarian position even though, as usual, Augustine was not mentioned by name. In his final argument against novelty, Vincent turned Celestine's own arguments against him: "Let [Celestine] speak himself, let him destroy the doubts of our readers himself. He said 'let novelty cease to assault tradition.'" The "inventors of novelty," whoever they might be, should be condemned.

Vincent concluded by arguing that because Pelagius, Coelestius (another Pelagian), and Nestorius, who had separated the human and divine natures of Christ, all had been condemned, it was necessary for Christians "to detest, pursue, and persecute the profane novelties of the profane." The doctrine of predestination also was novelty, and as such was to be condemned. By using

Celestine's own arguments, Vincent rejected Celestine's and Prosper's claims that the Gallic antipredestinarians were guilty of wrongdoing. Vincent and the Gauls showed that, however much they might respect authorities such as Augustine and the Bishop of Rome, they reserved final judgment for themselves. For the rest of the century, the Gallic theological establishment continued to reject predestination and to define ever more carefully its own conception of the interaction among grace, effort, and free will.

Vincent's treatise is the last extant evidence for the predestination controversy for nearly forty years. Prosper apparently gave up his efforts to influence the Gauls, admitted defeat, and permanently moved to Rome. His move did not mean, however, that there did not continue to be predestinarians in Gaul or that everyone agreed with the views expressed by Vincent. Gennadius of Marseilles reported that the reason the second book of *The Commonitory of Vincent of Lérins* survived only in outline form was that the complete version had been stolen. Vincent himself is not heard from again, and Gennadius states that he was dead by the year 450.

Summary

Vincent of Lérins wrote and taught at a time when the Western Church was in theological ferment. There was a growing concern with various kinds of heretical beliefs, their identification and suppression. One previously popular view, Pelagianism, had just been condemned. Another, more recent theory of Augustine, predestination, although accepted in other parts of the Roman Empire, in Gaul was considered heretical. This Gallic rejection of foreign influence was reflected in other spheres of the Church as well. Throughout the fifth century, for example, the Gauls, especially the monks of Lérins, refused to acknowledge any direct papal authority in Gaul.

Vincent was one of the primary figures in the Gallic theological discussions of the 420's and 430's. His articulate condemnation of predestination was accepted in Gaul for nearly a century. In the sixth century, however, after the fall of the Roman Empire in the West and the division of Gaul into barbarian kingdoms, the Gallic church no longer was able to maintain its independence. In 529, at the Second Council of Orange, the southern Gallic bishops, now under the influence of the pope and the Italian court, condemned the earlier rejection of strict predestination. Vincent's method for distinguishing orthodox from heretical beliefs, however, continued to be applied; it still provides the standard definition.

Bibliography

Brunetière, Ferdinand, and P. de Labriolle. *Saint Vincent de Lérins*. Paris: Bloud, 1906. Although rather dated, this work is one of the few biographies of Vincent ever written. In French.

Cooper-Marsdin, Arthur Cooper. *The History of the Islands of the Lérins*.

Cambridge: Cambridge University Press, 1913. The only English-language account devoted to the monastery where Vincent lived and worked. Includes an index.

Mathisen, R. W. *Ecclesiastical Factions and Religious Controversy in Fifth-Century Gaul*. Washington, D.C.: Catholic University of America Press, 1989. A detailed account of Vincent's ecclesiastical environment, including descriptions of the monastery at Lérins, Vincent's life and works, and the theological controversies in which Vincent became involved. Includes a detailed bibliography.

Vincentius Lerinensis, Saint. *The Commonitorium of Vincentius of Lérins*. Edited by Reginald Stewart Moxon. Cambridge: Cambridge University Press, 1915. This volume is considered by scholars to be the standard edition of Vincent's best-known work. In Latin.

_____. *The Commonitory of Vincent of Lérins*. Translated by C. A. Huertley. Vol. 11 in *A Select Library of Nicene and Post-Nicene Church Fathers*. Reprint. Grand Rapids, Mich.: Wm. B. Eerdmans Publishing Co., 1955. This English translation of Vincent's work includes a scholarly preface which discusses the background and context of Vincent's literary efforts in detail.

_____. *Vincent of Lérins: Commonitories*. Translated by Rudolph E. Morris. Vol. 7 in *Niceta of Remesiana*. New York: Fathers of the Church, 1949. An English translation of Vincent's most influential work. Includes critical commentary.

Ralph W. Mathisen

PHILIPPE DE VITRY

Born: October 31, 1291; Vitry, Champagne, France
Died: June 9, 1361; Meaux, France
Areas of Achievement: Music and literature
Contribution: De Vitry, whose reputation as a musician and poet was well-known among his contemporaries, is remembered as the author of the treatise *Ars nova*. De Vitry proposed a solution to notational problems that was ultimately adopted in France and Italy in the fourteenth century.

Early Life

Philippe was born in one of six towns named Vitry in the province of Champagne. His father was a member of the royal chancellery. In 1322, de Vitry became an officer in the French royal household, where he served as clerk and secretary to Charles IV in Paris.

Prior to the twentieth century, it had been generally believed that de Vitry was a musician and poet who had largely developed his skills through individual instruction and private study. Modern scholarship, however, suggests that de Vitry studied at the Sorbonne and was one of the important intellectuals of his day, with interests ranging from music to mathematics. Petrarch, who met de Vitry at the Avignonese court and who described him as an active seeker of truth and a great philosopher, was one among many prominent contemporaries who held de Vitry in high esteem.

Life's Work

De Vitry maintained his connection with the royal court throughout his life; in addition to serving Charles IV, he served Philip VI and Duke Jean of Normandy in the capacity of secretary. His association with Duke Jean was to prove particularly helpful. While in his service, de Vitry performed various functions and participated in at least one military campaign. He was in the service of the duke in 1350, when the duke became Jean II of France. De Vitry made several diplomatic journeys to the papal court at Avignon on behalf of Jean II. In addition to his royal posts, de Vitry held several ecclesiastical offices during his life; he was Canon of Soissons and Archbishop of Brie. In 1351, Pope Clement VI, acting upon Jean II's recommendation, appointed de Vitry Bishop of Meaux, a position he held until his death, in 1361.

De Vitry's most significant work is a treatise on music entitled *Ars nova* (English translation, 1961). There is some disagreement about the exact date of the manuscript; the most widely accepted date, however, is 1320, which means that de Vitry would have been twenty-nine years old at the time of its completion. His treatise, which proposed a new theory of mensural notation, was actually a response to the generally perceived shortcomings of the older

Franconian notational system that was used in the late thirteenth century.

Composers during this time pushed the older system beyond its limits, as they began to compose music using shorter note values than could be accommodated by the old Franconian system. The common compositional practice in use at that time dictated that the old notational system be revised or a new one be devised to allow the composer greater rhythmic flexibility. De Vitry's system, as outlined in his treatise *Ars nova*, was not the only solution proposed, but it was the one that ultimately prevailed.

There are several innovative features in de Vitry's treatise. He recognized the minim as the newest and shortest note value and added it to the maxim, long, breve, and semibreve already found in the older Franconian system. Thus, it became possible to notate shorter note values in a systematic way. Also, the notation and usage of the minim in compositions exerted a strong influence on overall notational practice, for, as increased usage of the minim came to be realized, the *tactus*, or unit of beat, slowed down and rendered the larger note values, such as maxims and longs, impractical in actual use. Further, de Vitry held that any note longer than the minim could be reduced to two or three shorter notes of equal value—for the first time placing duple meter on an equal footing with triple meter.

Before the fourteenth century, triple meter was regarded as perfect, the number three being symbolic of the Trinity and thus constituting a perfection. Duple meter was regarded as imperfect and was used sparingly. That began to change in the early fourteenth century, and de Vitry was actively involved in effecting this change.

The practical effect of de Vitry's system was to identify four commonly used mensurations. To assist the performer and to reduce the possibility of confusion as to which mensuration to apply, de Vitry introduced the idea of time signatures to indicate mode, the relationship between long and breve, and time, the relationship between breve and semibreve. Time signatures were not widely used until the last quarter of the fourteenth century. De Vitry also describes coloration in his treatise, the practice of using red ink notes to indicate changes in mensuration or value from those designated by the standard black notes.

De Vitry enjoyed a substantial reputation as a musician, particularly as a composer and most especially as a composer of motets. Fourteen motets are attributed to him. Five of the motets are found in the *Roman de Fauvel* (romance of Fauvel), a beautiful manuscript dating from around 1316 and containing thirty-three polyphonic motets. The other nine motets are found in the *Ivrea codex*, a manuscript containing a variety of sacred and secular compositions and dating from about 1360.

De Vitry's innovations are notable. His compositions reveal an extended range for the voices, and the added fourth voice to be found in the later motets reflects his increased interest in sonority. De Vitry's motets also reveal

Great Lives from History

one of the first uses of isorhythm, an important fourteenth century technique of repeating the same rhythm with different notes.

Isorhythm involved the *cantus prius factus*, a previously made melody, and was initially associated with the tenor voice, where the previously made melody was usually found. It featured the separation of the two elements always associated with melody: the pitch sequence of a given melody, which was called the color, and the rhythm pattern superimposed on that melody, which was called a *talea*. Once having been viewed separately, it was then possible to combine the color and *talea* in a variety of configurations. The color and *talea* could coincide or the two could be placed in a ratio; for example, two statements of one would be made equal to three of the other. The technique was a means of providing coherence to the composition. While de Vitry's creation of this technique cannot be irrefutably documented, the procedure, which was a logical outgrowth of the old repeated rhythm patterns commonly found in the tenors of thirteenth century clausulae (or ornamented cadences), was quite frequently used by him, as it was by some of his contemporaries. The principle was extended and came to be applied to the other voices as well.

Another compositional device found in de Vitry's motets, but not unique to him, is the use of hocket. Hocket was quite popular with French composers of the late thirteenth and the fourteenth century. The device consisted of the rapid alternation of notes between a pair of voices, each voice sounding and resting in turn. The desired result was a hiccuping effect.

Summary

Philippe de Vitry enjoyed a substantial reputation as a composer, theorist, poet, statesman, and ecclesiastic during his own lifetime. As a poet, he was as well-known and respected for the excellence of the Latin and French texts of his motets as he was for the composition of the music itself.

The paucity of de Vitry's musical output remains a puzzle, particularly in view of the fact that most of the extant motets and treatises for which he is known were completed while he was still a young man. It appears that de Vitry's responsibilities and interests led him in other directions during the mature part of his life.

Even so, it is clear that his impact upon the musical milieu of his time was significant, particularly with respect to the *Ars nova* treatise, which served to intensify the already long-standing concern about the proper use of music in church. Pope John XXII, in reaction to the treatise and the swelling tide of support for it, issued a bull in 1324 condemning the effect on sacred music of the new rhythmic procedures advocated by de Vitry. While it would be a mistake to credit de Vitry as the sole initiator and leader of the rhythmic and notational reform occurring in the fourteenth century, his was a prominent role.

Bibliography

Fuller, Sarah. "A Phantom Treatise of the Fourteenth Century? The *Ars nova*." *The Journal of Musicology* 4 (1985-1986): 23-50. Presents the original view that de Vitry did not write a definitive treatise entitled *Ars nova*. Fuller questions whether certain manuscripts traditionally attributed to de Vitry were actually his. She suggests that colleagues and students actually created a teaching tradition based on de Vitry's concepts.

Hoppin, Richard. *Medieval Music*. New York: W. W. Norton and Co., 1978. Provides an excellent survey of medieval music from chant to the music of the early fifteenth century. One chapter is devoted solely to the French *Ars nova* and the innovations of de Vitry. Also contains a discussion of isorhythm and important manuscript sources.

Plantinga, Leon. "Philippe de Vitry's *Ars nova*: A Translation." *Journal of Music Theory* 5, no. 2 (1961): 204-223. A translation into English from the single complete manuscript source of the *Ars nova*. Some variant readings have been used and are so noted.

Reaney, Gilbert. "*Ars Nova* in France." In *The New Oxford History of Music*. Vol. 3, *Ars Nova and the Renaissance, 1300-1540*. London: Oxford University Press, 1966. An excellent overview of the forms and composers of fourteenth century France. Contains information about major composers, such as de Vitry and Guillaume de Machaut. Also contains some information about minor composers of the period.

Sanders, Ernest Helmut. "The Early Motets of Philippe de Vitry." *Journal of the American Musicological Society* 28, no. 1 (1975): 24-45. An identification and careful study of motets composed by de Vitry as a young man.

_____. "Philippe de Vitry." In *New Grove Dictionary of Music and Musicians*, edited by Stanley Sadie, vol. 20. 6th ed. New York: Macmillan, 1980. Sanders' article provides important biographical information. De Vitry's theoretical writings and compositions are carefully discussed. A listing of de Vitry's compositions is provided at the end. The listing includes citations of sources where the compositions are found, listings of modern editions containing the works cited, as well as some brief commentary. Excellent bibliography.

Michael Hernon

VLADIMIR I

Born: 955?; Kiev (in modern Ukraine)
Died: July 15, 1015; Berestova, near Kiev
Areas of Achievement: Government, warfare, and religion
Contribution: Vladimir expanded the territorial base of Kiev, the first Russian state, to unite the East Slavs and Finno-Baltic peoples into a large nation. He linked the cultural fortunes of the Rus with the Byzantine world by his conversion of the East Slavs to Orthodox Christianity in 988.

Early Life

Born in Kiev sometime after 950, Vladimir Svyatoslavich was the son of Malusha (Malfried) and Svyatoslav I, Grand Prince of Kiev. Svyatoslav, as Prince of Novgorod, had fought bravely against Khazars, Volga Bulgars (Huns), and Viatichi. He later fought against the Byzantines and the Bulgarians of South Europe. Although Vladimir's grandmother, Grand Princess Olga, had converted to Christianity in Constantinople in 955 or 957, the principality remained pagan, as did her son, Svyatoslav. When he died in 972, civil wars erupted as his sons fought over the succession to the throne. Yaropolk, Prince of Kiev, defeated Oleg and compelled Vladimir to flee to Scandinavia. For a short time, Yaropolk united Novgorod and Kiev. Vladimir, however, recruited Viking armies, which liberated Novgorod and then Polotsk from Yaropolk's governance. Rogvold, the ruler of Polotsk, allowed his daughter, Ragneda, to marry Vladimir. Then Vladimir marched on Kiev, forcing his brother to flee. Soon after, Yaropolk died. Vladimir forged a new union of Novgorod and Kiev with the help of Scandinavian and Novgorodian forces. To maintain this empire, however, a common religious bond was required; thus the new grand prince considered a new religion for the nation.

Life's Work

Early in his reign, Vladimir considered the adoption of a new pagan cult to unify the realm. He had already created a pagan pantheon of gods, using regional cults in conjunction with the state cult of Perun. He soon realized, however, that the pagan cult could have little impact on the frontiers of the state. There were missionaries from Rome, Constantinople, the Volgan Islamic Bulgars, and the Jewish Khazars. Vladimir's grandmother Olga had been baptized in Constantinople, and there is evidence of Christian settlements in various parts of Rus.

Chroniclers relate the famous story of emissaries sent to investigate the various religions and the discussions which the grand prince had with each of them. There is undoubtedly some truth to the account of the prince's aversion to the abstinence from drink and the practice of circumcision among the Jews and Muslims as well as to his particular attraction to the beauty of the

Byzantine liturgy over that of the Roman and his aversion to the "foul-smelling" Islamic mosques. Yet it seems that the close political and economic ties between Kiev and Constantinople were decisive, as was the prince's apprehension of submitting to the central authority of Rome. His proposed marriage to the Byzantine emperor's sister, Anna, surely was another factor. The early chroniclers do not hesitate to reveal that the adoption of Byzantine Orthodoxy in 988 was a state decision enforced upon the community of Kiev, whose people were marched to the Dnieper River for baptism. Nor was there any doubt that the new church organization would be tied to the prince, whose elevation was invariably blessed by the clergy.

Vladimir is remembered for building the Kievan empire and expanding it in nearly all directions. His early concerns were toward the south and east, where the state was frequently attacked by nomads from the steppes. The internecine warfare that preceded his reign weakened the frontier defenses; thus, Vladimir began offensive operations. He began a number of expeditions against the Viatichi, forcing them into dependence upon Kiev in 981-982; he then did the same against the Radimichi in 984, thus uniting all the eastern Slavic peoples. Next he subdued the Volga Bulgars, descendants of the Huns, and the Khazars, their overlords. Making alliances with some Turkic tribes, Vladimir compelled the Bulgars to accept Kievan suzerainty over almost the entire Volga area, although his lieutenant Dobrynia told him that people who wore boots, as did the Bulgars, would never submit. Later campaigns in 994 and 997 were designed to reassert Kiev's control. The Khazar tribes, no longer the powerful empire of old, were weakened by the regime of Khorezm and so fell before Vladimir's armies in 985. As a result, the Black Sea port of Tmutorakan, with its link to the Volga, fell into Kievan hands. Vladimir also strengthened his presence in Sarkel, a former Khazar stronghold taken by Svyatoslav in 965. These successful operations in the east and southeast were supplemented by the grand prince's construction of a chain of fortifications in the southeast to check the raids of the Pechenegs. Divided into eight hordes, the Pechenegs sometimes wandered within a day's march of Kiev itself. The forts at the rivers Desna, Oster, Trubezh, Sula, and Stugna were constructed in 988-989. Manned by northerners, who sometimes resented service in the south, the forts in the steppes were linked by stockades and entrenchments. These measures enabled Vladimir to contain the nomad threat.

The seizure of Tmutorakan was a delicate matter, however, since that city was also within the influence of the Byzantine Empire. In 988, therefore, Vladimir sent a bodyguard of six thousand Varangian warriors to aid Basil II to quell a rebellion. This force was the origin of the famed Varangian Guard in Constantinople. When Basil refrained from sending his sister to Vladimir, however, an angry prince attacked the Byzantine port of Chersonesus. Soon after, the emperor sent Anna to marry Vladimir in Chersonesus and recognized the Kievan presence in the Black Sea.

Meanwhile, Vladimir paid attention to the lands to the north and west as well. In the borderlands between Kiev and Poland lived many peoples of uncertain ethnic identity; in 981, the Kievan forces moved to incorporate these regions within the state. This action did not cause irreparable damage to Kievan-Polish relations, since Vladimir's son Svyatopolk married the daughter of King Bolesław Chrobry early in the next century. Polish missionaries were even allowed to cross Kievan territory to preach to the Pechenegs, although little is known about the success of that mission. Vladimir also maintained friendly relations with Stephen I of Hungary and Udalrik of Bohemia. Troubles began with Poland only late in his reign, when Svyatopolk was suspected of trying to turn over his appanage of Turov-Pinsk to his father-in-law. When Vladimir imprisoned his son in 1012, the Poles invaded the Kievan state, supported by Pechenegs and Germans. The war continued after Vladimir's death in 1015, and three years later, Poland had regained the borderlands lost to Vladimir earlier.

Early in his reign, Vladimir sent Dobrynia to be Posadnik of Novgorod. His mission was to defend the northern borders. Under Dobrynia, Novgorod paid two thousand grivny each year to Kiev as tribute and another one thousand to cover its defense expenses. Novgorod often sent troops to the southern reaches but with increasing reluctance. In 988, Dobrynia was replaced by Vladimir's son Vycheslav, himself later replaced by another son, Yaroslav, later called "the Wise." In 1014, Yaroslav rebelled against the grand prince's financial exactions, an event that foreshadowed a new round of fratricidal warfare when Vladimir died in 1015.

Less is known of Vladimir's internal policies except for the matter of religion. By allying with the upper class, whose sons were the first students in his new religious schools, he provided its members with important posts in his newly created bureaucracy. By suppressing tribal boundaries, Vladimir set up a network of new administrative centers in Polotsk, Novgorod, Turov, Rostov, Murom, Vladimir, and Tmutorakan with his own sons and *druzhiny* as chieftains. He adopted the administrative organizations called the "hundreds" and "thousands" from tribal military practices, making their officers princely officials. Tribal leaders were treated lavishly and used by the grand prince within his administrative structure, as were many elders of the towns. Vladimir freely used Varangian mercenaries from the north; once, when they threatened to pillage Kiev, he simply sent them on an offensive mission to Constantinople. Vladimir also preceded Yaroslav's famed Russian Law Code by adopting the principle of fixed fines in the court of justice to replace the dependence upon blood feuds and vengeance. This unusual policy was not influenced by churchmen, who even had to convince him that it was proper to execute robbers. To support the construction of a new cathedral, Vladimir introduced the collection of the tithe, a Western church practice. The Metropolitan of Kiev, Ilarion (1051-1054), noted that Vladimir often consulted with the bishops on matters of state and security.

Summary

The religion adopted by Vladimir was to strengthen the princely class, to combat the centrifugal movements within the state, and to abet the state's need for ties to the West. Most important was the fact that Vladimir's decision to choose the Orthodox faith meant the adoption of an entire culture, replete with the artistic tradition of icon painting, Byzantine architecture, monasticism, religious education, legal principles, and other patterns of thought. It is worth noting that one feature was absent from the legacy of Byzantium—namely, the interest in theological speculation. Several modern authorities argue that Vladimir and the Kievan Rus were so entranced by the beauty of Orthodoxy that tampering with doctrinal formulations was thought to be tampering with perfection. Another modern analysis holds that the Russians were not really converted to Christianity so much as they overlaid a veneer of Christianity over a pagan base.

The extent to which Vladimir himself was converted is also disputed. Chroniclers make frequent mention of his weekly feasts, wherein he invited *druzhiny* and others to dine at court, while servants would distribute food to the poor in the streets. Notice is also made of his newfound aversion to capital punishment and the cessation of his harem. He continued to exercise little restraint in warfare, however, allowing his soldiers to pillage at will—the usual custom of the time.

It is strange to discover some Western elements in Vladimir's religious policies. Reference was made earlier to the introduction of the Western tithe to support the grand prince's designs for a church. In the matter of ecclesiastical law, Vladimir gave the Church a broad charter of immunity from civil law—so broad that it included many persons dependent upon the Church and even those without the protection of clan or class. The Church's own jurisdiction included not only moral and liturgical matters but also family disputes and inheritances. Such a situation corresponds more to Western than to Greek practices.

Unlike his Kievan predecessors, who were chiefly concerned with defending the frontiers, Vladimir wanted to expand those frontiers; consequently, he took an active interest in European affairs. To each of his twelve sons, Vladimir left a principality. His son Yaroslav of Novgorod eventually was to succeed him in Kiev. Vladimir was canonized two centuries after he died.

Bibliography

Cross, Samuel Hazzard, and Olgerd P. Sherbowitz-Wetzor, eds. and trans. *The Russian Primary Chronicle.* Cambridge, Mass.: Medieval Academy of America, 1953. This work contains the translation of *Povest vremennykh let*, the principal annals of Vladimir's era.

Fedotov, George P. *The Russian Religious Mind*. Vol. 1, *Kievan Christianity*. Cambridge, Mass.: Harvard University Press, 1946. A classic exploration of the historical roots of Russian Orthodoxy and its relations with the state by a writer who combines scholarship with beautiful prose.

Grekov, Boris D. "The Reign of Prince Vladimir Svyatoslavich." In *Kiev Rus*, translated by Y. Sdobnikov. Moscow: Foreign Languages Publishing House, 1959. The most noted work by a Soviet scholar on the Kievan era of Russian history. In it, he argues that paganism yielded to Christianity because the former was a tribal religion whereas the latter was essentially class oriented.

Grunwald, Constantin de. "Saint Vladimir." In *Saints of Russia*, translated by Roger Capel. New York: Macmillan, 1960. A concise, intelligent account of Vladimir's life, drawing on many Nordic sources and stressing his Scandinavian ties. Grunwald argues that the conversion of the Kievan people took place in 990.

Kluchevsky, Vasily O. *A History of Russia*. Translated by C. J. Hogarth. 5 vols. New York: Russell and Russell, 1960. An entertaining analysis by a great Russian historian. Though sparing of detail on Vladimir's career, it contains well-considered judgments on the grand prince's milieu.

Vernadsky, George. *Kievan Russia*. New Haven, Conn.: Yale University Press, 1948. The standard account of Vladimir's reign by a well-respected scholar whose discussion of the grand prince is still unchallenged.

Volkoff, Vladimir. *Vladimir, the Russian Viking*. Woodstock, N.Y.: Overlook Press, 1985. The first full-scale, twentieth century biography of the grand prince. Although the author is a novelist, the account is interesting, faithful to detail, and imaginatively constructed. Includes an index, maps, illustrations, and a select bibliography.

John D. Windhausen

WALTHER VON DER VOGELWEIDE

Born: c. 1170; probably lower Austria
Died: c. 1230; near Würzburg, Bavaria
Area of Achievement: Literature
Contribution: Walther von der Vogelweide was the greatest lyric poet of the
   German High Middle Ages; his writings set high standards of artistic qual-
   ity in the genre of the courtly love lyric as well as that of political poetry.

Early Life

Few details are known regarding Walther's life. He was born within the
area of Austria and was in Vienna around 1190 at the court of the Babenberg
rulers. At the death of his sponsor, Duke Frederick, in 1198, he wandered
around Austria in search of another wealthy patron. He resided at various
royal courts and finally settled in Würzburg at the court of the Emperor
Friedrick II, from whom he received a small stipend in 1220. Only one document exists that testifies to his life: a note that he was given money by
Wolfger, Bishop of Passau, in 1203 in order to purchase a winter coat. He is
depicted in a colorful illumination (from the famous *Manessische Handschrift*
manuscript) as the "king of poets," in a pose described in one of his most
famous poems.

Walther was born toward the end of the period of the German High
Middle Ages, when the culture and art of the royal courts were at their zenith. Courtly society was highly codified and stratified; hierarchies of rank
and authority were carefully observed. This period was the legendary age of
chivalry and knightly virtues, an era whose ideal knight combined the bravery of the Germanic warrior with the spiritual discipline of Christianity. The
knights were a class of soldiers who pledged fealty to a lord and were in
attendance at his court when not engaged in battle or a crusade. Since many
were literate, they were devoted to the arts of song and the lyric.

The knightly caste had strict rules of conduct that promoted certain primary social virtues. Honor, loyalty, and discipline were important qualities of
the warrior who served a lord in battle. Mildness and steadfastness of character and moderation in all behavior were social and psychological virtues
that complemented as well as moderated the more aggressive qualities of the
soldier. The goals of a knight were threefold: to attain worldly honor, material wealth, and, above all, the blessings of God.

Knights who were in attendance at a court often practiced devotion to a
noble woman of higher station (*Minnedienst*); the knight who undertook
such a commitment dedicated all of his heroic efforts to his lady and composed in her honor highly stylized love poetry (*Minnesang*). This idealized
love was thought to be a spiritual exercise that would ennoble the soul of the
knight. If the knight were dutiful in his service to the lady, she might grant

him the favor of a glance or a nod.

Since Walther both incorporated and transcended the conventions of the courtly love lyric in many of his poems, a closer look at the genre and its history is in order. The tradition of the love lyric in Germany was determined primarily by foreign influences, descending from the older cultural heritage of Arabic love poetry by way of the Moorish invasion of Spain and then subsequently from the Provençal area of France, where the tradition of Latin love poetry remained and where the ideals of knighthood also flourished. Provençal poetry reached its high point around 1100 in the songs of the troubadour. Prominent poets of the French tradition were Bertrand de Born, William of Poitou, and Bernard de Ventadour.

These Provençal poets devoted themselves and their poetry to an unreachable ideal, to the honor of a married lady of the court—which therefore (usually) excluded the possibility of physical love—and this striving for the ideal in attitude and behavior ennobled their souls. Love expressed to a young, unmarried woman was discouraged. The earlier Christian tradition of love poetry dedicated to the Virgin Mary is here also an obvious influence. Since this love service to the married woman was extremely passionate, in spirit at least, the affairs of the knight and his chosen lady were closely watched by others of the court. Secret meetings between the lovers were presumed by all, and such a clandestine rendezvous was a perennial theme in much of the poetry. The *alba*, or morning song, for example, celebrated the awakening of the two lovers after a night of secret passion. They were usually outdoors and romantically awakened by the singing of a bird. These motifs became highly stylized and were part of the poet's standard lyric repertoire.

The German reception of the French tradition of courtly poetry began in northern Germany and the Low Countries (by way of northern France) in the realistic love lyrics of Heinrich von Veldeke. From there, it was transmitted to the Rhineland area in the works of Friedrich von Hausen and to Middle Germany in the poetry of Heinrich von Morungen. These early German poets gave fresh inspiration to the conventions of the genre, writing lyrics which captured the passion and intensity of this spiritualized love experience in naturalistic imagery. By way of northern Italy, the tradition came to Austria, and at the Babenberg court in Vienna, the love lyric attained a high degree of formal stylization. The poet Reinmar von Hagenau (from the Franco-German area of Alsatia) produced poems in a folklike style and wrote of the sadness and melancholy longing of the lovers rather than the intensity and energy of their passion. The social prohibitions that denied the natural consummation of the love relationship had eventually produced an experience that was more form or gesture than content. This shift in theme toward the introspective suggests the waning of the genre. Reinmar was the major influence at the Babenberg court and was Walther's teacher. The German tradition of the love lyric became highly conventionalized and artificial at this stage. Numerous writers of lesser talent than Reinmar and Walther merely imitated the particulars of the style and form without entering into the original spirit of its early poets.

The impossibility of intimate union with the idealized lady gave rise to a variant of the courtly love genre, called "common love" (*niedere Minne*). This was a love lyric dedicated to the young and accessible girls of the local villages rather than the unapproachable, idealized ladies of the court. It was a poetry that celebrated the joys of reciprocal love and the simple village life, free of the formal and codified rules of courtly society. Its imagery was that of rural life and the simple pleasures of the village community. The rise of the common-love school again suggests that the tradition of the courtly love lyric had exhausted its thematic and stylistic possibilities.

The medieval courtly love lyric eventually devolved into a mere formal exercise during the fourteenth century, the period of the "master song" (*Meistergesang*). The meistersingers imitated the style of masters such as Walther in a mechanical and highly formalized manner. Singing schools (*Singschulen*), structured much like guilds, were organized in towns, and strict rules for composition were established. Competitions were held in which judges counted the syllables and assessed the rhymes in each line. Michel Beheim, a weaver, was one of the more famous meistersingers of the period.

Life's Work

Walther's career thus spanned the zenith and the decline of the courtly love genre. His poetry shunned the artificiality and conventionality so prominent in the works of others. His language and imagery were natural, spontaneous, and vital. Poems such as "Sô die Bluomen ûz dem Grase dringent" ("When the Flowers Spring out of the Grass") celebrate in natural images of spring the physical as well as the inner spiritual beauty of the beloved lady. In many of his texts, Walther questions the nature of the courtly love experience itself. Love is not the stylized and formal gestures of favor granted by the revered lady of the court to the dutiful knight, but the harmony of two hearts in delighted union. The poem "Saget mir ieman, waz ist Minne?" ("What Is Loving?"), for example, rejects the unequal relationship between a woman placed on an idealized pedestal and a subservient man kneeling before her. Love, Walther suggests, is a natural relation of equality between two lovers that enriches both participants. Consequently, Walther also composed poetry in the vein of the common love style. In texts such as "Herzeliebes Frou-welin" ("Dear Young Woman"), "Nemt, Frouwe, disen Kranz" ("Take, Young Woman, This Wreath"), as well as the well-known poem "Unter der Linden" ("Under the Linden-Tree"), he described the natural passions of the simple girl and his reciprocal affection for her.

Walther lived during a period of great political turmoil, and in many of his poems he gave voice to his concerns. After the death of Emperor Frederick I Barbarossa in 1190, conflicts ensued among the royal houses of the Guelphs and the Waiblingen. The Guelphs sought to assume leadership from the Hohenstaufen Dynasty. Friedrick II, son of Barbarossa, was finally crowned as emperor in 1220. This was also the era in which church and state vied for political hegemony in Europe, a conflict that extended over most of the thirteenth century. Walther was distressed at the loss of harmony and unity that had marked the earlier years of the Hohenstaufen empire. In many of his poems, he praised his German homeland, lauding its beautiful women, its landscapes, and its brave knights and chivalry. In his best-known poem, "Ich saz uf eine Steine" ("I Was Sitting upon a Rock"), he laments the violence and discord that had disrupted the land. He fears that the knightly ideals of honor, wealth, and God's blessings are threatened by the conflicts he sees around him. Unfortunately, the gradual process of disintegration within his beloved empire continued long after his death. The Hohenstaufen Dynasty came to an end in 1268 with the execution of Conradin in Naples.

Summary

If Johann Wolfgang von Goethe was the lyric genius of Germany's second Golden Age of literature (during the eighteenth century), then Walther von der Vogelweide was certainly the greatest genius of its first great era, during the Middle Ages. His poetry achieved a splendid union of form and content. He was able to infuse the conventions of the courtly love lyric with a freshness and vitality unequaled by others of his generation. His imagery is distinguished by a keen sense of realism combined with a genuine poetic sensibility. His love for his homeland, his concern for its future, and his egalitarian attitudes suggest a warm-spirited individual able to look beyond the parochial concerns that marked so many of his contemporaries.

If it can be said that the literary production of a society is the highest expression (in linguistic terms) of its values and ideals, then Walther's place in the history of German culture and civilization is assured. In certain respects, the tradition of the courtly love lyric manifested European (and especially Germanic) society's attempt to harmonize the virtues of two distinct cultural traditions, that of the strong and fearless tribal warrior and that of the humble Christian whose strength lay not in the physical but in the spiritual domain. As the foremost poet of this tradition, one who both epitomized and transcended its limits, Walther left a legacy that will continue to be examined by future generations.

Bibliography

Garland, Henry, and Mary Garland. *Oxford Companion to German Literature*. 2d ed. Oxford: Oxford University Press, 1986. Encyclopedic reference work with brief but informative section on Walther. Contains several important bibliographic references.

Heinen, Hubert. "Lofty and Base Love in Walther von der Vogelweide's 'So die bluomen' and 'Aller werdekeit.'" *The German Quarterly* 51 (1978): 465-475. Treats Walther's concept of love; includes quotes in German and English, notes, and bibliography.

O'Connell Walshe, Maurice. *Medieval German Literature*. Cambridge, Mass.: Harvard University Press, 1962. A good history of literature in the Middle Ages which contains a substantial section on Walther. Also includes a bibliography.

Reinhardt, Kurt Frank. *Germany: Two Thousand Years*. Milwaukee: Bruce Publishing Co., 1950. A very useful history of German civilization with a section on medieval culture, history, and literature including a discussion of Walther. Contains a bibliography.

Scheibe, Fred Karl. *Walther von der Vogelweide: Troubadour of the Middle Ages*. New York: Vantage Press, 1969. A good brief introduction to Walther's life and poetry that also surveys the reception of his works and lists English translations. Contains a bibliography.

Thomas F. Barry

WANG AN-SHIH

Born: 1021; Lin-ch'uan, China
Died: 1086; Nanking, China
Area of Achievement: Government
Contribution: A writer and statesman during the Northern Sung Dynasty, Wang An-shih introduced sweeping reforms in government, affecting particularly the state financial system and the bureaucracy.

Early Life

Wang An-shih was born in south central China in what is now Kiangsi Province, an area noted as a center of tea producers and merchants. His family first prospered in farming, although on a small scale, but later generations produced scholars, several holding the doctorate degree. Wang's father was a minor official who served in a variety of local government posts. His family thus instilled in Wang traditional Confucian values of education and of government service.

In 1042, Wang earned a doctorate, and for the next eighteen years, he served in local government posts. His experience, especially a year spent as a district magistrate, gave him insight into the conditions of the poor in the countryside and of the workers in the growing urban centers. His experience with incompetent bureaucrats led him, in 1058, to present to Emperor Jen-tsung (1023-1064) a memorial, the basis of his later reform proposals. In it, Wang showed how a well-trained, well-controlled bureaucracy could serve as the chief tool in bringing about a Confucian moral society.

Wang urged, among other things, that the emperor give highest consideration to the character and ability of candidates for government office. Further, he suggested "a prolonged period of probation as the best method of testing the appointees." Wang, as Chief Justice of the Circuit for one year, noted the scarcity of competent government employees and saw the need for securing capable officials. It was a theme he would repeat following his appointment to the court a few years later. No action was taken on his ideas at the time, but Wang's reputation as a scholar grew, and after 1060 he was called to the capital, where he served in a number of minor posts that brought him access to the emperor.

Life's Work

In 1067, Wang An-shih became Governor of Nanking, from which the new emperor, Shen-tsung (1067-1085), summoned him to court in early 1069. Wang was made second privy councillor, with responsibility for general administration. The emperor supported Wang's reform measures, which began to be implemented in 1069. Opposition built to the reforms, but the emperor reaffirmed Wang by appointing him first privy councillor in 1071, adding to Wang's prestige and power.

At the time Wang rose to eminence, the Sung Dynasty was experiencing heavy financial strains, a result of an enlarged military budget and the increase of great estates with their tax-evading landowners. According to John K. Fairbank, Edwin O. Reischauer, and Albert M. Craig in their *East Asia: Tradition and Transformation* (1973), government income by 1065 had fallen by nearly 25 percent. Northern barbarian tribes were a constant threat, and a sizable professional army to contain them proved very costly. The military alone accounted for close to 80 percent of the government revenue.

Along with financial distress, the dynasty, having become more centralized than at any previous time, suffered from the inertia of an inflexible bureaucracy. Officials were often divided over policies, and factionalism prevented easy resolutions. Most bureaucrats were traditionalists whose positions were threatened by Wang's reforms. Scholar-statesmen such as Ou-yang Hsiu (1007-1070), Ssu-ma Kuang (1019-1086), and Han Wei (1017-1098) led the antireform forces, leading to Wang's resignation, briefly, in 1074.

Wang's reforms, known as the New Laws, or the New Policies, covered several areas, all of them aiming at the creation—or restoration—of a Confucian moral society. Wang cast his reforms with continuity as well as change in mind. He argued that change was necessary because "the present system of administration is not in accordance with the principles and ideas of the ancient rulers." He was, therefore, advocating a return to the principles of a Golden Age. The reforms were intended to shape the behavior of the people and the bureaucracy, bringing about fundamental changes in political and social institutions.

The New Policies' areas were planning of state finance, state financing for farmers, state revenue and maintenance (for example, transportation and distribution of tribute items, a graduated cash tax, collective police duties, an equitable land tax), national defense, currency reform, trade expansion, and education and civil service (establishment of more prefectual schools, training in specialized fields such as law, medicine, military science, and emphasis on problem solving in the examination system). The majority of these New Policies tried to deal realistically with the problems of tax burden and state finance. Yet their success would depend on a competent bureaucracy.

The core of Wang's reforms was an improved bureaucracy. He advised the emperor to "search for and make use of the talented men who are capable of reviving the regulatory system of the ancient kings" before attempting to establish the regulatory systems for the country. The Sung Dynasty paid great respect to scholar-officials, some of whom were exempt from taxes and service to the state. Many scholars, however, especially those not stationed in the capital, received low pay and few privileges; morale therefore was low. Wang increased their salaries in the hope of raising morale and lessening corruption. Idealistic himself, Wang maintained high standards and demanded them of other scholar-officials as well. His criticism of what he considered an ill-prepared and impractical bureaucracy brought heated rejoinders, while his thinking on state finance was an additional irritation to many conventional Confucianists, who held a laissez-faire philosophy in the areas of business and industry.

Wang believed that the state could increase revenue by increasing productivity, primacy being given to agricultural productivity. He attacked the production of luxury goods, and extravagance in general. He reminded the emperor that "the good ruler maintains an economical standard in public life, extravagance being recognized as a great evil" and urged punishment for those producing articles of luxury. Wang wanted to force workers back into the fields so that "as more land is brought under cultivation, there will be no lack of food." To this end, Wang introduced state farming loans to rescue farmers from moneylenders, thereby enabling the farmers to keep their land. He also favored heavier taxation on merchants than on farmers.

Wang wanted the government to restrain and limit the powerful monopolizing families and to use its authority vigorously to aid the poor. He did not advocate revolution, the overthrow of the gentry and large landlords; rather, he feared that a peasant uprising would occur if poverty were not alleviated. Yet such reforms as remission of corvée (compulsory labor), a graduated land tax, and cheaper credit alienated large landowners, moneylenders, and merchants. They joined forces with conservative bureaucrats to condemn Wang and his program, forcing his resignation in 1074.

Although Wang returned to court in early 1075, his position was considerably weaker than before. The emperor was less open to his counsel, and previous supporters turned against him. Wang retired permanently in 1076. His reforms continued in effect until the death of Emperor Shen-tsung in 1085. Thereafter, they were gradually rescinded, although a brief revival of his system occurred between 1093 and 1125.

Summary

Many historians, assessing Wang's reforms, view him as a champion of small or middle landowners and small businesses. At the least, his efforts showed an interest in the broader sectors of society. In the long run, however, these efforts failed. A principal cause of this failure was Wang's inability to develop a dedicated and trustworthy official corps. Additionally, his opponents, in and out of government, succeeded in portraying him as a radical—and not truly Confucian at all. Ssu-ma Kuang, leader of the opposition until his death in 1086, accused Wang of being self-satisfied and opinionated and of setting his own ambition above the nation's interests; he added that Wang was impractical as well.

Wang did, however, have his defenders. Several decades after Wang's death, a Confucian philosopher, Liu Hsiang-shan (1113-1192), praised him as a man of "heroic mould and will." He attributed the failure of the New Policies to the intransigence of both Wang and his opponents, each side failing to make the necessary compromises. Certainly, Wang lacked sufficient tact to win over the traditionalists. At times, he was more theoretical than practical in political matters. Nevertheless, the New Policies did improve the financial situation for a time, and, as some twentieth century historians hold, perhaps Wang's reforms, as much as any other factor, enabled the Sung Dynasty to last another fifty years after his death.

Several of Wang's reforms, such as the militia organization—the Pao-chia system—and the graduated land tax, would be revived by later dynasties. His measures were not without defect. Still, as the centuries passed, aspects of them gained more approval, and Wang's reputation rose accordingly.

Bibliography
De Bary, William Theodore, Wing-tsit Chan, and Burton Watson, eds. *Sources of Chinese Tradition*. Vol. 1. New York: Columbia University Press, 1960. Contains translations of documents by and about Wang An-shih and his New Policies. Brief essays in each section. Several documents cover aspects of Sung society in general, giving a good framework for Wang's reforms. Includes an index but no bibliography.
Eberhard, Wolfram. *A History of China*. Translated by E. W. Dickes. Berkeley: University of California Press, 1950, 4th ed. 1977. Chapter 9 gives general characteristics of the Sung Dynasty, with much detail on such areas as military and administrative reform. Excellent notes and references for each chapter. Includes an index.
Eichhorn, Werner. *Chinese Civilization: An Introduction*. Translated by Janet Seligman. New York: Praeger Publishers, 1969. Chapter 9 is entirely on the Sung Dynasty, with nine pages given to Wang's reforms. His career is put into good perspective. Contains a bibliography, notes, and an index.
Fairbank, John King, Edwin O. Reischauer, and Albert M. Craig. *East Asia: Tradition and Transformation*. Boston: Houghton Mifflin Co., 1973. Chapter 6 is most pertinent. Contains an overall analysis of the Sung Dynasty with a brief but good summary of Wang An-shih's reforms. An index but no bibliography. Fine maps and illustrations.
Gernet, Jacques. *A History of Chinese Civilization*. Translated by J. R. Foster. New York: Cambridge University Press, 1982. Chapter 14 offers a thorough description of the Sung Dynasty. Most emphasis is given to the period before and after Wang's reform attempts. Contains chronological tables (pages 680-735), extensive bibliographies for each period in Chinese history, and an index.
Liu, James T. C. *Reform in Sung China: Wang An-shih (1021-1086) and His New Policies*. Cambridge, Mass.: Harvard University Press, 1959, 2d ed. 1968. A short volume synthesizing several contemporary Chinese and

Japanese scholars' work on the New Policies, with a reappraisal of them by Liu. Helpful notes for each chapter. Includes a glossary, an index, and a bibliography.

Liu, James T. C., and Peter J. Golas, eds. *Change in Sung China: Innovation or Renovation?* Lexington, Mass.: D. C. Heath and Co., 1969. A small volume which examines developments in Sung China, analyzing the nature of changes permeating that society. Two essays in particular are very good: "Change Within Tradition" and "Centralization, Conformity, and Absolution." Contains suggestions for additional reading.

Meskill, John Thomas, ed. *Wang An-shih: Practical Reformer?* Boston: D. C. Heath and Co., 1963. An excellent introduction leading into documents and essays by and about Wang An-shih and his reforms. Good variety of pro and con writers. One page of suggestions for additional reading.

Carol Berg

WANG CH'UNG

Born: 27; Shang-yü, K'uai-chi, China
Died: c. 100; Shang-yü, K'uai-chi, China
Area of Achievement: Philosophy
Contribution: During the later Han Dynasty, apocryphal literature became popular, supplementing humanistic and rationalistic Confucianism and supporting the belief in portents and prophecies. Amid this change, Wang Ch'ung became a rationalistic, naturalistic, and materialistic thinker; his philosophy subsequently contributed to clearing the atmosphere of superstition and occultism and to enhancing the spirit of skepticism, rationalism, and naturalism, which later bloomed in the form of Neo-Taoism during the Wei-Chin period.

Early Life

Wang Ch'ung was born in Shang-yü, K'uai-chi (now Chekiang Province), China, in 27; he lived during the period of transition from orthodox Confucianism to popular Neo-Taoism. During that time, China suffered a series of crop failures which resulted in widespread famine, and the country suffered from rebellions arising from the government's inability to find a solution to its people's problems. As a result, Confucianism, upon whose training advancement in the civil service was based, declined in popularity; the country began to search for another ideology. Without such a cohesive philosophy, the Chinese state and society would fragment and crumble.

While the country was going through this upheaval, Wang Ch'ung suffered his own difficulties, having been born into a family whose fortunes were already on the decline. His rebellious grandfather and father had less-than-successful careers in government service. Eventually, both were forced into an erratic life-style, moving from one job to the next. To compound matters, Wang Ch'ung was orphaned when he was very young.

Nevertheless, he always expressed an interest in learning. He continued to read, even in the most difficult of circumstances, in the local bookstores, going on to study at the national university in the capital city of Loyang. There he met Pan Piao, an eminent scholar and the father of Pan Ku, a noted historian. Much of Wang Ch'ung's education, however, was informal and irregular. In addition to teaching himself, he did not follow any of the traditional scholastic methods or values. Thus he has been classified as a member of the Miscellaneous school.

Like his grandfather and father before him, Wang Ch'ung worked as a government official, coming into conflict with his superiors as a result of his uncompromising personality. During the course of his career, he held a few minor official positions on the local level, serving without distinction. In 88 he retired from circuit government, a job he had obtained as a favor from

Tung Ch'in, a provincial official. He returned to his hometown and devoted the remainder of his life to teaching and writing.

Life's Work

The intellectual situation in Wang Ch'ung's lifetime was complex. Confucianism was supreme, yet it was being debased into a mysterious and superstitious doctrine. In addition, the belief in the unity of man and nature was changing: Man and nature were seen as mutually influencing each other, and these influences were thought to be exerted through strange phenomena and calamities. Heaven, though not anthropomorphic, was purposeful, asserting its will through prodigies which it used to warn mortals; on a smaller scale, spiritual beings exercised a similar influence.

Wang Ch'ung rejected these beliefs, declaring that Heaven takes no action; that natural events, including prodigies, occur spontaneously; that there is no such thing as teleology; that fortune and misfortune occur by chance; and that man does not become a ghost after death. In addition, he insisted that theories must be tested and supported by concrete evidence. He did not believe that the past is any sure guide with regard to the present, saying that there is no evidence that the past is better than the present, or vice versa. In short, he believed in human logic and nature's spontaneous manifestation.

Wang Ch'ung also wrote the following three books: the _Chi-su chieh-yi_ (ridiculing custom and decorum), in which he discussed the vagaries of politics and power. When he himself was out of power, he wrote the _Cheng-wu_ (political affairs), in which he discusses the defects of the political system, and the _Lun-hêng_ (c. 85; English translation, 1907-1911), in which he calls for a logic based on tangible evidence and rejects superstition and speculation without foundation. Only the _Lun-hêng_ has survived.

In the _Lun-hêng_, Wang Ch'ung presented a variety of views on human nature. In it, he first quoted Confucius, "By nature men are alike. Through practice they have become far apart," then turned to Mencius, one of Confucius' disciples, who saw mankind's nature as originally good, especially during childhood, and explained evil in terms of the circumstances of their lives. He also quoted Kao Tzu, Mencius' contemporary, who said that human nature is neither good nor evil: It is like the willow tree. Hsün-tzu, however, opposed Mencius, saying that "the nature of man is evil"; that is, just as a stone is hard as soon as it is produced, men are bad even in childhood. Tung Chung-shu read the works of both Mencius and Hsün-tzu and proposed eclectic theories of human nature and feelings: "Nature is born of yang and feelings are born of yin. The force of yin results in greed and that of yang results in humanity." He meant that human nature and feelings are both good and evil, for they are products of yin and yang. Liu Tzu-cheng concurred, saying that human nature is inborn and not expressed, but feelings are what come into contact with things; thus, human nature is yin (evil) and human feelings are yang (good).

Wang Ch'ung dealt with these theories eclectically. He considered that Mencius' doctrine of the goodness of human nature referred only to people above the average, that Hsün-tzu's doctrine of the evil of human nature applied to people below the average, and that the doctrine of Yang Hsiung— human nature is a mixture of good and evil—referred to average people. Although his statements seemingly indicate that Wang Ch'ung believed in three grades of human nature, he actually took this approach because he believed that human nature is neither good nor evil.

Nature and its spontaneity Wang Ch'ung explained in terms of skepticism and rationalism. He did not believe that nature (or heaven and earth) produces anything purposely; instead, all things are spontaneously created when the material force (*ch'i*) of heaven and earth come together. Specifically, the calamities and changes produced unexpectedly by nature are not for the purpose of reprimanding or rewarding humanity. Their occurrence is nothing but a spontaneous, natural manifestation, known as nonaction (*wu-wei*). Discussing this subject, he said, "What do we mean when we say that Heaven is spontaneous and takes no action? It is a matter of material force. It is tranquil, without desire, and is engaged in neither action nor business." Thus he rejected the teleological and anthropomorphic view of Heaven then popular among his contemporary Confucianists.

He developed his view of fate similarly. He believed that human nature and fate have nothing to do with a good or bad life: A good-natured man can be unlucky, and an evil-natured man can be lucky. He concluded that nature dictates its own course in and of itself.

Death he explained again in terms of skepticism and rationalism. First, he did not believe in the existence of spirits or ghosts because after people die they are not conscious and thus are not capable of doing anything for themselves, saying, "How can the dead be spiritual beings if such is the case?" He then continued, "When other creatures die, they do not become spiritual beings. Why should man alone become a spiritual being when he dies?" He gave further reason in terms of naturalism and rationalism: "Man can live because of his vital forces. At death his vital forces are extinct. What makes the vital forces possible is the blood. When a person dies, his blood becomes exhausted. With this his vital forces are extinct, and his body decays and becomes ashes and dust." In short, he believed in nothing after death. Human death, according to Wang Ch'ung, is like the extinction of fire: When a fire is extinguished, its light shines no longer, and when a man dies, his consciousness has no more understanding. Here Wang Ch'ung equated man (life) and matter (fire) in terms of material force (*ch'i*), which in turn is explained by nonaction (*wu-wei*). Thus he can be identified as a materialist and naturalist.

Wang Ch'ung also rejected the Confucian view that antiquity was a golden period in Chinese history. He believed in the equality of past and present, saying that the world was and is well governed because of sages and that it was and is ill governed because of unrighteous people; thus, good and bad governments, whether past or present, are not distinct. At times, however, he contradicted himself, saying that the present is better than the past. He came to this conclusion especially when the later Han Dynasty began. The Han empire's power and glory reached its pinnacle when it gained territorial expansion and political stability throughout the country; credit for these achievements was ascribed to the virtue of Han Dynasty rulers. Wang Ch'ung was neither anti-Confucian nor pro-Confucian. Although he gave the impression that he was no follower of Confucianism, he actually buttressed Confucianism through his rational skepticism and criticism.

Summary

Wang Ch'ung believed in the power of nature and its spontaneity and stressed the importance of skepticism and rationalism. Yet he did not propose any new ideas. Instead, he attacked and accommodated the old ideas in an eclectic fashion. As a result, he is generally credited with ushering in the era of Neo-Taoism which emphasized both the spontaneous power of nature (naturalism) and the critical ability of man (rationalism) during the Wei-Chin period. Orthodox Confucianism was severely challenged by such emergent unorthodox ideologies as Neo-Taoism; Wang Ch'ung, a typical Confucian scholar at heart, defended the basic Confucian tenets in his own unique way.

Bibliography

Chan, Wing-tsit. *A Source Book in Chinese Philosophy*. Princeton, N.J.: Princeton University Press, 1963. This book contains a chapter on Wang Ch'ung's life, together with extensive excerpts of his philosophical writings taken from the *Lun-hêng*.

De Bary, William T., Wing-tsit Chan, and Burton Watson, eds. *Sources of Chinese Tradition*. New York: Columbia University Press, 1960. 3d ed. 1964. A brief introduction to Wang Ch'ung's writings in relation to theories of the structure of the universe.

Fêng, Yu-lan. *A History of Chinese Philosophy*. Vol. 2. Princeton, N.J.: Princeton University Press, 1952-1953. An interpretative work on Wang Ch'ung's philosophy.

_____. *A Short History of Chinese Philosophy*. New York: Macmillan, 1948. A brief version of Wang Ch'ung's Confucianism is discussed in relation to yin-yang thought, Taoism, and Buddhism.

Forke, Alfred, trans. *Lun-hêng*. 2 vols. London: Leipzig, 1907-1911. An excellent, annotated translation of the *Lun-hêng*, the major result of Wang Ch'ung's philosophy.

————————. "Wang Ch'ung and Plato on Death and Immortality." *Journal of the North China Branch Royal Asiatic Society* 31 (1896-1897): 40-60. A critical comparative study of the two philosophers on life and death.

Li, Shi-yi. "Wang Ch'ung." *Tien Hsia Monthly* 5 (1937): 162-184, 209-307. Wang Ch'ung's life and philosophy are discussed, together with his contributions.

Needham, Joseph. *Science and Civilisation in China: History of Scientific Thought.* Vol. 2. Cambridge: Cambridge University Press, 1956. The scientific aspect of Wang Ch'ung's philosophy is discussed.

Key Ray Chong

WANG HSI-CHIH

Born: c. A.D. 307; Lang-ye, Lin-hsi, Shantung Province, China
Died: c. A.D. 379; near Shan-yin, Chekiang Province, China
Area of Achievement: Art
Contribution: By refining the styles of earlier calligraphers and developing new ones, Wang Hsi-chih, through his innovative brushwork, set the aesthetic standards for all subsequent calligraphers in China, Korea, and Japan.

Early Life

In 317, because of military onslaughts by non-Chinese "barbarians," the Western Chin (Tsin) Dynasty was forced to evacuate southward, reestablishing itself in refuge as the Eastern Chin (317-420). Wang Hsi-chih (Yi-shao was another given name he used) was born some years before this move in what is today the Province of Shantung, where the Wangs enjoyed the status of a leading aristocratic family. His father, Wang K'uang, was the cousin of Wang Tao, a prominent minister of the Western Chin, who advocated moving to the south. Both Wang K'uang and Wang Tao were praised for helping save the Chin through this fortuitous move.

Many of Wang Hsi-chih's relatives, besides being active in politics, were literati well versed in philosophy, literature, and the arts, especially calligraphy, the technique of writing characters with brush and ink. Chinese characters, the oldest continuous form of writing in the world, evolved from primitive markings on neolithic pottery, to first millennium B.C. graphs carved on tortoise shells and scapulae used in divination, and later to a complex script preserved on cast bronze ritual vessels and stone tablets. By the second century B.C., characters were being written on silk and bamboo slips using bamboo brushes with animal hair tips dipped in ink made from molded lampblack hardened with glue and dissolved in water on an ink slab.

As writing changed from carving, casting, and etching to a means of expressing through a flexible brush nuances of aesthetic feeling on a receptive surface such as silk or paper, the art of beautiful writing emerged. Writing had become not only a means of communication but indeed an expression of sentiment made manifest in ink. The ability to use the brush as both an artist's and a calligrapher's tool was a hallmark of the cultured gentleman. "A person's true character is revealed in one's calligraphy," according to a Chinese maxim; the facility to write Chinese characters in an elegant hand was judged to be a sign of talent and breeding.

Calligraphy is a discipline learned through practice and imitation. Wang was introduced to the "four treasures of the scholar's studio"—the brush, the ink stick, the ink stone, and paper or silk—in his youth by his father, who was adept in the "clerical" (*li*) style of writing, and an uncle, Wang Yi, a master of the "running" (*hsing*) style. These styles of writing had evolved from earlier calligraphers' experiments with character forms and the movement of writing implements over the ages. Beginning with the Shang period "oracle bone script" (*chia-gu-wen*), calligraphic styles progressed through the inscribed "ancient script" (*ku-wen*) on bronze implements, the "large seal script" (*ta-chuan*) on Warring States-era ritual vessels, and the "official" or "clerical" (*li*) style on Han Dynasty bamboo slips to the "block" script (*k'ai-shu*) of the first century or so. By Wang's time, the "running" style, aptly named since the strokes run together, along with "official grass" (*chang-ts'ao*), were new styles emerging out of these historical predecessors.

As a teenager, Wang became a disciple of the noted calligrapher Lady Wei. She was impressed with his talent, reportedly saying, "This child is destined to surpass my fame as a calligrapher." Later, to broaden his knowledge of past masters' brushwork, Wang traveled the land examining inscriptions preserved on stone stelae. In the south, he encountered specimens of Li Ssu, the Legalist prime minister of the Ch'in Dynasty (221-206 B.C.), whose decrees unified the scripts of the rival feudal states into a single one based on Ch'in models. He was also impressed by the "regular" script (*chen-shu*) works of Chung Yao, a Wei premier, and Liang Hu, noted for his large characters. The masterpieces of Ts'ao Hsi, Ts'ai Yung, and Chang Ch'ang also had an effect on him. From their examples he learned the theoretical and technical essences of calligraphy to enable him to go beyond imitation to creativity.

Awakened to new inspirations, he reportedly lamented that he had wasted years in studying under Lady Wei. "I [then] changed my master," he wrote, "and have been taking lessons from the monuments." He absorbed all the styles that he encountered, adapting them to create new versions. Besides the "running" style, he was especially proficient in the "grass" (*ts'ao*) style, an abstract, cursive form of writing whereby individual strokes of a character are effortlessly blended together while the brush rapidly moves across the writing surface, producing characters as flowing as "grass undulating in the breeze."

Life's Work

Wang Hsi-chih held several government positions, including Censor of K'uai-chi and "General of the Right Army" (*Yu-chün*), a title frequently affixed to his surname (Wang Yu-chün). He held posts in the provinces of Hupei and chekiang, but he was far better known as a calligrapher than as a government official.

Many anecdotes, perhaps apocryphal, but repeated nevertheless in most Chinese biographies of Wang, attest his brilliance and dedication to his art. One such legend relates that he would practice writing from morning until dusk beside a pond at the Chieh-chu Temple in Shao-hsing. Forgetting even to eat, he would copy characters repeatedly until he was satisfied. He washed out his brush and rinsed off the ink slab so frequently in the pond that its waters eventually turned black, and it became known as "Ink Pond."

Wang would practice even when he did not have paper, using his sleeve as a substitute. His writing was extremely forceful. Once, at Fen-yang, he asked a craftsman to carve out the characters he had written on a board; the worker reported that the power of his brush strokes had been impressed through three-quarters of the wood, giving rise to the phrase "penetrating three-fourths of the wood" as a metaphor for profundity and keenness. His wife, a noted calligrapher in her own right, often could not get him to stop writing even to eat; once she found him absorbed in his work, munching on sticks of ink which he absentmindedly had mistaken for food.

On another occasion, a Taoist monk, taking advantage of Wang's love of geese, connived to induce him to write out a Taoist text for him by arranging for a particularly fine gaggle to swim near the artist's boat. Instead of selling the geese to Wang, who wanted them badly and was willing to pay a high price, the monk asked him to write out the *Huang-t'ing ching* (Yellow Court Classic) in exchange for the fowl. Wang promptly obliged and sailed off with his beloved geese in tow, leaving the clever monk with an invaluable treasure. Wang's fascination with geese was rooted in his admiration of their gliding movement in the water and their bearing, traits he studied to improve his use of the brush.

On another occasion, Wang supposedly encountered an old lady selling fans beside a bridge in Shao-hsing. When she asked him to purchase one, he inquired as to how many she was able to sell each day. Admitting that her fans were out of fashion, the woman grumbled that she could barely make ends meet. Taking pity on her, Wang offered to write some poems on the fans and urged her to sell them at a high price. Though skeptical and thinking that her fans were spoiled by his writing, she followed his advice, and within a short period of time all the fans were sold. Now realizing the value of his calligraphy on her wares, she hounded Wang to decorate more, even pursuing him to his home. In desperation, he hid behind a stone grotto in the garden; later generations referred to this site as the "Old Woman Evading Stone." The bridge where the fans were reportedly inscribed is still popularly called the "Fan Writing Bridge."

The best-known event in Wang's life happened in 353. On the third day of the third lunar month, he joined a group of some forty men of letters, including Sun T'ung and Hsieh An, to celebrate the spring festival at a scenic spot near Shao-hsing, famous for the rare orchids supposedly planted there by a king of the fifth century B.C. There, at the Orchid Pavilion, they drank, challenged one another with word games, played chess, and composed poems. To commemorate the occasion, Wang wrote a preface to a collection of poetry created there by himself and his friends. This 324-character, twenty-eight-line masterpiece, the *Lan-t'ing hsu* (Orchid Pavilion preface), became treasured as one of Wang's greatest accomplishments.

This scroll's brushwork and composition were likened to "fairies flying among the clouds and dancing on the waves." Each character displayed his genius, and even where several characters, such as *chih* (repeated twenty times) and *pu* (used in seven places), were duplicated in the composition, calligraphic variations were employed to prevent any single character from being exactly like another. Wang later tried to duplicate this success by making copies, but he was forced to admit that even he could not surpass his original in beauty.

Eventually, he became dissatisfied with court intrigue and corruption, preferring to retire to a reclusive life in order to devote himself exclusively to study and calligraphy. His last days were spent secluded in the picturesque hills of Chekiang Province at the Jade Curtain Spring near Shan-yin, where he died, probably around 379 (some sources say 361).

Summary

Wang Hsi-chih is celebrated by connoisseurs of Chinese writing as the "Sage Calligrapher." His writing style was immortalized by the phrase "dragons leaping at the gate of heaven and tigers crouching before the phoenix hall," the words used by the sixth century Emperor Wu of the Liang Dynasty upon being shown Wang's works. Several of his seven sons, particularly Wang Hsien-chih (nicknamed the "Little Sage") carried on their father's legacy, becoming important calligraphers in their own right and producing equally talented progeny.

Wang Hsi-chih's holographs were greatly coveted. The *Lan-t'ing hsu*, for example, was passed on as a Wang family heirloom for seven generations, ending up in the possession of Chih Yung, a monk who was also well-known as a calligrapher. When Chih Yung died, the scroll was entrusted to his disciple, Pien Ts'ai. Emperor T'ang T'ai-tsung (reigned 626-649) wanted this scroll in order to complete his collection of Wang originals. Thrice the monk refused to give it up. Wei Cheng, the prime minister, then devised a scheme whereby a confidant named Hsiao Yi, pretending to be a kind host, disarmed the monk's suspicion by plying him with wine; taking advantage of his drunken stupor, Hsiao Yi was able to steal away the scroll, which had been hidden in a wooden temple beam. The emperor was overjoyed and ordered Chao Mu and Feng Ch'eng-su to make copies for distribution to his ministers for their enjoyment and study. On his death, T'ai-tsung ordered this scroll and all other original writings by Wang entombed with him so that he could enjoy them in the afterworld. The consensus of most experts is that none of Wang's originals exists today. Fortunately, many of his writings were carved in stone so that rubbings could be made for study, and other artists traced his originals to learn and to imitate his stroke style, thus preserving samples of Wang's genius for posterity.

Bibliography
Driscoll, Lucy, and Kenji Toda. *Chinese Calligraphy*. Chicago: University of
    Chicago Press, 1935. Has some references to Wang's theories on calligra-
    phy and his studies under Lady Wei.
Froncek, Thomas, ed. *The Horizon Book of the Arts of China*. New York:
    American Heritage Publishing Co., 1969. A concise biography of Wang is
    included under the heading "Wine, Weather, and Wang." Preceding page
    has a picture of Wang entitled "Wang Hsi-chi Writing on a Fan," painted
    by Liang K'ai (c. 1140-c. 1210).
Lee, H. T. *The Story of Chinese Culture*. Taipei, Taiwan: Literature House,
    1964. Contains an impressionistic essay, "Wang Hsi-chih and Chinese
    Calligraphy," giving anecdotal highlights of Wang's life.
Li, Dun J., ed. *The Essence of Chinese Civilization*. Princeton, N.J.: D. Van
    Nostrand Co., 1967. A partial translation of Wang's biography (supposedly
    written by Emperor T'ang T'ai-tsung) from the *Chin shu* (265-420; *History
    of the Chin*).
Nakata, Yujiro. *Chinese Calligraphy*. Tokyo: Weather Hill/Tankosha, 1983.
    Historical overview of Chinese calligraphy originally published in Japa-
    nese. Chapter 6, "The Masterpieces of Wang Xizhi [Wang Hsi-chih] and
    Wang Xianzhi [Wang Hsien-chih]," gives a short biographical account.
    Numerous examples of Wang's work are illustrated and analyzed. Appen-
    dix contains a chronology of calligraphers and their works.
Willetts, William. *Chinese Calligraphy: Its History and Aesthetic Motivation*.
    New York: Oxford University Press, 1981. Contains a short account of the
    writing of the *Lan-t'ing hsu* and reproduces a section of the scroll taken
    from a stone rubbing. Good bibliography on Chinese calligraphy in
    general.

William M. Zanella

WANG PI

Born: 226; possibly in modern Shantung Province, China
Died: 249; China
Area of Achievement: Philosophy
Contribution: Wang was a major creative force behind the most important philosophical school of his day, and his commentaries on some of the most revered Chinese classics still help shape their interpretation.

Early Life

Wang Pi (in Chinese fashion the family name, Wang, is given first) died at the age of twenty-three. It is therefore difficult to separate the story of his early life from that of his mature period of productivity. A further handicap to the student of Wang Pi is the fact that very little is actually known about the details of his life. In an uncharacteristic omission, the Chinese dynastic histories do not even contain a biography for him. Most of what is known about Wang Pi comes from a few short paragraphs appended as footnotes to the biography of another man and incorporated into a history called the *San-kuo chih* (third century; chronicles of the three kingdoms). Wang Pi's thought, however, survives in the commentaries he wrote to three Chinese classics: the *I Ching* (before the sixth century B.C.; *Book of Changes*), the *Tao-te Ching* (c. eighth to third century B.C.; also known as the *Lao-tzu*), and Confucius' *Lun-yü* (late sixth or early fifth century B.C.; *Analects*).

Wang Pi was a precocious child, and he soon proved himself remarkably adept at conversation—a skill that was much in vogue among the elite of third century China and which accounts for much of his contemporary reputation. He was a thorough master of the polite arts of the day, but, in keeping with his image as *enfant terrible*, he also was not quite sensitive enough to others' feelings and offended many of his acquaintances with his overly clever manner. He served in the relatively minor post of departmental secretary, which had also been his father's job, but failed to reach higher office because his patron, Ho Yen (190-249), was outmaneuvered at court in his efforts to have Wang appointed. Wang was not really interested in administration anyway, however, and preferred to devote his time and energy to philosophical speculation.

Wang flourished in the era of the Cheng-shih reign (240-249), which is often cited as the high point of the so-called Neo-Taoist movement in China. This period came to an abrupt end in 249, when a *coup d'état* stripped real power away from the ruling family of the Wei state in north China, where Wang lived, and placed it in the hands of a military dictator. Ho Yen perished in the wake of this coup, and Wang himself was dismissed from office, although his death later that same year came as a result of unknown natural causes.

Life's Work

Wang Pi and his patron, Ho Yen, are traditionally credited with founding the movement known in the West as Neo-Taoism. This name is misleading, however, since the movement really grew as much out of Confucianism as it did out of Taoism. It began with studies of the Confucian classic the *I Ching*, was enthusiastically discussed with reference to the Taoist *Tao-te Ching* and *Chuang-tzu* in the later third century, and in the fourth century finally merged into a newly triumphant Mahayana Buddhism. The movement is probably most accurately known by its Chinese name: *hsüan-hsüeh* (mysterious learning).

Wang himself stands accused of trying to interpret a Confucian classic, the *I Ching*, in Taoist terms, and, in the single most famous episode in Wang's life, of praising Confucius as the supreme Taoist because he knew better than to try and say anything about the ineffable Tao. The truth is that Wang was not much concerned with—indeed, he completely rejected—labels such as "Confucian" and "Taoist" and instead strove to unearth the ultimate truths concealed in each.

During the waning years of the Han Dynasty (207 B.C. to A.D. 220), various thinkers, notably the great Wang Ch'ung (27-c. 100), had become increasingly disillusioned with standard Confucian metaphysics, which in the mid-Han era had emphasized elaborate systems of correspondences between Heaven, Earth, and Man, cycles of the so-called Five Elements, and attempts to predict the future based on these. The desire to understand the basic principles of the universe was not lost, nor were the basic ideas entirely rejected, but the simplistic excesses—the teleology and the easy belief that Heaven was regular, purposeful, and concerned with humankind—were shaved away. At the same time, the so-called New Text versions of the Confucian classics which had supported the elaborate Han cosmological systems lost their standing and gradually were replaced by versions of the texts purporting to be older. These "Old Texts" did not fit neatly into vast cosmological systems and left a cosmological void in Confucian thought. By the end of the Han, the great pattern of the universe had seemingly dissolved into chaos.

In the third century, *hsüan-hsüeh* emerged to fill this metaphysical vacuum. *Hsüan-hsüeh* is predicated on the belief that the infinite phenomena of this universe are random, transitory, and without any meaningful pattern. Yet they all must, it was reasoned, be generated by one single, eternal verity. That was the "original nothingness" (*pen-wu*), or "nonbeing" (*wu*), the origin of all being.

Because of this emphasis on nonbeing as the root of al things, *hsüan-hsüeh* thinkers have sometimes been dismissed as nihilistic. This casual dismissal is reinforced by the explanation that they were escapist Neo-Taoists, who turned from the traditional social concerns of Confucianism because of political repression, the collapse of the established Han world order, or aristocratic indifference. In fact, *hsüan-hsüeh* was far more than mere escapism and represents an impassioned search for meaning in the universe by highly refined and critical intellects. The idea that nonbeing is the ontological foundation of the universe is similarly more than mere nihilism, since, in *hsüan-hsüeh* thought, nonbeing becomes the positive principle that renders the universe intelligible.

Being and nonbeing coexist and are fundamentally indivisible. This great unity of being and nonbeing is "The Mystery" (*hsüan*), also known as Tao, or the Way. It is the unifying principle of the universe, called a "mystery" because any name would be inadequate: It is absolute, and even to call it a mystery is to impose false and misleading limitations on it—better not to call it anything (but to call it "nothing" is not quite satisfactory either).

Wang's thought focused on this critical *hsüan-hsüeh* relationship between being and nonbeing. His work took the form of exegesis, an attempt to achieve an understanding of the classics of China's formative age. Wang's scholarship was solidly in the tradition of the Ching-chou school, a place in central China that had been a late Han center for Old Text scholarship and which was particularly famous for its study of the *T'ai-hsüan Ching* (contemporary with Jesus Christ; the classic of the great mystery). This book, in turn, was largely just an amplification of ideas to be found in the more venerable *I Ching*, and it was to the *I Ching* that Wang turned his principal interest.

Working with an Old Text edition of the *I Ching*, Wang rejected the Han tradition of interpreting it in terms of astrological symbols and numerology and sought instead to return to what he thought was the original meaning of the text. The *I Ching* consists of the set of all sixty-four possible combinations of six broken and unbroken lines; the resulting hexagrams were then assigned oracular values and used in divination. Later, a set of "wings," or commentaries, was added that recast this fortune-teller's manual into a kind of cosmological blueprint of the universe. Although Wang rejected the neat teleology of Han Confucianism, he was still searching for some abstract principle that would reconcile the apparent diversity and disorder of the material universe, and he found in the *I Ching* exactly the kind of cosmic diagram for which he was looking.

The *I Ching* spoke of a Great Ultimate (*t'ai-chi*) which gives rise to the twin poles, *yin* and *yang*, which in turn generate the multitude of phenomena in the world. This schema is the primordial unity which in the third century was called The Mystery. Unlike the elaborate systems and cycles of earlier Han cosmology, this principle is spontaneous and unpremeditated. Heaven and Earth move without obvious purpose, yet naturally accord with the Tao. This system is a truth beyond words which must be looked at holistically; any attempt at analytical description violates its absolute quality. Consequently, in a typically Taoist paradox, the subject of Wang's intense investigations was beyond the power of his words to describe.

Wang belonged to the side of a raging third century debate which believed in the inadequacy of language. Characteristically, this idea harked back to a passage in the *I Ching* which said that "words cannot exhaustively [convey] meaning" (*yen pu chin i*). Wang argued, therefore, that one should pay attention not to symbols or words but to their underlying, and more abstract, meanings. When you understand the meaning of a passage, you should forget the words.

Although the cosmic principle, or Tao, is unitary, it also has a binary extension—the dialectic between being and nonbeing. From these two, then, come the many. Wang liked to view the universe in terms of the interaction between a fundamental "substance" (*t'i*), and its "applications" (*yung*) in the phenomenal world. This schema is reminiscent of Plato's famous duality between ideals and physical appearances, but, more important, it also resembles the later Neo-Confucian duality between "principle" (*li*) and "matter" (*ch'i*). Wang, in fact, appears to have been one of the first Chinese thinkers to use *li* ("principle") in essentially this sense, and, although he cannot be given credit for fully conceiving these ideas, he clearly contributed to the ongoing development of an important theme in later Chinese thought.

Summary

In his short life, Wang Pi exerted a tremendous impact on philosophy. *Hsüan-hsüeh* was the dominant mode of thought for some two centuries, and Wang's commentaries on the *I Ching* and the *Tao-te Ching*, together with the commentary on the *Chuang-tzu* by Kuo Hsiang (died 312) and Hsiang Hsiu (c. 230-c. 280), were the central texts of *hsüan-hsüeh*. Later *hsüan-hsüeh* thinkers and conversationalists measured themselves against Wang.

Wang's scholarship, if not *hsüan-hsüeh* thought itself, also affects scholars even in the twentieth century. It is well-known that the *Tao-te Ching* has been the most translated of all Chinese books, and, of the literally hundreds of Chinese commentaries to the *Tao-te Ching* Wang's is considered to be the very best that still remains. Most translations of the *Tao-te Ching* are therefore based on Wang's edition of the text and commentary. To be sure, Wang profoundly influenced his own time, but he also exerts an influence on modern scholarship, as the *Tao-te Ching*, one of the most important books of all time, continues to be viewed partly through his eyes.

Bibliography
Balazs, Étienne. "Nihilistic Revolt or Mystical Escapism." In *Chinese Civilization and Bureaucracy: Variations on a Theme*, edited by Arthur F. Wright. New Haven, Conn.: Yale University Press, 1964. A brilliant, although highly unflattering, depiction of third century thought and society.
Fêng, Yu-lan. *A History of Chinese Philosophy*. Vol. 2, *The Period of Clas-*

sical Learning. Translated by Derk Bodde. London: Allen and Unwin, 1953. Although somewhat dated, and not without flaws, this work remains a classic. It is also virtually the only English language study of some of the lesser known Chinese thinkers, such as Wang Pi.

Hsiao, Kung-chuan. A History of Chinese Political Thought. Translated by F. W. Mote. Princeton, N.J.: Princeton University Press, 1979. This work contains a somewhat unsympathetic account of the political implications of Neo-Taoist thought.

Lin, Paul J. A Translation of Lao Tzu's "Tao-te Ching" and Wang Pi's Commentary. Ann Arbor: Center for Chinese Studies, University of Michigan, 1977. This book examines Wang's contribution to the study of the Tao-te Ching. It includes a complete translation of a brief third century biography of Wang.

Liu, I-ch'ing. Shih-shuo Hsin-yü: A New Account of Tales of the World. Translated by Richard B. Mather. Minneapolis: University of Minnesota Press, 1976. A fifth century collection of anecdotes, this book is one of the principal sources of information about Wang Pi. Mather has added an introduction and invaluable biographical sketches of all 626 persons mentioned in the text.

T'ang, Yung-t'ung. "Wang Pi's New Interpretation of the I-ching and Lun-yü." Harvard Journal of Asiatic Studies 10 (September, 1947): 124-161. An important essay by the foremost Chinese expert on the intellectual history of the period. This work may, however, be too technical for beginners, while experts would be better advised to consult the original Chinese text.

Yü, Ying-shih. "Individualism and the Neo-Taoist Movement in Wei-Chin China." In Individualism and Holism: The Confucian and Taoist Philosophical Perspectives, edited by Donald Munro. Ann Arbor: Center for Chinese Studies, University of Michigan, 1985. A fine scholarly description of Neo-Taoism viewed as an expression of Chinese individualism. The essay is marred somewhat by an insistence on the opposition between Neo-Taoism and Confucianism.

Zürcher, Erik. The Buddhist Conquest of China: The Spread and Adaptation of Buddhism in Early Medieval China. Leiden, Netherlands: E. J. Brill, 1959. While the focus of this authoritative study is on Buddhism, it also provides an overview of intellectual developments in the period and an excellent discussion of hsüan-hsüeh.

Charles W. Holcombe

WANG WEI

Born: 701; district of Ch'i, prefecture of T'ai-yuan, China
Died: 761; Ch'ang-an, prefecture of Ching-chao, China
Areas of Achievement: Literature, art, music, and government
Contribution: A major T'ang poet, Wang Wei left a body of some 370 poems
that can be considered authentic; his nature poetry has been particularly
admired, and it accounts for his preeminence in Chinese literature. He was
credited with founding the Southern school of landscape painting. Wang
Wei was also a highly skilled musician and an unusually competent government official.

Early Life

Not much is known about Wang Wei's early life and education. Born in
701, in the district of Ch'i, in the modern province of Shansi, China, he was
the eldest child of a family of aristocratic, middle-level officials. Wang Wei's
father, Wang Ch'u-lien, despite his middle-official rank, belonged to the
powerful T'ai-yuan Wang clan, while Wang Wei's mother belonged to the
prominent Po-ling Ts'ui clan. The Wangs and the Ts'uis were among the
"Seven Great Surnames" (*ch'i hsing*) and wielded much political power.

Wang Wei was a prodigy and evidently had the typical Confucian literary
education, which prepared him for the civil-service examinations. He began
to compose poetry at the age of nine and also showed talent in painting,
calligraphy, and music. At the age of fifteen, he went to the capitals of Lo-
yang and Ch'ang-an to prepare himself for the examinations and was warmly
welcomed at the courts of the imperial princes, especially that of Prince Ch'i
(Li Fan), the younger brother of the emperor. Known for his court poetry
and ability to play *p'i-p'a* (Chinese guitar), Wang Wei was an immediate success at court, where he shrewdly made important social and literary contacts.

Having taken first place in the provincial examination, he became qualified
to take the metropolitan examination. In 721, he was among the thirty-eight
successful candidates for the *chin-shih* degree out of the several thousand
who attempted it. As a result, he was soon appointed one of the court's associate secretaries of music. His future looked bright.

Life's Work

Nevertheless, at this time, Wang Wei's position as a literatus came to
overshadow his background as an aristocrat. When the Empress Wu had
usurped the throne in 690, she had initiated a conflict between the aristocracy and the literati by rejecting hereditary privilege in favor of the examination system for choosing high officials. Although Emperor Hsüan Tsung had
revived the hereditary privilege after ascending the throne in 712, he remained suspicious of political intrigues and kept a watch on the princes. Soon

after Wang Wei assumed his official position at the court of Prince Ch'i, the prince was suspected of conspiring against his brother. In 722 the emperor responded by breaking up the princely entourages. Wang Wei was charged with an indiscretion (allowing the performance of a tabooed dance). In 723 he was dismissed from court, demoted, and banished to the distant district of Chi-chou (in modern Shantung Province), thus beginning the early period of his literary development.

Wang Wei served in Chi-chou until 727, when he began a period of travel in the eastern provinces. These travels frequently provided inspiration for poems which are unusual in their perspectives. During his travels, Wang Wei made the acquaintance of Taoist and Buddhist masters and frequented their retreats. He also made important political friendships during his exile. His friendship with P'ei Yao-ch'ing, the prefect of Chi-chou, led to his introduction to the outstanding statesman and brilliant poet Chang Chiu-ling, the powerful imperial minister.

About 730 Wang Wei's wife died. He never remarried and chose to remain celibate the rest of his life, beginning a serious study of Ch'an Buddhism with the Ch'an master Tso-kuang. At this time, he also discovered his own poetic voice. In 733 he returned to Ch'ang-an. Now his acquaintance with Chang Chiu-ling paid off, for this powerful and highly ethical man sponsored his reentry into politics. In 734 Emperor Hsüan Tsung appointed him "reminder on the right" (*yu-shih-i*). True to his Confucian ideal, Wang Wei was in public service once again, thus ending his first stage of poetic development.

As reminder on the right, Wang Wei reminded the emperor of overlooked or forgotten matters. Such a position required much tact and subtle diplomacy; apparently Wang Wei was equal to it, for he maintained his position and continued to advance. Nevertheless, he found Hsuan Tsüng's new ministry dangerous. Although the triumvirate included Chang Chiu-ling and P'ei Yao-ching, the third member was the ambitious Li Lin-fu. Chang Chiu-ling and P'ei Yao-ching had both risen to positions of power through the examination system; they were literati. Li Lin-fu, however, was an aristocrat and a member of the imperial clan that supported hereditary privilege: Conflict was inevitable. When Chang Chiu-ling was banished and P'ei Yao-ching demoted in 737, Wang Wei also was in danger. Nevertheless, he survived, although he temporarily became investigating censor (*chien-ch'a yü-shih*) of Ho-hsi, a post on the northwest frontier in the province of Liang-chou (modern Kansu). Here he assisted the military governor, Ts'ui Hsi-i, from 737 until 738, when Ts'ui's forces were defeated by the Tibetans and the general was killed. Although not technically an exile, Wang Wei's frontier assignment gave Li Lin-fu time to consolidate his power without undue interference. He became a virtual dictator when the elderly emperor, preoccupied with his consort, Yang Kuei-fei, began to allow him a free hand in public affairs.

When Wang Wei returned to Ch'ang-an in 738, he was promoted to palace censor (*tien-chung shih-yü shih*). In 740 he was sent to the south to supervise the provincial examinations, returning to the capital and continuing his steady advancement. At about this time, he seems to have acquired his famous Wang-ch'uan estate, which was located in the foothills of the Chung-nan Mountains, some thirty miles south of Ch'ang-an; the estate was to prove important to his life and to his painting and poetry. About 750 his mother died, and he withdrew from court for the customary period of mourning, a little more than two years. Upon his return to Ch'an-an in 752, Wang Wei was appointed secretary of the civil office (*li-lu lang-chung*), which obliged him to nominate, examine, and evaluate civil officials. In 754 he became grand secretary of the imperial chancellery (*chi-shih-chung*), which represented a more prestigious rank. The following year, however, any further advance was abruptly curtailed by the onslaught of the An Lu-shan rebellion, which dispersed the entire court.

The years from 734 to 755 may be considered Wang Wei's middle period, his most productive and significant literary period. It includes his poem written to Chang Chiu-ling after the latter's exile to Hsing-chou in 739 and the frontier poems inspired by his military experience at Ho-shi. There are also such outstanding court poems as "Tseng ts'ung ti szǔ k'u yüan wai Ch'iu" ("Given to My Paternal Cousin, Military Supply Officer Qiu"), "Fêng ho shêng chih chung-yang-chieh tsai ch'en chi ch'un ch'en shang shou ying chih" ("Written at Imperial Command to Harmonize with His Majesty's Poem, 'On the Double Ninth Festival the Ministers and Assembled Officials Offer Their Wishes for Longevity'"), and "Ta-t'ung tien shêng yü chih Lung Ch'ih shang yu ch'ing yün; pai kuan kung tu; shêng en pien szǔ yen yüeh kan shu chi" ("At Datong Hall a Jade Iris Grew, and There Were Auspicious Clouds by Dragon Pond; the Hundred Officials Observed [These Phenomena] Together; Imperial Kindness Bestowed a Banquet with Music, so I Dared to Write on This Occasion"). The first court poem expresses Wang Wei's desire to withdraw from politics and celebrates the peace and serenity of reclusion. The latter two, however, celebrate imperial power. Finally, this period includes many fine Buddhist and nature poems, the latter often showing Taoist influences.

During the 740's and early 750's, Wang Wei apparently spent much of his time on his Wang-ch'uan estate. It is evident that he enjoyed this place immensely. His best-known companion was his friend P'ei Ti, a minor poet and official, who shared in the composition of the masterly "Wang-ch'uan chi" ("Wang River Collection"). Together they treated a series of topics whose order was determined simply by the geographical layout of the landscape. Wang Wei's continuous scroll on which he depicted the same twenty landscapes is no longer extant, but copies of it give a viewer some sense of what he must have done.

When Li Lin-fu died in 752, he had been replaced by Yan Kuo-chung, who although a man of little merit was the brother of the emperor's consort, Yang Kuei-fei. When the frontier general An Lu-shan rebelled in 755 and attempted to overthrow the emperor, Hsüan Tsung was caught unprepared. Fearing an attack on Ch'ang-an, he and his court fled at night to Szechwan. Some officials, however, remained behind, including Wang Wei.

Having almost immediately occupied Lo-yang, the rebels then attacked Ch'ang-an. Wang Wei attempted to join the emperor but was captured by the rebels. Although he pretended physical disability in an effort to escape having to serve the rebel government, he did not succeed and faced execution. Because An Lu-shan had been previously impressed with his abilities, however, he was imprisoned instead in the P'u-ti Monastery. Later he was compelled to collaborate with the rebel government.

Meanwhile, when Hsüan Tsung learned that his son had fled to Shensi in northwest China, he abdicated. His son proclaimed himself Emperor Sutsung and organized Uighur forces to help him overcome the rebels. After An Lu-shan was killed and Ch'ang-an was recaptured toward the end of 757, the new emperor and his court returned to the capital.

Debate now raged on what to do with the collaborators. Two of the emperor's ministers urged that they be killed; a third, Li Hsien, argued that the instability of the military and political situation demanded selective clemency. Most of the collaborators were punished by death, flogging, or banishment. Because of his brother's intercession and of a poem he had written from the monastery during the rebel occupation, however, Wang Wei was pardoned by the emperor. Wang Wei was then reinstated in the official ranks as vice-president of the grand secretariat of the crown prince (*t'ai-tzŭ chung-yun*) and later became its president. After again serving briefly as grand secretary of the imperial chancellery (*chi-shih-chung*), in 759 he was advanced to the highest position he ever attained, that of assistant secretary of state on the right (*shung-shu yu-ch'êng*).

Despite this honor, it appears that toward the end of his life Wang Wei became disheartened and increasingly inactive. He seldom stayed at his Wang-ch'uan estate but lived mostly just outside the capital. He wrote no more nature poems and on returning home from work spent his leisure hours reading Buddhist sutras. Lonely, old, weak, and with poor eyesight, he petitioned the emperor to recall his brother, Wang Chin, to court so the two could be near each other. The emperor did so, and Wang Chin was appointed grand counselor of the emperor on the left (*tso-san chi-ch'ang shih*). Wang Wei wrote a memorial thanking the emperor for his kindness; it is dated the fourth day of the fifth month of 761. Wang Wei died in the same year and was buried on his Wang-ch'uan estate.

Wang Chin survived Wang Wei to become a chief minister under the next emperor. The new emperor, who was fond of poetry, asked Wang Chin if enough of Wang Wei's poems had survived to make a collection for presentation to the throne. The poems that were extant, out of the several thousand written, were gathered together by Wang Chin and presented to the emperor in 763.

The years 756-761 may be considered Wang Wei's late period. The poems written during this time reflect his loneliness, his struggles with the infirmities of old age, and his growing awareness of death. In 756, as a prisoner of the rebels in the P'u-ti Monastery, awaiting a doubtful fate, Wang Wei was surprised by a visit from his friend P'ei Ti, who somehow had managed to slip into the monastery. P'ei Ti brought news of the outside world, especially about the behavior of the Pear Garden musicians when forced to celebrate the rebel victory. This event inspired Wang Wei to write a poem. Shortly thereafter, he addressed a poem directly to P'ei Ti. These two poems, as Professor Yu observes, "typify Wang Wei's ability to identify with both the committed official and the escapist recluse." At the time he wrote the poem about the Pear Garden musicians, Wang Wei could not have dreamed that it would play an important part in his rehabilitation and restoration, resulting in a pardon from the emperor and in his return to office.

Wang Wei's gratitude for the emperor's clemency is shown by his poem "Chi mêng yu-tsui hsüan fu fei kung fu kan shêng ên ch'ieh shu pi i chien fêng chien hsin hsü shih chün-têng chu-kung" ("Having Received Pardon for My Offense and Been Returned to Office, Humbly Moved by Imperial Kindness, I Write My Lowly Thoughts and Present Them to My Superiors"). Written in 758, the poem celebrates a return to the old order of stability and brilliance and predicts an even more glorious reign.

Summary

Wang Wei was the most prominent poet of his time. He knew the rigorous conventions of the court poetry of the Early T'ang, but he reacted against them and made his own way, becoming the premier capital poet, one who could hew to the rules and then go beyond them. Nevertheless, for centuries he has been best known as a nature poet. Indeed, he was a master at portraying tranquil landscapes, and he often composed such poems when he was away from court. Commonly admired for their concrete images and visual immediacy, they display at the same time an intuitive sense of the unreality of sensory experience. Such an impression is frequently supported by statements of a philosophical or religious character.

Wang Wei was politically a Confucian who dabbled in Taoism and who loved the Buddhist Way, and he studied for years under a Ch'an master. When away from court, he burned incense, practiced Ch'an meditation, and loved to associate with Buddhist and Taoist monks. His commitment to Buddhism inspired many of his poems.

As a poet Wang Wei was independent, daringly experimental, and original. He strove always for simplicity, integrity, and spiritual truth. Although interested in perception, he was not concerned with what the eye saw but with what the mind intuited, with the inner spirit of things. His own emotion was always restrained. His poetry is wide in scope both thematically and stylistically. His contributions to the development of genre by his treatment of the quatrain, which depended on proper closure, and his personal handling of the couplet were of major importance.

Wang Wei's influence on later Chinese poets began early. It is evident in the work of the later eighth century minor poets Liu Chang-ch'ing—whose poetry was written late in his life—and Wei Ying-wu. The great practitioners of the new *shih yü* poetry of the Northern Sung Dynasty (960-1127)— Ou-yang Hsiu, Wang An-shih, and above all Su Tung-p'o—looked to Wang Wei as their model. Indeed, it was Su Tung-p'o who elevated Wang's reputation as a painter to equal his reputation as a poet. He was also responsible, as Marsha Wagner has noted, for a remark about one of Wang's poems which, taken out of context and misinterpreted by others, led to his false reputation as the "painter-poet." This misunderstanding in turn led to the aesthetic ideal that a good poem was a "painting-poem" (*hua-shih*). Two prominent poets of the Ch'ing Dynasty (1644-1911)—Wang Shih-chêng and Shên Tê-ch'ien—who were also critics, formulated their poetic theories out of their admiration for Wang Wei's poetry. Wang Shih-chêng held that genuine poetry amounted to the immediate embodiment of spiritual inspiration in words. Shên Tê-ch'ien, a fine teacher of Chinese prosody, held that the technical proficiency of Wang Wei proved him the greatest of all Chinese poets.

Bibliography
Chou, Shan. "Beginning with Images in the Nature Poetry of Wang Wei." *Harvard Journal of Asiatic Studies* 42 (June, 1982): 117-137. Chou proposes that the solution to the problem of meaning in Wang Wei's nature poetry is to be found in understanding the Buddhist influence.
Gong, Shu. "The Function of Space and Time as Compositional Elements in Wang Wei's Poetry: A Study of Five Poems." *Literature East and West* 16 (April, 1975): 1168-1193. Gong believes that the evocation of solitude and transient human existence in Wang Wei's poetry is a function of his treatment of space and time.
Luk, Thomas Yuntong. "A Cinematic Interpretation of Wang Wei's Nature Poetry." *New Asia Academic Bulletin* 1 (1978): 151-161. Su Shih saw a Wang Wei poem as a pictograph; Walmsley saw it as a stereograph; Luk regards it as a cinematograph.
Owen, Stephen. "Wang Wei: The Artifice of Simplicity." In *The Great Age of Chinese Poetry: The High T'ang*. New Haven, Conn.: Yale University Press, 1981. Owen supplies an excellent short overview of Wang Wei as poetic technician and relates the poet's work to his life and historical context.

Wagner, Marsha L. *Wang Wei*. Boston: Twayne Publishers, 1982. Part of the Twayne World Authors series, this scholarly, well-written account of Wang Wei's life provides a balanced, perceptive appraisal of his contributions as poet, painter, and government official. Includes fine translations.

Wang Wei. *Poems by Wang Wei*. Translated by Yin-nan Chang and Lewis C. Walmsley. Rutland, Vt.: Charles E. Tuttle Co., 1958. Chang and Walmsley provide worthy translations of 136 of Wang Wei's poems. Includes a short critical introduction and a brief sketch of his life.

_____. *Poems of Wang Wei*. Translated by G. W. Robinson. Baltimore: Penguin Books, 1973. Fluid translations of 127 poems, with a brief introduction.

_____. *The Poetry of Wang Wei: New Translations and Commentary*. Translated by Pauline Yu. Bloomington: Indiana University Press, 1980. This study provides excellent, scholarly translations and notes as well as knowing critical appraisals of Wang Wei's poems. The effort to supply a framework of Western critical apparatus that might be applied to Wang Wei's poetry, however, appears dubious.

Richard P. Benton

WILLIAM OF AUVERGNE

Born: c. 1190; Aurillac, Auvergne, France
Died: March 30, 1249; Paris, France
Area of Achievement: Philosophy
Contribution: As the first European medieval scholar to attempt to integrate Aristotelian philosophy and Christian theology, William encouraged the growth of philosophy as a discipline distinct from theology and paved the way for the great synthesis of faith and reason of the later Middle Ages.

Early Life

The date of William of Auvergne's birth is unknown, as are most of the facts about his early life. Scholars have assumed that he was born before 1190, because in 1225, he was teaching theology at the University of Paris, a privilege not usually granted to those below the age of thirty-five. His birthplace was Aurillac, a village in the French province of Auvergne. A legend suggests that his parents were poor: As a child, William was begging one day on the street, when a woman offered him some money if he would promise never to become a bishop. Perhaps William had a sense of his own destiny, for he declined the offer.

Regardless of whether he was prescient, rich or poor, he must have shown enough intellectual promise to be sent to school, though where or when is unknown. In the Middle Ages, almost all elementary instruction was given in cathedral or monastic schools, and it was expected that most students would become candidates for the priesthood. William was not only ordained but also went to the University of Paris, the most prestigious school of higher learning in France. By 1223, he was a cathedral priest, or canon, of the Cathedral of Notre Dame, and was probably already teaching at the university.

In the early thirteenth century, the basic intellectual assumptions of the academic world were undergoing a rapid process of change, and William was to become an important part of this transformation. Until shortly before William went to Paris, most of the works of the Greek philosopher Aristotle had been unavailable to the Christian scholars of Europe. After the fall of the Roman Empire in the West, in A.D. 476, Europe had been virtually cut off from the more affluent and cultured East, and much of the heritage of Greek philosophy which had been passed to the Romans was lost. In the disruption that followed Rome's fall, the decline of the towns and the disappearance of secular schools left most education in the hands of the only well-organized institution that remained intact, the Church. While the flickering lamp of civilization was kept alight in the monasteries, it was necessarily colored by the viewpoint of religious faith. Thus for several centuries, philosophy, which then included all forms of inquiry about the universe, was taught as a part of Christian theology and remained firmly anchored to the views articulated by Saint Augustine early in the fifth century.

In the Augustinian universe, the knowledge of God obtained through the revelation of the Gospels and maintained in its purity by the Church was seen as inherently superior to the knowledge gained through reason and the senses. These faculties existed, in fact, simply to help human beings understand the revelation in which they already believed. Following Augustine, medieval philosophers had attempted to explain the phenomena of the world around them within a framework limited by such tenets of faith as God, His creation, and the Resurrection. This effort was seen as the whole purpose of Christian philosophy; ideas or observations which contradicted the structure of faith, as it had been revealed in the Bible and by the church fathers, were rejected as heresy.

Starting in the late twelfth century, however, the works of the Greek philosophers, particularly Aristotle, began to filter once more into Europe through Arabic translations and commentaries from Islamic Spain. As they were gradually translated into Latin, these works revealed a whole new (or, rather, very old) world of pre-Christian explanations of the universe based solely upon the use of reason. At first, the Church attempted to stamp out the Greek ideas, and, in 1228 and 1231, Pope Gregory IX condemned the use of Aristotle by the faculty at the University of Paris. Since Aristotle had addressed nearly every area of knowledge, however, the curiosity of the scholars could not be suppressed for long, and William was among the first to attempt to integrate Aristotelian ideas into Christian philosophy.

Life's Work

That William was a man of some prominence and ability, even early in his career, is evidenced by his appointments, in 1224 and 1225, to papal commissions assigned to investigate monasteries in need of reform. He was also, apparently, quite ambitious, as his actions following the death of Bartholomaeus, Bishop of Paris, in 1227 demonstrate. Church law provided that the canons of Notre Dame were to elect a new bishop, subject to papal approval. If the canons were not essentially unanimous in their choice, the right of selection would revert to the Pope. On April 10, 1228, the canons elected a candidate, but only by a slim majority. William proclaimed that the election was invalid and threatened to appeal the decision to Rome. The other canons, not wishing to lose their autonomy in the matter, accordingly held another election, but William was still unsatisfied and complained to Pope Gregory. The result was that William himself was appointed to the position, in which he remained for the rest of his life.

Though he is remembered today as a philosopher, among his contemporaries William was known primarily for his activities as Bishop of Paris. In fact, he was largely unknown to all but a few of the great philosophers who followed him, and Thomas Aquinas, John Duns Scotus, and William of Ockham seem not to have been familiar with his writings. Only Roger Bacon briefly mentions William, and even Bacon's brief note of praise seems more connected with William the bishop than with William the philosopher.

During William's tenure as prelate, the University of Paris was gradually gaining its independence from the Church. Since it had evolved out of the cathedral school of Notre Dame, the university remained under the jurisdiction of the bishop of Paris. By the early thirteenth century, however, it had become a largely autonomous body, governed not by the laws of the city or the kingdom but by its own teachers (called "masters") and students. The immunity of the university from either royal or municipal control set a precedent for other universities and became the basis of the centuries-long conflicts between "town and gown" which can still occasionally be seen. The only check on the often highly disruptive behavior of students and teachers was the bishop, who was himself often a former student and master. Nevertheless, both faculty and scholars chafed under even this usually sympathetic form of control and worked to end it.

William's relations with the university got off to an inauspicious start, for a famous strike of masters and students occurred in the spring of 1229. In February, the students had begun a riot in the course of celebrating the annual Carnival, and, after complaints from many citizens, royal troops were sent in to quell the disturbance. The resulting bloodshed outraged both masters and students, who demanded that William obtain redress from the king for this violation of their immunity. When William either refused or was unable to do anything, the students and faculty suspended all classes and dispersed to other cities. In response, William brought in some Dominican friars as substitutes; the striking masters appealed to the Pope, who ordered William to reinstate the strikers. In addition, the Pope created a commission to investigate the matter, which was decided in favor of the university. Masters and students then returned to Paris in triumph.

From this point onward, William seems to have been much more cautious in dealing with the university, and he frequently convoked the masters to seek their advice on issues which, technically, he could have decided on his own authority. The masters remained unsatisfied, though, and they demanded that William relinquish to them the authority to grant teaching licenses. The dispute over this issue, which dragged on from 1238 to 1245, may have arisen as a response to William's action in 1229, or it may simply have been part of the more general demand of the university for complete autonomy. The problem was not finally resolved until an agreement was drawn up, under pressure from Pope Innocent IV, among the masters, the university chancellor, and William.

Attempting to restrain the excesses of the university was not William's only function as bishop. In the Middle Ages, the Church was deeply involved in secular politics, and aside from his many purely religious duties William was often called upon to play a role in affairs of state as the French representative of the Papacy. In 1231, for example, he acted in this capacity in peace negotiations between France and England, and, in 1229, he was even asked to provide Pope Gregory IX with troops in a war against the Holy Roman Emperor, Frederick II. William sent money instead.

William also typifies the anti-Semitism of the Middle Ages, for he was responsible for the public condemnation and burning of the Talmud in June, 1242. Some four years previously, a converted Jew named Nicholas had compiled a list of heretical and anti-Christian doctrines contained in the Talmud and sent them to the Pope. Gregory wrote to William for advice, and the bishop recommended that strong measures be taken to suppress the Jewish sacred books. A papal bull (proclamation) was thus issued in 1240 through William as the papal representative ordering civil and ecclesiastical authorities to enter all French synagogues and confiscate copies of the Talmud. When the Jews understandably complained, a joint investigation by the royal and episcopal authorities into the contents of the Talmud resulted in its public incineration.

Despite such a busy schedule, William found time to write more than twenty treatises of varying lengths, most of which were to form a monumental *Magisterium divinale sive sapientale* (loosely, "on divine or philosophical wisdom"), which was completed about 1240. William's objective was to cover the whole field of theology and metaphysics and to answer questions of physics, logic, morals, and law through the application of reason, as well as through the learning of the past. In the *Magisterium divinale sive sapientale*, as well as in his other works, William shows that his attitude toward the newly rediscovered ideas of Aristotle is respectful without being slavish. While on the one hand the Church authorities had only recently condemned these ideas, many of the students and masters of Paris had gone to the opposite extreme of accepting them almost as if they were revealed truth. William preferred to follow a middle course: Whenever Aristotle presented a philosophical doctrine that disagreed with Christian belief, William would declare it erroneous, but, rather than simply appeal to tradition or authority, he would then go on to attempt to show by argument why the doctrine was incorrect.

While William often disagreed with positions taken by Aristotle, he knew that Christians could not ignore them. To attempt to dismiss Aristotle or reject his ideas without analyzing them, said William, would be ridiculous. He went even further, offering the nearly revolutionary advice that, in matters of philosophy, only philosophers should be consulted. While this may appear to suggest that William had adopted the modern view that philosophy is quite distinct from religion, his purpose was in fact theological: The theologian could only overcome the arguments of pagan philosophy by himself becoming a philosopher. In this view, he foreshadows the reasoning of Saint Thomas Aquinas.

For example, Aristotle had argued that the world was eternal and therefore uncreated. This idea contradicts the Christian belief that God created the world. In his treatise *De Universo* (c. 1247; on the universe), William not only gives the reasons behind Aristotle's point of view but also improves upon Aristotle's arguments—after which he refutes them by using elaborate and systematic proofs. Thus despite his willingness to accept some of Aristotle's views and methods of argument, William remains in the tradition of Augustine, using philosophy as the handmaiden of faith.

William died on March 30, 1249, of unknown causes, and he was buried in the Abbey of St. Victor. Though his relationship with the university was bumpy, he was apparently loved as a witty and eloquent preacher, an outstanding master of theology, and a conscientious servant of the Church.

Summary

William of Auvergne stands, unfortunately, in the shadows of his great successors. Because he took on Aristotle piecemeal rather than developing a coherent system and because his writing is often obscure and extremely complex, he has been largely ignored except by a few specialists in the field of medieval philosophy. Yet among these authorities, his achievement is very much respected. He is seen as a transitional figure, perhaps even a pioneer whose acceptance of some Aristotelian ideas paved the way for Saint Albertus Magnus and Thomas Aquinas, on the one hand, but whose rejection of the Aristotelian system as a whole also led to the anti-Aristotelian viewpoint of Saint Bonaventure. As the first of the great thirteenth century philosophers, his views might be symbolized as the twelfth century meeting the thirteenth, sympathetically, but not uncritically.

Since William appears to have had little direct influence upon his successors, it is fair to ask how he can be considered historically important. Perhaps this question can be answered best if attention is turned more directly upon his career as a teacher and bishop of Paris. Influence need not always be a matter of showing a direct relationship between two events, people, or sets of ideas; it can also be indirect and subtle. As a teacher and philosopher, William undoubtedly had some kind of effect upon each of his students. His congenial reception of new ideas allowed those ideas to be discussed, debated, and further developed. He realized the importance, if not all the implications, of the rediscovery of Aristotle, and he knew that the Church could not and should not simply attempt to ignore the tools of logic and reason that Aristotle offered. William insisted, in fact, that they be used to strengthen Christian faith. In this way, he made a positive contribution, not only to medieval philosophy but also to the freedom of inquiry that was, and is, the essence of the university.

Bibliography

Bréhier, Émile. *The History of Philosophy: The Middle Ages and the Renaissance.* Translated by Wade Baskin. Chicago: University of Chicago Press, 1965. Bréhier's work is considered a classic summary of medieval and Renaissance philosophy. Includes a section on William which concentrates on his doctrine of Being, and the way in which it relates to Aristotle and the Arabic philosopher Avicenna. It may be somewhat difficult for the reader unfamiliar with the study of philosophy.

Copleston, Frederick Charles. *A History of Philosophy.* Vol. 2, *Medieval Philosophy.* Rev. ed. Garden City, N.Y.: Doubleday and Co., 1962. Part of an extremely well-written series by a prominent Jesuit philosopher, this work emphasizes the importance of William as a transitional figure and offers the view that William not only foreshadows Thomas Aquinas and Bonaventure but also Duns Scotus. A clear introduction, not only to William but to the entire field of medieval philosophy as well.

Gilson, Étienne. *History of Christian Philosophy in the Middle Ages.* New York: Random House, 1955. Gilson's study is considered the most authoritative and scholarly work in the field and is a standard reference. Though extremely well written, it treats subjects intensively with many references to original works; it may therefore be difficult for the general reader. Covers the entire period from the earliest Christian philosophers to the beginning of the fourteenth century.

Kretzmann, Norman, Anthony Kenny, and Jan Pinborg, eds. *The Cambridge History of Later Medieval Philosophy: From the Rediscovery of Aristotle to the Disintegration of Scholasticism, 1100-1600.* Cambridge: Cambridge University Press, 1982. An immense compilation by many scholars, this work is organized topically. Contains several brief comparative discussions of William but no separate section. The study has a pronounced emphasis on English philosophers and is primarily useful as a reference, particularly for its outstanding bibliography.

Leff, Gordon. *Medieval Thought: St. Augustine to Ockham.* Harmondsworth, England: Penguin Books, 1958. An excellent, brief introduction to medieval philosophy, Leff's work divides the era into three periods, each with an introduction that offers some very helpful general comments. Includes a concise section on William. Especially useful for those with no background in the study of philosophy.

McInerny, Ralph M. *A History of Western Philosophy.* Vol. 2, *Philosophy from St. Augustine to Ockham.* Notre Dame, Ind.: University of Notre Dame Press, 1970. A very good text for those unfamiliar with philosophy. Several chapters of background information on related topics help to provide a solid context. Includes a separate section on William with a very clear and simple analysis of his theory of Being.

Marrone, Steven P. *William of Auvergne and Robert Grosseteste: New Ideas of Truth in the Early Thirteenth Century.* Princeton, N.J.: Princeton University Press, 1983. This is the only full-length study of William's philosophy, which is discussed in great depth and detail. Extremely readable for a scholarly work. As might be expected from the author of a major study, Marrone considers William a philosopher of the first rank and of great historical importance. Analyzes all William's work from the standpoint of the method by which truth can be perceived. Not for the beginner.

Moody, Ernest A. "William of Auvergne and His Treatise *De Anima.*" In *Studies in Medieval Philosophy, Science, and Logic: Collected Papers, 1933-1969.* Berkeley: University of California Press, 1975. This is a memorial volume containing fourteen articles by a renowned historian of medieval philosophy. The article on William, the first and by far the longest, was written as Moody's master's thesis in 1933; it is the most complete source on William, and the only one in English with any significant amount of biographical information. Interestingly, Moody concentrates the substantive portion of his discussion on *De Anima*, which was not a part of William's *Magisterium divinale sive sapientale*.

Thomas C. Schunk

WILLIAM OF AUXERRE

Born: c. 1150; Auxerre, France
Died: November 3, 1231; Rome
Areas of Achievement: Theology and philosophy
Contribution: As one of the first European medieval scholars to use the methods of philosophy to answer theological questions, William ranks as a pioneer in the growth of Scholasticism and the centuries-long attempt to harmonize Aristotelian philosophy with the theology of Saint Augustine.

Early Life

As is true of most medieval intellectuals, virtually nothing is known of William of Auxerre's origins or early career. Since it was customary in the twelfth century for young men planning for an academic life to enter the university at age thirteen or fourteen, he had probably already begun his studies by that age. The University of Paris, where William was to spend nearly all of his life, was Europe's most renowned center of learning, especially in the areas of theology and philosophy. A new student typically spent six years studying the "seven liberal arts"—grammar, rhetoric, logic (the trivium); and arithmetic, geometry, astronomy, and music (the quadrivium)—which had been inherited from the ancient world. The arts as a whole were often referred to as "philosophy." Following this generalized preparation, the scholar could become a teacher of the arts himself or begin specialized studies in theology, law, or medicine.

The greatest minds of the time chose theology, which was by far the most rigorous and respected discipline. That was natural, since the university itself was an outgrowth of the cathedral school of Notre-Dame de Paris and was still under the jurisdiction of the Church. Though many were never ordained as priests, students of the university were regarded as "clerics" and were subject to the discipline of the chancellor, an official of the cathedral.

After six years of attending lectures on the Bible and selected works of theology, the student received the baccalaureate and was then himself required to lecture for two years on two books of the Bible. After several more years of study, the apprentice teacher engaged in several "disputations," theological debates judged by a member of the faculty. If he successfully completed these tasks, the student was awarded the doctorate and, at age thirty-four, was allowed to teach theology. It is known that William made it through this arduous course for by 1189 he was already famous as a "master" (professor) of theology.

Life's Work

The thirteenth century was an age of intellectual ferment, particularly at the University of Paris. The university itself owed its existence to the revival of learning that had begun after about the year 1000. The gradual rediscovery of the literature of the pre-Christian world had increasingly challenged the relatively simple and dogmatic faith of the earlier Middle Ages, and scholars had begun to use the tools of logic to justify and explain their Christian beliefs and doctrine. By the end of the twelfth century, a flood of translations of the works of the Greek philosopher Aristotle as well as commentaries on him by Islamic philosophers such as Avicenna had begun to arrive in Paris from Moorish Spain. Aristotle's wide-ranging intellect had applied itself to virtually every area of human knowledge, from the creation of the universe and the nature of the soul to the proper structure of a logical argument. It was obvious that Aristotle was a genius, yet, as a pagan, he had arrived at conclusions and insights that often conflicted with the accepted doctrine of the Church.

From throughout Europe, scholars came to Paris to study the "new" learning; thus the cathedral school had expanded to become practically a separate institution, the university. By the time of William, famous medieval scholars such as Peter Abelard and Peter the Lombard had been developing for more than a century the techniques of intellectual inquiry that would later be called Scholasticism. The Scholastic approach involved the solution of an intellectual problem by posing it as a question, such as "Is the universe eternal?" The medieval scholar would respond to the question by juxtaposing answers derived from the Bible, or works of the church fathers, those offered by philosophy or reason, often as supplied by Aristotle. By constructing such a back-and-forth argument, called the "dialectic," the scholar hoped to reconcile the two positions, thus allowing reason to support faith. While Scholasticism clearly fostered a considerable amount of intellectual ingenuity, it later got a bad reputation because its practitioners always deferred to established authority, whether that of the Church or of the philosophers, rather than venturing to observe the real world or setting up empirical experiments. The reasoning of the Scholastics became increasingly abstract, and they often dealt with issues that were fantastically irrelevant. (The most famous of these is the old question, "How many angels can dance on the head of a pin?")

While it may seem strange, in the twentieth century, that the great intellectuals of the Middle Ages spent so much time trying to "marry" what today are considered the distinctly separate fields of philosophy and theology, the attempt itself represented a tremendous advance over the thinking of the early Christian period and the early Middle Ages, when many church authorities had disparaged the use of reason, insisting that, should philosophy and faith disagree, philosophy must always give way. Many of the church fathers had actually regarded study of the ancient authors as pernicious and sinful—one of the reasons that Aristotle's works had largely disappeared until the period of the Crusades. The efforts of the Scholastics to make philosophy and theology work together demonstrated that the processes of reason and logic had once again become respectable.

By the time of William, those works of Aristotle which had become available had themselves already gained the status of authority and threatened to dethrone church doctrine, at least as far as many of the students at the university were concerned, as the basis of theology. In the eyes of the church authorities, this threat was so dangerous that, in 1215, when the basic statutes of the university were drawn up, the papal legate (representative) at Paris prohibited the teaching of those works of Aristotle that dealt with "natural philosophy," meaning science. This decree apparently had little effect, for in 1231 Pope Gregory IX felt compelled to create a commission of three scholars to study and "correct" the works of Aristotle, so that they could be used at the university without contradicting church doctrine.

The head of the commission was William, who had by this time become famous both as a theologian and as a churchman. During the reign of Pope Honorius III (1216-1227), William had become archdeacon of Beauvais, a powerful and influential office, as well as a proctor of the University of Paris. In the latter capacity, he presented the interests of the university to the papal court at Rome; he had been sent there by King Louis IX in the spring of 1230 to advise the new pope, Gregory IX, on how to resolve a strike of teachers and students which had begun the year before. The Bishop of Paris, William of Auvergne, had failed to end the strike and may even have exacerbated the situation by bringing in Dominican friars to replace the striking teachers.

The strike had arisen out of a student riot that had occurred during the Shrove Tuesday festivities of February, 1229. Townsmen had requested the intervention of royal troops to quell this drunken rampage, and several students were killed in the ensuing melee. When demands by both students and masters for compensation went unsatisfied, the scholars voted to strike and return to their homes. By the time William of Auxerre left for Rome, however, the original issue had been subsumed in more general conflicts which had been brewing between the Church and the university for several years. The arts faculty, in particular, resented church hostility toward their growing acceptance of Aristotle, and the university faculty as a whole had long been seeking policy-making autonomy from the Church.

The pope now believed that his personal intervention was necessary, but he was unsure of the best course of action. William of Auxerre, who seems to have been a peaceful individual of very even temperament, apparently helped to craft Gregory's conciliatory response, which not only ordered the university authorities to reinstate the strikers but also promised to set up a commission to investigate the issues involved, including the position of Aristotle in the curriculum of the university. While the ban of 1215 on Aristotle's works on natural philosophy was maintained, it was only provisional, to be held until the papal commission had an opportunity to investigate Aristotle's works. Nowhere was it suggested that the use of Aristotelian logic to examine and analyze philosophical or theological questions be discontinued. Faculty and students returned triumphantly to Paris, regarding the papal decree as an academic bill of rights.

Unfortunately, the commission never really started work, probably because William of Auxerre died on November 3, 1231, only seven months after he was appointed to it. Why the pope did not appoint a successor is unclear: Possibly the commission had already decided that the effort to expurgate such a large and popular body of work would be impossible. The ban was allowed to expire without having much effect, and the process of attempting to reconcile philosophy and theology continued, leading eventually to the brilliant synthesis of Saint Thomas Aquinas later in the thirteenth century.

William of Auxerre himself contributed to this process in a work which had a considerable amount of influence upon his contemporaries, *Summa super quattuor libros sententiarum*, usually known as *Summa aurea* (golden summation), written between 1215 and 1220. This was a commentary on the compilation of Christian teachings created by Peter the Lombard in a series of four books used as basic texts in the fifth and sixth years of theological training at the university. Lombard had used the dialectic to address many questions of theology, but a host of new issues had been occasioned by the influx of translations of Aristotle and the Arabian philosophers. It was common practice among Scholastics of the twelfth and thirteenth centuries to write commentaries on earlier works regarded as authoritative and to bring them up to date, but *Summa aurea* is outstanding in that it not only looks back toward the pre-Aristotelian framework of theology but also comes to grips with some of the new questions addressed by Aristotle.

While the core of William's view of the relationship between reason and faith is derived from Saint Augustine and is therefore completely traditional, William also shows how some of the philosophy of Aristotle can be put to the service of Christian theology. Pre-Aristotelian Scholastics, for example, had discussed the nature of God and the Trinity at great length without ever seeing the need to prove God's existence. That, they believed, was self-evident, a matter of faith not to be questioned. Yet Aristotle, in *Metaphysica* (fourth century B.C.; *Metaphysics*) and other works, had attempted to understand the natural world around him by making direct observations and reasoning about them. Since God was not directly perceivable with the senses, Aristotle maintained that the answer to the question of his existence was unknowable. *Summa aurea* marks a break with the past because William addresses such questions and seeks to answer them with philosophical reasoning: He proves the existence of God, for example, by using the philosopher Avicenna's argument for the necessity of what was called a "prime cause," meaning an agency of creation from which everything else must ultimately originate.

In similar fashion, *Summa aurea* deals with problems such as natural law, free will, the nature of the soul, and the definition of virtue—issues seen by William's predecessors only in theological terms. William, however, often uses the tools of Aristotelian logic to substantiate the traditional answers of faith. Thus he asks, as Aristotle had, if the universe is eternal, but he disagrees with Aristotle's affirmative answer; since the universe was created by God, William reasons that it cannot have always existed. His general approach is thus to ask some of the questions which Aristotle's works necessitate but to use both reason and faith to prove the truth of the beliefs of the past. At the same time, though, William is inconsistent; he is often satisfied simply to repeat the doctrines of his predecessors, and he creates no new comprehensive system or approach to theological thinking. *Summa aurea* is, therefore, a work of transition, one which points the way to the future but is firmly rooted in the past.

Summary

William of Auxerre was the first medieval theologian to acknowledge explicitly the arguments of the philosophers, but he mixed them indiscriminately with those of earlier theologians. Yet even his reliance upon the past seemed to foreshadow the views of his better-known successors, for he insisted that theology is an "art" or "science"—rather than a simple matter of blind faith—because it argues from principles, even if these principles are themselves articles of faith. Further, he insisted that philosophy can be useful to theologians because they can use it to prove the articles of faith.

Such an argument, if offered today, might seem hopelessly backward, for science (philosophy) and religion (theology) have become completely separate; the idea of using logic to prove what faith believes appears to be a paradox. William of Auxerre's viewpoint may be viewed more sympathetically, however, if the context is considered. He was arguing for the validity and existence of philosophy against many who believed that all such approaches to knowledge should be suppressed. The university was a religious establishment; as an important member of the theological faculty, he could not, unlike some of the faculty in the arts, hope to escape intellectually the consequences of his position. In encouraging the integration of Aristotle into the teaching of theology, he demonstrated a courage and an open-mindedness, as well as an intellectual originality, that helped to make the University of Paris a bastion of academic freedom and intellectual growth. Until recently, the originality of William and his contemporaries and immediate successors, such as Philip the Chancellor and William of Auvergne, was largely ignored because these pioneers in religious philosophy did not attempt to create an entirely new system of thought. It is only now being realized by historians of medieval philosophy that the achievements of the great Scholastics who followed later, such as Thomas Aquinas and William of Ockham, were only possible because William of Auxerre was instrumental in clearing the path.

Bibliography

Copleston, Frederick Charles. *A History of Philosophy*. Vol. 2, *Medieval Philosophy*. New York: Image Books, 1962. Part of an extremely well-written series by a prominent Jesuit philosopher, this is an extremely informative discussion of the development of the University of Paris in its early years, as well as its curriculum, teaching methods, and student life during this period. Contains a short discussion of William and *Summa aurea*.

De Wulf, Maurice. *History of Medieval Philosophy*. 2 vols. New York: Longmans, Green and Co., 1926. One of the classic works of the history of philosophy. Extremely broad coverage, but somewhat difficult for the average reader today because it assumes a familiarity with Christian theology that is no longer common. Volume 1 contains a brief section on William, concentrating on his role as a master of theology at the University of Paris.

Gilson, Étienne. *History of Christian Philosophy in the Middle Ages*. New York: Random House, 1955. Considered the most authoritative and scholarly work in the field and a standard reference, this work includes a very thorough set of notes on nearly every philosopher of the period, including William, and works by or related to each. Though extremely well-written, it treats subjects intensively, with many references to original works; it may therefore be difficult for the general reader. Covers the entire period from the earliest Christian philosophers to the beginning of the fourteenth century.

Haren, Michael. *Medieval Thought: The Western Intellectual Tradition from Antiquity to the Thirteenth Century*. New York: St. Martin's Press, 1985. An excellent, brief summary which assumes a good deal of background on the reader's part, it contains one of the few discussions of any length on the views of William expressed in *Summa aurea* on specific questions.

Kretzmann, Norman, Anthony Kenny, and Jan Pinborg, eds. *The Cambridge History of Later Medieval Philosophy: From the Rediscovery of Aristotle to the Disintegration of Scholasticism, 1100-1600*. Cambridge: Cambridge University Press, 1982. An immense compilation by many scholars, organized topically, this study contains several brief comparative discussions of William but no separate section. Has a pronounced emphasis on English philosophers. Primarily useful as a reference, particularly for its outstanding bibliography.

Leff, Gordon. *Medieval Thought: St. Augustine to Ockham*. Harmondsworth, England: Penguin Books, 1958. An excellent, brief introduction to medieval philosophy. Divides the era into three periods, each with an introduction that offers some very helpful general comments. Notes the transitional role of William and the place of *Summa aurea* in the development of Scholasticism. Especially useful for those with no background in the study of philosophy.

McInerny, Ralph M. *A History of Western Philosophy*. Vol. 2, *Philosophy from St. Augustine to Ockham*. Notre Dame, Ind.: University of Notre Dame Press, 1970. A very good text for those unfamiliar with philosophy. Well organized by prominent scholars. Several chapters of background information on related topics help to provide a solid context.

Principe, Walter H. *William of Auxerre's Theology of the Hypostatic Union*. Rome: Pontifical Institute of Medieval Studies, 1963. This is the only book-length study of William of Auxerre and the only separate study of him in English. A useful introduction includes biographical information found nowhere else. An extremely difficult work by a specialist; very rare and difficult to obtain.

Thomas C. Schunk

WILLIAM OF MOERBEKE

Born: c. 1215; Moerbeke, near Gent, Flanders
Died: c. 1286; Corinth, Greece
Area of Achievement: Scholarship
Contribution: Along with many translations of classical works by other authors, William provided Europe with its first Latin translations from the Greek of Aristotle's major works.

Early Life

The enthusiasm of the Europeans for classical Greek works, particularly Aristotle, during the thirteenth century was overwhelming. The establishment of the Latin Empire in Constantinople in 1205 drove this enthusiasm because of the easy access to Greek manuscripts which it provided. Pope Innocent III encouraged the translation of these works into Latin. King Philip II of France founded a school in Paris for the purpose of teaching Latin to Byzantines residing in his country. Roger Bacon, the great medieval scientist, wrote a Greek grammar. The revival of Aristotle, in particular, led to renewed interest in science and a more accurate perspective on classical philosophy.

No one did more to reinforce this interest in the classics than Robert Grosseteste and William of Moerbeke, the two who did most of the translations from Greek into Latin. The effect of the translations was revolutionary, and Moerbeke was the hero of this effort. Only Gerard of Cremona, a great Arab-Latin translator of the twelfth century, matched William's productivity and range of material translated.

William was Flemish, born near Gent, then in the duchy of Brabant, in about 1215. Innocent III had just recognized the Dominican Order at the Fourth Lateran Council. William entered the Dominican priory in Gent, where his education began. Later, he studied in Paris and Cologne, where he probably knew Albertus Magnus, one of the great teachers of the century. The fact that William was a Neoplatonist reflected the dominant intellectual climate of both Paris and Germany; Albertus Magnus and his students, such as Ulrich of Strasbourg and the greatest of the medieval mystics, Meister Eckehart, were also Neoplatonists. Significantly, William contributed to this spirit of mysticism with his translation of Proclus, finished in 1268, which became the basis of Christian humanism. William joined the papal court of Urban IV, who patronized William and encouraged his translations. This support, which came at the beginning of the 1260's, marked the beginning of William's astoundingly productive career as a Greek translator.

Life's Work

At the same time, also at the papal court, William met Thomas Aquinas, who became his lifelong friend and who urged him to revise the existing

Arab-to-Latin Aristotelian texts and to translate previously unknown ones coming into Europe from Byzantium. Thomas believed that the direct translations would give European scholars, such as himself, a clearer understanding of Aristotle's philosophical intentions. The pope also wished to use the direct translations to curb Averroism, which conveyed Aristotle with Neoplatonic and Islamic overtones and was unacceptable—in part because of the strong undercurrent of superstition that ran through the Arabic texts.

Between 1260 and 1278, William revised and translated all Aristotle's major works, which were written from 335 to 323 B.C.: the *Politica* (*Politics*)—unknown even to the Arabs—*Metaphysica* (*Metaphysics*), *Physica* (*Physics*), and a number of his lesser works. He translated some of Plato's dialogues as well as works by Galen, Hippocrates, Archimedes, Hero of Alexandria, Simplicius, and Alexander of Aphrodisias. The *Politics* was picked up quickly by both church and state as a system of governance and a justification for the authority that each wished to exercise over the other.

In 1260, the pope sent William to Dominican priories, first in Thebes and then in Nicaea. As a result, William traveled widely throughout the Greek world, becoming even more proficient in Greek. In 1265, Pope Clement IV called William back to the papal court to serve as his confessor and chaplain. He held this position through the reigns of five additional popes. Papal confidence in William is further exemplified by the fact that he represented Pope Gregory X at the 1274 Council of Lyons called to reform the Church and to promote the reunion of the Eastern and Western halves of Christendom, for an optimistic attitude had been encouraged by the political existence of the Latin Empire. Having spent time in the East, William understood the Greek church better than many and was deeply committed to that reunion—a hope that was to remain unfulfilled.

Pope Nicholas III appointed him Archbishop of Corinth on April 9, 1278. That same year, William finished his translation of Aristotle's *Poetics*. The last eight years of William's life were spent in Corinth, where he continued to translate until his death around 1286.

Summary

Most of William of Moerbeke's translations made their way into European libraries through their use by the Dominicans, especially Thomas Aquinas, who used William's translations of Aristotle to construct his *Summa theologiae* (c. 1265-1273; *Summa Theologica*, 1911-1921), the epitome of the medieval synthesis of reason and faith. In addition, and as important, William's translations of other Greek authors opened the door to classical learning, especially in the sciences, that had been unknown or unavailable to Western scholars for centuries. The undeniable force of Aristotle's influence on the thirteenth century mind owed much of its vitality to the translations completed by William. The interest stimulated by these works intensified the impact of Aristotelian philosophy on medieval society and, by extension, on the whole intellectual tradition of Western civilization. William of Moerbeke stands as an indispensable component in the development of that tradition.

Bibliography
Crombie, A. C. *Medieval and Early Modern Science*. Vol. 1. Garden City, N.Y.: Doubleday and Co., 1959. Details the translation contributions made by William. It is also an excellent introduction to the history of science. The book is highly readable and contains an excellent bibliography.
Durant, Will. *The Story of Civilization*. Vol. 4, *The Age of Faith*. New York: Simon and Schuster, 1950. While sometimes considered a pedestrian popularization, it is good reading and an excellent source for little-known facts about William's life. This long work contains an extensive index, a standard bibliography, and a detailed table of contents.
Heer, Friedrich. *The Intellectual History of Europe*. Vol. 1. Garden City, N.Y.: Doubleday and Co., 1968. An excellent analysis of the development of Western thought. William is described as a crucial figure in the shaping of the medieval mind. This is a long, detailed study, and the sources must be culled from copious notes.
_____. *The Medieval World*. New York: Mentor Books, 1961. While this book does not discuss the work of William specifically, it is one of the best available historical surveys of the High Middle Ages. It is interpretive and provocative in tone and topical in arrangement, and it covers the standard medieval subjects. It includes chapters on intellectualism in the universities and the intellectual warfare in Paris, much of which centered on the works of Aristotle. The bibliography contains standard works in English, but most sources are in Latin.
Knowles, David. *The Evolution of Medieval Thought*. New York: Vintage Books, 1962. Knowles gives an excellent presentation of the philosophical and theological development of the Middle Ages, including the significance of William's translations in this development. A synthetic work of notable merit. The bibliographic essay, though brief, calls attention to standard, readily available works on medieval thought.
Leff, Gordon. *Medieval Thought: St. Augustine to Ockham*. Baltimore: Penguin Books, 1958. Like Knowles, Leff gives the reader an easily understood description of the development of medieval thought. He stresses the influence of William's translations upon the medieval mind. The bibliography is limited.
Marias, Julian. *History of Philosophy*. Mineola, N.Y.: Dover Publications, 1967. A detailed survey which includes some information about William but is more important for giving the reader an understanding of the major philosophical problems of the age.

Shirley F. Fredricks

WILLIAM OF RUBROUCK

Born: c. 1215; Rubrouck, French Flanders
Died: c. 1295; place unknown
Area of Achievement: Exploration
Contribution: William provided the first accurate account of the geography of Central Asia and of its people, the Mongols. He thus helped to fill in a blank space on the map and opened up a new era of exploration.

Early Life

The life of William of Rubrouck (Willem van Ruysbroeck) remains shrouded in mystery despite scholarly efforts to shed light on it. He appears on the stage of history between May, 1253, and August, 1255, the period during which he undertook a journey to the court of the Great Khan in Mongolia. Except for a brief stay in Paris during the late 1250's or early 1260's, nothing is known about his life before or after his historic journey.

Scholars assume that William was from the village of Rubrouck in Flanders, the northeasternmost corner of modern France. The date of his birth is unknown, though some historians place it as early as 1215. Similarly, the year of his death is unknown, though it is assumed that he was still alive when Marco Polo returned from his journey to China in 1295.

Nothing is known of William's educational background. When Louis IX commissioned him to go to Mongolia, William was a Franciscan friar serving at the king's court. The saintly Louis IX was fond of the mendicant (begging) orders of monks and so surrounded himself with friars. William's own narrative of his journey provides the only insight into his learning and character. Though the work is not written in the best Ciceronian Latin, the author reveals himself as a keen observer, one who was able to sift the relevant from the irrelevant and thus provide Europe with its first truly reliable information about the geography and peoples of inner Asia.

William reveals himself as a bold, even daring adventurer. The brazenness with which he preached the Christian faith shocked his Mongolian hosts, whose religious tolerance no doubt puzzled and angered William. He records in his narrative that several times the Great Khan urged him to be more diplomatic in his debates with Muslims, Buddhists, shamanists, and Nestorians. Fear that William was disrupting the religious peace may have been one reason that the Great Khan ordered him to return to his home.

Life's Work

It was only his journey to Mongolia that lifted William of Rubrouck from obscurity onto the pages of history. Hence, a discussion of his life's work must focus upon a period of roughly twenty-eight months. Beyond that, he is all but unknown.

William and Louis IX had similar yet different motives for a mission to Mongolia (Tartary). William's motives were primarily religious; Louis' motives were a mixture of religious and political. William was apparently deeply moved by reports of the plight of German slaves of the khan of the Golden Horde (Russia and Kazakhstan). The Germans were Catholics, and William felt burdened to go and minister the sacraments to them. He was encouraged by rumors that some of the Mongol rulers had already accepted, or were on the verge of accepting, Christianity.

Louis IX, noted for his piety, was similarly influenced by the rumors that certain of the khans were Christians. He was also encouraged, however, by the prospects of an alliance with the Mongols against the Muslims in the Middle East. Louis hoped to learn something about the intentions of the Mongol armies in Syria. Thus, he was persuaded to overcome his reluctance to send William. William was not to travel as an accredited envoy of the French king, however, but as a Christian missionary seeking permission to settle, found a mission, and preach the Gospel among the Mongols. Louis gave William a letter addressed to Prince Sartach, an alleged Christian and eldest son of Batu Khan, ruler of the Golden Horde, requesting that William be given safe conduct and permission to preach.

William was commissioned by Louis IX in the spring of 1252, while Louis was resident in Acre, Palestine, following a disastrous crusade in Egypt. From Acre, William journeyed to Constantinople, where he preached in the church of Hagia Sophia on Palm Sunday, 1253. On May 7, 1253, he departed from Constantinople on the first leg of his historic journey.

William's party consisted of four individuals. In addition to himself, there was a fellow Franciscan, Bartholomew of Cremona. Bartholomew was later to remain at the court of the Great Khan and become the first Catholic missionary to die in the East. There was also a clerk to look after the gifts Louis was sending and an interpreter, who proved unreliable.

William and his party reached Sartach's camp at Sarai, where the Volga River empties into the Caspian Sea, on July 31. During the three days he remained with Sartach, William learned that the Mongol prince was neither a Christian nor really interested in religious matters. Sartach ordered William to proceed to the court of his father, Batu Khan. Batu was encamped near Saratov, on the upper reaches of the Volga River, in modern eastern Russia.

Batu in turn sent William on to Mangu, the Great Khan himself, and provided two Nestorian Christian guides for the journey. They reached Mangu's encampment on the northeastern slopes of the Altai Mountains on December 27, 1253. They were treated courteously by Mangu, though he remained suspicious of William's true motives.

In the spring of 1254, Mangu returned to his capital at Karakorum, capital of the vast Mongol Empire. William and his party went with him and remained at Karakorum until July, when Mangu ordered him to return home. William was regularly questioned by Mangu's ministers, who apparently were never fully convinced that he was not an ambassador. Since he insisted that he was only a Christian missionary, he did not have the right to request an audience with the Great Khan; William had to wait for Mangu to summon him.

During his stay at Karakorum, William was housed with Nestorian monks. From time to time, Mangu himself arranged for disputations between William and representatives of the various religions of his subjects. Mangu was obviously very proud of the Mongols' tradition of religious toleration. William noted that the khan was careful not to show any preference for any one religion; he diplomatically spread his patronage equally among Buddhists, Taoists, shamanists, Muslims, and various Christian sects and attended all of their important ceremonies. William's dogmatic advocacy of his own Christian faith offended Mangu, apparently leading to Mangu's decision to send William back to Europe.

William departed Karakorum in July, 1254. He carried with him a letter from Mangu to Louis IX, calling upon the great lords and priests of Europe to go to Karakorum and do homage to the Great Khan. On June 16, 1255, he arrived in Cyprus, where he was disappointed to find that Louis IX had returned to France. Though he desired to go to Paris and report personally to Louis IX, he was ordered by his provincial vicar to return to Acre, where he became a lecturer in theology. This turn of events was fortuitous, for it forced William to write a narrative of his journey. All in all, William had traveled some ten thousand miles, much of it on horseback over harsh terrain.

Summary

William of Rubrouck's narrative of his journey provided a wealth of information for Europeans. His geographical revelations restored knowledge that had been lost to Western Europeans since the fall of the Roman Empire in the West (A.D. 476). He confirmed that the Caspian Sea was in fact an inland sea. He was the first European to recognize that Cathay was "Seres," the mythical city where ancient and medieval Westerners believed silk originated.

William was also the first European to describe an Asian city. Though he found Karakorum less impressive than Paris, what he described was a metropolitan capital of a vast, pluralistic empire. Not only did he note the existence in Karakorum of twelve Buddhist, Taoist, and shamanist temples, two Muslim mosques, and one Nestorian church, but he also provided the first descriptions of the religious rites and practices of those religions.

Karakorum was a meeting place of the various Asiatic peoples ruled over by the Mongols. William observed and recorded their life-styles, folklore, and customs. He was the first person to make Chinese writing known to Europeans. By his description of Karakorum and its varied residents, William dispelled the traditional belief that Asian cities contained palaces made of gold and precious gems. In the same way, his observations of Central Asia laid to rest the popular belief that the area was inhabited by mythical monsters.

After his return, William served as lecturer in theology at Acre. Perhaps as a result of the intervention of Louis IX, William was given permission by his vicar to return to Paris in the late 1250's or early 1260's. There he met the English scientist and philosopher Roger Bacon, a fellow Franciscan. Much of William's narrative was incorporated by Bacon in his *Opus majus* (1267; English translation, 1897-1900), which he acknowledges was written with William's help.

In a subsequent study, published in the mid-1260's, Bacon recorded the formula for gunpowder. Modern scholars believe that Bacon had obtained the formula from William, who in turn had learned of it while in Karakorum. Thus, William of Rubrouck's legacy was a mixed one. On the one hand, he opened up to Europeans a whole new world. On the other hand, he may well have given Europe gunpowder, thus helping usher in the era of modern warfare.

Bibliography
Chambers, James. *The Devil's Horsemen: The Mongol Invasion of Europe.* New York: Atheneum Publishers, 1979. Chambers provides a highly readable survey of the Mongolian invasion of Europe. Several clear maps help the reader locate geographical and battle sites mentioned in the text. Chapter 10 includes a summary of William of Rubrouck's journey, putting it in its historical context.
Dawson, Christopher, ed. *The Mongol Mission: Narratives and Letters of the Franciscan Missionaries in Mongolia and China in the Thirteenth and Fourteenth Centuries.* New York: Sheed and Ward, 1955. Part of the Makers of Christendom series. In addition to providing the text of William of Rubrouck's narrative in a very readable translation, Dawson's lengthy introduction includes all that is known about William and his mission. William's journey is placed in historical context with the other thirteenth century journeys of exploration to Mongolia.
Olschki, Leonardo. *Marco Polo's Asia: An Introduction to His "Description of the World" Called "Il Milione."* Translated by John A. Scott. Berkeley: University of California Press, 1960. Though this study focuses on Marco Polo, Olschki also deals with Polo's predecessors, including William of Rubrouck. It is a scholarly but readable discussion of the European discovery of Asia.
Prawdin, Michael. *The Mongol Empire: Its Rise and Legacy.* Translated by

Eden Paul and Cedar Paul. London: Allen and Unwin, 1961. Chapter 18 is especially helpful for its discussion of the Great Khan's religious tolerance.

Rockhill, William Woodville, ed. and trans. *The Journey of William of Rubruck to the Eastern Parts of the World, 1253-55, with Two Accounts of the Earlier Journey of John of Pian de Carpine.* London: Hakluyt Society, 1900. Reprint. Nedeln, Liechtenstein: Kraus Reprint Limited, 1967. This is the most authoritative English translation of William's narrative. The text is accompanied by rich explanatory footnotes, maps, and an itinerary of William's journey. A thirty-two-page introduction provides an excellent summary of Europe's relations with the Mongols in the thirteenth century, as well as the background to William's journey.

Paul R. Waibel

WILLIAM OF SAINT-AMOUR

Born: c. 1200; Saint-Amour, Jura, France
Died: September 13, 1272; Saint-Amour, Jura, France
Area of Achievement: Religion
Contribution: By opposing the papal and royal support of the newly created Franciscan and Dominican orders, William laid the foundations of later Gallican—and even Protestant—opposition to the Papacy.

Early Life

At the beginning of the thirteenth century, there were two clergies, seculars and regulars. The seculars served in the world (hence their name) as bishops and parish pastors; the regulars, on the other hand, submitted themselves to a regimen (from the Latin word *regula*) and lived as monks in a monastery or as members of a cathedral chapter. Many of the regulars were ordained and able to serve the sacraments, but ideally they restricted their use of these powers to their fellow regulars. William of Saint-Amour accepted this bipartite arrangement from his earliest school days and chose for himself the way of the seculars.

Probably given his basic education in the arts at Saint-Amour and Mâcon, William attended the University of Paris as a secular cleric, a subdeacon. He received in the course of his career the incomes of several ecclesiastical positions: By 1228 he was canon of Beauvais and rector of the church of Guerville, and in 1247 he was given the pastorate (though William was not an ordained priest) of the parish of Granville in the diocese of Coutances. These earnings supported William in his career as a master (teacher) at Paris. William distinguished himself by becoming one of the few persons of his age to take three advanced degrees, in liberal arts (1228), in canon law (1238), and in theology (c. 1250).

No doubt William was established as a young student-teacher when his university welcomed the Franciscans (in 1228) and the Dominicans (in 1231) into the Paris academic community. At first, William may have shared the popular estimate of these friars (from the Latin *fratres*, "brothers"), who exhibited admirable evangelical zeal. Officially recognized by the Papacy only a generation earlier, the friars were the most conspicuous ecclesiastical innovation of the thirteenth century. They operated outside the ordinary ecclesiastical hierarchy, preaching, serving sacraments, and performing various other services directly under the auspices of the pope. At Paris, as well as at other universities, both orders set up independent houses of study and recruited their students from their own outlying provincial schools. In time, however, the zeal of these newcomers attracted converts from the secular staff and student body of the university. Moreover, other orders imitated the friar convents. Consequently, by 1254, only three of the fifteen chairs of theology at the University of Paris were still occupied by seculars, and there was considerable sentiment among the remaining seculars in favor of halting further encroachment by the friars. Also, out in the parishes of France, secular priests and bishops had begun to resent the intrusion of the friars into their traditional spheres of ministry. Accordingly, one of the three remaining secular theologians emerged to provide brief but powerful leadership to the campaign against the friars—a campaign that brought upon him the condemnation of both Louis IX, known as Saint Louis, the King of France, and Pope Alexander IV. This man was William of Saint-Amour.

Life's Work

William argued that there was no biblical support for the mendicant orders. The bishops properly base their existence on the Apostles, and priests rightly trace their authority back to the seventy-two disciples commissioned by Christ. Similarly, deacons (such as William himself), and those in other minor orders, find biblical precedent for their ministry in the "helpers" who assisted the Apostles. Monks present no problem, because they simply reside in monasteries and seek after perfection, as Jesus directed those who "would be perfect." Yet where is the scriptural foundation for friars? William found none. The friars, in his view, were neither fish nor fowl. They could not be regarded as true seculars or as true regulars.

Further, William even claimed to have discovered biblical warnings to beware of the friars and to repulse them as heretics. Saint Paul prophesied that in the "last days" there would be corrupt men, proud and treacherous, who would "make their way into households and capture weak women, burdened with sins." Such are the friars, according to William. They steal their way into the consciences of laymen, hear their confessions, and absolve them without episcopal authority. They abduct the faithful parishioners away from the sheepfold. They build on other men's foundations, contrary to the precepts of Paul. They beg for their living, even though the Apostle commands manual labor. They are like the abominable Egyptian magicians Jannes and Jambres, who, according to medieval legend, were brothers (*fratres*). In short, friars lead students and faithful laity away from their proper bishops and teachers and therefore away from Christ.

By such arguments, William launched against the friars a polemic that went beyond simple criticism of friarly misbehavior. He called for the virtual suppression of both orders. At first glance, this argument appears motivated wholly by self-interested defense of traditional privileges. On close examination, however, it is clear that William was echoing the antipapal sentiments of the entire secular ecclesiastical hierarchy, which believed itself subverted from above. Could the pope justly send legions of friars, loyal only to himself, across diocesan boundaries, alongside long-established parish churches, and into the universities, to compete with the duly ordained and installed resident clerics? This century saw papal power greatly extended (for example, in taxation and legal review). This period was the age of "papal monarchy," when even kings were sometimes punished by excommunication and their lands subjected to the interdict. Thus William and his secular allies, in their attack on the friars, were protesting the papal assertion of *plenitudo potestatis* (fullness of power), first articulated by Pope Innocent III in 1198 and augmented throughout the 1200's.

The pope, the king, and the friars took offense at such criticism. In their view, Christendom was in need of renewal and reform, and the best corrective measure consisted in an evangelical "end run" around the vested interests of the complicated and complacent secular hierarchy. The friar movement, as they saw it, met the spiritual needs of parishioners long starved by poorly educated priests and absentee bishops. In the parishes, the Franciscans and Dominicans were usually the best preachers; in the universities, they were often the best teachers. At Paris, for example, Thomas Aquinas (a Dominican) and Bonaventure (a Franciscan) countered William's views. If William was distinguished for nothing else, he may be remembered as the man who was opposed by these scholars, both later canonized as saints and certainly the greatest theologians of the century.

This controversy between William's party and the friars lasted from 1250 to 1257. It passed through two phases. First, from 1250 to 1254, there were some encouraging developments for the seculars, and consequently they had some confidence that their side would prevail. Then, from 1255 to 1257, the contest turned in favor of the friars. The death of Pope Innocent IV in 1254 and his replacement by Alexander IV was the principal factor in this shift.

Innocent was originally disposed to favor the friars and had in fact ordered the secular masters to readmit the friar-masters as full members of the Paris theological faculty (in 1253 the seculars had ordered the friar-masters to confine their teaching to their own convents and friar-students). Innocent was alarmed, however, by the publication of a sensationalist Franciscan book, *Introductorius in evangelium aeternum* (1254; introduction to the everlasting Gospel), that made extravagant predictions of a coming Age of the Spirit in which the traditional structure of the Church would be dismantled. This writing did not reflect the sober judgment of the majority of the friars, but it was an effective pretext for William to secure papal support for the seculars. Thus, on November 21, 1254, the pope placed extensive restrictions on the ministries of the friars. This victory was to be short-lived, however, as Innocent died a few weeks later. Seculars at Paris lamented his passing and mockingly attributed his death to the influence of Dominican intercessions. Thus the seculars sang in the streets, "From the prayers of the Dominicans, good Lord deliver us." On December 22, 1254, Alexander annulled the decree of his predecessor and restored the privileges of the friars. Alexander, because he had been the cardinal-protector of the Franciscans before his elevation, could be relied on to support his own friar-dependents unreservedly.

William's party, undaunted, continued to disallow the readmittance of the friar-masters into the Paris faculty of theology. Thomas Aquinas, as a consequence, was forced to await his licensure to teach. (When Thomas eventually gave his inaugural lecture, in 1256, he and his audience had to be protected by soldiers of Louis IX.) The bishops of Orléans and Auxerre, under directives from the papacy, began proceedings in 1255 to bar William and his followers from the consolation of the Sacraments. Yet in the summer of that year, William successfully defended himself in the episcopal courts of Mâcon and Paris, and at Paris, he was supported by a sympathetic audience of four thousand clerics. Moreover, in October, the secular masters sought to annul the pope's directives, and thereby cancel their status of excommunication, by dissolving the university—and they threatened to leave the university altogether. Alexander obdurately insisted that they submit to him. In December, he instructed the chancellor of the university to license only those faculty who observed his pronouncement and demanded that William and his partisans be deprived of their teaching positions.

Throughout 1256, the dispute increasingly came to center on William himself. In the spring and early summer of that year, William composed in rapid succession three drafts of his best-known work, *De periculis novissimorum temporum* (1256; on the dangers of the last times), the third of which passed into the hands of king and pope.

In August, Alexander ordered the examination of *De periculis novissimorum temporum* by a commission that was dominated by the great Dominican biblical scholar, and William's rival at Paris, Hugh of Saint-Cher. The university, for William's defense, sent three theologians, the university rector, and a master of arts. Before this delegation arrived, however, the commission found the treatise to be scandalous and pernicious. Thus, by the time the seculars entered Rome, Alexander had condemned the treatise, and William and his supporters argued his case in vain. All other seculars at length submitted to the pope, but William stood alone and recalcitrant. In the winter of 1257, in ill health, William went into exile (by order of the king), where he remained despite numerous attempts by his colleagues at Paris to have his sentence overturned. He was later allowed to return to his native Saint-Amour, where he remained until his death in 1272. While in forced retirement, he composed his *Collectiones catholicae et canonicae scripturae* (1266; collections of Catholic and canonical writings), an extensive final warning to the Church to beware of the mounting dangers introduced by the friars.

Summary

Some scholars have dismissed William as an ultraconservative, a mere crank, who stood against the most progressive developments of the thirteenth century. Others have seriously suggested that William's biblical interpretation—that the "last days" were at hand—was actually a sophisticated farce designed to mock similar biblical exegeses by the more radical friars. Both views, however, are inaccurate. William is better understood as an early representative of the antipapal cause that reached its height in later centuries. Most striking is William's biblical interpretation of church ministry, exegesis which he certainly intended to be taken seriously, in which the thirteenth century clerical hierarchy is judged in the light of its apostolic first century antecedents. One can see here a precedent for the scriptural exegeses of John Wyclif (in the fourteenth century) and Martin Luther (in the sixteenth century). Indeed, Wyclif acknowledged his debt to William.

It is a matter of historical record that William's caricatures of the friars proved immensely popular. William was warmly remembered by many of his students and fellow clergy, and his rhetoric made its way into later literature. The poet Rutebeuf (fl. 1245-1285), vigorously defended William against both pope and king, whom he disparaged as Judases. Jean de Meung, author of the last part of *Le Roman de la rose* (thirteenth century; *The Romance of the Rose*, 1914-1924), devoted some thousand verses to praise of William and his ideas and depicted the friars by the type "False Semblance." William Langland, in the fourteenth century, portrayed the friars as "Doctor Friar Flatter," alias "Father Creep-into-Houses." Sixteenth century Protestants blessed William's memory and printed (in 1530) his *De periculis novissimorum temporum*. Perhaps there was even a dim echo as late as the eighteenth century, when Edmund Burke satirized the French radicals as "praters [who] effect to carry back the clergy to that primitive evangelical poverty. . . ."

Bibliography
Dawson, James D. "William of Saint-Amour and the Apostolic Tradition." *Mediaeval Studies* 40 (1978): 223-238. Dawson argues that William gave new meaning to the ancient ideal of apostolic tradition and therefore was one of the inventors of the primitive first century ideal that later would be used as a weapon against church institutions.
Douie, D. L. *The Conflict Between the Seculars and the Mendicants at the University of Paris in the Thirteenth Century*. London: Blackfriars, 1954. A brief survey, but the most complete in English, of the controversy between the seculars and the friars. Essential facts and names are provided, but there is little here in the way of interpretation.
——————. "St. Bonaventura's Part in the Conflict Between Seculars and Mendicants at Paris." In *S. Bonaventura, 1274-1974*, edited by J. G. Bougerol, vol. 2. Rome: Collegio S. Bonaventura Grottaferrata, n.d. Douie examines the controversy from 1252 to 1270 with special regard to the role of the Franciscan friar Saint Bonaventure. William figures prominently in this essay, which ends with observations regarding the implications of the controversy for the development of the medieval Papacy.

Lambert, Malcolm D. *Franciscan Poverty: The Doctrine of the Absolute Poverty of Christ and the Apostles in the Franciscan Order, 1210-1323*. London: Society for Promoting Christian Knowledge, 1961. An extensive study of the idea of poverty as conceived by Saint Francis of Assisi and developed by his order until the reign of Pope John XXII in the fourteenth century. Contains illuminating insights on the practical problems faced by the Franciscans and on the hostility they encountered from the seculars. Includes index.

Leff, Gordon. *Paris and Oxford Universities in the Thirteenth and Fourteenth Centuries: An Institutional and Intellectual History*. New York: John Wiley and Sons, 1968. A good introduction to the background of the friar-secular controversy. See especially Leff's treatment of the 1250's at Paris and his discussion of evangelical poverty.

Rosewein, Barbara H., and Lester K. Little. "Social Meaning in the Monastic and Mendicant Spiritualities." *Past and Present* 63 (May, 1974): 4-32. This article provides insight into the social and economic factors that augmented the spirituality of the friars. Notes the differences between the older Benedictines and the thirteenth century friars.

Larry C. Watkins

WILLIAM OF SAINT-THIERRY

Born: Probably between 1075 and 1080; Liège
Died: September 8, 1147 or 1148; Signy Abbey, Diocese of Reims, France
Area of Achievement: Religion
Contribution: William of Saint-Thierry, whose name is forever linked with that of Saint Bernard of Clairvaux, was one of the greatest of twelfth century monks, mystics, and theologians of the spiritual life. His writings on love, monastic friendship, and the Trinity were particularly influential.

Early Life

William was born at Liège of noble parentage; nothing else is known about his family. While still young, he left Liège, probably for Reims, where, it is thought, he studied between 1105 and 1115. Little is known with certainty about William's early life and education, but his writings give evidence of a good education.

Having decided to become a Benedictine monk, William joined the abbey of Saint-Nicaise of Reims, probably in 1113. Saint-Nicaise was a monastery of good reputation, and every indication is that from the beginning William practiced the monastic life with great seriousness and commitment. The quiet of the monastic cloister allowed him time for study of the church fathers, especially the works of Saint Augustine, Saint Ambrose, Saint Hilary of Poitiers, Boethius, and Gregory the Great. His growing reputation for learning and strictness of life led to his election in 1119 or 1120 as abbot of Saint-Thierry, northwest of Reims.

Saint-Thierry was a well-endowed monastery, and much of William's time was taken with administration of the monastic properties. At the time he became abbot, Saint-Thierry was not as well-known as the abbey of Saint-Nicaise. William's success in temporal administration and the spiritual guidance of the community, together with the respect accorded to his writings, was soon to make it one of the preeminent monasteries in the Benedictine Order.

Life's Work

If William was not already a priest by the time he became abbot of Saint-Thierry, at some unknown time he was so ordained. During his first three years as abbot, he wrote *De natura et dignitate amoris* (c. 1119-1128; *On the Nature and Dignity of Love*, 1956). This work envisioned the monastic life as a continuation of the communal life practiced at Jerusalem by the Apostles (see Acts 2:42-47 and 4:32-35), the goal of which was unity of mind from which love flows. For William, the monastery was a school of love. His interest in the contemplative life is also evident in another work from this period, *De contemplando Deo* (c. 1119-1128; *On Contemplating God*, 1955). As it was to turn out, these earliest of his writings were, along with his last two works, *Epistola ad fratres de Monte-Dei* (1144; *The Golden Epistle of Abbot William of St. Thierry*, 1930) and *Vite prima Bernardi abbatis* (c. 1147; *Saint Bernard of Clairvaux: The Story of His Life*, 1960), to have a significant influence on later generations. Yet these earliest two works were circulated in the thirteenth century under Saint Bernard's name.

William found the burdens of his position as abbot hard to bear. He was shy and sensitive, and commanding others did not come easily. Increasingly through the 1120's, he was troubled by the criticisms made by Saint Bernard of Clairvaux regarding the Cluniac form of Benedictinism, the usages of which had been adopted by William's own monastery. He had first met Bernard, who followed a stricter Cistercian reading of the Rule of Saint Benedict, in 1118. About 1125, Bernard addressed to William a pair of sharply written satirical works which created much controversy, for although on certain points Bernard was conciliatory, he persisted in many of his criticisms of the Cluniacs, hitherto the most influential monastic order, as lax and fond of luxury. Perceiving the justice of much of Bernard's criticism, William gave his approval to the work and subsequently cited it in some of his own writings. Beyond this, he became active in reform of his order in the province of Reims.

William had made journeys to Saint Bernard's monastery at Clairvaux for spiritual conversation, and by 1124 he told Bernard that he wished to resign his abbacy and move to Clairvaux. Bernard advised against it. For the time being, William accepted this advice and remained at Saint-Thierry, governing and writing.

In 1128, Bernard sent William a new work addressing the issues of grace and free will, asking for his criticism. In response, William composed *De sacramento altaris* (c. 1128; *On the Sacrament of the Altar*, 1970). This book on the meaning of the Eucharist is one of the first devoted solely to this subject. Probably about this time, William also began other works, for the most part dependent on his extensive knowledge of the Latin fathers, but with some use, through the Latin translation by Rufinus, of the Greek Christian writer Origen (c. 185-c. 254). Although both earlier and later Origen had fallen and was to fall under censure, in the twelfth century he was fairly widely read, and William was to adopt themes from Origen in several treatises. It is likely that many of the works of this period, including the *Meditativae orationes* (c. 1128-1135; *The Meditations*, 1954), were only begun at Saint-Thierry and were finished after William had moved to Signy.

The idea of becoming a Cistercian had never been abandoned by William, and in 1135 he resigned his abbacy and, as a simple monk, joined the new Cistercian monastery of Signy, also in the diocese of Reims. There followed a time of trial and self-doubt. William never had been particularly robust, and it may be that the very sparse diet of the Cistercians, who subsisted for the most part on bread and vegetables, weakened him further. In addition, doubts grew that he had made the right choice. He became so ill that he almost died. Even recovered, he remained frail and was thereafter exempted from the daily manual labor practiced by most Cistercians.

He returned to his writing. The *Expositio super Cantica Canticorum* (c. 1135-1138; *Exposition on the Song of Songs*, 1970) became a main preoccupation; in this work, William elaborated his teaching on man as the image of God and as possessing, as Augustine had taught, memory, intellect, and will. Beginning in 1138, a controversy whose repercussions were felt all across Europe arose. Certain of Peter Abelard's teachings had been condemned as early as 1121, but only in the mid-1130's did some of his later writings come into William's possession. William was outraged at what he took to be Abelard's contempt for tradition. He immediately took the attack and called Abelard's abuses to Bernard's attention. By 1140, the latter had seen to it that Abelard was condemned by Rome.

Abelard might have been condemned, but the issues he raised concerning the relation of faith and reason—of the role of reason in speaking of the things of God—remained. Like many others, William tried his hand at addressing these issues. Two works which have been preserved, *Speculum fidei* (1140; *The Mirror of Faith*, 1959) and *Aenigma fidei* (1144; *The Enigma of Faith*, 1974), were completed by 1144. These works both treat the problem of how man knows God; *The Mirror of Faith* is virtually an exposition of the theological virtues of faith, hope, and love, while *The Enigma of Faith* centers on the Trinity. William elsewhere attacked what he took to be a tendency of theologians such as William of Conches to undermine the unity of the Trinity, a theme taken up in *The Enigma of Faith*.

William gained a wide readership in the twelfth century (and even more in the thirteenth) from a work intended for hermits, *The Golden Epistle*. In about 1144, he had visited the recently founded Carthusian Charterhouse of Mont-Dieu, a community of hermits, also in the diocese of Reims. After William returned to Signy, his present to the hermits was a long epistle on the eremitic life. Like other of his works, this was to suffer at the hands of later medieval editors, who reshaped what had originally been a long letter into a formal treatise on the solitary life, eventually attributed to Saint Bernard.

William felt old and tired, but he had one final work to write: *Saint Bernard of Clairvaux*. Death intervened before he could finish, and he left the tale told only through about 1130. He died on September 8, 1147 or 1148, and was buried in his own cloister at Signy.

Summary

William of Saint-Thierry stands at the center of the twelfth century monastic impulse toward solitude, austerity, and contemplation. The movement of his life was from the less strict practices of Cluny to the more demanding life of the Cistercians, with an interest toward the end in the even more austere eremitic life of the Carthusians. Linked forever with his almost lifelong friend, Saint Bernard of Clairvaux, whose life he was writing at the time of his death, William was not the public figure that Bernard was. Although very much involved in monastic reform and always attentive to the threat of heresy, for the most part William lived a quiet life of solitude, a life of meditation and writing. It is here that his importance lies.

The revival of learning occurring all across Europe in the twelfth century had many aspects. One of these was an exploration of the reliability and limits of human reason, especially in understanding the nature of God. William considered that many of the scholars of the rapidly growing cities of his day were too audacious in speaking of God and too careless in abandoning established terminology for new ideas. His own interest lay elsewhere, in mystical theology, especially in elaborating for monks the manner in which, through love, the human soul becomes receptive to salvation and to God—indeed, in a certain sense becomes like God, who is Love.

At one level, William was one of the most conservative theologians of his day, siding with Saint Bernard against innovators such as Abelard and William of Conches. William of Saint-Thierry disliked the application of dialectic to theology: Better than the new Scholasticism was the prayer and contemplative theology of the church fathers, who attempted to reach God more by love and desire than by intellect and saw all understanding of God as rooted in love. In another sense, William can be said to evince a rather modern sensibility in his perception of inner peace and joy as signs of God's grace and consolation. The main point is that, by returning to the church fathers, William often recaptured ancient insights and expressed them in a contemplative synthesis built around access to God through love. This he offered as an alternative to the growing Scholastic attempt to turn theology into a science whose main instrument was intellect.

Bibliography
Anderson, John D. Introduction to *The Works of William of St. Thierry*. Vol. 3, *The Enigma of Faith*. Washington, D.C.: Cistercian Publications/ Consortium Press, 1974. One should consult all the introductions to the various volumes of translations of William's writings in this series, but this one is especially important because it corrects several errors repeated in many descriptions of William's life and downplays William's knowledge of the Greek church fathers. The introductions in this series contain some of the most recent bibliographical information on the particular works of William translated in each volume.
Bell, David N. *The Image and Likeness: The Augustinian Spirituality of William of St. Thierry*. Kalamazoo, Mich.: Cistercian Publications, 1984.

This is the best-informed and most up-to-date full-length study in English of William's spirituality and theology. The biographical comments in the introduction are sound, and it has a full bibliography and very useful indexes.

Brooke, Odo. *Studies in Monastic Theology*. Kalamazoo, Mich.: Cistercian Publications, 1980. Most of this volume is devoted to reprinting seven articles on William of Saint-Thierry originally published in various journals. It should be consulted by those interested in William's theology. It embodies many of the perspectives of Jean Marie Déchanet (see following entry) and needs to be corrected by those of John D. Anderson (see above).

Déchanet, Jean Marie. *William of St. Thierry: The Man and His Work*. Translated by Richard Strachan. Spencer, Mass.: Cistercian Publications, 1972. There is no definitive biography of the life and work of William, but this is the fullest biography in English. It is sometimes uncritical and sometimes overly speculative in advancing points of view for which there is little evidence. Its final chapter gives a useful survey of previous scholarship.

Gilson, Étienne. *The Mystical Theology of Saint Bernard*. Translated by A. C. Downes. New York: Sheed and Ward, 1940. A great work by one of the best twentieth century historians of medieval thought. Its fifth appendix, "Notes on William of St.-Thierry," gives an excellent outline of William's thought, clearly placing it in the Augustinian tradition.

Glenn W. Olsen

WŁADYSŁAW II JAGIEŁŁO and JADWIGA

Władysław II Jagiełło

Born: c. 1351; place unknown
Died: June 1, 1434; Gródek, near Lvov, Lithuania

Jadwiga

Born: 1373 or 1374; place unknown
Died: July 17, 1399; place unknown
Areas of Achievement: Government and religion
Contribution: Jagiełło and Jadwiga's marriage brought about the unification of Lithuania and Poland and the conversion of the Lithuanian people from paganism to the Roman Catholic faith.

Early Lives

Władysław II Jagiełło (Jogaila in Lithuanian) was the eldest son of Algirdas (also known as Olgierd), the grand duke of Lithuania, by his second marriage. Though Jagiełło's mother, Juliana of Tver, taught him Ukrainian and pushed him toward her Russian Orthodox Church and a Russian marriage, Jagiełło took after his cautious pagan father in most respects, even in the unusual practice of refusing to drink alcoholic beverages. Algirdas had shared power in Lithuania with his brother, Kęstutis, who had governed the western half of the country and fended off the eastern march of the Teutonic Knights and Kings Casimir the Great and Louis the Great. Algirdas had ruled over central Lithuania and the Russian dependencies.

Algirdas' death in 1377 precipitated a struggle between the sons of the two marriages. Jagiełło and his brothers overcame those rivals and, in 1382, they fought their uncle, Kęstutis, through secret alliances with the Teutonic Knights in which the brothers promised to convert the Lithuanians to the Roman Catholic Church. They found themselves in trouble, however, when Kęstutis' son, Vytautas, escaped to the Teutonic Knights and persuaded the Crusaders that he would be more likely to carry out his promises than Jagiełło. Soon, the baptized Vytautas threatened Jagiełło's hold on Lithuania so seriously that in 1385 Jagiełło looked abroad for help.

The kingdom of Poland was undergoing a serious crisis. Casimir the Great had expanded its frontiers to the east, but after his death in 1370 he left the country without a legitimate male heir. The crown had gone to Louis the Great, who was not in a position to defend them well. Confronted by the Turkish advance into the Balkans and in poor health, Louis ruled Poland through Hungarian and Silesian favorites. When Louis died in 1382, it appeared that foreigners would continue to dominate Poland, because his two young daughters were promised to prominent German princes.

Jadwiga, the daughter who became queen in 1384, had been married while still a child to Wilhelm von Habsburg. In 1385, young Wilhelm came to Kraków to urge his childhood playmate to consummate their marriage before the Polish bishops could arrange an annulment. The Polish nobles and clergy meanwhile looked hurriedly for an alternative bridegroom. The austere, clean-shaven, seemingly compliant Lithuanian grand duke was their choice.

Life's Work

The Treaty of Krewo, August 14, 1385, provided for Jagiełło to marry Jadwiga, for the conversion of the Lithuanian people, and for a dynastic union of the two states. Jadwiga was persuaded by the Polish bishops to marry the short, quiet, balding stranger, who would be known as her consort. She held the title "rex" and her advisers saw to it that Jagiełło's powers were strictly limited. The marriage does not seem to have been a love match (despite what has been written in nineteenth century Romantic novels) and only one child, a daughter, was born, in 1399. (Jadwiga died in childbirth, and the baby girl died three days later.)

The marriage took place on February 14, 1386, in Kraków. The following year, on February 1, Jagiełło established a bishopric in Vilnius (Vilna), his Lithuanian capital, and possibly wrote the Our Father and the Apostles' Creed in Lithuanian and led the converts in their first recitation. There were too few Lithuanian-speaking priests to make a great impact on the mass of the population, but that was perhaps just as well: The sincere pagans and the many Russian Orthodox believers were consequently left in peace until the new church was well established.

Jagiełło, meanwhile, had made his peace with Vytautas by promising to give him Kęstutis' lands. Failing to live up to that promise, he later had to fight Vytautas and the Teutonic Knights again—but without Polish help. Poland had lived in almost unbroken peace with the Teutonic Knights since the Treaty of Kalisz in 1343, and Jadwiga (supported strongly by her advisers) did not want war with them. Consequently, Jagiełło ultimately gave Vytautas all Lithuania, rescuing only a claim to ultimate sovereignty and a promise of help against the Mongols in the Ukraine, where Jadwiga's advisers had wanted Jagiełło to employ his talents all along.

The turning point in all Jagiełło's relationships came in 1399. Jadwiga's strong, independent personality had expressed itself largely in acts of piety and in curbing her husband's ambitions. Her death in childbirth made Jagiełło king in name and in fact. Vytautas, routed by the Mongols in pitched battle, pled for Polish help and two years later formally acknowledged Jagiełło as his overlord.

In all these endeavors Jagiełło had not demonstrated outstanding military skill. Instead, he was a master diplomat, a cautious but skillful politician, and a clever manipulator of personal and national weaknesses. Slowly, he made himself master of Poland, favoring that section of Polish nobility which had encouraged him to take the formal title of Władysław II, thus linking himself to Władysław I's lifelong efforts to recover Pomerelia (West Prussia) from the Teutonic Knights.

War with the Teutonic Knights came in 1410. On the battlefield of Tannenberg (Stębark), Jagiełło and Vytautas thoroughly crushed the grand master's army. Afterward, Jagiełło's brilliant statecraft isolated his enemy and, by forcing the knights to hire mercenaries year after year, drained their strength. In 1422, his armies laid Prussia to waste so thoroughly that the grand master renounced his last claims on Lithuanian territory. Jagiełło failed to recover Pomerelia, but his successors did so in the Thirteen Years' War (from 1454 to 1466), with the aid of West Prussian burghers and secular nobles.

Jagiełło restored royal authority over Masovia, reestablished control over the southeastern provinces, and worked closely with the Hussites in Bohemia to weaken German power along the Polish border. In 1413, Jagiełło and Vytautas confirmed the dynastic union of their states and defined the constitutional rights of the nobles of Poland and Lithuania, a major step toward limiting royal authority. Further steps came through concessions to Archbishop Oleśnicki.

Last, when Jagiełło's fourth wife produced two long-awaited sons (Władysław and Casimir), the king was unable to secure their succession without sacrificing more royal prerogatives. His authority over Lithuania was even weaker. Even though he frustrated Vytautas' ambitions to become king, Jagiełło was unable to secure the country for his own brother upon Vytautas' death in 1430. After Jagiełło died, Vytautas' brother, Sigismund, won the struggle for power, and regents ruled in Poland on behalf of the nobility and clergy.

Summary

When Władysław II Jagiełło defeated the Teutonic Knights, it was the most brilliant moment in Polish military history between 1200 and the victory of John III Sobieski over the Turks in 1683—at least from the point of view which prevailed after Poland had been divided among her neighbors. There is a tendency among an oppressed and divided people to simplify history and to remember and honor those moments when the country was militarily triumphant. This tradition has been a disservice to other glorious periods of Polish history and culture, and it has led to considerable distortion and romanticizing of the activities of Jagiełło and Jadwiga. Nationalist historians and novelists gave these figures all the virtues, their enemies all possible vices.

Lithuanians have always had an ambiguous attitude toward Jagiełło. They gave their real love to Vytautas, whose relationship with Jagiełło was rarely warmer than cautious mistrust. The Lithuanian attitude is most evident in nationalist analyses of the Battle of Tannenberg. The extreme Lithuanian point of view is that Jagiełło merely attended masses and prayed for victory, while Vytautas devised the brilliant feigned retreat which caused the Teutonic Knights to break their lines and open the way for the Polish attack. The extreme Polish view is that the Germans drove the Lithuanians from the field, so that victory was a result of Jagiełło's inspiring leadership and Polish courage alone. Germans have traditionally disliked Jagiełło, because his victory in Prussia dimmed the only brightness in their declining Holy Roman Empire. A recent change in this attitude reflects the disappearance of the generations which expected historical interpretations to support nationalistic aspirations.

Jadwiga was a strong figure in her lifetime, but she made only a small impression on history. In contrast, no one questions that Jagiełło was one of the great Polish monarchs. Although he was unable to reverse the decline of royal authority, for a short period he restored the unity of the kingdom and defeated or frustrated all enemies. Moreover, he extended Roman Christianity to Lithuania, founded the Jagiellonian University in Kraków (with a legacy from Jadwiga), and established a dynasty which lasted until 1572.

Bibliography

Christiansen, Eric. *The Northern Crusades: The Baltic and the Catholic Frontier, 1100-1525*. Minneapolis: University of Minnesota Press, 1980. The description of the Crusades of the Teutonic Knights from Prussia and Livonia provide helpful background to Jagiełło's conversion. Concise, witty, and well-written.

Davies, Norman. *God's Playground: A History of Poland*. 2 vols. New York: Columbia University Press, 1982. A well-written, scholarly account of medieval Polish history. Its somewhat ironic and rational interpretations are not likely to please romantic nationalists.

Evans, Geoffrey Charles. *Tannenberg: 1410-1914*. London: Hamilton, 1970. This volume, which describes Jagiełło's great victory, is strictly military. It predates archaeological work on the battlefield, providing important scholarship.

Halecki, Oskar. *Borderlands of Western Europe: A History of East Central Europe*. New York: Ronald Press, 1952. This work is the standard English-language survey of medieval Poland, Lithuania, and Russia. It has particularly strong coverage of the religious controversies.

Jasienica, Pawel. *Jagiellonian Poland*. Translated by Alexander Jordan. Miami: American Institute of Polish Culture, 1978. A well-recommended history of the dynasty which covers Jagiełło. This work is a translation from

Polish of a standard text from that country.

Reddaway, W. F., et al., eds. *The Cambridge History of Poland*. 2 vols. Cambridge: Cambridge University Press, 1950. Postwar scholarship has made advances beyond this long survey; nevertheless, this set remains a solid, useful work.

William L. Urban

WOLFRAM VON ESCHENBACH

Born: c. 1170; probably Eschenbach bei Ansbach, Franconia
Died: c. 1217; probably Eschenbach bei Ansbach, Franconia
Area of Achievement: Literature
Contribution: In the era of the High Middle Ages, Wolfram was a master in the tradition of the courtly epic; his works constitute one of the high points of the narrative writing produced during this first golden age of German literature.

Early Life

As is the case with many medieval figures, little is known about the life of Wolfram von Eschenbach. He was born and died in the town of Eschenbach bei Ansbach and was a Frankish knight in the service of the Count of Wertheim. He was married, had a child, and possessed a modest estate. His grave in the Frauenkirche of Eschenbach was unmarked and has become lost over the centuries. He was well-read but had received no formal education. Wolfram was a man who felt close to the common people and was deeply committed to the ideals of Christianity.

Wolfram lived during the reign of the Hohenstaufen dynasty—its most notable ruler being Fredrick I Barbarossa. It was the age of the Crusades and feudalism. European knighthood was in full bloom, especially in France, England, and Germany. The knights were the bearers of a culture which centered on the courts of the liege lords to whom they had sworn fealty. During a period when Christianity was in competition with the secular domain for political and cultural hegemony, the ethos of knighthood constituted an attempt to merge religious and profane values.

Since the courtly culture of the time was a formative influence on Wolfram and his writings, it would be helpful to summarize some major aspects. The knightly code of behavior was guided by a number of prominent formal virtues, some of which had descended from older Germanic tribal codes. Honor (*êre*) was foremost and meant that the knight would not do anything in thought or action to disgrace himself or the order of knighthood before God and the king. The courtly culture was concerned with proper form, and a knight's appearance before the world was of the greatest importance. Loyalty (*triuwe*) meant that the knight kept his oath of allegiance to his liege lord. Discipline (*zucht*) indicated that the knight must maintain his proper knightly attitude on the battlefield and in court. Moderation (*mâze*) suggested that he must avoid all extremes and maintain his formal bearing. A knight's goals in life were threefold: to own property (such as an estate), to maintain his honor before his peers, and to strive for God's blessing. As a landed knight, Wolfram was committed to the values of his class, and they are evident in his works. A deeply religious man, he regarded the institution of knighthood as a manifestation of God's will on earth.

The High Middle Ages was also the period of the highly formalized institution of courtly love (*Minnedienst*). Although occasional sexual liaisons undoubtedly occurred, courtly love was not an erotic affair but a form of spiritualized service in which the knight pledged his loyalty and honor to the defense of a lady of the court and thereby believed himself ennobled. The knight's adoration of his lady was most often manifested in the writing of love poetry (*Minnesang*). Wolfram did write some poetry, although he is not known primarily for this type of literary production.

Life's Work

Wolfram's greatest achievements were in the genre of the courtly heroic epic. Before turning to his individual works, a few words about this form of literature might be in order. The literary models for the German courtly epic came primarily from France in the *chansons de geste*, tales of great heroic deeds, such as the *Chanson de Roland* (c. 1100; *Song of Roland*), and especially in the tales of knightly glory that were associated with the legendary King Arthur and his Round Table. The French writer Chrétien de Troyes, who lived toward the end of the twelfth century, had given classic form to the genre with his Arthurian epics, and his works were an important influence on later German authors.

Wolfram's most famous text was his courtly epic *Parzifal* (c. 1200-1210; English translation, 1894), which consists of sixteen sections and was handed down in more than eighty manuscript versions and fragments. The text is written in rhymed couplets, the form characteristic of medieval German narrative poetry. It is based on Chrétien's *Perceval: Ou, Le Conte du Graal* (c. 1180; *Perceval: Or, The Story of the Grail*), stories surrounding the legendary chalice which was held by Christ at the Last Supper and was used by the disciple Joseph to catch Christ's blood. Wolfram's version is the story of the young and naïve Parzifal in his quest for the Holy Grail and for his true relationship to God and knighthood. Parzifal serves as a literary representative of his social class.

Since his father, the heroic knight Gachmuret, had been killed on a crusade, Parzifal's mother, Herzeloyde, rears her son alone in a secluded wood so that he might be saved from the worldly fate of his father. One day, however, the young boy, unfamiliar with the ways of the world, does meet three knights who advise him to go to the court of King Arthur. Since it was then believed that a knight's noble nature was inborn, Parzifal's true heroic heritage is awakened, and he leaves his mother, who dies, in order to pursue his dream of becoming a knight at Arthur's court. There he kills the Red Knight Ither and is instructed in the ways of courtly behavior by Gurnemanz. He is told to be humble and modest and not to ask too many questions.

After becoming betrothed to the beautiful Condwiramurs, he journeys to the Grail Castle, whose lord, Amfortas, lies suffering from a terrible wound. Naïvely following the advice he has received, Parzifal does not ask Amfortas about his suffering, and he is told that he shows no pity for his fellowman. Discouraged, he leaves Condwiramurs and Arthur's circle and sets forth into the world, resenting God, who he believes has abandoned him. Parzifal shows here that he lacks faith in God's wisdom, and such religious despair is considered a major sin within Christian thought.

Parzifal wanders in despair for four years and finally comes upon Trevrezent, the brother of Amfortas and the uncle that he has never known. From Trevrezent, he learns that his mother has died—as well as the secret of Amfortas' wound. He is instructed in the meaning of sin, grace, and faith in God's plan and comes to realize that his rejection of God was a result of his rage and pride. No longer naïve in the ways of God and man, Parzifal finally attains an inner peace. He leaves his uncle and engages in combat with a strange knight who turns out to be his friend Gawain. They return to Arthur's court, but Parzifal longs for Condwiramurs and the Grail and once more sets out upon a journey. He again engages in combat with an unknown knight, Feirefiz, who is his own half brother. They travel back to Arthur's court, where it is announced that Parzifal is to be king of the Grail Castle. He is also reunited with his love, Condwiramurs. Having finally attained worldly glory and God's blessing, Parzifal spends the remainder of his life committed to serving others in God's name.

Parzifal serves as a kind of Everyman figure. His individual destiny describes the road to ideal knighthood and is, broadly speaking, an idealized vision of the path of medieval education. As a boy he is an "innocent," unwise in the ways of the world, but he eventually attains a prowess in battle that defines his social status within the hierarchy of the court. He is on his way to reaching the three goals of the Christian knight (worldly honor, wealth, and God's blessing) but must embark upon an arduous journey in order to attain them. These ideals are symbolized by the Grail Castle, a union of secular values (knighthood) and religious faith (the guarding of the sacred chalice). His seeming lack of human compassion (not asking about Amfortas' wound) and his rejection of God during his years of self-imposed exile are symbolically illustrative of the difficulties the individual Christian knight would face in achieving the goals of his station.

Wolfram clearly indicates the Christian idea that despite man's good intentions, sin and guilt are an inevitable result of human existence. Parzifal's battles with strange knights who turn out to be friends (Gawain) or relatives (Feirefiz) suggest his "blindness" to those around him. His education must be directed at learning to recognize the truths of his faith and his society: that of the spirit (faith and the acceptance of God's will) and that of his class (learning how to conduct himself properly within courtly society). Parzifal's eventual appointment as king of the Grail Castle indicates that he finally does become the ideal knight. His journey moves him from the ignorance and naïveté of childhood to the wisdom and salvation of adulthood.

Wolfram worked on several other epics which remained uncompleted. In *Titurel* (c. 1217; *Schionatulander and Sigune*, 1960), he tells the tragic love story of Sigune and Schionatulander, two of the characters that had appeared briefly in the *Parzifal* text. This tale reflects the influence of the courtly love lyric tradition and its idealization of the love experience. Wolfram had also composed some poetry in this genre. In *Willehalm* (c. 1212-1217; English translation, 1977), written during his old age, he narrates the story of William of Toulouse and his battles against the heathen Saracens. This work owes its plot elements to the tradition of the heroic epic with its descriptions of battles and the bravery of the knights who fought them. Its theme focuses on the differences between the Christian and heathen worlds.

Summary

Along with Gottfried von Strassburg and Hartmann von Aue, Wolfram von Eschenbach is one of the greatest writers in the genre of the courtly epic, and his place within world literature is certain. His works indicate a talented artist with a well-developed sense of humor and fantasy, a visual and highly symbolic narrative style, and a deep concern with Christian values and the ideals of knighthood.

His *Parzifal* is one of the few great epics of the German Middle Ages. This tale of its hero's struggles to attain honor before his courtly peers, as well as the grace of God, presents a vision of ideal knighthood but is universal in its appeal. Such themes certainly relate to the individual's experience in the modern world as well as to the life of the medieval man. Whatever their historical time or belief, all human beings must seek at some point in their lives to balance the spiritual and the material, or social, sides of existence.

The story of Parzifal's journey through life, his learning of his own strengths and weaknesses as well as the ways of God and the world, has represented in certain respects a model of the maturation of the exemplary individual. This kind of narrative has become, in its later manifestations, a genre in itself, the so-called novel of education (*Bildungsroman*), in which the inner and outer development of the protagonist from youth through adulthood serves as the central theme of the text. Johann Wolfgang von Goethe's *Wilhelm Meisters Lehrjahre* (1795-1796; *Wilhelm Meister's Apprenticeship*, 1824) and Thomas Mann's *Der Zauberberg* (1924; *The Magic Mountain*, 1927) are later examples of this genre. Wolfram's *Parzifal* stands at the beginning of this tradition.

Bibliography

Poag, James F. *Wolfram von Eschenbach*. New York: Twayne Publishers, 1972. A very useful introduction with quotes in English and German. Contains index and bibliography.

Reinhardt, Kurt F. *Germany: 2000 Years*. Milwaukee, Wis.: Bruce, 1950. This survey of German civilization includes an excellent chapter on the Middle Ages, with a discussion of Wolfram and *Parzifal*. Contains bibliography and index.

Springer, Otto. "Wolfram's *Parzifal*." In *Arthurian Literature in the Middle Ages: A Collaborative History*, edited by Roger Loomis. Oxford: Clarendon Press, 1959. This chapter considers some of the central questions in *Parzifal* scholarship.

Walshe, Maurice O'Connell. *Medieval German Literature*. Cambridge, Mass.: Harvard University Press, 1962. Excellent introduction to the period, with a section on Wolfram. Contains a bibliography.

Weigand, Hermann J. *Wolfram's "Parzival."* Ithaca, N.Y.: Cornell University Press, 1969. General but very good introduction to Wolfram's text by a noted scholar. Contains bibliographic references and index.

Thomas F. Barry

XENOPHANES

Born: c. 570 B.C.; Colophon, near the coast of Asia Minor
Died: c. 478 B.C.; western Greece
Areas of Achievement: Philosophy, literature, and religion
Contribution: Xenophanes' critique of the Homeric gods marks the beginning of both systematic theology and the rational interpretation of myth in ancient Greek society.

Early Life

The childhood of Xenophanes, like that of most early Greek philosophers, is shrouded in mystery. By the time that Xenophanes himself appears in the literary record of ancient Greece, he is already a grown man, traveling from town to town as a professional poet. Scholars cannot even be certain of his father's name, since several ancient authorities have listed it as Dexius, others as Dexinus, and still others as Orthomenes. Scholars are certain, however, that Xenophanes was born in the city of Colophon (near the coast of Asia Minor) sometime during the middle of the sixth century B.C. Moreover, it is likely that he left this area in his youth, probably as the result of Persia's policy of imperial expansion. It was, then, during the very period of Xenophanes' youth that the Persian conquest of new territories began to lead, inevitably, to war between Persia and Greece.

Xenophanes himself would later allude to this stage of his life with these ambiguous words, taken from what is known as fragment 8:

Already there have been seven and sixty years tossing my thoughts up and down the land of Greece. And from my birth there were another twenty-five in addition to these, if indeed I know how to speak truly of such things.

Since in another fragment Xenophanes had mentioned "the coming of the Mede," it seems probable that he left Colophon at about the time that this city fell to Harpagus the Mede in 546. For the rest of his life, Xenophanes would support himself through his poetry. He became a traveling rhapsodist, composing songs on various topics as he journeyed throughout the Greek world. Unlike many other archaic rhapsodists, however, Xenophanes used only his own compositions in his performances. It is probably from these works that the extant fragments are derived.

Diogenes Laërtius states that Xenophanes spent much of his life in Sicily. Other authorities support this view, maintaining that Xenophanes had participated in founding the city of Elea, in what is modern Italy. Xenophanes, according to these scholars, is thus the spiritual forebear of the philosophers known as the Eleatics and one of the actual founders of Elea itself. The accuracy of this claim seems questionable, however, and the belief that

Xenophanes was instrumental in founding Elea may have arisen solely because the philosopher had written a poem commemorating the event. In fact, Xenophanes seems unlikely to have had any permanent residence; he must have spent most of his life traveling extensively throughout Greece and Sicily, pausing in each community only for brief periods.

Xenophanes' lifelong travels had a profound influence on his thought. For example, after he had observed fossils in a quarry near Syracuse, Xenophanes developed the theory that life on earth is cyclic: Those creatures who had lived in earlier eras, he believed, were repeatedly "dissolved" by the encroaching seas, and life had to develop all over again. Yet even more important than what Xenophanes observed during these travels was his contact with the intellectual revolution in Greek philosophy, which, by this time, was well under way. For example, Thales of Miletus, whose views about the composition of matter are regarded as the origin of Greek philosophy, had by then been active for more than forty years. Anaximander, who was Thales' successor and who had originated the notion of the *apeiron* (the "unbounded" or "unlimited" as the source of all creation), died in about the same year that Colophon fell. Anaximenes of Miletus, who had believed that all matter was composed of rarefied or contracted air, is also likely to have lived in roughly the same period as Xenophanes.

The ideas of these philosophers were of great importance in the Greek world where Xenophanes traveled, lived, and wrote his poetry. The young philosopher seems to have listened to the theories of his predecessors, considered them, and then combined their views with his own thought to create the subjects of his songs. Unlike many other pre-Socratics, however, Xenophanes has left the modern world substantial portions of his poetry, written down either by himself or by those who studied with him. It is from these surviving words of Xenophanes—about 120 lines in all—that modern readers are able to form their clearest picture of the philosopher and of his life's work.

Life's Work

As was common among the pre-Socratic philosophers, Xenophanes devoted a substantial portion of his thought to considering the nature of the physical universe. Although it is uncertain whether he actually wrote the work entitled *Peri phuseos* (on nature), which Stobaeus and Pollux attributed to him, a large number of Xenophanes' surviving fragments are concerned with matters of astronomy and the weather. In these passages, Xenophanes reveals that he was strongly influenced by Anaximenes, who had argued that clouds were merely condensed, or "thickened," masses of air. Xenophanes expressed a similar view, substituting only the notion of "sea" or "water" for that of air. In Xenophanes' theory, the sea gives rise to the clouds, winds, and rivers; the sun and heavenly bodies are created from thickened, or "ignited," bits of cloud. Rainbows, too, are said to be nothing more than colored fragments of cloud.

In two other passages, Xenophanes says that everything in the universe is made of earth and water. This theory is apparently an attempt to combine Thales' recognition that water is necessary to life and, as ice or steam, can change its shape with Anaximenes' belief that there must be some general process (condensation or rarefaction) which accounts for this change. That same general line of thought may also lie behind Xenophanes' belief that each day the sun is created anew, arising from fiery bits of dilated cloud.

Yet far more influential than these physical theories of Xenophanes were the philosopher's theological views and his statements about the nature of God. Xenophanes disagreed with earlier authors such as Homer and Hesiod who had presented the gods as immoral and had endowed them with the same physical traits and limitations as ordinary men. In two famous fragments, Xenophanes criticized the common assumption that the gods were merely immortal creatures similar in most ways to ordinary human beings:

> The Ethiopians claim that their gods are snub-nosed and black, the Thracians that theirs have blue eyes and blond hair. . . . But if cows and horses or lions had hands or could draw and do all the other things that men do, then horses would draw images of the gods which look like horses, and cows like cows, and they would depict the bodies of their gods in the same form as they had themselves.

The argument here is that all people wrongly assume the gods to be like themselves, in form and (it is suggested) in their vices and faults.

Xenophanes' own understanding of divinity was quite different. To begin with, Xenophanes was a monotheist, believing that there exists only a single god who is unlike humankind both in form and in character. Second, Xenophanes said that this deity perceives the universe differently from mankind, using all of its "body" simultaneously to think, to hear, and to see. Finally, in two important fragments, Xenophanes anticipated Aristotle's theory of the Prime Mover, asserting that this one god remains in a single place and guides the universe without movement, relying solely on the power of Mind.

Yet, by Xenophanes' own admission, even these statements about divinity are subject to debate. For "no man," he says, "either has known or will know the clear truth about the gods. . . . Belief [and not certain knowledge] is produced for all men." While not as general in focus as the skepticism of Plato's Academy, Xenophanes' remarks here do anticipate some of the views which would arise in later periods of Greek philosophy. His distinction between "believing" and "knowing," for example, was to have a crucial influence on the work of Plato himself. Moreover, Xenophanes' theory that human knowledge is necessarily limited would reappear in the works of many later Platonic scholars.

Summary

If Xenophanes' statements about his life in fragment 8 are to be believed, he had already reached the age of ninety-two when those words were written. Xenophanes' lifetime would have encompassed a period of Greek history which witnessed the birth of both tragedy and philosophy in the Western world. At the time of his death, the Persian Wars were drawing to a close and the classical period of Greek history was about to begin.

The picture of Xenophanes which emerges from his writings is thus that of a man who was representative of his day: diverse in his interests, immensely curious, and unwilling to remain content with the dogma of the past. These are traits which characterize many of the other pre-Socratic philosophers as well.

Yet Xenophanes was also important for the impact which he would have on later scholars. His perception of divinity would influence Aristotle and, ultimately, Saint Thomas Aquinas. His belief that human knowledge was inherently limited was to reemerge in the skepticism of the Academy. Xenophanes was, in other words, a pivotal figure who helped to transform the empirical philosophy of antiquity into the more metaphysical philosophy of the classical age.

Bibliography

Fraenkel, H. "Xenophanes' Empiricism and His Critique of Knowledge." In *The Pre-Socratics*, edited by Alexander P. D. Mourelatos. New York: Anchor Books, 1974. Fraenkel uses Xenophanes' theory of knowledge, and his rejection of earlier beliefs about the gods, as the basis for an exploration of the philosopher's worldview. Perhaps the best short summary available on the thought and contribution of Xenophanes to Greek philosophy.

Freeman, Kathleen. *Ancilla to the Pre-Socratic Philosophers*. Cambridge, Mass.: Harvard University Press, 1948. The most convenient source of information for anyone who is interested in examining the surviving texts of the pre-Socratics. Freeman translates, without commentary or interpretation, all the fragments included in Diels's exhaustive edition of the pre-Socratics.

_____. *The Pre-Socratic Philosophers*. Cambridge, Mass.: Harvard University Press, 1953. In this excellent survey, Freeman, taking each historical figure in turn, digests and summarizes all that is known about the philosophical views of the pre-Socratics. The fragments upon which she has based her information are all listed in concise footnotes. A very thorough summary of the philosopher's life begins each entry. At the end of the work is an invaluable list which presents, in a sentence or two, an encapsulated view of what is known about the authors who are the sources for the fragments.

Jaeger, W. W. "Xenophanes' Doctrine of God." In *The Theology of the Early Greek Philosophers*, translated by Edward S. Robinson. Oxford: Clarendon Press, 1947. The premise of Jaeger's book is that the pre-Socratics are important for their theological views as well as for their (more famous) doctrines on the physical universe. Xenophanes, as arguably the most theological of the pre-Socratics, naturally plays a central role in this work.

Kirk, Geoffrey S., and John E. Raven. *The Presocratic Philosophers*. New York: Cambridge University Press, 1957, rev. ed. 1983. A useful summary of pre-Socratic philosophers and their philosophy, containing both the major texts of the philosophers and reliable commentary on those texts. The extant fragments are grouped by topic rather than by number (as in many other editions). The 1983 edition contains more recent interpretations and a much-improved format: Translations follow Greek passages immediately, rather than in footnotes. Includes a short but important bibliography on each author.

Lesher, J. H. "Xenophanes' Scepticism." *Phronesis* 23 (1978): 1-21. A clear account of Xenophanes' views concerning the limitations of human knowledge. Lesher argues that it is Xenophanes' theological point of view—rejecting, for example, such traditional sources of knowledge about the gods as divination—which is revolutionary, not his skepticism per se.

Jeffrey L. Buller

XENOPHON

Born: c. 431 B.C.; near Athens
Died: c. 354 B.C.; probably Corinth or Athens
Areas of Achievement: Literature and philosophy
Contribution: Through his writings on subjects ranging from the practical to the philosophical, Xenophon, a pupil of Socrates, sought in the fourth century B.C. to instruct and improve Greek society. His works provide the modern reader with a clearer picture of the ancient world.

Early Life

Xenophon was born in or near Athens around 431 B.C. His father, Gryllus, was a wealthy Athenian aristocrat. Little is known of Xenophon's early life, but he would have come of age during the latter years of the Peloponnesian War (431-404), the great conflict between Athens and Sparta. He probably served in one of the crack Athenian cavalry units.

As a youth, Xenophon became a pupil of Socrates, joining an intellectual circle that included at various times such diverse personalities as Alcibiades and Plato. Socrates' teaching was frequently conducted out of doors and in an informal manner. No citizen was barred from listening to him or taking part in the discussions, and in a sense his pupils taught themselves. Each student thus developed his own concepts of who Socrates was and what he was saying; therefore, Xenophon should not be faulted because his views of Socrates were not those of Plato, who was gifted with an entirely different quality of mind.

Socrates' belief in moral purposes and his emphasis on the essential goodness of humankind would have appealed to Xenophon's sense of conventional morality. He was not a clever or brilliant pupil but a solid, practical person; probably he took some notes during Socrates' conversations, which would become in later years part of his *Apomnēmoneumata* (c. 381-355; *Memorabilia of Socrates*, 1712) and the *Apologia Sōcratous* (c. 384; *The Defense of Socrates*, 1832). The latter work was thought at one time to be by another author, but it is most likely genuine. Another brief work, the *Symposiou* (*The Banquet*, 1832), whose date, like much of Xenophon's writing, is unknown, places Socrates at an Athenian dinner party, where he discusses a variety of subjects, including the nature of love.

Athens was slipping beyond her golden age as the fifth century waned; Sparta's triumph and the political infighting between the parties of the right and left had tarnished the Athenian democracy. Socrates was increasingly viewed as a suspicious and even dangerous person, for he asked too many questions.

Xenophon was uncertain as to what career he should pursue. In 401, a friend and professional soldier, Proxenus, suggested that he join a band of mercenaries commanded by Prince Cyrus, son of King Darius II of Persia, on an expedition against his brother, Artaxerxes II. The lure of adventure, riches, and military glory was strong, but Xenophon hesitated and consulted Socrates, who advised him to seek counsel of the oracle at Delphi.

Xenophon went to Delphi but apparently had already made a decision before his arrival, since he asked Apollo not whether he should take service with the Persians, but how best the journey might be made. Returning home, he bade Socrates farewell, and the old man advised him to do the will of the god. They were never to meet again.

Life's Work

The high point of Xenophon's life was his military adventures in the Persian Empire, which he vividly describes in the *Kurou anabasis* (between 394 and 371; *The March up Country*, 1623, best known as *Anabasis*). In March, 401, Prince Cyrus led his mixed force of Greeks, Persians, and other troops from the city of Sardis in western Asia Minor to the Euphrates River and on toward Babylon. At Cunaxa on September 3 of that same year, a battle was fought between his and Artaxerxes' forces, and Cyrus was killed. Leaderless and isolated in hostile country, the Greeks were further devastated by the murder of their officers, who had been negotiating after the conflict with the Persians, under a flag of truce. Among the slain was Xenophon's friend Proxenus.

There could be no time for mourning; the ten thousand Greeks who survived elected new commanders, Xenophon being one, and hastily retreated northward into the mountains of Kurdistan and Armenia and fought their way back to civilization, the Greek colony of Trapezus on the Black Sea. The March of the Ten Thousand took approximately five months, and Xenophon undoubtedly played a vital role in its success. He kept a journal which he would use in writing the *Anabasis* decades later.

As Julius Caesar would later do, Xenophon told his story in the third person. Indeed, for reasons now unknown it was originally published under an assumed name. There is, however, no question of authorship; the writing style is Xenophon's, and several ancient authors, Plutarch being one, list the *Anabasis* among his works.

Lively and well written, the *Anabasis* is filled with details of army life, scenes of the countrysides through which the Greeks were passing, descriptions of strange animals and birds (such as ostriches, which ran too fast for the soldiers to catch), and the savage tribes which harassed the "Ten Thousand" on their long march to the sea. The *Anabasis* is Xenophon's most popular work.

The conclusion of these five months of danger and hardship was not as Xenophon had hoped. Denied the opportunity of enrichment and glory serving Prince Cyrus, he considered founding a colony on the Black Sea. Omens from the gods were unfavorable, however, and the Greeks were now divided in their aims. He and some of his friends were obliged to return to military life, first under the command of a petty Thracian king and then with a force of Spartans who had arrived in Asia Minor to defend the Ionian cities against a new Persian attack. During this latter campaign (399), Xenophon captured a wealthy Persian family and managed at last to make his fortune with the large ransom paid for their release.

The year 399 also saw the trial, condemnation, and execution of Socrates. Xenophon's initial reaction to this injustice is not known, but the death of his old teacher must have hastened his rejection of current Athenian democracy. To a professional military man, the order and discipline of the Spartans was more appealing.

During the campaign against the Persians and later in a war among the city-states which pitted Sparta against Athens and Thebes (395-391), Xenophon served on the staff of the Spartan king Agesilaus. In return, the Athenians banished him as a traitor. The Spartans then provided him with an estate at Scillus, near Olympia. Now married and with two sons, Xenophon had the leisure to pursue the life of a country gentleman, devoting his energies to hunting and entertaining his friends and guests, writing, and building a shrine to Artemis, the goddess of the hunt. It was probably during this period that his practical essays *Cynēgetikos* (394-371; *On Hunting*, c. 1832), *Peri hippikēs* (c. 380; *On Horsemanship*, c. 1832), and *Hipparchikos* (c. 357; *The Duties of a Cavalry Officer*, 1832) were composed.

An altogether different sort of work is the *Kyrou paideia* (after 371?; *The Institution and Life of Cyrus*, 1560-1567), a historical novel which treats not only the life and training of Cyrus the Great (not Prince Cyrus of the *Anabasis*) but also the history of the Persian Empire and Xenophon's views on what education and government should be. That the *The Institution and Life of Cyrus* is a complex work is evidenced by the fact that scholars still dispute what Xenophon hoped to accomplish. His contacts with Persians had given him a unique view of non-Greeks, whom many of his countrymen tended to dismiss as barbarians. Xenophon was both better informed and more appreciative of life outside Hellas than were most Greeks.

Local feeling against the Spartans and their allies after Sparta was defeated by Thebes at the Battle of Leuctra (371) obliged Xenophon and his family to leave Scillus and reside in Corinth. There is some question as to whether Xenophon returned to Athens after his banishment was revoked (369-365), but his sons were educated there, and the elder, Gryllus, enlisted in the cavalry as his father had done and died fighting for Athens at the Battle of Mantinea in 362.

In 361 or 360, King Agesilaus died, and Xenophon wrote the *Agēsilaos* as a tribute to him. Another of his major works was probably completed in Corinth at about this time. *Hellēnica* (411-362 B.C.; English translation, 1685) was intended to complement and complete Thucydides' unfinished history of the Peloponnesian War and carry the narrative into contemporary times, ending with the Battle of Mantinea. The *Hellēnica* is generally considered to be inferior to its predecessor, however, because of Xenophon's open expressions of admiration for Sparta and dislike of Thebes.

The *Peri porōn* (c. 355-353; *Ways and Means*, 1832) is probably Xenophon's last work; most scholars believe that he died within five years of its completion. This essay addressing the financial difficulties of Athens in the mid-fourth century offers various remedies to aid in the city's recovery, including such practical suggestions as ownership by the state of a merchant fleet, more efficient working of the silver mines, and improvement in the status of resident aliens. Xenophon eloquently cites the benefits of peace, suggesting that a board of guardians be set up to help maintain peace. In conclusion, he advises the Athenians to consult the gods, an echo of the counsel Socrates had given the young aristocratic cavalryman about to seek his fortune in Persia.

Summary

Although Xenophon was a staff officer of considerable talent and wrote several essays relative to his profession, his most lasting achievements were in the field of historical writing. One of the pleasures of Xenophon, quite apart from the readability of his prose, is his variety; he was genuinely interested in many things and eager to impart to his audience as much information as possible.

Socrates had taught his students to seek out and learn the good, and this advice is reflected throughout Xenophon's works, whether he is discussing the management of horses or a household (*Oikonomiko*, c. 361-362; *Estate Management*, 1532), describing constitutions, or exploring the nature of tyranny (*Hierōn*, date unknown; *Hiero*, 1832). At various times, it has been fashionable among scholars to dwell upon Xenophon's limitations and to compare him unfavorably to Thucydides or Plato. Such comparisons are unwise, however, and further study impresses one with his versatility.

It is of interest that writers discussing Xenophon seem to fall naturally into one of two camps: those who concentrate on his military career and his more practical works and those who focus on his more philosophical writings. It is a measure of his complexity that the definitive biography of Xenophon has yet to be written.

Bibliography

Anderson, J. K. *Military Theory and Practice in the Age of Xenophon.* Berkeley: University of California Press, 1970. The title gives the focus of the work. This lengthy study (more than four hundred pages, including index and bibliography) is enhanced by diagrams of formations and battle plans, as well as nineteen black-and-white plates illustrating military costumes and weapons.

Higgins, W. E. *Xenophon the Athenian: The Problem of the Individual and the Polis*. Albany: State University of New York Press, 1977. This sympathetic study deals with Xenophon as a writer and a pupil of Socrates. The style is pleasant and clear. In addition to the index, the author's notes are extensive and impressive.

Hirsch, Steven W. "1001 Iranian Nights: History and Fiction in Xenophon's *Cyropaedia*." In *The Greek Historians, Literature and History: Papers Presented to A. E. Raubitschek*. Saratoga, Calif.: ANMA Libri, 1985. The focus of this study is on *The Institution and Life of Cyrus* and how the author thinks that it has been misunderstood by scholars unfamiliar with Persian history and traditions.

Jacks, L. V. *Xenophon, Soldier of Fortune*. New York: Charles Scribner's Sons, 1930. Xenophon's life is covered in its entirety in this accessible work, beginning with his initial meeting with Socrates. There is no real effort at analysis of Xenophon's works, and the scholarship is somewhat dated. Jacks concentrates on the *Anabasis* and is primarily interested in Xenophon's military adventures, which he treats in considerable detail.

Richter, Gisela M. A. *The Portraits of the Greeks*. Vol. 2. London: Phaidon Press, 1965. This book is useful for its illustrations, notably the one of two pillars, each topped with a portrait bust of Xenophon, who was described by several ancient writers as a very handsome man.

Strauss, Leo. *On Tyranny*. Ithaca, N.Y.: Cornell University Press, 1968. Xenophon's *Hiero* (sometimes spelled *Hieron*) is interpreted in detail, with an analysis of the text as well as a translation. Also included is an essay by another scholar, Alexandre Kojève, not only on Xenophon and his views on tyranny but also on Strauss' own interpretations. This volume is for the serious student of Xenophon.

_____. *Xenophon's Socrates*. Ithaca, N.Y.: Cornell University Press, 1972. In this study, Strauss continues his interpretation of Xenophon as a man who wrote well and with wisdom, an important author who adds to the understanding of his teacher, Socrates. The book contains an appendix and an index and is intended for a scholarly audience.

_____. *Xenophon's Socratic Discourse: An Interpretation of the "Oeconomicus."* Ithaca, N.Y.: Cornell University Press, 1970. Xenophon's *Oikonomiko*, although in the form of a Socratic dialogue, is sometimes dismissed as an enjoyable essay on estate management, complete with a description of the character of the dutiful wife. Strauss writes that its purpose is misunderstood. As with previous references, this work is intended for the better understanding of Socrates as well as Xenophon.

Dorothy T. Potter

XERXES I

Born: c. 519 B.C.; place unknown
Died: 465 B.C.; Persepolis
Areas of Achievement: Warfare and architecture
Contribution: Xerxes mobilized the largest army ever assembled in ancient times and marched against Greece; he crossed Thessaly and annexed Attica to the Persian Empire. Posterity remembers him for capturing Athens and burning the Acropolis and for building the magnificent Palace of Xerxes at Persepolis.

Early Life

Among Darius the Great's seven sons, Xerxes was the youngest of two claimants to the throne of Persia. He was the eldest among the four children born to Atossa, the daughter of Cyrus the Great, whom Darius had married upon accession to the throne. The other claimant, Artabazanes, was Darius' eldest son by the daughter of Gobryas, born when Darius was still a private individual. Of the two, Xerxes had a stronger claim for succession, not only because he had been born into the royal house and his line continued that of Cyrus the Great but also because he was an able individual. In his mid-twenties, he was assigned the governorship of Babylonia in preference to Artabazanes. By the time the question of succession arose, he had already governed this kingdom for twelve years.

A bas-relief in the Archaeological Museum in Tehran depicts Xerxes as the heir apparent: He stands behind his father's throne. The father and son occupy the pinnacle of a symbolic pyramid; below them are the nobles, priests, generals, and dignitaries. The bas-relief, two versions of which are in existence, is part of a larger picture in which the king gives audience to his subject nations on the occasion of the Now Ruz (Persian new year). The participation of Xerxes in the ceremony signifies Darius' attempt to create a mutual bond between the prince and the representatives of many nations bringing gifts to the court at Persepolis.

Xerxes was about thirty-seven years old when he became king upon Darius' death in 486. His assumption of power did not represent an easy transition: His own brother, Aryamen the satrap of Bactria, rose up against him and had to be brought within the fold. Following that revolt, Xerxes marched on Egypt, where a usurper had been ruling since 484—two years prior to the death of Darius. The Persian army defeated the pretender and devastated the Nile Delta. After destroying all Egyptian fortifications, Xerxes appointed one of his brothers, Achaemenes, satrap and then left Egypt. As a result of this revolt, Egypt lost its autonomy within the empire; Egyptian citizens, however, continued to enjoy their previous rights and privileges.

While still in Egypt, Xerxes was informed of a revolt in Babylonia; by then the revolt of a first leader had given way to that of a second, Shamash-eriba. Xerxes marched on Babylonia, defeated Shamash-eriba, and then treated the kingdom in the same way as he had Egypt. He went so far as to break with Achaemenian tradition—he removed the statue of Marduk, the god who had welcomed Cyrus to Babylon, and took it to Persia. Removal of the much-adored golden statue was tantamount to the demotion of Babylonia to the rank of a satrapy. Under Xerxes, therefore, both Egypt and Babylonia lost their status as autonomous kingdoms in the empire. After his return from Babylon, Xerxes no longer called himself "Lord of Nations." He was now "King of the Persians and the Medes."

Life's Work

After his conquests in Egypt and Babylonia, Xerxes intended to live a tranquil life and attend to matters of state. Exiled Greeks and other ambitious individuals holding prominent positions in Persia, Lydia, and Athens recognized a Persian victory in Europe as the avenue to their own success. Their efforts, therefore, were expended upon convincing the king that Persia, ruled by a divine king, was superior and could easily defeat Greece. After giving the matter thought and keeping in mind his father's defeat at Marathon in 490, Xerxes assembled the notables of the empire and announced his intention to invade Greece. He proposed to build a bridge of boats across the Hellespont for the army to cross and further announced that he intended to set fire to the city of Athens in retaliation for the burning of the temple and sacred woods of Sardis by the Ionians.

The nobles, except for the king's uncle, Artabanus, agreed with the king and praised his foresight and might. Artabanus, speaking from experience, reminded the assembly of Darius' fruitless pursuit of the European Scythians in the steppes beyond the Danube. He reminded Xerxes of the enormous loss of life that had resulted from that futile endeavor. He further disagreed with those who claimed that the Persians could defeat the Athenians at sea. His advice to the king was to adjourn the meeting and continue with his plans to unify the empire.

Artabanus' words angered Xerxes. He shouted at the aged warrior that no Persian should sit idle while foreigners infringed upon his domain and set fire to his cities. He recounted the great deeds of his ancestors and pledged to surpass them. The assembly agreed with the king's views that war with Greece was inevitable and compromise impossible. Either Persia had to rule Greece or Greece would rule Persia. Over the next few days, Xerxes won Artabanus' agreement and began preparations for a major invasion of Europe. The king's next four years were devoted to military preparations and to diplomatic negotiations before the invasion. These preparations included marshaling forces, digging a major canal at Athos to prevent the kind of disaster experienced by Darius, and dispatching envoys to certain Greek cities to demand "water and soil," that is, recognition of Persian suzerainty without recourse to war. Drawing on the satrap system, a system of government initially installed by Cyrus and later expanded by Darius, Xerxes assembled an army the likes of which, according to Herodotus, no one had seen or remembered. This army gathered at Sardis in the spring of 480 and from there, led by the king himself, set out for Europe.

Among the obstacles that barred access to Europe, the most awesome was the formidable Hellespont. Ten years before, in his invasion of Europe, Darius had bypassed the Hellespont and built a bridge on the Bosporus. Xerxes, however, had decided to cross the Hellespont on a bridge made up of warships. The first array of boats was easily washed away by stormy seas. For the lost ships and the wasted time, Xerxes had the two engineers responsible beheaded. He also ordered the sea to be whipped three hundred lashes to calm it. The second bridge, built with reinforced materials and heavy ropes, held for the seven days that it took the Persian army (estimated as anywhere from 360,000 to two million) to cross. The bridge was not disassembled so that, in the event of a Persian defeat, the king could return to Asia and not be stranded in Europe.

From Thrace, Xerxes circled the Aegean Sea. He crossed Macedonia and Thessaly, where he stayed while the army deforested the land and built roads. He then headed for Attica, accompanied by his fleet, which remained a short distance offshore.

The Greek states, knowing of the enormity of the invading land army, set their internal squabbles aside so that they could put up a united front against the Persians. The alliance, led by Sparta, chose the narrow pass at Thermopylae for the initial meeting with Xerxes. The Greek navy at nearby Artemisium was in constant contact with the land force.

Initially, the battle at Thermopylae did not go well for the Persians. Xerxes sent in a contingent of Medes for the first day and fielded his ten thousand Immortals the second day. Both failed to turn the tide. Worse yet, a significant part of the Persian fleet was destroyed in a storm. Undaunted, however, Xerxes continued to fight. After the third day, a large contingent of Persians, guided through a hidden path the previous night by a Greek defector, appeared on the mountain overlooking the pass. Its defenders found themselves trapped. Leonidas, the Spartan king in charge of the Greek contingent, marshaled the troops of Sparta, Thespiae, and Thebes to continue the defense of the pass. He sent the rest of his men to reinforce the allied army that would fight Xerxes beyond Thermopylae. Leonidas and his three hundred men fought bravely and died to the last man, allowing their compatriots time to withdraw to the narrow strait of Salamis. Attica, and consequently Athens, was left defenseless.

The Persian army, having lost four of Darius' sons at Thermopylae, entered Athens. Most of the inhabitants had already been evacuated. Those who remained took refuge in the Acropolis, the home of Athena, the patron goddess of the city. Xerxes, as he had vowed, burned the city and celebrated his conquest. He was now the only Persian ruler, indeed the only Asian ruler up until that time, to have set foot in Athens as a victor. He dispatched a messenger to Susa to apprise Artabanus, his vice-regent, of the victory.

Xerxes' celebration, however, was premature. He had won the battle at Thermopylae, but the war raged on. Artabanus, had been right. The devastated Persian fleet was no match for the Athenian navy, especially when the latter was led by Themistocles, a general who had fought Darius at Marathon and who had spent his life building a formidable navy to match Persia's land army.

At Salamis, what had remained of the Persian fleet was dragged into narrow straits, outmaneuvered, and rammed by stout Greek ships. Witnessing the destruction of their fleet, the Persians fled the scene. Xerxes feared that he might become stranded in Europe. He immediately withdrew to Thessaly and from there to Asia. His hasty departure left the outcome of the war uncertain, especially when Mardonius, whom Xerxes had left in charge of the European campaign, was killed at Platae.

Henceforth, Xerxes became absolutely disinterested in the war and its outcome. Approaching forty, he returned to his palaces at Susa and Persepolis and watched from the sidelines as his appointees fought the war. The hostilities continued for another thirteen years.

At Persepolis, Xerxes devoted his time to the completion of Darius' Apadana and to the construction of his own palace, a magnificent complex erected southeast of Darius' palace. He also became involved in domestic politics and in the affairs of the court. A partial history of these involvements, especially in relation to the Jews of Persia, is found in the Book of Esther. Xerxes also became involved in harem intrigue. This latter involvement resulted in his death: Xerxes was murdered by his courtiers, among them Artabanus, his minister, in 465. He was fifty-four years old.

Summary

Xerxes stayed in the wings for twelve years, administering the affairs of the kingdom of Babylonia. He watched his father's rise in power and prestige and his fall at Marathon. As king, he found himself on the horns of a dilemma. He had to choose between witnessing the demise of a disunited empire and attempting to rejuvenate it through war. In addition, he needed to show his people that he was the son of Darius and that he could surpass the deeds of kings of the past. Having already decided on a course of action, he revealed his plans and spent much time and energy preparing to bring them to fruition.

The goal of his European campaign was the capture of Athens and the destruction of that city in retaliation for the burning of Sardis. This goal, however, was in conflict with a larger goal nurtured by Greece—the replacement of the absolutism of the East with the free institutions of the West. Thus the victory in Athens had a bittersweet taste for Xerxes, who was compelled by circumstances to fight at Salamis against his wishes. His defeat at Salamis demoralized him to the point that he no longer recognized the potential of his enormous land army and the possibility of an eventual victory.

Against this background, it is doubtful whether Xerxes, on his own, could have prepared the army so that it could capture and burn Athens. Behind Xerxes was the formidable war machine of Darius, a machine created for the single purpose of reducing Europe to a Persian colony. Xerxes merely guided this instrument to its destined end and then into the ground.

Furthermore, Xerxes greatly underestimated the seriousness of the fragmentation that had occurred during the final year of Darius' reign. The defeat at Marathon was closely related to the unhappiness of the peoples of such well-established kingdoms as Egypt and Babylonia. Yet Xerxes took it upon himself to further belittle these nations by reducing them to the rank of satrapies.

Rather than trying his hand at world conquest, Xerxes could have drawn on his forte, administration. Instead, he made the same mistake that his father had made: He took on Greece in Europe. Under Xerxes, therefore, the empire continued to disintegrate. Lack of leadership and squabbles among the future claimants further weakened the empire and caused its eventual demise.

Xerxes' view of himself was different. Like Darius, he attributed his success as king to Ahura Mazda, his god. He could do no wrong. Although he exercised great restraint in judgment, he allowed himself to be influenced and used by others. His inflexibility and self-confidence, both deriving from the incredible numbers he commanded rather than from the strength of his policies or that of his allies, played a major role in his demoralization and downfall. After Salamis, the man who had considered himself a good warrior, excelling in horsemanship, archery, and javelin throwing, became a womanizer and a manipulator of lowly lives at his own court.

Bibliography

Burn, A. R. *Persia and the Greeks: The Defense of the West, 546-478 B.C.* London: Minerva Press, 1962. This book contains detailed discussions of the various aspects of Xerxes' rule and an especially informative section on his campaign in Europe. Includes maps, charts illustrating battle formations, and genealogies for the major figures.

Cook, J. M. "The Rise of the Achaemenids and Establishment of Their Empire." In *The Cambridge History of Iran.* Vol. 2, *The Median and Achaemenian Period.* Cambridge: Cambridge University Press, 1985. This article examines the principal sources on ancient Iran and the extent and composition of the empire. Toward the end, Cook assesses the leadership that enabled the Persians to form a great empire.

Frye, Richard N. *The Heritage of Persia.* London: Weidenfeld and Nicolson, 1962. Frye's account of ancient Iran is unique. It focuses on the eastern provinces of the ancient kingdom, but, unlike similar accounts, it is based on cultural, religious, and literary sources. The book is illustrated; it includes an index, maps, genealogies, and an informative bibliography.

Ghirshman, Roman. *Iran.* Baltimore: Penguin Books, 1957, 2d ed. 1961. In this account of Iran's prehistory to Islamic times, Ghirshman juxtaposes textual information and archaeological data to place ancient Iran in its proper perspective. The book is illustrated with text figures as well as with plates. It includes an index and a selected bibliography.

Green, Peter. *Xerxes at Salamis.* New York: Praeger Publishers, 1970. This is a unique, though somewhat biased, account of the logistics of Xerxes' campaigns in Europe; it focuses on the leadership of Themistocles and on the divergent ideologies of the belligerents. The book has poor maps, an index, and a bibliography; it is sparsely illustrated.

Herodotus. *The Histories.* Translated by Aubrey de Sélincourt. Harmondsworth, England: Penguin Classics, 1954, rev. ed. 1972. In this comprehensive classical account, Herodotus discusses Xerxes' planned invasion of Europe, his long march in Asia and Europe, his capture and burning of Athens, and his retreat to Asia. This book should be read alongside other authoritative sources. It includes poor maps but has a good index.

Hignett, Charles. *Xerxes' Invasion of Greece.* Oxford: Clarendon Press, 1963. This work deals exclusively with Xerxes and his campaigns against Greece. It critically examines previous research on Xerxes and discusses Xerxes' fleet, the number of infantry the king commanded, and the topography of Thermopylae and Salamis. The book includes a bibliography, a good index, and eight maps.

Olmstead, Arthur T. *History of the Persian Empire.* Chicago: University of Chicago Press, 1948. This detailed history of the Achaemenid period remains the chief secondary source for the study of ancient Iran. The book includes a topographical index, maps, and many carefully selected illustrations.

Warner, Arthur G., et al. *The Shahnama of Firdausi.* 9 vols. London: Kegan Paul, Trench, Trübner, and Co., 1905. This translation of Iran's major epic provides a wealth of information on ancient Iranian religion, social hierarchy, and military organization. It especially underscores the role of the king—an absolute ruler carrying out a divine decree.

Iraj Bashiri

YAQUT

Born: 1179; probably Syria
Died: 1229; Aleppo, Syria
Area of Achievement: Historiography
Contribution: A major compiler of geographical, historical, and ethnographic information, Yaqut was the first Muslim scholar to use an encyclopedic organization for his material. His work gives modern scholars the most comprehensive insight on the state of knowledge in the thirteenth century Islamic world.

Early Life

Yaqut ibn 'Abdallah was born of Greek parents. He is known by two different sobriquets indicative of uncertainty about his origins: al-Rumi ("the Roman" or "the Byzantine") and al-Hamawi, in reference to his claimed place of birth in Hama, Syria. Yaqut's early life was one of slavery in the service of a prominent merchant in Hama. (The name Yaqut means "ruby"; slaves often received names of gems or other precious objects.) Slavery in medieval Islam, however, did not necessarily imply the dire fate usually assumed by Western students. Yaqut's master quickly recognized his servant's scholarly inclinations and gave him a solid, practical education, whereupon he became the merchant's personal secretary for several years.

Yaqut and his merchant master moved to Baghdad around 1199. According to some sources, Yaqut married in Baghdad and fathered several children. When Yaqut reached his majority, however, his master, rather than endowing him with property and a place in the family inheritance order—gestures expected in the middle-class culture of the time—released Yaqut from his service. Forced to make his own way in the world, Yaqut took to wandering, copying and selling manuscripts for a living.

Yaqut's travels took him first to Oman and the island of Qeshm at the mouth of the Persian Gulf, where he appears to have attempted some merchant ventures. He was seen in Tabrīz, in northwestern Iran, in 1213. During the next two years, he traveled through Egypt, Palestine, and Syria. In 1215, in Damascus, Yaqut ran afoul of politics. At this time, he was a follower of the Kharijites, a fervently democratic, almost anarchist movement which violently rejected the idea of a caliphate based on descent from Muhammad. The Kharijites argued that the caliph could be anyone, even a non-Arab (which is to say, from among the great majority of Muslims), and that selection should be based strictly on merit.

Yaqut's Kharijite views did not sit well in Damascus, and he became embroiled in a fierce public quarrel that forced him to flee the city with the police on his heels. He withdrew all the way to the important library center of Marw in northeastern Iran, where he spent the next two years combing libraries. By 1218, Yaqut had reached the city of Khiva in Khwarizm, south of the Aral Sea. There, hearing of the impending advance of Genghis Khan and the Mongols, he decided to beat a hasty retreat back to Iraq.

Life's Work

The scholarly fame of Yaqut rests principally on two works, the better known of which is his geographical dictionary *Kitab mu'jam al-buldan* (1224, 1228; partial translation as *The Introductory Chapters of Yaqut's "Mu'jam al-buldan,"* 1959). The manuscript comprises some four thousand pages, with an introductory section discussing various theories of the nature of the world, followed by more than fourteen thousand entries. The second work is a dictionary of learned scholars, *Mu'jam al-udaba'* (*Yaqut's Dictionary of Learned Men*, 1907-1913), which covers about twenty-seven hundred manuscript pages and includes about one thousand important biographical sketches.

Yaqut completed the first draft of *Kitab mu'jam al-buldan* in Mosul in 1224 and the final version in Aleppo in 1228. The work is of particular significance because Yaqut was one of the last scholars in medieval Islam to have access to libraries east of the Caspian Sea—many of which were in long-established intellectual centers—before the Mongol invasions of that region which resulted in the loss of large amounts of material. Yaqut acknowledges in his introductory remarks that it was the intellectual environment of Marw which inspired him to write the work. It affords an unrivaled synopsis of what was known about the world, its structure, and its place in the cosmos, in the twilight of caliphal times.

Kitab mu'jam al-buldan is a much more organized study than some of its rambling predecessors in the broad fields of history, geography, and ethnography. The entries are arranged alphabetically, and most follow a consistent internal structure in which historical, cultural, and scientific material on each location is discussed and evaluated. Particularly with respect to cosmography and related questions about the nature of the earth, Yaqut often presents conflicting theories developed by earlier scholars.

Yaqut was more a compiler than a synthesizer of knowledge. He lived at a time when most of the creative impulse of Islamic culture in its youth had been spent, and scholars contented themselves with assembling the enormous mass of information gathered by preceding generations. In composing *Kitab mu'jam al-buldan*, Yaqut worked without official patronage or, indeed, much encouragement of any kind, a circumstance which explains his numerous caustic comments on the state of scholarship in Syria.

The introductory portions of *Kitab mu'jam al-buldan* represent a mix of Greek and Islamic learning. The cosmographical schemes show heavy Hellenistic influence. On other matters, Yaqut made extensive use of his Muslim predecessors. His material on oceanography, for example, comes almost verbatim from the writing of the eleventh century scholar al-Biruni, who flourished in the lands east of the Caspian. References on eastern Asia derive from the tenth century historian al-Mas'udi. Many of Yaqut's primary sources, however, have been lost or remain undiscovered.

Yaqut's Dictionary of Learned Men is among several such compilations from various periods in medieval Islam which provide valuable data not only on individual scholars and intellectuals but also on the general state of learning and the scholarly environment in those times.

After his return from Khiva, Yaqut spent the remainder of his life in Mosul and in Aleppo, Syria. It is said that in later life he was in a position to offer financial assistance to the widow and children of his former master, who had been left destitute.

Summary

Kitab mu'jam al-buldan has been acclaimed as one of the most complete and comprehensive statements of geographical knowledge to survive from medieval Islam. Muslim scholars from later generations utilized it extensively. Many Arabic editions, some of them abridged, have appeared. Western scholars have also made extensive use of the work and in some cases have attempted to reconstruct the histories of whole periods or regions based on its authority.

Yaqut's work is a valuable artifact of the knowledge of his age and, as such, has assisted Orientalists in identifying and, in some cases, eventually tracking down surviving manuscripts of authors once known only through his references. As new manuscripts are discovered, they generally confirm Yaqut's accuracy of reference and breadth of learning.

Bibliography

De Slane, Baron MacGuckin, ed. and trans. *Ibn Khallikan's Biographical Dictionary*. Vol. 4. London: Oriental Translation Fund, 1871. Contains a traditional biography of Yaqut, describing some of the influences on his career and his various activities. A good example of traditional biographical treatment of the figure.

Elahie, R. M. *The Life and Works of Yaqut ibn 'Abd Allah al-Hamawi*. Lahore, Pakistan: Punjab University Press, 1965. A biographical sketch together with some translated passages; one of the few sources on Yaqut in English.

Rosenthal, Franz. *A History of Muslim Historiography*. 2d rev. ed. Leiden, Netherlands: E. J. Brill, 1968. A broad survey covering such topics as the Muslim concept of history, the forms of Muslim historiography—such as annals and genealogies—and the wide-ranging topics addressed by Muslim historians (from astrology to political science). The frequent references to Yaqut as a source attest his importance, but no extended study of individual historians or their works is included. Index, but no bibliography.

Yaqut. *The Introductory Chapters of Yaqut's "Mu'jam al-buldan."* Leiden, Netherlands: E. J. Brill, 1959. Virtually the only readily available source on Yaqut in English. An exhaustively annotated translation of the portion of the *Kitab mu'jam al-buldan* which lays out Yaqut's cosmographical scheme. The introductory section is an excellent example of his dependence on Greek paradigms and his methods of citation of earlier Muslim writers. The notes are rich in citations of German- and Arabic-language studies, which constitute the bulk of research on this figure.

Ronald W. Davis

YEN LI-PEN

Born: c. 600; Wan-nien, Shensi, China
Died: 673; Siking, China
Area of Achievement: Art
Contribution: Yen Li-pen introduced a new sense of realism to portrait painting, a genre which he did much to develop during the period of the T'ang Dynasty.

Early Life

Yen Li-pen was born to a distinguished family of artist-officials. His father, Yen P'i, was a famous Sui Dynasty painter, calligrapher, and official, holding the title Vice-Director of Construction. Apparently, Yen P'i spent much time with his two sons, Li-te and Li-pen, training them in art and calligraphy. Li-pen's older brother, Yen Li-te (c. 580-656), rose to become President of the Board of Public Works and held the title Grand Architect during the early years of the T'ang Dynasty.

The first half of the T'ang Dynasty is generally considered to be one of the two most glorious periods in Chinese history, the other being the Western Han (206 B.C.-8 A.D.). During the period between 618 and 750, the T'ang rulers were committed patrons of the arts as well as conquerors who expanded China's frontiers. By the end of the seventh century, the Chinese Empire was one of the largest in world history. During the second half of the seventh century, moreover, the capital city, Siking (modern Sian), would become the most cosmopolitan city of its day and one of the most sophisticated cities of all time.

The first ruler, Li Yuan—known to posterity as T'ang T'ai Tsu (reigned 618-627)—rose to power primarily through the efforts of his young son, Li Shih-min. The Lis had been a powerful aristocratic family which had served the Sui but later joined in the rebellion against them. Led by Shih-min, the Li family succeeded in ending the Sui Dynasty and eliminating other potential claimants to the Chinese throne. Just when it appeared that Li Yuan was about to choose a son other than Shih-min to succeed him, the emperor suddenly became ill and died, and Shih-min quickly ascended the throne in 627. Though his reign was relatively brief (twenty years), it was an active and rich period in Chinese history, and T'ai Tsung, as Shih-min would be posthumously called, is considered to have been one of the brightest and most capable rulers in Chinese history.

Even before becoming emperor, Li Shih-min, who was then Prince of Ch'in, surrounded himself with numerous scholars, poets, and painters, perhaps in anticipation of his ascension to the Dragon Throne. One of the people whom the future T'ai Tsung called upon to serve him was the young Yen Li-pen. In 626, Li-pen was commissioned to paint a picture of eighteen famous scholars who had gathered at the prince's palace five years before. Although a scroll titled *The Eighteen Scholars at the Palace of Ch'in* bearing Yen's name is in the Taipei Palace Museum, most scholars agree that it is probably a Sung Dynasty copy. The original was good enough to establish Yen as one of China's greatest portrait artists, with his speciality being the depiction of famous historical personages. In 642, for example, he was assigned to paint the official portraits of twenty-four meritorious officials, and these were then placed in a "Hall of Fame" situated in the palace. With these and several other works, Yen established himself as China's first truly great portraitist.

Life's Work

Of the paintings by Yen Li-pen which have survived, the most famous is probably the series depicting thirteen Chinese emperors, beginning with Han Wen Ti (reigned 179-157 B.C.) and ending with Sui Yang Ti (reigned A.D. 604-618). Located in the Chinese collection of the Boston Museum of Fine Arts, the first six that have survived are probably later copies, but the last seven are generally acknowledged to be by Li-pen himself. Clearly, Yen was able to capture the unique personalities of each of his subjects. Moreover, his limited use of color and his technique for drawing faces and setting them up with appropriate backgrounds established the guidelines for such painting in China. Many Chinese, Japanese, and Western art critics consider the *Scroll of the Emperors* to be among the greatest masterpieces in all Chinese art history.

Not all Yen Li-pen's works were devoted to historical portraiture. Although none of these works has survived, he painted Buddhist and Taoist subjects with such great mastery that the catalogs of imperial art holdings during the period of the Northern Sung (960-1126) mention numerous selections with religious motifs by Yen Li-pen. Another subject matter apparently popular with Yen was the depiction of tributary missions from "barbarian" lands. During the apogee of the T'ang Dynasty (the years between 625 and 755), foreigners from all over the world came to China bearing tribute to the throne. These "exotics" came with great pomp and circumstance to Siking, bringing with them native goods. The "barbarians" would offer some of the goods to the emperor but would also trade other wares in Siking and other Chinese cities. On one occasion, upon the request of T'ai Tsung in 635, Yen painted a lion brought as a tribute from Sogdiana. Several copies of barbarian-related paintings by Li-pen are located in the Beijing and Taipei palace museums. The tribute missions were important to the T'ang emperors not so much because of any economic benefits the Chinese rulers would derive but more as a testament to the claim that the Chinese emperor ruled everyone "under Heaven." Yen's paintings were, therefore, valuable visual recordings of such events, and the Chinese ruler clearly prized them.

T'ai Tsung may have treated Yen Li-pen well, but there was no question that the artist was still not much more than a servant to the throne. On one occasion, it is said that while Yen was sweating and dirty, in the midst of painting, T'ai Tsung peremptorily summoned him to sketch an unusual bird which had settled onto a lake in front of the emperor. Perhaps because of this incident, Yen Li-pen is reputed to have lamented that he was known "only by painting as if I were a menial." He is said to have discarded his brushes in anger and counseled his sons not to pursue an artistic career. Recently, pointing to his later honors, scholars have expressed doubt regarding the accuracy of this anecdote. The fact is, however, that Chinese intellectuals made the distinction between scholars who painted as a hobby and those who did so for a living, with the latter class suffering in reputation. Unquestionably, most of Yen's paintings were in fact court-commissioned works, and it may be that Yen was embarrassed by this.

Despite his purported chagrin, one of Yen's greatest achievements is still another commissioned work. The earliest and probably best example of funerary sculpture in China is that of a set of bas-reliefs of T'ai Tsung's six chargers which was based upon Li-pen's sketches. The T'ang emperor was particularly fond of horses, and it is likely that he commissioned Yen Li-pen to make a drawing of his horses to serve as the design for subsequent carving. Most art critics are in agreement that the reliefs are based on Yen's drawings; thus, he can be credited with originating the finest stone sculpture work of the T'ang. Four of the horses are in the Shensi Provincial Museum at Sian; the other two are at the University of Pennsylvania Museum in Philadelphia. It may also be that Li-pen painted some of the murals for T'ai Tsung's mausoleum, but they are now lost. That Yen's work was well received can be inferred from the fact that Yen himself is buried not far from the emperor's tomb at Chao-ling.

If Yen was humiliated by T'ai Tsung's use of him principally as a painter, then he must have been more satisfied during the period subsequent to T'ai Tsung's death in 649. Under the nominal rule of Emperor T'ang Kao Tsung (649-683)—in actuality power lay in the hands of Empress Wu—Yen Li-pen rose to important official positions. In 656, upon the death of his brother Yen Li-te, Li-pen became President of the Board of Public Works. While it is true that this position did not carry with it much political power, it certainly was beyond the reach of all but a few of China's scholar-official elite. In 668, Li-pen became prime minister of the right (there were two prime ministers at the time), and in 670 he was appointed secretary general of the secretariat. It is possible, however, that despite these honors the stigma of being a "commissioned painter" never quite left Yen Li-pen, for a saying of that time derided the minister of the left as being incompetent and the minister of the right as getting his job through the use of "cinnabar and blue."

In 673, Yen Li-pen died and was buried with the highest possible honors, obtaining the posthumous title of *Wen Chen*, or True Scholar. As noted above, his burial in the vicinity of T'ai Tsung's tomb is an indication that he was highly respected by Empress Wu. Such honors were enough to guarantee wealth and prestige to the Li family for several generations, but none of his children or grandchildren enjoyed any particular fame. Perhaps they had heeded Li-pen's admonition against pursuing a career in art. The legacy of Yen Li-pen, however, has endured and grown.

Summary

Yen Li-pen was one of the great luminaries of the culturally resplendent T'ang Dynasty. Perhaps in order to downplay the T'ang imperial family's Turkic and therefore "barbarian" origins, the imperial court tended to be a very active sponsor of the arts. Being great patrons of Chinese culture may have been an attempt to compensate somehow for such questionable heritage. During the early years, however, such support was not without limitations. The T'ang rulers—in particular T'ai Tsung—handled Chinese artists and poets as if they were hirelings who were at the beck and call of the Dragon Throne. This must have rankled men of great artistic ability, and no doubt Yen Li-pen must at least on occasion have felt maligned and insulted.

One wonders, however, whether Yen's scholarship alone would have been enough to earn for him the very high official positions he attained. At the time he was being rewarded with such honors, the Chinese court, under Empress Wu's prodding, was moving increasingly toward a very rationalized system of bureaucracy, one which rewarded scholarship and knowledge of the Confucian Classics. There is no record or even indication that Yen Li-pen was subjected to rigorous civil service examinations. One can therefore assume that Yen arose to his position primarily by virtue of his reputation as an artist. Being a commissioned painter, therefore, led to a career success which few other painters in Chinese history would enjoy.

It was court sponsorship which enabled Yen to paint and develop his unique style of portraiture, a style which would be emulated but not equaled by subsequent Chinese portrait painters. In several cases, it was also court action which guaranteed that his works would survive. What the artist's sensitivity could not well endure his admirers, and those who are grateful that Yen's works are still extant, can understand and forgive.

Bibliography

Bush, Susan. *The Chinese Literati on Painting: Su Shih (1037-1101) to Tung Ch'i-ch'ang (1555-1636)*. Cambridge, Mass.: Harvard University Press, 1971. This study, based on the author's Harvard thesis, quotes several Chinese scholars' views of Yen Li-pen. Includes illustrations and a bibliography. Part of the Harvard-Yenching Institute Studies series.

Cahill, James. *An Index of Early Chinese Painters and Paintings*. Vol. 1,

T'ang, Sung, and Yuan. Berkeley: University of California Press, 1980. Contains a lengthy list of paintings and other works by Yen Li-pen which are held in museums and private collections. Includes a twelve-page bibliography.

Loehr, Max. *The Great Painters of China*. New York: Harper and Row, Publishers, 1980. Contains an excellent account of Yen Li-pen's career together with several photographs of paintings and works which are attributed to him. Includes an index and a bibliography.

Sirén, Osvald. *Chinese Painting: Leading Masters and Principles*. Vol. 1, *The First Millennium: Early Chinese Painting*. New York: Ronald Press, 1956. This volume, by a leading historian of Oriental art, contains a glowing assessment of Yen's work. Illustrated, with a bibliography.

——————. *A History of Early Chinese Painting*. New York: E. Weyhe, 1932. Volume 1 contains a fairly lengthy account of Yen's career and impact on Chinese painting, together with examples of his work. The bibliography, naturally, is dated.

Sullivan, Michael. *A Short History of Chinese Art*. London: Thames and Hudson, 1973. Contains a brief passage about Yen Li-pen with an example of his work. The volume includes seventy-two pages of plates and maps.

Waley, Arthur. *An Introduction to the Study of Chinese Painting*. New York: Grove Press, 1958. Excellent discussion of Yen Li-pen and his impact on Chinese art. The volume contains forty-nine plates. Brief bibliography. Author has also written on Chinese history, philosophy, poetry, and plays.

Hilel B. Salomon

YO FEI

Born: 1103; China
Died: 1141; Hangchow, China
Area of Achievement: Warfare
Contribution: The Chinese general Yo Fei was killed in prison by members of his own government during a war against an external army. Since that time he has been hailed as a symbol of patriotic resistance to foreign invaders.

Early Life

One of the exemplary heroes of Chinese civilization is Yo Fei, also known as Yüeh Fei. The many myths and legends surrounding his life make it difficult to see the real man, and not much is known of his early life. Modern biographers accept that his father, Yo Ho, was a farmer of modest wealth. The family property was damaged by a flood when Yo Fei was an infant, and his mother narrowly escaped with her child by floating to safety in a large water jar.

Although he did not pursue a career in the civil service, Yo Fei was apparently well educated by his father in the literary, historical, and military classics. The discipline and dedication of the young student and devoted father can be seen in the formation of an impressive writing style, evidenced by the extant specimens of his calligraphy. In addition to his scholarly interests, the young Yo Fei had unusual physical strength and became highly skilled in archery, swordsmanship, and the use of the lance.

At age nineteen, Yo chose the military route to prominence when he volunteered to serve in a special force that sought to seize Peking from the Khitan state (Liao Dynasty) in the northeast. Although the campaign failed in its objective, Yo was impressed with the great city to the north and remained with his commander, Liu Chia, in what amounted to police action on the frontier between their Sung regions and the Khitan, a federation of nomadic Mongolian tribes. During this campaign, Yo demonstrated a remarkable military skill, which prompted many tales of courage and daring. Prior to the end of his nineteenth year, however, as a result of his father's death, he returned home to attend to the needs of his mother and family. During the four years that he remained with his family, 1122-1126, one foreign invader replaced another in China. In 1123, the Juchen from Manchuria overthrew the Khitan with some assistance from the Sung. This move was soon recognized as an error, and the Sung withdrew southward, establishing the Southern Sung Dynasty (1127-1279) and seeking to hold the area north of the Yangtze River to the Huai River. This action resulted in a fierce and extended war between the Sung and the Juchen and prompted Yo Fei's return to military service.

Life's Work

From his return to the field in 1126 until his death in 1141, Yo Fei occupied a prominent place in the military history of the Southern Sung Dynasty. Personality conflicts among the ambitious officers complicated the command system, however, and for a brief period Yo moved out of the official army to become the commander of an independent army unit on the frontier. Eventually he would return to the ranks and establish an army that enjoyed a wide and prestigious reputation for its spirit, discipline, and striking power. Under his leadership, his army was reported to have never suffered a defeat. According to his grandson, Yo built his army upon the following principles: careful selection, careful training, justice in rewards and punishments, clear orders, strict discipline, and community of both pleasure and toil. Yo was widely known for sharing with his troops the fortunes and misfortunes of war. He slept where they slept, ate what they ate, and inflicted a fair but severe justice. On one occasion he sentenced his son to be decapitated for permitting his horse to stumble during military exercises. His son was spared only by the pleadings of the other generals.

Yo's early education led him to welcome scholars and civilians to his various camps. He reportedly sought their advice and used them to relate tales of past military heroics to the troops. A portion of his spare time was spent in the writing of poetry and music, some of which survives as early symbols of Chinese nationalism and patriotism. His goal was a unified China under an emperor who would be a scholar, warrior, and statesman; undoubtedly, he saw himself in that role. With the confidence of success behind him, Yo went so far as to recommend to Emperor Kao Tsung that he seek to meet that ideal more effectively. From 1129 to 1134, Yo Fei's army operated in the valley of the Yangtze River and on the frontier between the Southern Sung Dynasty and the Juchen, who were now identified as the Chin Dynasty. This period was marked by Yo Fei's struggles against independent military units similar to those he had previously commanded and by general frontier lawlessness. In 1134, Yo was named regional commandant and directed a number of major campaigns against the Chin and their Ch'i buffer state, which had been established between themselves and the Southern Sung. Here he achieved his greatest military reputation, directing large forces and coordinating with other armies to drive forcefully into northern China, his target being Peking. The rallying cry of the campaign—"Give us back our rivers and mountains!"—came from one of his poems, an expression that remains symbolic as a cry of Chinese nationalism.

It may have been Yo's great successes, however, that contributed to his downfall and death. The campaign of 1140 proved especially effective, with his army driving far north into Chin areas along the Yellow River. This invasion encouraged the Chin to establish negotiations with the government of the Southern Sung, an opportunity that the latter seemed eager to pursue if for no other reason than to slow the successes of an ambitious and powerful general. While the army was in the field, a treaty was concluded that provided for the withdrawal of the Sung army from the Chin areas in the north. Emperor Kao Tsung had decided upon retrenchment rather than restoration. This decision may have been motivated by the fact that the Chin were holding the emperor's older brother captive; should the army of Yo Fei have proven too successful, the emperor would probably have been forced to surrender his throne. The emperor used his chief councillor, Ch'in Kuei, to negotiate a settlement with the Chin that effectively made the Southern Sung a vassal state of the Chin. Yo had little choice except to withdraw or lose his command. The army pulled back but protested what was widely regarded as a traitorous peace. As a result of this protest, a number of leading generals, Yo Fei included, were removed from military command and relocated to civilian posts. Loyal subordinate officers objected to this action, and rumors of plots began to emerge, including one alleged plan by Yo's principal lieutenant, Chang Hsien, and Yo's son Yo Yun, which resulted in their arrest and public execution. Yo Fei was himself soon identified as having been a party to the rumored plot and was imprisoned. Two days before the end of the year, he was murdered.

Summary

Although the details of Yo Fei's death are obscure, the traditional account relates that the arrangements for his murder were included in the negotiations and agreement between the Chin and Ch'in Kuei. The Chinese therefore universally view Ch'in Kuei as the quintessential traitor, while Yo Fei is depicted as the ideal patriot and national hero. Late nineteenth and early twentieth century groups which organized to oppose foreign exploitation of China took his name as the symbol of their cause. As the Chinese depend heavily upon models, imitation, and precedent to teach, Yo Fei has been an enduring subject, combining those values that are so much a part of Confucian China: discipline, courage, loyalty to parents, self-sacrifice, harmony with one's community members, intense dedication to vocation, scholarship, and strength. Yo Fei is the subject of numerous plays, novels, and poems, and there are many temples that stand in celebration of his defense of his country. He remains a powerful symbol of Chinese nationalism and resistance to foreign invaders.

Bibliography

Eberhard, Wolfram. *Conquerors and Rulers: Social Forces in Medieval China*. Leiden, Netherlands: E. J. Brill, 1952. An excellent study of the social aspects of medieval China. Eberhard is the leading Western scholar of Chinese folklore and in this study provides insight into a society receptive to myth, legend, and heroics.

Latourette, Kenneth Scott. *The Chinese: Their History and Culture*. 4th ed. New York: Macmillan, 1962. An outstanding overview of Chinese history and culture that places Yo Fei in a historical perspective. Features a valuable bibliographical format.

Rodzinski, Witold. *The Walled Kingdom: A History of China From Antiquity to the Present*. New York: Macmillan, 1984. A recent history of China which contains an excellent chapter on the Sung dynasties and the northern invaders. Briefly discusses Yo Fei's role in the wars between the Sung and the Chin and the significance of Yo's historical image.

Ruhlmann, Robert. "Traditional Heroes in Chinese Popular Fiction." In *The Confucian Persuasion*, edited by Arthur F. Wright. Stanford, Calif.: Stanford University Press, 1960. An important study of selected heroes in Chinese fiction. Places emphasis on historical and legendary examples of princes, scholars, and swordsmen. Stresses that Yo Fei's achievements are important to the Chinese because they are humanly possible, not miraculous.

Wilhelm, Hellmut. "From Myth to Myth: The Case of Yüeh Fei's Biography." In *Confucian Personalities*, edited by Arthur F. Wright and Denis Twitchett. Stanford, Calif.: Stanford University Press, 1962. A brilliant analysis of Yo Fei's role in Chinese history. This essay is the best English-language source of information on Yo. Compares the historical and mythical factors surrounding his life and career and explains how he created a myth of himself, his army, and his cause for later generations.

Frank Nickell

YUNG-LO
Chu Ti

Born: 1363; Nanking, China
Died: 1424; Peking, China
Area of Achievement: Government
Contribution: Combining traditional Chinese and Mongol ideas of imperial
rule, Yung-lo brought the Ming Dynasty to its height, making it notable
for the caliber of its ministers, internal improvements, support of the arts,
and domestic stability.

Early Life

Chu Ti, who upon ascension to the throne in 1402 took the reign name
Yung-lo (meaning "eternal joy") and later received the temple name Ch'eng-
tsu ("completing ancestor"), was born in the Imperial Palace in Nanking, China, in 1363. He was the fourth son of Chu Yüan-chang, known as
Hung-wu, who was shortly to become the first Ming emperor, and a Korean
palace concubine. A northerner and a commoner whose family background
included lower-class Yangtze artisans and Huai River (northern Anhwei
Province) tenant farmers, Chu Yüan-chang had emerged from a background
of abysmal poverty, seeking refuge for a time in a Buddhist monastery where
he received a rudimentary education. Subsequently, he lived by his wits,
eventually establishing a rebel power base in his northern home district.
Before he was forty, by adroit selection of comrades and great military skill,
he became the master of Han lands along the Yangtze, successfully expelled
the Mongols (thus causing the collapse of the Yüan Dynasty), and seized
power.

Chu Ti's early years were shaped by his father's sometimes savage efforts
to found and stabilize what he designated as the Ming, or "brilliant,"
Dynasty—which would, in fact, last until 1644. Conscious of the internal
dynastic rivalries of his Yüan predecessors, Chu Ti's father centralized
authority in his own hands, maintained the loyalty of ministers and other officials by frequent bloody purges, and dispatched all of his sons to separate
princely fiefs, except the heir apparent.

As Prince of Yen, Chu Ti ruled over Peking, not then the capital, and the
region surrounding it. It was essentially a northern border post, and although
the princes were not entrusted with civil administration, they were responsible to their father for the military security of their regions. Meanwhile, they
were further educated both by members of the military aristocracy and by
Confucian scholars. Nevertheless, military exigencies proved the dominant
formative influence, for Chu Ti spent much of his early life in military campaigns and earned his initial reputation from them.

Placed in command in 1390 and again in 1391, he led notable expeditions against the Mongols, who—although previously defeated by his father—were not quiescent. Following his father's massive purges of allegedly subversive nobles and military officials during the early 1390's, designed further to concentrate power in his own hands, Chu Ti, as a result of the shake-up, was given command over all troops within his fiefdom, along with generous subsidies of land and grain, a substantial administrative staff, and a body of princely guards. Thus, Chu Ti developed a powerful base for himself in a northern region, a region not only preferred by his father but also considered by most Chinese to be the heart of their civilization.

The final years of his father's reign were pacific ones. Chu Ti's last victorious patrol north of the Great Wall was in 1396, and thereafter there was a general stacking of arms. Still, the problem of succession was seriously unsettled when Chu Ti's father died in June, 1398. The chief difficulty, as he himself had feared, was the power of Chu Ti and the other princes, whom—with prospects of their plotting in mind—he had previously banned from attending his funeral.

Twenty-one, gentle, scholarly, and eager to profit from his elders' excesses, the dead emperor's grandson and heir Chien-wen nevertheless immediately sought to impose his authority over his uncles, the princes. Five of the leading princes were systematically stripped of their support while another died, leaving Chu Ti the oldest survivor, the most dangerously situated strategically and the most popular and powerful.

Seeking to isolate him too, Chien-wen and his advisers hoped to provoke him into a rebellion they believed they could crush. Overconfident, they rashly sent a force against Chu Ti in the summer of 1399 which Chu Ti ambushed and destroyed. Declaring that he was merely trying to liberate the new emperor from bad advisers, Chu Ti, as the Prince of Yen, took to the field, and for the next three years civil war raged in North China, essentially a conflict between north and south.

Notwithstanding serious handicaps, Chu Ti maintained himself against imperial forces, generally defeated them, and, in January of 1402, was able to commence precarious drives south across the Hwang River toward the Yangtze River, Soochow, and Nanking. In July, 1402, Nanking capitulated. The emperor and empress purportedly died in the blaze of the Imperial Palace, and the northern rebel, the Prince of Yen, assumed the Ming throne.

Life's Work

Hung-wu, the first Ming emperor, was forty when, as a rebel, he seized the throne; Yung-lo was forty-two and, like his father, a rebel destined to rule for two decades (from 1402 to 1424). A large, strong, active man, Yung-lo profited from his physical presence, his military reputation, and his capacity for ruthless action, and in these respects he also resembled his father. Yet he evinced a greater confidence, more control of his temper, and a more sensitive ability to work effectively with subordinates.

Nevertheless, Yung-lo's reign opened with a bloody purge of Chien-wen's supporters. He reduced the remaining princes to mere figureheads and precluded any future threats to the stability of government from imperial family members or from within either the civil or the military establishment. Inevitably, this meant a further concentration of power in his own hands, but it was precisely that which permitted a resumption of the sounder policies of his predecessors and encouraged the return of stability within the empire.

Because his own power base had always been in the north, Yung-lo transferred the capital from Nanking to Peking in 1407, gradually leaving only the heir apparent and his entourage in Nanking. Peip'ing Province was transformed into a metropolitan area and given a functional importance as the seat of government which was confirmed when it was officially designated the capital in 1421. The recovering Mongols also lent impetus to Yung-lo's shift of power to Peking. To counter their perpetual menace, he made Peip'ing Province the mainstay of his northern, hence major, defense system. After 1407, therefore, both personal predilection as well as security considerations kept him continuously based in his new capital.

Relocation northward brought substantial logistical problems. Previous establishment of sizable mercantile colonies along the northern frontier, plus his predecessors' upgrading of regional agriculture, meant that the transport of grain by sea around the Shantung Peninsula—for generations a costly expedient because of losses from pirates, rebels, and weather—had become unnecessary. The presence of officials and the growing military establishment in the Peip'ing metropolitan area required new, assured avenues of supply.

To develop these avenues, Yung-lo mobilized the Yangtze naval command to reinstitute sea transport of the capital's grain supplies while simultaneously reconstructing inland waterways that were inadequate or had fallen into desuetude. His Minister of Works, Sung Li, and Ch'en Hsüan, the Yangtze commander who had surrendered to Yung-lo in 1402, began reconstruction of the Grand Canal, which had silted so badly that it was unnavigable. A system of forty-seven locks was brilliantly engineered so that after 1415 grain shipments could be delivered directly into the Hwang River, precluding further perilous sea journeys around Shantung and ensuring the capital's sustenance.

Yung-lo dealt with potentially menacing or factious neighbors by resorting both to diplomacy and to force. In the north, he was able to extend indirect Chinese influence by successfully wooing Jurchen tribesmen, who, although previously under Mongol influence, had by 1402 come more under the influence of Korea. Offering them commercial inducements and incorporating them into Ming militia units, he brought them under Chinese overlordship by 1415. In addition, Mongols who had been settled between the Great Wall and the Liao River while retaining their own chieftains were encouraged to assimilate to Chinese organization; others, such as the Urianghad Mongols, were rewarded for having served as Yung-lo's cavalry by a grant of independence within the Peip'ing regional military organization. Still other such tribes were relocated farther in the interior under Chinese supervision.

More important were the menacing remnants of the Yüan Dynasty's forces composed of Eastern Mongols, or Tatars, and the Western Mongols, or Oirats. Since far to the west Tamerlane had conquered much of the Middle East, Syria, and parts of India, the great danger to Yung-lo was Tamerlane's potential for deploying various of these Mongol peoples against him. Indeed, Tamerlane had been preparing such a campaign when, fortunately for Yung-lo, he died in 1405. Taking no chances, however, Yung-lo personally led forces beyond the Great Wall into the Gobi Desert in attempts to keep various Mongol chieftains, particularly the Tatar Arughtai, divided and off balance.

Northern frontiers solicited no more of his attention than did those to the south. Since the 1370's, Annam had been rent by dynastic quarrels which by Yung-lo's ascension involved his government. Annamese refugees in China urged Yung-lo to intervene in the restoration of their legitimate ruler, and in anticipation of Chinese interference, Le Qui-ly, the Annamese usurper, launched spoiling attacks along China's southern border. Chinese envoys dispatched to seek a peaceful solution to the problem in 1406 were murdered.

Retaliating, Yung-lo, from bases in Kwangsi and Yunnan, invaded Annam, crushed the opposition, and, failing to discover an acceptable replacement for Le Qui-ly, absorbed Annam as a new Chinese province in 1407. Thousands of well-educated Annamese, many of them possessing superior knowledge about firearms, were brought into the employment of Yung-lo's government. Such actions did not stabilize the situation, and not even the best Chinese administrative and military talents could prevent the outbreak of guerrilla resistance, the deterioration of China's position, and, after Yung-lo's death, the loss of the province.

Despite his background, events make it clear that Yung-lo preferred the extension of Chinese influence through diplomacy, commerce, and other peaceful means. After years of tensions between his father and a Japan torn by political tumults, Yung-lo was pleasantly confronted by the new Ashikaga shogunate, which had reunified Japan in 1392 and which sought amicable relations. In 1403, Japanese plenipotentiaries arrived in Peking to announce that the shogun recognized himself as a subject of Yung-lo and was eager for close commercial relations. These were sanctified the following year, with the result that Japanese fleets were permitted periodic visitations to Ningpo to trade and deliver tribute. The shogun even hunted down Japanese pirates who for generations had scourged the China littoral and delivered them for punishment to Peking. Such idyllic conditions dissipated with the succession of a new shogun in 1408, and thereafter relations cooled. The shogun rejected a tributary position and ignored the pirates' return to their enterprises.

Two of Yung-lo's remarkable eunuchs acted as emissaries and spread his influence into other parts of Asia. Beginning in 1403, when several fleets were sent to ports in Southeast Asia and Javanese and southern Indian ports, an unprecedented extension of China's naval activities commenced. A number of expeditions were led by Hou Hsien, who had previously journeyed to Tibet and Nepal, and by the famed Muslim admiral (also a eunuch) Cheng Ho, who had been in Yung-lo's service since he was a boy. Between them, Hou and Cheng, often with great fleets, tens of thousands of personnel, and vessels of immense size (440 feet in length, 186 in beam), traveled to thirty-seven countries, including a number on Africa's west coast, in Zanzibar, and in the Persian Gulf—the last being Mecca.

These voyages were indisputably profitable in terms of tribute, commerce, and the emperor's prestige. Occasionally these voyages encouraged the use of Chinese force: the suppression of pirates in Sumatra, intervention in a Javanese civil war, the capture of a hostile Ceylonese ruler for imprisonment in Peking, and assistance to local rulers in quelling domestic rebellions. Yet they were mostly peaceful and instructive, exotic adventures that lasted from 1403 until Yung-lo's death although the indefatigable Cheng Ho continued voyaging after 1424.

After a vigorous reign generally marked by domestic stability and prosperity, Yung-lo died in the autumn of 1424 as the result of an illness contracted on a campaign waged north of the Great Wall against Mongol tribesmen.

Summary

Yung-lo's two decades of rule consolidated Ming power. In many ways, his reign was the apogee of the Ming Dynasty. He persisted in concentrating authority in his own hands, thus ensuring continuation of an absolutism characteristic of his father, the dynasty's founder. Yung-lo was, however, less barbarous. There were fewer sanguinary purges during his reign, and a stabler environment developed in which his ministers could work more effectively. By relying heavily upon eunuchs and military officers to implement his initiatives, he permitted the civil service to function somewhat apart and to cohere around Confucian principles: to recruit and indoctrinate through the *chin shih* examination system and to serve according to it, thus allowing it to evolve its own institutional ideology and esprit.

In part, these developments account for the unusual official longevity of Yung-lo's secretaries and ministers in their posts. There were two vitally important long-term consequences of these conditions. First, in a positive sense, the civil service was rendered more capable of removing from the emperor the daily burdens of administering justice, handling financial problems, and attending to the routines of governing. Second, in the process of assuming such responsibilities, the civil service became—although not during Yung-lo's regime—a powerful political force that was able to control and even thwart emperors.

Without question, Yung-lo's military and diplomatic actions aggressively secured China's borders, even extended them somewhat, while establishing China's presence throughout Asia and parts of the Middle East in an unprecedented fashion. In the fifteenth century no other power could claim influence over such vast areas and numerous populations. The immediate import of this was domestic security and tranquillity. China ceased for a time to be torn by dynastic successions, warlords, powerful rebellions, and governmental incompetence. Inevitably, after Yung-lo's death, there was an erosion of some achievements: Annam fought its way out of the Ming grasp, Japan's shoguns withdrew from their subjection to Peking, and the several major Asian tribes to the north, west, and southwest remained actual or potential menaces and kept Ming borders in constant jeopardy.

More lasting was Yung-lo's consolidation of the Yüan absolutism that had characterized the rule overthrown by his father with an evolving Confucian, or scholars', bureaucracy. Together, they defined much of the character of Chinese government for centuries.

Bibliography

Dreyer, Edward L. *Early Ming China: A Political History, 1355-1435*. Stanford, Calif.: Stanford University Press, 1982. Scholarly and eminently readable, this volume is one of the most extensive English-language studies of its subject. While lacking maps, it has detailed notes, an excellent annotated bibliography, a standard character list, and a very useful index.

Hucker, Charles O. *The Censorial System of Ming China*. Stanford, Calif.: Stanford University Press, 1966. A detailed scholarly examination of a central Ming political institution. Essential reading for those wishing more than a survey of the Ming Dynasty. With an adequate glossary, notes, and an index.

_____. "Governmental Organization of the Ming Dynasty." *Harvard Journal of Asiatic Studies* 21 (1958): 25-73. A scholarly, interpretive overview, very useful for understanding conflicting perspectives on early Ming institutions. Includes useful footnotes.

_____. *The Ming Dynasty: Its Origins and Evolving Institutions*. Ann Arbor, Mich.: Center for Chinese Studies, 1978. Written originally for *The Cambridge History of China*, this extended essay by a leading scholar of the Ming Dynasty is both readable and clearly organized. With brief but useful notes.

_____, ed. *Chinese Government in Ming Times: Seven Studies*. New York: Columbia University Press, 1969. Excellent scholarly essays on various aspects of Ming development, such as Ray Huang's "Fiscal Administration During the Ming Dynasty." Contains useful notes and an index.

Needham, Joseph. *Science and Civilisation in China*. Vol. 4, *Physics and Physical Technology*. Cambridge: Cambridge University Press, 1971. This work is part of a classic scholarly series. The third part of this volume, *Civil Engineering and Nautics*, contains wonderful coverage of the technology underlying Yung-lo's overseas adventures, such as naval architecture, navigation, astronomy, and cartography. Includes excellent notes, a bibliography, and an index.

Clifton K. Yearley
Kerrie L. MacPherson

ZEAMI MOTOKIYO

Born: 1363; Nagaoka, Yamishiro Province, Japan
Died: 1443; Kyoto, Honshū Province, Japan
Areas of Achievement: Theater and drama
Contribution: A great actor and a great dramatist, Zeami was also an outstanding teacher of acting and a theoretician of theatrical aesthetics. He established the Nō (*sarugaku*) form of drama, which has survived to modern times.

Early Life

Little is known of Zeami Motokiyo's birth and early life. His great-grandfather was the lay priest Keishin, Kamajima Kagemori, the lord of the fief of Asada in Iga Province. Zeami was the son of Kan'ami, an actor, playwright, teacher, and leader of the Yamato *sarugaku* troupe. His mother was Yasaburō Ukikujo, the daughter of a priest who was the lord of the fief of Obata. At a tender age, Zeami was put into the hands of Yasaburō Katsukiyo, the leader of the Konparu troupe, to be trained as an actor.

During the late 1360's and early 1370's, Kan'ami's genius began to be recognized, and he and his troupe became very popular in Kyoto and its environs. Soon Zeami was acting on the stage with his father, and the precocious youngster was attracting unusual attention. In 1374, the troupe gave a performance at the Daigoji Buddhist temple, southeast of the capital, that was witnessed by Ashikaga Yoshimitsu (1358-1408), who had become the shogun (generalissimo, or military dictator) at the age of ten. Almost seventeen years old and already an important patron of the arts, Yoshimitsu was amazed and enchanted by the beauty, charm, and talent of the eleven-year-old Zeami. As a result, the shogun became Zeami's patron, as well as his friend and companion.

Yoshimitsu's affection for Zeami was so openly displayed that some of the court nobility (*kuge*) were annoyed. They were particularly critical of the military nobility (daimyo) for trying to please the shogun by giving expensive presents to Zeami. Their objection to the intimate relationship between Yoshimitsu and the boy actor was not, as one might suppose, to any homoerotic possibilities in it but simply to Zeami's low-class status as a commoner and an actor.

Ironically, Zeami was actually the descendant of feudal lords of the Ōta clan and of royal blood. This family of daimyo had descended from Minamoto Yorimasa (1106-1180), who was famous both as a poet and as a warrior. The Minamoto branch had descended from Sadazumi-shinno (874-916), the son of the emperor Seiwa. It had produced the three shogun families of Minamoto, Ashikaga, and Tokugawa. Kan'ami, however, had deliberately kept his family line secret from Ashikaga Yoshimitsu when he had founded his *sarugaku* dramatic troupe.

At least one old aristocrat was not repelled by the mixing of social classes at the court: the poet Nijō Yoshimoto, who proved an enthusiastic admirer of the young actor. A letter exists in which Yoshimoto expresses his delight in the company of Zeami, referring to him, however, by the name "Fujiwaka," which had been conferred on him by Yoshimoto himself:

Should Fujiwaka have time, please bring him over with you once again. The entire day was wonderful, and I quite lost my heart. A boy like this is rare— why look at his *renga* and court kickball [*kemari*], not to mention his own particular art! Such a charming manner and such poise! I don't know where such a marvelous boy can have come from.

In the same year (1378), the retired emperor Sukō, who had reigned at Kyoto from 1349 to 1352, was informed of a *renga* session held at Yoshimoto's residence in which Zeami was a participant. As host, Yoshimoto would produce the first two lines of a proposed five-line poem. As guest, Zeami was obliged to produce the final three lines and link them to the first two. The emperor recorded his opinion of Zeami's skill in his diary, stating that the boy's linkages were "inspired" and copying a pair of the poems the two composed as examples. However inspired Zeami's linkages may have been, they show that he understood thoroughly the rules for *renga* compositions and sought to adhere strictly to them. This contest between a common teenager and a senior court noble required much self-confidence and poise on Zeami's part.

In 1384, Kan'ami died at the age of fifty-one. Zeami, who was then twenty-one, was obliged to assume the responsibility of the leadership of the Kanze troupe.

Life's Work

As leader of the Kanze *sarugaku* troupe, Zeami proved highly successful. Although he lost an important supporter with the death of Yoshimoto in 1388, he retained the patronage of Yoshimitsu. The first documented reference to Zeami—he was then known as Kanze Saburo—as an adult performer occurred in 1394, when it was said that he gave a performance during Yoshimitsu's pilgrimage to Nara. In 1399, he gave two performances, both witnessed by Yoshimitsu. From 1400 to 1402, Zeami wrote his first treatise on the aesthetics of the Nō, *Fūshikaden* (also known as *Kadensho*; English translation, 1968), which purported to transmit the teachings of his father. In this work, he introduced the concept of *ka*, or *hana*, literally meaning "flower." In his aesthetics, however, the symbol of the flower referred to the freshness and charm evoked by the actor's performance. Zeami followed the lead of Kan'ami, who had chosen his stage name by selecting the first character of the name of the bodhisattva Kanzeon. Zeami selected the second character of the same name. The sound of this character was unvoiced as "se," but, according to tradition, Yoshimitsu advised Zeami to voice the sound as "ze"; therefore, his name became "Zeami," instead of "Seami."

Yoshimitsu had abdicated the shogunate in 1395 in favor of his son Yoshimochi, who was then nine years old. Nevertheless, he continued to rule under the title of prime minister. Even when a year or so later he had his head shaved and became a bonze at Toji-in, a Buddhist temple of the Shingon sect, he still ruled from the splendid palace at Kitayama, which the people called Kinkakuji, or Golden Temple. During an emperor's visit there in 1408, a *sarugaku* performance was given in which the Kanze troupe no doubt took part. Not long after this performance, Yoshimitsu died (1408), at the age of fifty. Thus Zeami lost the powerful ruler who had been his friend and patron for so long.

Although Zeami faced competition for the shogun's favor from other acting troupes, he and his Kanze players fared well during most of Yoshimochi's rule (1408-1428). In 1422, at the age of fifty-nine, Zeami retired as leader of the Kanze troupe. He immediately took Sōtō Zen vows to become a lay Buddhist priest. His gifted son Kanze Motomasa succeeded his father as the leader of the Kanze troupe. At this time, also, Konparu Zenchiku (1405-1468) must have married one of Zeami's daughters. Actor, playwright, and critic, he was to become a model son-in-law to the aging Zeami. It should be recalled that Zeami had a connection with the Konparu troupe as a young child, a tie which no doubt accounted for his daughter's marriage to Zenchiku.

Upon the death of Yoshimochi, his brother Yoshinori was chosen to succeed him. With the advent of Yoshinori's shogunate, Zeami and his sons began to be treated badly. In 1429, Yoshinori sponsored a grand *sarugaku* performance at the Kasakake Riding Grounds. Two Kanze troupes participated in this competition against two other troupes. This performance was odd in that it was done in the style of Tōnomine, the mounted characters riding live horses and wearing real armor. Motomasa and Zeami in some way displeased and angered Yoshinori. Not long afterward, the shogun retaliated. He ordered that both of them be excluded from the Sentō Imperial Palace, which was the residence of the retired emperor. No sooner had they been banned from the palace than Onnami, the son of Zeami's brother Shirō, began to perform there. Further, in 1430, Motomasa had the musical directorship at the Kiyotaki shrine taken from him. It was then conferred on Onnami. Motomasa was now apparently forced from the capital. He retired to Ōchi, in the province of Yamato.

Zeami's troubles continued. Later in the year 1430, his second son, Motoyoshi, who had been acting with the Kanze troupe, became discouraged with his career as an actor, apparently believing himself lacking in talent. He thereupon retired and took Buddhist orders. Worst of all for Zeami was the death of Motomasa in 1432. It seems probable that Motomasa had been banished from the capital because of suspected ties with the southern dynasty. Perhaps fear for his life made him retire to the protection of the lord of Ōchi. Shortly before his death, he gave a performance at the Tennokawa shrine, not far from Yoshima, where the southern dynasty had established its court. Following his performance, he said a prayer and left a mask at the shrine. Afterward, he died in the province of Ise, possibly the victim of murder. Zeami not only grieved for his dead son but also worried that no one would carry on the Nō tradition and the subtle art he had made of it.

Perhaps as important as any political factors that might have made Yoshinori reject Zeami and his sons was the refusal of Zeami to recognize the shogun's favorite as Motomasa's legitimate successor. Yoshinori was deficient in elegant, stylish knowledge (*yabo*). He lacked the connoisseurship (*tsū*) required to appreciate the kind of artistry practiced by Zeami. Before he became shogun, his favorite theatrical performer had been Enami. After Enami died in 1424, Yoshinori supported Onnami, because he liked the demonic plays he regularly presented. Demonic plays depended more on realistic miming than on symbolically significant acting, dancing, and words. Zeami rejected demon characters altogether in his Nō drama. Furthermore, he rigidly opposed Onnami's becoming leader of the Kanze school and refused to turn over the Kanze secret treatises to him, giving them to his son-in-law Konparu Zenchiku instead. Onnami considered himself a legitimate member of the Kanze school. He had chosen his stage name by selecting the third syllable of the Kanzeon name, just as Kan'ami had taken the first and Zeami the second. Zeami once stated that the Kan'ami-Zeami artistic line had been brought to an end with Motomasa's death, and, in his short treatise *Kyakuraika* (1433; the flower of returning), Zeami was even more adamant on this point. Zeami's opposition to Yoshinori's will must have angered the shogun considerably. Despite Zeami's resistance, Onnami eventually became leader of the Kanze school.

At any rate, in 1434, Yoshinori banished Zeami (then seventy-one years old) to Sado, a large island on the west coast of Japan which for years had been a place of exile for important personages. How long he lived on Sado and when he returned to the mainland—if he did return—is unknown. It is certain that he was exiled for at least two years, for he left a record of his exile in *Kintōsho* (1436; the book of the golden isle). This work consists of eight pieces meant to be recited and sung in the Nō style, and their formal character keeps the reader at some distance from Zeami's personal experience. He discloses no bitterness over his fate and views himself as part of the tradition of the personages who had also been exiled on Sado. Toward the end of his collection, he even adopts a hopeful and lighthearted tone. One tradition affirms that Zeami sent this collection to his friend Ikkyū (Sōjun), a notable Renzai Zen Buddhist priest and poet in Chinese, for editing. Ikkyū, also a friend of Konparu Zenchiku, is said to have given Zeami's pieces to the emperor, who was so impressed by them that he pardoned Zeami. If this legend is true (it appears plausible enough), then Zeami probably returned to the mainland about 1437. According to tradition, he died in Kyoto in 1443.

Zeami had a high reputation as an actor in his time, but his acting method and style can only be imagined from his plays. As a playwright, he excelled. Not only are his plays well received in modern time but they are also superior in literary value to other extant Nō plays. Although some ninety Nō dramas have been attributed to Zeami, only about twenty can be specifically identified as his; about thirty-five others, however, can be considered almost certainly his. Occasionally Zeami did adapt the plays of others to suit his own purposes. Also, the sources of Nō plays were strictly conventional, and the playwrights typically chose material from specific classic Japanese narratives (which often included poems), as well as from certain ancient Chinese and Japanese verse.

Typical of those plays which are specifically identified as Zeami's or which can reasonably be considered his are *Atsumori* (English translation, 1921), *Hanjo* (*Lady Han*, 1970), *Kinuta* (English translation, 1917), *Kiyotsune* (English translation, 1955), *Oimatsu* (*The Old Pine Tree*, 1962), *Sekidera Komachi* (*Komachi at Sekidera*, 1970), *Tadanori* (English translation, 1934), *Takasago* (English translation, 1955), and *Izutsu* (*The Well Curb*, 1917).

Practically nothing was known of Zeami's important contributions to aesthetics until the beginning of the twentieth century. Between 1908 and 1909, Yoshida Tōgo discovered sixteen of Zeami's critical treatises. He published these as *Nōgaku koten: Zeami jūrokubushū* (1909; "Zeami's Sixteen Treatises," 1941-1942). In 1945, Kawase Kazuma discovered seven additional Zeami texts, which he published as *Tōchū Zeami nijūsambushū* (prologue to Zeami). Two of these texts are spurious, and one is fragmentary. A more accurate version of one of these, *Shūgyoku tokka* (finding gems and gaining the flower), was discovered in 1956, and a full version of the partial text, *Go on* (five sounds), was published in 1963. In 1984, J. Thomas Rimer and Yamazaki Masakazu published an excellent English translation of seven of Zeami's better-known texts that treat the essentials of acting.

Zeami used the term "flower" (*ka*, or *hana*) as one of his central concepts and "mystical beauty" (*yūgen*) as another. By *hana*, he meant the effect the actor ought to have on his audience. By *yūgen*, he meant the ideal beauty the actor ought to exude from within himself. *Yūgen* would be evident in the grace of his movements, in the elegance of his clothing, and in the gentleness of his voice. The word Nō literally meant "ability," or "talent." As a dramatic form, Nō grew out of both *dengaku*, or field music, and *sarugaku*, or comic entertainment, to become *sarugaku no nō*, or Nō. There are two types of *sarugaku*: Nō, a kind of opera combining acting, dancing, and singing, and *kyōgen*, an improvised comic drama with some singing and dancing. Nō employs a stylized literary language; *kyōgen* uses colloquial language. The actors in Nō wear masks, but in *kyōgen* they do not. In Nō the characters are supernatural beings, famous men and women of the Heian period, and celebrated warriors. In *kyōgen*, the characters range from daimyo and their followers to monks, thieves, artisans, and peasants.

It was Zeami who developed Nō in a direction different from the *sarugaku* of his father, Kan'ami. He avoided the confrontation of two characters and developed dramatic tension from the anguished self-examination of one. He developed an economy of presentation that amounted to asceticism, since it was a transposition of aesthetic values through the medium of secularized Buddhism. His critical treatises were designed to pass on his tradition to his heirs. To Zeami, art was a way toward human perfection.

Summary

Building on his father's work, Zeami Motokiyo revolutionized the Nō drama. He made it respectable, an entertainment for the elite. He also pointed the way to its perfection. The idea of *yūgen* figured more prominently in his Nō than in Kan'ami's. The severe training that Zeami demanded of his students derived from the "difficult practice" of secularized Zen Buddhism as opposed to the "easy practice" of Pure Land Buddhism—burning incense, prayer, recitation of the Buddha's name, and reading of Scripture—so popular with the masses. This difficult practice required discipline, asceticism, composure of body and mind through silent meditation, and the disappearance of the self. It appealed to the samurai class. Zeami replaced the traditional heroes of the masses with the warrior heroes—Atsumori, Tadanori, Yorimasa—or with the classical figures of Heian court culture.

In addition to his fine plays, Zeami left critical treatises both on the aesthetics of Nō and on the art of acting. Although he inherited the affective-aesthetic poetics of Ki no Tsurayuki's preface to the *Kokinshū* (c. 905), with Tsurayuki's terms *kokoro* (heart), *tane* (seed), and *kokoba* (words), he went beyond Tsurayuki's idea that Japanese poetry takes the human heart as its seed, or effecting cause. Zeami held that in Nō the seed was artistic performance (*waza*). In Nō performance, the *yūgen* (mystic beauty) issued from the human heart and produced the *hana* (flower). Zeami replaced Kan'ami's *monomane*, or realistic miming, with the idea of the actor fulfilling a role by intuitive feeling and artistic acting.

The Nō drama survives in present-day Japan, and even the Kanze school is still existent (a Nō performance in modern times, however, is much slower than it was in the medieval era). Nevertheless, some 250 plays constitute the present repertoire. There are god plays, warrior plays, woman plays, lunatic plays, revenge plays, and some other kinds. Further, the Nō has influenced twentieth century Western drama, most notably through the works of William Butler Yeats and Ezra Pound.

Bibliography

Hare, Thomas Blenman. *Zeami's Style: The Noh Plays of Zeami Motokiyo.* Stanford, Calif.: Stanford University Press, 1986. Superb study of Zeami's career and artistic contributions.

Ishibashi, Hiro. *Yeats and the Noh: Types of Japanese Beauty and Their Reflection in Yeats' Plays.* Edited by Anthony Kerrigan. Dublin: Dolmen Press, 1966. An interesting study of Japanese aesthetic influence.

Keene, Donald, ed. *Nō: The Classical Theatre of Japan.* Palo Alto, Calif.: Kodansha International, 1966. An authoritative, substantial study of the Nō drama. With photographs by Kaneko Hiroshi.

——————. *Twenty Plays of the Nō Theatre.* New York: Columbia University Press, 1970. Includes good translations of Zeami's work.

Nippon Gakujutsu Shinkokai, trans. *The Noh Drama: Ten Plays from the Japanese.* Rutland, Vt.: Charles E. Tuttle Co., 1960. Excellent translations by the Japanese Classics Translation Committee.

Nogami, Toyoichiro. *Zeami and His Theories of Noh.* Translated by Matsumoto Ryozo. Tokyo: Hinoki Shoten, 1955. Deals with the ideas of Zeami's *Fūshikaden*, or *Kadensho*.

O'Neill, P. G. *Early Nō Drama: Its Background, Character, and Development, 1300-1450.* London: Lund Humphries, 1958. Important treatment of early Nō drama essential for understanding how Nō survives today.

Pound, Ezra, and Ernest Fenollosa, trans. *The Classic Noh Theatre of Japan.* New York: New Directions, 1959. One of the landmarks in the introduction of Japanese theater in the West. Despite Pound's lack of knowledge of Japanese, he had an intuitive understanding of and sensitivity to the spirit and form of Nō.

Ryūsaku, Tsunoda, et al., eds. *Sources of Japanese Tradition.* Vol. 1. New York: Columbia University Press, 1958. Includes excellent translations of important Zeami treatises, such as "On Attaining the Stage of *Yūgen*," "On the One Mind Linking All Powers," "The Nine Stages of Nō in Order," and "The Book of the Way of the Highest Flower."

Yeats, William Butler. *Plays and Controversies.* Rev. ed. New York: Macmillan, 1924. Contains Yeats's four plays for dancers and the music for *At the Hawk's Well* (1916) and *The Dreaming of the Bones* (1919). The influence of Zeami is clearly present in these works.

Zeami, Motokiyo. *Kadensho.* Translated by Sakurai Chuichi, Hayashi Shuseki, Satoi Rokurō, and Miyai Bin. Kyoto: Sumiya Shinobe Publishing Institute, 1968. One of Zeami's most influential treatises.

——————. *On the Art of the No Drama: The Major Treatises of Zeami.* Translated by J. Thomas Rimer and Yamazaki Masakazu. Princeton, N.J.: Princeton University Press, 1984. Excellent translations of nine of Zeami's treatises that deal with the essentials of acting.

                                                                                  Richard P. Benton

ZENO OF CITIUM

Born: c. 335 B.C.; Citium (modern Larnaca), Cyprus
Died: Probably fall, 261 B.C.; Athens
Area of Achievement: Philosophy
Contribution: Zeno founded Stoicism, the leading Hellenistic school of philosophy. Though not the school's greatest thinker, he created its unified, systematic teaching and guided it to prominence.

Early Life

While a full biography of Zeno of Citium cannot be written from the anecdotes and sayings collected in late antiquity, principally available in the work of Diogenes Laërtius, much can be learned from a critical reading of them. Diogenes quotes the honorific inscription that dates Zeno's death as well as the statement of Zeno's disciple Persaeus of Citium that the master lived to be seventy-two, which dates his birth. Nevertheless, there is no information about his childhood; even the name of his mother no longer survives. Mnaseas, his father, has a name ambiguously meaningful both in Phoenician (equivalent to the Hebrew Manasseh, "one causing to forget") and in Greek ("mindful," a strong opposition). Mnaseas, contemporary with Citium's last Phoenician king, under whom the town was besieged and burned by Ptolemy Soter of Egypt in 312 B.C., may have initiated the family's break from Phoenician and commercial to Greek and philosophical culture: The name he gave his son has no Semitic meaning but refers to the Greek god Zeus and was celebrated in a famous syncretic hymn by Zeno's disciple Cleanthes. In one story, Mnaseas brought many books by Socratic writers back from Athens for Zeno. In another story, Zeno himself, shipwrecked on a commercial trip to Athens, consoled himself in a bookstore with Xenophon's *Apomnēmoneumata* (c. 381-355 B.C.; *Memorabilia*) and rushed to follow the Cynic philosopher Crates of Thebes, when Crates was pointed out as a living Socratic teacher. Persaeus said that Zeno was twenty-two when he came to Athens; he never seems to have left. His arrival would have been in 311, the year after Citium fell to Ptolemy.

The failure of the records to mention close relationships with his parents or others may be significant: Stoicism was to teach, as Cynicism had, individual self-sufficiency and rational discipline of the emotions. Socrates was the type of this life: Personally ugly but desirable, ethically committed but unwilling to be called a teacher or to write anything, sealing his commitment to philosophy with his death at the hands of democratic Athens, Socrates was publicized by his followers, including Plato and Xenophon, and became the personal inspiration of all the fourth century schools of philosophy. Plato's Academy was almost a formal alternative to the city-state which had killed its greatest thinker, and Aristotle's Lyceum was modeled on it. The Cynics, on the other hand, avoided institutional encumbrances, living and teaching in public to a scandalous degree: Their name means "doglike." In a symbolic story, Zeno, soon after he became Crates' follower, modestly covered his teacher and Crates' student-bride Hipparchia with a cloak as they consummated their "dog-wedding" in public in the Stoa Poikile. Cynics, including the young Zeno, maintained the ill-dressed, voluntarily poor, and combatively questioning, even anti-intellectual stance they claimed to derive from Socrates' teachings.

Zeno's Cynic period culminated before 300 in the publication of his most notorious book, *Politeia* (the republic), a short work denouncing then current methods of education and calling for a city of wise men and women without temples, courts, or gymnasiums, with the god Eros to be honored by friendship and polymorphous, unrestricted sex. Zeno also studied and perhaps enrolled in the Academy (studying Plato's dialogues, dialectical method, and metaphysics—including incorporeal ideas as causes for physical events, which he rejected) and followed the dialectical teachers Diodorus Cronus and Stilpo, who arrived from Megara about 307. Their advanced modal logic, however, proved a form of determinism Zeno found unacceptable. By about 300, Zeno, in his early thirties, was able to declare his independence from other teachers and begin his regular strolls up and down the Stoa Poikile with his own students.

Life's Work

The professional career of a philosopher is rich not so much in public as in internal events, and Zeno's development is hard to follow in the absence of extensive or datable writings. *Politeia* came early, and it was widely enough quoted that a dozen or more of the extant fragments of his writings can be identified as belonging to it; none of the other twenty-four titles of his canon allows for as definite a reconstruction. He was a powerful teacher, famous for an epistemological demonstration in which he closed one extended hand by stages and then steadied the fist with his other hand while he named the corresponding stages of knowledge: "An impression is like this; assent is like this; cognitive grasp is like this; and science is like this; and only the wise man has it." He established, for all Stoics except his unorthodox pupil Aristo of Chios, the three-part division of philosophy into logic (philosophy of language and meaning), physics (philosophy of nature—including theology, since spirit as breath and *logos* as creative word are bodies and also divine), and ethics (the famous division of things into good, bad, and indifferent; the development of the Cynic's "life according to nature" as the only virtuous and happy way of life). To a degree not approached by Plato, by Aristotle, or by his contemporaries the Cynics, Megarians, Epicureans, and Skeptics, Zeno made of these subjects a single, unified whole, giving priority neither to metaphysics—as with Plato and Aristotle—nor to ethics—as with the

Epicureans. The system was seen as dogmatic, and debate with Stoicism played a large part in the Academy's move into skepticism from the 270's. The dogmatic system was not perfected by Zeno himself: He left his logic rudimentary, to be developed by his successor's successor, Chrysippus; among other changes, later Stoics softened the antisocial side of his ethics toward a propriety more acceptable to dignified Roman adherents such as the Gracchi, Seneca the Younger, and Marcus Aurelius.

Zeno was remembered for his pithy comments about and to his students; these observations were perhaps made more pointed by his Phoenician accent and manners, which he never tried to overcome. During his thirty-nine years leading the school, his oval face hardened into the philosophic persona visible in surviving portraits. It is not a handsome face: The forehead recedes, the frown lines are pronounced, the expression seems severe or even morose; the neck bends forward, and Diogenes says that it crooked also to one side, adding that Zeno was rather tall, thin but flabby, and dark-complected. Self-control was the main attribute he projected. He lived on bread, water, and "a little wine of good bouquet"—coming from a commercial family, he seems never to have been really in want—avoiding dinners and drinking parties except when his pupil and patron, the Macedonian prince Antigonus Gonatas, the future King of Macedon, insisted. Zeno is said to have had a weak constitution—justifying his abstemiousness—but also to have been in good health until his death, which was voluntary and in response to a trivial fall that he took as a divine sign. As for his pleasures, they included green figs and sunbaths and boy slave-prostitutes, whom he "used sparingly." He did, to be sure, state in *Politeia* that Eros is a god of constructive political friendship, and he is recorded to have been in love with Chremonides, later the instigator of Athens' last, ill-starred war against the dominion of Macedon.

Zeno's school had a different sort of corporate existence from the more settled Academy, Lyceum, and Epicurean "Garden," of which the first two were technically sodalities of the Muses and Apollo meeting in public gymnasiums (religiously consecrated exercise grounds particularly used by Athenian *ephebes* in their compulsory military and civic-religious training), the last Epicurus' private house and garden, later inherited by the school's leaders. Zeno, barred as a foreigner from owning property and perhaps drawn to the Stoa Poikile from his studies with Crates, chose that public facility for his lessons. The Stoa Poikile was a sizable building (accommodating meetings of at least five hundred people) on the northwest corner of the Athenian civic center (Agora), with an open colonnade facing south across the Agora toward the Acropolis temple complex; the structure was roofed, with walls on three sides hung with paintings (hence the name Poikile, "decorated"), by Polygnotus and other masters, of great historical and mythic battles, which often suggested reason defeating emotion. It was fitting that this should be the scene for what amounted to a radical shift of the city from historical, civic excellence to philosophy. Since the building did not belong to them in any sense, the Stoics (as they came to be called in preference to "Zenoneans") must have done their administrative and library work elsewhere. In Zeno's time, given his Cynic background, administration must have been slight, though books were always important to this scholarly sect.

One sort of student was easy to find at the Stoa Poikile: The years after 307 marked the end of the compulsory *ephebeia*, and eighteen- to twenty-year-olds would have found themselves drawn to public lounging areas such as the Stoa Poikile. As a philosophical organization, however, the Stoa was formidably professional, and Zeno seems, according to remarks such as his threat to charge passersby for listening, to have discouraged random crowds. Most of his known disciples came from abroad—including non-Greek places such as Citium, Zeno's own home—drawn, as Zeno had been, by published books and Athens' educational reputation. The most illustrious of these people was Antigonus Gonatas, who was in Athens as overlord but who thought of himself as a Stoic and employed Zeno's fellow Citiote, housemate, and disciple Persaeus as a tutor for his son and even as a general. Of the more modest sort were Persaeus himself (sometimes rumored to have been Zeno's slave); Cleanthes of Assos, who made a living at the waterworks so as to be in Athens to hear Zeno lecture and who inherited Zeno's position as leader of the school; Aristo of Chios, who set up a rival school teaching ethics; and Sphaerus, the specialist in definition who advised Sparta's revolutionary, land-reforming king, Cleomenes III.

Summary

Athens, during Zeno of Citium's fifty years there, passed through upheavals that largely left him untouched: Demetrius Eukairos, the philosopher-tyrant, was succeeded by a rivalry of democrats (who initially illegalized philosophy schools), oligarchs, and moderates, while the port of Piraeus was constantly garrisoned by Macedon. William Scott Ferguson counts seven changes of government and four of constitution, three bloody uprisings, and four sieges during this period—with Zeno, though the teacher of a major warlord, never taking any prominent part. The turmoil may already have had for him the unreal quality it acquires in retrospect; the impassive Stoic (and stoic) remains.

Zeno did influence Hellenistic politics, however, contributing some enlightenment to what would in any case have been despotisms. It is important that he did not solve all the questions he addressed but left the school with room for future development over several generations: Forward-looking, even arrogant, thinkers liked the dynamic and the sense that human action is cosmically purposeful and significant, though Epicureans and Skeptics demurred. The detailed contributions of the Stoic thought that Zeno either began or left for great successors to begin are great. Finally, Athens honored him after his death with statues in the Academy and Lyceum, a public tomb, and a resolution praising him as a teacher of virtue and temperance who had lived the morality he taught.

Bibliography

Arnold, E. Vernon. *Roman Stoicism: Being Lectures on the History of the Stoic Philosophy with Special Reference to Its Development Within the Roman Empire*. Cambridge: Cambridge University Press, 1911. The fourteen pages on Zeno are nearly the longest essay on him in English, and the book—in spite of its title—is a classic treatment of Greek Stoicism in a religious context that was deemphasized in later English philosophical treatments. The chronology needs to be revised from later works.

Camp, John M. *The Athenian Agora: Excavations in the Heart of Classical Athens*. London: Thames and Hudson, 1986. Photographs and discussion of the Stoa Poikile, where excavation began in 1981, in the context of extended archaeological presentation of the city center. A good background for the narratives of Ferguson, Tarn, and Walbank.

Diogenes Laërtius. *Lives of Eminent Philosophers*. Translated by R. D. Hicks. Cambridge, Mass.: Harvard University Press, 1925. The only English translation in print of the main source of information on Zeno. Includes symbolic anecdotes and apothegms in the same relation to Zeno as the Gospels are to Jesus. Hicks's terminology is not always philosophically sophisticated and should be compared to that of Long and Sedley.

Dudley, Donald R. *A History of Cynicism from Diogenes to the Sixth Century* A.D. London: Methuen and Co., 1937. Reprint. Hildesheim, West Germany: Olms, 1967. The most vivid historical presentation in English of the philosophical environment in which Zeno studied. Includes bibliographical notes and appendices.

Ferguson, William Scott. *Hellenistic Athens: An Historical Essay*. London: Macmillan, 1911. A classic narrative, never superseded though Walbank and others have improved the chronology and updated the bibliography. Chapters 2 through 4 constitute the history of Athens in Zeno's time and pointedly end with his death. In the absence of a modern biography of Zeno, this work and Tarn's study are the two most extensive substitutes.

Hunt, H. A. K. *A Physical Interpretation of the Universe: The Doctrines of Zeno the Stoic*. Melbourne, Australia: Melbourne University Press, 1976. Though philosophically and historically naïve, this is the only English monograph on Zeno. Not a biography, it presents 105 of the fragments of his teaching in acceptable translations, with commentary and a limited bibliography.

Karageorghis, Vassos. *Kition: Mycenaean and Phoenician Discoveries in Cyprus*. London: Thames and Hudson, 1976. The dean of Cypriot archaeologists surveys Zeno's hometown with photographs, references, and bibliography. Useful as background, although no treatment of Zeno himself.

Long, A. A., and D. N. Sedley. *The Hellenistic Philosophers.* Vol. 1, *Translation and Principal Sources with Philosophical Commentary.* Cambridge: Cambridge University Press, 1987. The results of a generation's study of Stoicism are presented in the central 280 pages. Philosophically illuminating, not concentrating on the philosophers' personality or history. Contains a good glossary of technical terms, lists of philosophers and ancient sources, and a panorama of Athens showing the locations of the schools. Short bibliography.

Richter, Gisela M. A. *The Portraits of the Greeks.* 3 vols. London: Phaidon Press, 1965. Volume 2 presents the known ancient portraits of Zeno (except for a group of carved gems) and supports the author's detailed description of Zeno's physiognomy, which, absent further data, must stand for his character to some extent.

Sandbach, F. H. *The Stoics.* New York: W. W. Norton and Co., 1975. The short opening chapter mentions most of the data, though the death date should be brought down probably to 261. The volume is competent, though not as vivid as Dudley's (whose coverage it does not duplicate).

Tarn, William Woodthorpe. *Antigonos Gonatas.* Oxford: Oxford University Press, 1913. A classic biography by an admirer of Alexander the Great and Hellenism, fitting Antigonus into the mold of adventurous, enlightened prince and featuring Zeno as one of his teachers and a member of his circle. Chronology and bibliography to be supplemented from Walbank.

Walbank, F. W., A. E. Astin, M. W. Frederiksen, and R. M. Ogilvie, eds. *The Cambridge Ancient History.* Vol. 7, *The Hellenistic World.* 2d ed. Cambridge: Cambridge University Press, 1984. A useful, long chapter on the period of Antigonus places Zeno's adopted home in perspective with his princely student. Includes chronological improvements on Tarn's and Ferguson's works. Chronological chart, immense bibliography.

Owen C. Cramer

ZENO OF ELEA

Born: c. 490 B.C.; Elea
Died: c. 440 B.C.; Elea
Area of Achievement: Philosophy
Contribution: Although Zeno cannot be said to have succeeded in defending Parmenides' doctrine of the one, his paradoxes are still remembered, and his method of argument influenced all later philosophy.

Early Life

Little is known of Zeno's life. In the early fifth century, when he was young, Greek philosophy was still in its cruder, experimental form, sometimes mythological, even borrowing from Oriental lore, sometimes resembling primitive science by trying to explain the physical world and basing its conclusions on observation if not on experiment. One tendency was to try to explain all material phenomena as variations on one particular element. Thus, Thales of Miletus taught that all material things were derived from water; Anaximenes of Miletus taught that all things were derived from air; and Heraclitus of Ephesus, though his philosophy was by no means as simple as those of his predecessors, thought that all things were derived from fire. Empedocles, on the other hand, rejected the idea of any single element as the source of all and saw the material world as the result of the mixture and separation of four elements: earth, air, fire, and water.

Zeno's master, Parmenides, rejected this notion of multiplicity in favor of a fundamental unity. His arguments, which were placed in a mythological setting and expressed in hexameter verse, have survived only in fragments; they are exceedingly involved and hard to follow but perhaps can best be summarized as saying that multiplicity is illogical, self-contradictory, or merely unthinkable. This leaves the one, which is not water or air or fire but simply is "being"—"individual, changeless, featureless, motionless, rock-solid being." Multiplicity, however, if contrary to logic, is nevertheless a fact of experience, and Parmenides apparently undertook to give a systematic account of it. A modern thinker might say that the world of reason and the world of experience were mutually exclusive and could never be reconciled.

Life's Work

Despite the paucity of biographical information about Zeno, Plato's dialogue *Parmenides* (c. 360 B.C.) reports the conversation of Socrates—then a young man—and the visiting Parmenides and Zeno. In that account, Zeno is described as "nearly forty years of age, tall and fair to look upon; in the days of his youth he was reported to have been beloved by Parmenides." In the dialogue, having finished reading aloud from his works, written in his youth, Zeno frankly explains their origin and his motive:

The truth is, that these writings of mine were meant to protect the arguments of Parmenides against those who make fun of him and seek to show the many ridiculous and contradictory results which they suppose to follow from the affirmation of the one. My answer is addressed to partisans of the many, whose attack I return with interest by retorting upon them that their hypothesis of the being of many, if carried out, appears to be still more ridiculous than the hypothesis of the being of one.

After Zeno confesses that his arguments were motivated not by "the ambition of an older man, but the pugnacity of a young one," Socrates endeavors to sum up Zeno's arguments:

Do you maintain that if being is many, it must be both like and unlike, and that this is impossible, for neither can the like be unlike, nor the unlike like . . . ? And if the unlike cannot be like, or the like unlike, then according to you, being could not be many, for this would involve an impossibility. In all that you say have you any other purpose except to disprove the being of the many? And is not each division of your treatise intended to furnish a separate proof of this, there being as many proofs of the not-being of the many, as you have composed arguments?

In the dialogue, Zeno acknowledges that Socrates has correctly understood him. Zeno's defense of Parmenides thus consists not of evidence supporting Parmenides' position nor even of positive arguments; rather, Zeno demonstrates that the opposite position is self-contradictory.

These proofs of the being of the one by proving the not-being of the many might not seem relevant in a scientific age, but some have survived and are known to those who are not otherwise learned in pre-Socratic philosophy. The most famous of Zeno's arguments, called the "Achilles," is summed up by Aristotle: "In a race, the quickest runner can never overtake the slowest, since the pursuer must first reach the point where the pursued started, so that the slower must always hold a lead." Almost as famous is the paradox of the arrow, which can never reach its target. According to Zeno's argument, at each point of its flight, the arrow must be at that point and at rest at that point. Thus, all motion, and therefore all change, is illusory.

Zeno's famed pugnacity was not limited to philosophy. After a plot in which he was involved against the tyrant Nearchus of Elea was discovered, the philosopher died under torture, and his death became the subject of various anecdotes. Some claim that he revealed the names of the tyrant's own friends as conspirators. Another story states that Zeno bit off his tongue and spit it out at the tyrant; in another, he bit off the tyrant's ear or nose.

Summary

Plato recognized in *Sophist* (after 360 B.C.) that there is something futile about such arguments as those of Zeno and that those who make them may simply be showing off:

> Thus we provide a rich feast for tyros, whether young or old; for there is nothing easier than to argue that the one cannot be many, or the many one: and great is their delight in denying that a man is good; for man, they insist, is man and good is good. I dare say that you have met with persons who take an interest in such matters—they are often elderly men, whose meagre sense is thrown into amazement by these discoveries of theirs, which they believe to be the height of wisdom.

Zeno can be defended in a number of ways. One could argue that his motives were good—that he wanted only to defend Parmenides. In doing so, he simply showed that trait of loyalty which brought about his death. More seriously, one could argue that his position in the history of philosophy excuses his failures and could praise him for raising issues and developing methods of argument which Aristotle took seriously. In Zeno's arguments a recurring theme in philosophy can be seen: the conflict of reason and common sense. Periodically in philosophy, thinkers prove by logic things that ordinary people cannot accept. The British empiricists—John Locke, George Berkeley, and David Hume—did this by stripping away the qualities of objects until the real world had to be defended as an illusion. More recently, the poststructuralists have denounced the logocentric view of the world and have written *sous rature*—the world may be described rationally, but that analysis must be voided, since any logocentric analysis of the world by definition must be faulty. Periodically, it seems, logic and common sense must be at odds.

Nevertheless, in the twentieth century, Zeno has found one eminent and eloquent defender, Bertrand Russell. Zeno, he says, for two thousand years had been pronounced an ingenious juggler and his arguments had been considered sophisms, when "these sophisms were reinstated, and made the foundations of a mathematical renaissance, by a German professor," Karl Weierstrass. Russell concludes, "The only point where Zeno probably erred was in inferring (if he did infer) that, because there is no change, therefore the world must be in the same state at one time as at another." Thus, at the dawn of philosophy, when philosophers sometimes wrote in hexameters and were executed for their politics, Zeno expressed certain philosophical problems in a form which still amuses ordinary people and which still occasions profound debates among professional philosophers.

Bibliography

Aristotle. *The Physics*. Translated by Phillip H. Wicksteed and Francis Macdonald Cornford. 2 vols. London: Heinemann, 1929-1934. The sixth book contains an analysis of Zeno's arguments. Important because Zeno's extant texts are so fragmentary. This translation is part of the Loeb Classical Library series.

Freeman, Kathleen. *The Pre-Socratic Philosophers: A Companion to Diels' "Fragmente der Vorsokratiker."* Cambridge, Mass.: Harvard University Press, 1946. Freeman's work contains translations of the extant fragments of Zeno's work, interspersed with analysis and commentary.

Fuller, B. A. G. *A History of Philosophy*. New York: Henry Holt, 1938. Fuller gives a brief but helpful summary of Zeno's philosophy. Includes an extensive bibliography.

Hussey, Edward. *The Pre-Socratics*. London: Duckworth, 1972. This volume contains a sympathetic analysis of Parmenides and Zeno. According to Hussey, "What is historically most important here is the logical analysis of such concepts as *time, change, diversity, separation, completeness.*"

Plato. *Parmenides*. In *Plato and Parmenides*, translated by Francis Macdonald Cornford. London: Routledge and Kegan Paul, 1958. Plato provides a glimpse of Zeno as a person as well as some idea of the thought of Parmenides. It is not certain that the dialogue form Plato favors was actually employed by Zeno. An "Eleatic stranger," said to be a disciple of Parmenides and Zeno, takes part in two of the dialogues, but it is not certain whether he expresses their thoughts.

West, Martin. "Early Greek Philosophy." In *The Oxford History of the Classical World*, edited by John Boardman, Jasper Griffin, and Oswyn Murray. Oxford: Oxford University Press, 1986. Although this essay does not give much detail on Zeno, it is nevertheless useful in placing him in his historical and cultural context. The volume itself is illustrated and includes an index and bibliographies.

John C. Sherwood

COUNT JAN ŽIŽKA

Born: c. 1360; Trocnov, Bohemia
Died: October 11, 1424; Přibyslav, Bohemia
Area of Achievement: Warfare
Contribution: Žižka's innovations in military organization and weapons were directly responsible for the success of the Hussite revolution; they spelled the end of the medieval system of mounted knights.

Early Life

Jan Žižka was born in Trocnov, Bohemia, probably sometime around 1360. Trocnov was twelve miles southeast of Budweis (modern České Budějovice), in Czechoslovakia, and only a few miles north of the modern Austrian border. The region south of Trocnov was populated mostly by Germans, and Budweis was controlled by them. Žižka was thus brought up in an essentially bilingual culture. Žižka (pronounced Zhīshka, with z's like that in "azure") meant "one-eyed" and was a nickname derived from his early loss of an eye. His family was impecunious, and Žižka was apparently reared in the royal court, gaining military experience in its service.

From about 1380 to 1392, Žižka's activities are a mystery, except that he was apparently the royal hunter in the town of Zahorany near the royal castle of Orlik for Wenceslas IV. About 1405 Žižka returned to his homeland. Sometime during this period, he left the king's service to fight as a mercenary in one of the guerrilla bands employed by barons who sided with either the Bohemians or the Moravians in their protracted struggle. In 1409 King Wenceslas pardoned Žižka for his renegade military adventures, and Žižka was soon fighting with Sokol of Lamberg for the Polish king against the Teutonic Knights. From this campaign Žižka derived considerable valuable military experience.

The court register of Prague's New Town (which was established in the mid-fourteenth century) reveals that Žižka bought a house there in 1414. Two years later, he sold this house and bought another one closer to the king's residence, at the same time apparently assuming some official position in the city palace. It is quite probable that during these years Žižka met Jan Hus and heard him preach.

Hus became dean of the faculty of arts at the university in Prague in 1401, and in the same year, he began an outstanding career preaching at Bethlehem Chapel. In many ways, he was a follower of John Wycliffe, and in 1408 he was censured for ignoring an order from cathedral officials to reject a list of forty-five articles drawn up from Wycliffe's writings. Hus's continued defense of Wycliffe and defiance of the Church led to his being burned at the stake in 1415. A similar fate met Jerome of Prague the next year.

These events created a furor. Hus approved of the custom of administering

Holy Communion in both forms—wine as well as bread—as expressed in the phrase "sub utraque specie," and soon after Hus's death, many nobles and university men took up the custom in what became known as the "Utraquist" revolt. By 1420, they were also demanding punishment for simony, freedom to preach the Word of God, and a halt to the venality rampant among priests and monks. These three points, along with the demand for both forms of Communion, became known as the "Four Articles of Prague." Thus, the Hussite revolt can be seen as a precursor to the Reformation.

Life's Work

After an angry crowd threw the members of the Prague council out of the council building's windows in 1419, King Wenceslas accepted a new council made up of Hussites. He died shortly thereafter. It is at that time that Žižka entered the complicated political and religious maneuvering, often in the service of the Taborites.

The Taborites were a radical, chiliastic sect who took their name from the biblical Mount Tabor. In November, 1419, when various Taborite groups approached Prague, several were ambushed by royalist supporters. Then Žižka took up arms for the Taborites and led them in capturing the royal castle, the Vyšehrad.

Following this triumph, Žižka left Prague to settle in Pilsen as the resident Hussite leader; in February, 1420, he received a call for help from Tabor (the home community of the Taborites). Thus, in late March, 1420, Žižka set out with a small group and twelve wagons, armed with cannon, determined to assist the Taborites against the royalists. When his forces were ambushed in the village of Sudomer, Žižka led them to a stunning victory over superior numbers and thereby kept radical Hussitism alive in the Tabor community. Žižka was soon elected one of the four captains of the Taborites, and during this period he carried out many terrorist campaigns against both castles and towns. He was also instrumental in building up the defenses around Tabor.

In the aftermath, King Sigismund of Hungary (Wenceslas' half brother) in 1420 led a military force against Prague; the Hussites quickly mustered an army to meet him. Žižka was called back to Prague, where he trained and commanded a force that completely routed Sigismund's men. Important to Žižka's success against Sigismund was the placement of his war wagons in a quadrangle surrounded by a moat. The decisive battle was fought on July 14, 1420, on the hill of Vitkov near New Town, where Žižka defeated a huge army that outnumbered the Hussites four or five to one.

The struggle between the royalists and the Hussites continued for several more years, with Žižka winning numerous important engagements; by the autumn of 1420, the Taborites of the south had become a potent national faction, which often disagreed with the moderate Utraquists in Prague. By the spring of 1421, the Hussites were in command of Hradčany Castle, forcing the Utraquists to sign an armistice on May 21.

The ceaseless haggling over theological and ecclesiastical issues soon brought Žižka back into combat, however, and in June, 1421, while directing an assault on the castle at Bor, Žižka was hit in his remaining eye by an arrow and blinded permanently. Nevertheless, his greatest victories were yet to come. He helped drive the Misnians out of Bohemia, and he purified the Taborite faith of what he considered the evil influence of Martin Houska and his heretical teachings about the Eucharist. Žižka also defeated in pitched battle the Adamite wing of the Taborites. The Adamites were radicals who taught that one should succumb completely to one's impulses, leading to nudity, the prohibition of marriage, and group orgies. Žižka's campaign against them in October, 1421, finished the Adamite movement. Of his military conquests after his blindness, his defeat of Sigismund at Kutna Hora in December, 1421, and his victory at the Battle of Malesov on June 7, 1423, stand out.

Žižka's death came in October, 1424, when he fell ill—perhaps of the plague—during the siege of Přibyslav. After his death, his followers called themselves "Orphans" in acknowledgment of their bereavement.

Summary

Much of Count Jan Žižka's fervor was generated by his dedication to the Four Articles of Prague. He strongly supported the third of the articles—that which deprived monks and priests of their accumulation of earthly possessions—and he even more strongly supported the fourth:

> All mortal sins and especially those that are committed publicly, as well as other disorders offending against the Law of God, shall be properly and sensibly prohibited and punished in each estate by those who have the authority to do so; and . . . evil and slanderous rumors about this country [shall] be cleansed away, thus insuring the general welfare of the Bohemian Kingdom and Nation.

A long list of sins accompanied this article. Laymen were condemned for adultery, gluttony, and the like, while the members of the clergy were called to task for simony, selling indulgences, taking money for saying Mass, as well as for whoring, brawling, and many other faults. For the many pious Christians such as Žižka, this list of human failings threatened the foundation of God's Kingdom: Žižka clearly saw himself as a "severe avenger" (as he was described in the inscription to a sixteenth century portrait of him) whose duty it was to purify the church membership. According to Frederick G. Heymann, Žižka regarded himself as

> the legitimate prosecutor, judge, and executor in implementing the Fourth Article. He never had any doubt that this was his office, that he was fully au-

thorized by God and Christ, as was any true Christian with enough power on his hands, to destroy the deadly sins wherever he met them.

This conception explains the ruthlessness of many of Žižka's actions.

Žižka's success as leader of the Taborite military force can hardly be overestimated. The strategy that produced his enormous successes was his deployment of his wagons, and these were his major contribution to military science. Their use made obsolete the medieval style of military combat with mounted knights. In addition, Žižka's deployment of his peasant warriors surpassed in discipline and flexibility any previous approach to military tactics. Finally, when Žižka mounted guns on his wagons, he created his own field artillery, an invention that proved to be psychologically as well as materially devastating to his enemies.

Bibliography

Durant, Will. "The Western Slavs: 1300-1517." In *The Story of Civilization*, vol. 6. New York: Simon and Schuster, 1957. This chapter gives an excellent, succinct overview of the period, with sections on Bohemia, Jan Hus, and the Bohemian Revolution. A good essay with which to begin.

Heymann, Frederick G. *John Žižka and the Hussite Revolution*. Princeton, N.J.: Princeton University Press, 1955. A detailed, five-hundred-page study of its topic. Heymann is especially good at clarifying the role of the Taborites in the Hussite revolution and explaining what the Taborites meant to Žižka. The military campaigns are recounted in detail. The appendices and bibliography are especially useful, though most of the entries are in Czech.

Kaminsky, Howard. *A History of the Hussite Revolution*. Berkeley: University of California Press, 1967. A long scholarly study with an excellent bibliography. There are frequent references to Žižka, and the discussion of the Taborite movement is very good.

Urbanek, R. "Jan Žižka, the Hussite." *Slavonic Review* 8 (December, 1924): 272-284. A glowing survey of Žižka's career written for his quincentenary. Adds no new information, but traces the key events in Žižka's life. Assumes some acquaintance with Žižka's life.

Frank Day

ZOROASTER

Born: c. 628 B.C.; probably Rhages, northeastern Iran
Died: c. 551 B.C.; probably northern Iran
Area of Achievement: Religion
Contribution: The founder of one of the great ethical religions of the ancient world, Zoroaster exerted direct and indirect influence on the development of three other great religions: Judaism, Christianity, and Islam.

Early Life

Zoroaster (the corrupt Greek form of the Persian name Zarathustra) was one of the most important religious reformers of the ancient world and the founder of a new religion which took his name: Zoroastrianism. Since very little is known about his life, the dates of his birth and death are disputed. According to tradition, he "lived 258 years before Alexander" the Great. This has been interpreted as 258 years before Alexander's conquest of Persia in 330 B.C. The date has also been interpreted not as a birth date but as the date of one of three principal events in his life: his vision and revelation at the age of thirty, the beginning of his preaching at age forty, or the conversion of King Vishtaspa (or Hystaspas) two years later. Since, according to tradition, Zoroaster lived for seventy-seven years, he lived between 630 and 553, 628 and 551, or 618 and 541.

Although he was never deified, legends and pious embellishments began to grow about Zoroaster after his death. Such legends have both clarified and obscured modern knowledge about him. It was said that he was the product of a miraculous birth and that at birth he laughed aloud, thus driving away evil spirits. As an adult, he became a great lover of wisdom and righteousness, withdrawing to an isolated mountain wilderness, where he survived on cheese and wild fruit. There he was tempted by the Devil but successfully resisted. He was then subjected to intense physical torture, which he endured by clinging to his faith in Ahura Mazda, the true god and the Lord of Light. He received a revelation from Ahura Mazda in the form of the *Avesta*, the holy book of his religion, and was commissioned to preach to mankind. After suffering ridicule and persecution for many years, he at last found a convert and patron in King Vishtaspa. Married and a father of a daughter and two sons, Zoroaster appears to have enjoyed a degree of local prominence at his patron's court. His daughter apparently married a leading minister of the king.

Life's Work

Like the other great ethical religions, Zoroastrianism had its origins in its founder's reaction to the religious beliefs and practices of his people. The religion of the pre-Zoroastrian Persians displays many features in common with Hinduism. This is understandable, because the ancient settlers of Persia and India came from the same Aryan tribes which had invaded Persia and India a millennium before Zoroaster's birth. Persian religion before Zoroaster was polytheistic, with specific deities attached to the three major classes of society: chiefs and priests, warriors, and farmers and cattle breeders. The deities known as *asuras* (lords), who alone were endowed with an ethical character, were attached exclusively to the first class. Two forms of sacrifice were practiced: animal sacrifice, apparently to propitiate the gods, and the drinking of the fermented juice of the sacred *haoma* plant, which, through the intoxication it induced, supplied a foretaste of immortality. To perform the sacrifices and the other rituals, a priestly class, the *magi*, rose to a position of great power in early Persian society.

Basing his teachings on the *Avesta*, a book of revelations from Ahura Mazda, Zoroaster conceived it as his mission to purify the traditional beliefs of his people by eradicating polytheism, animal sacrifice, and magic and to establish a new, more ethical and spiritual religion. Ultimately, Zoroastrianism succeeded because of its founder's and early followers' ability to accommodate their teachings with certain features of traditional Persian religion.

It is impossible to determine how many of the teachings of Zoroastrianism originated with its founder. The *Avesta*, as it has come down to the present, is composed of several divisions, including two liturgical texts, prayers, and two sets of hymns, only one of which, the *Gathas*, is definitely ascribed to Zoroaster. Much of the *Avesta* has been destroyed or lost. Zoroaster probably made additional contributions, as did his later followers. There is, however, general agreement that it was Zoroaster who provided the central teachings of his religion.

According to Zoroaster, the history of the world was the ongoing conflict between the forces of good and evil. God, Ahura Mazda, represented the former; the Devil, Ahriman, the latter. Ahura Mazda, one of several of the *asuras* of traditional Persian religion, was elevated by Zoroaster to the place of the one high god; Zoroastrianism was originally a distinctly monotheistic religion, although later it absorbed polytheistic features. Zoroaster divided history into four three-thousand-year periods, during which Ahura Mazda and Ahriman competed for men's souls and the ultimate victory of their respective causes. At the end of the final stage, which some Zoroastrians interpreted as beginning with the birth of Zoroaster, Ahura Mazda would overpower Ahriman and his minions in a great conflagration and cast them into the abyss. This would be followed by a resurrection of the dead, a last judgment, and the beginning of a new life for all good souls (believers in Ahura Mazda) in a world free of evil, darkness, pain, and death. Zoroastrianism included concepts of a hell and purgatory as well as a paradise. At death, all souls would have to cross the narrow Sifting Bridge (also known as the Bridge of the Requiter), which was like a long sword. The good would be offered the broad (flat) side of the bridge and would be welcomed into Paradise by a beautiful young maiden. There they would reside with Ahura Mazda throughout eternity. The evil souls—the followers of Ahriman— would be forced to walk along the razor's edge of the sword-bridge and would fall into a hell which would be their abode of darkness and terror forever. For the souls who had sinned but whose good works outweighed their bad, there would be a short period of temporary punishment to cleanse them in preparation for entrance into Paradise. For sinners of greater degree, who had nevertheless performed some good works, suffering in Hell would last until God's final victory and the last judgment, when they also would be welcomed into Paradise. Those who subscribed to Zoroaster's teachings, therefore, could face death unafraid in anticipation of a blissful afterlife, if not immediately at least ultimately.

The religion of Zoraster was ethical. Man's duty was threefold: to befriend his enemy, to lead the wicked to righteousness, and to educate the ignorant. The greatest virtue toward which the believer must strive was piety, followed by honor and honesty in both word and deed. The worst sin was unbelief, which was not only a denial of Ahura Mazda but also a rejection of his ethical code of conduct and an acceptance of evil. Since piety was the greatest virtue, the first obligation of the believer was to worship God through purification, sacrifice, and prayer. Although Zoroaster rejected blood sacrifices, he retained the sacrifice of fire, which was a symbol of Ahura Mazda and thus of purity and truth. Although Zoroaster decried the drinking of the fermented juice of the *haoma* plant for its intoxicating qualities, it was retained as a medium of Holy Communion. Historically, the fire ritual became the central feature of Zoroastrian worship. Sacred fires are tended and preserved by priests in fire temples, where the king of fires, Bahram, is crowned and enthroned. Modern Zoroastrians (Parsees) have also retained the practices of wearing the *sadre*, the shirt which symbolizes their religion, and the daily untying and reknotting of the *kushti*, the sacred thread whose seventy-two strands symbolize the chapters of the *Yasna*, one of the sacred liturgical texts. The final act of piety is proper provision for the disposition of one's body after death. The corpse is neither cremated nor buried, since the first method would defile fire and the second method the earth, both of which are regarded as good creations of God. Instead, the dead are exposed to the elements, where their flesh is consumed by vultures. This practice survives today in the famous Towers of Silence in Bombay among the Parsees (Persians), virtually the last significant surviving community of Zoroastrians.

Although Zoroaster was a monotheist, he nevertheless sought to accommodate his religion with Persian religious traditions. Surrounding Ahura Mazda are the six "Beneficent (or Holy) Immortal Ones" and the *yazads* (the worshipped ones), who probably had their origins in the deities worshipped by the lesser orders of ancient Persian society. These beings have been compared to the archangels and angels of Christianity. Because of the exalted nature of Ahura Mazda, it came to be believed that he should be approached indirectly through these servants, who came to personify certain facets of God's creation and qualities. The *yazad* Mithra, keeper of the sacred fire (the fire temples came to be called the courts of Mithra), who represented justice and friendship and who was Ahura Mazda's chief lieutenant in the struggle against evil, was himself to become the deity in a religious offshoot of Zoroastrianism, Mithraism, which was one of Christianity's chief competitors in the Roman Empire. Opposed to the servants of God were Ahriman and his hordes of demons, who were also associated with lesser ancient Persian demigods. They brought evil into the world in its various forms and worked to deny humans their blissful afterlife with Ahura Mazda and his servants.

Zoroaster is thought to have died at the age of seventy-seven; legend states that he was murdered.

Summary

The history of Zoroastrianism following the death of its founder was characterized by change, accommodation, decline, and revival. The most notable changes were the emergence of dualism, with the deification of Ahriman and the conception of history as the struggle between separate gods of good and evil, and the emergence of an increasingly powerful priestly class, the *magi*, who introduced elements of magic, astrology, and blood sacrifice in a perversion of Zoroaster's ideals. Following the Muslim conquest of Persia in the seventh century, Zoroastrians were alternately tolerated, persecuted, and forcibly converted to Islam. In the eleventh century, all but a small remnant left Persia and emigrated to India, where most of them settled in the area around Bombay. There they have remained, and, known as the Parsees, they have become among the wealthiest, best-educated, and most charitable members of Indian society, all the while holding fast to their religious beliefs and practices. In the nineteenth century, they reestablished contact with the remaining Zoroastrians in Iran, the Gabars.

There are significant parallels between Zoroastrianism and three of the world's great religions, Judaism, Christianity, and Islam, although the extent of Zoroastrianism's direct influence remains a subject of debate. Perhaps Zoroaster's greatest contribution, both to his own age and to later civilizations, was the elevation of religion from debasement, magic, blood sacrifice, and pessimism to a scheme which optimistically promises rewards to those who conform in word and deed to a high, but realizable, code of ethical conduct.

Bibliography

Duchesne-Guillemin, Jacques. *The Western Response to Zoroaster*. Oxford:

Oxford University Press, 1958. This is a valuable introduction to scholarship on Zoroaster and Zoroastrianism by one of the leading twentieth century scholars on the subject.

Durant, Will. *Our Oriental Heritage*. New York: Simon and Schuster, 1954. This first volume in the Durants' multivolume popular classic, The Story of Civilization, contains an especially helpful and perceptive account of Zoroaster and Zoroastrianism. Durant considers the subject both in its ancient Persian context and as a powerful influence on later religions.

Masani, Rustom. *The Religion of the Good Life*. London: Allen and Unwin, 1938, 2d ed. 1968. This is a useful account by a Parsee of the teachings and practices of Zoroastrianism.

Olmstead, A. T. *History of the Persian Empire*. Chicago: University of Chicago Press, 1948, reprint 1959. This classic history of ancient Persia is useful in placing Zoroaster in his historical context.

Parrinder, Geoffrey, ed. *World Religions from Ancient History to the Present*, New York: Facts on File Publications, 1983. In this revised and enlarged edition of a book first published in 1971 as *Man and His Gods* in Great Britain and as *Religions of the World* in the United States, Zoroastrianism is traced from its origins to the present, including material on its most important offshoots, Mithraism and Manichaeanism.

Zoroaster. *The Hymns of Zarathustra*. Translated with an introduction by Jacques Duchesne-Guillemin. London: J. Murray, 1952, reprint 1963. This translation of the *Gathas*, which contains the only teachings of Zoroastrianism which can definitely be attributed to its founder, is indispensable to serious study of the subject.

J. Stewart Alverson

ZOSER

Born: c. 2700 B.C.; probably Memphis, Egypt
Died: c. 2650 B.C.; Memphis, Egypt
Areas of Achievement: Government and architecture
Contribution: Zoser was the first great king of the epoch known as the Old
  Kingdom, Third through Sixth dynasties. His outstanding achievement was
  the construction of the Step Pyramid at Saqqara near Memphis, the earli-
  est of the great pyramids.

Early Life

Zoser's brother Sanekht preceded him to the throne as the first king of the
Third Dynasty. Since both Sanekht and Zoser were sons of Khasekhemwy,
the last king of the Second Dynasty, it is not clear why Sanekht's accession
should have caused a change of dynasties. It may be that their mother,
Nymaathap, was not a legitimate wife but a concubine of Khasekhemwy and
the only one to produce suitable male offspring for the king. Upon his brother's death, Zoser assumed the throne and ruled for nineteen years.

Zoser's physical description is known from several reliefs found in the Step
Pyramid complex and from a seated limestone statue, thought to be the
oldest life-sized statue found in Egypt. This portrayal of the king was discovered in a small, doorless room near his pyramid, positioned to look out of
two eyeholes in the wall so that the king could view food offerings brought to
him by his funerary priests each day. Although the inlaid eyes have been
gouged out and the nose has been damaged, the massive head, with its high
cheekbones and prominent mouth, has lost none of its intimidating majesty.
This is no idealized portrait, but the likeness of Zoser himself.

Apart from the members of his immediate family, only a few others can be
linked to Zoser by name. Hesyra and Khabausokar have left impressive funerary monuments which testify to their importance in Zoser's court. Although his tomb remains to be discovered, there is one man, Imhotep, whose
name must rank with that of the great king. In later antiquity he was credited
with every kind of wisdom and was even accorded divine status as a god of
healing. It is as Zoser's chief architect, however, that Imhotep has ensured
his place in history, for the king entrusted to this innovative genius the construction of the Step Pyramid.

Life's Work

The ancient Egyptian believed that his king was a god, the incarnation of
the falcon god Horus, source of all goods and prosperity for the entire land.
During his life on earth, the king displayed his effectiveness as a ruler by the
wealth and beauty of his royal residence; after his death, he proclaimed his

ability to continue to perform good services for his subjects by the magnificence of his tomb. When the king departed this life he became one with his father, Osiris, god of the land's fertility, and continued to bestow prosperity on his subjects through the new incarnation of the god Horus, that is, the king's son and successor.

From the very beginning, royal tombs were built on the analogy of the royal residence, for the king's tomb was his "house of eternity," in the common Egyptian expression. Thus, in very early times when the king lived in a circular hut, his tomb was circular; when the royal residence became rectangular in shape, the royal tomb became rectangular. The royal tomb, despite some changes, remained essentially the same until the time of Zoser. It consisted of a subterranean structure where the dead king was buried with his most valuable possessions, topped by a brick superstructure in the form of a rectangular platform, which Egyptologists refer to as a mastaba (Arabic for "bench").

When Zoser came to the throne, he had the same assumptions about his role as his predecessors. He was the god Horus, or rather a temporary incarnation of that god, whose special name for this particular incarnation was Netjerykhet (divine of body). It was by this name that the king identified himself everywhere in the Step Pyramid complex and not by the familiar Zoser (found only in later writings together with the name Netjerykhet). Like his predecessors, Zoser assumed that one of his most important duties as king was to undertake the preparation of his "house of eternity." Fortunately, he had in his service the brilliant Imhotep.

Zoser's decision to construct a mastaba for his monument was dictated by tradition, but instead of employing the usual rectangular shape, he directed Imhotep to build it as a square, with each side facing the four cardinal points and measuring approximately 207 feet. In addition, he ordered that the monument be constructed of limestone and not brick, the material used in all previous constructions of this sort. Rising to a height of twenty-six feet, this square stone mastaba was enclosed in a rectangular area by a wall thirty-three feet high and more than a mile long.

Even as it stood, Zoser's monument displayed a number of bold innovations. Simply in point of size, it dwarfed anything in Egyptian experience, since the area enclosed by the girdle wall was more than sixty times larger than any built so far. Almost immediately, however, Zoser began to rethink the plan of his monument. In the end, the original mastaba underwent six major reconstructions and eventually emerged as a white stone pyramid rising in six unequal steps to a height of 204 feet and measuring at the base 411 by 358 feet. Instead of viewing his tomb simply as his royal residence in death, Zoser had come to think of it also as a colossal staircase by which his transfigured body might climb up into the sky and join the sun god Re in his solar barge as he passed through the sky each day (this according to information discovered in pyramids of the Fifth Dynasty).

Not until after the pyramid was finished did Zoser complete the numerous other temples and courts which he considered essential to the complex, for he envisioned it as a true necropolis, a city of the dead. Except for the Mortuary Temple and the smaller building in which Zoser's statue was found, none of the other buildings surrounding the Step Pyramid has any known precedent or parallel, and the purpose that many were intended to serve remains obscure. One group of buildings, partially restored, whose function is reasonably clear, relates to the celebration of the Sed or Jubilee Festival and requires special attention.

In earlier times, when the king's physical vigor was observed to weaken he was put to death and replaced by a younger man, since nature's bounty was thought to depend on the king's virility. In later times, this custom was supplanted by the Sed Festival, which enabled the aging king to renew his power through magic and thus ensure the welfare of his kingdom. Zoser most likely had celebrated this festival during his life and had intended that the complex of buildings south of his pyramid should provide him with the setting necessary for repeating this ceremony throughout eternity. One of the most important rites was the reenactment of the king's double coronation as King of Upper and Lower Egypt, during which he was presented with the white crown of the south and the red crown of the north. In another rite, which is depicted in a fine relief, the king is shown running a fixed course, apparently to display his renewed strength to his subjects. An area was set aside for Zoser's eternal run.

Archaeologists have carefully examined the subterranean part of Zoser's tomb, where he was buried with his most valuable possessions. Despite having been plundered by tomb robbers over the course of some four thousand years, the storage rooms have yielded to excavators some ninety tons of stone vessels made of such costly stones as alabaster, porphyry, and quartz. It is clear that Zoser was lavishly equipped for eternity, on a scale never attempted before.

Summary

Menes, the legendary first king of the First Dynasty, unified Upper and Lower Egypt in approximately 3200 B.C. An Egypt with a strong central government was able to undertake large hydraulic projects to control the annual inundations of the Nile. Under one king, the obedient army and conscripted peasants could increase the amount of arable land by draining swamps and irrigating the desert margins. During the first two dynasties, despite periods of civil strife, a unified Egypt was able to make enormous strides forward in every way. The invention of writing made it possible to conduct censuses of people and animals, make records of more complicated data, and communicate easily over long distances. Leisure provided the intelligentsia with an opportunity for speculative thought and for the fine arts as well as the practical.

Roughly five hundred years of progress culminated in Zoser's reign. Although written documents are generally lacking for this period, the Step Pyramid itself is very reliable testimony to the great prosperity and self-confidence which characterized Zoser's tenure. The size of his funerary monument alone implies much about the economic and political status of Egypt during this period. More important than mere size, however, are the architectural innovations, especially Zoser's decision to build his monument in the revolutionary shape of a pyramid and to use quarried stone for its material, the first large structure to be so raised. The Step Pyramid represents Zoser's vision of himself as king, able literally to ascend into the heavens by a stairway that would never perish. Zoser's vision was fully realized about one hundred years later in the Great Pyramid of Cheops, still a wonder to the world.

Bibliography

Aldred, Cyril. *Egyptian Art in the Days of the Pharaohs, 3100-320 B.C.* New York: Oxford University Press, 1980. Primarily trained as an art historian, Aldred has produced perhaps the most elegant and lucid descriptions of Egypt's art treasures available in any language. The chapter on the Third Dynasty is particularly informative on the precise nature and significance of the architectural innovations of Zoser's reign.

Edwards, I. E. S. *The Pyramids of Egypt.* Harmondsworth, England: Penguin Books, 1947, rev. ed. 1961. Edwards has written the classic account of the pyramids. His chapter on Zoser's Step Pyramid includes a very helpful discussion of the king's successors, who tried to follow Zoser's example in building their tombs in step-pyramid form. The pyramid of Sekhemkhet, Zoser's son, was planned on a more lavish scale than his father's, but it was never finished.

Firth, C. M., and J. E. Quibell. *Excavations at Saqqara, the Step Pyramid.* Architectural plans by J. Ph. Lauer. 2 vols. Cairo: L'Institut Français d'Archéologie Orientale, 1935-1936. Serious excavations around the Step Pyramid did not begin until after World War I, when Firth took charge of the work from 1920 until his death in 1931. Lauer joined Firth in 1927 as architect and is responsible for the extensive restoration work on the pyramid and surrounding buildings which is still in progress. This book is the fundamental work on the Step Pyramid complex.

Lichtheim, Miriam. *Ancient Egyptian Literature: A Book of Readings.* Vol. 3, *The Late Period.* Berkeley: University of California Press, 1980. Lichtheim translates and comments on the famous rock inscription called the "Famine Stela." It purports to be the record of an order given by Zoser himself during a time of famine to appease the god Khnum, who controlled the floodwaters of the Nile. Many scholars doubt the authenticity of the inscription.

Smith, W. S. *The Art and Architecture of Ancient Egypt.* Harmondsworth, England: Penguin Books, 1958, rev. ed. 1981. The chapter on the Third Dynasty is generously illustrated with black-and-white photographs. Although the bibliography cited for the chapter is much less extensive than that cited in *The Cambridge Ancient History*, it is quite sufficient for practical purposes. Smith provides a compendious and serviceable account of the major art forms of Zoser's time, excluding pottery, for which no adequate account has yet been written.

_____. "The Old Kingdom in Egypt." In *The Cambridge Ancient History*, vol. 1, edited by I. E. S. Edwards, C. J. Gadd, and N. G. L. Hammond. 3d ed. Cambridge: Cambridge University Press, 1971. Smith's discussion of the Third Dynasty includes all the minutiae pertaining to Zoser's lineage and the chief monuments of officials of his court. In general, this admirable series of volumes is written by scholars for scholars, and Smith's account is no exception. Each chapter is furnished with an extensive bibliography, an indispensable guide to further study.

H. J. Shey

INDEXES

BIOGRAPHICAL INDEX

I

BIOGRAPHICAL INDEX

BIOGRAPHICAL INDEX

V

AREAS OF ACHIEVEMENT

X

AREAS OF ACHIEVEMENT

Henry the Lion II-930
Heraclius II-948
Herod the Great II-958
János Hunyadi III-1039
Innocent III III-1086
Innocent IV III-1092
Itzcóatl III-1115
James I the Conqueror III-1131
Joan of Arc III-1157
Justinian I III-1204
Kanishka III-1222
Khosrow I III-1228
Kublai Khan III-1239
Saint László I III-1253
Louis II the German III-1293
Louis IX III-1299
Gaius Maecenas III-1331
Mansa Mūsā III-1341
Marcus Aurelius III-1345
Margaret of Denmark, Norway, and Sweden III-1350
Gaius Marius III-1360
Menander (Indian king) III-1385
Miltiades the Younger III-1398
Mithradates the Great III-1404
Muhammad III-1422
Nebuchadnezzar II III-1444
Nezahualcóyotl III-1454
Nizam al-Mulk IV-1477
Saint Olaf IV-1484
Osman IV-1504
Otto the Great IV-1510
Ou-yang Hsiu IV-1515
Pachacuti IV-1525
Peisistratus IV-1557
Pericles IV-1569
Philip II IV-1598
Philip II of Macedonia IV-1603
Philip IV the Fair IV-1609
Philip the Good IV-1614
Piankhi IV-1624
Pittacus of Mytilene IV-1644
Pompey the Great IV-1689
Psamtik I IV-1737
Michael Psellus IV-1741
Ptolemy Philadelphus IV-1752
Ptolemy Soter IV-1757
Rabanus Maurus IV-1784
Ramses II IV-1795
Cola di Rienzo IV-1815
Rudolf I IV-1820
Saladin IV-1835
Samuel IV-1851
Sargon II IV-1861
Scipio Aemilianus IV-1871
Scipio Africanus IV-1876
Seleucus I Nicator IV-1885

Seneca the Younger IV-1890
Sesostris III IV-1906
Shapur II IV-1910
Shōtoku Taishi IV-1918
Solomon V-1956
Solon V-1962
Ssu-ma Kuang V-1983
Stefan Dušan V-1987
Stephen I V-1998
Su Tung-p'o V-2014
Suger V-2020
Lucius Cornelius Sulla V-2026
Sundjata V-2032
Sylvester II V-2037
Cornelius Tacitus V-2047
T'ai Tsung V-2053
Taira Kiyomori V-2059
Tamerlane V-2065
Themistocles V-2092
Theodoric the Great V-2108
Theodosius the Great V-2115
Thutmose III V-2164
Tiberius V-2169
Tigranes the Great V-2175
Trajan V-2180
Urban II V-2197
Valdemar II V-2202
Vespasian V-2237
Vladimir I V-2274
Wang An-shih V-2284
Wang Wei V-2304
Władysław II Jagiełło and Jadwiga V-2344
Yung-lo V-2383
Zoser V-2416

HISTORIOGRAPHY. *See also*
EDUCATION and SCHOLARSHIP
Alfonso X I-124
Saint Athanasius I-269
al-Biruni I-332
Giovanni da Pian del Carpini I-400
Cassiodorus I-413
Aulus Cornelius Celsus I-438
Eusebius of Caesarea II-715
Jean Froissart II-760
Gregory of Tours II-832
Herodotus II-964
Ibn Khaldun III-1066
Joachim of Fiore III-1152
Flavius Josephus III-1189
Livy III-1283
al-Mas'udi III-1376
Pan Ku IV-1530
Polybius IV-1681
Michael Psellus IV-1741
Sallust IV-1845
Saxo Grammaticus IV-1866

XI

GREAT LIVES FROM HISTORY

AREAS OF ACHIEVEMENT

AREAS OF ACHIEVEMENT

XV

AREAS OF ACHIEVEMENT

GEOGRAPHICAL INDEX

GEOGRAPHICAL INDEX

XXI

GEOGRAPHICAL INDEX

78368